The Decade *of* Power Politics

INDIA'S STRATEGY AND LEADS

The Decade *of* Power Politics

INDIA'S STRATEGY AND LEADS

Edited by
Manasi Sinha
Vishal Rajput

KNOWLEDGE WORLD
KW Publishers Pvt Ltd
New Delhi

ISBN 978-93-91490-83-6 Hardback
ISBN 978-93-91490-84-3 ebook

Published in India by Kalpana Shukla

KNOWLEDGE WORLD

KW Publishers Pvt Ltd
4676/21, First Floor, Ansari Road
Daryaganj, New Delhi 110002
Phone: +91 11 43528107
Marketing: kw@kwpub.in
Editorial: production@kwpub.in
Website: www.kwpub.in

Printed and Bound in India

*For the undaunted spirit that
never stops giving up...*

R. Indus
Kuen Lun
Lucknow
Allahabad

R. Brahmaputra
BURMA

CONTENTS

FOREWORD

The world is facing global challenges that, without a doubt, are easier to solve together, with the help of the international community. But not all states quickly cope with large-scale problems that undermine their economy and social sphere, as well as negatively affect the internal political structure and foreign policy image. The COVID-19 pandemic has become one of such global challenges of our time, exposing trouble not only in healthcare but also in other realms, thereby forcing the international community to take a different look at universal global and regional issues.

In addition, stability and well-functioning institutes for responding to such challenges in the Asian countries have become obvious. The authorities of these states quickly interacted not only with their citizens to address a number of key issues during the pandemic, but also with other countries, including the West. It is also interesting that the effect of the pandemic on the economies of the Asian region was not as negative as for the EU and US economies. The pandemic also altered the balance of power and put forward such actors as China and India that started playing more influential roles in global politics and economics.

It is difficult to consider the spread of Western political ideas and institutions as a universal positive phenomenon that needs to be promoted in Asian countries. For sure, the East is inhomogeneous. However, it can be observed general trends in the development of a number of political and economic areas. Consequently, today many experts are considering the possibility that the Asian countries will be able to promote their rules of global integration and their vision of the future of the world already in the West.

In this backdrop of the changing complexities, 'Decade of Power Politics' is a timely literature to understand the latest development in the changing geopolitics and give an insight into the future course from a scholarly perspective.

Therefore, I highly recommend taking a closer look at Decade of Power Politics, edited by Dr. Manasi Sinha and Vishal Rajput. The book covers extremely up-to-date topics in geopolitics and international relations such as the rise of China; India's strategic engagement with today's global politics; geopolitical competition in the Arctic; key actors of the contemporary system of international relations and so on and so forth. I am sure that the book can be interesting not only for the experts and scholars but also for students and people who are really concerned with geopolitics, international relations, and global economics.

Liudmila A. Pechishcheva, PhD,
Associate professor at the Russian State University
for the Humanities (RSUH), Moscow, Russia.
E-mail: mayflower-85@inbox.ru

PREFACE

As we enter into a new dawn of the 21st century, it encased a 'new normal'—a condition that has permanently changed the lives and behaviour of people, society and nations at large. Impacting widely on society and people across the world, the COVID-19 pandemic has also excavated the precarious conditions of international politics. On the one hand, where relentless efforts by all the nations continue to ensure that this pandemic does not exacerbate, on the other, nations are becoming more inward oriented, ultra-protective, more competitive and conflictual and in pursuit of their own national interests only. The return of 'realpolitik' is what defines the contemporary world system. The Liberal values, democratic institutions, values of global solidarity, cooperation, collective security, peace and development that became the norm for all the international actors and institutions during the 20th century seem to be fading away as we paddle into a new era. The visionary goals and objectives to set up an international system that will direct more towards humanitarian concerns and sustainable goals, could not wipe out the inherent lust for power politics among the nations. Morgenthau's *Politics among Nations* still bears a resemblance to what the world politics appear to us today. The growing tensions and debates about the rise of China and its expansionist policies, the waning hegemony of USA, Israel's devouring Palestine, the setting off the Taliban regime in Afghanistan, the surge of digital supremacy, the echoing tensions in the Indo-Pacific, the imminent existential challenges of the European Union, the unprecedented geopolitics in the global north and south, the bandwagoning of developing states allying with powerful states for security and survival—all these pressing issues and challenges continue to construct the discourse and reality of contemporary global politics. In addition to this, the COVID-19 pandemic struck the world like never before as it exposed these structural and fundamental changes that define international politics today.

While India has been grappling with these challenges, it aspires to become a resilient strategic actor that aspires to define, lead and shape the global politics. In spite of constant geopolitical tensions posed by China and Pakistan in many ways in and around its vicinity, India stands out alone to decide its rules to balance the political scores and not be driven by others in the international arena.

It is some of these pressing concerns and the imminent power transitions persisting in the global order that we seek to put forth in this collection of essays. The decade of power politics therefore is an attempt to map out the trajectory of contemporary world politics and situate India in a constant flux where rapid transformations and transitions continue to surface in the international politics and how strategically India stands out to respond to this tumultuous environment. With the contribution of some young scholars and illuminating minds and experts from India, we have brought together a kaleidoscopic view of the contemporary world politics. This eclectic collection discusses the issues India has been grappling with in contemporary global politics and in what strategic ways it articulates and responds to such rapid changes in the international order. This edited book will be of interest to undergraduates, post-graduate scholars and researchers of international relations and specifically Area Studies to a large extent. The book is written in a comprehensive manner to make it also readable by laypersons and any seeker of knowledge in international relations.

Dr. Manasi Sinha
New Delhi

ACKNOWLEDGEMENTS

Thank you, the mystical universe, for letting there be so much light, hope, music, children and enlightening minds as life gets easier with them. It's a wonderful experience to create one's own creation, but encasing the work of others, shaping it slowly to bring out its finest elements is what makes an editor proud and honoured. The last few months have been extremely tiring, yet memorable for me as I lived my life as editor only, using a needle's eye to all the diverse ideas and perspectives of the authors, reviewing, modifying, editing and everything to give shape to this edited volume. And this remarkable journey would not have been possible without Vishal (co-editor), who relentlessly assisted me in accomplishing this project. Thank you so much, Vishal, for all your great support and elaborated work.

This book has developed out of a series of lectures and project-based learnings on international relations and global politics that I delivered for undergraduate and post-graduate students at Galgotias University, over the last three years. For, I had some bright energetic minds in my department who absorbed all my theoretical inputs on IR and global politics with high spirit and intensely engaged in critical debates and discussions with me and other faculty in the department for further explorations into the field of contemporary global politics. It was the sight of their zeal to exchange and share ideas and open up to critical outlook on contemporary international issues that prompted me to come up with this project that intends to capture some of these ideas on contemporary politics that popped up in our debates and discussions.

I am indebted to these young scholars who agreed to share their academic work with me and help me in making this book a grand success. Thank you so much, Rashmi, Payal, Priya, Sarthak, Shazad, Nawid for being so wonderful all the time. Thank you, Megha and Alakh for your brilliant contributions. Most of all, I want to thank my forever best friend, Pratyush, for the most delightful of beverages, invaluable support and expert comments. It really helped me in refining the ideas and construct for the book.

Last, but not the least, my parents and brothers and my extended family members, you are always special and close to my heart. I thank you all for everything that you have done for me.

LIST OF FIGURES

ABBREVIATIONS

CCP	Chinese Communist Party
PRC	People's Republic of China
GDP	Gross Domestic Product
IMF	International Monetary Fund
PPP	Purchasing Power Parity
IPR	Intellectual Property Rights
BRI	Belt and Road Initiative
OECD	Organization for Economic Cooperation and Development
PLA	People's Liberation Army
ASBM	Anti- Ship Ballistic Missiles
PLAN	People's Liberation Army Navy
PLAAF	People's Liberation Army Air Force
PLARF	People's Liberation Army Rocket Force
PLASSF	People's Liberation Army Strategic Support Force
SIPRI	Stockholm International Peace Research Institute
USSR	Union of Soviet Socialist Republics
WTO	World Trade Organisation
UNESCO	United Nations Educational, Scientific and Cultural Organization
UN	United Nations
RAW	Research and Analysis Wing
FATA	Federally Administered Tribal Areas

NATO	North Atlantic Treaty Organisation
TAPI	Turkmenistan, Afghanistan, Pakistan and India
SAARC	South Asian Association for regional cooperation
UNAMA	United Nations Assistance Mission in Afghanistan
NWFP	North-West Frontier Province
LAC	Line of Actual Control
CPI	Communist Party of India
USA	United States of America
UK	United Kingdom
SSN	Sub Sector North
CBM	Confidence Building Measures
CPEC	China-Pakistan Economic Corridor
NSG	Nuclear Supplier's Group
NAM	Non-Aligned Movement
EU	European Union
ASEAN	Association of Southeast Asian Nations
NDA	National Democratic Alliance
UPA	United Progressive Alliance
SAU	South Asian University
B2B	Bharat to Bhutan
OTPC	ONGC Tripura Power Company
BBIN	Bhutan-Bangladesh-India-Nepal
JeM	Jaish-e-Mohammad
AC	Arctic Council
EEZ	Exclusive Economic Zone
UNCLOS	United Nations Convention on the Law of the Sea
IMO	International Maritime Organization
GPS	Global Positioning System
LNG	Liquified Natural Gas

EODEX	Explosives Ordnance Disposal Exercise
JSF	Joint Strike Fighter
INSTC	International North South Transport Corridor
PLO	Palestine Liberation Organization
DRDO	Defence Research and Development Organization
BJP	Bharatiya Janata Party
IAI	Israeli Aerospace Industries
UAV	Unmanned Aerial Vehicles
IMI	Israeli Military Industry
SAM	Surface-to-Air Missiles
JWG	Joint Working Group
BVRAAM	Beyond Visual Range Air-to-Air Missile
IIAP	Indo-Israel Agricultural Project
UNHRC	UN Human Rights Commission
ISA	Israel Space Agency
ISRO	Indian Space Research Organisation
ORF	Observer Research Foundation
AESA	Active Electronically Scanned Array
EW	Electronic Warfare
MIDH	Mission for Integrated Development of Horticulture
ATGM	Anti-Tank Guided Missile
UNECOSOC	United Nations Economic and Social Council
SIS	Small Island States
IOR	Indian Ocean Region
WP	Western Pacific
AEP	Act East Policy
EIA	Energy Information Administration
SCS	South China Sea
SAGAR	Security and Growth for All in the Region

IPOI	Indo-Pacific Oceans Initiative
BIMSTEC	Bay of Bengal Initiative for Multi-Sectoral Technical and Economic Cooperation
IORA	Indian Ocean Rim Association
IOC	Indian Ocean Commission
IFC-IOR	Information Fusion Centre—Indian Ocean Region
HADR	Humanitarian Assistance and Disaster Relief
EAMF	Expanded ASEAN Maritime Forum
IFR	Indian Fleet Review
EAF	East Asia Forum
PIC	Pacific Island Countries
FIPIC	Forum for India-Pacific Island Cooperation
SLOC	Sea Lines Of Communication
UNSC	United Nations Security Council
RCEP	Regional Comprehensive Economic Partnership
ADB	Asian Development Bank
MSR	Maritime Silk Road
BDN	Blue Dot Network
FOIP	Free and Open Indo-Pacific
IOTC	Indian Ocean Tuna Commission
EAM	External Affairs Minister
IORIS	Indian Ocean Regional Information Sharing
VBSS	Visit, Board, Search and Seizure
EEC	Eastern Economic Corridor
BRICS	Brazil, Russia, India, China, South Africa
SCO	Shanghai Cooperation Organisation
CAR	Central Asian Region
IMU	Islamic Movement of Uzbekistan
TIP	Turkestan Islamic Party
IS	Islamic State
RCTS	Regional Counter-Terrorism Structure

ITEC	Indian Technical and Economic Cooperation Programme
JCPOA	Joint Comprehensive Plan of Action
WHO	World Health Organisation
ICC	Indian Culture Centre
NER	North East Region
AADMER	ASEAN Agreement on Disaster Management and Emergency Response
DIREX	Disaster Relief Exercises
ICCR	Indian Council for Cultural Relations

INTRODUCTION

INDIA'S STRATEGIC ENGAGEMENT WITH CONTEMPORARY GLOBAL POLITICS

MANASI SINHA

If anyone is much speculative about what constitutes India's new strategy towards contemporary world politics, Aditya Dhar's recent movie 'Uri: The Surgical Strike' could be a relevant signal in that direction. The movie Uri is potentially packaged with pointers towards what narratives 'New India' or Naya Hindustan aspires to project in the international arena. *The Hindu* (January 11, 2019) spells out this as 'Triumph of the will', delineating a new India "that doesn't believe in offering the other cheek when slapped on one—that believes in the policy of 'eent ka jawab patthar se (tit for tat)'—articulating power over peace and for paying back than being a pacifist." The movie is poised with a narrative that portrays India as an active player on the chessboard of the international matrix, unlike its past when it would cautiously design its defensive strategies to protect its sovereign polity and territorial integrity. Today, it engages more effectively to voice out its strategic importance to the world, stand out invincible to its potential enemy to wreak vengeance for any real or anticipated attacks rather than offering olive branches of negotiations to its neighbours that keep on snooping around its borders with malicious intentions of capturing Indian terrain or harbouring deadly militants.

Over the decade, India's position in global politics has been extensively articulated not only in terms of its structural transformations gained through economic and military calculations but also through ideational elements interlacing with soft-power politics. Albeit China's rise in global politics as an invincible force over the decade, to a large extent has served as a realistic ground for India to sharpen its global competence, but at the very least, the canvas of everchanging global politics thrust it further to shape its diplomatic strategies with global actors. The aspiration to become not only a 'rising power' but a 'leading power' in world politics resonates to a large extent with India's new strategic track that plays out diverse diplomatic strategies to make its presence felt and substantiated not only around its peripheral countries, but also the far-off seas and lands. This is symptomatic of what India's Prime Minister Narendra Modi spoke about a year after his entry into government in May 2014, when he declared India to be positioning itself in a leading role, rather than just a balancing force, globally. Modi's relentless interaction with international initiatives since then reflected this ever-growing self-confidence of India and its aspirations to become a leading power in international politics.

Raising itself from the shackles of colonialism, the newly independent India's foreign policy was primarily guided by the Nehruvian outlook of non-alignment. Throughout the Cold War period, India's position remained non-aligned, even though it made limited strategic engagement with either of the two superpowers in different circumstances. India's vantage point at that time was to lead through its moral leadership of the newly decolonised world. Although the end of the Cold War induced adjustment in India's foreign policy calculations, the philosophy of non-alignment remains unaltered throughout, and until the 1990s it was still designing its foreign policy around this wider philosophy to shape India's outlook towards the global world. While the Western nations were largely shaped through the principle of liberal internationalism, India found its solace in what it calls 'Westphalian internationalism'.

Major changes took place in India's conception of national interests and its engagement with global politics as the decade-long phase of the Cold War came to an end with the disintegration of the Soviet Union. The contemporary world order that demanded more of an extensive engagement with global institutions and new political actors in the international arena, had India making a move not as a dissident but as a proactive engager, dramatically shifting its strategic decision from its old stance on non-alignment. Major thrust under the Modi government to secure its national interests, strategic positions, and aspirations to become a key leader in global politics added further to this direction. Over the decade, India boosted its economy and forayed into multiple engagements with international actors on diverse avenues, adding up to diverse regional blocs, showcasing the strength of politico-cultural diplomacy, maritime politics, and scientific innovations—all that featured to engage in a multipolar world. Drawing its new outlook towards international politics, Jaishankar rightly spelled out that new India appears "more energetic and participative as compared to an earlier posture of abstention or non-involvement." To his view, after decades of non-alignment strategy, India seemingly has engaged more proactively to shape global outcomes and with the growing demands in the global order, India's shift in its stance on foreign policy in the last quarter of a decade has been momentous. Shedding some of its traditional reservations from a 'receiver' to 'actor' in global order enormously has defined the meaning of an expanded and embracing outlook that India holds towards the world.

To his view, the decade-long non-alignment policy no longer captures the needs of an international system and has outlived its utility for now. As such, Narendra Modi's decisive stand to not attend significant NAM summits in 2016 in Caracas and Baku, Azerbaijan in 2019, strongly is symbolic of contemporary India's estrangement from non-alignment as a strategic tool to pursue national interests. Responding to the needs of contemporary global politics, new strategic decisions and security initiatives are at play to shape India's foreign policy discourse at present. India's engagement in the Indo-Pacific and the QUAD dialogue becoming strategic initiatives that not only collaborate with global powers in balancing regional geopolitics in South Asia, but addressing diverse needs and interests in the region, significantly impact and enrich the coalesced actors. New Delhi's global engagement is perhaps more robust today than it has ever been before. India's willingness to step up to its global responsibilities, from climate change to global health, from institutional balancer to humanitarian crisis, to promoting values of democratic and cultural cooperation largely has turned its image as a 'leader' in global politics. India's humanitarian response to stave off COVID-19 pandemic and reaching out to its neighbours through its pharmaceuticals products and medicines seemingly have added to its leadership skills and ambitions.

Indian policymakers—pursuing the interests of India as a "leading power" with its aspirations and capabilities—seemingly have captured central attention in global political discourse in recent times. Washington's challenge to balance the power equation in South Asia and prioritising India to be an indispensable ally in confronting China in the region to balance it partly, have answered to the hitherto inertia the world has shown to India so far. The latter's emerging leadership in Asian geopolitics along with new regional architecture like QUAD and AUKUS transpires of what India as a leading power is becoming to transform and restructure the prevailing geopolitical churn in global politics. While spelling out India's strategic autonomy in global politics, Jaishankar opines that more than institutional bindings, what could drive India's engine in world politics is its move beyond formal alliance and taking advantage of various regional groupings depending on interests. Reiterating this, he spelled out that, "a more transactional ethos will promote *ad hoc* groupings of disparate nations who have a shared interest on a particular issue. This would be supported by requirements of working together and reaching out beyond alliances. The combination of these developments will encourage more regional and global balances with less global influence on their working (Jaishankar, *India Way*[1]). The reaffirmation of India-France commitment to the Indo-Pacific partnership is part of India's new strategic outreach to Europe in parallel with its deeper commitment to engaging Australia, Japan and the United States in the region. India's leadership vision for Indo-Pacific is strengthened by its effort to act as a potential bridge between different parts of the West and transatlantic initiatives. For the West, too, India has been seen as a leading voice of the Global South that brings more political legitimacy and sustainable power equations.

The nature of contemporary global politics is in a constant state of flux. Global actors are multiplying, even as rules are weakening. The old order is visibly changing, but the new one is not yet in sight. Unlike previous eras, where alliances seem to dominate the political discourse, at present, stable and bonding partnerships among global actors are laid down with common interests and nurturing transnational linkages. While the 20th century was largely shaped by the changing relations of the world's great powers, the 21st century is constantly becoming a political theatre of rebalancing the great powers, restructuring global economic and regional structures vis-à-vis geopolitical needs and interests. The last decade witnessed a repositioning of power centres, with the rise of China; the relative decline of American hegemony; the surge of populism in the Western democracies—all rendering the international system with much of uncertainty and disproportionate adjustments of global powers.

Unlike Morgenthau's state actors, although modern political actors seemingly have drawn away from deploying war and violence as a tool to exert power over each other, they seek to exercise their interests and agendas through diplomatic relations and forming strategic alliances based on common interests. More than a drive for the relentless struggle for power, the contemporary global powers operate through strategic instruments like bargaining with like-minded state actors to delimit the rise of a single power structure in the system, channelising resources to meet common goals and interests, creating norms to meet sustainable agendas, etc. At this juncture, India's rise to the horizon of a multipolar world as a 'balancer' or 'manager' in which global actors sought to have new aspirations and agendas to take control over the international power structure, was timely and significant. Today, as China rises, India cannot be oblivious to its geopolitical consequences, and as such India finds it imperative to sharpen its competitive instincts and strategic ambitions to become a global leader. In May 2014, India's Prime Minister Narendra Modi vociferously spelled out the nature of emerging global politics and the new role India was going to play in global politics. Positioning India's new avatar, he spelled out, "to help India position itself in a leading role, rather than just a balancing force, globally." The eventual international development reflected India's growing self-confidence, declaring that the country now "aspires to be a leading power, rather than just a balancing power." Modi's clarion call for India to assume a leading, rather than merely a balancing, role signifies larger ambitions. Unlike 'Great powers' that polarise the system, India as a 'leading power' exists within the dispositions created and defined by the great powers and shapes the politics in the system. The same is reiterated further when Indian Foreign Secretary, S. Jaishankar expressed, "India looks to transforming itself from a balancing power to a leading power" (Jaishankar 2015), in one of his maiden lectures at the International Institute for Strategic Studies on 'India, the United States and China'.

S. Jaishankar's exemplary work, *The India Way*, significantly sketches out how India should forge a foreign policy in a world that is mostly driven towards China's rise and assertiveness of major global powers. Contemplating the needs of a contemporary world, Jaishankar spells out that contemporary world politics demands a policy that does not believe in achieving peace by distancing from power dynamics but engaging deeply into it. For him "political romanticism", faith in the Non-Aligned Movement, is not much relevant today to deal with contemporary world politics as such India seeks to engage more closely with the permanent Five (US, Russia, China, UK and France) of the secutiy council as the council largely influences, scrutinizes and shapes the contemporary global politics more than institutional norms and rules. For S. Jaishankar, India has paced up its global position through diplomatic milestones in the last decade through "nuclear tests, nuclear deal and a tougher national security posture" and a closer engagement with the significant global actors.

India's leading role is fairly evident in diverse debates that figure around contemporary international politics. India has been vociferous about issues pertaining to existing disorder in global governance, in matters of required expansion of the United Nations Security Council (UNSC) and the Nuclear Suppliers Group (NSG), about the unsystematic factors of power transition and balancing the formidable challenge in the global order, etc., and has increasingly shown an affinity towards common global issues like climate change, counterterrorism, maritime security, military cooperation, non-proliferation of nuclear powers, digital connectivity among others. The realisation that bonding over issue-based cooperation is more effective and long-lasting is what drives the modern aspect of India's foreign diplomacy. As such in pursuit of its significant strategic ventures India has been constantly putting efforts to go beyond the traditional alliances and reaching out to the needs and interests of political actors over the decades. In a nutshell, India's willingness to engage and contribute to the geopolitical conundrum and the wider global interests of peace, security and governance extensively defines India's unique role in contemporary times. However, while venturing out to become a leading power in global politics, India has a few bottlenecks within and around its periphery. Notwithstanding India's stake in global leadership and progress in economic strides experienced in the post-Cold War period, poverty remains a stark reality, as a significant number of its population still remains below the poverty line. More so, traditional threats posed by issues of terrorism, and hostile neighbours along with in-house populist culture, inequality in socio-economic and political domains continue to overshadow India's strategic goals to be at par with global strategic interests.

While profound changes are taking place in contemporary world politics, with the relative decline of American supremacy over global governance, the rise of populist regimes in the West, and China's expansionist agenda to manoeuvre power structure of global politics, India's role is becoming notably demanding in the matrix of regional and global governance. Unlike its relatively passive role in matters of global governance and regional security issues in the past, it has started to project itself more as an assertive player (Pant 2016: 197-211). With the foci of contemporary international politics shifting from the West towards the South with pressing challenges from China and Pakistan, India is keen to lead the discourse in strengthening regional forces and governance structure to keep a check on any rising hegemon in South Asia, thus offering more stability and creditability to the world governance. At present, when the US is seemingly retreating from its global commitments and an emerging China gaining more power, and international institutions and norms are coming under massive pressure, India's leadership role becomes even more decisive and significant.

It is to put forth some of these pressing concerns and the imminent power transitions persisting in the global order and India's strategic decisions, that we seek to put forth in this collection of essays called **'The Decade of Power Politics'**. With the help of some young scholars and experts from India, we have brought together a kaleidoscopic view of contemporary world politics. It is an attempt to foray into the dynamic contours of contemporary power politics and its implications for India's international trajectory.

The rapid rise of China in the world system as an alternative hegemonic power considerably challenges the hitherto US hegemony. Over the decades, China has rapidly strengthened its economic, technological and military power with resultant changes in the geopolitical and strategic landscape of the world. This has major implications for the world order and India as well. In balancing the global ecology system and countering a rising China, no nation is more important to the USA than India. The compelling chapter **'Rising China as a Superpower: A Global Challenge to US Hegemony'** elaborates in great depth on the evolution of the People's Republic of China and its exemplary accomplishments over the decades within its territory and beyond. With its burgeoning power in South Asia, the chapter explains how China has been creating a security dilemma in the region and continues to pose wider challenges and complexities for India to deal with. As such it has become imperative for India and the US to engage in more effective strategic relations despite their own issues and challenges. This strategic relationship is significant for both actors. The USA sought to bolster India as a counterbalance to China to maintain the power balance in the South. And for India, coinciding with US interests and shared values possibly make its foreign policy more effective to run in the South Asia region and in the global arena.

With China's ever-growing expansion and strategic control in and around its neighbouring states, India seemingly has been caught up in an alarming situation. India's engagement as an active actor is more desired unlike in the past. As S. Jaishankar writes, "this is a time to engage America, manage China, cultivate Europe, reassure Russia, bring Japan into play"(2020). India's aspiration to manage global politics as well as counter China is what decides the future of India at present. India has a larger stake in the region not only in terms of preserving a democratic space with smaller states with which it shares inclusivity and freedom of navigation, but also a heavy traffic route that may get impassable in presence of any skirmishes or hegemonistic influence. For smaller states' claims and contestations over the South China Sea continue to shape the geopolitical discourse in the region. The chapter on '**The Periphery at Stake: India's Fight against China's Expansionist Policy**' has extensively framed around the dynamics at play that capture India's strategic interventions to counter China's expansionist policy in South Asia as well as narratives of small states and the existing operational complexities that shape the wider strategic environment in the region.

India's intensified strategic interests in South Asia got a setback as a tumultuous situation engulfs Afghanistan shaking its power structure in Kabul and setting up a new regime by the Taliban. This has profound consequences for the region. Not only is the multireligious and multi-ethnic region confronted with imminent threats of religious extremism and diktats of conservative governance, but there are also issues of gender violence and human rights violations which may challenge the overall stability in the region in the long run. The withdrawal of the American troops from Afghanistan, led to fissures in the new geopolitical theatre in the region with the confluence of multiple actors pulling the string in their own favour. An axis of regional powers such as China, Pakistan, Russia and the Taliban seemingly have captured the vacuum already resulting in a larger geopolitical nexus shaping the future in the region. What makes the matter one of concern is how the rise of an anti-America axis (China, Russia, Iran, Pakistan and a Taliban-led Afghanistan) and anti-American sentiments in the region would impact India's regional interests given that it has become closer to the US than ever before in history. In whatever scenario, India needs to ensure that it does not become a casualty on the South-Western Asian geopolitical chessboard. There are pressing issues and challenges including an increase in terrorism and a humanitarian crisis that India may get infected within the region. The region's terror ecosystem that was lessened by America's presence in the region is bound to change as the Taliban takes over the system. The chapter **'The Geopolitics in Afghanistan: Echoing the Tensions in South Asia'** discusses the most significant geopolitical catastrophic event of Afghanistan War. The author looks at the trajectory of Afghanistan's foreign policy transitioning from Cold War to post-Cold War till the present time and how the country shapes through different political regimes over the decades particularly in the wake of the recent crisis. The chapter anticipates the future of Afghanistan as it jostled with pressing conditions that may worsen with the Taliban regime coming into power. Because of the ongoing developments, India's strategic and regional ambitions may take a major hit in the years ahead.

Moving beyond South Asia, India has a great deal of interest in the Middle East and New Delhi is crafting strategies to strengthen its ties with Israel particularly after the Modi government came to power in 2014. Israel too is looking forward to strengthening its relations with India to gain more legitimacy and leverage to direct its actions in global politics. The chapter **'Strategic Partners: Mapping out the key issues and challenges between India and Israel'** examines Indo-Israel relations through different phases and how it has shaped and transformed the formal bilateral relations into a comprehensive and strategic relationship over the decade. The chapter underscores the new dynamics and avenues the duo are exploring including maritime security, intelligence, and digital governance in order to strengthen their relations.

Indo-Pacific geography is a new nomenclature that has emerged recently yet has gained major significance in twenty-first-century power politics. Albeit lately, with China starting to rise and exerting its power from Oceania to Middle East and beyond to the coast of Africa, the Indo-Pacific region becoming a focal point for global actors so as to maintain the balance of power in the region, and as such India was necessarily seen as a balancer in the region. India's role as a natural ally is linked with its cultural-historical relations with South Asian countries where India had played an active role historically. Despite the weakening of India's historical commitment towards these countries in the last few decades, India sought to restore the same recently through inclusive economic and maritime engagements with South Asian countries. Diverse studies indicate Indo-Pacific region becoming a political theatre of both opportunities and conflicts. While partnerships with the big powers are evident and crucial, India's focus on the Island nations in the Pacific and Indian ocean arrest imminent needs and concerns. The chapter, **'The Tryst between India and Small Islands Nations: A Nautical Dimension of India's Indo-Pacific Policy'** looks at the rise of Indo-Pacific narrative vis-à-vis small islands and inherent issues pertaining to them. It offers an account of how the politics of Small Islands in the Indo-Pacific regions has implications for India's strategic, geopolitical and security interests in the region. How the exisitng instability, the power transition, and the structural shift in the region largely impacts India's Indo-Pacific policy towards these Indo-Pacific Island nations. The author argues here that India's partnership with small islands is imperative as it forms the bedrock that shapes India's Indo-Pacific approach. The foreign policy choices of these Small Island nations will have a bearing impact on India's security environment in the region.

As the Indo-Pacific region turns into a major geopolitical theatre for major powers, it demands more of India's increased strategic position in the region. While issues and challenges persist in the Indo-Pacific, the absence of substantive and robust institutions had resulted in distressing power transition in the region. Over the years, the formation of QUAD—India, US, Japan, and Australia—has meted out the emerging needs of an effective and impactful mix of soft-power dynamics and hard-ball measures as necessary in ensuring shared progress, peace and security, territorial integrity, and economic prosperity in the sensitive Indo-Pacific and beyond. The idea behind the cooperation among these like-minded democracies is to contain destabilising forces manifested by coercive economic practices together with unsettling military manoeuvring in the Indo-Pacific in a more effective manner. The QUAD acts as a power equilibrium in the region as it is encased with strategic issues that not only dealing with regional developments but also involve in securing free and open access to Indo-Pacific, partnering on emerging technologies and cyberspace, enhacing Vaccine diplomacy to tackle COVID 19 pandemic, issues related to climate change among other imminent problems. Additionally India constantly advocates an enhanced multidimensional role of the QUAD in synergising and strengthening maritime security and territorial sovereignty in the Indo-Pacific region. All these initiatives seemingly have deepen the shared vision and priorities and glued these four democracies together by an urgent need to cope with China's rising economic, technological and military might. The chapter **'India's Soft Power in Consolidating QUAD'** is compelling research illustrating the dynamics of QUAD and its strategic interests and ambitions in the region. The chapter extensively spells out the close cooperation of QUAD partners in diverse strategic areas like culture, pharmaceuticals, medical tourism, human assistance, disaster relief and digital connectivity, etc. What the chapter offers is an exploration of new strategic areas that are enhancing cooperation, and wholly address pressing multilateral, security and geopolitical concerns.

The Arctic region has recently assumed considerable geopolitical significance in global politics. With multiple power centres putting their influence in the region as legitimate members of the Arctic Council, India's strategic engagement is timely and significant. Its current observer status in the Arctic Council has received some political mileage, although it has to find more avenues to serve its purpose. There are potentials and constraints too. While India's newly drafted Arctic Policy (IAP), 2021 is a striking tool to boost India's scientific diplomacy in the Arctic region, it has also come as a shot for India to balance the geopolitics in the region. With its global ranking (currently at third) in scientific research and development, it has not only been able to support climatic concerns but also has placed itself in the strategic milieu of the big powers, the USA, China, Russia, etc. The draft also acts as a balancing factor against the expansionist and ambitious China in the region. Although through its 'Polar Silk Road' (part of Belt and Road Initiative), initiative, China is spanning and influencing its geopolitical and geo-economic posture in the region, India's 'sustainable engagement' diplomacy and 'SciTech' initiatives have been far-reaching and more effective in reaching out to the Arctic circle nations and its allies in the region. The scientific engagement through Himadri station in particular has been a great initiative that balances existing terrain of power and competition exerted by China which has reasonably worried the strong players like Russia, Canada and Norway in the region for a while now. The chapter **'Geopolitical Competition in the Arctic Circle'** helps the readers to understand the prevailing geopolitical contestation and competition of various regional powers and how rapidly it is also becoming a turf of another great game. It also explores the implications of India's engagement with the region as a newcomer. The chapter considers diverse issues ranging from energy, climate change, security issues and all that form the dynamic aspects of what great powers seek to engage in as part of their Arctic exploration and diplomatic relations and how this has wider implications for global politics and governance.

India's consistent engagement with multilateral international institutions, particularly the United Nations (UN), is one of the trademarks of its soft power as a rising force in the international community. Historically, India's non-aligned stand has frustrated Western powers by what they believed India's repugnance to conform to unique global issues of climate change and nuclear proliferation. The perception of India as a multilateral naysayer and obstructionist has long influenced India's stability in global politics. However, India has been able to overcome such claims and has created new realities in contemporary times. Over the decade India has integrated itself within the global order through its phenomenal economic growth, strategic steps, diplomatic functions and engagement in multilateral issues and institutions. The values of interdependence and cooperation with global players define the core interests of India's nature of multilateral engagement. India's proactive engagement in global trade, climate change, and development policy debates are reflective of some of India's global commitments in contemporary times. **'India's Foreign Policy towards Multilateral Institutions'** explores how India's engagement in multilateral institutions has shaped India's wider geopolitical reality. The chapter discusses in great detail India's engagement with multilateral actors beyond traditionally defined bilateral ones. Examples like India-China cooperation at BRICS are exemplary of India's larger commitment and responsibility towards multilateral blocs despite pressing challenges between the countries. The chapter puts forth the significance of multilateral institutions in global politics and India's greater responsibility towards the same.

Notwithstanding India's aspirations and extensive engagements in world politics, there are conflicting views that refute India's leading position in global politics and corroborate reasons that considerably express India as a reticent nation. Considering India's tenacious problems of development and other disadvantages like nuclear power, military, population size, combined growing economic growth, John Garver (2002)[2] predicted twenty years ago, that India may not make a rising power and China would probably supersede India in the run-up to regional power game, notably in South Asia. Reiterating the same, Manjari Chatterjee Miller has engaged in this discussion with her fascinating book, *Why Nations Rise: Narratives and the Path to Great Power* (2021),[3] in which she spelled out thought-provoking arguments about why some rising powers, like China, could become great powers while others, like India, do not. Assessing this, Miller argued that, besides material capabilities, what significantly creates rising great powers are the ways in which different states direct their own role in global politics—this is what Millar terms 'national narratives'—and become integral to the assessment of state power. She holds that "if a country seeks to increase its relative material power without attempting either to acquire global authority or to court both external and internal recognition of itself as a great power in the making, it is unlikely to become a great power" (p. 10). For her, rising powers that constantly approve and materialise ideas and initiatives of great-powers, seemingly have emerged as great powers, while those lacking such adaptation remain what Miller terms 'reticent' nations on the global stage.

Miller argues that while India's potential to emerge as a great power in the post-Cold War world was laden with opportunities and prospects, India could not seize upon such opportunities as it remained rooted in ideas that it propounded during the Cold War. Additionally, India's reluctance to embrace multilateralism the way China did, and not reaching out to its peripheral neighbours and to the far-off nations to contain China's rising status initially put India in a relatively weaker position than China. In her words, "although India was rapidly increasing in both military and economic strength,

Indian officials did not seem to have consistent and concrete narratives about what that could mean, how India could use its rise for leverage, or what kind of great power India could become" (p. 3). However, Harsh V. Pant, poses a different opinion against such a narrow perception about India's status as a reticent nation. Rebutting Miller's idea, he highlights how the comparison between China and India in terms of their rising power status neglects India's strength in democratic institutions that have largely shaped and created narratives of India as a rising power over the decades, and the same has been substantially missing in the case of the authoritarian state, China. To him, India's engagement with the global world is perhaps more robust today than ever before. While China's position has been more belligerent and less multilateral in nature over the decade, India scored its position better by openly embracing the West. Most of India's efforts mirror its willingness to share global responsibilities and governance structure. The recent engagement of India in the United Nations as a non-permanent member of the UNSC, and the humanitarian assistance that is provided through the global pharmacy hub during COVID-19 translate its aspirations to becoming a leading global power. Although China's hegemonic influence in South Asia decides most of India's geopolitical necessity and partnership with like-minded countries for greater security, stability and peace, it is more of India's stand on democratic, shared global values and cooperative governance that strengthen its image at the global level. Notwithstanding pressing issues and challenges within, India continues to strive to craft and recrafting its narratives to reach out to the larger global audience for gaining legitimacy to lead at the global level. And the new discourse on India's foreign policy aspires to evolve around these newly defined goals to shape India's new image for a new world.

Notes

1. S. Jaishankar, *The India Way: Strategies for an uncertain world* (New Delhi: Harper Collins India, 2020).
2. Also see J. Garver "Asymmetrical Indian and Chinese Threat Perceptions", *Journal of Strategic Studies*, 25/4 (2002), pp. 109-34.
3. Manjari Chatterjee Miller, *Why Nations Rise: Narratives and the Path to Great Power* (USA: Oxford University Press, 2021).

RISING CHINA AS A SUPERPOWER STATE: A GLOBAL CHALLENGE TO US HEGEMONY

RASHMI SINGH

Introduction

In international history, the Chinese history is found to be very attractive as well as complicated in nature. The culture of China has been observed as peace and like a war. China was formed after winning many wars and ruled by several kings. However, China has faced a period of peace as well as trading with the neighbours too. There was a time period when China isolated itself from external influences which made it a closed society. This phase and experience are reflected in the culture of China and in its strategic thinking.

The past hundred years were easy-going for China. Japanese rule during the time period of the 1930s as well as the 1940s, along with Civil War, had been the reason for Mao Zedong and the Chinese Communist Party (CCP) to come into power in the year 1949. It was a very volatile period in the history of China. The Civil War led to the formation of the People's Republic of China (PRC). However, this was the advent of the next phase of isolation in which China tried to make itself stronger. When Mao ruled, China managed to become independent with every kind of resource along with technology, Still, it was lagging behind two or three decades in achieving modern standards of technology at par with other Western nations.

When the period of globalisation, liberalisation and privatisation started, China kept up approaches which made the Chinese economy exceptionally destitute, and development was not happening. There was the control of central government, and the Chinese economy was not connected with the economy of the world. The primary reason for isolating itself was the Chinese communist ideology where the market is under the control of the state. Subsequently, when Deng Xiaoping became the chief person of Chinese modernisation, China started trading with foreign countries and actualised free-market changes in 1979. Over a period of time, with the average growth of 9.5% in the Gross Domestic product (GDP) in 2018, China became the fastest growing economy, as depicted by the World Bank, *"the fastest sustained expansion by a major economy in history"* (Service, 2019). This development helped in empowering China to double its GDP in the time period of eight years which made a difference in uplifting around 800 million individuals from destitution. China got the chance to be the biggest economic producer, stock dealer, and holder of foreign traders in the world. China became a major commercial partner of the USA.

China is the largest trading partner of the United States, and third largest trade market for the United States. In addition to this, China is the main foreign holder of the depository securities of America, that help to store the obligation of the government and keep the interest rates of the US low.

As the economy of China developed, the growth in its GDP has now fallen from 14.2% in 2007 to 6.6% in 2018, and the International Monetary Fund (IMF) projected this development to tumble to 5.5% by 2024 (EveryCRSReport, 2019). The Chinese government has accepted lower monetary development, calling it the "new normal", and realised the need to accept a new model for development, which would not be dependent much on fixed trade and investment, but would focus more on private utilisation, administration, and advancement for financial development. Such changes are required for China to try not to hit the "middle-income trap" when nations accomplish a specific financial level yet start to encounter forcefully decreasing monetary development rates since they can't embrace new wellsprings of financial development.

The government of China has focused on development in its monetary planning through various activities, for example, "*Made in China 2025*" (Kania, 2019), an arrangement which was declared in 2015 to update and modernise manufacturing of China in ten key areas through broad government assistance which can help the country to become a significant worldwide player among these areas. Although, such kinds of measures have progressively created worries that China means to utilise modern strategies to diminish the country's dependence on foreign innovation and eventually rule worldwide business sectors.

The increasing worldwide monetary influence of China and the financial arrangements it follows for trade produce are of critical impact for the United States and, consequently, of significant interest to Congress. China is a developing business area for US firms, however, its fragmented changes to the economy considered as free market have brought about financial strategies which may have negative impacts on the financial interests of the United States, such as industrial policies and theft of US licensed innovation.

China's ascent from a developing agricultural nation to a significant financial power in around forty years has been praiseworthy. From 1979 (when financial changes started) to 2017, China's genuine Gross Domestic Product (GDP) developed at a normal yearly pace of almost 10%. As per World Bank, "China has experienced the fastest sustained expansion by a major economy in history, and has lifted more than 800 million people out of poverty" (Bank). China has arisen as a significant worldwide monetary force. For instance, it positions first in respect of monetary size on a Purchasing Power Parity (PPP) premise, stock exchange, and its foreign trade reserves.

The sudden financial development of China has prompted a significant expansion in bilateral business ties with the United States. As per US exchange information, complete exchange between both the nations developed from $5 billion in 1980 to $660 billion in 2018. China is right now the United States' largest product exchanging accomplice, its third largest fare market, and its biggest wellspring of imports. Numerous US organisations have broad tasks to sell their items in the flourishing market and for China to make cheap labour advantageous for trade arranged manufacturing. Those activities have encouraged several industries of the US to be competitive at the global level and have provided US buyers with an assortment of merchandise. China's huge acquisition of US treasury securities, which added up to $1.1 trillion as of April 2019, have empowered the national government to finance its budget deficits, and its help keep interest rates of US generally low.

Nonetheless, the development of China as a significant financial power has created tensions among US policymakers. Many opine that China uses unfair trade practices (for example, an underestimated money and endowments given to domestic manufacturers) to flood markets of the US with minimal cost products. Many claim that the utilisation of modern strategies by China to develop Chinese firms with government support, and its inability to take positive steps against violation of and threat to Intellectual Property Rights (IPR) of Americans in China, subvert the competitive nature of intensive ventures of the US. Likewise, as China is becoming an enormous and developing business sector for US products, critics claim that various exchange and venture obstructions limit openings for US companies to trade in the Chinese market, or force them to create production facilities in China as the cost of working there.

The Chinese authorities see a developing economy as crucial to keeping up friendly steadiness. Nonetheless, China faces various major financial difficulties that could halt development in future, including twisted monetary strategies that have brought about over-belief on fixed venture and fares for monetary development (as opposed to buyer interest), government support for state-owned firms, weak system of banking, enlarging pay holes, population growth, and the general absence of law and order in China. The government of China has recognised these issues and has promised to manage them by carrying out arrangements to build the market at the economic level, support advancement, attract consumers to spend the main impetus of the economy, extend social well-being net coverage, empower the improvement of less-contaminating enterprises (like administrations), and get serious about true corruption by government. The capability of the Chinese authorities to execute such changes will probably decide if China keeps on increasing general rates of quick monetary development, or otherwise keeps on encountering lower rates of development.

China's developing financial power has driven it to be progressively associated with worldwide financial arrangements and undertakings, particularly framework improvement. China's "Belt and Road Initiative" (BRI) addresses a great technique by China to back foundation all through Asia, Africa, and Europe. If successful, China's financial activities could fundamentally extend fare and venture markets for China and enhance its "soft power" at the international level

Economic and Military Reforms of China

- The History of Economic Development of China: Chinese Economy Prior to Reforms

Before 1979, during the administration of Chairman Mao Zedong, China kept a centrally governed economy. An enormous portion of the nation's financial yield was coordinated and constrained by the Central government, that planned production objectives, controlled costs, and distributed assets all through the majority of its economy. At the time of the 1950s, the entirety of the household firms in China were organised into huge communities. To speed up industrialisation, the government invested on a large scale on both physical as well as human resources during the 1960s and 1970s. Subsequently, by 1978 almost three-fourths of the production of industries was manufactured by centrally administered and state-owned enterprises (SOEs), as indicated by centrally arranged yield targets. Private endeavours and foreign contributed firms were by and large banned. The main aim of the Chinese authorities was to make the economy of China moderately independent. Foreign exchange was restricted to getting those products that couldn't be produced or manufactured in China. These policies produced contortions inside the economy of the country. Since a large portion of the economy was overseen and managed by the government, there was no mechanism in the market to proficiently designate assets, and hence there were few incentives for firms, labourers, and ranchers to be more gainful or under stress on what they have created as well as about its quality (since they were chiefly centred around creation objectives set by the public authority).

As indicated by Chinese government measurements, China's genuine Gross Domestic Product (GDP) developed at a normal yearly pace of 6.7% from 1953 to 1978, however, the accuracy of this information has been questioned by numerous examiners, many of them claiming that at this time, Chinese authorities (particularly at the local levels) frequently overstated the levels of production for various political reasons. According to financial specialist Angus Maddison, China's real average annual Gross Domestic Product

(GDP) growth at this time was about 4.4% (Maddison, 2007). Likewise, China's economy endured a huge financial decline at the time of Chairman Mao Zedong. From 1950 to 1978, the per capita GDP of China on the basis of Purchasing Power Parity (PPP), a typical estimate of a nation's expectations for everyday comforts, doubled. In any case, from 1958 to 1962, Chinese expectations for everyday comforts decreased around 20.3%, and between 1966 and 1968, they decreased by 9.6% (see Figure 2.1). Moreover, the development in Chinese expectations for everyday comforts pales when compared to those in the West, such as Japan.

In 1978, soon after the passing of Chairman Mao, the Chinese authorities chose to give up its Soviet-style financial strategies by progressively making positive changes in the economy as per free-market principles in consonance with Chinese communist ideology, and starting up investment and trade along with the West, with the expectation that it may fundamentally enhance growth at the financial level as well as living conditions. Chinese pioneer, Deng Xiaoping, the planner of economic reforms, said: "*Black cat, white cat, what does it matter what colour the cat is as long as it catches mice?*" (Buckle, 2018).

Chinese's Economic Reforms: An Introduction

With the advent of the year 1979, various financial reforms were launched by China. The government started providing ownership as well as subsidies to farmers in order to keep them motivated, that empowered them to sell a part of their harvests in the free market. Also, the government set up four uncommon monetary zones at the side of coast to pull in and attract foreign ventures, enhance exports, and bring in high innovation items into China. Extra changes, which continued, looked to decentralise financial policymaking in various areas, particularly in trade. Financial control of different ventures was taken by local authorities, and were permitted to work and contend on principles of free market, and were free from following and bearing principles of state planning. Likewise, residents were urged to begin their own businesses. Extra waterfront districts and urban areas were assigned as open urban communities and improvement zones, which permitted them to explore different avenues regarding reforms of free market and to draw in investments by foreigners by providing subsidies in trade to motivate them. Likewise, state control of the prices of a wide range of items was eliminated slowly. A significant key to China's financial success was trade exchange and liberalisation too. Eliminating trade obstructions supported more competition. China's continuous application of monetary changes looked to recognise which policies delivered positive outcomes financially (and which didn't) with the goal that they can be applied in different regions of China. Deng Xiaoping allegedly called this process "crossing the river by touching the stones" (Chunsheng, 2018).

Reforms and Growth of Chinese Economy: 1979 to Present

Right from the introduction of financial changes, China's economy has developed significantly quicker if compared to the period before reforms in economic policies, and, generally, has dodged major monetary disruptions. Between 1979 and 2018, the average annual GDP of China was 9.5%. This has proved China's ability to double its economy after eight years on an average. The worldwide financial decline, which started in 2008, essentially influenced the Chinese economy in a negative manner. China's media detailed in 2009 that 20 million transient labourers had returned as they lost their professional work because of the economic crisis, and GDP in the final quarter of 2008 had tumbled to 6.8% year after year. The Chinese government reacted by executing a $586 billion financial package, focused to a great extent at funding foundation and slackening money related policies to expand bank lending. Such strategies enabled China to face the impacts of the worldwide decline in demand for Chinese goods. From 2008 to 2010, GDP development of China was 9.7% on average. Although, GDP growth rate declined for the next six years. According to the IMF's April 2019 World Economic Outlook, China's genuine GDP development will moderate every year throughout the following six years, tumbling to 5.5% in 2024 (Figure 2.2). Financial experts caution that China's monetary development may be moderated more if China and the United States keep on overwhelming reformatory monetary measures against one another, such tariff climbs that have come about because of the action of the US under Section 301 and counter of China. According to the Organization for Economic

Figure 1: China's Annual GDP Growth: 2007-2018 and Projections through 2024

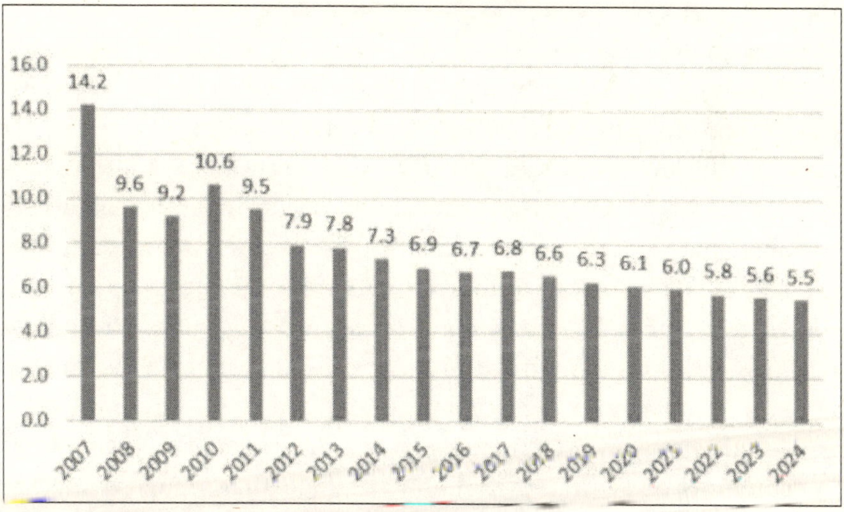

Source: https://www.researchgate.net/publication/348135738_The_Big_Boom_of_Chinese_Economy_How_Did_China_Succeded_An_Analysis_of_Chinese_Growth_For_40_Years_1980-2020 and Projections through 2024

Cooperation and Development (OECD), expanded taxes on all exchanges in-between China and the United States could decrease China's GDP by 1.1% in 2021-2022 compared with the OECD's baseline monetary projections.

Military Reforms in China

The government of China is attempting to build its military stronger, more effective, and technologically advanced to turn into a top-level power in 30 years. With the budget of the past ten years, the People's Liberation Army (PLA) as of now is positioned among the world's top militaries in areas which include anti-ship ballistic missiles (ASBM) and artificial intelligence.

The advanced Chinese military started functioning during the time of civil war (1927-1949) in between Nationalist Kuomintang powers and Chinese Communist Party (CCP). The guerrilla-style armed force depended on a mass activation of Chinese residents, and the PLA generally saved this hierarchical design in the coming ten years to secure its boundaries.

A defining moment came during the 1990s, when the CCP saw two exhibitions of US military force in the Eastern regions, "the Gulf War and the Taiwan Strait Crisis". Struck by the refinement of US powers, Chinese pioneers recognised that China did not have the capability to wage an advanced war and keep foreign forces from mediating in the region. The Chinese Authorities pushed to get up to speed with top-level militaries by expanding defence spending, putting resources into new weapons to improve Anti-Acess/Area Denial, and setting up projects to support the defence industry of China.

Another move started in 2012, when the leadership powers went in the hands of President Xi Jinping. Supporting what he referred to as the Chinese Dream, a dream to re-establish China's status as a great power. President Jinping has pushed military reforms too, compared to his predecessors. The Central Military Commission was led by President Xi, which is the top most decision making entity of PLA, and he has focused on delivering a "world- class force" that can overwhelm the Asia-Pacific and "fight and win" worldwide conflicts by 2049.

The focus of Xi Jinping was on making huge, primary reforms. Among his most critical changes are new joint theatre orders, profound staff cuts, and enhancements to military-citizen coordinated efforts. He is pushing to change the PLA from a generally regional power into a significant maritime force.

People's Liberation Army (PLA)

The PLA is the biggest force and was considered the most significant, yet its prominence has faded as Beijing tries to build up a coordinated battling power with top-notch maritime and air capacities. As different administrations extended, the Army has 2,183,000 active personnel and 510,000 reserve troops, as indicated by the *Global Firepower* (Shukla, 2020). Over a period of time, changes have aimed at smoothing out its cumbersome order structure, making more modest, more dexterous units, and engaging lower-level authorities. The military is additionally redesigning its weapons. Its 'lightweight Type 15 tank', for instance, came into administration in 2018 and considers commitment in high-elevation zones, like Tibet and Xinjiang.

People's Liberation Army Navy (PLAN)

The PLA naval force has overhauled and modernised at an amazing rate to turn into the world's biggest maritime power as to numbers of ships and submarines. In 2016, it authorised 18 boats, while the Naval force of US dispatched five. The PLA's boat quality has likewise improved significantly, and at par with the US's.

Regional experts say the naval force, which has an expected 250,000 dynamic service individuals, has become the prevailing power in China's close proximity's oceans and is directing more tasks at more noteworthy distances. Its modernisation needs to incorporate more atomic submarines and aircraft carriers. China has two aircraft carriers, against the United States' eleven. A third carrier is relied upon to be operational by 2022, which is being manufactured domestically.

People's Liberation Army Air Force (PLAAF)

Additionally, the PLAAF has developed, with 395,000 dynamic help individuals in 2018. It has procured advanced hardware, some ideas to be duplicated from taken US plans, which include airborne warning and control frameworks, aircraft, and automated flying vehicles. The aviation-based armed forces also have an assortment of stealth aircraft, which include J-20 warriors. In 2015, RAND Corporation assessed that a good proportion of China's warriors and fighter planes were modern.

People's Liberation Army Rocket Force (PLARF)

PLARF is responsible for keeping up conventional and atomic rockets of China. The rocket power was raised to an autonomous assistance during changes in 2015. It has almost 120,000 dynamic soldiers. China has consistently expanded its atomic arsenal, as per estimations it had 290 warheads in 2019 with modernised capabilities, which includes the advancement of "Anti-Ship Ballistic Missiles (ASBM)" which could target warships of the US in the Western Pacific, as it is a feature of its A2/AD methodology. China apparently owns cruise missiles, and weapons that as of not long ago the United States and Russia were restricted from manufacturing. The PLA is manufacturing hypersonic rockets too, which travel at speeds quicker than the speed of sound and hence are difficult for enemies to safeguard against.

People's Liberation Army Strategic Support Force (PLASSF)

Set up during the reforms of 2015, the Strategic Support Force deals with the electronic warfare of PLA, its cyberwarfare, psychological activities, among other innovative and technological missions. With an expected 145,000 help individuals, it is additionally answerable for the military's space activities, incorporating those with satellites.

Figure 2: China's Military Regions

Areas of responsibility

Central Command
Beijing, security for CCP leadership, and support to other theaters

Northern Command
Korean Peninsula, borders with Russia and Mongolia, and Yellow Sea

Western Command
Border with India and counterterrorism

Eastern Command
Taiwan, East China Sea and the Senkaku/Diaoyu Islands, and Japan

Southern Command
South China Sea and borders with Southeast Asian countries

Source: Stratfor, US Department of Defense

How Much Does PRC Spend on Its Military?

The Finance Ministry of PRC stated that the 2021 budget of defence is $210 billion (Char, 2021); nonetheless, experts estimate that Beijing exaggerates what they actually spend. The PLA developed a taking off financial plan as the economy of China boomed in the recent decade. The investment on defense expanded more than seven times, from $88 billion in 1998 to $189 billion in 2018, as per the Stockholm International Peace Research Institute (SIPRI), which makes it the second-biggest investor in the world, after the United States.

Challenges to US Hegemony with China's Burgeoning

"When China awakes it will shake the world".

—Napoleon Bonaparte

In just a period of thirty years, China emerged from an ineptitude and backward nation to the dominant position in international politics. China is obviously en route to recapturing its historic place as the largest economy in the whole world, replacing the United States. The possibility of predominant wealth of China and its influence, combined with the downgrading of the financial as well as political prestige of the United States, has prompted mounting theory about China's rise as a worldwide hegemon to challenge and, maybe, outperform the United States.

Not long before, during the Cold War, the system of the world was characterised with the connection of the Soviet Union and USA as the masters of adversary alliances of countries. Reviewing this, a few intellectuals anticipate the reappearance of a bipolar world wherein the United States and China practise joint initiative in a so-called "G-2" (Bush, 2011). With the break-up of the Soviet Union, American leadership left with no rivals after Washington became the dominating power. The United States, that is the largest investor in its military in comparison to the other nations in the world, has a military presence in each part of the world. Some envision China as a "peer competitor" to dominate at the global level.

When Deng Xiaoping spoke at the General Assembly of the United Nations in New York in 1974, since then, China has been careful to deny any likelihood that it may look for any kind of dominance. 'White paper', as a Chinese defence, stated, "*China will never seek hegemony or engage in military expansion now or in the future, no matter how developed it becomes.*" With this statement, China is unintentionally repeating the American non-interventionists of the 19th as well as early 20th century. After then, the United States didn't try to rule or control the global system of nations, nor did it seek military solutions for issues which were a long way from its shores. However, as time passed and in response to various situations, the United States did both.

China is back after a few terrible centuries. It accepts, with some defence, that for the greater part in its history, it was the biggest, richest, well governed, and innovatively most progressed society on Earth. China overflows with certainty that it may recapture this status, which it thinks to be characteristic of international affairs, and it will do as such in this century. In comparison other emerging powers with shorter histories such as France, Germany, the United States, the USSR, Japan, are not useful in foreseeing the outcome of the rise of China. China does not have any messianic philosophy to trade, no beliefs of "manifest destiny" to propel, no faith in social Darwinism or basis of expansion of territory to follow up on, no clique of the champion to energise militarism or praise war, no avoidance from present worldwide administration to survive, no settlements abroad or philosophical conditions to ensure, no set of experiences of projection of power or military mediation beyond its boundaries nearby, no twisted coalitions or bases abroad.

China has an extremely interesting clarification about its national interests. According to China, it requires domestic serenity and tranquillity at its borders to seek its modernisation and financial development. It appears to be entirely fine with a multipolar world order, in which harmony and financial development prevail. However, anyone having the experience of negotiating with China can confirm that it has capability for both haughtiness and irritability. This appears to have been shown at Copenhagen. How an even more advanced China behaves later on will be evident to some degree by Chinese real factors as transformed with the history of China. However, Chinese conduct will depend upon how the other nations in the world, along with the eminently occupant hegemon, the United States, respond and interface with China as it rises. Furthermore, Chinese behaviour in future can't be isolated from the personality of China's domestic governmental issues. An autocracy that doesn't hesitate to overlook rule of law at domestic level is probably not going to concede to international law and system at global level.

Whatever the significance of China's affirmations that it doesn't seek hegemony or take part in military expansionism in coming times, we can't be sure that it won't. There is reason for hope, particularly concerning China's utilisation of military force. The history of China includes instances of forceful activities at its borders, particularly in Vietnam and Korea. Yet, generally, China has been known for its mindful, careful, and internal public safety act. The Great Wall symbolises an image of abandoning of Ming fleet in 1437. In spite of a considerable history of development in military innovation and warfare on a comparable scale with its tremendous population and immense size, Chinese diplomatic custom emphasises that armaments are hazardous devices to be utilised when the utilisation of power is not avoidable.

China has utilised power when estimates short of war have proved ineffective to save its borders or basic profits (such as in Korea, Vietnam and India), at the same time, by stamped appear differently in relation to India in Goa or with Indonesia in Timor-

Leste, this allowed diplomacy the many years expected for the resolution of the Hong Kong as well as Macau conflicts without any bloodshed. China was inclined towards negotiations instead of utilising power to resolve the Taiwan issue. Tensions at Cross-Strait are reducing. China has demanded United Nations approval for its military exercises at international level, which are aimed at keeping peace and preventing theft.

China is still developing its military at an unconventional state of time. The United States acquired overall military prevalence after the break-up of the USSR. It has accepted the neo-traditionalist plan of supporting this predominance no matter what. However, the rising defence abilities of China disintegrate the supremacy of the United States. China's new weapons imperil US power projection abilities in Western Pacific. China's anti-satellite projects jeopardise US worldwide reconnaissance and communications abilities, its developing operations on the internet hazard the operations of the US government and its economy. These are serious threats not just for the hegemony of the US but for its core interests as well. They have now started to cause a reaction.

The outcome is a profoundly bad military relationship between the US and China in spite of reducing possibilities of battle across the Strait of Taiwan. China will persist in its endeavours to assemble a tenable response to American pressure. The United States won't withdraw its obsession with outright military presence all over the world. A less domineering target would permit the US to oblige a more remarkable China while holding the capacity to exist in any conflict with it. Military conflict between China and the United States is possible if conclude the present conditions.

These intrinsic anxieties, alongside those emerging because of much more imbalance of bilateral trade in favour of China, are the reasons why US-China duopoly such as G-2 is not feasible regardless of whether it was desirable, which it wasn't. However, the economy of the world is going to observe the uprooting of the United States from its twentieth-century transcendence. China will come together with the US, Japan and the EU in the top list. Others in G-20 such as India, Russia and Brazil will follow. The hegemony of a couple of nations is not what is in prospect, however, it is opposite, economic power in the multipolar world.

Like Japan, China is, obviously, a nation with the population which is much more than it can support prosperously through its own resources, enormous as they are. Also, China is behind in the quest to get raw materials for its expanding ventures. China's vital interests are within the propagation of a worldwide financial order open for investment and trade. China is presently tangled with multilateral associations in which it should show its devotion daily to the sovereign uniformity of countries, small or big. This authorises the regard for comity which is the quintessence of a "responsible stakeholder". It enlightened Chinese bank of people about Governor Zhou Xiaochuan's wary idea that it is smarter to deal against the dollar being down to a reasonable global job than to make it break down.

However, Americans are clumsy at managing autonomous centres of power. For as far back as twenty years the United States was the undisputed worldwide hegemon. For a time period of 40 years prior to this, the USA was the vital referee of the coalition of countries known as the "free world". Politicians of the USA are not accustomed to making policy by making multilateral consultations with different countries. China is not good in this either, however it appears to be more open-minded to this in comparison with the United States. America will, as usual, perform what should be performed, after it has depleted the entirety of the other options. However, it will require significant time period and cost and further impact and prestige of the United States. In the meantime, China's worldwide job will develop, particularly if Beijing beholds the humility and ability to what its representatives or diplomats have gotten known, instead of the arrogant nature which a few domestic authorities of China progressively epitomise.

The Communist Party of China has conveyed success to common Chinese, that is the reason they support it. No less than 86% of Chinese believe their nation is in the correct direction. China observes evidence of the prevalence of it's political-economy in evident adequacy of its reaction to the economic smash and the consequences of the same. The policies of Chinese government have so far prospered with regard to sustaining high rates of financial growth with the help of programmes which upgrade long-lasting financial as well as rational competitiveness. So far, Americans have contracted with the hard choices important to re-establish monetary trustworthiness towards their government or to invert genuine rot in their country's human as well as physical infrastructure. This downturn has contributed to the foreign conflicts and proceeding with decay in relationship to the Islamic nations as an elementary reason speeding up the decline of Americans.

China appears to be sure to rise up out of the problem with a much bigger and stronger economy. People who were brought into the world under the policy of single-child are growing. It is definitely more slanted to utilisation than its economic predecessors. A quicker progress to development operates by domestic utilisation than many have suspected conceivable appears to be in prospect. Imports of China are presently rising substantially more quickly than its exports. Its equilibrium of instalments excess, immense as it actually is, fell considerably in 2009. Proceeding with financial development, extended bonds with Asian neighbours, the reformist globalisation of a yuan which is ascending in value, all guarantee stability at domestic level and, more noteworthy worldwide, height of China in upcoming time period.

The present self-congratulatory mindset in China is hence totally justifiable. However, it covers the fundamental shortcoming of the political system of the Chinese. The contemporary Chinese government infers its authenticity primarily from its capacity to convey rapid monetary development. It represents no reliable qualities, it does not trust and is not even believed by those whom it rules, experiences an undeniable degree of corruption, and doesn't have any reasonable goal for personal growth. If the politics of the United States is broadly seen as so dishonest as to be useless, the system of China is viewed as pessimistically shrewd and with legitimacy being questionable. Not having any reforms at political level, China will stay helpless against agitation should the economy flounder. If rule of law is not there in China, Beijing's statement will be questioned internationally. Even after having monetary triumphs and developing defence abilities, China's global impact will stay restricted until it neglects to advance an appealing political framework. It isn't unimaginable that it might do as such, however there is no proof currently to recommend that it will.

The perception of the Chinese about the United States that it is endeavouring to use its military prevalence over to hold down China may urge Beijing into endeavours to oust the United States from its place of worldwide predominance. With the consistent inequalities in power at national level, the struggle in future would not be a short struggle. The cause would presumably be the one derived with the incidents from military operations of the United States near China or the issue of Taiwan, because of which the relations between the US and China remain hostile. This is far-fetched, however, unfortunately, it isn't difficult to envision.

China is effectively thinking about how to put pressure effectively on the United States for putting a stop to its arms deals with Taiwan. China desires that Washington confine itself to Ronald Reagan's obligation to limit and lessen such deals in order to get a reliable pursuit by China for a settlement of peace in its disparities with Taipei. Sanctions on a few companies of America, modelled on those which have been imposed on the companies of China by the US Congress for selling objectionable things to other people, are evidently among the choices before the leaders of China. In the present financial environment, any step taken by China may cause a frightful encounter and release a host of American protectionist reprisals that would probably start a trade war. However, the potential consequences of any miscalculation by either China or the United States represent the global stake in proceeding with judicious administration of the relations between China and the United States by both sides.

China's quick financial development and rise as a significant financial power have given the leadership of China expanded trust in its model for economic policies. Many accept that the major difficulties confronting the United States to persuade China are as follows:

- It has contributed in keeping up the worldwide system of trade, that is generally the major factor in its financial ascent, and needs to play a dynamic role as a leader in keeping up that framework.
- Additional monetary as we change in the exchange policies arc the definite route in front of China to modernise and develop its economy.

Bringing down barriers of both investment and trade would uplift the level of competition inside China, enhance financial productivity, minimum costs for buyers and spur development. But numerous stakeholders of the US are in tension about the efforts of China for enhancing the growth of local technology and innovation as it could bring about more prominent intercession by the state (like endowments, exchange and barriers in investments and biased policies), which may adversely influence intensive firms of the US.

Opinions vary regarding the best method on how to treat China over big problems at economic level. A few suggest a strategy of commitment with China through different platforms. Others suggest a kind of mixed strategy for utilising commitment whenever the situation allows, combined along with more forceful utilisation of various procedures for the settlements of disputes used by WTO for addressing unjust policies for trade of China. At the same time, those who consider China to be a developing danger for the economy of the US and the system of global trade, support a strategy of attempting to hold economic power of China and following corrective actions, like increased taxes under consideration of Section 301, for either countering the negative impacts of industrial policies of China on US companies, or force China to make changes in its twisted and unfair strategies (for example, the initiative of Made in China 2025). Reacting to the BRI of China is seen by many as a significant threat for the worldwide financial interests of the US. While the monetary help of China in several infrastructural projects in various nations can create beneficial financial outcomes, policymakers of the US have shown worries that China will make the use of BRI to primarily take advantage for its organisations, that the procedure of execution of schemes or plans won't be straightforward, that involvement of BRI can burden nations in huge indebtedness, and China will make the use of BRI to expand its financial and strategic framework in different nations.

Conclusion

It is important to consider China to be as it is, not as what we want or dread it to be. In 1943, an announcement was made by President Franklin Roosevelt, *"China has become one of the great democracies of the world"*. Obviously, it did not make sense. However, there are several incidents about China that it is rising as an anti-democratic power. The almost certain possibility is that in future, China can secure its position along with the United States and other nations on the top of a multilateral structure of worldwide administration.

In this kind of world system, China will experience extraordinary status, however it will not have monopoly of power as compared to that which has been recently enjoyed by the United States.

The global political hegemony of America has already been lost. However, China is not capable of succeeding for this role. The financial model of Anglo-Americans is quite discoloured because of recent events. Yet, no option in contrast to it has arisen. It appears to be sure that whatever replaces it would be made through numerous assistances, just a few of which would be Chinese. Utilisation by Americans, at this point, is not the only factor which is running the worldwide economy. Chinese market now has a significant impact in supporting world development. However, China isn't just one and the only economy which is rising. China will be predominant in certain territories of worldwide trade and investment, but it would not be in others. In the military field, regardless of whether monetary constraints force retrenchment, the only power with worldwide command would be the United States, for a long time to come.

Americans will have it hard to adjust to a world in which it is not all-powerful in every sphere. However, neither Americans nor Chinese would stop to seek their own national interests or advantages as they seek for them now. In numerous examples, such perspectives would pretty much overlap. If others agree on such matters, there will be worldwide advancement. Where we do not agree, we go under stress by the rest of the people to look for a common sphere. Not any one of them would be that much strong to overlook such pressure.

The rise of China can't be underestimated. First, China is a long way from being a Superpower as Britain and the US were in the past, which means military force, economic power, social and cultural power, legal power, capabilities to impose its commands and norms altogether in these areas.

Military forces of China are yet extremely feeble in front of the United States' military. It possesses just two aircraft carriers, rather than twenty in comparison to the United States with its land bases in almost 40 nations, instead of only three for China. Atomic force of China is generally insignificant despite the fact that its computerised warfare capacity is challenged just by Russia. China doesn't possess the agrarian fields which are required to fulfil its people's needs, neither does it have the rural land expected to take care of its populace, nor the social framework to secure aging people. Dictatorship can only decelerate the development.

The United States becomes the only leading economic nation in the world and has capabilities for enforcing its laws on a large portion of the Earth. Technological organisations of the United States remain experts of data.

In fact, in the 21st century, the United States as well as China, both will be big and influencing powers, however, master of the world will be neither of them. And the world will remain a multipolar one. China experiences dictatorship which constrained it to deceive itself during the start of the epidemic, even prior to misleading the whole world. The past proves that no country can really become a superpower if it does not possess the capability to withstand criticism.

The US will have an excessive number of internal issues to manage the world and for being a model for it. Both the United States and China have much to do first at the domestic level to administer the whole world.

Hence, in coming years, the world would be much "democratic" and most probably, much tangled comparable to the past, as numerous nations, not only China and the United States, would exercise command on the world. There would be plentiful opportunities in front of nations to impact how they engage in worldwide issues. There will be not be only one global hegemon, and there will not be any "G-2".

References

Bank, T. W. (n.d.). *The World Bank In China*. Retrieved from The World Bank: https://www.worldbank.org/en/country/china/overview

Buckle, M. (2018, August 2). *Black cat, white cat*. Retrieved from *China Daily*, at http://www.chinadaily.com.cn/a/201808/02/WS5b728ae4a310add14f385b4a.html

Bush, R. C. (2011, October 11). *The United States and China: A G-2 in the Making?* Retrieved from Brookings at https://www.brookings.edu/articles/the-united-states-and-china-a-g-2-in-the-making/

Char, J. (2021, April 22). *China's military budget: no need for alarm yet*. Retrieved from *East Asia Forum*, at https://www.eastasiaforum.org/2021/04/22/chinas-military-budget-no-need-for-alarm-yet/

Chunsheng, L. (2018, 12 18). *Opinion: "Cross the river by feeling the stone": a valuable lesson after 40 years*. Retrieved from CGTN, at https://news.cgtn.com/news/3d3d514d336b7a4d31457a6333566d54/share_p.html

EveryCRSReport. (2019, June 25). *China's Economic Rise: History, Trends, Challenges, and Implications for the United States*. Retrieved from EveryCRSReport, at https://www.everycrsreport.com/reports/RL33534.html

Kania, E. B. (2019, Feburary 1). *Made in China 2025, Explained*. Retrieved from The Diplomat, at https://thediplomat.com/2019/02/made-in-china-2025-explained/

Maddison, A. (2007). *Chinese Economic Performance in the Long Run, 960-2030 AD*, Second Edition, Revised and Updated. OECD. doi:https://doi.org/10.1787/9789264037632-en

Service, C. R. (2019). *China's Economic Rise: History, Trends, Challenges, and Implications for the United States*. Congressional Research Service.

Shukla, S. (2020, June 18). *How India and China stack up in terms of military capability*. Retrieved from *The Print*, at https://theprint.in/defence/how-india-and-china-stack-up-in-terms-of-military-capability/443991/

State, U. D. (n.d.). *The Chinese Revolution of 1949*. Retrieved from Office of the Hisotrian, at https://history.state.gov/milestones/1945-1952/chinese-rev

THE PERIPHERY AT STAKE: INDIA'S FIGHT AGAINST CHINA'S EXPANSIONIST POLICY

PRIYA KUMARI

A Historical Overview of Border Conflict

In the history of sovereign nations and their territorial demarcation, the Sino-Indian border is the largest border in the world. On Indian side, there are four states, Himachal Pradesh, Sikkim, Uttarakhand and Arunachal Pradesh, and one Indian union territory, Ladakh, which share the periphery with China. After the Sino-Indian War of 1962, line of actual control (LAC) came up in dividing the Chinese and Indian territory (Joshi, 2021). However, we must understand the line of actual control is a loose demarcation line. In contemporary times, this is the effective border between India and China. In toto, the total boundary length of the Sino-Indian border is 4,056 km and it is divided in three sectors, which are, the 'eastern sector' which includes the borders of Arunachal Pradesh and Sikkim, the middle sector, including the states of Himachal Pradesh and Uttarakhand, and the last one which is the western sector of Ladakh.

Both the countries' troops in the past have been engaged in the border conflict and skirmishes on the peripheries of Ladakh,

Figure 3: LAC Boundary

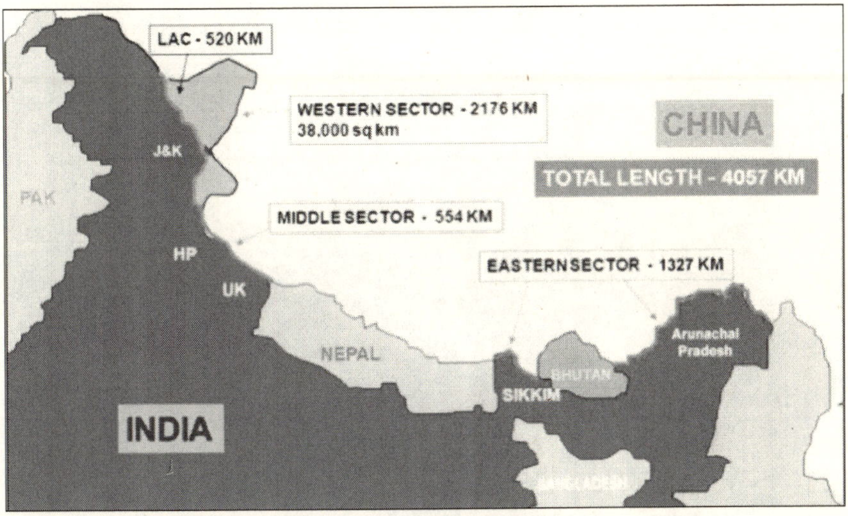

Source: https://www.drishtiias.com/pdf/1614425942.pdf

Sikkim, and Arunachal Pradesh, which has often triggered the fear of war. But the stand of China in Ladakh and Arunachal Pradesh is India's worst border tension between the two because the 1962 India-China war took place in both states of India. As far as the middle sector is concerned, no dispute has ever been reported because India has an advantage of altitude and in the situation of war, any country having the height advantage is strategically at the upper hand to its adversaries.

If we analyse the history of Chinese strategic policy, on October 19, Mao Tse-tung gave message to the communist party of India (CPI) and said that *"I firmly believe that relying on the brave communist party of India and the unity and struggle of all Indian patriots, India will certainly not remain long under the yoke of imperialism and its collaborators. Like liberated China, free India will one day emerge in the socialist and people's democratic family; that day will end the imperialist reactionary era in the history of mankind"* (Gupta, 2009).

Figure 4: Disputed Border between India and China

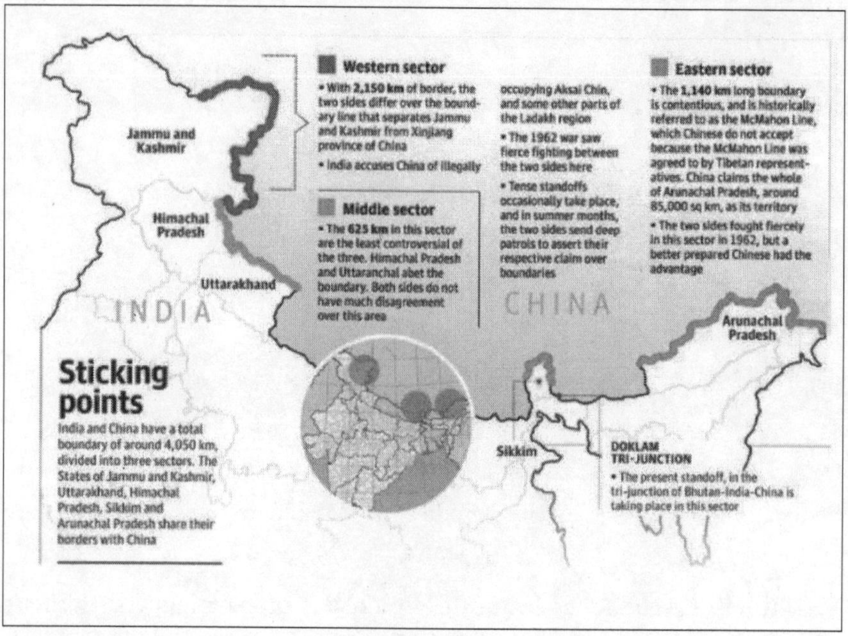

Source: https://www.drishtiias.com/to-the-points/Paper2/disputed-territories-of-india

The assertion indicates that India is still not so-called independent like China, according to China's legendary revolutionary leader Mao Zedong. According to his right-hand palm and five fingers strategy in the 1950s, Tibet is the right palm, which is detached from its five figures of Indian states: Ladakh, Nepal, Sikkim, Bhutan, and Arunachal (China's five-finger punch, 2020). Through this geopolitical strategy, Mao from the very beginning wanted to control Tibet, and at the same time formulated the Chinese priority of taking over the rest of the territory. This is the main reason behind Chinese attempt of invading Indian territory repeatedly. On the contrary, India, under the guidance of then PM Jawaharlal Nehru, follows the

Panchsheel Principles on peaceful coexistence with respect to China (MEA, Panchsheel).

The western region of border dispute is basically over an Aksai Chin and is over 3,800 km north of the range of Karakoram. This sector in the area included the Shaksgam valley north of Kashmir.

This section affords the classical background and development of both sectors to light up the vastly delicate historical vindications used in both countries of border claims and describe how the border debate first emerged and became incurable.

Beginning with the western sector, it explores how the interplay between the British Raj, Tibet and Imperial (later Republican) China left current China and India with undefended borders. I then move

Figure 5: Current Border Claimed by Both Countries

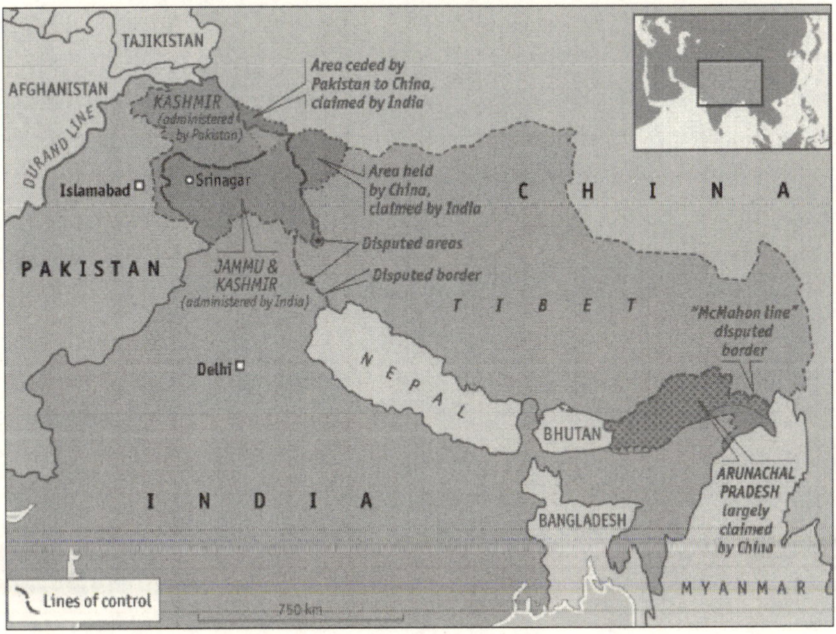

Source: https://www.researchgate.net/figure/Figure-1-Current-and-Claimed-borders-of-both-China-and-India_fig2_301607858

on to talk about how this uncertain border pivoted into a plumage border dispute between China and India during the 1950s as far as tensions and misinterpretations.

So, the war of 1962 origins in the relations of India and China since their independence and establishment so in the year of 1947 India gets. Following the civil war with the Kuomintang government, Mao Zedong proclaimed the People's Republic of China from the Tiananmen on October 1, 1949 (*Guardian*, 2019). Initially both India and China had very good relations because all the countries were coming out of long periods of disturbance, one was coming from a long period of war with Japan and civil war in the mainland. On the other hand, India was under the shackles of the British empire. With the proclamation of People's Republic of China, the coming into being of PRC was not acceptable to the USA, UK and many other Western countries because it was a communist country so they did not recognise it. China wasn't allowed to join the United Nations but remarkably India was one of the first countries to recognise China as well as it favoured its admission to the United Nations (Harder).

At that time, Nehru proposed that China should join us as soon as possible. In fact, in 1960 Jawaharlal Nehru gave up the power of veto which was offered to India and it was given away to China (Ayoob, 2019). Nehru said that India will never require veto power because we are a non-aligned country, and paved the way for permanent seat to People's Republic of China. Mao Zedong was the chairman of China and he was also the architect of the Chinese revolution for the Chinese civil war because he was a leader of the party from a long time and along with Zhou En-lai, Premier, he was also a leader of the Communist party and held the post for ten years. The position of chairman is more like president so although Mao was the president but he was the main ideological force behind China's policy.

Afterwards, in 1950 China annexed the independent country of Tibet (Tibet). Historically, it was not independent and type of kingdom since long, even during Chinese empire of Ming dynasty, and had their own ruler, Dalai Lama. I will be discussing later but China, the newly established country, said that traditionally and historically, Tibet was part of Chinese empires in the past and so this has to be a part of the newly formed China as well. So, Mao ordered the communist army to annex Tibet, and the next area adjacent to Tibet was India. Earlier, India did not share a direct boundary with China but after it annexed Tibet, India and China now have a direct boundary. When this event took place, some concerned stakeholders in India said that China could now possibly come to war with India or it could threaten India, but Nehru had good friendship with the leadership of China and was reassured that China can never invade India. Over a period of time, and with Nehru's optimism, India and China signed the Panchsheel Agreement. It was the treaty according to its five principles that mainly dealt with peaceful coexistence between the two states. According to this peace treaty, India said that we will not interfere in each other's internal affairs and such it was an open knowledge mind that is now under Chinese control the entire many countries in the world that is the control of by China against this annexation of China was having was the Chinese army was doing many atrocities against the local population but India did not say anything. In fact, government of India explicitly accepted that Tibet was traditionally a part of China (Chellaney, 2003) and it will remain a part of China.

Now we come to the boundary dispute between the two countries, not the spot between India and China that has been un-demarcated for a long time since the British time period and then the time period of Chinese empire. So, it was mostly based on local traditional areas of dominance and the natural barriers mainly the Himalayas had found between the many umpires on both sides in thousands of years there was a small agreement called the Shimla agreement was signed in 1914 between British government and government of Tibet and the

Chinese government (Kalha, *The McMahon Line: A hundred years on*, 2014). These three have participated in Shimla to demarcate the disputed border.

Chinese government had participated in a small conference in Shimla. Later there was a dispute after the revolution in China, and the communist government denied acceptance of the borders which were agreed by the two parties according to the Shimla agreement of 1914.

The war was also called in the Eastern sector of Ladakh. It was called the Western sector of India as this is situated on the eastern part and the part here in Ladakh in Jammu and Kashmir. Another disputed area was Aksai Chin, this was found as the Western sector of India. It is a plain which is important as it is situated at great heights in the Ladakh plateau. Aksai Chin is inhabited people's land and is an important land route from ancient times. It is also used by people who go there, and it is not permanently inhabited by a large population, but a small scattered population here and there.

The Himalayan border dispute originates from both countries and their area of study are for a combination of all aspects of ground, that is technology and also the absence of a map making in Tibet region in this situation British map-making is clear. In 1913, the Shimla conference was beginning and in the year 1914 took place the "Anglo-Tibetan Shimla Conference" (Karackattu, 2014). In this conference British authorities drew the McMahon Line, named after the chief negotiator, Sir Henry McMahon, which established the boundary between British India and Tibet. Besides, the Chinese representatives present at Shimla refused to recognise the accords on the basis that Tibet was under Chinese jurisdiction and therefore did not have the power to conclude a treaty. Under the McMahon plan, India will get Tawang region and Tibet will be divided into outer and inner, that means the red line is outer Tibet and blue line is inner Tibet. Outer Tibet has a boundary with India. The inner Tibet will be an area separate from the outer Tibet, and outer Tibet is an area which is separating it from the inner Tibet will be blue and red in McMahon plan. At present, Tibet is an autonomous region which is currently occupied by China.

India after getting independence in 1947 considered the McMahon line as the official border with Tibet territories. Afterwards in 1950 China invaded India, and now Tibet and China share a common border. After the newly established People's Republic of China took over Tibetan territories and India was defeated by the People's Army, China saw the McMahon Line as illegal (BASU, 2020), because in the Shimla Convention China was not party to the agreement.

A brief period of improvement in the relationship between both the countries came in 1950. Indian Prime Minister Jawaharlal Nehru and Chinese President Chairman Mao signed the treaty in 1954, China and India agreement on Trade between Tibet region (Baruah, 2016). Nehru imagined it as a trade-off between the border of Tibet but from a China perspective, there was no trade-off and China did not follow the McMahon line.

In the year of 1962 armed conflict between the two nations, during the period of war Chinese troops advanced, capturing territory of India in sector of western region in Ladakh and eastern sector, or take back to their previous location that was named as Line of Actual Control (LAC) (Lidarev, 2012). The war left India with a difficult border dispute with China which still is a major reason of conflict between the two countries.

Western Sector

The western sectors starting with the range of Karakoram in Ladakh and Aksai Chin in the region is a disputed area, where Chinese military is occupying about 33,500 sq. km of land, and this area is claimed by India largely based on the "Johnson Line" (BHONSALE, 2018). In 1856, British strategy secured the northern part of India and played a critical role in annexation in Kashmir. In 1856 border claim, W. H. Johnson was sent to the area, and he proposed the Johnson Line and putting Aksai Chin as a part of Kashmir. While Aksai Chin is an eastern part, and it is a point between Tibet and Xinjiang, it has also high strategic value to China. China and India border disputes are complex historical issues and as both countries cannot agree on border delimitation, there has never been an official boundary in both countries.

Eastern Sector

In independent India, the government inherited the British territorial policy and followed McMahon line as the border between India and Tibet. Till the existence of Tibet, boundaries were peaceful, but with the China invasion of Tibet, India and China directly came to share a border. After the newly established People's Republic of

Figure 6: India and China Border in Western Sector

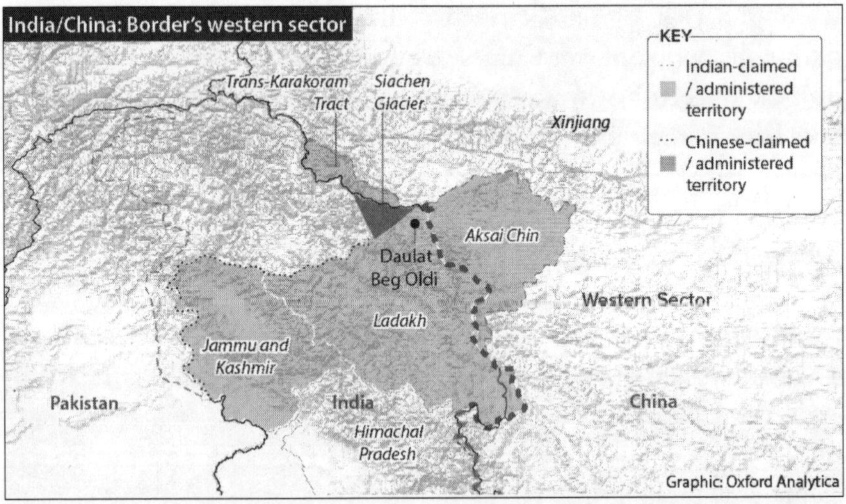

Source: https://dailybrief.oxan.com/Analysis/GI253474/India-China-Borders-western-sector

Figure 7: Border of India and China in Eastern Sector

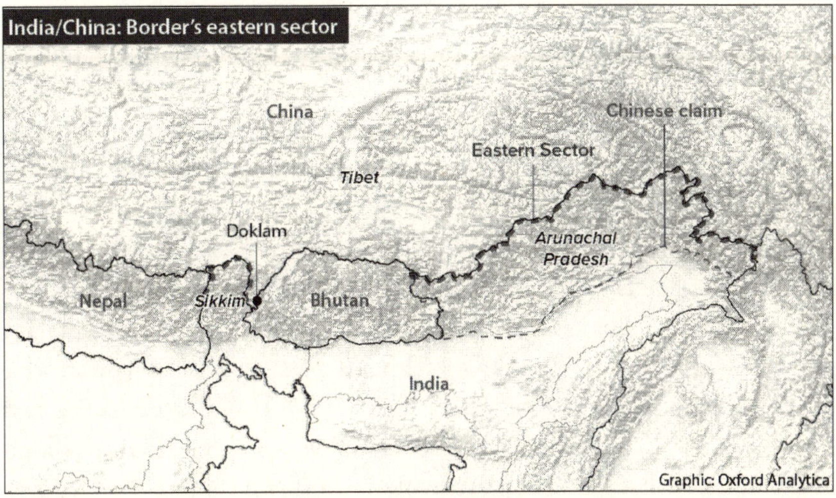

Source: https://dailybrief.oxan.com/Analysis/GI253477/India-China-Borders-eastern-sector

China took over the Tibetan territories and India was threatened by the Chinese army presence in Tibet, India quickly strengthened its administrative and military control in the eastern sector. China viewed the McMahon Line as an illegal demarcation because in Shimla Convention China did not sign and considered it as a colonial attempt of dividing China. Meanwhile India considered the line as an international boundary. And in the same year, China took the control over the Tawang (Kalha, *What did China Gain at the End of the Fighting in November 1962?*, 2012).

Military Stand-offs and India's Strategic Position

Galwan stand-off

India has a history of violent boundary clash with China, and the recent stand-off came at Galwan Valley. The conflict occurred at

Galwan due to long-standing bitterness of both sides to claim their territorial lands at Aksai Chin region. There are multiple factors for the direct confrontation. I am highlighting some of those crucial factors.

In 2019 the BJP government reconstituted the state of Jammu and Kashmir, and it has now two separate union territories, Jammu and Kashmir and Ladakh (Rai, 2019).

If we see figure 4 this much would be Ladakh and the last corner is a north-eastern part of Ladakh, which today is under China's control, and is called Aksai Chin, although it is a part of Ladakh. But India lost this part of Ladakh to China in the 1962 India-China war.

The Galwan river originates from the Aksai Chin region, and the Galwan river area comes under sub-sector north (SSN), which is a military forward area that provides a direct axis to Aksai Chin from India. For the Indian army this point is crucial for the defence

Figure 8: India and China Galwan Stand-off

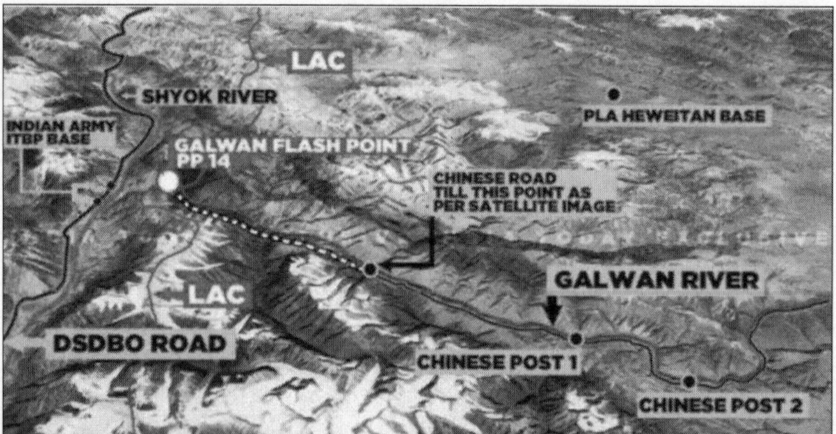

Source: https://www.businesstoday.in/latest/economy-politics/story/india-china-border-dispute-why-are-both-nations-fighting-over-galwan-valley-eastern-ladakh-261442-2020-06-17

of the Siachen and Leh. If we see figure 3, the north-eastern portion of Ladakh black boundary line basically is the actual border line claimed by India, that is how Aksai Chin is considered a part of Ladakh. The 1962 India-China war took place here in the Galwan valley, from October 28 to November 21, 1962, that means in the month of September 1962, the Chinese army illegally occupied this much of the Indian territory; see figure 4 along the Karakoram range.

By the end of the 1962 war, that is, the month of November, the Chinese forces reached further inside and had in a sense then claimed that Galwan valley is a part of China. In 1957 China built the national highway called G219 (Ying, 2014) that passes right through the disputed area of Aksai Chin. It connects the regions of Xinjiang with Tibet. The construction of this road is also set to be a reason behind the 1962 India China war, because that road was built without India's consent. If we look at the average elevation of mountains in the Karakoram range, it is about 6,000 metres, almost twice the height where altitude sickness occurs, that means any humans in this area have to undergo gradual acclimatisation or suffer crippling headache, nausea and phatic and the Chinese knew this and to control any movement by the Indian army from west from the Ladakh side the Chinese made LAC goes through the highest crest line of the Karakoram mountains.

So that India does not control the dominating heights, there is more depth and distance between LAC and the Chinese G219 highway. The Galwan river is the only way to provide a direct axis to Aksai Chin from Ladakh. The Chinese want to control this area as they fear the Indian site could be threatened by the position of Aksai Chin by the use of river and valley. India is trying to construct the feeder road to Darbuk-Shyok village to Daulat Beg Oldie Road (BDO) (Subramanian, 2020). It is the 255-km-long road that runs along the Shayok river and the most critical line of communication close to Line of Actual Control. This road basically connects Leh to Daulat Beg Oldie Road. This road is an important supply route which serves the Indian troops, and this road runs parallel to LAC at the Aksai Chin.

If we see the conflict from a non-partisan point of view, India and China have border disputes due to lack of maps in the area along LAC. The Galwan valley region of Aksai Chin and LAC has never been demarcated, that means no maps have been exchanged in this area between both the countries. "The Line of Actual Control has to be properly demarcated and simultaneously confidence building measures (CBMs) have to be conducted", said the military expert, Shaurya Karanbir Gurung (Gurung, 2018).

Doklam Stand-off

Technically the Doklam dispute is not a part of India and China but between Bhutan and China; the Sino-Indian border is a trijunction, that means the border of Sikkim, Bhutan, and Tibet meet at this disputed area. Indian and Chinese troops have confronted one another in a stand-off and it has aggravated the already tense relations and is considered the most intense crisis between the Asian powers in the last three decades; however, what is less clear are the geopolitical motives behind the stand-off.

We know that India and China share a boundary and it was demarcated and so from time to time there has been friction, but the Doklam situation is slightly more complicated. The current stalemate isn't even a dispute between Beijing and New Delhi; rather it stems from a discord between China and Bhutan. The incident started on June 16 when a group of Chinese military engineers began construction work in the area of Doklam, which is one of the seven disputed territories between Bhutan and China (*The Hindu*, "Timeline: the story of the Doklam stand-off", 2017). Beijing had been operating freely in the Doklam territory since 2005 and the work appears to be an effort to extend a road closer to India's border

Figure 9: Bhutan Trijunction Area

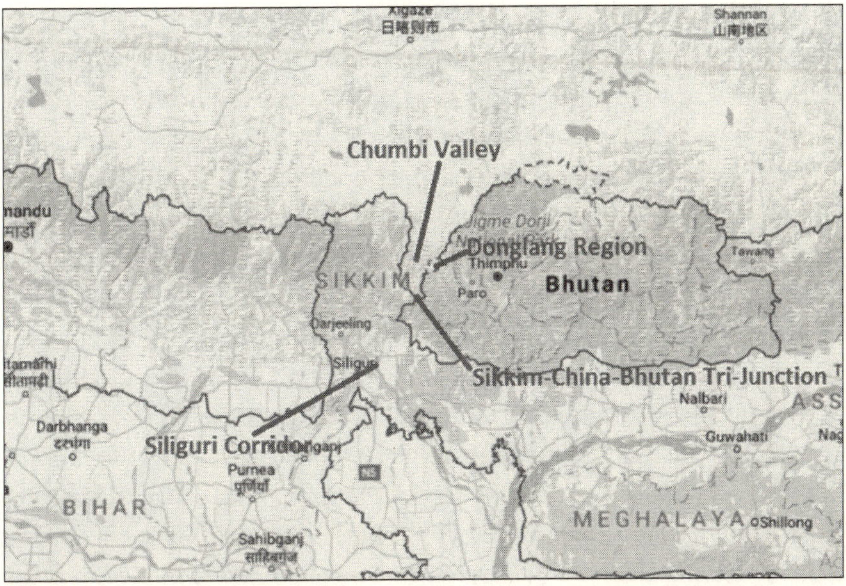

Source: https://www.iasparliament.com/current-affairs/tension-at-the-tri-junction

through the Doklam plateau. On June 18 Indian military forces crossed the Bhutan border and barricaded the Chinese project which led to a counter-response of authorities in Beijing deploying their own forces to confront the Indian army (Philip, 2019).

Although the details of the security situation are unclear, most sources claim that roughly 400 soldiers on both sides have been locked in near the Dhokla plateau. The region of contention revolves around the three areas of Doklam, which is the point at which India, China and Bhutan meet. Officials in Bhutan claim that the boundary point is situated about four km north of the Dhokla plateau, where the real stand-off between Indian and Chinese troops is ongoing. Meanwhile China claims that the points near mount hip mochi across Li 2.5 km south of the Dhokla pass.

India has significant influence over Bhutan's foreign policy. The treaty was revised in 2007 (*The Hindu*, "Why Bhutan is special to India", 2017) and gave Bhutan greater autonomy but it retains the clause that neither government shall allow the use of its territory for activities harmful to the national security and interest of the other. Essentially due to this treaty China and Bhutan have no formal relations. Moreover, it is also the reason why the crossing of Indian troops into Bhutan is not considered a violation of international law. The details of the Bhutanese-Chinese dispute are slightly obscure but the disagreement lies in the interpretation of the Calcutta convention of 1890 between British India and Chin dynasty (Ahamed, 2017). That treaty is known as a convention between Great Britain and China relating to Sikkim and Tibet. The treaty highlights in first Articles that *"The boundary of Sikkim and Tibet shall be the crest of the mountains range separating the waters flowing into the Sikkim Teesta and its affluents from the waters flowing into the Tibetan Mochu and northwards into other rivers of Tibet. The line commences at mount Grip Mochi on the Bhutan frontier, and follows the above-mentioned water parting to the points where it meets Nepal territory"* (Patranobis, 2017).

The statement confirms China's territorial claims to mount hip Module some 2.5 km south of the Dhokla Plateau. In this regard Beijing sees the Bhutanese-Chinese borderline already determined by the Calcutta convention; however, in historical relations, in the 19th and 20th centuries Himalayan border limitations were established on the basis of the highest mountain ridgeline. The disputed area of their ridgeline runs from the three borders of China, India and Nepal to the area of current stand-off. However, topographically the ridgeline ends at the points which India and Bhutan claim as the three boundary points, which is some 4 km north of the Dhokla plateau so even though the convention clearly mentions China's claim over mount hit Motu and thus reaffirms Beijing's position, it's equally important to mention that the document contains a topographic error which is likely the result of survey work in the 19th century, but as interesting as topography and Central 3 30 may be, the governments in New Delhi and Beijing merely use the technicalities to adjust the narrative to their design. The true nature of the conflict is geopolitical what makes mount keep mojo.

For instance, a Chinese road through the Dhokla plateau towards the Hippo chi mountains and by extension an observation post would give a clear view of the local area. The mountain sits near the jump area which descends into the foothills of Bhutan and then leads to the Siliguri corridor also known as "chicken neck". This corridor is the

Figure 10: Sikkim Trijunction from June to August

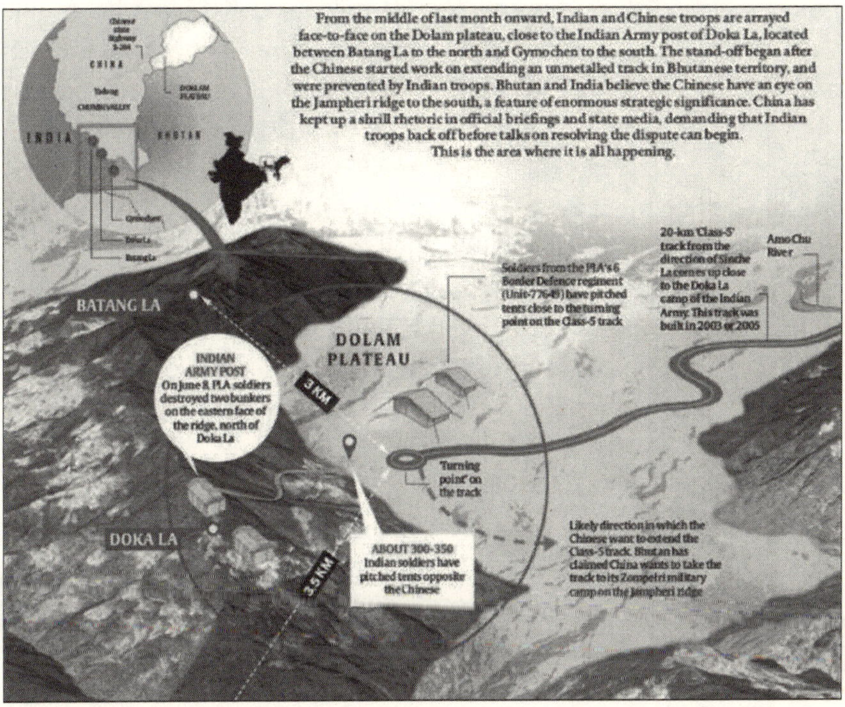

Source: https://indianexpress.com/article/explained/india-china-standoff-sikkim-doka-la-simply-put-where-things-stand-on-the-dolam-plateau-4763892/

primary supply line physically connecting India to its North Eastern territories. At the narrowest point Siliguri corridor is measured at 27 km and thus forms a strategic choke point and core vulnerability of India. The capture of the location of the Siliguri corridor would detach northeast India (Srivastava, 2017) which is home to about 45 million people from the rest of the country. To that end whoever controls northeast India controls the upstream of the Brahmaputra River which flows through Bangladesh and drains into the Indian Ocean.

Now the relationship between China in India has never been good but in recent years it has declined sharply because of the former's support for Pakistan. Beijing sees its relationship with Islamabad as a means to contain India from becoming a regional contender. In this context Beijing's construction of the China-Pakistan Economic Corridor (CPEC) as well as many other economic projects of the Belt and Road Initiative (BRI) runs counter to Indian interest, besides the grand scheme of things. China has repeatedly undermined India's diplomatic efforts; for instance, Beijing has used its UN veto power to deny India from imposing sanctions on Pakistani militants (Tay, 2019) and keeping New Delhi from entering the Nuclear Supplier's Group (NSG) (Aneja, 2017) which denies India access to modern technology. India in the meantime returns the favours by, among other things, boycotting the inauguration of Belt and Road Initiative, although both countries are roughly the same in terms of population size.

Chinese military, economic and diplomatic resources outstrip that of India and for this reason India cannot afford a military skirmish with China. Therefore, Prime Minister Narendra Modi has sought to reach out to a diplomatic resolution to the stand-off and ask China to return to the status quo before the incident. However, since China outperforms India, the Chinese leadership is confident of its ability to come out on top which is why Beijing has given an ultimatum that diplomacy can only be possible after New Delhi unilaterally withdraws its troops as the backdrop of the crisis. The kingdom of Bhutan has been left in an awkward position, siding with New Delhi would invite retaliation from Beijing, and wall distancing itself from India would cost Bhutan more than it would gain with China. Despite the exchange of nationalist rhetoric, neither China nor India wants to initiate hostilities.

India's Border Disputes Under Different Regimes

1. Jawaharlal Nehru

Jawaharlal Nehru became the first PM of Independent India and was a notable PM in the history of Indian political system. Nehru proposed that China should join UN as soon as possible. In fact, in 1960 Jawaharlal Nehru gave the power of veto to China, which was initially offered to India. Nehru said that India will never need veto power because it is a non-aligned country.

After that great tension occurred in the western region. In the years between 1953 and 1957, China built up massive projects and construction to support its presence in Tibet. Also, the most important projects started in the year of 1953 in the area of Aksai Chin, a motorable road from Xinjiang. This road was completed in 1957.

On October 18, 1958, Indian government sent a memo to the Chinese government officially claiming Aksai Chin as a part of Indian territory (Raghavan, 2006). In this memo to Zhou Enlai, Nehru wrote that "there can be no question of these large parts of India [shown as within China on the Chinese map] being anything but India and there is no dispute about it". In January 1959, Zhou's reply highlighted some points such as:

1. Border had never been demarcated in both countries.
2. Border disputes do exist between both the countries.
3. Aksai Chin was a part of China and had always been under Chinese jurisdiction, and

4. McMahon line was illegal, China considered as India modified its claim to Aksa Chin (Center, 1959).

This proposal was rejected by Nehru and he sent Indian troops into all claimed territories in India. After the Kongka pass incident, Zhou visited India to solve the border tension peacefully through negotiations.

However, India rejected this proposal, and claimed that there should be no standstill, no compromise, no negotiations. After the summit failed, India implemented its Forward Policy between the years 1961 to 1962 (Noorani). At the same time, China increased its army in all of these disputed regions. And tension was high in all sectors of Sino-Indian border. On October 20, 1962, China launched a pre-emptive offensive marking and started the first war that is known as Sino-Indo border war (Abadi, 1998). This war ended with China's victory, and after the war the border became quiet, but still India refused to negotiate with China on border issues. And the border tension remained the same in the late 1970s. In 1971, India renamed NEFA (North East Frontier Agency, the disputed eastern sector) as Arunachal Pradesh (Pradesh).

2. **Rajiv Gandhi**

Rajiv Gandhi was a young leader to join Indian politics, after his mother was assassinated and younger brother Sanjay died in an aircrash in the year 1980. He was the voice of India during the time of the Cold War. He improved relations with many countries. However, it was starting a new chapter with China. He said China is an important neighbour country to India but relations with the latter strained after the year 1962 and the India-China war.

In the year 1988, he became the first Indian Prime minister to visit China in over 30 years (ICS, "Prime Minister Rajiv Gandhi's Visit to

Figure 11: Paper Article Shows China Attack on Disputed Area

Chinese attack on both fronts

Forward posts fall in NEFA, Ladakh after stiff fight

NO MILITARY PLANES IN OPERATION: MENON

Relations with China: official view in Delhi

Reference to UN not yet, says Menon

Mystery over

Source: Wikimedia Commons

China", 1989). His meetings transformed the relations between the two neighbouring countries.

He changed Indian border policy slightly, then China's Vice Premier and Chinese Foreign Minister Huang Hua visited India in 1981 for the first time (ICS, "India-China Relations April-June 1981", 1981) and it led to talks about the border tension between both countries. From 1981 to 1987, there were eight rounds on this topic but these talks didn't yield any fruitful results. From 1986 to 1987, an army stand-off occurred in the area of Sumdorong Chu Valley between India and China (Nayanima Basu, 2020).

But this military stand-off did not escalate into another war between India and China. Rajiv Gandhi's visit to China was the reason of ongoing border talks between the countries. After bilateral relations improved both the parties signed an agreement for peace over LAC in both countries in 1993.

The Majority Government (1989-2014)

After Rajiv Gandhi, there were no stable governments. Unstable minority governments were formed between 1989 and 2014. The

INC dominance over the Indian political system broke down after the new political system came up and parties joined it, such as regional parties and Hindu nationalist party.

Narasimha Rao was the first Prime Minister of the minority government at this time. This shift of power in geopolitics and India headed NAM policy. The most important foreign policy was Rao's Look East policy, and this is related to India's focus on South Asian region to engage economically and strategically with Southeast Asian countries. This reform had impact for a breakthrough in the war of border disputes between China and India. The Narasimha Rao government decided to maintain the status quo and maintain peace on the border dispute issues, and hence the signing of an agreement in 1993 on peace (MEA G. , 2005).

Atal Bihari Vajpayee was the next prime minister of note during this period of minority governments, and he led the main opposition party, that is, Hindu nationalist BJP. He became prime minister of India in the year 1996. In 1998 elections Vajpayee managed to form a coalition known as National Democratic Alliance. After the testing of nuclear bomb in 1998, many countries were not in support of India and tension rose. Hence the only approach was status quo policy. Vajpayee visited China in 2003 and India agreed to SRP, Special Representative Meetings and an agreed framework for border resolution (Kulkarni, 2018).

Manmohan Singh was the last prime minster in this period. He had served asFinance Minister in the Narasimha Rao administration. Under the Manmohan Singh-led UPA government, the main strategic objective was to improve economic power.

Tension over India and China dispute emerged in 2006. This time, China was more aggressive. Under Manmohan Singh SRMs and events both the countries signed two agreements in 2012 and 2013 on border issues (MEA, "India-China Agreement on the Establishment of a Working Mechanism for Consultation and Coordination on India-China Border Affairs", 2012).

Narendra Modi became the prime minister of India. Modi basically made objectives of tackling corruption and promoting the development of the economy based upon his past experience as the chief minister of Gujarat. Also, he has consolidated India's most dominant state. Modi's administration also boosts our military power. The most important step taken by Modi was converting "Look East" policy into "Act East" policy; in 2021 these goals were achieved, and there was increase in acquisition of weapons and equipment for the Indian armed forces.

The Modi regime faced the Doklam stand-off in 2017, and both countries maintained peace. In 2018, Modi and Chinese president held the first summit in Wuhan, China. In this meeting, they exchanged views on issues of bilateral and national development. This informal meeting was a milestone in the history of bilateral relation between the two leaders.

After this informal meeting, in 2019, Chinese president visited India and held second informal meeting in Chennai (*The Hindu*, "Modi-Xi Jinping summit at Mamallapuram, Day 1 | Modi and Xi conclude 'highly productive day' with private dinner", 2019). This meeting was also based on how to maintain bilateral relations, development and especially in the year 2020, which completes the 70th anniversary of established diplomatic relations between India and China. However, after a while Ladakh stand-off happened and, at the same time, the whole world faced the pandemic of COVID-19.

Conclusion

In my whole research the main idea was to establish that both the sides need to find solutions to our bilateral issues because our primary aim is to diffuse tension in this frightening situation. Undoubtedly, neither side wants the situation to be turned into a battleground because that will have enormous ramifications not only for India and China but also for regional stability.

I don't believe either government would like a situation of prolonged conflict which all the more points to the need to sit down and arrive at some middle ground because diplomacy is all about reaching middle ground. In that context, I believe we need to be sensible. We need to be cool-headed. Nationalism certainly infuses the public imagination in both countries much more than before but this boundary dispute between the two countries is a legacy dispute. It's a 20th-century legacy dispute which we see unfolding before us today in the current situation.

So, it will require much political perspective on both sides to reach a solution. I don't believe I will be able to resolve the boundary dispute. But I think the primary focus should be to see how we can ensure a regime that holds the peace along the Line of Actual Control, not only in Ladakh but also in the middle sector in Sikkim and Arunachal Pradesh.

References

Abadi, J. (1998). The Sino-Indian Conflict of 1962—A Test Case for India's Policy of Non-Alignment. *Journal of Third World Studies*, 15(2), 11-29. Retrieved from https://www.jstor.org/stable/45193761

Ahamed, A. N. (2017, July 4). *Did Nehru really accept the Sino-British Treaty as final word on the border issue?* Retrieved from *The Hindu*, at https://www.thehindu.com/news/national/did-nehru-really-accept-the-sino-british-treaty-as-final-word-on-the-sikkim-border-issue/article19210128.ece

Aneja, A. (2017, May 22). *No room yet for India in NSG, says China*. Retrieved from *The Hindu*, at https://www.thehindu.com/news/international/no-room-for-india-yet-in-nsg-says-china/article18523724.ece

Ayoob, M. (2019, March 18). *Nehru, China, and the Security Council seat*. Retrieved from *The Hindu*, at https://www.thehindu.com/opinion/op-ed/nehru-china-and-the-security-council-seat/article26561751.ece

Baruah, A. (2016, May 23). *When Nehru and Mao met.* Retrieved from *The Hindu*, at https://www.thehindu.com/opinion/op-ed/comment-piece-on-the-maonehru-conversation/article7202352.ece

Basu, N. (2020, September 30). *What's the 1959 claim line? The one China says it's following in the Ladakh stand-off.* Retrieved from *The Print*, at https://theprint.in/theprint-essential/whats-the-1959-claim-line-the-one-china-says-its-following-in-the-ladakh-stand-off/513878/

Bhonsale, M. (2018). *Understanding Sino-Indian border issues: An analysis of incidents reported in the Indian media.* New Delhi: ORF. Retrieved from: https://www.orfonline.org/research/understanding-sino-indian-border-issues-an-analysis-of-incidents-reported-in-the-indian-media/

Center, W. (1959). *Premier Chou En-lai's [Zhou Enlai's] Letter to Prime Minister Nehru.* Washington, D.C.: Wilson Center. Retrieved from: https://digitalarchive.wilsoncenter.org/document/175959.pdf?v=1e8bdb140ea9671eecba1c252bca0865

Chellaney, B. (2003, July 28). *India's Betrayal of Tibet.* Retrieved from *The Wall Street Journal,* at https://www.wsj.com/articles/SB105934174617047500

China's five-finger punch. (2020, July 22). Retrieved from *The Strategist,* at https://www.aspistrategist.org.au/chinas-five-finger-punch/

Guardian, T. (2019, October 1). *Mao Zedong proclaims the establishment of the People's Republic of China—archive, 1949.* Retrieved from *The Guardian*, at https://www.theguardian.com/world/from-the-archive-blog/2019/oct/01/mao-zedong-proclaims-establishment-of-peoples-republic-of-china-1949

Gupta, B. S. (2009). "China and Indian Communism". *The China Quartely*, 272-94. doi:https://doi.org/10.1017/S0305741000050311

Gurung, S. K. (2018, July 12). Behind China's Sikkim aggression, a plan to isolate Northeast from rest of India. Retrieved from The Economic Times, at https://economictimes.indiatimes.com/news/defence/border-face-off-why-china-tries-to-break-chickens-neck-to-isolate-northeast/articleshow/59420472.cms

Harder, A. (n.d.). *Not at the Cost of China: India and the United Nations Security Council, 1950.* Wilson Center. Retrieved from: https://www.wilsoncenter.org/publication/not-the-cost-china-india-and the-united-nations-security-council-1950

Hindu, The. (2017, August 28). *Timeline: the story of the Doklam stand-off.* Retrieved from *The Hindu*, at https://www.thehindu.com/news/national/timeline-the-story-of-the-doklam-stand-off/article19576380.ece

Hindu, The. (2017, July 1). *Why Bhutan is special to India*. Retrieved from *The Hindu*, at https://www.thehindu.com/news/national/why-bhutan-is-special-to-india/article19195034.ece

Hindu, The. (2019, October 11). *Modi-Xi Jinping summit at Mamallapuram, Day 1 | Modi and Xi conclude 'highly productive day' with private dinner.* Retrieved from *The Hindu*, at https://www.thehindu.com/news/national/modi-xi-jinping-meet-in-mamallapuram-live-updates/article29653752.ece

ICS. (1981). "India-China Relations April-June 1981. *China Short*. Retrieved from: https://journals.sagepub.com/doi/abs/10.1177/000944558101700608?journalCode=chra

ICS. (1989). "Prime Minister Rajiv Gandhi's Visit to China". *China Report*, 187-200. doi:https://doi.org/10.1177%2F000944558902500209

Joshi, M. (2021). Eastern Ladakh, the Longer Perspective. New Delhi: Observer Research Foundation. Retrieved from: https://www.orfonline.org/research/eastern-ladakh-the-longer-perspective/

Kalha, R. (2012, November 21). *What did China Gain at the End of the Fighting in November 1962?* Retrieved from MP-PDSA, at https://idsa.in/idsacomments/WhatdidChinaGain%20attheEndoftheFighting_RSKalha_211112

Kalha, R. (2014, July 3). *The McMahon Line: A hundred years on.* Retrieved from MP-IDSA, at https://www.idsa.in/idsacomments/TheMcMahonLine_rskalha_030714

Karackattu, J. T. (2014, March 27). *How Britain, Tibet and China actually chalked out claim lines at the 1914 Simla conference.* Retrieved from T*he Economic Times,* at https://economictimes.indiatimes.com/opinion/et-commentary/how-britain-tibet-and-china-actually-chalked-out-claim-lines-at-the-1914-simla-conference/articleshow/32769125.cms?from=mdr

Kulkarni, S. (2018, September 11). *The one who reached out to China: On Atal Bihari Vajpayee.* Retrieved from *The Hindu*, at https://www.thehindu.com/opinion/op-ed/the-one-who-reached-out-to-china/article24918999.ece

Lidarev, I. (2012, August 21). *History's Hostage: China, India and the War of 1962.* Retrieved from *The Diplomat,* at https://thediplomat.com/2012/08/historys-hostage-china-india-and-the-war-of-1962/

MEA. (2012, January 17). *India-China Agreement on the Establishment of a Working Mechanism for Consultation and Coordination on India-China Border Affairs.* Retrieved from MEA, GOI, at https://mea.gov.in/bilateral-documents.htm?dtl/17963/IndiaChina+Agreement+on+the+Establishment+of+a+Working+Mechanism+for+Consultation+and+Coordination+on+IndiaChina+Border+Affairs

MEA. (n.d.). *Panchsheel.* New Delhi: MEA, GOI. Retrieved from: http://www.mea.gov.in/Uploads/PublicationDocs/191_panchsheel.pdf

MEA, G. (2005, April 11). *Agreement between the Government of the Republic of India and the Government of the People's Republic of China on the Political Parameters and Guiding Principles for the Settlement of the India-China Boundary Question.* Retrieved from Ministry of External Affairs, at https://mea.gov.in/bilateral-documents.htm?dtl/6534/Agreement+between+the+Government+of+the+Republic+of+India+and+the+Government+of+the+Peoples+Republic+of+China+on+the+Political+Parameters+and+Guiding+Principles+for+the+Settlement+of+the+IndiaChina+Bound

Nayanima Basu, S. S. (2020, June 30). *Sumdorong Chu, Ladakh-like India-China face-off which took 9 yrs to end but without violence.* Retrieved from *The Print*, at https://theprint.in/past-forward/sumdorong-chu-ladakh-like-india-china-face-off-which-took-9-yrs-to-end-but-without-violence/451517/

Noorani, N. M. (n.d.). "India's Forward Policy". *The China Quarterly*, 45, 157-63. Retrieved from: https://www.jstor.org/stable/651889

Patranobis, S. (2017, July 1). *Sikkim standoff: The historic treaty at the heart of India-China border problem.* Retrieved from *Hindustan Times*, at https://www.hindustantimes.com/world-news/sikkim-standoff-the-historic-treaty-at-the-heart-of-the-problem/story-OUCHMdRFuKh4cfVo53h9lI.html

Philip, S. A. (2019, October 17). *Operation Juniper—inside story of how Indian Army pushed China back from Doklam.* Retrieved from *The Print*, at https://theprint.in/defence/operation-juniper-indian-armys-human-wall-china-doklam/307332/

Pradesh, G. O. (n.d.). *Government: The Past and Present.* Retrieved from Government of Arunachal Pradesh, at https://www.arunachalpradesh.gov.in/655-2/

Raghavan, S. (2006). "Sino-Indian Boundary Dispute, 1948-60: A Reappraisal". *Economic and Political Weekly*, 41(36). Retrieved from: https://www.jstor.org/stable/4418679

Rai, V. (2019, August 8). *India Amends Article 370—A Constitutional Perspective*. Retrieved from ISAS, NUS, at https://www.isas.nus.edu.sg/papers/india-amends-article-370-a-constitutional-perspective/

Srivastava, U. (2017, July 7). *Sikkim standoff: Strategic importance of Siliguri corridor and why India should be wary of China*. Retrieved from *Firstpost*, at https://www.firstpost.com/india/sikkim-standoff-strategic-importance-of-siliguri-corridor-and-why-india-should-be-wary-of-china-3785967.html

Subramanian, N. (2020, June 16). *Explained: The strategic road to DBO*. Retrieved from *The Indian Express*, at https://indianexpress.com/article/explained/lac-stand-off-india-china-darbuk-shyok-daulat-beg-oldie-dsdbo-road-6452997/

Tay, S. (2019, March 13). *Beijing has used its UN veto power to deny India from imposing sanctions on Pakistani militants*. Retrieved from CNBC, at https://www.cnbc.com/2019/03/13/un-is-set-to-blacklist-jems-azhar--but-china-hinders-this.html

Tibet, F. (n.d.). *Tibet's History*. Retrieved from *Free Tibet*, at https://freetibet.org/about/history

Ying, L. (2014, September 24). *A road in the sky*. Retrieved from *Global Times*, at https://www.globaltimes.cn/content/883229.shtml

THE GEOPOLITICS IN AFGHANISTAN: ECHOING THE TENSIONS IN SOUTH ASIA

NAWID FAZLY

Introduction

For the controlling and governing of a state, making of government or state is important and there is no country that can maintain its governance in isolation without having external relations with countries and global community or that can maintain its authority alone. In international system the presence of states or countries defines on the basis of objectives and principles of foreign relations, where at end every country has to make or formulate its own foreign policy with respect to every involved nation which defines the nature of bilateral relationship.

Foreign policy according to Charles P. Schleicher refers to the state's official member activities that impact the human manners apart from their own state's authority. Also, he defines foreign policy in a broad sense that "the interaction of a country to another country by its plans, objectives"(International Relations by Vinay Kumar Malhotra, n.d.).

A successful foreign policy (which includes basic determinants, like general and objective determinants, includes sovereignty and integrity of the state, promotion of national interest, internal and external conditions. Also, external factors like international organisations (UNESCO, UNO), world public opinion, other states' reaction, etc.) increase a state's power and also increase government's trustworthiness or value in the eyes of citizens.

As far as Afghanistan is concerned, it is a Muslim nation settled as a bridge not only between Middle East and Central Asia, but also between the Islamic world and the West. Afghanistan's foreign policy is based on important beliefs, goals and values, wherein Afghanistan's constitution in articles 7 and 8 determines: "Foreign policy of country should formulate with the saving of independence, territorial integrity, national interest essentially non-interference, equality of rights, good neighbouring and mutual respect (article 8). The United Nations Charter, inter-state agreements, international treaties to which Afghanistan has membership and the Universal Declaration of Human Rights should notice or keep in mind by Afghanistan's government". We saw that it shows the determinant of foreign policy of Afghanistan, where its foreign policy made or derived from three main important factors which are geopolitics, economic needs and racial structure that play animportant role in formulating Afghanistan's foreign policy.

India and Pakistan had ties with different Afghan governments from the time of the British colonial empire break-up in 1947, where both countries emerged and got their independence, where I am going to discuss the Afghanistan foreign policy with India and Pakistan during different Afghan governments.

Afghanistan Foreign Policy During Cold War

As we mentioned above when India and Pakistan got their independence from the British colonial empire, it has affected Afghan foreign policy or brought changes in Afghan foreign policy because of conflict over 'Durand line' where Afghanistan never accepted or recognised that border line which was marked by the British empire (The Tangled History of the Afghanistan-India-Pakistan Triangle, n.d.). The South Asian Map and politics and also internal and external politics of Afghanistan changed by the emergence of Pakistan, where from 1947 Afghanistan's foreign policy towards India and Pakistan is the most debatable topic that Afghanistan had to maintain a balance between India and Pakistan.

India was one of the countries in 1979 that recognised the Soviet Union-supported communist government in Afghanistan, and did not oppose publicly the invasion by the Soviet Union in 1979. India had better relations with the communist government during the Cold War than Pakistan (Prospects for Indian-Pakistani Cooperation in Afghanistan, n.d.).

India was one of the founders of the non-alignment movement, and also supported the Soviet invasion, because of which the non-alignment movement got divided, and at the same time Pakistan created difficulties in Jammu and Kashmir, so India supported Pakistan's opponent or adversary and stopped supporting Afghanistan until 1992 till Pakistan backed the Mujahideen to win the war. During the Cold War Pakistan supported Afghan Mujahideen groups who fought against the Soviet Union on behalf of the United States where Pakistan was the ally of the United States of America (Ganguly & Howenstein, 2009).

Afghanistan's Foreign Policy in the Post-Cold War

When the Soviet Union withdrew from Afghanistan or was defeated by Afghan Mujahideen groups, India had also good relations till 1996. But with the victory of the Taliban, India got isolated whereas Pakistan developed good relations with the Taliban and gained "strategic depth". Also, India was forced to leave its embassy and withdraw its diplomatic staff from Afghanistan (Ganguly & Howenstein, 2009).

Figure 12: The Map of Soviet War or Invasion in Afghanistan

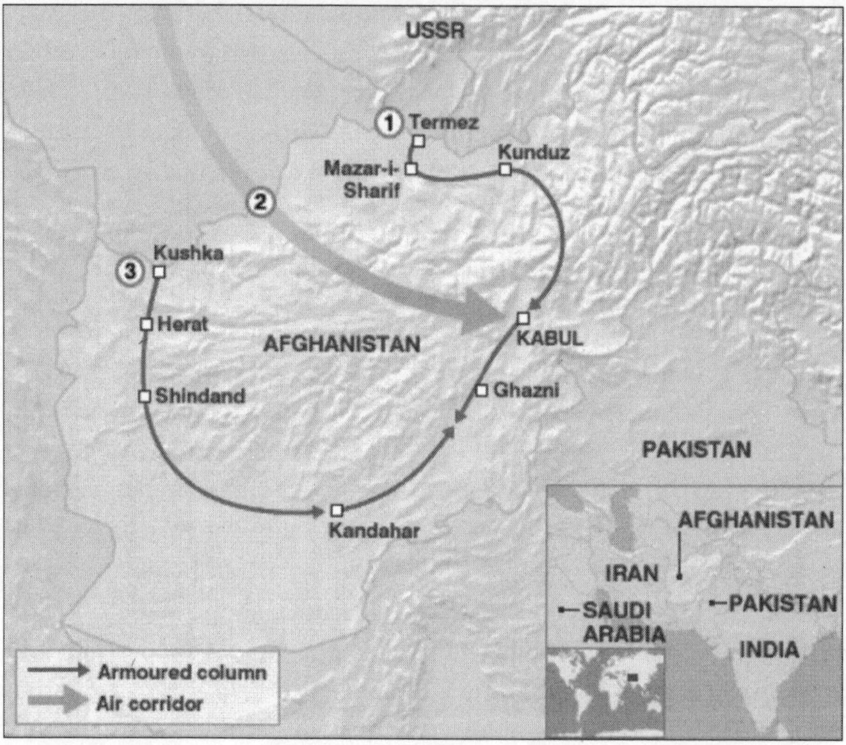

Source: http://news.bbc.co.uk/2/hi/7883532.stm

India also had less contact with Afghan Mujahideen during Afghan Jihad (1979-1989) but when Burhanuddin Rabbani became president of Afghanistan, India had good relation with Afghanistan. At that time Rabbani thought that Pakistan supported Gulbuddin Hekmatyar's Party Hezb-e- Islami which brought civil war in Afghanistan. Riaz Ahmed Khan, a former Pakistani foreign secretary in his book, Afghanistan and Pakistan: Conflict, Extremism and Resistance to Modernity, wrote that when Rabbani led Jamiat-e-Islami and at that time defence minister Ahmad shah Massoud became "Shura-e-Nazar" to fight against Soviet invasion and Pakistan was sceptical about this group as it feared that they could brought things against Pakistan's interest, where Pakistan was dissatisfied with Rabbani's government.

When the Taliban took the control or came into power in 1996 under the helm of Mullah Mohammad Omar, India lost its support and cooperation. But India maintained support to the Northern Alliance militarily and financially during the Taliban regime (India's Challenge in Afghanistan, 2014).

When the Taliban took power in 1996 it was for the first time that Pakistan improved its bilateral relation with the Taliban regime. In contrast, India supported the Jamiat-e-Islami (the party that was led by Rabbani where India supported this group during the civil war against the Hizb-i-Islami lead by Gulbuddin Hekmatyar) and the Northern Alliance which was established by one of the commanders of Jamiat-e-Islami Ahmad Shah Massoud when the Taliban took power in 1996. This support of India influenced the Taliban's mindset, because of this they never tried to have connection or improve their diplomatic relations with India. (The Tangled History of the Afghanistan-India-Pakistan Triangle, n.d.).

Afghanistan's Foreign Policy with India and Pakistan during Hamid Karzai Presidency Period

After the US toppled the Taliban government, Hamid Karzai became Afghanistan's new president. During this entire period, from 2001 to 2014, Afghanistan-Pakistan relations moved toward chaos rather than harmony. Generally, Kabul's Indo-Pak policy was very much pro-India. This was influenced by the fact that both countries had provided sanctuary to the groups opposing each other's government in the Cold War period. This affected the strategic mindsets in both Afghanistan and Pakistan.

These Cold War-type fears and nightmares were relived in the post-2001 period. Pakistan blamed Kabul, for—along with Indian intelligence agency RAW—destabilising Balochistan, the Federally Administered Tribal Areas (FATA), and other Pakistani territories. Afghanistan, on the other hand, claimed that Pakistan provided sanctuary to the ousted Taliban and supported them. Therefore, another proxy war started between India-Afghanistan-Pakistan in the Af-Pak region during the Karzai era, and continues today. (For more information about the proxy war in Afghanistan see William Dalrymple's essay, "A Deadly Triangle: Afghanistan, Pakistan and India.")

During the beginning of Hamid Karzai's first term, Afghanistan was largely secure and peaceful; therefore, Kabul's Indo-Pak policy was somewhere between neutrality and an overtly pro-India stance. Though military relations between Kabul-Delhi started in 2007 with the deployment of a military team, the interaction was only "limited to train[ing] Afghan security forces in weapons handling, map reading, and battalion-level staff work."

However, in 2009, Karzai's relations with the new US President Barack Obama fell flat. As a result, Kabul sought to improve relations with regional countries such as India, China, and Russia. It was in this period that Afghanistan signed one of its first strategic agreements with India, which included the acceptance of Afghanistan's nearly six-year-old request for India to train Afghan security forces. Moreover, ahead of 2014 US-NATO troop withdrawal, Kabul approached India with a weapons wish-list, including "150 battle tanks, 120 (105 mm) field guns, a large number of 82 mm mortars, one medium lift transport aircraft (AN-32), two squadrons of medium lift and attack helicopters and a large number of trucks." In addition, more than 1,400 Afghans were sent to India for military training.

The motive behind Karzai's multilateralism and regionalism was very much influenced by his relations with the United States, which labelled him "not an adequate strategic partner", combined with the perception that Pakistan was behind the rise in insecurity in Afghanistan and the announcement of US-NATO withdrawal.

Kabul's relations with Pakistan deteriorated in Karzai's second term because of insecurity in Afghanistan, and Kabul's romanticised vision of Delhi (particularly when it came to security and strategic relations). Meanwhile, Pakistani security forces arrested those Taliban leaders who had opened "peace talks" with Kabul, such as Mullah Baradar, the second in command in the Taliban hierarchy, and provided sanctuary to fighters involved in militancy and insurgency in Afghanistan. That is why, in this period, Kabul's policies became more pro-India compared to Karzai's first term.

Also, in the beginning of 2006 president of Pakistan Pervez Musharraf said that Afghanistan's president Hamid Karzai was unaware of what was happening in his government, where also Pakistan's president or Pakistani sides said that Hamid Karzai blamed Pakistan to hide his government's failure to draw away the attention of the people (Ahmed & Bhatnagar, 2007).

Afghanistan and India Relations and Challenges for Pakistan

Afghanistan has the attention of the international community because of its strategic location and mineral resources. After Hamid Karzai became the president of Afghanistan, India and Afghanistan shared a good relationship. India helped Afghanistan in reconstruction of the nation and also trained and gave scholarships to Afghan students. India increased its influence and impact in Afghanistan which annoyed Pakistan, where the frequent security dilemmas created misunderstandings between Pakistan and India.

Indo-Afghan Political Relations

In 2011 both India and Afghanistan signed the strategic friendship treaty which was the continuation of their partnership treaty of 1950 which they had signed and where it was written that the two countries would be friends and live in peace. With the signing of this treaty India locally and internationally achieved a lot of benefits.

India got the chance to train Afghan forces who also served for a long period for India. In the economic domain, India also got access to Afghan natural resources and mines (Amjad & Mustafa, 2019).

This agreement also gave chance to India to operate freely in every part of Afghanistan for its own security and strategic benefits.

With the signing of the 2011 strategic friendship treaty, India and Afghanistan also signed two more agreements, which are:

1. MoU (Memorandum of Understanding) for the improvement of hydrocarbons.
2. Giving back or help for the improvement of minerals by MoU (Memorandum of Understanding).

India's purpose was fulfilled in the shadow of these agreements that India had waited for a long time for this achievement. India

Figure 13: Afghanistan and India Signed Strategic Partnership Agreement in 2011

Source: Press Information Bureau / ID 36903

was protecting the strategic interests of both countries, Afghanistan and India, from Farkhor airbase, which was located 130 km from its capital. India provided weapons to the Northern Alliance at the time of Taliban regime, and India also constructed hospitals for Northern Alliance armies to provide medical facilities to them (Amjad & Mustafa, 2019).

India many times accused Pakistan of training terroristic groups in tribal areas of Pakistan and also requested the international community to put pressure on Pakistan to stop these activities in the tribal areas. Pakistan could not digest the presence of India in Afghanistan, as it would harm its own interest. Pakistan was also sceptic of India's intentions as, in the garb of development, India was securing its national interests (Mustafa et al., 2019).

Objectives of India in Afghanistan

India's purpose in Afghanistan has derived from the idea or writing of Kautilya, also known as the Indian Machiavelli, which said, *"Every neighbouring state is enemy and enemy's enemy is a friend"*, where Afghanistan because of its geopolitical and important strategic place became important for India. Its purpose in Afghanistan is multidimensional, such as limiting the Taliban's activity, helping Afghanistan to be democratic, also decreasing Pakistan's impact in Afghanistan and gaining the leading role in central Asia. (Amjad & Mustafa, 2019).

India seeks to have wide interest in Afghanistan by decreasing the influence of Pakistan in Afghanistan. The major objectives of India in Afghanistan are:

1. *Stop Anti-India Terrorism*

India's major purpose is to stop and avoid the terrorist groups, which are supported by Pakistan, from using Afghanistan as a place against India, for example, against its economic, diplomatic operation or interests. India in the United Nations in July 2008 asserted that our priority must be to stop the terrorist activity in Afghanistan's border and help that country with her security. After four months the terrorists, members of Lashakr-e-Taiba that supported by Pakistan, attacked at different parts of Mumbai city (Hanauer & Chalk, 2012).

2. *Increase Presence in Central Asia*

An important objective of India in Afghanistan is to gain or take advantage of Central Asian energy resources. India spends a lot of money building roads for increasing its presence in Central Asia. For the growth of their economies both India and Pakistan need energy resources like the TAPI (Turkmenistan, Afghanistan, Pakistan and India) pipeline, one of the important projects which cost 1.4 billion transit fees for Afghanistan. This pipeline will motivate both India and Pakistan to promote its security and also insist on stability in Afghanistan (Hanauer & Chalk, 2012).

3. *Project Power and Indicate Global Interests*

In India's foreign policy, India's improvement and integration in world economy increases the value and aim of trade and commercial purposes of India. India's armed forces play an active role, where India built an airbase in Tajikistan through which India sent humanitarian help and goods into Afghanistan. India also sent a small number of troops to Afghanistan to protect reconstruction projects and its diplomatic missions. For India, Afghanistan is a test to present itself as a global power.

Afghanistan and India Economic Relations

After the falling of the Taliban regime, when Hamid Karzai became the president of Afghanistan, India helped a lot for reconstruction and development of Afghanistan. In the conference (Heart of Asia) in Kabul in 2012, India promised to assist and integrate Afghanistan in regional economy. Also, India promised that it would lead Afghanistan in facilitating regional trade and business. Afghanistan can be important for trade and energy in the region if it has good economic relations with Pakistan. India helped Afghanistan in 2007 in becoming the member of SAARC (South Asian Association for Regional Cooperation (Price, n.d.).

Social and economic improvement is essential for regional security as India has recognised in Afghanistan. Afghanistan and India signed a strategic partnership agreement in 2011 when Hamid Karzai visited India, and that agreement includes: trade and economic cooperation, political and security assistance, help in education, cultural and people-to-people relations, whereby India became one of the big five donors in Afghanistan.

For assuring the stability of Afghanistan, the region must improve socially and economically. Indian government's help and assistance to Afghanistan with its economic policies include, promotion of trade, investment in private sectors to increase its impact in Afghanistan. In improvement assistance that India supports the Karzai government and accepts the Karzai administration, and also assist in development of Afghanistan such as assistance in improvement or providing of education, healthcare, generation of power, telecommunications training. Also in trade assistance, India and Afghanistan signed a trade agreement in 2003. India also invests in private sectors, where Indian companies invest in agriculture and mining fields (Hanauer & Chalk, 2012).

Indian help is mainly in three domains such as humanitarian help, infrastructure and capacity building, and the most important are:

- With the help of world food programming organisation, India helps with distribution of food and biscuits to primary school children and also reintegration of schools.
- Salma Dam power project construction.
- 3,500 tonnes wheat assistance for Afghanistan.

- Parliament building construction.
- Reintegration of Zaranj-Delaram road.

As mentioned above, India helped Afghanistan a lot and this is why India is the fifth largest donor of Afghanistan (Price, n.d.). India also assisted Afghanistan in reconstruction of social sectors, where the government of India built a children's hospital in Kabul called Indira Gandhi Children Hospital which has 150 beds for patients (Amjad & Mustafa, 2019).

India, with its economic and trade assistance, wants to increase her political influence in Afghanistan and at the same time wants to decrease or undermine the impact of Pakistan. India constructed the road between Zaranj and Delaram, which is 220 km long. Also,

Figure 14: Afghanistan Parliament Building Built with the Help of India in Afghanistan

Source: Twitter

India made the leading routes of Chabahar port which is important to Afghanistan, connecting Herat and Kandahar highways.

This route made by India will save Afghanistan from wastage of time in reaching the main ports. It will also decrease the importance of Pakistan's Gwadar port and prevent Pakistan from stopping Indian exports to Afghanistan.

India's Humanitarian Assistance to Afghanistan

India helped Afghanistan on many an occasion as one of its assistance is humanitarian assistance, where the officials of the

Figure 15: Chabahar Leading Routes with the Connection of Herat-Kandahar Highways

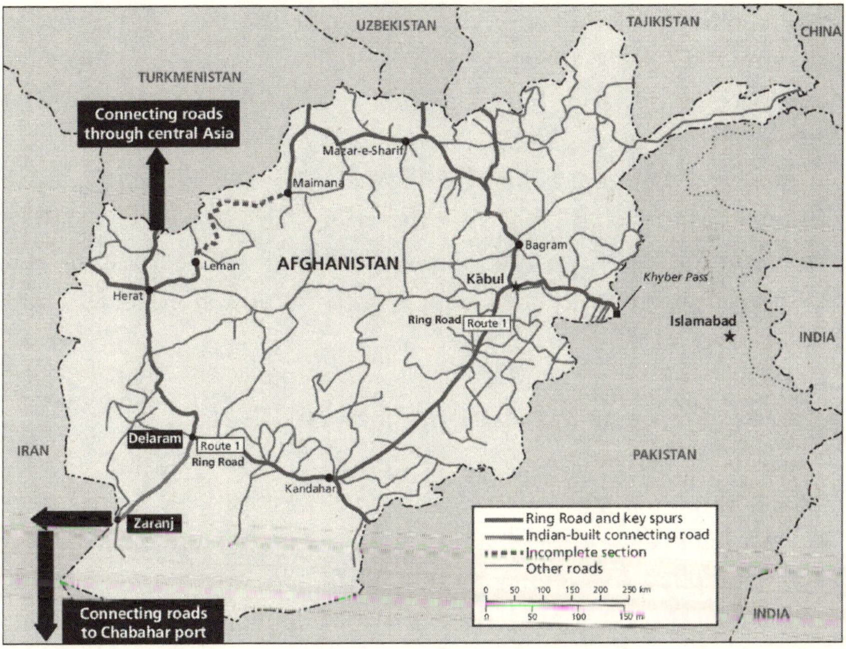

Source: https://www.semanticscholar.org/paper/India%27s-and-Pakistan%27s-Strategies-in-Afghanistan-Hanauer-Chalk/4433429c5f2bce4212f70f53ae216f9bc53dd763

United Nations appreciated India for providing Covid-19 vaccines to Afghanistan at this time of pandemic. In Afghanistan the head of the United Nations Assistance Mission in Afghanistan (UNAMA), and Deborah Lyons the UN Security Council said that it looks that Afghanistan has suffered a second wave of Covid-19; she also said, in a meeting that "we thank India for its assistance of vaccines to Afghanistan and we have to be careful about the third wave of Covid-19 virus where the vaccination has begun. Also, Adela Raz, Afghanistan's permanent representative at the United Nations, says thanks to India's humanitarian assistance and said that we have to fight against this virus and recover the Afghans from this pandemic by vaccination." T. S. Tirumutri, India's permanent representative, also stated that India helped Afghanistan with 75,000 Mt of wheat through Chahbahar port because of the food insecurity in the time of COVID-19; also India helped with providing 968,000 doses to Afghanistan ("India's Donation of COVID-19 Vaccines to Afghanistan Lauded", 2021).

Embassy of India in Kabul also mentioned in its brief bilateral relationship that in the time of pandemic, India's humanitarian assistance was that in 2020 India helped with 5 lakh Hydroxychloroquine tablets and 1 lakh Paracetamol tablets and 50,000 surgical gloves to Afghanistan.

Analysis of Foreign Policy of Afghanistan Towards India and Pakistan

Afghanistan's foreign policy is based on important beliefs, goals and values, where Afghanistan's constitution in article 7 and 8 determine: "Foreign policy of country should formulate with the saving of independence, territorial integrity, national interest essentially non-interference, equality of rights, good neighbouring and mutual respect (article 8). The United Nations Charter, inter-state agreements, international treaties to which Afghanistan has membership and the Universal Declaration of Human Rights should notice or keep in mind by Afghanistan's government." Afghanistan's foreign policy is made or derived from three main factors, which are geopolitics, economic needs and racial structure.

India and Pakistan have good relations with Afghanistan and want to increase their influence and achieve their goals in Afghanistan

Figure 16: After the Emergence of Pakistan, Political Division Map of South Asia from 1947 to 1971

Source: https://www.researchgate.net/figure/A-map-of-political-divisions-in-South-Asia-From-1947-until-1971-East-Pakistan-was-part_fig1_267629390

from the time of the partition of British India and mainly from the time of Hamid Karzai's government. (Ganguly & Howenstein, 2009) There are reasons for Afghanistan being pro India, and its relations not so good with Pakistan, from the time of the emergence of Pakistan that changed the map of South Asian politics and also changed the internal and external politics.

As mentioned above, Pakistan's emergence in 1947 changed the south Asian map and also changed the foreign policy of Afghanistan toward Pakistan. The main reason was the dispute over Durand line that Afghanistan never recognised. Afghanistan's relations with India were mostly good after the falling of Taliban's regime. India had not had good relations with the Taliban. India supported the Northern Alliance against the Taliban. When Hamid Karzai became President of Afghanistan and Northern Alliance members got high government posts, India made its presence strong.

India and Pakistan both countries want to have their presence and influence in Afghanistan and undermine each other's influence. Three countries (Afghanistan, Pakistan and India) bear militant violence, where India fears that if civil war happened in Afghanistan, Afghanistan will be used by extremist groups against India, and also Pakistan fears that the inflammation of civil war will result in riots by Afghan refugees in Pakistan. So, Afghanistan should maintain a balance between the two countries and accordingly that Afghanistan must formulate its foreign policy.

Afghanistan has been the transit for the silk route, where Afghanistan's relationship with its neighbour countries, India and Pakistan are of prime importance. When Afghanistan wants to formulate its foreign policy, she should not see the bilateral relations, it means it is not enough. There are essential relations and connections that impact Afghanistan's policies, and Afghanistan should keep in mind that there is not only one country. Afghanistan differs its relations with India and Pakistan with the paying cost for one side and with having closeness to another side ("A See-Saw Relationship", 2020).

Conclusion

Afghanistan as a Muslim nation settles as a bridge between not only the Middle East, Central Asia, the subcontinent, but also is the gateway between Islamic world and the West. Afghanistan's foreign policy is based on important beliefs, goals and values, where Afghanistan's constitution in article 7 and 8 determine: "Foreign policy of country should formulate with the saving of independence, territorial integrity, national interest essentially non-interference, equality of rights, good neighbouring and mutual respect (article 8). The United Nations Charter, inter-state agreements, international treaties to which Afghanistan has membership and the Universal Declaration of Human Rights should notice or keep in mind by Afghanistan's government."

We saw that it shows the determinant of foreign policy of Afghanistan, where its foreign policy is made or derived from three main important factors which are geopolitics, economic needs and racial structure that play an important role in formulating of Afghan foreign policy.

India and Pakistan had ties with different Afghan governments from the time of the break-up of the British colonial empire in 1947, when both countries emerged and got their independence. Afghanistan's relationship with its neighbour countries India and Pakistan are of prime importance. When Afghanistan wants to formulate its foreign policy, she should not see the bilateral relations, it means it is not enough.

There are essential relations and connections that impact Afghanistan's policies, where Afghanistan should keep in mind that there is not only one country. Afghanistan differs its relations with India and Pakistan with the paying cost for one side and with having closeness to another side.

With different governments emerging in Afghanistan, Afghanistan differs its relations with India and Pakistan for some reasons. The emergence of Pakistan in 1947 brought changes in the south Asian map, especially changes in Afghanistan's internal and external politics.

As we see both countries, India and Pakistan, have competition in Afghanistan in having close relations with Afghan government, undermining each other's influence in Afghanistan. Afghanistan had better relations with India than Pakistan during upcoming of different governments. If we see from the time of the Cold War when the Soviet Union invaded Afghanistan, India was the first country that did not publicly oppose the Soviet Union's intervention in Afghanistan. At the same time, India formed the non-alignment movement. Whereas Pakistan did not have good relations with Afghanistan at that time.

During the time of the Taliban, it was the first time that India lost its relations with Afghanistan, whereas Pakistan had good relations with the Taliban's regime. India supported the Northern Alliance against the Taliban.

After the fall of the Taliban's regime, when Hamid Karzai became the president of Afghanistan, the Northern Alliance members got high posts in government, so India took advantage of this and strengthened its presence in Afghanistan.

At the time of Karzai's government, India had good relations with Afghanistan, where also India supported Karzai's government and helped Afghanistan financially, politically.

Afghanistan and Pakistan did not have good relations in Hamid Karzai's time, when both countries many times blamed each other.

Karzai blamed Pakistan for creating instability in Afghanistan with the support of the Taliban and giving them safe haven. Pakistan blamed Afghanistan for supporting Baluch liberals.

Afghanistan and Pakistan did not have good relations from the start because of their dispute over the Durand line, the border line that was signed in 1893 between Amir Abdur Rahman Khan and the British Empire. Afghanistan did not recognise or accept this border line until now, which divides the Pashtun people who have the same culture and live on both sides of the border.

Afghanistan also opened the Pashtunistan homeland reason with Pakistan that Pakistan has to give the right to self-determination to the Pashtun people who live in its territory.

The Pashtunistan problem became the main dispute between Afghanistan and Pakistan, and every Afghan government that came to power has maintained the demand of Pashtunistan. Pakistan behaves carefully with both its domestic Pashtuns and with Afghan Pashtuns. Pakistan manages carefully the Pashtun idea, where the NWFP (North West Frontier Province) is not named for the majority of its ethnic that most of time requested by Pashtuns to renamed as Pashtunistan, but Pakistan government has refused the request. Pashtunistan for Afghanistan and for the Pashtuns who live outside of Pakistan mean a lot, which covers from Indian ocean to Gilgit Northern areas of Pakistan, and from Durand line to Kashmir.

Afghanistan was the first country to oppose membership of Pakistan to United Nations, where Afghanistan said in Assembly of United Nations: "In this great organization, Afghanistan envoy does not oppose to membership of Pakistan, but in this time, we have no ability and we have repented to vote for Pakistan. This is for that Pakistan should determine them whether they want to be independent or want to be part of Pakistan."

The common Objectives of South Asian countries are to grow their economies, live in peace, cultural development, develop the quality of life, where the common interest of the three countries (Afghanistan, India and Pakistan) are also the same to grow their economies, with a stability of having good relations with each other.

References

"A See-Saw Relationship: An Overview of Afghanistan's Ties with India and Pakistan", *E-International Relations*, August 6, 2020, at https://www.e-ir.info/2020/08/06/a-see-saw-relationship-an-overview-of-afghanistans-ties-with-india-and-pakistan/

Ahmed, Z. S. and S. Bhatnagar (2007). "Pakistan-Afghanistan Relations and the Indian Factor", *Pakistan Horizon*, 60(2), 159-74.

Amjad, M. and G. Mustafa (2019). Indo-Afghan Relations: Implications for Pakistan, 84, 53-79.

Ganguly, S. and N. Howenstein (2009). India-Pakistan Rivalry in Afghanistan", *Journal of International Affairs*, 63(1), 127-40.

Hanauer, L. and and P. Chalk (2012). *India's and Pakistan's Strategies in Afghanistan: Implications for the United States and the Region,* at https://www.rand.org/pubs/occasional_papers/OP387.html

Pant, Harsh V., "India's Challenge in Afghanistan: With Power Comes Responsibility", January 14, 2014, Centre for the Advanced Study of India (CASI), at https://casi.sas.upenn.edu/content/indias-challenge-afghanistan-power-comes-responsibility-harsh-v-pant

"India's donation of COVID-19 vaccines to Afghanistan lauded", *The Hindu*, March 21, 2021, at https://www.thehindu.com/news/international/indias-donation-of-covid-19-vaccines-to-afghanistan-lauded/article34148051.ece

Malhotra, Vinay Kumar, *International Relations,* (2012), Fourth Revised and Enlarged Edition, Vedams eBooks (P) Ltd. (n.d.). Retrieved June 20, 2021, from https://www.abebooks.com/first-edition/International-Relations-Vinay-Kumar-Malhotra-Anmol/7577938487/bd

Mustafa, G., M. Asif and M. Arslan (2019). *Indo-Afghanistan Relations: Challenges for Pakistan*, 59-69.

Price, G. (n.d.). *India's Policy towards Afghanistan,* 10.

"Prospects for Indian-Pakistani Cooperation in Afghanistan". (n.d.). Retrieved June 22, 2021, from https://www.csis.org/analysis/prospects-indian-pakistani-cooperation-afghanistan

"The Tangled History of the Afghanistan-India-Pakistan Triangle". (n.d.). Retrieved June 22, 2021, from https://thediplomat.com/2016/12/the-tangled-history-of-the-afghanistan-india-pakistan-triangle/

STRATEGIC PARTNERS: MAPPING OUT THE KEY ISSUES AND CHALLENGES BETWEEN INDIA AND ISRAEL

SHAZAD

Introduction

With the independence of India from British suzerainty, there was the dawn of the nation having the potential of significant military, economic, and geographical capabilities and charting a new course in the history of international relations. India has ushered itself as the nation emerged from the fight against colonialism, imperialism and the leader of the third world. Moral ethical rhetoric has laid the foundation of the nation under the helm of first Prime Minister of India, Jawaharlal Nehru, who implicitly was sympathetic to socialism and was having the dream of putting India in the centre of the international politics as a responsible and emerging power. When the whole world was engulfed in the Cold War politics and choosing either sides of US or Soviet camps, India was carving its own trajectory of not joining either, and formed the Non-Aligned Movement (NAM). According to some scholars, the establishment of NAM was indeed a remarkable and daring step from the third world countries, consisting of more nation-states than either of the aforementioned camps. And, the recent independence of their nations would have been threatened if they would have engaged themselves in Cold War politics. However, the NAM had also its limitations where it sometimes seems a bogus multilateral platform and tilts more often towards the Soviet Union. India, at those times, was recovering from the trauma of partition and its culminated religious riots and many of its parliamentarians were appeasing its minority Muslim population because they have been targeted by the Hindu chauvinists over the treatment of Hindus in Pakistan. One the one hand, Jawaharlal Nehru was aiming to creating a socialist independent nation free from the religious divisions, and on the other, the Indian leaders were struggling to convince the royal kingdoms to join India and had faced enormous difficulties as well.

As far as the foreign policy is concerned, India started establishing the diplomatic relations with various countries and engaged itself in international business. India vigorously took part in the activities of the UN and manifested itself as the major power. Under his leadership, Asian Relations Conference was organised in 1947 where many leaders of the independence movements of various countries came together and the juncture asserted a first ever "Asian Unity" (Nehru, 1947).

In the backdrop of the overwhelming Muslim population in India, he established the diplomatic relations with the Arab Nations and the historical and cultural linkages of the Arab World with India has strengthened the diplomatic and strategic relationship with them. Most of the Arab nations became members of the NAM over a period of time. When India was establishing its footprint in the International World Order, there was long conflict between the Palestinians and Israelis over the establishment of the State of Israel from the British mandate territory. On May 14, 1948, Israel was created.

The establishment of Israel has completed changed the regional geopolitical dynamics of the Arab World in particular and the whole international politics in general. The creation of Israel has also the implication on India as it has multifaceted relations with the Arab World and its response on the events had defined the course of its foreign policy towards the Arab World and Israel.

I am trying to look into the India-Israel relations through the historical lens and see the various trends in their relations and the contemporary developments in it. Moreover, I am looking into the future course of action in the backdrop of their relations and engagements at various levels. In addition to this, I will try to discover the impact of India-Israel relations over the regional security paradigm in South Asia and the Middle East and the overall International World Order in general.

I am looking into their relations through four different phases from the defining period to have a better understanding of the events that took place and led to the changing course of the action by the stakeholders of India and Israel in their diplomatic relationship.

Defining Period in Indo-Israel Relations: 1947-1962

Since the Congress party was at the forefront of India's Independence struggle, Jawaharlal Nehru, after India's Independence, took the responsibility of the formulation of India's Foreign Policy and his ideals of anti-imperialism, anti-colonialism and socialism, formulated over the course of India's independence struggle, led to the foundation of India's initial foreign policy objectives. He called to offer support to other countries fighting imperialism and colonialism under the domain of NAM. In the Arab World, he viewed then ongoing conflict between Arabs and Jews as a matter of colonialism and asserted that, *"Palestine is not an empty land waiting to be settled by foreigners, there are Arabs who live there and pressed for creating a democratic and federal state of Palestine where Jews and Arabs will live together"* (Hadass, 2002, pp. 95-106). He viewed the

Zionists collaborating with the Britain, one of the colonial powers, to colonise and create a religious division in Palestine. He acknowledged the Jewish connection to Palestine but viewed their aspiration to establish Israel, a Jewish state, as a matter of great conflict between the existing Arab and Jewish populations and a piece of land for the colonial powers to colonialise (Inbar, 2017, pp. 369-383). In 1974, India recognised the Palestine Liberation Organization as the sole, legitimate representative of the Palestinians; it was the first non-Arab country do so.

With the unfolding of various international events concerning the Cold War, both the US and Soviet Union supported the creation of Israel as they viewed this opportunity to further expand their influence in favour of them, and could be used as a strategic option in the near future. However, India, being in a nascent stage of nation-building and a new player in international politics, stuck to its idealism to favour Palestine and didn't anticipated the coming waves of developments in favour of Israel. Moreover, India, being a Member of United Nations Special Committee on Palestine, voted in favour on Federal Plan instead the two-state solution, supporting the latter by a majority of the nations. Though India's move didn't yield any result in resolving the conflict, there was a sudden incident with the creation of Israel in 1948, without acknowledging the consequent establishment of the State of Palestine. The establishment of Israel didn't happen in consonance with the India's idea of Israel-Palestine conflict. Therefore, when the voting took place regarding the recognition of Israel in the UN, India declined to recognise it in the United Nations in June 1949.

Several theories came up at that time on the decision of India not recognising Israel but some convincing arguments emerged which analysed Nehru's move on the basis of pragmatism. There were several reasons behind it. India was facing a very tough time with the accession of Kashmir in the India Union and the ensuing war with

Pakistan over its claim. Moreover, the case of Kashmir had already being dragged in the UN Security Council and India feared that if it were going to recognise Israel, it would cost the discord of Arab world in supporting Pakistan on Kashmir. During those times, India's Ambassador to United States, Vijaya Lakshmi Pandit, met with the Israeli counterpart and shared that the tense situation in Kashmir postponed recognition of Israel (Blarel, 2017, pp. 384-400). In 1950 Nehru wrote a letter to his Chief Ministers of the Indian Union *"we refrained from recognizing Israel because of our desire not to offend the sentiments of our friends in the Arab countries"* (Falk, 2009, pp. 1-6). In addition to this, India during those times was appeasing its Muslim population, in the aftermath of partition, and this decision could have isolated them and its strategic interests in West Asia. Acknowledging the discourse over the recognition of Israel, one of the Muslim parliamentarians said in the Indian Parliament:

> "...will the Honourable Prime Minister keep in mind the fact [that] there are a large number of people living in the Indian Dominion whose wishes and sentiments in this regard should be kept in view regarding the recognition of the State of Israel as they are definitely opposed to it."

In the international community, there was a wave of support for Israel, partly due to the sympathetic cause of Jews and partly due to their strategic interest in favour of Israel in the near future. Majority of the regional powers such as Iran, Turkey, China had de jure recognised Israel. In the meantime, India was observing those events and took the decision of following suit and extended de jure recognition of Israel in September 1950. Israel welcomed this move and was very much receptive to strengthening relations with India. Israel aided India with sophisticated weapons and ammunition which immensely helped India in Kargil War with Pakistan in 1999. Moreover, Israel also provided humanitarian relief to India. Following a devastating earthquake in 2001, Israel sent an IDF emergency response delegation to India for two weeks to provide humanitarian relief and treatment for the victims. *It opened its consulate in Mumbai in 1953 to facilitate the immigration of thousands of Jews to Israel, but India was still obscure of its relationship with Israel and had the priority to appease the Arab world. Both Israel and the United States appealed to India for further strengthening the relations with the former, but India was adamant on sticking on its realist-cum-moral principles and failed to see the future and India's stakes over its foreign policy decision.*

In contrast, India was quick to establish relationship and offered friendship to the newly born secular regime of Nasser in Egypt. PM Jawaharlal Nehru even visited Cairo in 1953 and discussed various issues from Arab-Israel conflict to US neo-imperialism. Moreover, when the Baghdad Pact was founded with support of the US, both India and Egypt denounced the military alliance as they were of the opinion that it would lead to regional instability and will provide a strategic location for the US to encircle Soviet Union's influence. Not only this, when the Suez Crisis occurred, India stood by the side of Egypt and called Israel the 'aggressor'. India also sent its forces as peacekeepers to Egypt under the United Nations Emergency Force, in the aftermath of the Suez Crisis.

Interestingly, in the backdrop of India's support to Egypt during Suez Crisis and supporting Palestine in Arab-Israel conflict, its Middle East Policy has been able to yield some favourable outcomes by isolating Pakistan in its attempt to create a pan-Islamism ideology and countering India's influence in West Asia. At the same time, it muddles through limited engagement with the Jewish State. Over a period of time, India steadily engaged with Israel by taking all accounts in consideration. On one stance, Defence Minister, V. K. Krishna Menon said in the parliament that "we have no hostility whatsoever so far as the State of Israel is concerned, and we declare its existence as a sovereign state" (Srivastava, 1970, pp. 238-264). However, the Indian government refrained from establishing full diplomatic relations with Israel as its stake of moral and strategic costs were very high and being a nascent country in nation-building, India could not afford to take such significant decisions where any strategic blunder could hamper India's growth and development.

Transition Phase: 1962 to 1990

By the time, India had not been involved in any major military conflict. Though, it won its war with Pakistan in 1948, as Pakistan didn't match the military capabilities with India then. However, India under Nehru's leadership was in the hang-over of idealism and looking forward its ties with China under the realm of 'Panchsheel Agreement'.

The winning of war by China over its border conflict with India in 1962 exposed India's flaws in its military capabilities to fight a full-fledged war with China. India's idealism and NAM showed the limitations to deal with hegemony and living in the realist world order. During the War of 1962, the Israeli Prime Minister David Ben-Gurion expressed his "fullest sympathy and understanding" and, on the request of Prime Minister Jawaharlal Nehru, supplied weapons to India (SEN, 2020). India sourced Israeli weapons during the India-Pakistan wars of 1965 and 1971. *India faced a humiliating defeat and realised the utmost need of overhauling its military apparatus and state-of-the-art weapons in its fight with China. In the aftermath of war, India was looking for some partner states to modernise its weapons and army. And, at the same time, Israel saw this as an opportunity to accommodate India's need at its crucial and tough phase. Israel extended its limited arms support to India, but this goodwill gesture didn't yield any changes in India's posture toward Israel vis-à-vis thePalestinian conflict. In fact, India joined other Arab states in criticising Israel's invasion of Egypt, culminating in the Six-*

Day War of 1967. The victory of Israel resulted in the conquering of territories allotted by the UN action plan for the Palestinian state. Many states came out harshly against Israel, including India. In October 1967, the Indian Defence Minister proposed that "Israel must withdraw from occupied territories, all states should respect the territorial integrity of each other, resolution of the dispute by peaceful method and safeguarding of right of Palestine refugees" (Ward, 1992).

On the UN platform, Indian representative to UNSC put forward the "four-point formula", which asserted that the aggressive party should not enjoy the fruits of aggression, and both the parties should go back to June 4, 1967 position.

The impressive victory of Israel in the conflict with collective Arab nations was perplexing, with its military burgeoning in such a short span of time. Afterwards, Israel became the regional military power and came at the geopolitical desk to bargain peace and maintain strategic relationship with it. In the West, overwhelming number of the nations were willing to establish strategic and security ties with Israel. When the world was discussing Israel's victory, it appealed to India as well to establish security and strategic ties with it. Under those geopolitical settings, India established intelligence ties with Israel. At the behest of then PM Indira Gandhi, who was seen was a realist stateswoman in the strategic and military circles, India's Research and Analysis Wing established relations with Mossad, Israel's intelligence wing, in 1968. Meantime, in South Asia, East Pakistan's Mukti Bahini under Sheikh Mujibur Rehman demanded separation from West Pakistan and called to establish an independent nation. Long years of protest and killings of protestors by Pakistan Army severed the situation and many regional powers took note of the changing scenarios in East Pakistan. India specifically was facing a very tough time during those phases because of the atrocities meted out by Pakistan Army against Hindus and other minorities creating an influx of millions of refugees in India's West Bengal and the North East. It led to 'Operation Searchlight' by the Pakistan Army and the subsequent 'Operation Chengis Khan' which dragged India into the conflict and both India and Pakistan came to war with each other. Pakistan was getting support from the both the US and China and had the strategic military superiority over India in the initial times. Taking this point into consideration, India asked for military supplies from Israel among which India received heavy 160 mm mortars from the latter (Mumtaz Ahmad Shah, 2020).

In international politics, the Soviet Union's position was also diminished due to its internal rift and was retreating from the Middle East. Most of the Arab nations were introspecting and revising their national security, amidst the strategic interest in the region. The Iranian Revolution threatened many Arab states and they saw Iran as a bigger threat than Israel. This condition withered away the possible Arab bloc behind the Palestinian cause. Egypt realised the reality of its militarist inferiority against Israel and took the decisive step of normalising relations with the US and Israel. After consistent efforts, President Jimmy Carter too brokered a deal between Israel and Egypt, he managed to convince President Anwar Sadat to normalise relations with Israel and no longer support any sort of confrontation and antagonism against Israel. Keeping in mind the drain of resources in the war with Israel, Egypt signed "Camp David Accord" with Israel in the presence of US President Jimmy Carter. Following this event, many realised that taking sides with Israel will at least keep their regime safe from the same sort of revolution that happened in Iran.

When this strategic paradigm shift was happening, India wanted to take advantage of these fault lines and with restraint moving towards Israel. When Rajiv Gandhi became the Prime Minister, he offered goodwill gestures to Israel. One of the manifestations of India's getting closer to Israel was witnessed when a United Arab resolution came in UN Assembly concerning the expulsion of Israel from the UN for besieging the Palestine Liberation Organization (PLO) in Tunis in 1985. Indian Minister of External Affairs, Bali Ram Bhagat, criticised Israel's aggressive policies, but India abstained from backing the Arab sponsored resolution in the UN General Assembly (Ward, 1992). For the very first time, PM Rajiv Gandhi met with Israeli PM Shimon Peres on sidelines of the 40th UN General Assembly session. Moreover, during his visit to the US in 1988, PM Gandhi met American Jewish stakeholders and pro-Zionist US Congressmen and discussed various issues from Israel-Palestine issue to Pakistan's sponsored terrorism (Blarel, 2017). Hence, all these moves helped in strengthening and normalising the relations between Israel and India. Moreover, time helped India in testing Israel as a reliable strategic partner in the changing world order.

Constructive Engagement: From 1990 to 2014

Towards the early 1990s, the Soviet Union dramatically collapsed, resulting in the victory of the United States and the emergence of a unipolar world order. Geopolitical settings around the world suddenly changed and every nation-state was preserving their national interests. In South Asia, India during Bangladesh Liberation War, sided with the Soviet Union, due to imminent threat of US if India engaged in war with East Pakistan, and signed the 'Friendship Treaty' in 1971. This action strategically shifted India from NAM trajectory to socialist one along with the Soviet Union. And with the disintegration of the Soviet Union, India was left to change its foreign policy attitude and get ready to engage with the sole Superpower, the United States. And if it is going to engage with the US, then it had to establish war relations with its close allies. In Middle East, the US's closest ally was Israel. In strategic circles, there was a realisation that the road to Washington passes through Tel Aviv (Kumaraswamy, 2010). Moreover, the disintegration of the Soviet Union, which happened to be one of the major arms suppliers to India, forced India to look out for new partners for modern weapons acquisition. And Israel was one of choice. It had achieved the global status of being an innovative state, capable of producing high-end surveillance technology, missile systems of different range and electronic equipment to upgrade heavy defence hardware.

With the changing head of the states in India, PM Narasimha Rao decided to get away with the persistent outlook of India towards Israel as the Jewish state and looked forward to treat it as a normal state. India then finally joined the US-backed move to revoke UNGA Resolution 3379 that equated Zionism with racism in December 1991. Under his prime ministership, India took the decisive decision to liberalise its economy and paved the way for Globalisation, Privatisation and Liberalisation. In its pursuit to economic liberalism, it followed the United States and strengthened its ties with it. Under the sway of the US, India started thinking about further consolidating its relations with Israel.

And finally, the biggest decision came from Delhi's South Block in the history of India-Israel relations, where India established full diplomatic relations with Israel on January 29, 1992.

Afterwards, both countries started looking into areas of cooperation between each other and normalised diplomatic exchanges. For the first time, India's top diplomat Foreign Secretary, J.N. Dixit, travelled to Israel in 1993. In the same year, the Israeli Foreign Minister Shimon Peres was hosted in New Delhi. During his visit, he assured his New Delhi counterpart of supporting India on Shimla Accord as the basis for resolving the highly contentious Kashmir issue with Pakistan (Iqbal, 2014). As far as the pacts are concerned, India and Israel signed an agreement on Science and Technology. A US$3 million joint science and technology fund was set up to facilitate research and development (R&D) collaboration between the two states. After this agreement, most of the researchers and scientists started visiting each other's country for further better collaborating and cooperating on research projects. In addition of this, various Israeli universities started offering special scholarships to Indian students to pursue courses on science and technology and other fields and disciplines. Further, in December 1994, the two sides signed an agreement on trade and commerce, which granted the most favoured nation status to each other.

However, cooperation in military and security was paramount in India-Israel relations because of the immediate threat to their national security from their neighbours. Defence cooperation between India and Israel was started with the visit of Israel's air force commander to in India in 1994. Two years later, then the chief of the Indian Defence Research and Development Organisation (DRDO), A.P.J. Abdul Kalam, visited Israel for further exchange of defence agreement and to discuss matters of defence cooperation between India and Israel. Afterwards, defence cooperation was further discussed when Israeli President, Ezer Weizman came to India in December 1996. On his visit, he was warmly greeted by the government and the two sides agreed to establish the Defence Attaché's Office in Tel Aviv and New Delhi in 1997.

Meanwhile it was important to note that most of the time, the centre or centre-left parties have formed the government in India which has a bigger section of Muslim minorities as their biggest vote bank towards them. Therefore, before taking any foreign policy decision, it was essential for them to take into account the suggestions/reservations of Muslims and made sure that any policy or bill hadn't upset this section of society because their political fortune depends upon former's blessings. And as far as the India-Israel relations are concerned, those parties didn't want to fully engage and support Israel because of the antagonism of Muslims towards Israel and those parties didn't want to offend them. And this particular convention was being followed from various governments to governments and a consistent restraint was shown from the Indian sides towards Israel.

However, the coming of right-wing party, Bhartiya Janata Party (BJP), under Atal Bihari Vajpayee into national politics got the chance of forming the government in 1998. A far as the foreign policy is concerned, it has made national security paramount before any religious and sectarian fault lines. They didn't bother about the views or antagonism of Muslims towards Israel as they have witnessed the relevance of Israel in preserving India's national security. In both 1962 and 1999, India realised the importance of Israel and its sophisticated weapons if further conflict occurs between India and its neighbours.

Under Atal Bihari Vajpayee, India showed its political will to make national security paramount and, in need of preserving it, Israel is a vital ally. So, when India tested its nuclear test in 1999, the whole world came against and criticised India and almost all the major powers put sanctions upon India. However, during the same time, Israel neither criticised nor uphold international sanctions upon India and didn't care about them while strengthening its relations with India. Israel truly realised the need of nuclear weapons to India as the latter is also facing the same difficult situation to preserve its national security when it is getting threatened by its immediate neighbours, alike Israel. Israel believed, it is not wrong to possess nuclear weapons when national security was at stake.

Moreover, amidst the nuclear tests by India, most of the major powers put off all the major agreements signed between them. However, Israel assured India that all contracts and joint ventures which had been negotiated before the tests would be respected. A few days after the tests, a delegation from Israeli Aerospace Industries (IAI) visited India to accelerate the defence cooperation (Cowshish, 2017, pp. 401-412).

During Kargil War between India and Pakistan in 1999, when the whole world put sanctions on India in the wake of nuclear tests in 1998, Israel provided LITENING electro-optical targeting pods on urgent basis and a few Israeli technicians flew to work with IAF's Aircraft System Testing Establishment in Bengaluru (Singh, 2017). Moreover, it supplied ammunition drones, and satellite pictures, all that was considered by Indian military establishment the valuable asset at a critical time. And when the war was over, the crucial meeting of PM Atal Bihari Vajpayee with close ministers and bureaucrats decided to import sophisticated weapons and arms from Israel and amongst them the prominent ones were Unmanned Aerial Vehicles (UAVs) Searcher-I and Searcher-II supplied by Israeli Military Industry (IMI). IAI supplied advanced medium-range Heron drones. Moreover, New Delhi imported from Israel, fast attack Super Dvora Mk-2 boats, 160 mm mortars, Griffin guided bombs, and Spice guided bombs, and various types of radars, among others. The deal for 200 units of Barak-I vertically launched Surface-to-Air Missiles (SAMs) was concluded in 2000. Those missiles were equipped on the INS Viraat aircraft carrier, Godavari class frigates, two Kashin class destroyers, three Brahmaputra class frigates, and a Godavari class frigate (SIPRI).

In international politics, the United States embraced the improving India-Israeli relations. Moreover, the US was willing to encourage Israel to help India in modernising its armed forces and weapons acquisition. It intended to alienate Russia as the top defence supplier to India and was putting all forward to make Israel India's top defence partner along with it. Consequently, the US didn't object to Israel's selling technology to India. However, the US indeed objected to Israel's selling technology to China through joint venture in 1998, while India received from Israel three Phalcon AEW&C systems in 2004 (Kumaraswamy P. , 2010).

In the security domain, cooperation was further expanded to such a level that it led to the advent of national security level dialogue in 1999. The tradition started from this year has been followed every year where the dialogue organises alternately in Tel Aviv and New Delhi. Since every visit of political leaders, there were negotiations to solidify defence cooperation and, in this backdrop, on the visit of India Home Minister in 2000, Israel and India agreed to establish Joint Working Group (JWG) to strengthen their defence deals, military ties, and coordination in the security and intelligence sectors. After a while, Israeli leadership thought to pave the way for the first ever visit of Israeli PM to India.

There was a sense of displeasure amongst the Indian Muslim circles and leftist parties on the visit of Israeli PM to India. In 2003, Ariel Sharon, became the first Israeli Prime Minister to visit India. He was welcomed in right-wing circles and was warmly welcomed by Bharatiya Janata Party. Moreover, a Hindi language newspaper, *Navbharat Times*, called Israel "an important friend of India". On his visit, Ariel Sharon asserted that Israelis *"regard India to be one of the most important countries in the world."*

From the Vajpayee government there was a paradigm shift in the strategy to deal with Israel vis-à-vis Palestine. Earlier governments used to engage with Israel along with Palestinian issues of self-determination and India's foreign policy towards Israel was not de-hyphenated to Palestine. However, from BJP's government there was the usage of de-hyphenation in dealing with Israel and Palestine as two different matters of concern. Before hosting the Israeli Prime Minister, India hosted Palestinian Foreign Minister Nabil Shaath in September 2003. Thus, Vajpayee's policy of disembodying the issue of the Israeli occupation of Palestinian territories from mutually shared interests with the Jewish State paved the way for strategic level cooperation between the two states in defence, technology, trade, and agriculture sectors.

And there came the setback in the India-Israel relations with the coming of UPA alliance government in India. As the alliance was supported by the left parties, the government was not interested in whooping its relationship with Israel. So, when Israel invaded Lebanon in 2006, India supported the newly formed goldstone fact-finding commission to investigate the war crimes in the conflict. Moreover, when there was a call for upgradation of status of Palestine as a full member in United Nations Educational, Scientific and Cultural Organization (UNESCO), India joined the cohorts of advocating nation states on 31st October 2011. Again, in the 67th session of the UNGA, India supported the resolution to give Palestine a non-member observer status. These steps restrained the diplomatic exchange between India and Israel.

In fact, the then defence minister, Pranab Mukherjee was supposed to visit Israel in 2006 and later on it was reportedly cancelled due to some unforeseeable reasons. In the span of ten years of Prime Minister Manmohan Singh's government, foreign minister S. M. Krishna's trip was the only high-profile official trip to Israel.

Although, India could not bolster the ties with Israel, it could not avoid its inevitable cooperation in the defence sector. PM Manmohan Singh himself cultivated closer ties with Israel in defence and agriculture sectors. India's key interest became Israeli missile technology. It brought three Barak-1 SAM systems for Delhi class destroyers in 2005. Next, New Delhi concluded a deal for eighteen Spyder-MR air defence systems, 750 units of Python-5 missiles and 750 units of Derby BVRAAM (beyond visual range (BVR) air-to-air missile (AAM)) in 2008. These systems were pertinent and essential to keep India's aerial superiority with Pakistan in the event of any militaristic adventure. The two sides also entered into joint venture programmes. Since 2006, Barak-8 is jointly developed by IAI, Elta Systems, Rafael, with their Indian counterpart, DRDO, and Bharat Dynamics Limited (AHRONHEIM, 2017).

India's relationship with Israel wasn't purely strategic and defence-centric. India since a very long time is facing acute food security and it desperately needed the partnership or collaboration with a nation having the advanced technology in the food and sustainable development. And Israel was that nation which could help India in its food security. An MOU was signed between the agricultural ministers of the two states in 2006. The MOU led to the advent of Indo-Israel Agricultural Project (IIAP) in 2008, which operates through centre for excellence (CoE). Under this project the major objectives to be achieved are: post-harvest management, irrigation and fustigation technologies, introduction of new varieties, plant protection, pollination technologies, and water management technologies for agriculture. These CoE were set up in the first phase in Haryana, Maharashtra, Gujarat, Karnataka, Punjab, Tamil Nadu, and West Bengal (MIDH, 2020). It has been evident through the Karnal district project under CoE that Haryana's Chief Minister order to replicate the practice of poly-house cultivation and micro-irrigation and grow off-season vegetables in all districts of the states in 2011. All these initiatives are being welcomed by the people on the ground level and helping in changing the perception towards Israel as a 'helping nation' to their country.

Strategic Level Cooperation: From 2014 Onwards

The year 2014 doesn't only surprise the Indian nationals with the resulting victory of BJP-led NDA alliance in the 2014 general Lok Sabha elections, but also to some nation-states and Israel in particular. With the coming of right-wing regime, after a long span of Congress rule, it gave the hope of reinvigoration of earlier strengthened ties between India and Israel. Moreover, PM Benjamin Netanyahu was more optimistic with the coming of PM Narendra Modi at the helm of India.

In Middle East, it was the time when there was the fierce rivalry between Iran, Saudi Arabia, Turkey over the leadership of Muslim World and the ideologies of each other. Israel was able to make itself politically, economically and strategically strong in the meantime.

And for India, it realised that a distracted Muslim coalition won't be able to become a counterweight to Israel. The government realised that it must take a decision in the midst of changing waves of regional order. Notably, PM Narendra Modi himself showed resolve to carry forward the strategy of de-hyphenating the two bilateral relationships of Israel and Palestine, to demonstrate that India's ties with Israel are independent, special, and strong (Kaur, 2019, pp. 1-17). From his government, the foreign ministry started changing its attitude towards the conflict. Therefore, in the war between Israel and Hamas in 2014, India's Foreign Ministry expressed its concern over the overwhelming loss of innocent lives but concurrently asserted its concerns over cross-border provocations resulting from rocket attacks targeting Israel. In the aftermath of the attack, in the Indian parliament, BJP government blocked the opposition resolution of condemning Israel's invasion of Gaza Strip.

When the UN Human Rights Commission (UNHRC) decided to launch a probe into the human rights violation in Gaza City, India on record supported it but abstained from participation in passing the McGowan Davis Commission's report.

Subsequently, government started showing sympathy towards Zionism as well and looked forward to see any common points between Indian and Zionist civilisation. So, for instance, Indian Embassy, with the support of immigrant Jewish community, organised the Second Indian Jewish National Convention in Yeruham on October 14, 2014.

As far as the political relations are concerned, after the long gap of fourteen years, an Indian Home Minister visited Israel in November 2014. In the earlier visits of Indian delegates of ministers, there was political custom being followed to visit both Tel Aviv and Palestine. However, during the visit of Home Minister Rajnath Singh, he broke the custom of visiting both and kept his visit limited to Tel Aviv only. This move reflected the government's detachment to address Palestine's issue along with its bilateral relationship with Tel Aviv. And the relationship became significant in international politics, with the first ever visit of the Indian head of state, President Pranab Mukherjee in 2015. He acknowledged the contribution and help made by Israel when India needed it most in its difficult times. He said, *"Israel's technological advances could help India increase its industrial production, and create jobs in both countries"* (Johny, 2015).

On the occasion of the completion of 25 years of their diplomatic relations, Prime Minister Narendra Modi himself visited Israel in 2017. It was a historic moment in the history of India-Israel bilateral relations with the visit of PM himself and was applauded by the media houses and strategic circles in India. On his visit, he visited Haifa and paid homage to the British Indian soldiers who died in the Battle of Haifa by fighting against the Ottoman Empire in the World War I. He also visited the grave of Theodore Herzl, the founder of the Zionist movement, and paid his homage there also. Moreover, when the Mumbai attack happened on November 26, 2008, many Israeli Jews lost their lives in that attack, but one Israeli boy was saved from the terrorists. He was also met by Narendra Modi during his visit. From his visit, his message was evident that India does, indeed, recognise the existence of Israel as a Jewish nation, and found a major correlation of victimisation by terrorism between them. He said, *"India has suffered first-hand the violence and hatred spread by terror, so has Israel"* (Wire, 2017). Along with PM Netanyahu, he issued the joint statement on terrorism and reiterated the commitment to fight terrorism together and recognised it as a major component in establishing regional peace.

However, the major accomplishment with his visit was the upgradation of bilateral relationship to strategic level partnership. It includes promoting commercially viable business models, planting material, and the transfer of post-harvest technical know-how.

In addition to this, it was agreed between them about the joint manufacturing of defence products and the subsequent transfer of technology. They also agreed to formulate a strategic framework for cooperation in cybersecurity. Both states also signed the MOU on the establishment of India-Israel Industrial R&D and Innovation Fund. They also acknowledged the persistent cooperation between the Israel Space Agency (ISA) and the Indian Space Research Organisation (ISRO) (India, 2018), and were optimistic for further cooperation in outer space.

After his visit, several ministers of both states visited each other for inking various agreements and pacts. President Reuven Rivlin toured India for a week-long period in November 2016. In India, Rivlin visited the CoE Vegetables in Haryana, where he said: "India could learn from Israeli experience and know-how in the fields of agriculture, water-saving, and water cleaning techniques." Back home, President Rivlin told the newspaper, *"India assures us, they will never, never, ever let anyone act against the existence of Israel"* (LAZAROFF, 2016).

After a while, when India's highest security and diplomatic conference, Raisina Dialogue, was organised by the ORF think tank, he accompanied the 130 members delegation to India where he was the guest of honour of the event in 2018. During the conference, he said:

> "...the strong survive, the weak don't survive, you make peace and alliances with the strong. I like soft power, but hard power is usually better. You need F-35s, you need cyber, you need a lot of intelligence especially for a country like Israel" *(News18, 2018).*

During his visit, he paid homage to Indian soldiers died in Second World War in Palestine, and in his honour, Teen Murti Chowk was renamed as "Teen Murti Haifa Chowk". He also participated in the Second India-Israel CEO forum. With his presence, Israel signed nine MOUs with India in the fields of cybersecurity, oil and gas production, air transport, homeopathic medicine, film production, space technology, and innovation.

In the changing regional security architecture, they also discussed various security and defence level cooperation in the meetings of JWG on Defence Cooperation, India-Israel Forum and JWG on Border Management. For instance, the inaugural meeting of the India-Israel Joint Steering Committee on Homeland Security was held in Israel from September 21 to 23, 2014. The fourteenth meeting of the India-Israel JWG on Defence Cooperation was held in New Delhi on July 3, 2018. Moreover, the eighth India-Israel Forum was held in Israel in October 2015. The fourth meeting of JWG on Border Management between India and Israel took place in November 2018 in Israel.

In the military side, there is a continuing tradition of promoting military to military cooperation between India and Israel, and in this backdrop, Israel's Naval and Air Force Chiefs visited India in 2015. When the second edition of the International Air Force Commanders' Convention held in May 2018, Indian Chief of Air Staff, Air Chief Marshal Shri B. S. Dhanoa, participated in Israel. Moreover, Director-General of the Indian Coast Guard Shri Rajendra Singh visited Israel to explore the potential for cooperation in the areas of coastal security and maritime law enforcement in July 2018. Not only this, when the first Indo-Israel military drill was organised, a contingent of Indian forces participated in the Israeli Blue Flag drill in 2018. In addition to this, there is a pact between Sardar Patel National Police Academy and National Police Academy to train the officers selected in Indian Police Service by the Israeli officers in counterterrorism and national security. These initiatives and cooperation helped both the countries in deepening the strategic relationship and building the trust between each other.

PM Narendra Modi was having the dream of producing goods and products in India itself and no longer purchase it from other countries. In this pursuit, he put forward the "Make in India" programme where countries will be invited to invest in India. In this initiative, Israel became the partner of India in 'Make in India' vision. In the defence sector, Israeli Rafael, Israel Weapon Industries and Elbit Advanced Systems have formed joint ventures with their Indian counterparts of Kalyani Strategic Systems Ltd., Astra Microwave Products, Adani Group's Aero Defence Systems & Technologies, Alpha Design Technologies, Punj Lloyd and Reliance Defence Ltd. to produce Barak-8 MRSAM missile kits, drones, radio communication systems and small arms. Israel is also a partner to India's Light Combat Aircraft Tejas programme. HAL has signed two contracts with the Elta Systems for the supply of 83 units of ELM-2052 active electronically scanned array (AESA) radars and ELL-8222WB electronic warfare (EW) for its upgraded version of Tejas Mark-IA on October 26, 2018. Elta was selected over two European defence contractors, Thales and Saab. Moreover, the Tejas Mark-IA is slated to be armed with Rafael's supplied Litening pods and Derby missile defence system.

These developments helped India immensely modernising its armed forces and military assets and made the Indo-Israel relationship deeper and more strategic in nature. With the passing of years, Israel became the second largest defence partner of India after Russia.

Partnership was further intensified in non-defence sector as well. "Indo-Israel Development Cooperation: Three Year Work Programme in Agriculture" (2018-2020) was signed in 2017. In the action plan, it was supposed to accomplish the completion of CoE as agreed upon Phase 1 and 2 of the IIAP, and will bring them to full operational stage and will implement Phase 3 of IIAP. The participating states were decided to be Haryana, Maharashtra, Rajasthan, Punjab, Karnataka, Gujarat, Bihar, Uttar Pradesh, Tamil Nadu, Jharkhand, Uttarakhand, Kerala, Andhra Pradesh, Madhya Pradesh, Odisha, Chhattisgarh, Tripura, Mizoram, Himachal Pradesh, Telangana, and

West Bengal. According to the Mission for Integrated Development of Horticulture (MIDH) Government of India, so far, twenty-eight CoE centres have been completed, and two are under-process.

In toto, the bilateral trade between India and Israel had increased from US$1.5 billion in 2000 to US$ 4.52 billion in 2014 and from there to $5,431.9 million in 2018. Although India's bilateral trade is not much at par with Iran and Saudi Arabia, the level of deep cooperation has surpassed those nations, when the political and defence cooperation of Israel with India came into being. Their defence trade in the first decade of the twenty-first century had progressed with the acceleration of about US$1 billion per year. Israel's share in India's total arms import had jumped from 7.2 per cent in 2014 to 8.48 per cent in 2018. That makes Israel the second-largest military supplier to India, and later the largest importer of Israeli defence products.

As far as India's bilateral relation with Israel is concerned, defence comprises the major and core component of their relationship. The advantage for India with enhancing its strategic relationship with Pakistan is that Israel doesn't have to balance its South Asia Policy because India's arch rival, Pakistan, has not recognised Israel hitherto and therefore, Israel is supporting India in its acquisition of sophisticated military technology. Israel, from the very start, didn't bother to balance its relationship with India with other south Asian nations and therefore didn't bother to provide arms when India was in dire need of it. Israel has emerged as India's key defence partner and has shown a willingness to sell its advanced weapons with a provision of transfer of technology. Those weapons act as ears and eyes to Indian heavy weapons, which it imported mostly from Russia and in increasing volume from the US. Due to advanced weapons acquisition by India from Israel, Pakistan didn't dare to make a pre-emptive attack on India. For instance, when India and Pakistan got engaged in a short military stand-off in February 2019, Indian defence forces were laced with Israeli supplied AC&WS radars, guided bombs, and drones.

Indian Army in its latest budget has created an emergency procurement funds and, in that conflict with Pakistan, India used that fund to purchase Israeli spike anti-tank guided missile (ATGM) systems. Although this decision created some friction in the defence ministry as it was suggested that the same sort of missiles could be produced by DRDO as well (Now, 2019). Since then, Indian army has deployed those missiles on the its border with Pakistan.

In the bilateral relationship of India and Israel, we have analysed it from more from a political and strategic point of view. However, we are missing an important linkage of close affinity between Hindu nationalists and the Jewish state. Since the establishment of the state of Israel, both India and Israel have shared the sentimental feelings of the oppression of terrorism by a few unreligious persons emanating from the Islamic World. This has warned India about the rise of political Islam and that's why India abstained from voting against the UN body's call for the violation of human rights by Israel in Palestinian territories. And for the first time, India voted alongside Israel in the UNECOSOC to oppose the grant of observer status to a Palestinian human rights organisation named Shahed in 2019.

However, from the Modi government there is a praxis of more realist and pragmatism vis-à-vis India's Middle East Policy and India is finally getting over from the emotional and idealist foreign policy. However, India at the same time, is not leaving its moral grounds of long unwavering support to Palestinian cause. When PM Narendra Modi was about to visit Israel, he hosted Palestinian President Mahmud Abbas in New Delhi. He assured him of India's "unwavering support" to the Palestinian cause, saying it hopes to see a sovereign, united, and an independent Palestine, coexisting peacefully with Israel. Moreover, on February 11, 2018 he travelled via Jordan to Palestine and offered his compliments on the exemplary courage of Palestinians living in such a chaotic environment. PM Narendra Modi with his Palestinian counterparts signed agreements worth around US$50 million that included setting up a US$30 million super-speciality hospital in Palestine.

Moreover, India has defied the bandwagoning of western nations in supporting Israel in all forms. So, when the US announced its decision to recognise Jerusalem as the Israeli capital, India joined 128 states in opposing the US's decision and stayed with their persistent diplomatic relations from Tel Aviv. Not only this, India offered 5 million dollars support to UN Relief and Work Agency, higher from till now 1.25 million dollars support to them, amidst the financial issues from the Trump Administration to the agency.

Conclusion

In toto, India's foreign policy is the legacy of PM Nehru and its early relations with Israel were also attributed to him as well. Although, India had recognised Israel as a nation-state, it kept itself apart from Israel as far as diplomatic and political relations are concerned. While Indira Gandhi realised the dilemma between India's value position and national interests. She preferred to cultivate clandestine security ties with Israel. Meanwhile, the rise of Indian neo-liberal and Hindu nationals was a departure movement in India's foreign policy outlook. Both these domestic perspectives share policy consensus on working closely with Israel in the areas of mutual interest, but both differ in political language. As such, the rise of the new political elite in India, in the post-1990s era, explains that opportunities were translated into diplomatic actions to bring about a balance in India's Israel policy vis-a-vis Palestinian issue and with other regional powers. There emerged a new consensus that India, as an emerging global power, should, like other global powers, engage both Arabs and Israel. This shift towards pragmatic policy changed India's interests to bring about a balance and elevated the marginal status of Israel. Over the years, the Indian government has also toned down its reaction to Israel's policy towards the Palestinian territories. Interestingly, PM Modi resolved that New Delhi should accord priority to strengthening ties with Israel while maintaining a stand that Palestinians deserve their state. Today India and Israel collaborate in defence, trade, strategic, and intelligence and security-related areas. Notably, the mutually beneficial defence cooperation is giving Israel access to one of the world's largest defence markets, which optimises its defence research and India has gained access to critical defence technology of Israel to increase its surveillance and reconnaissance capacities and ability to deal with challenges posed by Pakistan. Both sides have come to follow a pragmatic approach by not pushing each other to take their respective stand on third-party issues and understand the limits arising from their domestic politics, international security environment. This explains why in a short span of 25 years, India and Israel have come to call their bilateral engagement the strategic partnership.

References

Johny, S. (October 15, 2015). Ties with Israel on upswing: Pranab. Retrieved from *The Hindu*, at http://www.thehindu.com/news/international/president-pranab-mukherjee-sixday-trination-tour-ties-with-israel-on-upswing-pranab/article7762301.ece

Ahronheim, A. (August 29, 2017). Indian Navy receives first missile jointly developed with Israel. Retrieved from *The Jerusalem Post*, at https://www.jpost.com/Israel-News/Israel-sells-India-their-first-long-range-surface-to-air-missile-503696

Blarel. (2017). reference no., 20.

Blarel, N. (2017). "Assessing US Influence over India–Israel Relations: A Difficult Equation to Balance?", *Strategic*, 41(4).

Cowshish, A. (2017). "India–Israel Defence Trade: Issues and Challenges. *Strategic Analysis.*

Falk, J. (2009). "India's Israel Policy: The Merits of a Pragmatic Approach. *Stanford Journal of International Relations*, 2(1).

Hadass, J. (2002). Indo-Israeli Relations. *India International Centre Quarterly*, 29(2).

Inbar, E. (2017). Israel and India: Looking Back and Ahead. *Strategic Analysis*, 41(4).

India, T. M. (2018). *Annual Report 2017-18*. New Delhi: The Ministry of External Affairs India.

Iqbal, J. (2014). "Palestine as a Factor in Indo-Israel". In F. M. Azmi, *Foreign Policy of India and West Asia: Change and Continuity*. New Delhi, India: New Century Publications.

Kaur, V. (2019). "India's Israel Relations in the Modi Era: A Transformative Shift". *Israeli Affairs*.

Kumaraswamy, P. (2010). *India's Israel policy*. New York: Columbia University Press.

Lazaroff, T. (November 23, 2016). *Rivlin to JPost: India won't let anyone threaten Israel's right to exist*. Retrieved from *The Jerusalem Post*, at https://www.jpost.com/Israel-News/Politics-And-Diplomacy/Rivlin-to-Post-India-wont-let-anyone-threaten-Israels-right-to-exist-473410

MIDH, T. (2020). *"Countries Core: Israel"*. New Delhi: Integrated Development of Horticulture (MIDH) Government of India. Retrieved from https://midh.gov.in/CoE/aboutus.html

Mumtaz Ahmad Shah, D. T. (2020). "India's Israel Policy: From Nehru to Modi". *Journal of Critical Reviews*, 7(9).

Nehru, J. (1947). *Pt. Jawaharlal Nehru's speech at Asian Relations Conference*. Delhi: Tibet Sun. Retrieved from https://www.tibetsun.com/news/1947/03/24/pt-jawaharlal-nehrus-speech-at-asian-relations-conference-1947.

News18, T. (2018, Janurary 16). *Netanyahu Live in India: Israeli PM lauds Modi, Says Astonished to see India's rise in the Ease of Doing Business*. Retrieved from The News18 at http://www.news18.com/news/india/netanyahu-in-india-live-israeli-pm-lauds-modi-says-astonished-to-see-indias-rise-in-ease-of-business-rankings-1633193.html

Now, T. T. (Feburary 26, 2019). *Israeli Spyder Hits Pakistani Drone: India*. Retrieved from The Times Now, at https://www.timesnownews.com/india/article/israeli-spyder-pakistani-spy-drone-abdasa-village-kutch-gujarat-balakot-air-strike-rafale-advance-defense-system-derby-missile/372979

Sen, S. (September 10, 2020). *India's Alliance With Israel Is a Model for the World's Illiberal Leaders*. Retrieved from Foreign Policy, at https://

foreignpolicy.com/2020/09/10/indias-alliance-with-israel-is-a-model-for-the-worlds-illiberal-leaders/

Singh, S. (July 5, 2017). *Israeli help and Indian jugaad in recapture of Tiger Hill.* Retrieved from *The Indian Express,* at https://indianexpress.com/article/explained/israeli-help-and-indian-jugaad-in-recapture-of-tiger-hill-4735806/

SIPRI, T. (n.d.). *Transfers of Major Weapons from Israel to India: Deals with Deliveries or Orders made for 1990 to 2018*. The Stockholm International Peace Research Institute. Retrieved from https://www.sipri.org/databases/armstransfers.

Srivastava, R. (1970). "India-Israel Relations". *The Indian Journal*, 31(3).

Ward. (1992). reference no. 27.

Ward, E. R. (1992). "India's Pro-Arab Policy: A Study in Continuity". UK: British Congress Library.

Wire, T. (July 6, 2017). *Focus on Water and Terror as Modi Makes Israel India's 31st Strategic Partner*. Retrieved from *The Wire*, at https://thewire.in/154777/modi-israel-water-terror/

THE TRYST BETWEEN INDIA AND SMALL ISLANDS NATIONS: A NAUTICAL DIMENSION OF INDIA'S INDO-PACIFIC POLICY

MEGHA SRIVASTAVA

The Indo-Pacific region has gained serious ground in twenty-first century power politics. Through various scholarships, it has been made evident that it is the theatre of both opportunities and conflicts in the times to come. While partnerships with the big powers are evident and crucial, India's focus on the Island nations in the Pacific and Indian oceans needs further scrutiny. Instead of pressing on the power balancing of big states, this chapter accounts for the politics of small Islands and what it means for India's Indo-Pacific approach. It discusses India's strategic and functional approach towards Island nations in its Indo-Pacific policy. This analysis focuses on three main policy areas: India's Indo-Pacific thrust in its Act East policy by understanding its enhanced engagement with countries like Indonesia and Vietnam; India's approach in the Indian Ocean region focusing on Sri Lanka, Mauritius, Maldives; and India's Oceania approach including the three core islands groups in the South Pacific. While examining these three domains of India's Indo-Pacific policy, the chapter also sheds light on the strategic challenges and implications of the politics of small Island states on India's geopolitical and security interests in the region. I argue that India's partnerships with these small islands will form the bedrock to shape India's Indo-Pacific approach and that their foreign policy choices will have a bearing impact on India's security environment in the region. I also argue that, though India's new venture on reprioritising and reorienting Act East Policy towards the South Pacific Island nations will see the test of time, its significant investments will keep Indian Ocean Islands in priority.

Introduction

The twenty-first century geopolitics has brought new paradigms to deal with. At the turn of the century and in the coming decades, world politics is much more surrounded by the seas. This becomes evident with the reprioritisation of the concept of Asia-Pacific to the Indo-Pacific and the reorientation of foreign policies of major actors towards the Indo-Pacific for several reasons. The transformation from the geopolitical concept of Asia-Pacific to Indo-Pacific was conceived by the then-Japanese Policymakers in 2007 when they referred to a region called Indo-Pacific as "The Confluence of Two Seas—The Indian Ocean and the Pacific Ocean". Since then, the concept has reinforced the foreign policies and geopolitical priorities of almost all major actors in the region and beyond where countries like the UK, France, and the Gulf are involved in the geopolitical and security scenario of the region. The concept became more coherent when it was discussed by the Australian Defence White Paper in 2013 and when the US redirected India as the pivot to the region's geopolitics in 2017 during the Trump administration.

The conventional pillars in Indian foreign policy, namely, strategic autonomy, non-alignment, etc., play a vital role in formulating India's conception of the region. India's concept of Indo-Pacific was highlighted with PM Narendra Modi's speech at the 2018 Shangrila Dialogue with the main idea highlighting "openness", "ASEAN Centrality", "inclusiveness", "not directed against any country" (2018). Defining the region, India's Foreign Secretary Harsha Vardhan Shringla, said that Indo-Pacific geography for India can be divided into three semi-circles. The first circle includes India's closest neighbours that share coastlines with the Indian Ocean waters. The second arc includes the countries of the Gulf and the countries towards India's east. The third circle moving outward includes countries from the Pacific Islands to the archipelagos of the western Indian Ocean and off the eastern coast of Africa, also including alliances like the QUAD countries. (Chaudhary, 2020) Thus, the Indo-Pacific concept has moved beyond economic, and historical linkages to include strategic imperative that showcases Indian foreign policy's transformation into expansive hard power attributes.

India has accelerated its engagement with countries throughout the Indo-Pacific while balancing between China and Russia on the one side, and proactively cooperating with the USA, Australia, and Japan on the other, to maintain its strategic autonomy and to gain the stature of a rising competitive power as well as a security provider in the region. To analyse its role in the Indo-Pacific region concerning the Small Island States (SIS), this chapter aims to dig down on India's approach towards Small Island States in the region and look forward to studying the challenges and implications for India's Indo-Pacific policy. The geopolitics and geo-economics of the Indian Ocean Region (IOR) and the Western Pacific (WP) differ to a great extent in both economic and security environments. Also, in recent times, India's strategic policy priorities like Act East Policy (AEP) have started to reorient towards the Indo-Pacific concept. Thus, the chapter analyses the priorities and approaches of India towards these nations by studying the following three wings in India's Indo-Pacific policy. First, it analyses the significant engagement and approach of India with islands in the IOR. Second, it studies the extended approach of India's Act East policy and analyses how the AEP inculcates and expands towards the Indo-Pacific approach except for the extension towards South Pacific. Third, it separately studies the enhanced and refurbished relationship of India with islands in the South Pacific region under India's Oceania approach and as an extension of AEP. It further identifies the importance of Island nations in India's Indo-Pacific approach both towards building individual partnerships or to counter China's growing influence. It upholds the position of Island nations in helping middle powers like India to find strategic leverage in their efforts to maintain multi-polarity in the region. It also explores the challenges for India in way of materialising its position among these nations and further guides on the ways cooperation can be enhanced. It concludes by advocating the role of small Islands, which were previously considered pawns for big powers as "strategic assets" to build influence in the region.

India's Strategic Stakes in the Indo-Pacific

It is said that Indo-Pacific is what you make of it. (Phillips, 2018) The hype around the significance of this region is attributed to the maritime checkpoints, large-volume trade, rising non-traditional threats, vast natural resources, revisionist tendencies of China, increasing militarisation by traditional powers, and so on. Despite being small in size, SIS holds an immense area in their Exclusive Economic Zones (EEZ). Though they are small land states in area, they were referred to as "The Big Ocean States". (Pacific Islands Forum, 2012) The 2007 Annual report of the Ministry of Defence stated that South Asia is too small an economic space for India and its strategic interests lie beyond the "traditional and claustrophobic South Asia approach". (Ministry of Defence, 2007) This was further made clear in the 2009 Indian maritime doctrine that India's strategic interests lie beyond South Asia and the Indian Ocean. (Ministry of Defence, 2009)

In the 21st century, Oceans will act as a core source of power and maritime control seems to have threatened the world order already concerning China's increasing nautical footprints and influence in the littorals. China's control on major trade routes, ports, presence of a submarine fleet in the region is causing discomfort to India and thereby threatening her maritime interests. To protect and ensure fair trade and freedom of navigation, India's proactive presence in the region becomes crucial. India's prime interest is safety at sea to ensure trade, investments, and energy resources. Indo-Pacific politics offers India to project its geopolitical and naval power to the world. Its ability to ensure freedom of navigation in the high seas, to effectively manage the transnational security threats will reshape India's geopolitical influence and its maritime power. Indian Navy is the third-largest in the Indo-Pacific region and thus lies in an ideal position to counter Beijing's growing revisionist tendencies. (Sakhuja, 2011) Its strategic interests being extended to the Indo-Pacific region is significant to address the growing role of India in the extended neighbourhood as well as its position in altering world order.

India is moving towards diversifying its energy extraction and resource exploration priorities and SCS in this respect can turn out to be a lifeline for India. According to the records of the US Energy Information Administration (EIA), South China Sea contains approximately 11 billion barrels of oil and 190 trillion cubic feet of natural gas. (USEIA, 2013) SCS also belongs to one of the busiest trade routes involving the strategically important Strait of Malacca. Through this region, India alone has approximately 50 per cent of trade export and 40 per cent of trade imports (Purushothaman, 2015). The Strait annually hosts 60,000 to 94,000 cargo ships containing oil and gas, which are transported to the littoral states in the region. India is looking forward to collaborating with the littorals in the SEA mainly Vietnam and the Philippines regarding oil exploration. Thus, conflicts arising in the SCS are not only of geopolitical significance but make a great deal for the geo-economics of major actors. If India is successful in harnessing vital resources in the Indo-Pacific, it would be able to bypass the complexity in the West Asian resource politics to an extent.

While India's immediate interest lies in maintaining safety and security in the Indian Ocean, its long-term geopolitical interests extend to the eastern flank including the Pacific islands. India aims to garner support and goodwill among the littorals by engaging in cooperation on matters of non-traditional threats like climate change, combating marine pollution, deep-sea mineral exploration, regulating illegal, unregulated, and unreported (IUU) fishing, and effective disaster risk management.

Leveraging Through the Indian Ocean Approach

The geopolitics of the Island nations are often defined and dominated by the narrative on great power politics. While the traditional powers are continuing to gain crucial positions in shaping Indian Ocean Region (IOR), Island nations have often been overlooked in the debates regarding changing security architecture in the region. As C. Rajamohan puts it, *"Nothing has undermined the geographical thinking and outreach of India as much as the idea of South Asia"*, the regional infatuation of India within its heartland neighbourhood had kept India surrendering historic ties with the littorals. (RajaMohan, 2019) This section will explore the areas where Island nations in the Indian Ocean region are critical to secure India's Indo-Pacific policy and analyse how India perceives small islands in her Indo-Pacific approach.

Recent elections in almost all island nations witnessed strong mandates for debates around maritime security while recognising the island's importance in regional security and geopolitics. Thus, the foreign policy of these island nations is increasingly turning more conscious towards regional dynamics rather than simply bearing

Asian or African identity. Regional aspirations in these countries signify their desire to emerge as important players in the geopolitics of the region. For example, Maldives may well be considered falling under the Indian sphere of influence, however, Male's strategic importance as an island of IOR is increasingly taking bigger postures in the region's trade and maritime security. Thus, the force structure in the Indian Ocean region is changing gradually due to national sentiments, regional aspirations, and power balancing by traditional powers. The naval capabilities of the littorals, as a result, are growing. They are building effective maritime zones and increasingly embracing investments from big powers. It also becomes important for the traditional powers to reckon that the SIS is coming out of the shackles of sub-regional identity and are seeking a greater role in balancing the strategic geopolitical dynamics by embracing positive developments by major powers in their region of influence.

India's efforts are aimed at prioritising the local needs and equity of ethics towards the host community while advancing its efforts to build economic projects, infrastructure, connectivity, and enhance the supply chain in the region. India's foreign secretary Harsha Vardhan Shringla, while describing India's clear sights of the region and its approach towards building prosperity in the region, puts that "India while developing connectivity focuses on facilitating fair competition to avoid over-indebtedness by the receiving country and thereby aims at ensuring sustainability and transparency through its efforts". (Chaudhary, 2020) Unlike China's approach of disrupting the local economies and political cultures, India views its strengthening ties through the prism of localisation, democratisation, transparency, and trust.

India has envisioned the region's prosperity through its idea of Security and Growth for All in the Region (SAGAR) and Indo-Pacific Ocean's Initiative (IPOI). Indian PM Narendra Modi coined the term 'SAGAR' at Mauritius in 2015. (India Writes, 2016) This was conceptualised to represent the enhanced importance of IOR island nations in India's maritime diplomacy which is now looking towards 'issue-based' alignments. The five important approaches under the SAGAR (which means 'sea' in Hindi) are: strengthening maritime security cooperation, utilising multilateral platforms like IONS for building naval capabilities, strengthening the concept of blue economy by utilising IORA, primary responsibility for peace and security in the region remains with the island nations themselves. India demands transparency in operations and adherence to international best practices based on international Maritime law. Later in 2019, PM Modi revealed the Indo-Pacific Ocean's Initiative (IPOI) at the East Asia Summit in Bangkok, which is based on the amalgamation of India's Act East and Act West concerning littorals in the Indo-Pacific region. (Chaudhary, 2019) It is one such initiative taken to manifest the whole idea of 'free and open' and 'rule-based' Indo-Pacific. India is also engaging with IOR Nations through multilateral platforms like BIMSTEC (Bay of Bengal Initiative for Multi-Sectoral, and Economic Cooperation), IORA, IONS, etc., to give a holistic and wider scope to cooperation and developmental efforts.

Recognising the importance of island nations in India's naval ambitions and towards strengthening its Indo-Pacific concept, the Indian government has recently set up an Indian Ocean division in its Ministry of External Affairs (MEA) that includes the islands in the Western and Southern Indian Ocean. (The Wire, 2019) India has also joined the Indian Ocean Commission (IOC)—an international organisation representing the interest of five western Indian ocean countries, as an observer country. (The Wire, 2020) India has also signed a defence agreement with Comoros and Madagascar in 2018 and is expected to be appointed as the defence attaché to its mission in Madagascar. (Parashar, 2021) India, in its next, is eyeing to include the activities of the Indian Coast Guard to engage in maritime wellness of the strategically located Vanilla islands. This will enhance

India's maritime ties with the nations and boost India's capability to monitor security developments in the region.

Indian Navy has the strongest presence in the region in recent times and is also increasingly challenged by China. India has showcased systematic defence and policing capabilities in the region through coordinated patrols with the island nations. India's deployment of a nuclear-based submarine in the Bay of Bengal has changed the geostrategic picture in the region as well as India's image as a hard power among the littorals. India's efforts towards capacity building in the region are directed towards fulfilling the emerging needs of the maritime defence system and ensuring coastal security. The National Maritime Strategy also aims to picture India in the form of a 'Net Security Provider' in the region. (Defense, 2015) Delhi's Information Management and Analysis Centre are laid out to help secure safety and stability by providing maritime domain awareness to the Indian Ocean littorals. Another initiative called IFC-IOR (Information Fusion Centre-Indian Ocean Region) by India has sought to set up links between 18 countries in the region with 15 maritime security agencies. India has also placed many coastal surveillance radar systems and naval patrol boats for many countries like Myanmar, Bangladesh, Sri Lanka, Seychelles, Mauritius, etc., in the past six years. India is dedicated to provide and strengthen its defence training programmes and capability measures by sending mobile training teams to the islands. Within the region, India has established itself as an unstinted leader in the field of Humanitarian Assistance and Disaster Relief (HADR) by building holistic technological and emergency facilities.

Through historical overturns, we may no further stumble upon the importance of SIS in being favourable to great power to secure their maritime influence. Baruah puts forward that "Rising nations have always sought to control strategic island to project hard power tactics". (Baruah, 2018) Highlighting India's increasing role, Donald

Berlin, in 2006, said that the "Rise of India" in Asia and as a growing maritime power in the region plays a vital role in enhancing the vitality of the Indian Ocean Region itself. (D. L. Berlin, 2006) Referring to Chinese increasing dominance in the region, John Power noted, "China has tipped the balance of power in the Indo-Pacific region through an island-building campaign". (Power, 2020) If India does not manifest the narrative of Indo-Pacific involving the SIS of Indian Ocean littorals, it may well be losing an opportunity standing on its doorstep.

Deepening Thrusts in India's Act East Policy

The increased salience of the Indo-Pacific region and it is becoming the hotbed of great power conflict makes India extend its Act East to go beyond its earlier horizons to manifest more than what the name suggests. India's motivation to expand its outreach in the region beyond Southeast Asia is driven by multiple reasons including the sheer size, economy, natural resources, security architecture, and great power influence. Considering India's vision of turning itself into a maritime powerhouse and natural security provider for the littoral states, India more than ever seeks to enlarge the vision of its AEP to include its perspectives and outlook on the Indo-Pacific region. There can be three significant ways in which the Act East is being promoted from the Look East: security realms have become significant moving beyond the economic engagement; sustained priority and urgency in efforts towards cementing ties bilaterally and regionally; and moving beyond Southeast Asia and Northeast Asia to include Indo-Pacific region. That is the reason Pranab De says, the Act 'East' is now getting transformed into Act 'Indo-Pacific'. (De, 2020)

With a renowned focus, AEP aims to secure the greater influence of India in the Indo-Pacific regions by gaining more attention towards security and maritime spheres. Historically, though the Indian Ocean has been a core area of function, the Pacific front has faced benign neglect in the strategic thinking of the Indian Navy. The "Coupling of the two seas" made India stretch its scope of bilateral as well as the regional approach to the ASEAN nations towards building a sustainable maritime partnership that can ensure India's maritime interests in the region and can enhance India's role as a security provider for the littoral against China's hawkish adventures. The 25th ASEAN-India dialogue held in New Delhi in 2018 declared that India aims to "Strengthen maritime cooperation through the existing mechanism and through Expanded ASEAN Maritime Forum (EAMF) to address the common challenges faced by both in the region". (MEA, 2018) Thus, 'Acting East' with a newly manifested 'Nautical lens' is what India seeks to nurture through its Indo-Pacific approach.

The concept of the maritime economy in India's Indo-Pacific approach and also manifested through Act east is also referred to as 'Blue Economy'. The increasing significance of 'Blue Economy' for India's economy and strategic ties with the region was also emphasised by Prime minister Modi at the inaugural function of the IFR (Indian Fleet Review) as he said, "An important part of India's transformation is my vision of 'Blue Economy' in its widest sense." (Modi, 2016) This approach seems to have been accelerating in the past few years, especially considering India's strategic tie-up with Vietnam, Singapore, and Indonesia. The value of India as a reliable maritime partner is upheld by the Asian maritime partners time and again and that is the reason Walter Ladwig III says, "India's expanding role in the Asia-Pacific has been facilitated by countries such as Singapore, Vietnam, and Indonesia that looks towards India to help hedge against Beijing's growing regional influence." (Ladwig III, 2009) Also, C. Raja Mohan argued, "So long as Indian economic growth is accelerating, and New Delhi is dedicated to building on its blue water policy along with modernizing its military capabilities, Asian littorals will continue to rely on India as a valuable partner". (Mohan, 2009)

India's thrusts in the Indo-Pacific are also reflected through its interest in the South China Sea (SCS) region. The maritime zone around the SCS acts as a strategic left flank for India considering its connectivity with the Indian Ocean. India, neither being a part of the littoral zone of the maritime sphere nor having any disputed territory, holds strategic interest in the region for ensuring long-term stability. Since India's trade with East Asia is linked through the same sea lines of communication, India has security, economic and maritime interests in the region. India hopes to ensure rule-based order in the region to manifest the objectives of its AEP and to support its evolving advocacy and narrative of inclusiveness and transparency in the Indo-Pacific region to ensure shared prosperity and cultivation of resources by all.

India's close engagement approach with certain big members of ASEAN is also a priority plan. India is closely engaging in maritime, defence, and diplomatic matters with countries like Vietnam, Indonesia, and Singapore. India's concept of Indo-Pacific is similar to Indonesia's vision of Indo-Pacific. The term "Global Maritime Fulcrum" coined by Indonesian President Joko Widodo explains India's role in the region. It comprises five core pillars—Maritime connectivity and infrastructure, Maritime culture, Maritime Resources preservation, Maritime diplomacy, and Maritime defence. India and Indonesia have also shared a vision document on the Indo-Pacific. These countries are strategically located at the intersection of the two seas, controlling military and strategic commodities, and are facing crucial choke points. Being a sizeable archipelago, they also possess greater potential to emerge as a major maritime power in the region. India's maritime cooperation and partnership with these countries will play a crucial role in bridging the divide between the Indian Ocean region and Western Pacific and thus will reinforce the narrative Indo-Pacific in line with India's framework. On a multilateral level, ASEAN and East Asia Forum (EAF) will help

India in managing the changing geopolitical scenario in the Indo-Pacific region. Also, if India envisions to have a greater presence and goodwill among the countries beyond ASEAN in the wider Pacific Ocean, the platform of ASEAN and EAF will be instrumental in materialising the benefits of India's Indo-Pacific vision.

Traditionally, Indian foreign policy through 'Panchsheel' has shared similar features with the ASEAN Way. In terms of responses to rivalry, both have prioritised dialogue rather than conflict. India's inclination for an ASEAN Way to handle the Chinese challenge in the Indo-Pacific region is an obvious affair. India has traditionally pursued a 'to engage to contain' strategy vis-à-vis China. Additionally, PM Narendra Modi at the 2018 India-ASEAN Summit in Jakarta said, "The partnership between India and ASEAN can guarantee peace and prosperity in the Indo-Pacific region and beyond". (ET, 2018) At the 2018 ASEAN summit held in Singapore, the President of Indonesia Joko Widodo also emphasised the role of ASEAN in 'developing Indo-Pacific cooperation' to maintain the 'relevance and centrality of the Southeast Asian Association'. (Jakarta Post, 2018) Facing a common aggressor and rival in the region, i.e., China, both India and ASEAN are mired in a series of dynamism and disputes. And both choose to counter China's growing clout in the region through diplomacy, trade, and connectivity. In the words of Bhattacharya, ASEAN and India are together in an attempt to defer the conflict which seems inevitable in a power transition phase between rising but dissatisfied power and the dominant one. (Bhattacharya, 2019) To secure this, India's policy set four major goals: to minimise differences with China, accelerating integration with Southeast Asia, gaining more influence in the Indian Ocean region and connecting sea lanes with the SEA region, strengthening strategic partnerships with balancing powers (the USA, Australia, Japan, South Korea, Taiwan, and France). Also, if key partnerships with Australia, Japan, the USA, and South Korea is the realist vision of India's vision, then placing ASEAN to the centrality of its Indo-Pacific approach is vital to materialise the concept of India's Indo-Pacific policy.

Catching the South Pacific Wave

Southwest Pacific is the lower flank of the Indo-Pacific region. It is a region that faced long-standing neglect in India's geostrategic thinking as they were considered as Western backwaters "managed by" Australia and New Zealand. In recent years, with the global theatres shifting towards the Asia-Pacific, the role of these countries in harnessing India's energy resources, as a network of maritime markets, and within its geostrategic position in the Indo-Pacific has become prominent. The region comprises 14 countries called Pacific Island Countries (PIC), namely, Cook Islands, Kiribati, Marshall Islands, Micronesia, Nauru, Fiji, Niue, Palau, Papua New

Figure 17: Pacific Islands

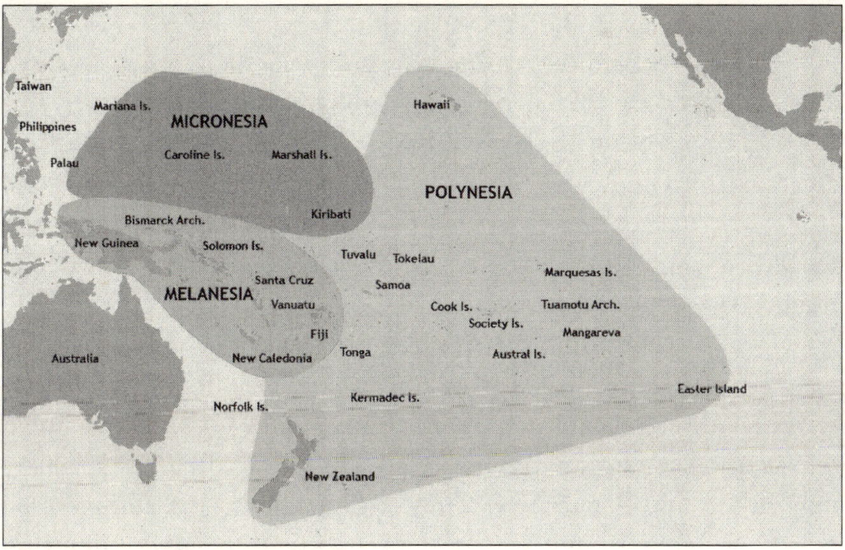

Source: commons.wikimedia.org

Guinea, Solomon Islands, Tonga, Tuvalu, Samoa, and Vanuatu. These countries form three major groups—Micronesia, Polynesia, and Melanesia.

India does not hold any South Pacific policy to manifest its engagement with the PIC. India's approach towards this region is mainly guided by its AEP. PM Modi, stating the importance of PIC in his visit to Fiji in 2014, formulated the concept of Forum for India-Pacific Island Cooperation (FIPIC). This summit is a step towards extending the AEP to redefine the core geographical interests of India to portray herself as a leading player in the Indo-Pacific region. According to the 2015 Maritime Strategy of India, sea routes to the Pacific littorals come under the secondary area of Maritime importance to India. (Defense, 2015) India can get access to important SLOCs, fisheries, military, and naval bases and a sizeable number of countries to support India's bid for UNSC reforms. Thus, India also looks forward to accelerating its engagement with the PIC under the spirit of South-South cooperation. Also, PIC is eager to have a stronger Indian presence in the region. PIC's Look North Policy gives recognition to India's vitality in their effort towards diversification of foreign relations above traditional actors like Australia and New Zealand. India and PIC carry huge scope for diversification and close engagement in the political, economic, and strategic domains. Major areas of convergence between India and the PIC include climate change and security, maritime resources, trade, space cooperation, etc.

Notably, when India is hustling to check the western pacific waters under its strategic dimension, China has already entered the region with significant economic clout. While China maintains a diplomatic presence in almost all PIC, India has diplomatic offices only in Fiji and Papua New Guinea. Opposite to the ethnic-based policy of India routed in diaspora presence in some countries, China's presence is evenly distributed among all PIC and gives an impression of nation-to-nation engagement. Also, PIC countries seem to have embraced China's BRI when the Fijian ambassador to China rejected the notion of the debt trap and rather called it Chinese efforts to help Fiji better. (Ministry of Foreign Affairs, 2017) Moreover, according to reports in 2018, there are apprehensions that China could build a military base at Vanuatu which could strengthen China's clout in the region. (Wroe, 2018) The aid diplomacy of countries like China, New Zealand, and Australia is successful and way ahead of India. However, to be economically sustainable and strategically more vital in the region, trade is needier to the PIC than aid. Other than commercial ties, India has no significant trade investments in PIC except Fiji and Papua New Guinea. Thus, India needs to focus on the intensification of trade and commerce making India contributing greatly to the economy of these nations. However, China, being a member of RCEP and India being out of it, will significantly give an edge to China's trade closeness with PIC. One area where India might gain a significant edge in leveraging China's politically tensed relations with most of the PIC as 12 out of 14 maintain relations with Taiwan. India's presence in the vicinity with more strategic engagement with the PIC will also counter China's dominance in the region. On the strategic naval imperative of the traditional powers in the Pacific waters, the region is increasingly becoming a new venture for securing military and naval cooperation. The US has its military base in the Marshall Islands and Paris controls bases in New Caledonia and French Polynesia. India, to make sense of its naval strategy in the greater Indo-Pacific and to counter unfavourable adventurism, needs to ensure greater naval cooperation.

The South Pacific lies at the pivot of the pacific rebalancing. Closer and more cooperative ties with PIC are crucial to take over the vision of a safe and secure Indo-Pacific. India has much to gain through PIC small-scale economies which are very much compatible with India's economic spaces and village-scale societies. This was showcased by two Tongan old ladies who went to the Barefoot College for their solar training in Rajasthan. Thus, having a remarkable synergy, it can be said that India's approach towards the PIC should be much different from China, Australia, etc., as India could emphasise well newer economic models, diaspora, and democratic approach. The question remains that how would India garner significant goodwill among the PIC as India cannot match China's "Dollar Diplomacy". Chris Anderson's book, "The Long Tail: Why the future of business is selling less of more?" published in 2006, suggested a model which can work to strengthen unique ties between Indian and PIC relations. (Anderson, 2006) Practising the long-tail economics in investments and trade engagements with the pacific nations will give more weightage to Indian efforts. (Motulalo, 2013) India should take advantage of PIC capitalising on service-based and knowledge-based investments something that India is known for. The immediate step should be to launch the model of Long-tailed economics in one PIC, or preferably Tonga, as it is well-positioned to be the regional leader. Once it is successful in Tonga, greater markets can be sought in other PIC.

Though India has a natural affinity with the region, India has been slow to capitalise on that. India's approach towards PIC was largely driven by its Fiji lens and Oceania approach focusing on Australia and New Zealand. India has not been successful in leveraging on its diaspora as its economic and political ties have remained limited. Early in 2011, Ambassador Rajiv Bhatia noted that the time is ripe for India to bring a comprehensive Policy for the Pacific Island Countries. (Bhatia, 2011) India's lack of diplomatic representation should not reflect its lack of interest in the region. The sub-regional approach that India follows towards the PIC as an extension of its AEP should not make China look a more serious alternative for the PIC.

Strategic Challenges in India's Indo-Pacific Littoral Approach

The Asian Development Bank (ADB) Report on Asian Century published in 2011 says that, "The rise of Asia is preordained and is fraught with multiple risks and challenges in the coming years." (Asia 2050: Realising the Asian Century, 2011) This explains the multitude of issues that are ahead in terms of power balancing as well as cooperation on the concept of Indo-Pacific for almost all powers. The emerging maritime order faces grim challenging factors like China's revisionist tendencies and traditional threats like seaborne terrorism; piracy in the waters, climate change; natural and man-made disasters; illegal fishing; and maritime disputes and flashpoints like in the South China Sea (SCS).

The foremost issue is the conception of Indo-Pacific being in an ambiguous viewpoint. There is an absence of uniformity in the definition of the region when it comes to the strategic ambition behind framing the narrative. While countries like India, Australia, Indonesia claim regional prosperity and non-containment strategy, the USA's motivation behind reframing the Asia-Pacific is to enhance the role of regional players in the containment of China's rise. Chinese conception of Indo-Pacific is also different from the overall objectives of the concept. In 2018, the foreign Minister of PRC condemned the idea of Indo-Pacific as "an attention-grabbing idea" that would "dissipate like ocean foam." (Emmerson, 2018) Beijing considers the QUAD (which is a minus China concept) an anti-China containment strategy led by the USA. However, China lately seems to have evolved its strategic thinking towards Indo-Pacific to see it as an opportunity rather than adversity. The Indo-Pacific concept has further pushed the naval strategy of PLAN towards increasing its presence in both the oceans. Chinese scholars have referred to China's Maritime Silk Road (MSR) as "Indo-Pacific with Chinese Characteristics". (Medcalf, 2019) Moreover, the Chinese Communist Party (CCP) sanctioned project, the Hainan Free Trade Zone and Port is hailed by Chinese scholars as "The Gateway of Indo-Pacific". (Shaomin, 2017) Thus, China is materialising its position throughout the Indo-Pacific and beyond by recalibrating its conscious efforts to enhance its leverage on the island nations especially in the Indian Ocean nations and the SCS. Also, the challenge is to balance its vision of ASEAN Centrality with the QUAD initiative, to fulfil its Indo-Pacific perception, and to materialise its enhanced role recognised by the US as a regional player to contain China's rise in the region. Lots of apprehensions are encircled around how the power rivalry can dilute the inclusivity and transparency of the concept.

China in the last decade has increased its footprints and naval presence trying to revise the traditional power balance and its sphere of influence in the whole wide region. This does not only threaten the existent world order but also diminishes India's traditional presence in its strategic backyard—IOR. According to C. Raja Mohan, as given in his book, Samudramanthan, "India-China maritime rivalry finds its sharpest expression in the Bay of Bengal, the South China Sea, and the Malacca Strait...", that seems to be at the intersection of the Indo-Pacific. (Mohan, 2012) According to Indian Naval Chief Admiral Karambir Singh, "Four to six Chinese research vessels in addition to over 600 Chinese fishing vessels are operating in the IOR beyond India's EEZ for every year since 2015". (Gurung, 2020) China's long-term vision, the Belt and Road Initiative (BRI), further supports increasing commercial shipping giving a boost to China's trade relations with littorals as well as enhancing maritime partnerships with them. China's increasing proximity with island nations, traditionally being under India's influence, including Sri Lanka, Myanmar, Seychelles, Maldives, Mauritius, etc., is causing discomfort to New Delhi. India perceives China's infrastructure and naval adventures as unsustainable and rather disruptive for the region's prosperity. The strategic perspective of both countries concerning their policies and actions in both the oceans has failed to find convergence. This puts forward one of the biggest challenges of the 21st century—How India and China will coexist as competitors and dependents on each other, especially in the Naval sphere. The geopolitical and naval confrontation between India and China will set up a stage in the theatre of Indo-Pacific geopolitical rivalry.

India's strategic interests are expanding towards the SCS, not only in terms of trade and secure SLOCs but also in terms of procuring mineral resources. India is investing in its ties with Vietnam and Indonesia to secure its investments in oil and gas fields, however, China's objection to the same while disputing the territories held by the ASEAN nations is dodging India's economic interests. China's arbitrary claims on SCS as its 'Natural Territory' are against India's norms on the high seas and international maritime law. Some important arbitrary disputes led by China are The Pratas island between Taiwan and China; the Scarborough Shoal between China and the Philippines, the Spratly between China, Vietnam, Malaysia, and the Philippines; the Senkaku islands between Japan and China, etc. These disputes not only bring mutual conflict between nations but also diminish the scope for mutual collaboration and international agreements of cooperation in various domains. India increasingly fears that China's increasing naval and economic footprint in the region is undermining the freedom of navigation in the high seas which is disrupting the economy and geopolitics of the region. It hampers India's vision of ASEAN Centrality in the Indo-Pacific as it downsizes India's close engagements with these nations.

Other bottlenecks are the problems of connectivity, long-term funding, and sustainable infrastructure against ensuring prosperity in the region. Big regional players have envisioned regional connectivity plans in the form of ASEAN Connectivity 2025 of ASEAN, Quality Infrastructure of Japan, Blue Dot Network (BDN) of the US, and SAGAR, IPOI of India. However, India's exit from RCEP and the

USA's revocation of TPP have given some halt to plans on regional trade and connectivity. The anti-China approach of some players may cause the plans of regional connectivity to falter as China has key stakes and investments encircling the whole Indo-Pacific region. Moreover, forming a common master plan to finance the massive investments is one of the things seeming to be at a stalemate.

To resolve the streak of crisis in the region, India at last, faces the challenge of formulating a grand strategy involving cooperation on the political, economic, and strategic level. Our strategic interest and ability to maintain regional stability in the Indo-Pacific is dependent on the way India responds to these challenges.

Leveraging Existing Mechanism for Cooperation

India, so far, has been successful in establishing itself as a major player and a naval power in the region. However, there are factors where India's approach has been termed as lack-sided and that its perception of the Indo-Pacific region lacks coherence. This section will cater to the factors where India can develop strategically important capabilities to enhance its positions as a reliable partner for the littorals and to materialise its Indo-Pacific vision.

India lacks institutional mechanisms in the region to showcase its leadership and to fructify its Indo-Pacific vision. While in the Eastern Indian Ocean and the Pacific, FOIP, EAS, ASEAN, ASEAN Regional Forum (ARF), Expanded ASEAN Maritime Forum (AMF) to deliberate and seek cooperation on Indo-Pacific, the western Indian Ocean works with IORA as the only regional institutional framework. India as a regional power and geographically closest partner to major Indian Ocean littorals should take the leadership to build cooperative mechanisms via available institutional platforms like IORA, BIMSTEC, Indian Ocean Commission, Indian Ocean Tuna Commission (IOTC), etc. Additionally, India can venture upon forming a grouping with the Vanilla Island nations to secure more effective outcomes in the WIOR. This will enhance India's potential as a regional and resilient partner avoiding the reliance on China or the US-led frameworks. In the SEA, India can engage better with the SEA countries through Masterplan on ASEAN Connectivity 2025. India needs to work proactively and materialise most from connectivity projects like Asia-Africa Growth Corridor (India's joint initiative with Japan) and Sagarmala Project (Indian port connectivity project).

Since maritime security has emerged as an important dimension of India's bilateral engagement with the littorals, India needs to upgrade its vital data sharing and information system. At the Indian Ocean Dialogue Forum meet, India's External Affairs Minister, S. Jaishankar mentioned that India's information-sharing centres are mostly located towards the east and are sporadic in the WIOR. In this domain, India needs to forge meaningful partnerships with the countries having excellent technical know-how like Japan, the US, France, etc. There is a need to set tandem between the currently dedicated networks—IFC-IOR and IORIS that can cover a wider area within the IOR. In the domain of disaster management and blue economy, India should enhance cooperation in port connectivity projects to minimise the dumping of waste in the Indian Ocean region. Such port connectivity projects can potentially curb the dumping of marine plastic debris from travelling throughout the oceans and disturbing key ecosystems.

India can utilise the platform of IONS for providing professional inputs on maritime security to India and the IORA. Maintaining synergy between both organisations is vital to ensure maritime safety and security in the IOR. To make the littorals the upholder of the maritime order, India needs to fill the currently existing capacity gap in all spheres including political, administrative, operational, and judicial. India should involve the proactive participation of the littoral navies, coastal police, and coast guards towards building capacity with a holistic design. India's IFC at Gurugram can help to coordinate among various navies on maritime awareness and institutionalise relevant cooperative mechanisms. According to Indian Naval Strategic Publication, the Indian Navy plans to deploy ships to exercise its presence and conduct surveillance in areas of maritime interests. (Defense, 2015) Thus, a well-planned mechanism for our Navy's Presence and Surveillance Mission (PSM) should be formulated and aimed at enhancing the Indian Navy's eyes in the Indian Ocean region. Other than building a holistic naval strategy, India needs to strengthen its capacity and work in interoperability, tackling piracy, and building maritime security and safety on a priority basis. For this, again India's SAGAR should be materialised to cover the entire spectrum of challenges and offer India's hard and soft power capabilities to the littoral nations. Indian Navy should gear up to pace with the growing narrative of Indo-Pacific by developing coordination in Visit, Board, Search and Seizure (VBSS) operations. These collaborative capacity-building practices by all the littorals in the region will contribute towards preparing them to neutralise the impact of non-state actors in the region.

Competition from external players, and that too disruptive, can dilute the efforts of India towards protecting her stakes in the littorals. There is a growing consciousness among IOR littorals regarding Chinese disruptive footprints and successful leasing of their ports leading to vulnerable and dependent economies in the long run. In the last decade, this has been demonstrated through the naval occupation of Oman's Duqm, Pakistan's Gwadar, Iran's Chabahar, Sri Lanka's Hambantota, Seychelles' Assumption Island, Myanmar's Kyaukpyu, and so on. India, vociferously, has supported the sustainable development of island nations without the intrusive presence of external powers. Thus, there is an urgent need to ensure criteria and set ground rules for the use of littoral harbours by extra-regional navies for which platforms like IONS should be utilised. Need also arises to build trust among the major navies including the extra-regional players to establish long-term force stabilisation.

For this, India's SAGAR can provide opportunities to strengthen its multilateral diplomacy with regional and extra-regional players.

India needs to explore innovative measures to enhance her engagement with the littorals like green or blue bond. There is a good scope that the Indian market can generate such investment mechanism which is beneficial to boost home as well as the economies of the littorals. India's Sagarmala project should target collaborating with other regional connectivity projects like ASEAN Masterplan on ASEAN Connectivity 2025, Thailand's Eastern Economic Corridor (EEC), and Indonesia's Sea Toll Highway to manifest the aim of building resilience and sustainability through regional infrastructure and connectivity.

Some of the most crucial threats that the small Island states face are non-traditional. For India, nurturing their relationship in a true sense will require India's efforts to be directed towards addressing non-traditional threats like Climate Change. For this, strengthen the pan-regional protective mechanism and effective maritime diplomacy will boost the resilience of island nations.

Prognosis and Implications for Future

David Brewster, an Australian Professor, and an eminent strategist, said that the concept of the Indo-Pacific may lead to a change in popular "mental maps" of how the world is understood in strategic terms. (David Brewster, 2014) This may have multiple connotations for both traditional powers and the littorals. The world likely sees a different picture of littorals in strategic and geopolitical terms. Littorals seem not only to play the role of mere pawns in the emerging Indo-Pacific order. No doubt, the littorals will continue to look towards regional power centres for maritime assistance and addressing security challenges, however, their strategic importance in building a hegemonic position in the Asian Century will see more colours.

They are likely to become crucial players in the geopolitics, trade, and maritime security of the region with increasing bandwagoning among the traditional powers for strategically important ports and naval bases.

In the times to come, the role of littorals is going to be even more relevant as Indian Ocean Region (IOR) and the Western Pacific (WP) are interlinked in the Indo-Pacific concept. The events happening in the IOR are likely to impact the geopolitics of WP. Geopolitically induced investments by the traditional powers will encourage economic growth and prosperity in the shattered tourism-centred economies. The most significant of such development will be the naval power structures of these nations especially bigger archipelagos like Indonesia.

China's strategically formulated plan MSR will further manifest its 'Two-Ocean Strategy'. (Robert D. Kaplan, 2009) Beijing's leasing of ports in Sri Lanka and the Maldives inflicts serious apprehensions on their future, making them more vulnerable. The mutual rift of the big powers is likely to reinvigorate the hitherto dormant maritime disputes in the region. India-China, China-Japan, China-Australia, and China-US geopolitical rivalry for resources in the region is likely to enhance the maritime-military confrontations leading to insecurities.

Though a non-containment strategy and inclusiveness will remain the foundation of the Indo-Pacific vision, the looming threat of Chinese hegemony cannot be ignored. The role of ASEAN centrality needs to be supplemented by groupings like QUAD. However, the involvement of the US's anti-China stand and extra-regional players like France should not bring exclusivity and cooperation having military focus. Military alliances among the QUAD and QUAD plus countries will further tense the atmosphere in the Indo-Pacific geopolitical rivalry. Thus, the cooperation of like-minded nations should be based on sustainable development, maritime cooperation, safety, geo-economics, and openness at high seas. At this, the role of India and the Indian navy is crucial as a middle power to not only balance the regional power dynamics but also to secure its positions as a dominant player in the region. Khurana states that to maintain a stable balance of power in the region, the proactive role of regional players like India, Australia, and Japan is necessary. (Khurana, 2019) Keshav Balkrishna Vaidya, an exponent of India's sea power, suggested the creation of a ring of Indian naval bases, outside India, including the Vanilla Islands, Southern Chains, Chagos Islands, etc. (Scott, 2006) Admiral Prakash also suggested that India must take all endeavours to reflect itself as a "Comprehensive national power" including the maritime capabilities and create its image as a strong negotiator. (Prakash, 2020)

Conclusion

It can be said that 21st Century can become the Indo-Pacific century. And in that century, Oceania will act as a lynchpin towards securing cooperation as well as rebalancing. SIS are expected to emerge as a significant force generator holding the immense potential to push both power politics and economic prosperity in the region. Through, the narrative of Indo-Pacific, India sees an opportunity to fill the vacuum in the great power politics. India's efforts to ensure non-compartmentalization of Asia in favour of any hegemonic structure will require India to gain sufficient Asian Outreach which is not possible without the SIS. Being a middle power and an excellent negotiator among the small states, India lies in an ideal position to endorse the role of littorals in fulfilling the vision of an inclusive Indo-Pacific. India's closer ties with ASEAN and traditional influence in the Indian Ocean region will strengthen its position as an upholder of a desirable regional order. Moreover, its efforts to manoeuvre goodwill among the pacific island nations will enhance its potential to reap the benefits of the expanded regime for India.

India's evolving requirements in the region desperately need a more coherent maritime strategy. Such a successful maritime strategy should look out to inculcate the role of SIS and sub-regions more comprehensively. If India has to follow its bottom-up strategy to reconstruct the regional order, India needs to forge priority engagement with smaller nations that lack military and economic power. This also comes as part of India's role as a pivot to the Indo-Pacific region. It is expected that, as a result, these nations will also take India's leadership as a more viable alternative. Thus, partnership with SIS should stand at the core of India's Indo-Pacific policy. This way, a confident India with a workable bond with China and push from the USA and other major powers in the region will contribute to a greater quest for maintaining stability in the region. With fierce challenges and limited capacity to confront them, India needs to limit the gap between the two by encouraging stronger cooperative alignment with big powers and benevolent partnership with the SIS to advance our values and interests in the region.

To realize the vision of Indo-Pacific, only concerted efforts of like-minded countries can secure maritime and geopolitical tranquillity. Further, India continues to believe in refurbished statecraft, conducive bilateral engagement, garnering cooperation through multilateral platforms, forward presence of Indian navy, and constructive engagement with alliances including QUAD and QUAD plus initiative to promote the inclusive, peaceful and resilient Indo-Pacific vital to ensure India's security and prosperity.

References

(2011). *Asia 2050: Realising the Asian Century*. Asian Development Bank, p. 3.

"India, Asean can ensure peace, prosperity in Indo-Pacific: Narendra Modi. (May 30, 2018). *The Economic Times*.

Administration, U. E. (2013). *South China Sea*. Washington, USA: USEIA.

Affairs, M. o. (2016). Prime Minister's address at the International Fleet Review. New Delhi: Government of India.

Affairs, M. o. (2018). *Prime Minister's Keynote Address at Shangri La Dialogue. Shangri La Dialogue*, p. 1. New Delhi: Government of India.

Agency, U. S. (2013). *Contested areas of South China Sea likely have few conventional oil and gas resources*. Washington: USEIA.

Agency, U. S. (2017). *World Oil Transit Checkpoints*. Washington: USEIA.

Anderson, C. (2006). *The Long Tail: Why the future of business is selling less of more?*. New York City: Hyperion.

Baruah, D. M. (2018). "Islands as Game Changers in the Indian Ocean". *Asia Maritime Transparency Initiative*.

Bhatia, R. (February 3, 2011). "Engaging India's Far East". *The Hindu*.

Bhattacharya, S. (2019). "India, ASEAN and Indo-Pacific Geopolitics". *UNISCI Journal*, pp. 253-54.

Chaudhary, D. R. (November 3, 2020). "More & more countries are aligning their definition of the Indo-Pacific with India's: Foreign Secretary". *The Economic Times*.

D. L. Berlin. (2006). India in the Indian Ocean. *Naval War College Review*, vol. 59, no. 2.

David Brewster, (2014). "Dividing Lines: Evolving Mental Maps of the Bay of Bengal". *Asian Security*, vol. 10(2), 151-67.

De, P. (2020). *Act East to Act Indo-Pacific: India's Expanding Neighbourhood*. New Delhi: Knowledge World.

Defence, M. o. (2007). *Annual Report 2006-07*. New Delhi: Government of India.

Defence, M. o. (2009). *Indian Maritime Doctrine, Naval Strategic Publication 1.1*. New Delhi: Government of India.

Defense, M. o. (2015). *Ensuring Secure Seas: Indian Maritime Security Strategy*. New Delhi: Government of India.

Emmerson, D. (2018, June 14). "In Search for the Real Indo-Pacific". *YaleGlobal Online*.

G. S. Khurana. (2008). "China's 'String of Pearls' in the Indian Ocean and Its Security Implications". *Strategic Analysis*, vol. 32, no. 1.

Ghosh, Y. K. (2020). "The 'Indo' in the 'Indo-Pacific'—An Indian View". *Naval War College Review*, vol. 73, article 7.

Gurung, S. K. (January 30, 2020). "Alarm over Chinese research ships in Indian Ocean Region". *The Economic Times*.

IFR 2016: PM Modi unveils 'Sagar' doctrine of transforming India via maritime security. (February 8, 2016). *India Writes*.

III, W. C. (2009). "Delhi's Pacific Ambition: Naval Power, 'Look East', and India's Emerging Influence in the Asia-Pacific". *Asian Century*, 5: 2, 87-113.

"India Approved as Observer of Indian Ocean Commission". (March 6, 2020). *The Wire*.

"Indonesia wants ASEAN to take central role in developing Indo-Pacific cooperation". (April 24, 2018). *The Jakarta Post*.

Khurana, G. (2019). "What is the Indo-Pacific?". In S. M. Axel Berkofsky, *Geopolitics by Other Means. The Indo-Pacific Reality*, p. 32. Milano, Italy: Ledizioni LediPublishing.

Khurana, G. S. (2017). *The Indo-Pacific Concept: The Retrospect and Prospect.* New Delhi, India: National Maritime Foundation.

"MEA Expands Indian Ocean Division to Include Islands off African Coast". (December 20, 2019). *The Wire*.

Medcalf, R. (2019). "Indo-Pacific with Chinese Characterstics". *Politique étrangère*.

Ministry of Foreign Affairs, P. R. (2017). *Closer Cooperation under Belt and Roat win-win for Fiji, China. Beijing*: Ministry of Foreign Affairs.

"Modi address's Putin's Quad concerns in Singapore". (June 5, 2018). *The Economic Times*.

Mohan, C. R. (2009). "Is India an East Asian Power? Explaining New Delhi's Security Politics in the Western Pacific". *SAS Working Paper*, p. 1.

Mohan., C. R. (2012). *Samudramanthan: Sino-Indian Rivalry in the Indo-Pacific.* New Delhi: Carnegie Endowment.

Motulalo, T. (2013). *India's Strategic Imperative in the South Pacific*. Mumbai: Gateway House.

Parashar, S. (January 31, 2021). "Eye on China, India woos Madagascar and Comoros". *The Times of India*.

Power, J. (January 18, 2020). "Has the US already lost the battle for the South China Sea?". *South China Morning Post*.

Prakash, A. (July 22, 2020). "India must formally revive Quad, seek its expansion". *Indian Express*.

Press Information Bureau. (2018). *Delhi Declaration of the ASEAN-India Commemorative Summit to mark the 25th Anniversary of ASEAN-India*

Dialogue Relations. New Delhi: Government of India, Prime Minister's Office.

Puna, H. (2012). "Large Ocean Island States: The Pacific Challenge". *43rd Pacific Islands Leaders Forum*. Cook Islands.

Raja Mohan, C. (June 7, 2019). "Modi's visit to Male, Colombo can affirm the salience of the Indian Ocean island states". *The Indian Express*.

Robert D. Kaplan. (2009). "China's Two Ocean Strategy". In Abraham Denmark and Nirav Patel (eds.), *China's Arrival: A Strategic Relationship for a Global Relationship*. Washington: Center for New American Strategy.

Saha, A. M. (January 13, 2020). "India's Indo-Pacific strategy must take along the neglected side: Eastern nations". *The Print*.

Sakhuja, V. (2011). *Asian Maritime Power in the 21st Century: Strategic Transactions China, India, and Southeast Asia*. New Delhi: Pentagon Press.

Scott, D. (2006). "India's 'Grand Strategy' for the Indian Ocean: Mahanian Visions". *Asia-Pacific Review*, pp. 1-3.

Shaomin, X. (November 21, 2017). "Geography is not destiny: Rise of Indo-Pacific". *The Global Times*.

Speech by Deng Xiaoping at the Communist Youth League conference. (August 20, 2014). *China Daily*.

Wroe, D. (April 9, 2018). "China eyes Vanuatu military base in plan with global ramifications". *Sydney Morning Herald*.

"Foreign Trade (North East Asia)", Ministry of Commerce and Industry, Government of India, at http://commerce.gov.in/InnerContent.aspx?Id=75

"Annual Report 2017-18", Ministry of Commerce and Industry, Government of India, at http://commerce.gov.in/writereaddata/uploadedfile/MOC_636626711232248483_Annual%20Report%20%202017-18%20English.pdf, p. 49.

"US looking for partnership, not dominance in Indo-Pacific", *The Statesman*, August 1, 2018, p. 9.

INDIA'S SOFT POWER IN CONSOLIDATING QUAD

ALAKH RANJAN

Introduction

India's engagement with the world has always shown an inclination towards soft power over hard power. It has never tried to conquer any territory by the use of force, and believed in the idea of 'Vasudhaiva Kutumbakam' which regards the world as one family and has followed this noble principle all through its history. These values have been the guiding principle of India's foreign policy as it has always worked towards building alliances through cooperation and mutual agreement. Starting from hosting Asian Relations Conference, NAM to G-77, it has always tried to build synergy among the nations through soft power tools. The international relations and global politics have changed dynamically in the twentieth century due to which hard power tools will no longer be sufficient to pursue national interest and alliances in the present world. Indian soft power engagement could be a value addition to global politics, and more so for the QUAD.

The precursor to the QUAD was a Tsunami Core group which was formed to carry out humanitarian assistance and relief work after the region was hit by the 2004 Boxing Day Tsunami. It later developed as a security alliance. Since its revival in 2017 it has also been trying to expand its working area beyond traditional security issues. With the changing geopolitics, the grouping has been trying to adapt to the needs of the region.

The COVID-19 pandemic which made health security as one of the paramount issues for all the governments across the globe has also made the QUAD realise the importance of non-traditional security issues. This was clearly visible in the recently issued joint statement in March 2021. The statement emphasised its commitment towards non-traditional security issues such as climate change, health security and disaster management in the Indo-Pacific region. As one of the QUAD members, India has started working towards achieving the agendas. India has gone beyond its cultural engagement with the region as a soft power tool and has contributed to the health sector by exporting medical equipment and pharmaceuticals to the region. New Delhi has been the first responder to the disaster in the region and has been at the forefront in relief aid and assistance during natural disasters.

The chapter is going to discuss the role of India's soft power in consolidating the QUAD in the Indo-Pacific region. It will explore India's engagements in the Indo-Pacific region in general, and ASEAN in particular, in the areas of health, culture, disaster management and relief initiatives. The paper looks into the significance of the soft power in strengthening the grouping influence in the region and how India can be the pivotal state in releasing this motive.

QUAD: Past, Present and Future

The QUAD, a group of four countries: the United States of America (USA), Japan, Australia and India which came first into existence as an ad hoc group, "Tsunami Core Group" to help the countries of the Indo-Pacific which were hit by the devastating 2004 Tsunami. (West, 2021) The first QUAD meeting was held in May 2007 on the margins of ASEAN Regional Forum. It was then termed an 'informal dialogue'. It was Japanese President Shinzo Abe who conceptualised the idea of QUAD and laid down the ideological foundation of this grouping during his address titled "*Confluence of the Two Seas*" at the Central Hall of Indian Parliament. (Abe, 2007) During his speech he talked about how the coming together of Japan and India will lead to "broader Asia" which will form a network spanning the whole of Pacific and will incorporate the USA and Australia, ensuring a free open and transparent network which will facilitate free flow of goods, people, capital and knowledge.

The first 'informal meeting' was followed by a joint multilevel military exercise called the Malabar Exercise between the four countries along Singapore in the Bay of Bengal. (Kaushik, 2020) But the grouping fell apart within a year of its formation when in 2008, Australia pulled out of this grouping. The two major reasons which led to the abrupt end of this grouping was first, the Chinese pressure. In July 2008, after his visit to China, Australian Defence Minister Brendan Nelson stated "Australia was only interested in peacekeeping and economic issues in the quadrilateral engagement and doesn't want to do anything unnecessarily that upsets any other country." Secondly, Prime Minister Shinzo Abe resigned in September 2007, which was a big blow for the grouping as he was the chief architect of this grouping. The grouping also ended abruptly because the objectives and purposes of this were not clearly defined and each country had different objectives to form QUAD.

After a decade the grouping revived in 2017 due to the changing geopolitics and increased coercive behaviour of China in the Indo-Pacific region, and also against the four countries of the QUAD. India faced a stand-off with China at the Doklam trijunction and its entry into Nuclear Suppliers Group (NSG) was blocked by China; Australia discovered active Chinese interference in its politics and universities; Japan nationalised three Senkaku island in 2012 which resulted in China sending 11 ships to East China Sea. (Khan, 2012) In the USA, reports emerged about economic espionage by Chinese citizens. (Grossman, 2015) All this led to the resumption of QUAD with the assistant-secretary level meeting of four countries in Manila in November 2017. (Australia-India-Japan-U.S. Consultations on the Indo-Pacific , 2017) In this meeting, discussions were held about cooperating for promotion of a "free, open, prosperous and inclusive Indo-Pacific region". (Release, 2017) Post this meeting there have been regular meetings that have continued at senior official levels biannually. (Rimland, 2020) This built momentum for QUAD which finally resulted in the virtual meeting between the heads of four countries. This shows that QUAD as a grouping will consolidate as an organisation and grow in its scope and area.

After the meeting a joint statement was issued. The statement clearly stated two things: first, ASEAN's centrality in QUAD, and second, the push for soft power agenda. The QUAD countries understand ASEAN's apprehensiveness towards QUAD. The ASEAN major concern is with a new multilateral group being formed whose area of operation overlaps with its area of operation which might lead to its side lining. The QUAD has been sensitive towards this concern and has always endorsed the 'centrality of ASEAN' in all its meeting reports since its beginnings and this was followed in the Joint Statement. The statement reads that, "We reaffirm our strong support for ASEAN's unity and centrality as well as the ASEAN Outlook on the Indo-Pacific." (Affairs, Quad Leaders' Joint Statement: "The Spirit of the Quad", 2021) Thus, reaffirming its support to ASEAN's centrality.

The push for 'soft-power' agenda was mentioned implicitly in the Joint Statement. The statement read, "We strive for a region that is free, open, inclusive, healthy, anchored by democratic values, and unconstrained by coercion."

The statement also talked about jointly manufacturing vaccines and ensuring 'equitable access' among the countries of the region through international organisations such as World Health Organisation (WHO) and COVAX to ensure health security. The USA president stressed more on the soft power agenda with a focus on areas such as climate change, health security and technology. (Bochkov, 2021) The statement also mentioned cooperation to fight the challenges of climate change, cyberspace, critical technologies, counterterrorism, quality infrastructure investment, and humanitarian-assistance and disaster-relief as well as maritime domains.

The emphasis on ASEAN's centrality and soft power clearly shows that QUAD understands that the answer to China's coercive action and aggressive policies will require taking into confidence the countries of the ASEAN. In these troubling times of pandemic, health security has been paramount for every country and by providing affordable vaccines to the countries of the SEA will surely win many supporters of the QUAD in these countries. Along with this emphasising on climate change and assuring that the QUAD will work "to strengthen the climate actions of all nations, including to keep a Paris-aligned temperature limit within reach" will help in garnering support among the countries of the ASEAN. Rising temperatures and sea levels are one of the biggest threats for these countries as it will cause multiple problems, such as reduced land area, increased salinity of soil in the coastal area and climate migration.

The QUAD realises the fact that if it wants to become a strong and sustainable organisation in this region, it will need the complete support of the ASEAN countries, and hard power tools such as military support and weapon export cannot be the only solutions. Soft power tools will be crucial to win the confidence of these countries.

Soft Power and India

Soft power, a term coined by Professor Joseph Nye, is relatively new in international discourse but it has been in application since ages. This term was first mentioned by Nye in his book *Bound to Lead*:

The Changing Nature of American Power where he writes, "*When one country gets other countries to want what it wants might be called co-optive or soft power in contrast with the hard or command power of ordering others to do what it wants." He further defines soft power in his book The Means to Success in World Politics as, "Soft Power is the ability to get what you want through attraction rather than coercion or payments."*

After being coined by Nye, this term has been actively used by politicians, academicians, researchers in international relations all across the globe. The key component of soft power is that a country can gain influence through attraction. He identified three main sources of soft power: culture (in places where it is attractive to others), its political values (when it lives up to them at home and abroad), and its foreign policy (when they are seen as legitimate and having moral authority) (Jr.).

The term Soft Power in its sense has been practised in world politics and diplomacy even before it was coined by Nye. India has been practising soft power since centuries. Culturally speaking, in ancient and medieval history, India was perceived as the land of knowledge and wisdom. (Basham, 2019) Nalanda University, a Buddhist monastic centre in eastern India had students and scholars from Greece, Persia, Tibet, China and Korea. (Bisht, 2020) In terms of political values and foreign policies, an Indian philosopher, Vishnugupta or Kautilya in third century BC, very well elucidated the concept of power "as a means to achieve political ends" in his book Arthashastra. (Rangarajan, Kautilya - The Arthashastra, 1992) In the book along with tools of hard power and coercion he has discussed various facets of soft power. While discussing coercion as means to achieve the ends, he also used the terms such as *sana* (reconciliation) and *dana* (gifts) as tools to achieve the goals. (Ibid.)

Being the first democracy in the non-western world enhanced India's soft power position and the non-alignment as a foreign policy appealed to the newly independent countries of Africa and Asia. Under the leadership of Jawaharlal Nehru, India started to develop furthermore on its soft power sources. To take its culture to the world, it opened up Indian Culture Centres (ICCs). The first ICC was opened in 1989 in Moscow, and at present India has 38 cultural centres dotted across the world. (Relations) The success of India as a democracy was predicted by few in the West but its success attracted the world towards it.

In foreign policy, India's clout has grown over the years. India's desires and efforts to be seen as a global soft power dates back to the time when India was not even independent. India hosted Asia Relations Conference in March-April in 1947 and invited several countries such as Afghanistan, Myanmar, Sri Lanka, Turkey, Soviet, Asian Republics, Indonesia, China, Korea, Mongolia, and Vietnam. It played a pivotal role in forming an 'Afro-Asian alliance' by participating in the Bandung Conference.

After Independence, the world also witnessed Delhi's leading role in creation of the third bloc under the Non-Alignment Movement (NAM), the G-77, BRICS. It is today the member of several regional and international multilateral organisations such as South Asian Association for Regional Cooperation (SAARC), Bay of Bengal Initiative for Multi-Sectoral Technical and Economic Cooperation (BIMSTEC), Shanghai Cooperation Organization, The Indian Ocean Rim Association (IORA), to name a few. Over the years, India has been voicing the issues of the global south on all of these platforms. Such as, reforms in United Nations Security Council (UNSC), international economic order, including concerns related to the World Bank and International Monetary Fund. (Pande, 2017) After liberalisation, India has grown its economic power and is now being considered one of the 'emerging powers' in world politics. The twenty-first century has been termed as the Asian Century and India has been the third largest economy in Asia and will play a leading role in the world.

The geopolitics of the world has been changing over the years and COVID-19 accelerated it. Today, the theatre of world politics has shifted from the Atlantic to Indo-Pacific. This gives India a chance to strengthen its position in the region as well in the world and emerge as a reliable power. It has the potential to be one as it possesses the right combination of both hard power (military capabilities and economy) and soft power (culture, civilisational connect, free and open society) to win the hearts and minds of the countries of the Association of Southeast Asian Nations (ASEAN) and the whole of Indo-Pacific.

Soft Power Tools: Bringing South-East Asia and QUAD Closer

India's soft power capabilities have been enhanced over the years, which makes it an essential partner in realising the soft power goals of QUAD. India has several tools which can help bring SEA closer to the QUAD and weave a close-knit bond between them. The three major soft power tools of India which can aid in consolidating the QUAD and bring SEA closer to QUAD are cultural connect, medical and pharma and human assistance and disaster relief (HADR).

Cultural Connection

As an ancient civilisation, India has been the powerhouse of soft power and always possessed a key resource of soft power, i.e., its attractive culture, for centuries before the term came into existence. It has influenced cultures across the globe across history. Jawaharlal Nehru in his book has expressed about the origins and richness of Indian culture and civilisation where he has written, "Thus in these very early days we find the beginnings of the civilization and culture which were to flower so abundantly and richly in subsequent ages, and which have continued, in spite of many changes, to our own day." Many other scholars have also written about how early the Indian culture was inchoate in the ancient times. Professor Macdonell wrote about this in his book, *A History of Sanskrit Literature* that

"When the Greeks towards the end of the fourth century BC invaded the north-west, the Indians had already worked out a national culture of their own, unaffected by foreign influences .... No other country except China can trace back its language and literature, its religious beliefs and rites, its dramatic and social customs through an uninterrupted development of more than 3,000 years."

India shares close civilisational ties with the countries of SEA. Indian ships from the beginning of history had sailed as far as Borneo, and flourishing Indian colonies had existed for over 1,200 years in Malaya, the islands of Indonesia, in Cambodia, Champa and other areas of the coast. (Nehru, *The Discovery of India*, 2008) Monsoon wind patterns were the main facilitators of these civilisational connections. These winds created the navigational routes for sailors to the SEA region. The sailors sailed with one monsoon wind and returned with the next year's monsoon wind. This gave them the time to settle in these countries. With these monsoons, not only the products travelled, along with them travelled the different facets of culture such as Ramayana, Buddhism, music, dance, cuisines, etc.

From the first century of the Christian Era onwards wave after wave of Indian colonists spread East and South East Asia reaching Ceylon, Burma, Malaya, Java, Sumatra, Borneo, Siam, Cambodia and India-China. (Ibid.) The cultural overlapping between India with this region can be stated by the fact that the Java is clearly from 'Yavadvipa' or the Island of Millet and even today java means barley or millet in India. In Thailand, even today the kings are crowned by Brahmin priests, Cambodia has one of the largest Hindu temples in the world, Angkor Wat, its legislations are based on the Laws of Manu, the ancient law giver of India, Indonesian national airline is called Garuda and a ballet has been produced in the Philippines narrating the stories of Ramayana (Shashi Tharoor, 2011).

The depth of the civilisational relations that India shares with the region can be inferred from the article written by the first Indonesian

President, Sukarno in The Hindu in 1947 where he said that "In the veins of every one of my people flows the blood of Indian ancestors and the culture that we possess is steeped through and through with Indian influences. Two thousand years ago, people from your country came to Jawadvipa and Suvarnadvipa in the spirit of brotherly love. They gave the initiative to found powerful kingdoms such as those of Sri Vijaya, Mataram and Majapahit. We then learnt to worship the very Gods that you now worship still and we fashioned a culture that even today is largely identical with your own. Later, we turned to Islam but that religion too was brought by people coming from both sides of India." (Amit Singh, 2017)

The culture connect is the strongest soft power tool which India can employ to win over the hearts and minds of the people of this region. In terms of the cultural connect, Buddhism is one thread which closely binds India and SEA. India under Prime Minister Modi truly realises this and this is the reason, in his 'Act East' policy he has worked to forge a closer connection. India has been trying to market its Buddhist circuit to attract the tourists from the SEA region which is the home to the highest number of Buddhist population. The free flow of cultural travel and tourism between India and countries of the SEA will help in building strong and sustainable relations between India and SEA region which will lead to greater confidence and trust among the people of this region towards India. The tourism and cultural exchanges will bring the hearts of people together which will generate goodwill for India which in turn can lead to bringing the QUAD closer to ASEAN.

Pharmaceuticals and Medical Tourism

With health security becoming paramount for every country in the world, India is now seen as a valuable ally as it is the manufacturing pharmaceutical hub of the world. It is also one of the largest manufacturers of COVID-19 vaccines and has exported vaccines to over 91 countries under its '*Vaccine Maitri*' programme before it was hit by the second wave of COVID-19 virus in the month of March due to which it had to curtail the export of vaccines. It is expected that the situation will improve in India in the second half of the year which will lead to India again exporting the vaccines to the world.

The QUAD in its joint statement has announced that the four countries will pool in resources to manufacture up to one billion vaccine doses by 2022. Under this partnership one billion doses will be manufactured in India by a Hyderabad based Biological E Limited including the Johnson & Johnson vaccine. (Fact Sheet: Quad Summit, 2021) In the press release, it was also implicitly mentioned that the focus area of these manufactured vaccines will be South-East Asia. This clearly shows that vaccine diplomacy will be a key mechanism in strengthening the relationship between QUAD and the SEA countries and India being the production centre of these vaccines will play an important role.

Apart from COVID-19 vaccines and generic drug manufacture, India is also a major medical tourism destination for developing countries due to its affordable world-class medical services. India has been catering to a large number of medical tourists from across the group and it has also been receiving a large number of them from the SEA countries. The medical tourists from SEA to India has increased from 2,82,427 in 2017 (Tourism, 2017); p. 53) to 5,95,546 in 2020 (Ministry of Tourism, India Tourism Statistics, 2020); p. 46) and it is expected that these numbers will grow in the coming years.

This is another area which India can utilise to boost its relationship with the people of the SEA region. The QUAD is funding the vaccine manufacturing in India by providing concessional loans from Japan, in the same manner it can help in ramping up the medical facilities in India which will help the citizens of the SEA, the access to better health care services. In this regard, hospitals and other medical infrastructure can be developed in India's North-East Region (NER) which has also been termed as the gateway to SEA. NER being closer to the SEA region is the ideal place for developing it as the medical tourist hub for the people of the SEA due to its close proximity with the region.

Human Assistance and Disaster Relief (HADR)

HADR was the reason which initially brought the four countries of the QUAD together. The four countries brought together their military capabilities to carry out the relief work of Tsunami 2004 in the Indo-Pacific region. India in 2004 responded to the crisis within 24 hours. (Bhaskar, 2005) India's swift response during this devastating crisis transformed India's image at the world stage. The world recognised its military capacity and political commitment by inviting it to be the part of "Tsunami Core Group" which was a USA-led initiative. The initiative initially had Australia, India, Japan and the USA. It was later expanded to include Canada, the European Union (EU) and the United Nations. (Mohan C. R., 2014) This group was formed to undertake a coordinated effort to tackle the crisis. The forming of this group was the first instance when these four countries came together which later materialised into the idea of Quad Security Dialogue.

Post 2004, New Delhi has always been at the forefront in the last decade and a half to every crisis in the region, and has emerged as the 'first responder' (G. o. Ministry of External Affairs) to every natural disaster and crisis in the Indian Ocean Region. It contributed to the relief work in Bangladesh during its Cyclone Sidr in 2007 (Press Information Bureau I., November), in 2008, during cyclone Nargis in Myanmar, India was the first external country to arrive (Bureau P. I., Indian Armed Forces Launch Operation Sahayata: IAF, Navy Rush Relief to Myanmar, 2007). In 2017, when Sri Lanka and Bangladesh were hit by a devastating flood, at that time too, the Indian armed forces were the first to respond to the crisis. (G. o. Ministry of External Affairs) The quick response by India shows its capability, and willingness to mitigate regional and international crises.

Disaster management is one area which has been at the top in India's engagement with the ASEAN region. The leaders from the ASEAN also requested India to work together in implementation of the ASEAN Agreement on Disaster Management and Emergency Response (AADMER) Work Programme and to Collaborate with the ASEAN Coordinating Centre for Humanitarian Assistance on disaster management (AHA Centre). (Ministry of External Affairs, Governement of India., Chairman's Statement of the 11th ASEAN-India Summit, Bandar Seri Begawan, October 10, 2013) New Delhi's concept of human assistance comes from its cultural and spiritual values that "espouse solidarity with suffering and giving without expectations in return".(Ibid) This has aided in boosting the alliance with the countries of the Indo-Pacific region.

ASEAN, which is central to QUAD, is a disaster-prone region and India's HADR capabilities have been useful to them in the past, and due to its close proximity and HADR competence will always be the first to reach them. India and ASEAN share profound relationships in this area and New Delhi has been participating in the Disaster Relief Exercises (DiRex) since 2011. The proven record of India over the years in HADR has enhanced India's soft power capability. It has assisted the countries in the region and across the globe without expecting anything or with any strings attached. India along with the QUAD countries should work towards strengthening its capabilities in the HADR area because China, which has till now been reluctant to venture into HADR beyond its borders, is heavily investing in its naval capabilities and has been expanding its human assistance activities in the region. With rising China, QUAD's answer to China in HADR cannot materialise without India.

The need of the hour is to boost the soft power capabilities in close partnership with India. The QUAD has started working in this area. India's soft power concepts has been even endorsed by the American president and other leaders of the QUAD. In his statement during the

QUAD meeting, President Biden said, "Our agenda today—covering areas like vaccines, climate change, and emerging technologies—make the Quad a force for global good. I see this positive vision as an extension of India's ancient philosophy of Vasudhaiva Kutumbakam, which regards the world as one family. We will work together, closer than ever before, for advancing our shared values and promoting a secure, stable, and prosperous Indo-Pacific."

The QUAD has formed three expert working groups to deal with soft power issues along with security related problems which was announced after the 2021 QUAD meeting. The groups are: the QUAD vaccine working group, the QUAD climate working group and the QUAD Critical and Emerging Technology Working Group. This balanced approach from the grouping will surely enhance the confidence in it among the countries of Indo-Pacific and also aid in removing apprehensiveness towards QUAD in the ASEAN region.

Conclusion

The four countries of QUAD came together for a humanitarian cause and later developed the security dialogue. This security dialogue in its first version or QUAD 1.0 failed with a whimper only to return after a decade. The major reason for this was as in its first version, it seemed as a security alliance because the first joint event after the May 2007 meeting was the joint military exercise. The grouping was viewed as an 'Asian NATO' with an aim to contain China. This caused tensions among the ASEAN countries as they feared that they might get caught in the great game and lose their centrality in the region. In QUAD 2.0, the group became more sensitive about the concerns of the ASEAN region and regularly mentioned about ASEAN's centrality in all its oral statements and written documents. This helped in building confidence about the grouping.

In the joint statement which was released after the meetings, the heads of the four states mentioned about the objectives of the QUAD and the working areas. Soft issues such as climate change, vaccination, health security, HADR, quality infrastructure, restoration and strengthening of democracy were mentioned in the joint statement along with security issues such as counterterrorism, cyberspace and critical technologies. The joint statement clearly shows that the four countries are now treading a path of smart power[1] by striking a balance between the hard power issues and soft power issues. As soft power is now being given importance under the grouping, India could play a vital role in it.

To develop the QUAD into a successful and sustainable organisation in the region, it needs to work on several things to avert the fate which it suffered in 2008. The QUAD needs to have a clear geographical demarcation of the area because at present each of the four countries of the QUAD have different geographical understanding and definition of the Indo-Pacific region. This is a problem which needs to be addressed to have an effective presence in the region. Since India's soft power resources are vital for the consolidation of this grouping, it should play a leading role in demarcating it as per its strengths. Second, division and delegation of the working area. The QUAD in its vaccine partnership decided to draw upon the strengths of each country in implementing the vaccine programme. This is the reason that India has been given the role of manufacturing the vaccine. Continuing with this policy, the QUAD should work towards combining the resources and give India a primary role in areas such as cultural and medical tourism. It shares a common thread of Buddhism along with deep historical ties in terms of cuisine, architecture, mythology, etc., which can be used to develop cultural and religious ties across the region. The Indo-Pacific region is a culturally connected region and to constitute a durable organisation a continued effort should be put in place to ensure regular exchanges among the people of the regions.

In this age where protectionism is on the rise across the world and countries are becoming inward looking, soft power is the best way for the QUAD to make inroads in the Indo-Pacific region. To succeed in this region and to win over the confidence of the government in the ASEAN region along with the Indo-Pacific, soft power tools will aid in gaining the backing of the government. In this regard, India is in the best position to foster soft power relationship as it shares a historical and cultural relationship, and lately under Prime Minister Modi has been tirelessly working to build strong relations by implying soft power tools. By backing India in this region with its engagements in the soft power with the ASEAN countries and the whole Indo-Pacific will help the QUAD grouping also gain legitimacy from the region and outside.

Note

1. Smart power is the ability to combine hard and soft power resources into effective strategies. Unlike soft power, smart power is an evaluative as well as a descriptive concept. —Jospeh Nye Jr.

References

West, J. (2021, April 3). *What Does the QUAD Summit Signal For US's Relationships With Asian Countries?* Retrieved June 2021, from Asia Century Institute: https://asiancenturyinstitute.com/international/1666-what-does-the-quad-summit-signal-for-us-s-relationships-with-asian-countries

Abe, H. S. (2007, August 22). *Confluence of the Two Seas.* Retrieved April 2021, from Ministry of Foreign Affairs Japan: https://www.mofa.go.jp/region/asia-paci/pmv0708/speech-2.html

Kaushik, K. (2020, November 3). *Expalined.* Retrieved May 2021, from The Indian Express: https://indianexpress.com/article/explained/malabar-naval-exercise-india-6915447/

Khan, S. A. (2012, September 25). *Japan's "Nationalisation" of Senkaku: Internal and External Determinants.* Retrieved May 2021, from Manohar Parrikar Institute for Defence Studies and Analyses: https://idsa.in/idsacomments/JapansNationalisationofSenkaku_sakhan_250912

Grossman, A. (2015, May 19). *U.S. Charges Six Chinese Citizens With Economic Espionage.* Retrieved May 2022, from The Wall Street Journal: https://

www.wsj.com/articles/u-s-charges-six-chinese-citizens-with-economic-espionage-1432046527

Australia-India-Japan-U.S. Consultations on the Indo-Pacific. (2017, November 12). Retrieved June 2021, from Ministry of Foreign Affairs of Japan : https://www.mofa.go.jp/press/release/press4e_001789.html

Release, P. (2017, November 12). *India-Australia-Japan-U.S. Consultations on Indo-Pacific (November 12, 2017)*. Retrieved May 2021, from Ministry of External Affairs, Government of India: https://mea.gov.in/press-releases.htm?dtl/29110/IndiaAustraliaJapanUS_Consultations_on_IndoPacific_November_12_2017

Rimland, P. G. (2020, March). *Defining the Diamond The Past, Present, and Future of the Quadrilateral Security Dialogue*. Retrieved April 2021, from Center for Strategic and International Studies : https://www.csis.org/analysis/defining-diamond-past-present-and-future-quadrilateral-security-dialogue.

Affairs, M. o. (2021, March 12). *Quad Leaders' Joint Statement: "The Spirit of the Quad"*. Retrieved June 2021, from Ministry of External Affairs, Government of India: https://www.mea.gov.in/bilateral-documents.htm?dtl/33620/Quad_Leaders_Joint_Statement_The_Spirit_of_the_Quad

Bochkov, D. (2021, March 23). *Hard power or soft power? Quad opts for 'smart' power.* Retrieved June 2021, from Asia Times: https://asiatimes.com/2021/03/hard-power-or-soft-power-quad-opts-for-smart-power/

Basham, A. L. (2019). *The Wonder That Was India Vol. 1: A survey of the history and culture of the Indian sub-continent before the coming of the Muslims*. Picador India.

Bisht, M. (2020). *Kautilya's Arthashastra: Philosphy of Strategy*. New York: Routledge.

Rangarajan, L. N. (1992). *Kautilya - The Arthashastra*. Penguin Books India.

Pande, A. (2017). *From Chanakya to Modi. The Evolution of India's Foreign Policy.* Harper Collins Publishers India.

Nehru, J. (2008). *The Discovery of India*. Penguin India; New edition (1 February 2008).

Shashi Tharoor. (2011). India as a Soft Power, Author(s):. *India International Centre Quarterly*, 330-343.

Amit Singh, A. S. (2017, October). Paraspara, Encounters, and Confluences: India's Soft Power Objective in the Indo-Pacific Region. *Politics & Policy*, 45(5), 733-761.

Fact Sheet: Quad Summit. (2021, March 12). Retrieved June 2022, from The White House: https://www.whitehouse.gov/briefing-room/statements-releases/2021/03/12/fact-sheet-quad-summit/

Tourism, M. o. (2017). India Tourism Statistics. Governemnt of India, Ministry of Tourism. Governemnt of India.

Ministry of Tourism, G. o. (2020). *India Tourism Statistics.* Government of India, Ministry of Tourism. Government of India.

Bhaskar, C. U. (2005, January 08). *Tsunami Reveals Indian Military's Humanitarian Response Capability.* Retrieved June 2021, from Manohar Parrikar Institute for Defence Studies and Analyses (MP-IDSA): https://idsa.in/idsastrategiccomments/TsunamiRevealsIndianMilitarysHumanitarianResponseCapability_CUBhaskar_080105

Mohan, C. R. (2014, March). *Indian Military Diplomacy: Humanitarian Assistance and Disaster Relief.* Retrieved March 2020, from ISAS Working Papers, NUS: https://www.isas.nus.edu.sg/papers/184-indian-military-diplomacy-humanitarian-assistance-and-disaster-relief/

Affairs, M. o. (n.d.). *https://www.mea.gov.in/Portal/IndiaArticleAll/636548962666860480_Responding_First_Leading_Power.pdf. Retrieved May 2021, from Ministry of External Affairs, Government of India: https://www.mea.gov.in/Portal/IndiaArticleAll/636548962666860480_Responding_First_Leading_Power.pdf*

Nye, J. S. (2004). *Soft power: The means to success in world politics.* New York: Public Affairs.

ICCR. (n.d.). *Indian Cultural Centers Abroad List View.* Retrieved May 2021, from Indian Council for Cultural Relations: https://www.iccr.gov.in/indian-cultural-center-map-list-view

GEOPOLITICAL COMPETITION IN THE ARCTIC CIRCLE

PAYAL BANSAL

Introduction

In the core geographical sense, there were always the domination of mainland tropical areas in the politics, history, culture, society and others. Less inhabited areas such as Polar region, Antarctica and others didn't receive much attention of the people in the mainland. However, over a period of time, there is a major voice amongst the scientists, geopolitical analysts, leaders and other concerned stakeholders that those regions should be give due consideration as they have ample importance of the countries and societies. Development over there is definitely going to affect the livelihood of the people in tropical region. Hence, the region can't be overlooked. As far as the Arctic region is concerned, it has many different meanings, which is often used depending on the context and time and space. The Arctic comprises all of the northern sections of the Arctic Circle and their eight associated territories, namely, Canada, Denmark/Greenland, Finland, Iceland, Norway, Russia, the United States, and Sweden.

Figure 18: Arctic Region of Alaska as defined by ARPA

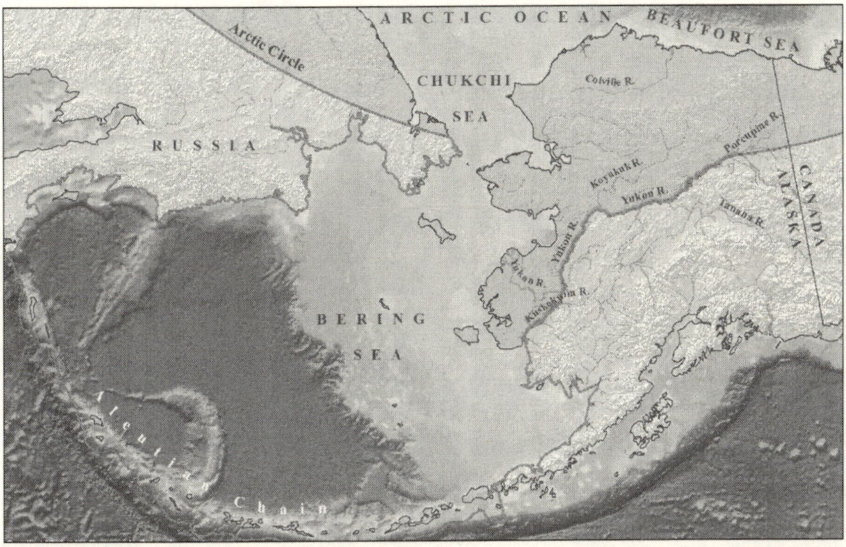

Source: https://www.arctic.gov/maps/

Other definitions might include regions north of the 10 centigrade July isotherm, as well as the Arctic Ocean boundary up to 801.31 degrees. Some Arctic governments define the territory differently to promote their own interests; for example, the Arctic Ocean and adjacent areas are included in Russia's strategy. Apart from other Arctic nations' definitions, the fact that they are all Arctic Council members demonstrates that they all recognise the same concept of the Arctic Circle.

According to the US Coast Guard, "the U.S. The Arctic Circle spans 2,521 miles, including a transnational river near the Russian Federation and 647 miles above the Canadian border. The Arctic Exclusive Economic Zone (EEZ) covers roughly 889,000 square miles of water in the United States."

Some Arctic definitions are based on factors such as moderate temperature, the northern line of the tree, the size of the ground ice, the size of the sea ice, or the limits of control or control. Climate-based data can fall into various areas over time due to climate change.

Legal Facet of the Arctic

The Arctic is widely regarded as a calm and tranquil environment. Although there is no official Arctic treaty like the Antarctic Treaty of 1959, there are a number of papers that serve as the foundation for local law. The United Nations Convention on the Law of the Sea is without a doubt the most significant (UNCLOS). The Ilulissat Declaration (2008), the International Maritime Organization (IMO), the Polar Code (2014), and the Arctic Council Declaration (although the Arctic Council is a high-level business on behalf of international legal business and thus rarely raises legal obligations, consider regional cooperation and governing body) are other important Arctic texts. The varying interests and aspirations of many countries drive the problem of Arctic administration. Some nations, such as the Antarctic, believe the Arctic to be an autonomous organisation, and some countries consider the Arctic to be an independent organisation.

The UN Convention on the Law of the Sea was signed at Montego Bay, Jamaica, in 1982 and came into force in 1994. There are 17 terms in this agreement, each split into parts and clauses. For the purposes of this work, the most important factors include: the effects of international migration (part III); special economic zone (part V); Continental shelf (section VI); maritime protection and conservation (section XII); and dispute resolution (paragraph XV).

The Convention establishes the limits for the states' marine jurisdiction for the territorial waters.

Rise of 'New' Economic Interests in Arctic Energy

Annual reduction of Arctic Ocean ice reaches 45,000 sq. km, which is larger than the size of Denmark. Since 1978, the total reduction of sea ice has been more than 10 per cent. In 1976-1990 the sea level dropped by one million miles, much higher than combined Norway, Denmark and Sweden. This reduction is most evident in the Arctic Ocean. The melting of ice accelerates and opens large clusters of the front shelves of the 'frozen' continent for testing and use.

In its quest for oil and gas, the oil industry is expected to follow the ice north and the slope of the continent, but not to advance the maritime strategy. The discovery of Arctic resources continues to emerge and the involved nations are keeping a sharp eye to claim which will certainly lead to a resource conflict.

These countries are looking for alternatives to politically stable water supply. This also draws attention to the official establishment of the North Pacific Tunnel, North Sea Corridor and Road Corridor, which could highlight the role of Arctic transport routes in international trade in tropical sands and crime zones in the Indian Ocean and East China Sea. As one geopolitical analyst suggested, "The prospect of western maritime ships will one day cross the Arctic, instead of the Suez Canal, may be seen as one good reason to open dialogue (with the Russian counterparts) in navigation technology."

Former President of the Norwegian Shipowners' Association, Rolf Saether, asserted that, "We must all work together to promote sustainable development (NSR), development that can stimulate the economy and improve living conditions, become a source of international trade and exports. "North will eventually emerge as a new and important global trade route. . . We would all like that to happen."

Ambassadors' mediation mechanisms, such as the Arctic Council, exist, but questions remain about their ability to resolve disputes and negotiate agreements. The decade of 2020 could be a pivotal moment in the impact of the Arctic Council on the region and provide hope for international cooperation. The results of a successful Arctic Council decision could boost the credibility, in the minds of sceptics, of other sceptical organisations such as the North Atlantic Treaty Organization (NATO) and the United Nations (UN). On the other hand, the pessimistic side of a regional war can escalate beyond the region to a major war in many regions. Although the Arctic Circle is known for its elevation, it is now become the epicentre of regional power's geopolitics.

Therefore, in investigating the exploitation of Arctic and marine resources in the transformation of the energy sector, this study has a dual agenda. It contributes to understanding the exploitation of Arctic oil and gas resources by promoting a different analytical view of hitherto traditional perspective of Arctic scholars.

The study builds on the MLP framework in the major social and technology programmes (LTS). Hughes describes LTS as a business of diversity, physical, management, science and art. It works in many sizes and is a very complex organisation. During the communication process, changes occur in the system, while its components are adapted to new conditions. In the framework of this study, LTS is a global energy industry, including the use of Arctic oil and marine resources and natural gas resources with all incorporated companies, scientific, technical and legal entities.

We aimed to investigate the complex interactions of various elements during the exploitation of oil and natural gas resources in the context of global energy transformation, promoted by the MLP and similar studies focusing on energy issues and other non-LTS energy. The MLP was originally developed to define and understand the transformation processes in complex systems. It sets up maps and analyses them at two levels closest to the building management category—social and technical space and niche level.

Geography is an external environment that incorporates good economics, politics and culture. Applied in the Arctic context, land development resources include external macroeconomic resources, energy systems, international law and global energy system regulatory frameworks.

The meso level is called 'social and technological status'. It represents the practices of the engineering community and incorporates the virtues of technology, as well as the 'social' aspects—the methods and approaches of scientists, policymakers and other related groups. All of these connections keep the system stable and do not like to change. In the case of the Arctic, those are the current trends of the oil and gas sector, as well as related national policies, and other construction, industrial, and political markets.

A niche level is a small level at which new things come up. MLP studies pay close attention to niches because they are seen as the key to producing new products and supporting their spread. In the case of the exploitation of oil resources and natural gas in the Arctic, something new is happening to national and international energy companies.

Contested Claims of the Arctic Countries

During the Cold War, most of the scholars who published had a productive connection in the Arctic, described by "Arctic uniqueness", which may have seemed to be important regional power struggles as well as traditional ones. And its reputation as a province near the Arctic, the Russian Arctic Ship, rising integration between Russia and China, political tensions between Russia and the United States, and the global struggle between the United States and China are all odd Arctics in the big race for renewable energy.

United States Secretary of State Michael R. Pompeo referred to the Arctic as "global power and competitiveness" in his virginity speech at the two-year Arctic Council conference in Rovaniemi, Finland. In 2018, China published a page white paper on the Arctic system, referring to it as an "Arctic nation," and introducing the Belt and Road Initiative's outstanding "Solar Road" (BRI). Russia is bolstering its military and commercial presence in the Arctic by increasing its huge fleet of ships and submarines, as well as establishing new military and naval sites and repairing old ones.

Common Arctic security, according to neorealists, is the job of determining how great powers will cooperate and how big power conflicts will occur. The historic security of the Arctic is described in this paper as a mix of three facts: First, China's limited influence is being transformed at the global and regional (Arctic) levels. Second, tensions between the US and Russia are on the rise. Third, Russia and China's strategic partnerships are expanding.

Shifting Balance of Power: China's Rise and America's Decline

China is the world's most stable power. The United States' share in global commerce and GDP is decreasing. China continues to be challenged by American heroism, while the United States has returned to its international duties and is going ahead.

In a bipolar, or better-written, colourless country, Beijing is quickly narrowing the military gap with Washington, and world order is going ahead. China acquires both bravery and determination as a result of the shift of power. China is a sovereign Arctic nation with a policy of gradual evaluation. China's economic, military, and communications position have all advanced considerably in the last two decades, and the country's most dependable and affluent China desires a voice that is heard throughout the world, not just in the Indo-Pacific but also elsewhere. While a military conflict with the United States is improbable, China's salami-cutting methods and debt consolidation raise concerns about the Arctic's tremendous stability, and the United States in particular. In the United States and China, Greenland and Iceland are foci of unification. In its policy papers and political ethics, the US expresses worry over Chinese involvement in mining in Greenland, global warming in Iceland, and Finland's joint venture initiative to create a "data silk road". Greenland is a good example of the region's competing American and Chinese interests. China's efforts to purchase an underused port and its ambition to build a new airport in Nuuk, Greenland's capital, have gained such traction in Washington that US Secretary of Defence James Mattis has had to intervene to exert pressure on the Danish government.

Furthermore, US authorities are always concerned that Chinese money would bolster Greenland's economy and aid the country's bid for independence from Denmark. This will have a substantial influence on the US's regional obligations, particularly at its military station in Thule.

The strength of the security crisis—in which one state's efforts to strengthen its security are characterised by systematic mistrust in another state, evoking a bad spirit of bad relations leading to security, conflict, and war—intensifies the struggle for power created by the transformation of power. As the great power struggle between China and the United States progresses, tensions, disputes, and competitiveness from one area of the world are likely to spread to other parts of the world. These "strategic spillovers" are always a threat to the Arctic.

New Cold War in the Arctic

During the Cold War, the Arctic Ocean was a key battleground. Nuclear sanctions were imposed on the North Arctic by the Soviet Union and the United States. Because of its proximity to the territory between the United States and the Soviet Union (now Russia), archers can attack the enemy by flying over the Arctic, ensuring that the old ones do not vanish. Russia has always been a power that has always beaten beyond its own weight, even if its economy is in decline. Although the United States and China can compete in constructing the globe, Russia is an unquestionable military and economic force in the Arctic. In the Arctic war, the Russian people have put in a lot of work. Russian Arctic forces are now very guarded, but their invading strength is evident. Russia established a new Unified Strategic Command, nicknamed "OSK Sever", in 2014 to improve the security of its vast Arctic boundaries and safeguard its Arctic interests. The Kola Peninsula continues to serve as the foundation of Russia's military infrastructure in the western Arctic, safeguarding the country's interests and magical powers in the Atlantic Ocean and beyond. Russia is constructing 475 new military sites, including bases north of the Arctic Circle, as well as 16 new deep ports, according to the Russian government. It confirms its presence by employing innovative wind-blocking techniques and anti-ship missiles.

The origins of Russian military action cannot be traced back to natural development or the emergence of systematic conflicts between Moscow and Washington. Following Russia's annexation of Crimea in 2014, the US and other Western nations placed economic and financial sanctions on the Russian government. Russia was kicked out of the Arctic Security Forces Roundtable in the same year. These incidents, along with a slew of others, serve to explain Russia's increasing military presence in the Arctic. Political tensions along the Black Sea impacted Arctic security both directly and indirectly, validating the concept of strategic spillovers. "Despite its nature, the Arctic is not isolated from the rest of the world, nor is it removed from the demands of personal connections with Russia and the West," Mathieu Boulègue describes his account about the status of Russian forces.

The joint deployment of NATO and Russian warships between the Barents Sea and Norway has increased the risk of a catastrophic military conflict between the two countries. Russian forces debuted in 2018. During the NATO exercise "Tribe Juncture" in Norway, GPS communications channels were used. Furthermore, the distance between Russian sites on the Kola Peninsula and NATO bases in Norway is only a few kilometres. The fact that five of the seven Arctic nations outside of Russia are NATO members (the United States, Canada, Denmark, Iceland, and Norway) and two (Finland and Sweden) are NATO partners in improved opportunities adds to the risk of future war. Therefore, the 100-year conflict between Russia and the United States will continue to threaten Arctic stability.

The United Nations Declaration on International Development and the creation of the New International Order in 1997 paved the way for Russia-China collaboration. Fears of American instability emerged with the collapse of the Soviet Union, prompting the statement. Following that, in 2001, the Neighborhood and Cooperation Agreement was signed. Russia and China have undertaken several military exercises since 2005. "Military collaboration between Russia and China", according to David Scott, is a "clear indicator" of politics rather than opposition to US-led power.

The ongoing political struggle between the United States and Russia and China, on the one hand, has driven the two countries' development. Russian military analyst Alexander Shirokorad wrote to the Independent Military Review("The Return of Great Power Competition to the Arctic," 2020), speculating on a probable collision between Russian and Chinese planes and Arctic missiles. Some people are worried since comforting notions are already floating around.

The perceived desire to offset the United States dominates strategic integration between Russia and China. The desire for balance is exacerbated by Russia's need for infrastructure and investment, as well as a scarcity of Chinese resources. The energy industry is the clearest example of integration. The Chinese government silk fund holds a 9.9% interest in the Yamal Liquified Natural Gas (LNG) projects, while China's National Petroleum Corporation controls 20% of the shares. When Washington was outlawed, cooperation grew. The impact of the sanctions on Russia's export economy and China's energy security has been significant. Because of the tight political situation between China and the United States, Russia will become a key province, and the extent of its collaboration with China will determine the fate of the Arctic and the rest of the globe.

In the Arctic battle, how did the US-China-Russia initiative succeed in establishing goals for peace and stability, or conflict? Predicting the future is always risky and difficult, but current political and regional research hint to a complicated, unpredictable, and contradictory future.

As an unexpected increase in the tendency to increase competition for Arctic control, the region continues to struggle in many areas.

The Arctic power, for starters, boosted its military presence in the region. The number of Russian, American, and Norwegian ships and Russian Arctic planes has increased dramatically in recent years. As a result, Russian land mines brought 87 planes to the region in 2008. In retaliation, the US and Norway launched anti-aircraft missiles. In the Arctic, Western countries intend to enhance their military relations. Former Norwegian Foreign Minister Thorvald Stoltenberg offered recommendations for collaboration between the five Northern European nations (Norway, Sweden, Finland, Denmark, and Iceland) in the fields of military and foreign affairs in a study issued in early February 2009. Construction of an integrated naval fleet, an icebreaker, a submarine, a humanitarian aid system, and an integrated personnel training programme are among the report's highlights. According to Stoltenberg, the implementation of these measures may result in considerable security savings for five nations.

This relationship should include an increase in the number of military exercises in the Arctic. In 2008, Canada conducted the most extensive military exercises in the region's history. Two Los Angeles-class American submarines took part in the Ice Exercise 2009, which was meant to evaluate performance in Arctic conditions and assure the safety of scientific investigations. During NATO patrols near Norway's northern coast in January 2009, a huge explosion of bombs and explosives occurred. Experts from 10 nations are involved in the EODEX (Explosives Ordnance Disposal Exercise) project: Norway, Sweden, Denmark, Lithuania, Germany, the Netherlands, France, Belgium, Estonia, and Turkey. Its goal was to prepare teams to work in difficult winter circumstances. The participants climbed through the cold, slid through the snow, and destroyed the submerged installation. The NATO Cold Response Test, which took place in March 2009, examined integrated techniques for preventing enemy aggression.

The development of the Arctic troops' armed forces was expedited. By the end of 2007, there were only around five construction ships operating off the coast of Norway. In 2008, the Norwegian government chose to replace the Norwegian F-16 pilot with an American Joint Strike Fighter (JSF). For these objectives, it intends to invest $150 billion on the Norwegian krone. In 2008, a Finnish airline received a grant of 200 million euros to construct a new radar system to track its presence in Russia. Long bombs (TU-95MS, TU-160, and TU-22MZ), as well as the deployment of less than three ships north of Fleet in Borei. As previously stated, the US Coast Guard intends to upgrade its heavy boats, which are seen as an essential instrument for dealing with northern challenges and maintaining the availability of Arctic natural resources.

The Arctic is attracting increasing attention from key regional entities as well as people all around the world. Here is a stunning natural resource that is devoted to the benefit of all humanity in the future. The region may be home to the world's busiest transportation corridor. At the same time, the Arctic has a number of issues, including environmental issues, unsolved regional disputes, and, in some cases, a disastrous indigenous world. Regrettably, numerous international actors still prefer to compete in this sector rather than collaborate. Parties frequently use force to settle disputes rather than using political and legal means. There is a worrisome trend in Arctic power. It is critical that Russia and the rest of the international community consider developing acceptable solutions to both prevent the spread of hazardous behaviours and to prevent the spread of bad practices themselves. A location built on collaboration and love, in our opinion, is better at strengthening the ongoing conflict in this region, which will be crucial in the near future.

As the Arctic approaches the second half of the twenty-first century, Russian imperialism and military strength continue to develop not just swiftly, but also with Russia's aid, as a result of climate change.

Scholarly journals, politicians, and the media have all pointed out that Putin's actions in the Arctic, like those in Ukraine, the Baltic States, and the Cold War, plainly demonstrate military force. Unlike Crimea, Georgia, or other former Soviet republics, the Arctic Circle is a worldwide ocean that is fast changing and expanding into an area with new consequences. As a result, in order to determine if Russia's operations in the Arctic are defensive or offensive, we must consider its goals and ambitions, as well as Soviet events, economic initiatives, climate change, and geopolitics in the future region. Working with the legislation to offer openness and consultation with international groups from NATO to the Arctic and Russia would be the only way to prevent a security crisis or deal with the military.

Dispute between Countries Over Arctic

The emergence of maritime resources and new shipping routes from global warming has created a great deal of interest in trade in the Arctic region. The proposed profile also invites speculation—"the global spread of Arctic politics since 2007 has fueled popular myths about the possibility of conflict in the region". The first event to allay concerns about the Russian strike is two submarines that will raise the Russian flag (Arctic 2007) at the North Pole seeking Lomonosov Ridge as part of Russia's shelf. This was a manifestation of Russia's application for rights to marine hydrocarbons. According to the 1982 Convention on the Law of the Sea (UNCLOS) 1982, coastal countries have the right to explore and transport maritime resources in their exclusive economic zone (EEZ), up to 200 nautical miles from their coast. Outside the EEZ area it is open to negotiations as sections 4-7 if the state can prove that the maritime zone is an extension of its continental shelf. The Russian Ministry of Environment said in 2007 that the ship's shell adheres to the cover of the Russian continent, and should therefore be considered part of the shelf of the Russian continent. Russia's claim on Lomonosov Ridge is still being challenged by Canada and Denmark, which filed a complaint with the UN Commission in 2014 over relations between Greenland and Lomonosov. Russia filed another application in 2015. The legal status of the shelf remains controversial because research that is often seen at sea is not available. The US is currently signed but not authorised by UNCLOS, and cannot submit any claims.

The controversial situation of Lomonosov Ridge has failed to create much controversy. Significant progress has been made in resolving the Arctic Empire, and many sources are at hand. The remaining disputed or unwanted areas in the Arctic where the provinces wish to be acquired by the US compared to the Russian Federation in the Bering Sea, the US compared to Canada in the Beaufort Sea and Canada compared to Denmark in Davis Strait. Canada and Denmark were involved in a dispute over Hans Island on Nares Strait. Canada also views the North West Tunnel as part of its flow while other states view the area as a global problem, but have never implemented a legal process. Russia and Norway resolved the dispute over the Barents Sea in 2010, but still oppose fishing rights in the exclusive economic zone (EEZ) around the island of Svalbard. In the post-2007 period scholars generally agree that Arctic formation is not possible. The Arctic Center determines that there are no major political conflicts at sea and in the remaining areas after the settlement of the Barents Sea dispute.

India and the Arctic

In 2008, India opened its 'Himadari' research station in Svalbard, Norway, representing the first time an Asian country and a growing power had entered the Arctic. Five years later, it was awarded the status of 'Observer' at the Arctic Council, piquing the attention of countries and Arctic stakeholders in what New Delhi could accomplish in the north. India released its tentative Arctic policy after seven years, when the momentum does seem to have slowed and reached a standstill. If India intends to be recognised as a stakeholder in the Arctic, it must maintain advancement now that it has resolved to reinvigorate its approach.

The rationale for a state's excursion into unchartered environment is decided by its rationale. One can wonder and be inquisitive about India's participation in the Arctic, with the main question being, "What brought India to the Arctic?"

India's connections to the Arctic, contrary to the common assumption, are not new. The Svalbard Treaty of 1920, which maintained Norwegian sovereignty over the archipelago, was ratified by the United Kingdom. British India was a signatory by virtue of being administered by the colonial power. However, a newly independent India, preoccupied in the challenging work of nation-building, saw no reason to continue and pursue an Arctic policy. Notwithstanding a three-decade history of conducting research in the Antarctic, the Arctic continued to remain overlooked.

The ramifications of changes in the Arctic environment are gradually appearing evident on the Indian weather system, with the capacity to influence the entire planet. The scientific community considers that Arctic climate conditions and monsoons are interrelated. Monsoon is the lifeblood of agriculture in the Indian subcontinent, supporting millions of community livelihoods. One of the primary reasons for India to forge forwards in the Arctic in 2007 seems to be this. In the same year, it initiated its Arctic Research Programme and its first research expedition. The major purpose is to understand more about the Arctic's connection with monsoons, assess the North's flora and fauna and compare it with those of the Antarctic, and research the effects of climate change in the Arctic using the country's technological expertise in the outer space sphere. The scientific community aggressively pushed for the study's scope to be broadened to also include the Arctic. The imperative for India's active participation in all three poles was felt as debates about Himalayas as the "Third Pole" gained traction, considering the common characteristics prevalent in the Arctic, Antarctic, and Himalayas.

Since the advent of Westphalian nations, the current world order has been hierarchical, with both the West as the norm giver and the East as the norm taker. Following WWII, two blocs evolved, with countries embracing one or the other. India followed the non-alignment course and primarily pushed its ideas in the developing world. Multipolarity and the resurgence of Asian nations, notably India and China, characterised the post-Cold War world. They have a significant voice in the world system and have developed unique value systems based on their history, culture, and social experiences. Asian nations came to popularity in 2013, particularly in the Arctic, after becoming designated as "observers" at the Kiruna Ministerial Meeting.

The unveiling of India's proposed Arctic policy may therefore be considered in the context of the changing world order. First, India is a burgeoning great power with formidable military and economic capability, as well as international goodwill. Its own great power objectives necessitate that Russia play a much bigger role in the twenty-first century globe, including previously unfamiliar territory including the Arctic. Shyam Saran, India's former foreign secretary, argued in 2011 that emerging world powers like India and China must "put this region on the international agenda" in a geopolitically changing Arctic.

New Delhi, as a significant economic power, seeks to diversify its energy sources. Since 2018, India has focused on leveraging the Russian Arctic's oil and gas reserves, along with collaborating with Denmark, Norway, and Sweden on environmental protection and polar research collaboration.

Second, China's increased involvement in Arctic concerns. The release of a white paper by Beijing, as well as its emergence as a strong external power in the Arctic, may have placed strain on New Delhi to broaden its operations. Third, India was one of the few countries with an Arctic presence that did not release an Arctic policy. A policy document that outlines the wider objectives will influence a country's approach to the Arctic.

In January 2021, India released a proposal of their Arctic policy. India's policy, such as that of other non-Arctic nations, explains the rationale and seeks to contextualise its identity inside the broader Arctic framework. India has underlined the connection to monsoon and the persuasion of the concept of the Himalayas being the "Third Pole" when discussing science as a tool for addressing the Arctic. It's worth mentioning that, through the policy, India has positioned itself as being a country that is a part of one of the polar areas, emphasising its identity while intending to actively connect with the Arctic. It's analogous to China's attempt to project its Arctic identity by referring to itself as a "near Arctic state".

The 'five pillars' of science and research, economic and human development cooperation, transportation and connectivity, governance and international cooperation, and national capacity building all emphasise 'sustainable involvement'. India's objective to involve and engage with the Arctic consists of learning about the Arctic and developing a better understanding of climatic changes, and also contributing to international efforts as an Observer in the Arctic Council. The policy also highlights the need to reinforce 'Himadri', establish partnerships with polar science research institutes, and acquire and build ice class vessels to assist India's scientific research in the north.

Transportation and connectivity are a relatively new area of interest for India in the Arctic, and they've been mentioned as one of the policy's five pillars. It aims at investigating the possibility of reaching the Arctic through the International North South Transport Corridor (INSTC), which would be a faster and so more direct route. Integration of the INSTC with European rail networks including the North Sea-Baltic TEN-T Core Network Corridor, the Baltic-Adriatic

TEN-T Core Network Corridor, or the Scandinavian-Mediterranean TEN-T Core Network Corridor may be advantageous in this aspect. India is also contemplating building a marine link between the two key port towns by establishing the Chennai-Vladivostok Maritime Corridor. In 2019, Prime Minister Modi and President Putin signed a memorandum of understanding after the former became the first Indian Prime Minister to visit Russia's Far East. In the long term, the idea may offer a counterpoint to China's Polar Silk Road.

The proposed policy describes why and how it intends to engage with the Arctic by incorporating the government, civil society (think tanks, academicians, scientists, and other professionals), and forming partnerships with Arctic institutions like the University of the Arctic (UArctic). Nevertheless, it falls short of articulating what India would contribute to the Arctic table, particularly how it will leverage its enormous potential and expertise to make a significant contribution to the region.

The draught policy cautiously alludes to the Arctic as a "common legacy of mankind," reinvigorating the global commons debate. India, on either hand, is a member of the Council as an observer and has agreed to the Ottawa Declaration, which preserves the Arctic states' sovereignty. As a result, this fundamental paradox should be addressed.

India must also appoint an official "Arctic ambassador/ representative" to represent and express India's opinions on Arctic concerns. Developing a dedicated expert committee to formulate, monitor, steer, implement, and evaluate New Delhi's Arctic strategy could enhance the country's approach. Lastly, given the wide variety of interwoven challenges that the Arctic faces today, a multidisciplinary framework for understanding the region is required.

Conclusion

The thought of a society without government appears daunting in today's world of globalisation. If there has been any significant or little influence, it has now occurred in the United States of America, which might be considered the world's obvious leader. The world views of Mahan and Mackinder were established at different eras and so do not apply immediately. When applied to a new area, such as the Arctic, the Heartland hypothesis remains a viable notion with numerous hurdles to national expansion today (such as people and economic power, sustainable and efficient infrastructure and resources, and technology).

Because of the consequences of climate change and the potential it offers, the Arctic has garnered a lot of attention. Regardless of future Arctic plans, provinces and their national interests will ultimately determine the region's future, implying the region's importance and nature and natural resources, while non-governmental actors continue to take a back seat in any discussions and decisions.

When it comes to Arctic cooperation, the unique Arctic Five group and the path they are on continue to be a key cause of concern. If the Arctic Council continues to make unique decisions on the Arctic, its power and relevance will be weakened, and the Arctic Five and the rest of the world will be divided (Arctic countries, non-Arctic countries and actors). Given that each situation in the Arctic has far-reaching implications (whether it affects climate change, environmental protection, exports, or power generation), inclusive interactions should be felt rather being restricted to a small group.

The energy issue in the Arctic is equally crucial. The law of the sea is encased in its shell, and while the United Nations Convention on the Law of the Sea (UNCLOS) cannot be applied in the United States at this time, international customary law governs it. Other legal texts have been developed on specific Arctic concerns (for example, the polar IMO code for exports), but there is no higher degree of consensus in the region. While establishing a permanent agreement would not take much time or effort, it would require a high level of commitment from the provinces. A full agreement, as the Antarctic

Treaty illustrates, may be more successful and efficient if the world community chooses to construct it. The Arctic landscape, on the other hand, is distinct from the Antarctic landscape not only in terms of geographical diversity (the Arctic has no place, whereas Antarctica is a continent), but also in terms of its stunning scenery, which is surrounded by independent countries and their continental shelves and exclusive economic zones (EEZ). This piques the provinces' interest in splitting their individual portions, but it leaves the Arctic as a human legacy with little prospect of survival.

Several problems will need to be solved if the Arctic becomes a future global sport. To begin, any economic growth in the region, whether in the energy or shipping sectors, would necessitate the melting of sea ice. However, this will not be enough; to make the exploration and exploitation of Arctic resources more economical, either a significant technological development or a significant increase in hydrocarbon prices would be necessary. If sea ice continues to melt and ports are developed, the NSR may help Russia and its northern regions, as well as the Euro-Asian commercial sector and enterprises. The melting of the oceans, however, has a detrimental influence on the Arctic ecosystem and global climate as a consequence of biological and man-made disasters, necessitating a larger need for environmental protection, which has become a key component of international relations.

As a result, a complete conquest of the Arctic is unlikely. Long-term exports may continue to contaminate the waters beyond what is necessary if short Arctic routes are discovered, even if the effects of climate change are minimised and Arctic water conservation is prioritised. Even if all Arctic exploration and exploitation is forbidden, if the energy sector does not grow, it may be difficult to benefit from it in the future, particularly in Russia, but also in Canada, Norway, and the United States. Furthermore, the region and maybe ecosystems would suffer if the Arctic spacecraft and energy industry were not developed.

Despite continuous developments in the energy market and the significant difficulties posed by climate change, conventional oil and natural gas resources are still extensively utilised. Exploitation of oil and natural resources in the Arctic Ocean is one of the unusual circumstances. Norway and Russia have been two of the most active countries in developing these resources.

We utilised the MLP framework in this research to examine the utilisation of Arctic oil and natural resources in Norway and Russia. It has contributed in gaining a better understanding of these countries' origins and objectives, as well as analysing the interaction between face-to-face levels. Rising energy demand, oil pricing, geopolitics, and climate change are the four geological variables that both generate and impede the development of Arctic and marine resources, as well as natural gas resources. Regardless of the fact that they are both sufferers of local oppression, they are not the same, and their results at the political level are significantly different.

MLP analysis performed shows that local pressures cannot penetrate and evenly shape the state level. In addition, research shows that artistic goals control the formation of the earth. The results of the study lead to the conclusion that the current concept of spatial function and energy is incomplete and needs to be revised. All in all, this confuses the transformation processes in the energy industry

References

Albert Ferrero, J. (November 2011). Incidencia del Deshieloen la Geopolítica del Ártico.

General Revista de Marina, 681-90.

The Return of Great Power Competition to the Arctic. (2020, October 22). *The Arctic Institute.* https://www.thearcticinstitute.org/return-great-power-competition-arctic/

Baev, P. (October 2007). "Russian Arctic Race and New Geopolitics of the North Pole". Retrieved from https://jamestown.org/wp- content / uploaded / 2007/10 / Jamestown-BaevarusArctic_02.pdf

Beauregard-Tellier, F. (October 24, 2008). "Arctic Resources: Hydrocarbon". Retrieved from the Canadian Parliament, at http://www.lop.parl.gc.ca/content/lop/researchpublications/prb0807-e.html

Christopher, J., and E. Fast. (October 24, 2008). "Arctic: Transport, infrastructure and communications". Retrieved May 30, 2016, from Parliament of Canada, at http://www.lop.parl.gc.ca/content/lop/researchpublications/prb0808-e.htm

Green Peace. (June 2014). "Arctic Sanctuary". Retrieved September 20, 2016, from http://www.greenpeace.org/international/en/publications/Campaign-reports / Oceans-Reports / arctic-sanctuary /

Heinininninen, L. (2011). "Arctic Strategies and Policies: Inventory and Comparative Study". Retrieved August 7, 2016, from the Northern Research Forum, at http://www.rha.is/nrf/publications/books-and-publications/arctic-strategies

Hepple, L. W. (2000). "Hepple, L. W. (2000). "Géopolitiques de Gauche. French radical geopolitics

K. Dodds and D. Atkinson, *Georgian culture. A century of world thought*, pp. 268-301. New York: Routledge.

Lacoste, Y. (1976). "Geography: Arma para la Guerra". Retrieved from http://www.lectulandia.com/book/la-geografia-un-arma-para-la-guerra/

Mackinder, H. J. (1942). "*Democratic and Reality Ideas*". London: Constable Publishers.

Mahan, A. T. (1890). "Influence of Marine Power on History", 1660-1783. Retrieved September 30, 2016, from the Project Gutenberg, at http://www.gutenberg.org/files/13529/13529-h/13529-h.htm

Mayor, M. (n.d.). "What Is Geopolitics?". Retrieved October 5, 2016, from *Geopolitics North*.

Palacián de Inza, B., and I. G. Sánchez. (July/August 2013). "Geopolitics del deshieloen el Ártico".

Quinn, E. (December 18, 2015). "The Arctic is not part of the Paris climate agreement". Retrieved October 20, 2016, from Radio Canada International.

Scholvin, S. (April 2016). "Geopolitics: Summary of Ideas and Examples from International Relations". Retrieved August 13, 2016, from The Finnish Institute for International Affairs, at http://www.fiia.fi/fi/publication/586/geopolitics/

Scarphédinsson, Ö. (May 14, 2010). "Iceland Interests and relevant foreign policy". Retrieved from https://www.mfa.is/publications/

Seeking, B. B. (2008). "Ilulissat Declaration: Background and Impact on Arctic Rule". Retrieved from http://www.arcticgovernance.org/the-ilulissat-declaration-background-and-implications-for-arctic-governance.4626039-137746

Alexeeva, O., and F. Lasserre. (2014). "La Chine en Arctique: genèse et évolution d'une politique". KuM. Foucher, *L'Arctique: la nouvelle frontière* pp. 111-28. Paris: CNRS additions.

Borgerson, S. G. (2008). "Arctic melting". Outside (March/April). Retrieved May 1, 2016, from https://www.foreignafrogram.com/articles/arctic-antarctic / 2008-03-02 / arctic-meltdown

Borgerson, S. G. (2013). "The explosion of the Arctic Boom". Foreign (July/August).

Buchanan, E. (January 21, 2016). "Arctic Thaw". Foreign. Retrieved June 2, 2016, from https://www.foreignafrogram.com/articles/russian-federation/2016-01- 21 / arctic-thaw

Dodds, K. (October 2010). A Polar Mediterranean? "Discovery, Resources and Sovereignty in the Arctic Ocean". *International Policy*, 1 (3), 303-11. Retrieved June 15, 2016, from http://onlinelibrary.wiley.com/doi/10.1111/j.1758- 5899.2010.00038.x / pdf

Ebinger, C.K., and E. Zambetakis. (November 2009). "Arctic Melt geopolitics". *International News*, 85 (6), 1215-1232. Retrieved May 25, 2016, from http://onlinelibrary.wiley.com/doi/10.1111/inta.2009.85.issue-6/issuetoc

Foucher, M. (2014). *"L'Arctique: a new frontier"*. Paris: CNRS additions.

Giok, K. K. (2015). "Sea Power as a Strategic Domain". Identity, 41 (3). Retrieved from https://www.mindef.gov.sg/content/dam/imindef_media_library/graphics/po inter / PDF / 2015 / Vol. 41% 20No.3 / Sea% 20Power% 20As% 20A% 20Strategy

% 20Domain.pdf

IGómez de Ágreda, Á. (March 2014). "Arctic Climate Change: Beyond the North Pole". *Spanish Institute of Strategic Study*, 3. Retrieved from https://dialnet.unirioja.es/servlet/articulo?codigo=4729395

Heinininen, L. (2012). "Status of Arctic Strategies and Policies—Summary". *Arctic Yearbook*.

Jakobson, L. (March 2010). "China is preparing for the frozen Arctic". *Sipri Insights for Peace and Security.*

Kuersten, A. (August 20, 2015). "Lost Arctic race". Foreign. Retrieved May 1, 2016, from https://www.foreignafrogram.com/reviews/2015-08- 20/ arctic-race-wasnt

Liow, J. C. (June 21, 2014). "Arctic summer". Foreign. Retrieved June 2, 2016, from https://www.foreignafrogram.com/articles/arctic-antarctic/2014-06-21 / arctic-summer

Jain, M. (September 2, 2014). "Geopolitics: The Foundations of Geography". Retrieved September 7, 2016, from YouTube, at https://www.youtube.com/watch?v=6e0DIrbhpjo

Maré, C. (2014). "Réchauffement climatique en Arctique: la fin de l'Age de glace". In

M. Foucher, *L'Arctique: la nouvelle frontière*, pp. 147-63. Paris: CNRS additions.

Moltó, Á. (March 10, 2011). El Ártico y la política is outside Canada. Estudios de Política. Outside.

Pancracio, J.-P. (2014). "Navigating en Arctique". KuM. Foucher, *L'Arctique: la nouvelle frontière*, pp. 91-109. Paris: CNRS additions.

Althingi. (March 28, 2011). "Parliamentary decision on Iceland's Arctic policy". Retrieved September 3, 2016, from the Department of Foreign Affairs, at https://www.mfa.is/news-and-publications/nr/6275

Arctic Council. (2009). "Exploring Arctic Ocean Shipping". Retrieved June 27, 2016, from http://www.pame.is/index.php/projects/arctic-marine-shipping/amsa

Arctic Council. (April 2015). "Arctic Marine Strategic Plan". Retrieved October 2, 2016, from https://oaarchive.arctic-council.org/handle/11374/413

Council of the European Union. (May 12, 2014). "Council's conclusions on the development of the European Union Arctic Regional Policy". Retrieved September 3, 2016, from http://ec.europa.eu/maritimeaferals/policy/sea_basins/arctic_ocean_en

European Commission. (June 26, 2012). "European Union policy framework in the Arctic region is being developed: progress since 2008 and the following steps". Retrieved September 3, 2016, from http://ec.europa.eu/maritimeaferals/policy/sea_basins/arctic_ocean_en

European Commission. (April 27, 2016). "Integrated European Union Arctic Policy". Retrieved September 3, 2016, from http://ec.europa.eu/maritimeaferals/policy/sea_basins/arctic_ocean_en

European Union External Action. (June 15, 2016). "EU Arctic policy". Retrieved October 13, 2016, from https://eeas.europa.eu/topics/eu-arctic-policy/418/eu-arctic- policy_en

Government of Canada. (2009). "Northern Canada Strategy: Our North, Our Heritage, Our Future". Retrieved July 26, 2016, from http://www.northernstr Strategy.gc.ca/cns/cns-eng.as

Government of Canada. (2010). "Canada Arctic Foreign Policy Statement". Retrieved July 26, 2016, from http://www.international.gc.ca/arctic-arctique / arctic_policy-canada-politique_arctique.aspx? Line = what

Department of Foreign Affairs of Denmark. (August 2011). "Danish Empire Arctic Plan 2011-2020". Retrieved July 26, 2016, from http://um.dk/en/foreign-policy/the-arctic

Norway Department of Foreign Affairs. (February 21, 2007). "Northern Government Strategy. Norway". Retrieved September 16, 2016, from https://www.regjeringen.no/en/find-document/reports-and- plans/ id438817 /? Documenttype = dokumenter / planer and ownerid = 833 and title = 9 19

Norway Department of Foreign Affairs. (April 7, 2009). "New Buildings in the North. Norway". Retrieved from https://www.regjeringen.no/en/find-document/reports-and- plans / id438817 /? documenttype = dokumenter / planer & ownerid = 833 & title = 9 19

Office of the Prime Minister. (June 7, 2010). "Suomen Arktinen Strategia". Retrieved from http://vnk.fi/julkaisut?p_p_id=publicationssearch_WAR_publicationsportlet & p_p_lifecycle = 0 & p_p_state = standard & p_p_mode = view & p_p_col_id = 2 columns & p_p_col_pos = 1 & p

Swedish Foreign Ministry. (October 2011). "Swedish Arctic regional strategy. Sweden". Retrieved from http://www.government.se/country-and- regional-strategies / 2011/10 / Swedish-i-arctic-regional / strategy

Ilulissat announcement. (May 28, 2008). Retrieved June 16, 2016, from http://www.arcticgovernance.org/the-ilulissat-declaration.4872424.html

White House. (January 9, 2009). Presidential Guidelines for National Security/ NSPD-66. Office of the Secretary of News. Retrieved September 4, 2016, from http://www.state.gov/e/oes/ocns/opa/arc/

White House. (May 2010). "Arctic Regional National Strategy". Retrieved September 4, 2016, from http://www.state.gov/e/oes/ocns/opa/arc/

United Nations. (1982). "United Nations Convention on the Law of the Sea". Retrieved June 3, 2016, from http://www.un.org/depts/los/index.htm

United Nations. (1959). "Antarctic Treaty". Retrieved November 2, 2016, from https://treaties.un.org/Pages/showDetails.aspx?objid=0800000280136dbc

Arctic Council Website. Accessed September 26, 2016, at http: //www.arctic-council.org/index.php/en/

Briney, A. "Overview of Political Geography". Accessed September 30, 2016. *About Education*, at http://geography.about.com/od/politicalgeography/a/View All Views- Political Website-Geography.htm Greenpeace.

ICC website. Accessed July 8, 2016, at http://www.inuitcircumpolar.com/

IMO website. Accessed October 5, 2016, at http://www.imo.org/EN/Pages/Default.aspx

International Permafrost Association website. Accessed November 20, 2016, at http://ipa.arcticportal.org/

Lossan, A. (June 23, 2016). "Gazprom delays overseas gas production: Will prices rise in Europe? Russia surpasses news headlines". Accessed October 25, 2016, at https://rbth.com/business/2016/06/23/gazprom-postpones-offshore-gas- production-will-prices-rise-in-europe_605715

OGJ editors. (August 2, 2010). "Shtokman's partners delayed the start of production". *Oil and Gas Journal*, at http://www.ogj.com/articles/2010/02/shtokman-partners.html

Total. (n.d.) "Yamm LNG: Cold gas". Accessed October 25, 2016, at http://www.total.com/en/energy-expertise/projects/oil-gas/lng/yamal- lng-cold-environment-gas

BUDDHIST DIPLOMACY: SOFT POWER POLITICS OF INDIA AND CHINA

VISHAL RAJPUT AND SARTHAK DUNEJA

A Historical Epistemology of Indic Civilisation

Ab initio, the human settlement in Indian Subcontinent beheld the *"First Urbanization"* ever through the advancement of Indus Valley Civilisation, amongst one of the oldest civilisations of Old World, where the burgeoning of it laid the dichotomy between symmetric and asymmetric standard of living wherein prominent cities, unlike in villages, proper drainage and system, discoveries in metallurgy and handicraft materials, double-storeyed houses specially built of bricks, systematic urban town planning (Jha, 2004, p. 31) could be manifested. The Pictures below had shown some early development in Indus Valley Civilisation.

In the meantime, from 2600 to 1900 BCE, the major cities of Indus Valley Civilisation which flourished as the major urban centres were Dholavira, Kalibangan, Ropar, Rakhigarhi, and Lothal in India as well as Harappa, Ganeriwala and Mohenjo-Daro in Pakistan; as still these were preserved with the help of archaeologists of both the states and not-so-subtle UNESCO. However, around 1600 BCE, it

Figure 19: Early Development in Indus Valley Civilisation

Source: commons.wikimedia.org

gradually started declining as witnessed through the violence among the native groups alongside the rise of infectious diseases like Leprosy and Tuberculosis which consequently instigated the migration of natives (Robbins Schug G, pp. 136–147). The withdrawal of the Indus Valley Civilisation led to the advent of the *Vedic Period* as its name was adopted from the Indo-Aryan Culture of North-West India. Accounts of Vedic Society were mentioned in Rig Veda and at the end of Indus Valley Civilisation, Aryan Society started expanding its influence on western Ganges Plain. The Second Wave of Urbanisation ushered the expansionism of Indic Civilisation, which resulted in the advent of Kingdom of Magadha under the aegis of Mauryan Empire, and for society, agriculture became the primary occupation and its societal framework centred on the *Varna System* (Samuel, 2008). Meanwhile, the early settlement on Ganges Plain simultaneously formed the *Sramana* Movement from which Jainism and Buddhism originated and flourished later all over the world.

One the one hand, the theoretical base of Classical Hinduism was laid down through the composition of Upanishads and on the other, the burgeoning urbanisation in India led to the rise of new ascetic movements, Jainism and Buddhism, which were in disagreement with the orthodoxy of rituals. (Flood, p. 82) (Mascaró, p. 7) (Olivelle, pp. xxiv–xxix)

Moreover, as far as the Buddhism is concerned, it attracted a favourable size of preachers, unlikely Jainism as it was the first religion, which appealed upon using the reason and insight that initially laid the path for enlightenment.

Buddhism: A Facet of Indic Civilisation and Its Advent in South-East Asia

In the midst of majoritarian prevailing religion in the mainland, Buddhism enchanted the masses as it called for using reason and not go around with the orthodox rituals in order to appease the privileged class. The origin of Buddhism is believed to be initiated through the teachings of Siddhartha Gautama, a Kshatriya by birth, who renounced his life to find the reasons of pain and suffering in life and finally attained enlightenment became the "Awakened One" and then popularly known as "Buddha".

From the outset, the religious experts have the pretensions that Buddhism was a missionary religion, alike Islam and Christianity but the essential difference is that it was not burgeoning with swords. Buddha himself travelled to many places to spread his teachings and asked his disciples the words:

> "Go monks, and wander for the good and welfare of the communities".

However, when the Ashoka Maurya came to be emperor of India, the dissemination of Buddhism was given a substantial boost in 3rd century BC. The reason behind the dissemination is the catastrophe brought with the bloody war in the east coast of India, the present-day Odisha, in the form of extreme death and suffering upon the civilians, which deeply influenced him to turn to Buddhism. His remorse for havoc being done under the aegis of his empire led to many humanitarian works like building wells, houses for poor, hospitals for ailing people, and abolished death penalty and torture of prisoners. (Harvey, p. 101) The shrewdness of Ashoka was appreciated in his leadership by relinquishing violence and initiating governance in statecraft on the teachings of Buddhism.

Under his patronage, Buddhism burgeoned to the extent that he dispatched ambassadors to the courts of rulers, as many literature texts in Sinhalese language mentioned, in South-East Asia and Macedonia. (Keown, D., p. 76) Many critics believed Ashoka promoted Buddhism at the cost of other faiths, Hinduism and Jainism, but there is some testimony that comes up with the idea that Ashoka also supported other faiths as well, which did not discriminate on account of his personal faith in Buddhism. (Harvey, p. 102)

On the other hand, in the South, the other facet of Buddhism, Theravada, reached to the island nation, Ceylon, present-day Sri Lanka. Historians believe that a Buddhist monk named Mahinda brought Buddhism there. He played a significant role in developing Buddhist culture by writing Pali Cannon around 80 BC. An Indian monk, Buddhaghosa, also played the key role by accumulating the early discourses and edited them into Pali language mainly for the convenience to understand the text of highest scholarship in Buddhism (Keown, D., pp. 78-79)

Traces of Buddhism are evident early from the times of the reign of Emperor Ashoka. The southeast region is so complex in nature that it had the influence of both Mahayana and Theravada. The latter form developed by Ceylon Bhikkus who travelled from Sri Lanka and Burma into major Southeast Asian nations—Laos, Cambodia,

Thailand, and Malaysia and beyond. Nevertheless, it also manifested the Mahayana tradition in the way of advancement from North India to Tibet and China and influenced Indonesia and Vietnam with it (Nguyen, pp. 2-9).

During the initial times of the expansion being carried out, analysts believe that there were many measures through which Buddhism reached the shores of South-East Asia. For comprehensively understanding the advent, we need to critically analyse the major factor behind this, which I categorically mention in this paper.

First, the wave of expansionism of Buddhism was attributed, through the efforts of ambassadors being sent out by the kings where Emperor Ashoka, initially, commenced the process, which has influenced the intellectual elites and subsequently disseminated within the society.

Second, the insightful work of scholars and intellectuals with the highest scholarship provided the rich heritage of ideas and theories, which intrigued the then progressive stakeholders of the society. Third, one of the paramount pursuits of transmission was the ancient trade route that passes through Asia. The feudal class had always the curiosity to indulge in knowing the new set of ideas, and donated for religious activities. Nonetheless, the overwhelming efforts of the artisans needs to be mentioned here, where they produced works of religious art, in the form of statues of Buddha and bodhisattvas and carving of Buddhist images in caves. (Keown, D., pp. 81-83)

Therefore, the advent of Buddhism had the imperative impact upon the relations of India with South-East Asian Nations where it laid down the similar set of cultural and religious ways of living which made the consensus of strengthening the relations between the two in the near future. The common link of familiarity based on Buddhism established the close link of cooperation in all facets of relations, which has the emphasis on the relations of modern nation-state in contemporary times. The mainstream stakeholders of the governmental apparatus of India has put their serious concern on using the Buddhist Card for making the basis of economic policies which is very significant for their North-Eastern Region, as it shares the land boundary with South-East Asian countries and where government had in the past turned the Nelson's eye, to become the patron of India's standpoint which has been culminated with the "Look East Policy" of India, where it is particularly focusing upon establishing the ties which will enhance the strategic relations of India through North-East with the South-East Asian nations.

Look East Policy: A Way Forward to South East Asia

When the whole world witnessed the disintegration of the Soviet Union into many republics, the major powers started the paradigm shifts in their foreign policies. India was no different to experience the wave of neo-liberalism where the then Narasimha Rao Government took major steps to liberalise, globalise and privatise the country under the intense pressure of economic and political realities concerning with shrinking foreign exchange reserves at just $1.3 billion. In due course, they took the observation of the fact of the resurgence of economic ties with countries of South-East Asia. While in the past, India had the relationship with South-East Asia based on the common struggle for decolonisation from western imperialism and by organising two pan-Asian Conferences concerning with national freedom movements, intra-Asian migration and so on and so forth. However, this time the driving force was quite different as reiterated by Yashwant Singh, then foreign Minister of Government of India, who outlined the difference while giving the speech at

Harvard University, which is also considered as the government's position on it:

> In the past, India's engagement with much of Asia, including South East and East Asia, was built on an idealistic conception of Asian brotherhood, based on shared experiences of colonialism and of cultural ties. The rhythm of the region today is determined, however, as much by trade, investment and production as by history and culture. That is what motivates our decade-old 'Look East' policy. (Zhang, D., 2006)

The objective set for the Look East Policy by the Narasimha Rao Government was *"to draw, as much as possible, investment and cooperation from the Asia-Pacific countries, in consonance with our common concept and solidarity and my faith in our common destiny"* (Nanda, 2003). However, we also cannot neglect the fact that the Look East Policy framework was initially focused upon South-East Asia and ASEAN. Arguably the reason behind this is the proximity of India with South-East Asian countries.

If we envisage the whole scenario of India's relationship with South-East Asia, India is acquainted in a much more favourable place in contrast to any other nation in the region. Strategists highlighted the trajectory for India's policymakers, which was followed to culminate in the 'balancer' of the region in toto. Therefore, in the backdrop of this concern, 'Look East Policy' was the opening gambit for the multifaceted relationship and considered as the cornerstone for furthering the relations to the new phase of cooperation in the 21st century.

On the other hand, India started participating in "Shangri La Dialogue" and "ASEAN Defence Ministers Meeting Plus" where it rested the common consensus on the issue of fighting Terrorism, enhancing International Trade, having strategic partnership with other countries, securing Justice in Global Affairs, promoting Democracy in the society and reducing the chances of conflict and tussle, which partially resulted in enhancing its diplomatic position. However, its balancing role was equally shortened and limited in nature through the 'Look East' approach. While, then Indian strategists were equally concerned with the trade prospects with South-East Asia and advancement of China's position in South and South-East Asia, there were little efforts on the part of framing any grand strategy for securing 'protagonist' role in Asian affairs. Under the leadership of US President Barak Obama, who outlined the strategy of redeployment of significant strategic assets of the US from the Persian Gulf and the Middle East to the region of Indo-Pacific under its 'Pivot' strategy in Asia. However, the ambiguous posture of India showed unwillingness in any form of engagement with the advantage of its improving relations with the US to counterbalance Chinese assertiveness. It was also circumspect of any pre-emptive strategy of the US for the containment of China, which would have complicated the Sino-India Relations. (Acharya, pp. 552-53)

Albeit, Look East policy proved to be very fruitful for India as it helped in joining India as the sectoral partner with ASEAN in 1992 and the much larger platform of ASEAN regional forum as the dialogue partner and member in 1992, and registered great diplomatic victory in South-East Asian Region. It also led to enhancement of bilateral trade with the remarkable rise from $2 billion in 1992 to $12 billion in 2002. However, in the past few decades, the government could not maintain the same pace through which it had been going as usual. This pretension has been endorsed by then US Secretary of State, Hillary Clinton, who suggested the Indian leadership to not only 'look' towards east but also 'act' with east which will intensify India's position and reflect the high priority of the eastern region in its foreign policy. (Sajjanhar, 2016) Likewise, the stagnant and moribund behaviour of the Indian political leadership left the Look East Policy achieving very little progress to which policymakers could have made more inclusive in nature by turning around from economic and strategic to people-to-people connectivity. The pretensions of strategists were to explore the earlier common linkage of Buddhism which had made the steadfast relations between India and South-East Asia which could be used in the contemporary times to reinvigorate the ties in a more comprehensive manner and impeccable in nature.

During the course of time, when the NDA alliance came into power in 2014 general elections and Narendra Modi came at the helm of the country as the Prime Minister, he gave his serious concern on engaging more comprehensively and looking beyond just the counter-intuitive economic and military dimension of diplomacy. His government's concern paved the way for transforming Look East Policy into more serious "Act East Policy" with manifold dimensions, which will offer great swathes with imperative of making an oasis of engagements. In the initial stage, Act East Policy overwhelmingly gained the admiration and capitalised the opportunity by projecting India's Soft Power through 'Buddhist Diplomacy' in the Global Politics.

Paradigm Shift from Look East to Act East Policy

Ab initio, India's Prime Minister, Narendra Modi, reckoned with the idea of initially having strong relations with the neighbourhood and pledged to intensify the engagement with eastern and south-eastern countries. In August 2014, under the backdrop of the *"Neighbourhood First Policy"* through which Indian leadership wants to assert more proactive and integrated approach, the incumbent Minister of External Affairs, Sushma Swaraj, pledged to turn around from 'Look East' to more assertive and holistic policy of 'Act East' which would enhance the engagement on manifold dimensions for the diplomatic discourse. (Narayan, 2014) Within the short span of time, Act East Policy was formally announced in November 2014 when PM Narendra Modi attended the 12th ASEAN-India Summit in Myanmar. (MEA, 2015, p. xvi)

The sober outlook of NDA government for Act East Policy was reflected through establishing separate Indian Mission for the ASEAN just after taking over the power at the centre in April 2014.

Moreover, they posted an ambassador to manage the affairs of ASEAN and East Asian Summit (EAS) at the ASEAN Secretariat in Jakarta, Indonesia.

Act East Policy prompted many key developments, which need to be categorically analysed to understand the progress on the following projects.

1. **Moreh border.** It is a place on India-Myanmar Border in Manipur. Economically, this place plays a very significant role as it is already functioning as commercial hub. Economists believe that it is the financial capital of Manipur, which could serve as India's Gateway to South-East Asia. The incumbent Chief Minister of Manipur, Nongthombam Biren Singh, is of the opinion that Moreh could play the role of linkage for the promotion of trade activities by establishing multi-speciality hospitals, educational institutions and by improving banking facilities which will cater to the needs of upper Myanmar for the implementation of Act East policy.

   The establishment of ASEAN-India Free Trade Area paved the way for India-Myanmar-Thailand Trilateral Highway, a quid pro quo for both the stakeholders, which was constructed under the framework of Look East Policy but could not achieve the desired result. And in post-2014 era, it finally culminated in much more reinvigorated policy of 'Act East' that effectively accelerated the economic development of the North-Eastern India. Biren

Singh asserted that the formation of high-level inter-Ministerial body be constituted by entrusting the Manipur and Mizoram governments to devise the kosher strategy for the Act East Policy to reach its zenith. (India, 2018)

2. **Kaladan Multi-Modal Transit Project.** This project will connect the far eastern seaport of Kolkata with the Myanmar's Sittwe Seaport located in Rakhine State. In Myanmar, it will be connected to Paletwa in Chin State through the narrow passage of Kaladan River route which will be further linked by road from Paletwa to Mizoram of North-East India. It will strengthen the relations by encompassing the development of the neighbouring countries for facilitating the cross-cultural relations with each other. This project will reduce the dependency of India's mainland transport route, Siliguri Corridor, and will nurture the trade cooperation with Myanmar by helping the government over there in building key assets for their nation building.

There are many more manifestations of economic developments taking place or rejuvenation of the old projects of Look East Policy, but Act East Policy encompasses more than the economic facet where the policy also gave priority to cultural links between the two stakeholders, which could be strengthened to reach its new zenith in 21st Century. NDA government takes a leaf out of historical epistemology of Buddhism in India and uses it as a sheer opportunity to further nourish the relations of India with the Eastern hemisphere. "Buddhist Diplomacy", arguably, helped India to project its soft power by following the trajectory on the lines of Buddhism where it had been left out.

Buddhist Diplomacy in Act East Policy

> "India has a new top Cultural Diplomat—and he is called the Buddha."

Among all the incredible things produced in India, undoubtedly the most captivating was the advent of the religious philosophy of Buddhism. It facilitated the wave of enlightenment and reformation that appealed extensively to the natives through its integrated philosophical text encompassing manifold ways to guide humanity for centuries, which is still persistent in the lives of millions for realising the perfection with the ultimate aim to attain the enlightenment. In the history of Asia, Buddhism is believed by many as an important foundation for sociocultural transformation in Asia. One could argue the reflection of Asian identity under the purview of Buddhism and the emergence of pan-Asian importance as far as spiritual linkages between nations are concerned. (Stobdan, P., 2016) One of the reasons for losing the momentum of Look East Policy was the absence of any strategy on the sidelines of Buddhism. Thus, with due concern, the NDA government took it as the priority to formulate the strategies to reinvigorate the old cultural linkages of Buddhism.

India's Foreign Policy demonstrates an impressive outlook as, economically, it is the seventh largest economy in the world according to the statistics of nominal GDP. (IMF, 2018) In terms of Military features, it is the fourth strongest army in the world. (Agnihotri, 2018) However, with the paradigm shifts in International Relations and Diplomatic posture, nation-states turn around to take leverage of Soft Power to achieve the desired results, which do not demonstrate any sign of force and domination but assimilation within each other's culture and initiating people-to-people connectivity. When the world started witnessing the emergence of Soft Power, India was already in a very advantageous position because of its historical ties with the nations swayed under cultural and religious aspects. Along with economic growth, India has sought to foster its soft power in the international realm. China's proactive efforts in advancing its Buddhist Diplomacy has drawn India into the competition where, eventually, it asserts the dominant position as the centre of Buddhism. (Overdorf, 2012)

Albeit, Buddhism declined in the 6th century, just after the Muslim invasion in India, but its principles hitherto cast a spell over India's Foreign Policy. In fact, the essence of Buddhist principles could be manifested with regard to the co-optive power where it allows the nation-states to pursue their ambitions without heading to the crossroads in pursuit of national interests. Even the Buddhist principle of Madhyamika is believed to be the foundation for India's democratic inclusivity, pluralistic nature of the society and the non-alignment contour of the foreign policy at the times of Cold War. The inheritance of such principles and doctrines exemplifies India as not the dominant power in the region. In this background, India is not in the position to avoid any leverage of Buddhist Diplomacy in the current foreign policymaking scenario. For using the Buddhist Card as its diplomatic tool to reach out to the eastern region, government to focus upon these following aspects.

Accommodating Tibetan Refugees and Hosting the Dalai Lama

In 1959, when the uprising took place in Tibet, 14th Dalai Lama fled with his thousands of Tibetans in India to take refuge where then Prime Minister, Pandit Jawaharlal Nehru, allowed him along with his cohorts to settle down in the region of inner Himalayas. However, realists took the different standpoint where this helping hand was offered with the motive of projecting India's image as the defender of human rights of the Tibetans that helped in strengthening Indo-US Relations. (Wales, 2003, pp. 294-95) However, arguably, India's efforts of supporting the Tibetan cause at the cost of its multifaceted engagement with China left some serious setback. In contrast, it has received overwhelming appreciation from Global Buddhist Community. Dalai Lama's activities in India always crisscross with China. As evident through one event that happened in the month of March where Dalai Lama was invited for the inauguration of the seminar on 'Buddhism in the 21st Century' in Rajgir, Bihar.

This act came at a very critical juncture in Sino-India relationship where China categorically condemned and urged India to *"respect China's core concerns and avoid China-India relations from being further disrupted and undermined."* (Times, 2017) In April also, they objected to the visit of Dalai Lama in Tawang. (Parthasarathy, 2017) Way back from his advent in India, he accelerated the development of Buddhist Diplomacy by joining the events as manifested through the one a few years back, where he delivered the keynote address in one of the programmes of India's Soft Power.

Revivalism of Nalanda: School of All Buddhist Schools of Thought

Rejuvenation took place in two phases where on the one hand, commencement of Indian Buddhist Conferences had happened as evident through the series mentioning the Meaning of Nalanda organised in April 2003, the Heritage of Nalanda in February 2006. It was initiated to acknowledge the contribution of this school of thought to disseminate the literature gained from the enlightenment of Buddha. The Conference was presided over by the Dalai Lama. (Mission, 2011) In 2015, a New Delhi-based Think Tank, Vivekananda International Foundation, in collaboration with Tokyo Foundation organised *'Hindu-Buddhist Initiative on Conflict Avoidance and Environment Consciousness'* in Bodh Gaya which was inaugurated by Prime Minister Narendra Modi where he reiterated the message of Lord Buddha avoiding conflict and move towards a constructive discourse and dialogue. (Bureau N., 2015) This conference was one of the manifestations of shared cultural bond between Hinduism and Buddhism where they reiterated the message of peace and harmony to the world and projection of mutual benefit and not antagonism toward each other.

On the other, the Indian Government for reviving the lost legacy responded by establishing the *'Nalanda Mentor Group'* where Noble Laureate Amartya Sen was presiding over to frame the strategy for

Nalanda University. He was assisted by former Singapore Foreign Minister George Yeo, who was also the member of board, believed this project as the "the icon of Asian renaissance" and his positive response helped India to approach the intellectual elites of Buddhism to work with India experts for the noble cause. (Nation, 2011) (Lee, 2007)

Religious Tourism

Albeit, Lord Buddha was born in Nepal, but it is no surprise that all the major events in his life range from his enlightenment, delivering of first sermon, acquiring nirvana and all other activities concerned with his life took place in India. (Zhang J., p. 26) All the major Buddhist sites in India are the priorities for world Buddhists as far as their tourism is concerned, as India is the home to seven of the eight most important Buddhist sites in the world. However, the annual footfalls of Buddhist pilgrims and tourists to these sites were not up to the anticipation of the leaders over here. To remedy this ongoing issue and reflect the sincere approach for the revivalism, Ministry of Tourism planned to transgress the national borders for the promotion of their tourist circuits where they identified the sites—Lumbini and Kapilavastu in Nepal to be included in their Buddhist Circuit. Moreover, on the international juncture on the sidelines of BIMSTEC Summit, India asked for the cooperation to come together to establish the Organization for Buddhist Circuit which was successfully ratified in their joint statement. (Bureau P. I., 2015) (Bureau P. I., 2016)

Narendra Modi has gone out with the conventional contour by appointing Lokesh Chandra, served until 2017, who essentially aimed at the outreach programme of Act East Policy by Prime Minister as evident through his symbolic gestures. Chandra said to *The Telegraph*, "*It's about time we invest in tapping into Buddhism as a key arm of our cultural diplomacy, there's incredible potential and interest overseas—we need to capitalise on that.*" As Buddhism is the heart of Sino-India Relations, ICCR is planning to host an exhibition based on Chinese Buddhist paintings and on the other hand, Modi Government will organise a conference for Chinese monks and scholars on *Aparigraha* where with insightful discourse with the Indian scholars they will reach common consensus for the promotion of Buddhist School of Thought around the world.

Narendra Modi is no different to his predecessor for leveraging Buddhism Card in his Foreign Policy but unlike Manmohan Singh, his zeal offered more than Singh's action in his tenure by taking up the legacy just after coming at the helm of the nation. Amongst his foreign visits, he made his first foreign visit to Bhutan, a Buddhist dominated country in South Asia, whereas when the Chinese counterpart, President Xi Jinping, paid his visit to India, he was warmly greeted in Ahmedabad with an exhibition centred around the cultural linkages between Gujarat and China. His initiative of gifting the sapling of the original Bodhi tree as the symbolic gifts to East Asian Nations astonished his counterparts for his outreach.

Therefore, with the last year of his tenure in the political spectrum, we cannot ignore to acknowledge his efforts by shifting the paradigm from Look East to Act East and making Buddhist Diplomacy as its priority in the policy for the multifaceted engagement with East and South-East Asian Nations to enlarge the national interest of India and reach out to the diaspora as well for helping their home country to strengthen the relations with their host country.

Conundrums in the Trajectory of India

In the aforementioned initiative of academic redevelopment in the form of Nalanda University, the complex bureaucratic apparatus and biases of the domestic politics affected its development projects. The apparent delays in the project are plaguing the vision of revivalism of Buddhist School of Thought and creating a setback of India's Buddhist Diplomacy in particular and Act East Policy in larger terms. (Mitra, 2016) Moreover, the not so far involvement of Dalai Lama in this project isn't showing a good sign of its inclusiveness. His absence will create a sceptic thought in the minds of Buddhist academic community and intellectuals. (Kishwar, 2018) In contrast, China took the leverage by establishing the Nanhai Buddhist College as the replication of Nalanda University with the close cooperation of various Buddhist intellectual centres of its neighbouring countries, except India, which is seen as an attempt to bypass India's Soft Power. (Yadav, 2017) Likewise, Indian Government is lacking on the part to move beyond the Tibetan Buddhist School of Thought and explore other areas of Buddhist influence to expand Buddhist Scholarship. In fact, the antagonism that has been developed between India and China to become the protagonist of Buddhism is marginalising the idea of Asian Century and giving the positive sign for the third country to fuel the tussle further.

As far as the economic facet of Act East Policy is concerned, which has also one way or other a direct impact upon Buddhist Diplomacy, the perpetual delays in the aforementioned key projects is also hampering the development of its North-Eastern region where the concerned states are keenly waiting for initiating the trade with the Eastern Neighbours. Many scholars espoused the paradoxical posture in *"Delhi's ability to convert words into deeds"*.

Hence, Act East Policy needs to more comprehensive and proactive in its role to seriously engage with East and South-East Asia. Policymakers have to introspect the progress being made on its key policy measures and speed development for promoting trade, tourism and political engagement.

Religious Power Politics between India and China

"Rajapaksa had reiterated through his election manifesto titled 'Mahinda Chinthanaya' that he would follow a non-aligned foreign policy. Yet Rajapaksa's Sri Lanka was clearly tilted more towards

China. A multitude of factors, including hostile policies adopted by the West, pressures exerted by the United Nations Human Rights Council, India's lack of participation in Sri Lanka's infrastructural developments projects, and the machinations of the Tamil diaspora pushed Colombo towards Beijing." (Peshan Gunaratne, 2015)

In short, Mahinda Rajapaksa in his administration (2005-2015) had developed very close ties with China. The Chinese investments and financial aid helped Sri Lanka to recover its economy after the hostile, protracted war. Significantly, both countries give the foremost place to Buddhism, and thus Beijing used it as a foreign policy strategy to strengthen Sino-Sri Lanka relations with its religious neighbours. On the other hand, India embraces Buddhism to balance the Chinese Soft Power advantage. India's soft power bridge of Buddhism was invoked during the administration of Narendra Modi.

The Lotus tower project is one of the significant religious projects undertaken by the Chinese in Sri Lanka's largest city, Colombo. It is 350 metres high that emblematise the lotus sutra, one of Buddhism's sacred scriptures. (Sharma, 2020) The Chinese have funded $100 million for constructing the tower. (Mendis, 2013) This project reflects one of the Chinese core foreign policy interests of peaceful rising. Besides that, Chinese delegates visit Buddhist clergies and leaders on the island, such as, the Chinese ambassador met monks of the Asgiriya Chapter in 2015. Notably, in October 2015 Sri Lankan Buddhist delegation participated in the 4th World Buddhist Forum which was organised by the Buddhist Association of China and China Religious Cultural Communication Association in Wuxi, China. (Lanka, 2015)

The Chinese further developing ties with Pakistan, Myanmar, Bangladesh, Maldives, Sri Lanka indicates that China is strategically encircling India to reduce its sphere of influence in South Asia. Thereby, India has revamped its foreign policy with its neighbours and given priority towards cooperation and an amicable relationship with them. In Sri Lanka, particularly in Narendra Modi's administration, India incorporated Buddhism as one of the soft power tools. Both countries have hosted diplomats to Buddhist religious sites. Such as, in 2020 Mahinda Rajapaksa visited various religious places in India, including Bodh Gaya (PTI, 2020). Moreover, in September 2020, India announced grant assistance of $15 million to Sri Lanka to strengthen Buddhist ties between both countries. (Chaudhury, 2020)

Though both countries have embraced Buddhism in their bilateral relations with Sri Lanka, Sri Lanka tends to be tilted towards Beijing due to extensive economic assistance. Notably, island politics ensures that Sinhalese identity is protected from external influence. This can be a significant reason to engage minimally with India because it is a Hindu majority country. Therefore, as a foreign policy tool, Buddhism cannot be ignored in Sri Lanka, and the Chinese have successfully used it compared to India. Thus, irrespective of India using Buddhism as a soft power tool to counterbalance the Chinese influence on the island, India has to strengthen its relationship with Sri Lanka in other strategic fields such as maritime cooperation, financial assistance, diplomatic relations, and others.

Conclusion

Albeit the challenges, India has the opportunities too where it has the potential to take leverage to resolve those challenges and could possibly wither away in its trajectory. Buddhism could be acted as the catalyst for initiating dialogue for peace, development and eradication of major issues like poverty, climate change and terrorism between Asian Leaders. The incumbent Prime Minister is not so subtle about the significance of Buddhism to reach out to the rest of Asia. It could be manifested through his pretention that *"the 21st Century will be Asia's century and without Buddha, this cannot be Asia's century."* (Stobdan P., 2016) In fact, China could help India by assisting in Act East Policy by serving its own economic interests. One of the finest examples of Sino-India

Cooperation is the development of Bangladesh-China-India-Myanmar Corridor which will provide greater access to each other's market for shared economic growth and services. (Bart Gaens, 2017) The incumbent government has definitely shown a decisive role in transforming India's Foreign Policy outlook and worked at the grassroots level to secure its national interest with the close cooperation with the regional partners by even assisting them under certain circumstances. However, India cannot go so far by just organising various conferences, seminars and workshops for Buddhist monks and tourists but multifaceted engagement with East and South-East Asia and overcome its shortcoming in achieving the desired results. But certainly, Act East Policy will completely change the paradigm of cultural, economic, and most importantly, people-to-people connectivity of the region in the forthcoming years.

References

Acharya, A. (2015). "India's 'Look East' Policy". In David M. Malone et al., *The Oxford Handbook of Indian Foreign Policy* (1st edn.). Oxford, UK: Oxford University Press.

Agnihotri, A. (March 7, 2018). *Indian Military Ranked Fourth Strongest in World, Pakistan at 13*. Retrieved from *The Quint*, at https://www.thequint.com/news/india/indian-military-power-fourth-strongest-in-the-world

Bart Gaens, O. R. (2017). *India's "Look East"-"Act East" Policy: Hedging as a Foreign Policy Tool. Helsinki:* The Finnish Institute of International Affairs.

Bureau, N. (September 3, 2015). *PM stresses need to shift from ideology to philosophy*. Retrieved from *The Hindu*, at https://www.thehindu.com/news/national/intolerant-nonstate-actors-unleashing-barbaric-violence-on-innocent-people-modi/article7611348.ece

Bureau, P. I. (2015). *3 Buddhist Circuits identified by the Ministry of Tourism*. Ministry of Culture, Government of India. New Delhi: Press Information Bureau. Retrieved from http://pib.nic.in/newsite/PrintRelease.aspx?relid=116398

Bureau, P. I. (2016). *BIMSTEC Leaders' Retreat 2016 Outcome Document*. Prime Minister's Office. New Delhi: Press Information Bureau. Retrieved from http://pib.nic.in/newsite/PrintRelease.aspx?relid=151717

Bureau, P. I. (2018). *President inaugurates "International Buddhist Conclave 2018"*. Ministry of Tourism, Government of India, Press Information Bureau. New Delhi: Press Information Bureau.

Chaudhury, D. R. (September 26, 2020). *India extends $15 million grant for promotion of Buddhist ties with Sri Lanka*. Retrieved from *The Economic Times*, at https://economictimes.indiatimes.com/news/politics-and-nation/india-extends-15-million-grant-for-promotion-of-buddhist-ties-with-sri-lanka/articleshow/78334018.cms

Flood, G. D. (1996). *An Introduction to Hinduism*. Cambridge: Cambridge University Press.

Harvey, P. (2003). *An Introduction to Buddhism: Teachings, History and Practices* (2nd edn.). Cambridge, UK: Cambridge University Press.

Harvey, P. (2013). *An Introduction to Buddhism: Teachings, History and Practices* (2nd edn.). Cambridge, UK: Cambridge University Press.

IMF. (October 1, 2018). *World Economic Outlook Database*. Retrieved from International Monetary Fund, at https://www.imf.org/external/pubs/ft/weo/2018/02/weodata/weorept.aspx?pr.x=44&pr.y=11&sy=2018&ey=2018&scsm=1&ssd=1&sort=country&ds=.&br=1&c=512%2C668% 2C914%2C672%2C612%2C946%2C614%2C137%2C311%2C546%2C213%2C962%2C911%2C674%2C314%2C676%2C193%2C548%2C122%2C5

India, U. N. (May 4, 2018). *Moreh an important hub to make Act East Policy materialise*. Retrieved from United News of India, at http://www.uniindia.com/moreh-an-important-hub-to-make-act-east-policy-materialise-cm-biren/states/news/1221034.html

Jha, D. (2004). *Early India: A Concise History*. New Delhi: Manohar Publishers and Distributors.

Keown, D. (2013). *Buddhism: A very short introduction* (2013 edn.). Oxford, UK: Oxford University Press.

Kishwar, S. (2018). *The Rising Role of Buddhism in India's Soft Power Strategy*. Observer Research Foundation. New Delhi: Observer Research Foundation.

Lanka, E. O. (November 2, 2015). *Sri Lankan Buddhist delegation participating in the 4th World Buddhist Forum in China*. Retrieved from Embassy of PRC, at http://lk.china-embassy.org/eng/xwdt/t1311063.htm

Lee, S. (June 20, 2007). *George Yeo Joins Panel to Revive Historic Indian Varsity*. Retrieved from *The Straits Times*, Singapore.

Mascaró, J. (November 30, 1965). *The Upanishads.* London, UK: Penguin Classics; Later Printing Edition.

MEA. (2015). Annual Report 2014-15. Ministry of External Affairs. New Delhi: Policy Planning and Research Division, Ministry of External Affairs.

MEA. (2015). *Annual Report 2014-15. Ministry of External Affairs.* New Delhi: Policy Planning and Research Division, Ministry of External Affairs.

MEA. (2016). *MEA Annual Report 2015-16. Ministry of External Afairs.* New Delhi: Policy Planning and Research Division, Ministry of External Affairs.

Mendis, P. (2013). "China's Buddhist Diplomacy: Why Do America and India Entangle with Tiny Sri Lanka?", *Journal of International Affairs.*

Mission, A. (2011). *Brochure in English.* New Delhi: Asoka Mission. Retrieved from http://asokamission.in/sites/default/files/Brochure%20-%20GBC.pdf

Mitra, D. (May 23, 2016). *Nalanda University Campus Construction Likely to Be Delayed as MEA Claims 'Anomalies' in Tender.* Retrieved from The Wire, at https://thewire.in/education/nalanda-university-campus-construction-likely-to-be-delayed-as-mea-claims-anomalies-in-tender

Nanda, P. (2003). *Rediscovering Asia: Evolution of India's Look-East Policy.* New Delhi, India: Lancer.

Narayan, R. (August 24, 2014). *Modi government to give greater push to Look East Policy: Sushma.* Retrieved from Yahoo News, at https://in.news.yahoo.com/modi-government-greater-push-look-east-policy-sushma-140619223.html

Nation, T. (November 24, 2011). Revival of ancient Buddhist university hits funds hurdle. Retrieved from The Nation Thailand.

Nguyen, T. T. (2008). *The History of Buddhism in Vietnam.* Washington, DC, USA: Council for Research in Values & Philosophy.

Olivelle, P. (2008). *Upanishads.* Oxford: Oxford University Press.

Overdorf, J. (January 19, 2012). *China vs. India: The Battle for Buddha: China and India seek to leverage their ties to Buddhism for soft power in the region.* Retrieved from *Global Post*, at http://mobile.globalpost.com/dispatch/news/regions/asia-pacific/india/120118/nepal-buddhism-dalai-lama-china-tibet

Parthasarathy, G. (April 19, 2017). *When the Dalai Lama visited Tawang.* Retrieved from *The Hindu Business Line*, at https://www.thehindubusinessline.com/opinion/columns/g-parthasarathy/when-the-dalai-lama-visited-tawang/article21976373.ece1

Patidar, S. (August 13, 2016). *Town planning of Indus valley civilization & its contributions*. Retrieved Febuary 2, 2019, from http://indiansatglance.blogspot.com: http://indiansatglance.blogspot.com/2016/08/town-planning-of-indus-valley.html

Peshan Gunaratne, J. B. (May 26, 2015). *Sri Lanka: Balancing Ties Between China and the West*. Retrieved from *The Diplomat*, at https://thediplomat.com/2015/05/sri-lanka-balancing-ties-between-china-and-the-west/

PTI. (Feburary 11, 2020). *Sri Lankan PM Mahinda Rajapaksa offers prayers at Tirumala*. Retrieved from *The Hindu Business Line*, at https://www.thehindubusinessline.com/news/variety/sri-lankan-pm-mahinda-rajapaksa-offers-prayers-at-tirumala/article30792335.ece

Robbins Schug, G. et al. (2012). "A peaceful realm? Trauma and Social Differentiation at Harappa". *Int J Paleopathol* 2.

Sajjanhar, A. (2016). *Taking Stock of India's 'Act East Policy'*. Observer Research Foundation. New Delhi: Observer Research Foundation. Retrieved from https://www.orfonline.org/wp-content/uploads/2016/05/ORF_Issue_Brief_142_A_Sajjanhar.pdf

Samuel, G. (2008). *The Origins of Yoga and Tantra: Indic Religions to the Thirteenth Century*. New York, USA: Cambridge University Press.

Sharma, P. (July 30, 2020). *As Polls Approach in Sri Lanka China Begins Cultivating Buddhist Clergy*. Retrieved from WION, at https://www.wionews.com/south-asia/as-polls-approach-in-sri-lanka-china-begins-cultivating-buddhist-clergy-317068

Singh, N. K. (July 21, 2007). *Reviving the open society*. Retrieved from *The Indian Express*, at http://archive.indianexpress.com/news/reviving-the-open-society/206144

Stobdan, P. (February 19, 2016). *Asia's Buddhist Connectivity and India's Role*. Retrieved from Institute for Defence Studies and Analyses, at https://idsa.in/issuebrief/asias-buddhist-connectivity-and-indias-role_pstobdan_190216

Times, T. E. (March 20, 2017). China warns India over invite to Dalai Lama to Buddhist meet . Retrieved from The Economic Times, at https://economictimes.indiatimes.com/news/politics-and-nation/china-slams-india-for-inviting-dalai-lama-to-buddhist-seminar/articleshow/57731676.cms

Wales, T. C. (January 2003), *The CIA's Secret War in Tibet*. *The Journal of Military History*, 67(1), 294-95.

Yadav. (n.d.). *"Look East" to "Act East"*.

Yadav, Y. (June 5, 2017). *Soft power: China gets its own Nalanda university, shames India.* Retrieved from *The Indian Express*, at http://www.newindianexpress.com/nation/2017/jun/05/soft-power-china-gets-its-own-nalanda-university-shames-india-1612915.html

Zhang, D. (2006). *India Looks East: Strategies and Impacts.* Canberra: AusAID Working Paper.

Zhang, J. (2012). *Buddhist Diplomacy: History and Status Quo.* University of Southern California, USC Center on Public Diplomacy at the Annenberg School. Los Angeles: Figueroa Press. Retrieved from https://www.uscpublicdiplomacy.org/sites/uscpublicdiplomacy.org/files/useruploads/u35361/2012%20Paper%208.pdf

INDIA'S FOREIGN POLICY TOWARDS MULTILATERAL INSTITUTIONS

VISHAL RAJPUT

Introduction

In international politics, there is a well-documented history of the usage of diplomatic tactics to counterbalance or dominate rival powers and ultimately win the wars. One of those tactics is collaborating with friendly powers to dominate their common opponents. As far as the wars are concerned, two world wars are the detailed accounts of how different regimes and powers collaborated against their opponents and engulfed the whole world directly or indirectly in fighting the wars. With the coming of the Westphalia world order and the internationalisation of democracy and liberalism, the monarchy became obsolete, and democracy became the polity of an overwhelming number of nations. In accordance with the realist theory, nations became the key player in forging alliances so that the national interest could be preserved. The asymmetrical division of power and resources compels the nation-states to get help and collaborate with friendly nations to keep a check and counterbalance any expansionist plan of their opponents. Hence, in a contemporary globalised world, there is a significant reliance upon like-minded countries and multilateral alliances as far as nations' pursuit of power expansionism or existential survival is concerned.

One of the early alliances being made was in two world wars where the 'Allies' alliances in the later war resulted in the culmination of the United States becoming the sole superpower, and the cooperation amongst the allies resulted in the political, ideological, and strategic defeat of the Soviet Union. Another form of seeing the multilateral alliance is NATO. The organisation was established to support the member countries and perceived the threat to any particular nation as a common threat. Through this regional strategic mechanism, it helped the smaller nations to protect their sovereignty and freedom from the communist threat of the Soviet Union. With the success of these regional alliances, many countries started forging their alliances with primarily but not necessarily the neighbouring countries as they shared the same concerns and similarities of culture and society helped them better cooperate with each other on trade, defence, culture and connectivity.

Moreover, the significance of multilateralism has started reflected through the inclusion of foreign policy. Nations started taking a particular viewpoint while engaging with the multilateral institutions and their members, in isolation while engaging bilaterally with those members. Initially, the global north was the first to establish such sorts of regional alliances, but with the decolonisation, many countries became independent and sovereign and started coming together with other nations with the aim of developing their region in toto. In this paper, I will be looking into India's Foreign Policy towards multilateral institutions with an overview of its engagement with varied institutions in general but with a specific focus on NAM, SAARC, BIMSTEC, BRICS, and QUAD which received significant attention in its foreign policymaking from the advent to hitherto. In addition to this, I will be analysing the impact of India's engagement with those institutions in making the international order a multipolar one. Moreover, the research also looks into yielding any significant progress in burgeoning India's position on the one hand, and helping the country in resolving pertinent issues primarily with its immediate neighbours.

Analysing India's Multilateral Engagements and Its Foreign Policy

Idealist Diplomacy: An Establishment of India-NAM Relations

In South Asia, when India got independent from the decades-long British colonialism, the charismatic leadership of Jawaharlal Nehru started showing global leaders when he took India to the center of global politics with the establishment of the Non-Aligned Movement (NAM). It was a time when the small and newly independent nations were worried about bitter ideological competition between the two camps and get wary if they chose either camp, India was one of those few countries who chose to not join either camp and established NAM for primarily third world countries. (Patrick, 2012)

It was the defining moment in the history of India's International Relations where both the camps often came for help in breaking deals with their opponents. In addition to this, newly independent nations were given the option to not receive the wrath of the two Superpowers and their allies. In those times, Nehru was perceived as a great statesman overriding the prestige of its Asian competitor, Mao Zedong. In another sense, India's foreign policy was overwhelmingly laid down by Jawaharlal Nehru, who stressed the immense importance of forging alliances with alike countries. However, critics give a very reasonable criticism of his foreign policy on multilateralism where his morality guided his decisions, unlike realpolitik. He established and supported NAM primarily with the aim of expanding the decolonisation movement as India suffered the same from Britishers. He didn't actually intend to change the course of Cold War politics and as per US lawmakers, Nehru was a socialist and was favourably inclined towards the Soviet Union. Therefore, according to them, NAM was another tool for the socialist bloc to expand its influence in the member countries. Another reason for their criticism is that major colonial powers sided with the United States and all the third world countries wanted to oppose their colonisers at the international level and hence were more friendly to the socialist bloc.

In contemporary times, it has become fashionable to treat non-alignment as nothing more (or less) than the rational outcome of a calculated approach to maximising national interests in a context shaped above all by Cold War bipolarity where countries were helpless to choose either side. In the backdrop of this rationale, the policy of non-alignment was the best possible strategy to keep its economic and political power independent from the influence and coercion of the two Superpowers where both were seeking to attract newly independent countries to their side.

While there are undoubtedly moments in the history of Indian foreign policy when the appearance of such a fence-sitting strategy paid great dividends, it would be a considerable historical mistake to reduce the complex history of non-alignment to such a narrow, if omniscient, perspective. In particular, this line of argument would predict that a non-aligned India would never have joined a non-aligned grouping of countries. The rational calculation would assess that the uncertainties and costs of maintaining group cohesion of a heterogeneous and militarily weak group of countries in a highly unequal international system would far outweigh the benefits of going it alone—yet that is exactly what India did from 1955 to 1960, taking the lead in helping to create a bloc of countries that have both grown and nominally continued this identification to this day (Abraham, 2008, p. 196).

Over a period of time, with the disintegration of the Soviet Union and the world becoming a unipolar one, NAM started losing its significance, and India along with others started engaging with the US and looked forward to strengthening political, economic, and strategic ties with the nation. At the same time, India started looking beyond the NAM and engaged with several other regional multilateral institutions. The end of the Cold War was the vantage point of the transformation in India's foreign policy towards multilateral institutions by shifting from an idealist pursuit to the realist one while engaging with the alliances. Since then, the Indian government started engaging with multifaceted multilateral institutions, from the EU to BRICS to ASEAN and SCO depending on the regional interests of India.

With the final ending of the Cold War, India took the first step of liberalising its economy and allowed globalisation in India. In the following move, it started privatising major PSUs and allowed private entities to take over businesses that were administered by government entities. As the country took the mega-economic initiative, India started looking into the rising economic multilateral institutions to do business and help in its economic burgeoning. And the first institution India started engaging with—Association of South East Asian Nations (ASEAN).

Praxis of Act East Policy: The Foundation of India-ASEAN Relations

Under the Narasimha Rao government, India's 'Look East Policy' provided the nation with a dedicated policy framework to engage with primarily ASEAN nations. The Look East Policy has today revamped into a dynamic and action-oriented 'Act East Policy'. PM Narendra Modi at the 12th ASEAN India Summit and the 9th East Asia Summit held in Nay Pyi Taw, Myanmar, in November 2014, formally enunciated the Act East Policy. (Dewan, 2021)

India's relationship with ASEAN is the major pillar of Indian Foreign Policy since the foundation of their bilateral ties with India became a Sectoral partner in 1992, then upgraded into the Dialogue partner in 1996, and finally established the strategic relationship in 2012. In order to strengthen its ties with ASEAN, India established a permanent mission in Jakarta, Indonesia in 2015 for engaging with both ASEAN and EAS. Over a period of time, with the changing strategic equations in the Indo-Pacific region and the evolving US-China geopolitical competition, India and ASEAN took the initiative to identify cooperation in maritime domain under the strategic partnership at the ASEAN-India Commemorative Summit. Moreover, India is actively taking part and attending annual meetings in the security dialogue platform of ASEAN, ASEAN Regional Forum. They have initiated the historic track 1.5 'Delhi Dialogue' to discuss political, economic, and security cooperation between India and ASEAN. (Kesavan, 2020)

In addition to their political security cooperation, ASEAN is the fourth largest trading partner of India and its trade stands at $81.33 billion. Not only this, they have a comprehensive social and cultural exchange such as the ASEAN student exchange programme in India, Special Training Course for ASEAN diplomats, Exchange of Parliamentarians, Participation of ASEAN students in the National Children's Science Congress, ASEAN-India Network of Think Tanks, ASEAN-India Eminent Persons Lecture Series, amongst others. India and ASEAN have expanded their bilateral relationship to many other facets beyond the conventional political, social, economic and strategic. In contemporary Indian foreign policy, we cannot ignore the greater significance of ASEAN in burgeoning India's economic and strategic leverage in the Indo-Pacific region. As the great game is evolving in the Indo-Pacific, India position ASEAN at the center of the Indo-Pacific. (MEA, India-ASEAN Relations)

South Asian Regional Integration: Deconstructing India-SAARC Relations

Though the historical reasoning for the creation of a SAARC goes back to the pre-independence era of India when, in 1928, the Indian National Congress passed a resolution on the creation of an 'Asian Federation'. (Jain, 2005, p. 56) In this context, PM Nehru once said in 1945, *"Small states of the world tomorrow have no future in store and they are sure to be reduced to the status of satellite states ... I stand for a South Asian Federation of India, Iraq, Afghanistan and Burma"*.

However, with the consequent nation-state remaking and various deliberations of the heads of the South Asian states, at the first summit held in Dhaka on December 7-8, 1985, the Charter establishing the South Asian Association for Regional Cooperation (SAARC) was adopted. The main objectives laid down in the charter are: to promote the welfare of the people of South Asia, to accelerate economic growth and social progress, promote active collaboration in economic growth and social progress, to promote active collaboration in the economic, social, cultural, technical and scientific fields, to strengthen cooperation in international forums on matters of common interest and to cooperate with international and regional organisations with similar aims and purposes. (Ibid., p. 61)

However, the infamous historical conflict between the two member states, India and Pakistan, has rocked the sanctity of the institution and has impeded its progress. As SAARC aims at promoting economic ties through free trade, the strategic conflict between India and Pakistan has reduced the volume of intra-regional trade unlike other institutions like EU, ASEAN, MERCOSUR, etc. (Ahmed, 2012)

A few years back, with the coming of PM Narendra Modi at the helm of India, he participated in the last summit in 2014 held at Kathmandu. Nevertheless, he was supposed to attend the next scheduled summit in Islamabad, but in the wake of a tragic terrorist attack on the Uri Base camp of the Indian Army by Pakistan-based cross-border terrorists affiliated with Jaish-e-Mohammad, India declined to participate in the 19th SAARC Summit scheduled to be held in Islamabad. (PTI, India, "Pakistan enmity main reason why SAARC is not prospering: Bangladesh FM", 2019) Unsurprisingly, the enmity between the two is well known in international circles, but the Uri incident worsened the diplomatic ties. In fact, in one meeting, Bangladesh Foreign Minister, A. K. Abdul Momen asserted that SAARC is not prospering due to continuous enmity between India and Pakistan, but, at the same time, showed optimism for BIMSTEC. (Ibid., n.d.) In another sense, we can say, the domestic nationalistic fervour of the BJP government in India doesn't want to look forward to engaging with Pakistan and aims to diplomatically isolate the latter at the international level. According to several foreign policy analysts, PM Modi has decided to leave SAARC alone due to inevitable disagreements with Pakistan and aims to put India's multilateral efforts in another alternative south Asian organisation, BIMSTEC, at the cost of SAARC. Joyeeta Bhattacharjee, Senior Fellow with Observer Research Foundation (ORF), however, wrote in a paper in January 2018: "Since the SAARC summit has only been postponed, not canceled, the possibility of revival remains. The success of BIMSTEC does not render SAARC pointless; it only adds a new chapter in regional cooperation in South Asia." Probably, the change in guard in the national government of both India and Pakistan could yield some progress and growth. Although, there are several ups and downs in the progress of SAARC, as far as the regional development and stability are concerned, India, on the one hand, cannot ignore the influence of Pakistan in South Asian politics and the potential to challenge India's adverse action against it, and therefore the need of the former to restart its diplomatic channel with the latter and the pursuit of dialogue to figure out the pragmatic solution to their long-term conflict and divisions. On the other, Pakistan has to seriously take into their consideration India's concern regarding terrorism as it has become a threat to the national security of both countries, and providing safe refuge to terrorist outfits is not going to threaten India and its national interest. Its battle against terrorism will help in clearing the path of India's friendship and its assurance in fighting terrorism on the same side. But Pakistan has to be clear that the path of terrorism and unconventional warfare won't yield any great success in threatening India's position, but will further deteriorate its relations with India.

As far as other Indian initiatives towards SAARC are concerned, SAARC countries got special focus under its 'Neighbourhood First' Policy and the primary manifestation was through inviting SAARC leaders to the swearing-in ceremony of Narendra Modi's government. His government's first diplomatic move was to reiterate the importance of SAARC in the Indian foreign policy and assured seriousness in establishing the regional integrated zone in South Asia through the SAARC trajectory. However, the bilateral diffusion between India and Pakistan is impacting the whole institution and cannot realise its objective until both the countries diffuse their regional tensions and create an atmosphere of trust amongst themselves for each other.

An Establishment of Multipolar World Order: Analysing India-BRICS Relations

The unparalleled global dominance of the United States is challenged by the rise of other great powers such as China, India, Russia, Brazil and South Africa. These days, the United States doesn't have the authority to shape the world order, and its liberal posture is challenged by the establishment of BRICS (Brazil, Russia, India, China, and South Africa). Initially, they aimed to improve the global economic situation and reform financial institutions.

From an Indian perspective, BRICS has emerged as the voice of developing countries on diverse issues like WTO, climate change, inclusive development and mutual cooperation in areas including trade, finance, health, agriculture, energy, space, culture, education, technology and IT.

The juncture of BRICS allows India and China to diffuse their bilateral disagreements/tensions with the support of other member states. It was clearly manifested through the Doklam stand-off and the recent Galwan clashes where both India and China met during the 12th BRICS Summit. (PTI, "PM Modi to attend virtual summit of BRICS on November 17, 2020") Moreover, Russia discreetly helped in releasing captured Indian soldiers during the Galwan Valley clashes with the Chinese army. (Chaudhary, 2020) Groupings like the BRICS and SCO afford both India and China the opportunity to "decouple" their strategic contest from the other dimensions of the relationship. Moreover, as close observers of the India-China standoff in Ladakh will attest, Moscow continues to play an important though discreet role in bringing both sides to the negotiating table. India's dependence on Russian weaponry is deep enough for New Delhi to be not able to offend Russian sensibilities directly. The very fact that Russia is chairing the BRICS this year almost axiomatically implied that India would participate in the BRICS activities despite everything else.

As many scholars of Indian foreign policy have persuasively argued, a lot of India's behaviour on the world stage can be explained by its quest for international status. While this was most pronounced during the Cold War, when a materially enfeebled India continued to lecture the West and sought to lead Third World coalitions, status-seeking hasn't disappeared, despite the country's newfound advocacy of a realist foreign policy. BRICS is a case in point. Moreover, as India's External Affairs Minister, S. Jaishankar recently described it, BRICS provides India a transcontinental reach by virtue of Brazil and South Africa's presence. While one can rightly litigate what, in fact, has concretely materialised from this reach, the fact of the matter is that India's presence in BRICS looks good, presenting the country as a truly international player. In fact, New Delhi's participation in a variety of informal arrangements is a low-cost way for it to signal its aspirations as a global power, even though—in the strict material sense—its equities, say in South America, remain limited.

In addition to this, India is a proudly revisionist power when it comes to the extant structure of international organisations and the United Nations system. It continues to maintain that the international system does not recognise the country's economic and political heft and demands top-down reform, beginning with the UN Security Council (UNSC) where it seeks permanent membership. Even a casual look at BRICS joint statements from the past reveals that reform of the international multilateral architecture remains the key political issue for the BRICS. New Delhi is not naive enough to believe that China, for example, would substantially advocate a greater role for India, especially where it matters—the UNSC. But that said, the BRICS' repeated calls for reform boost India's own assertions in this direction, acting as a multiplier to the country's own demands for reform. (Rej, 2020)

BRICS, which in many ways is redefining multilateralism and multiculturalism, has emerged as a template for cooperation between emerging powers and a useful instrument for India to fight the agenda-setting monopoly of Atlantic powers, in its quest for a greater role in global governance.

Over a period of time, there will be a crucial point in international politics when BRICS will provide a viable economic and security alternative to the international community and, with India's involvement in it, it will give immense legitimacy to the group as the latter has earned international prestige as a responsible power with great track record of multipolar world order and rule-based global governance with equal economic opportunity to all countries.

Hence, in the coming times, India will have a crucial role in shaping the world order and in the effort of international legitimisation of alternative financial institutions.

India's Presence in Eurasian Security Architecture: Its relationship with Shanghai Cooperation Organization

With the collapse of the Soviet Union, the security apparatus also disappeared with it leaving the vacuum to be filled by other regional actors. At that point in time, both Russia and China were looking to fill that vacuum for their strategic interests. For Russia, it wanted to retain its dominant position and avoid getting Western powers involved in the region. And as far as China is concerned, it wanted to enlarge its influence beyond the South Asian region, and the Central Asian region was indeed a space where China could grow and play greater power politics. With this strategy, China, Russia, Kazakhstan, Kyrgyzstan and Tajikistan established the Shanghai Cooperation Organization (SCO), founded on 15th June 2001 (SCO).

Over a period of time, they developed their cooperation in several domains but they primarily focused on the political, economic and security sectors. Besides, many other countries developed their interest in joining it, and with their participation, SCO further developed as an extensive multilateral organisation in the Eurasian region. Though China and Russia have their sway over the organisation and due to this, it was perceived as an anti-Western alliance. With this perception, it could not receive much legitimacy in Western circles and remained limited in its operation and collaboration.

However, after a while, India developed its interest in joining it and after intense negotiation amongst the members, India joined it with the strong support of Russia on June 9, 2017. In order to counterbalance India in SCO, Pakistan too joined it in China's favour. (Bhattacherjee, 2017)

India's induction was a huge accomplishment in making SCO more inclusive and it brings greater legitimacy to international politics. Afterward, SCO started gaining attention as a responsible alliance with a greater role in regional development and events. India too gained a larger exposure in international affairs. With the ascendancy of Prime Minister Modi, there was a shift in India's approach in its relationship with Eurasia. As India has started reaching out to Central Asian nations and aims at building political, economic and strategic relationships, SCO provided the platform where it can play a major role in its development, peace and security. At the same time, India wanted to deepen its cooperation with Russia beyond its military products acquisition and its bilateral exercises. In these times, New Delhi has a clear three-pronged policy approach—deepen ties with Russia; monitor and counter the influence of China and Pakistan; and expand cooperation with CARs.

Moreover, as India is facing religious extremism in the Kashmir region due to the involvement of non-state actors, SCO will enable India, as an integral part of the Eurasian security grouping, to neutralise centrifugal forces arising from religious extremism and terrorism in the region. Besides, when India is looking to build cooperation in areas of energy, building trade, and transportation, SCO could facilitate these for India at its juncture. Also, India is advancing its 'Connect Central Asia Policy', SCO will be the best viable option for India to reach out to Central Asian countries through it. India's ongoing engagement with SCO can be seen through the prism of reconnecting and re-energising ties with a region with which India has shared civilisational linkages, and is considered the country's extended neighbourhood. The SCO provides India with a convenient channel for its outreach—trade and strategic ties—to Central Asian countries. In addition to this, by acknowledging the strategic importance emanating from the region and SCO, the Indian Prime Minister had articulated the foundational dimension of Eurasia being 'SECURE'. The letters in the word SECURE are (Meena Singh Roy, 2019):

- S for Security of our citizens,
- E for Economic development for all,
- C for Connecting the region,
- U for Unite our people,
- R for Respect for Sovereignty and Integrity, and
- E for Environment protection.

If we deeply analyse the terrorism facet, it is not limited to one particular area, having spread its tentacles to South, Central and West Asian region. It has also morphed—new actors and forces connect more easily through terror networks, and use social media to recruit, train and finance their extremist activities.

In this context, the drawdown of Western forces from Afghanistan and the rise of the Islamic State (IS) with its stated intention to create *'Khorasan'* have added a new explosive dimension to the region's security landscape. In many ways, security and stability of Eurasia are linked to peace in Afghanistan. The Islamic Movement of Uzbekistan (IMU) has shown signs of revival while the Taliban and IS have expanded their presence in northern parts of the country bordering CARs. Similarly, the Al Qaeda linked Turkestan Islamic Party (TIP), comprising largely of Uyghur jihadist members, has indicated its willingness to join the Afghan Taliban, apart from being active in Syria. This raises the prospect of spillover of violence in the Eurasian heartland, given the regional terror groups' linkages. Central Asia also remains vulnerable due to the many drug trafficking routes that traverse the region. This assumes even greater significance given the ties between drug trafficking, terrorism and organised crime. Notably, the largely secular CARs have witnessed a growing shift toward Political Islam. Several fault lines, ranging from weakened socio-economic state structures to inter-ethnic discords, have led to increased radicalisation, particularly among the regional youth. This has seen more than 2,000 Central Asians joining the IS. The Ferghana Valley remains a hotbed of religious extremism.

Similarly, the potential base of Khorasan in the Af-Pak area can be the pivot to spread IS influence in Kashmir. IS has already threatened to attack India, kidnapped Indians in the Middle East and indoctrinated a few. As such, the prospect of IMU, IS, Taliban, TIP and other extremist outfits coordinating their militant activities in Eurasia raises the spectre of an arc of regional instability. It is, therefore, in India's and SCO's interest that Afghanistan does not regress into a hub of terrorism.

India, as a victim of terrorism, has been developing its skills at the national and state level and cooperating with other countries at the regional and international levels to fight this menace. It has articulated the belief that no country can fight terrorism alone, and that only a well-coordinated, multilateral and integrated effort can tackle this problem. To counter these threats and challenges, India can share its experience with the region. In the post 26/11 phase, India's counterterrorism infrastructure has been strengthened. India can offer expertise on policy aspects, train people and provide technological solutions. India has niche capabilities in satellite, bio and information technologies which can help in collecting and analysing intelligence that can, in turn, be employed for counterterrorism and human development. Thus, India can offer customised solutions if required.

India's desire to strengthen its security cooperation with SCO was noted by its External Affairs Minister during the 2014 SC summit meeting, where she said, "we are keen to deepen our security-related cooperation with the SCO in general and with the Regional Counter-Terrorism Structure, in particular". (MEA, Statement by External Affairs Minister at the Shanghai Cooperation Organization (SCO) Heads of State Summit 2014 in Dushanbe, 2014) In this context, India has actively supported the SCO Qingdao Summit Leaders 'Appeal to

Youth' against radicalisation of youth, participated in the SCO Peace Mission 2018 counterterrorism exercises and attempted to strengthen its coordination with RATS. It is also likely to co-host the next meeting of the SCO-Afghanistan Contact Group along with Afghanistan.

As far as trade and connectivity are concerned, the foundation of India's economic outreach to Inner Asia is based on its 2012 Connect Central Asia Policy (Jha, 2016) with its focus on the 4 C's—Commerce, Connectivity, Consular, and Community. These are aimed at building long-term partnerships, both bilaterally and collectively. India's willingness to share its unique experience in banking, finance, Information Technology (IT), education, telecommunications, health and agriculture with CARs can be leveraged to build mutually beneficial development partnerships. Given the regional economic slowdown, brought on by the devaluation of the rouble, India, with its long-term positive economic outlook, can help stabilise the region. India has implemented several projects involving IT excellence, entrepreneurship development and industrial training centers in Central Asia. Some of India's core strengths that can be leveraged to expand India's engagement with SCO involve:

1. **Pharmaceutical and Health Care.** One of India's biggest strengths is its niche capabilities in the pharma, healthcare, and hospitality sectors. Its pharmaceutical companies have much to offer to the Eurasian region, including affordable medicines. Other areas of collaboration can include telemedicine and medical tourism. Notably, India has emerged as an attractive destination for medical tourism for regional countries.
2. **Green Technology and Bio-Fuels.** Green technology is an area where India is investing heavily, particularly in solar, bio, and wind energy. India is a founding member of the International Solar Alliance with its secretariat based in the outskirts of New Delhi. India can contribute, collaborate and share its experience with the regional countries on adopting clean, renewable energy.

These capabilities can gain traction on account of environmental issues being a serious cause of concern for the entire region. Given the successful India-Russia cooperation on ash damps, it has been suggested that this project could become one of the pilot projects for India to cooperate with SCO.

3. **Education.** India has a robust education and training curriculum that can be offered to the SCO member states. Its technology institutes, business schools, and banking and financial institutions can be of relevance to the region. In this context, India's successful tele-education and telemedicine initiatives in Africa can be a model for the Eurasian region as well. Similarly, New Delhi's Indian Technical and Economic Cooperation Programme (ITEC), a program with the Central Asian countries, which seeks to build capacity in the region, can be further expanded.
4. **Culture.** Given India's historical and civilisational linkages with the Eurasian countries, culture can be a vital area where India can contribute to the SCO processes. Old regional links can be revived in order to frame confidence-building measures. Cultural exchange programmes, in the mould of 'SCO Our Common Home', 'Days of Open Doors', SCO Film Festival and SCO World Heritage Exhibition, that foster greater people-to-people contacts and exchange of ideas can be expanded. Indian art, music, dance and movies continue to be popular in the region. India's proposal to host the SCO exhibition on 'Shared Buddhist Heritage' in 2019 is a step in the right direction. Notably, Buddhism had spread from India to Central Asia with Buddhist stupas being discovered at Dalvarzintepe near Bukhara and Tashkent being named after a local Buddha altar.
5. **Infrastructure and Energy.** India and SCO members share a similar objective of developing multi-modal transport and transit routes, effectively linking markets of Central Asia to South Asia, South East Asia and Europe, to boost intra and inter-regional trade and

investment. The need of the hour, therefore, is to build pan-Asian cooperation. India is already working to enhance its connectivity with the region through the International North-South Transport Corridor (INSTC). The present government has recently outlined its vision for unified connectivity among the South Asian countries. In this context, cooperation between SAARC and SCO to enhance connectivity and build energy pipelines will go a long way in bridging distances. The first meeting of the Heads of Railways of the SCO Member States held in September 2018 highlights the endless possibilities of shortening the prevailing distances. Indian companies have, meanwhile, built considerable expertise in building refineries. Indian infrastructure and oil companies can cooperate with CARs, China, Russia, Iran, Mongolia and other member states to boost ties in the regional framework. The SCO's deliberations on forming an Energy Club, in order to bring together the regional producers and consumers, hold strategic relevance for an energy-deficit India.

6. **Disaster Management.** Given the multiple disasters, both natural and man-made, that India has faced, the country has developed robust disaster management practices covering a broad spectrum of worst-case scenarios. These are being further augmented by niche Indian advancements in space with satellite mapping and weather forecasting helping prevent and mitigate disasters. India's skills can be of relevance for SCO members who have had to tackle critical environmental challenges in the past.

Above all, the SCO has been seen as a grouping worth pursuing as it retains India's geopolitical balance, a useful counterpoint to New Delhi's otherwise much more robust relations with the Western world.

If we look into the geopolitical arena, the US's power struggle with China, exit from the Iran nuclear deal JCPOA, and adversarial attitude towards Russia have forced India to choose sides. While Washington's stance against Islamabad after the Pulwama attack was evidence of its support for New Delhi, India has had a strained relationship with China after the Doklam stand-off, followed by attempts to reset relations in Wuhan.

In the SCO, India's sitting down with less-than-free regimes, Russia and China have always had the West worried. India, however, has always been tactful in not aligning with these countries on governance issues. What draws India to SCO is the "Shanghai spirit", which emphasises harmony, non-interference in others' internal affairs, and non-alignment. The bottom line is that it helps India keep all options open in terms of international partnerships. (Roy, 2019)

Moreover, as far as the prospects are concerned, in the absence of the SAARC summit, the SCO summit gives an opportunity for Indian and Pakistani leaders to meet informally, on the sidelines. Both sides have the obligation not to bring in bilateral disputes but can cooperate on issues of mutual interest and importance. Signing off on joint counterterrorism exercises will be a new form of engagement between the two militaries. With China, it is yet another opening, like the BRICS summit last year, to bring down tensions, and ahead of the next informal summit in October in India.

Conclusion

India's International Relations have transformed significantly and its posture towards multilateral institutions has been shaped from time to time by various international and national events, domestic political ideologies, its historical background, and national interests. And after analysing its foreign policy towards different multilateral institutions, it is evident that India has significantly risen in stature in international politics. Moreover, when SCO brings brighter opportunities for India, it also comes with a baggage of several challenges too.

As China was skeptical to inducting India into SCO, it now perceives India's involvement as a challenge to its hegemonic position and certainly, its bilateral disputes on border conflict which has often taken shape in a hard conflict between the two, the progress of SCO will be affected due to bipartisan issues. Moreover, at the same time, Pakistan's presence in SCO is another important challenge as it will attempt by every possible means to hamper India's strategy in achieving its objective on counterterrorism, energy, trade, and security. India has already indicated that most of the non-state terrorist organisations have a safe haven in Pakistan, which will be detrimental to the former's seriousness in tackling terrorism and establishing stability in the region. Therefore, Pakistan won't be more interested in working with India on these domains by keeping its position clear and intact.

Nonetheless, the changing scenario in Afghanistan is going to directly impact India in SCO as most of the members have developed their individual understanding that the Taliban are going to establish their rule over there. And keeping in mind the sour relationship of India with the Taliban, the former is on the backfoot in shaping the contemporary events in Afghanistan, unlike countries like China, Russia, and Pakistan. Moreover, when it comes to SCO, there is an unexplicit consensus amongst the members that working against the Taliban will impact the stability of both Central Asia and Afghanistan. Therefore, in order to keep its influencing position in SCO intact, it is necessary for India to change its trajectory while dealing with the Taliban and develop its foreign policy towards Afghanistan based on realpolitik.

However, at the global level, there is an edge for India as SCO aims at establishing a multipolar world order, India's presence in SCO, BRICS and ASEAN will help in gaining legitimacy for both institutions and ultimately a multipolar world order.

Hence, it is imperative for India to deepen its cooperation and collaboration with those multilateral institutions because its endeavour to put India at the center of the global stage, its collaboration with multilateral institutions will help in achieving its political, strategic, economic, and security objectives and safeguarding its larger national interests.

References

Abraham, I. (2008). "From Bandung to NAM: Non-alignment and Indian Foreign Policy, 1947–65". *Commonwealth & Comparative Politics*. Retrieved from https://indiachinainstitute.org/wp-content/uploads/2011/02/Abraham.pdf

Ahmed, Z. S. (Janurary 16, 2012). *India-Pakistan relations and SAARC.* Retrieved from *Peace Insight*, at https://www.peaceinsight.org/en/articles/india-pakistan-saarc/?location=pakistan&theme=mediation-dialogue

Bhattacherjee, K. (June 9, 2017). *India, Pakistan become full members of SCO*. Retrieved from *The Hindu*, at https://www.thehindu.com/news/national/india-pakistan-become-full-members-of-shanghai-cooperation-organisation-sco/article18912600.ece

Chaudhary, D. R. (July 6, 2020). *How Russia's Quiet Diplomacy helped in reducing tensions between India and China.* Retrieved from *The Economic Times*, at https://m.economictimes.com/news/defence/how-russias-quiet-diplomacy-helped-in-reducing-tensions-between-delhi-and-beijing/articleshow/76802915.cms?_oref=cook

Dewan, V. (May 31, 2021). *India's Act East Policy: Strategic Rationales and Maritime Strategy.* Retrieved from *Strategic Distillery*, at https://thesecuritydistillery.org/all-articles/indias-act-east-policy-strategic-rationales-and-maritime-strategy

Ibid. (n.d.).

Ibid. (n.d.).

Jain, R. (December 2005). *"India and SAARC: An Analysis". Indian Journal of Asian Affairs*, 18(2), 55-74. Retrieved from http://dcac.du.ac.in/documents/E-Resource/2020/Metrial/505CihnnitaBaruah1.pdf

Jha, M. (December 2, 2016). *India's Connect Central Asia Policy*. Retrieved from *The Diplomat,* at https://thediplomat.com/2016/12/indias-connect-central-asia-policy-2/

Kesavan, K. V. (Feburary 14, 2020). *India's 'Act East' policy and regional cooperation*. Retrieved from ORF: https://www.orfonline.org/expert-speak/indias-act-east-policy-and-regional-cooperation-61375/

MEA. (September 12, 2014). *Statement by External Affairs Minister at the Shanghai Cooperation Organization (SCO) Heads of State Summit 2014 in Dushanbe*. Retrieved from Ministry of External Affais, Government of India, at https://mea.gov.in/Speeches-Statements.htm?dtl/23993/Statement+by+External+Affairs+Minister+at+the+Shanghai+Cooperation+Organization+SCO+Heads+of+State+Summit+2014+in+Dushanbe

MEA. (n.d.). *India-ASEAN Relations*. New Delhi: Ministry of External Affairs, Government of India. Retrieved from https://www.mea.gov.in/Portal/ForeignRelation/India-ASEAN-Relations-August-2018.pdf

Meena Singh Roy, R. R. (December 4, 2019). *India and the SCO: A Vision for Expanding New Delhi's Engagement*. Retrieved from RIAC: https://russiancouncil.ru/en/analytics-and-comments/analytics/india-and-the-sco-a-vision-for-expanding-new-delhi-s-engagement/

Patrick, S. M. (August 30, 2012). *The Nonaligned Movement's Crisis*. Retrieved from *Council on Foreign Relations*, at https://www.cfr.org/blog/nonaligned-movements-crisis

PTI. (December 24, 2019). *India, Pakistan enmity main reason why SAARC is not prospering: Bangladesh FM*. Retrieved from *The Economic Times*, at https://economictimes.indiatimes.com/news/politics-and-nation/india-pakistan-enmity-main-reason-why-saarc-is-not-prospering-bangladesh-fm/articleshow/72954461.cms?from=mdr

PTI. (November 16, 2020). *PM Modi to attend virtual summit of BRICS on November 17*. Retrieved from *The Hindu*, at https://www.thehindu.com/news/national/pm-modi-to-attend-virtual-summit-of-brics-on-november-17/article33108563.ece

Rej, A. (October 12, 2020). *4 Reasons Why India Supports the BRICS*. Retrieved from *The Diplomat*, at https://thediplomat.com/2020/10/4-reasons-why-india-support-the-brics/

Roy, S. (June 13, 2019). *What SCO summit means for India's global and regional interests*. Retrieved from *The Indian Express*, at https://indianexpress.com/article/explained/what-sco-summit-means-for-indias-global-and-regional-interests-5777804/

SCO. (n.d.). *What is the SCO?*. Retrieved from Shanghai Cooperation Organisation, at http://eng.sectsco.org/docs/about/faq.html

EDITORS AND CONTRIBUTORS

Editors

Dr. **Manasi Sinha** (PhD, JNU) is Associate Professor and Programme Chair (Division of Political Science), in the School of Liberal Education, Galgotias University. She is currently teaching Political Science (International Relations) and Gender Studies to undergraduate/post-graduate and Ph.D research scholars in Galgotias University. Her major research areas include Global Politics & IR (Theories & Issues), Culture, Politics and Society in Europe, European Union and Gender Policy Discourse, Gender and Politics of Violence (India/Sweden/Europe). Her research work has been widely published across Academic and Peer Reviewed Journals and books across National and International Platforms. She has been awarded IBIES Erasmus Mundus Fellowship for contributing to higher research in Indo-European studies in the University of Warsaw, Poland (2013-2014). She is a member for the Editorial Research Committee at EuropeNow (Open Journal for Council for European Studies, Columbia University). Her recent work involves an Edited Book on 'Socio-political landscape in India's Democracy: Sailing or Sinking?' by Disha International Publications (2022).

Vishal Rajput is a researcher at Nehru Memorial Museum and Library working on the Border History Project of the Ministry of Defence, Government of India. He was formerly associated with the National Security Council and United Service Institution of India. He did post-graduation in International Relations and Area Studies from MMAJ Academy of International Studies, Jamia Millia Islamia University. He has also attended BRICS Summer School at Fudan University, X International Russian Chinese Summer School on International Relations at Higher School of Economics, and Tsinghua Global Summer School at Tsinghua University. In addition, he was a Pakistan studies scholar at the National Institute of Advanced Studies. He has written articles and research papers for the Australian Institute of International Affairs, Diplomatist Magazine, The Citizen, United Service Institution of India, Centre for Strategic and International Studies (CSIS Indonesia), IJOPEC Publications (UK), Pakistan Reader, South Asia Monitor and The Quint. His research focuses on Maritime Geopolitics, Russian Foreign Policy, Chinese Foreign Policy, and Politics and Development in the North-East. He can be contacted at vishal.rajput@stud-mail.uni-wuerzburg.de

Contributors

Megha Shrivastava is a Dr. TMA Pai Fellow and Doctoral Research Scholar at the Department of Geopolitics and International Relations, Manipal Academy of Higher Education, Manipal, Karnataka (India). She has earlier received her post-graduation in International Relations from the School of International Studies, Jawaharlal Nehru University (JNU), New Delhi and a Bachelor's in Political Science from the University of Delhi, India. She has also been associated with various think tanks including the Institute of Chinese Studies, Foreign Policy Research Centre, Yogya Empowering Society, and Centre for Legislative Research and Advocacy, New

Delhi. Her research focuses on the intersection of technology and international relations, state and private big-tech corporations in China, and China's technology policy. She has earlier contributed her work on China's foreign policy and the Indo-pacific region in journals like Indian Journal of Law and International Affairs, Journal of Communication, Politics and Society, ICS Analysis, Foreign Policy Research Centre Journal, The Diplomatist Magazine, Science Technology and Security Forum, etc.

Alakh Ranjan is a research scholar. He has previously worked as Research Assistant with Centre for Land Warfare Studies (CLAWS) and Vivekananda International Foundations as Young Professional. He has done his Masters in International Relations and Area Studies from Jamia Millia Islamia University. His area of interest includes soft power diplomacy and foreign policy in the Indo-Pacific region.

Nawid Fazly hails from Faryab province of Afghanistan. He graduated in law and political science from Kabul university in 2017. He has done an internship in Asia foundation as a legal advisor. He is now working as an editor in a committee of journals in a private University in Afghanistan. In 2019, he undertook Masters programme in Political Science at Galgotias University, Greater Noida. His area of research includes International Relations in South Asia with specific focus on Afghanistan's relations with India and Pakistan.

Rashmi Singh has completed her graduation in Political Science (Hons) from Galgotias University, Greater Noida. She is currently pursuing Masters in Political Science from IGNOU. Her research interest includes Geopolitics of China, Conflicts in Global Politics, Society and Politics in India

Priya Kumari has completed her graduation in Political Science (Hons.) from Galgotias University, Greater Noida. She is pursuing Masters in Political Science from IGNOU and is preparing for competitive exams. Her research focuses on Border Studies with respect to India and China and the South Asian Geopolitics.

Shahzad has completed his graduation in Political Science (Hons.) from Galgotias University, Greater Noida. He is also pursuing MA in Political Science and His research is focuses on India-Israel relations, Contemporary politics in South Asia, India's Foreign Policy.

Payal Bansal has completed her graduation in Political Science (Hons.) from Galgotias University, Greater Noida. She is also pursuing MA in Political Science and is currently preparing for combined defence service examination. Her research interest focuses on the Geopolitics of Arctic region, Northern Sea Route and Russia's power in Arctic region.

Sarthak Duneja has completed his graduation in Political Science (Hons.) from Galgotias University, Greater Noida and is currently pursuing MA in Political Science. He is currently working as freelancer in content writing and preparing. His research interest primarily focuses on the India-US relations, Gender in Global Politics, India's Foreign Policy, etc.

Volume 2

Manual of Chest X-ray

Modules 3 and 4

Module 3

- LUNG PARENCHYMA II
  Miliary Lesions
  Nodular Lesions
  Mass Lesions
  Calcified Lesions
- PLEURA

Module 4

- RADIOLOGY OF TUBERCULOSIS
- RADIOLOGY OF BRONCHIECTASIS
- RADIOLOGY OF CHRONIC OBSTRUCTIVE PULMONARY DISEASE (COPD)
- RADIOLOGY OF ALLERGIC BRONCHO-PULMONARY ASPERGILLOSIS (ABPA)
- RADIOLOGY OF LUNG CANCER
- RADIOLOGY OF INTERSTITIAL LUNG DISEASE (ILD)
- RADIOLOGY OF SARCOIDOSIS
- RADIOLOGY OF COVID-19
- RADIOLOGY QUIZ

Volume 1

Modules 1 and 2

Module 1

- HOW TO READ NORMAL CHEST X-RAY
- SOFT TISSUE SHADOWS
- BONY CAGE
- DIAPHRAGM

Module 2

- TRACHEA
- HEART
- HILUM
- MEDIASTINUM
- LUNG PARENCHYMA I
  Zones, Lobes and Segments
  Radiopaque Shadows
  Infiltrative Lesions
  Cavity

Volume 2

Manual of Chest X-ray

Rajendra Prasad
MD DTCD FAMS FCCP (USA) FRCP (Glasgow) FRCP (London)
FNCCP FICS FCAI FIAB FIMSA FCCS DSc (Honoris Causa)

Director, Medical Education and
Professor, Department of Pulmonary Medicine
Era's Lucknow Medical College and Hospital
Era University, Lucknow, India

Emeritus Professor
National Academy of Medical Sciences (India)

Former
Director, Vallabhbhai Patel Chest Institute
University of Delhi, New Delhi, India

Professor and Head
Department of Pulmonary Medicine
King George's Medical University
Lucknow, Uttar Pradesh, India

Director, UP Rural Institute of Medical Sciences and Research
Saifai, Etawah, Uttar Pradesh, India

Nikhil Gupta
MBBS MD (Medicine) MAMS FIMSA
DAA, DFID (CMC Vellore)
Associate Professor
Department of General Medicine
Dr. Ram Manohar Lohia Institute
of Medical Sciences
Lucknow, Uttar Pradesh, India

Kiran Vishnu Narayan
MD DNB DM
Associate Professor
Department of
Pulmonary Medicine
Government Medical College
Thiruvananthapuram
Kerala, India

CBSPD

CBS Publishers & Distributors Pvt Ltd

New Delhi • Bengaluru • Chennai • Kochi • Kolkata • Lucknow • Mumbai
Hyderabad • Jharkhand • Nagpur • Patna • Pune • Uttarakhand

Volume 2

Manual of
Chest X-rays

ISBN: 978-93-5466-617-9

First Edition: 2024
Reprint: 2025

Published by Satish Kumar Jain and produced by Varun Jain for

CBS Publishers & Distributors Pvt Ltd
4819/XI Prahlad Street, 24 Ansari Road, Daryaganj, New Delhi 110 002, India
Ph: 011-23289259, 011-23266861, 011-23266867 Fax: 011-23243014 Website: www.cbspd.com
e-mail: delhi@cbspd.com

Corporate Office: 204 FIE, Industrial Area, Patparganj, Delhi 110 092, India
Ph: 011-4934 4934 Fax: 011-4934 4935 e-mail: publishing@cbspd.com; publicity@cbspd.com

Branches

- **Bengaluru:** Seema House 2975, 17th Cross, K.R. Road, Banasankari 2nd Stage, Bengaluru 560 070, Karnataka, India
  Ph: +91-80-26771678/79 Fax: +91-80-26771680 e-mail: bangalore@cbspd.com
- **Chennai:** 7, Subbaraya Street, Shenoy Nagar, Chennai 600 030, Tamil Nadu, India.
  Ph: +91-44-26680620, 26681266 Fax: +91-44-42032115 e-mail: chennai@cbspd.com
- **Kochi:** 42/1325, 1326, Power House Road, Opposite KSEB, Ernakulam, Kochi-682 018, Kerala, India.
  Ph: +91-484-4059061-67 Fax: +91-484-4059065 e-mail: kochi@cbspd.com
- **Kolkata:** 147, Hind Ceramics Compound, 1st Floor, Nilgunj Road, Belghoria, Kolkata-700 056, West Bengal, India
  Ph: 033-25633055/56 e-mail: kolkata@cbspd.com
- **Lucknow:** Basement, Khushnuma Complex, 7-Meerabai Marg (Behind Jawahar Bhawan), Lucknow-226 001, Uttar Pradesh, India.
  Ph: +0522-4000032 e-mail:tiwari.lucknow@cbspd.com
- **Mumbai:** PWD Shed, Gala No. 25/26, Ramchandra Bhatt Marg, Next to JJ Hospital Gate No. 2, Opp Union Bank of India, Noorbaug, Mumbai-400009, Maharashtra, India
  Ph: +91-22-66661880, 66661889 e-mail: mumbai@cbspd.com

Representatives

- **Hyderabad** 0-9885175004
- **Jharkhand** 0-9811541605
- **Nagpur** 0-9421945513
- **Patna** 0-9334159340
- **Pune** 0-9923910676
- **Uttarakhand** 0-9716462459

Printed at HT Media Ltd., Greater Noida, UP, India

to

my teachers for their guidance, wisdom and inspiration

and

my parents, wife and children for their love and patience

Foreword

Chest X-ray is an important diagnostic tool in virtually every discipline of medicine and skill in reading chest X-ray is certainly required by everyone treating the patients. In this context, the *Manual of Chest X-ray* in 4 modules is a timely and useful addition to the existing literature on chest X-ray interpretation. This is a comprehensive manual on chest X-ray in which Dr Rajendra Prasad has presented reading of normal chest X-ray and various lesions in soft tissues, bony cage, diaphragm, hilum, mediastinum, heart and different types of radiological lesions in lung parenchyma and pleura. There is a large number of chest X-ray images, which make its reading extremely interesting.

Prof Rajendra Prasad is a nationally acclaimed chest physician and tuberculosis expert, possessing more than four decades of illustrious teaching, research and administrative experience with proven excellence in teaching, research and administrative activity. He is also a very popular medical teacher. He is currently Director, Medical Education and Professor, Department of Pulmonary Medicine, Era's Lucknow Medical College and Hospital, Era University, Lucknow, Uttar Pradesh. He has earlier served as Director, Vallabhbhai Patel Chest Institute, University of Delhi, New Delhi, Professor and Head, Department of Pulmonary Medicine, King George's Medical University, Lucknow and Director, UP Rural Institute of Medical Sciences and Research, Saifai, Etawah, Uttar Pradesh. He has devoted all his energy in promoting medical education, patient care and research. His contribution in teaching of pulmonary medicine, tuberculosis and chest X-rays is widely acclaimed. He is the recipient of a large number of awards from various international and national scientific societies including prestigious Dr BC Roy National Award for his dynamic leadership in academic, patient care and administrative areas.

This comprehensive manual in print as well as in electronic versions in 4 modules contains plethora of knowledge and would be a valuable source for undergraduate and postgraduate medical students, radiologist, physicians, surgeons involved in interpretation of chest X-rays in day-to-day clinical practice. I am quite hopeful that this manual will be used by everyone who wishes to strengthen chest X-ray interpretation. This manual deserves a place in the library of every clinician, medical colleges and healthcare institutions.

D Behera
Former Professor and Head
Department of Pulmonary Medicine
Postgraduate Institute of Medical Education
and Research, Chandigarh

Foreword

The chest radiograph remains the cornerstone of thoracic imaging and radiology. Despite the advent of newer modalities and artificial intelligence (AI), the Covid-19 outbreak has taught us that simple, inexpensive tools like the chest radiograph can still make a difference to the diagnosis and management of diseases in patients. Interpreting chest radiograph well has always been an art. It needs both experience and expertise and I sometimes believe that reading a CT scan is perhaps a shade simpler. I have learnt to be better at chest radiographs after seeing the pathology on cross-sectional imaging and then going back to the radiographs to understand the patterns more clearly.

While a chest radiograph, normal or abnormal, does not obviate the need to do a CT scan or ultrasound depending on the symptoms and signs, it helps directly the next mode of diagnosis and serves as a quick, cheap modality for follow-up. Dr Rajendra Prasad's *Manual of Chest X-ray* in 4 modules is a timely addition, given the "hyposkillia" that pervades radiologists and non-radiologists alike worldwide. Between now and a time when AI will take over most of chest X-ray evaluation, Dr Prasad's manual serves as an excellent guide for younger doctors to learn and understand how to interpret chest X-rays and a quick refresher for more senior doctors.

I am honored to be writing the *Foreword* to this manual written by Dr Prasad, who is a nationally acclaimed chest physician and tuberculosis expert, possessing more than four decades of illustrious teaching, research and administrative experience. He is also a very popular medical teacher and has taught chest X-ray interpretation to undergraduate and postgraduate students for more than four decades. It is this teaching that he has now distilled into this project. He is currently Director, Medical Education and Professor, Department of Pulmonary Medicine, Era's Lucknow Medical College and Hospital, Era University, Lucknow, Uttar Pradesh. I congratulate him for seeing this manual through to fruition and I am sure that many doctors will benefit from his experience and expertise.

Bhavin Jankharia MD
Partner and Consultant
Picture This: Imaging and Beyond
Mumbai

Foreword

Chest X-ray is still the backbone of the thoracic radiology despite the advent of newer and more exciting imaging techniques. In contrast to many of newer methods, conventional chest X-ray is interpreted not only by radiologists but also by a large number of physicians and surgeons. With each examination, one is confronted with radiological findings that require interpretation in order to arrive at a radiological diagnosis and differential diagnosis. Therefore, skill in interpreting the chest X-ray will certainly be required by everyone treating the patients. In this context, *Manual of Chest X-ray* in 4 modules is a timely and useful addition in the existing literature on chest X-ray interpretation. This is a comprehensive manual on chest X-ray in which Dr Rajendra Prasad has presented reading of normal chest X-ray and various lesions in soft tissues, bony cage, diaphragm, hilum, mediastinum, heart and different types of radiological lesions in lung parenchyma and pleura.

Prof Rajendra Prasad is a nationally acclaimed chest physician and tuberculosis expert, possessing more than four decades of illustrious teaching, research and administrative experience. He is also a very popular medical teacher in pulmonary medicine, and also extremely popular in teaching chest X-rays to undergraduate and postgraduate students for more than four decades. He is currently Director, Medical Education and Professor, Department of Pulmonary Medicine, Era's Lucknow Medical College and Hospital, Era University, Lucknow, Uttar Pradesh. He has earlier served as Director, Vallabhbhai Patel Chest Institute, New Delhi, Professor and Head, Department of Pulmonary Medicine, King George's Medical University, Lucknow and Director, UP Rural Institute of Medical Sciences and Research, Saifai, Etawah, Uttar Pradesh.

This comprehensive manual in print as well as in electronic versions in 4 modules contains plethora of knowledge and would be a valuable source for undergraduate and post-graduate medical students, radiologists, physicians, surgeons involved in interpretation of chest X-rays in day-to-day clinical practice. I am quite hopeful that this manual will be used by everyone who wishes to strengthen chest X-ray interpretation.

Neera Kohli
Professor and Head
Department of Radiology
King George's Medical University, Lucknow

Foreword

Despite the advent of newer and more exciting imaging techniques such as computed tomography (MDCT and HRCT), magnetic resonance imaging (MRI) and positron emission tomography (PET), chest X-ray is stll the backbone of the thoracic radiology. Conventional chest X-ray is interpreted not only by radiologists but also by a large number of physicians and surgeons. Therefore, skill in interpreting the chest X-ray will certainly be required by everyone treating the patients. In this context, the *Manual of Chest X-ray* in 4 modules is a timely and useful addition in the existing literature on chest X-ray interpretation. This is a comprehensive manual on chest X-ray in which Dr Rajendra Prasad has presented reading of normal chest X-ray and various lesions in soft tissues, bony cage, diaphragm, hilum, mediastinum, heart, lung parenchyma and pleura. There are a large number of chest X-ray images, which make its reading extremely interesting.

Prof Rajendra Prasad is a nationally acclaimed chest physician and tuberculosis expert, possessing more than four decades of illustrious teaching, research and administrative experience. He is also a very popular medical teacher in pulmonary medicine, and also extremely popular in teaching chest X-rays to undergraduate and postgraduate students for more than four decades. He is currently Director, Medical Education and Professor, Department of Pulmonary Medicine, Era's Lucknow Medical College and Hospital, Era University, Lucknow, Uttar Pradesh. He has earlier served as Director, Vallabhbhai Patel Chest Institute, New Delhi, Professor and Head, Department of Pulmonary Medicine, King George's Medical University, Lucknow and Director, UP Rural Institute of Medical Sciences and Research, Saifal, Etawah, Uttar Pradesh. He is the recipient of a large number of awards including prestigious Dr BC Roy National Award for his dynamic leadership in academic, patient care and administrative areas.

This comprehensive manual in print as well as in electronic versions in 4 modules contains plethora of knowledge and would be a valuable source for undergraduate and postgraduate medical students, radiologists, physicians, surgeons involved in interpretation of chest X-rays in day-to-day clinical practice. I am quite hopeful that this manual will be useful to everyone who wishes to strengthen chest X-ray interpretation. This manual deserves a place in the library of every clinician, medical colleges and healthcare institutions.

Sachin Khanduri
Professor and Head
Department of Radio-diagnosis
Era's Lucknow Medical College and Hospital
Era University, Lucknow

Preface

Traditional chest X-ray remains the most commonly obtained chest-imaging tool since its discovery by Wilhelm Röntgen in 1895 and it is commonly used in virtually every discipline of medicine. Chest X-ray is still the backbone of the thoracic radiology despite the advent of newer and more exciting imaging techniques such as computed tomography (CT), magnetic resonance imaging (MRI) and more recently positron emission tomography (PET). In contrast to many of these newer methods, conventional chest X-ray is interpreted not only by radiologists but also by a large number of physicians and surgeons. With each examination, one is confronted with radiological findings that require interpretation in order to arrive at a general diagnostic impression and a reasonable differential diagnosis. Therefore, skill in interpreting the chest X-ray will certainly be required by everyone treating the patients. To assist the treating clinicians and radiologists for correct interpretation of chest X-rays, this manual is based upon various radiographic findings unlike most other books in radiology that are disease-oriented.

As a senior author of this manual, I have been involved in teaching chest X-rays to undergraduate as well as postgraduate students and treating patients for more than four decades and have come across many interesting chest X-rays while treating them which I have tried to share in this manual. Volumes 1 and 2 of this manual comprise four modules and are available in print as well as in electronic versions. Module one comprises reading normal chest X-rays, lesions of soft tissues, bony cage and diaphragm. Module two comprises lesions of trachea, heart, hilum, mediastinum, infiltrations and cavity. Module three comprises miliary, nodular, mass, calcified and various pleural lesions. Module four comprises various chest X-ray findings of tuberculosis, bronchiectasis, COPD, allergic bronchopulmonary aspergillosis (ABPA), lung cancer, interstitial lung diseases (ILD), sarcoidosis and covid-19.

I hope that this manual will be useful to all medical students, residents, radiologists, physicians and surgeons involved in the interpretation of chest X-rays in day-to-day clinical practice.

Rajendra Prasad

Acknowledgements

As a senior author of this manual, I wish to acknowledge my indebtedness to a number of people who have significantly contributed to the publication of this manual. The individual whom I would like to acknowledge first is Late Prof BK Khanna who was the Head, Department of Tuberculosis, King George's Medical College, Lucknow, Uttar Pradesh. While I was a postgraduate student in that department, markedly stimulated my interest in chest X-ray and other chest diseases. His own tremendous knowledge and wisdom in reading chest X-ray, set an example of thoughtfulness and meticulousness which I have always tried to emulate.

I am also indebted to Late Prof PK Mukherjee, Late Dr MS Agnihotri, Late Dr Jafar Jameel and Late Dr J Nath, for their great inspiration as teachers during my postgraduate days. I am greatly indebted to many postgraduate students who have been trained under me in the department at King George's Medical College, Lucknow; Vallabhbhai Patel Chest Institute, New Delhi, and Era's Lucknow Medical College and Hospital, Lucknow, especially Dr Suryakant, Dr RAS Kushwaha, Dr Rajiv Garg, Dr Sanjay Verma, Dr Suneesh C Anand, Dr Ved Prakash, Dr Darshan Bajaj, Dr Giridhar BH, Dr Abhijeet, Dr Abhishek Agrawal, Dr Saurabh Karmakar, Dr Rachit Sharma, Dr Mandeep Singh, Dr Pawan Gupta, Dr Visweswaran Balasubramanian, Dr Faizan Ahmad, Dr Amitabh Banka, Dr Sakshi Batra, Dr Ronal Naorem, and Dr Asna Khan, Dr Harsh Saxena, Dr Rishabh Kacker, Dr Huda Shamim, Dr Syed Ahmed Hussain Kazmi, Dr Mohammad Tanzeem, Dr Tanmay Bhargava, Dr Ravikant Pandey, Dr Prashant Mishra, Dr Harshita Rani, Dr Apoorva Singh, Dr Dhruv Raj Singh, Dr Jay Manchanda, Dr Anshita Chabra and Dr Deepak Maheshwari. The effort of these postgraduate students in part is responsible for generating much of the data that has been incorporated in making the chapters in manual more evidence-based.

I also wish to express my appreciation to Dr Nikhil Gupta and Dr Kiran Vishnu Narayan, co-authors of this manual, for helping me in preparing and correcting the manuscript. I also wish to express my thanks to Mr PP Sharma, Mr Ashish Yadav, Miss Seema Shukla, Mr Gyan Prakash and Mr Mithun, for their invaluable help in the preparation and typing of the manuscript. I am also thankful to all my patients who gave me experience in the field of pulmonary medicine during their treatment.

I am very grateful to the whole team of Help U Educational and Charitable Trust and Chest Care and Research Society, Lucknow, for all their support to work in this manual and make it a success. Without their co-operation, I could not have completed this manual.

I am extremely thankful to Mr SK Jain, CMD, Mr Varun Jain, Director, Mr YN Arjuna, Senior Vice-President—Publishing, Editorial and Publicity and other supporting staff of CBS Publishers and Distributors for their help and guidance in completing this manual.

Rajendra Prasad

Contents

PLATE I

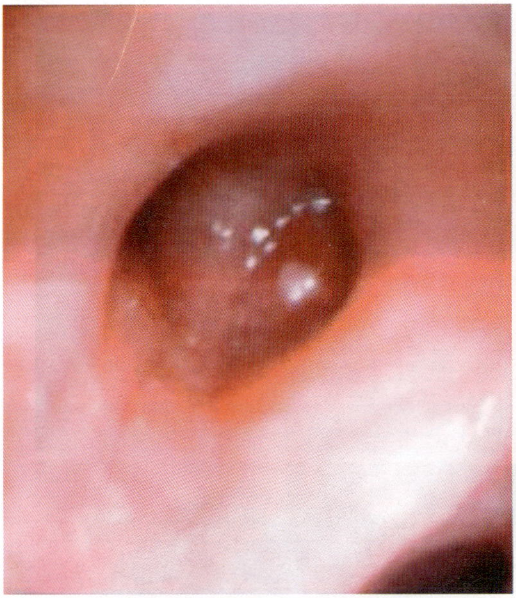

Fiberoptic bronchoscopy shows endobronchial growth

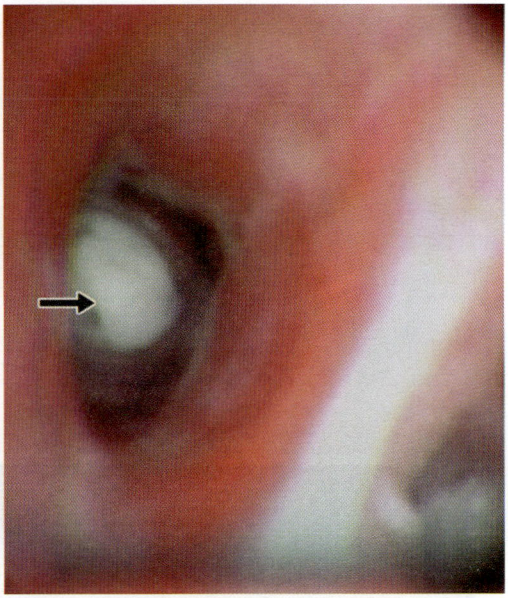

Fiberoptic bronchoscopy showed whitish material in right lower lobe bronchus

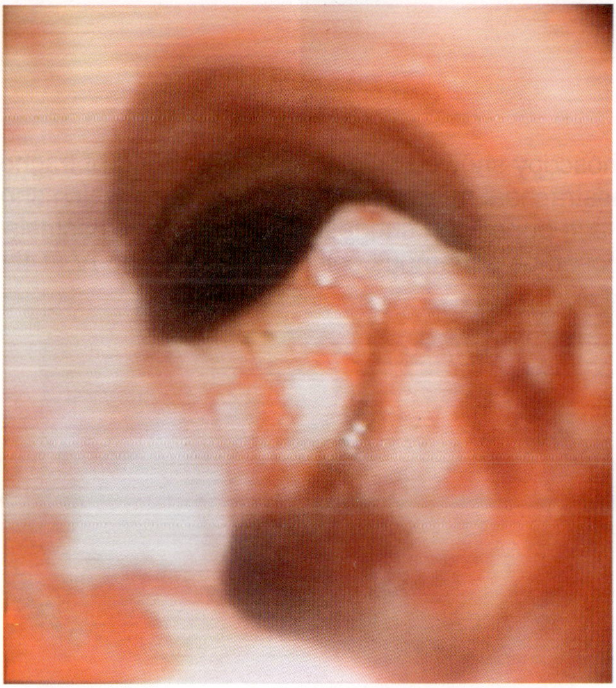

Bronchoscopy shows mass in oesophagus protruding in trachea

PLATE II

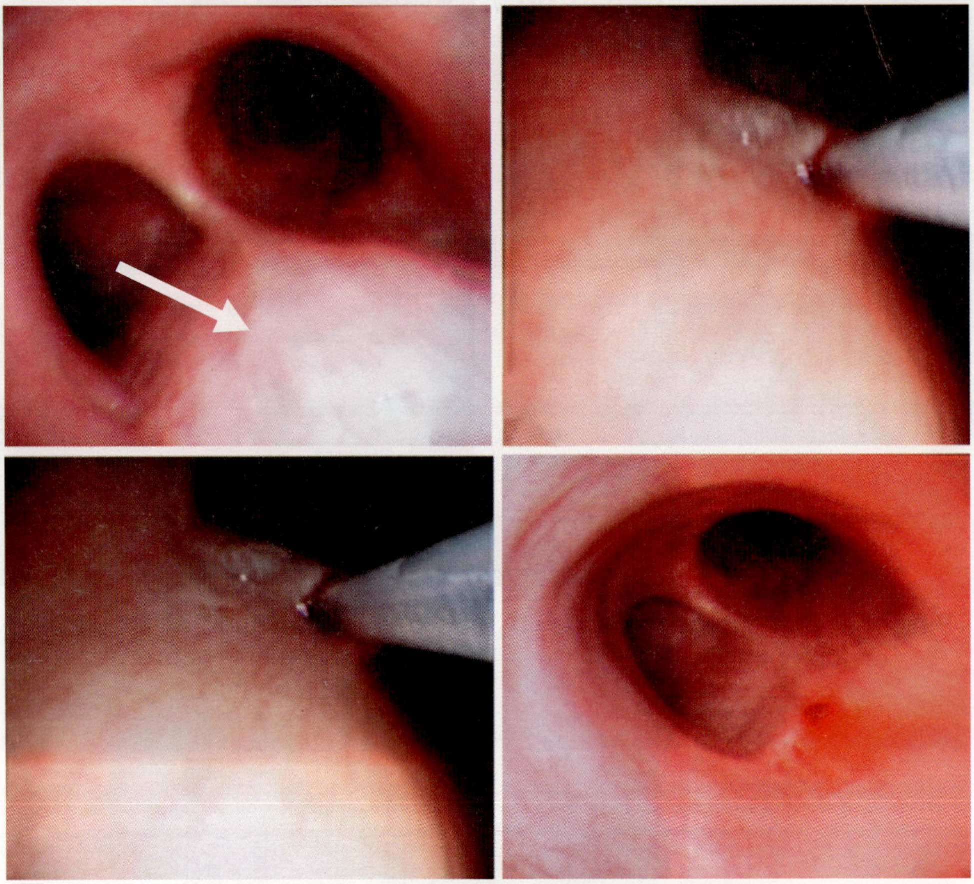

Fiberoptic bronchoscopy showed bulging near lower end of trachea just before the main carina, transtracheal needle aspiration was done which showed squamous cell carcinoma and bone scan suggestive of skeletal metastasis in sacrum and patient was diagnosed as squamous cell carcinoma stage IV (T4N2M1) with COPD

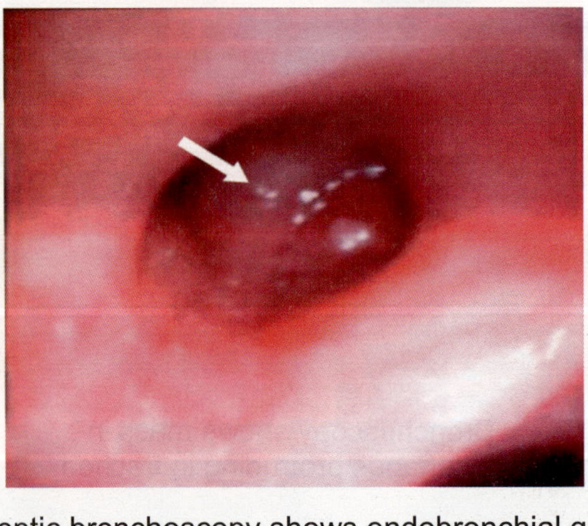

Fiberoptic bronchoscopy shows endobronchial growth

PLATE III

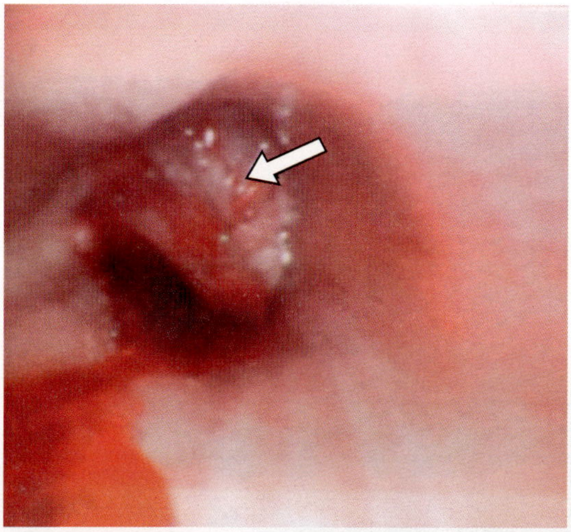

Bronchoscopy shows endobronchial growth

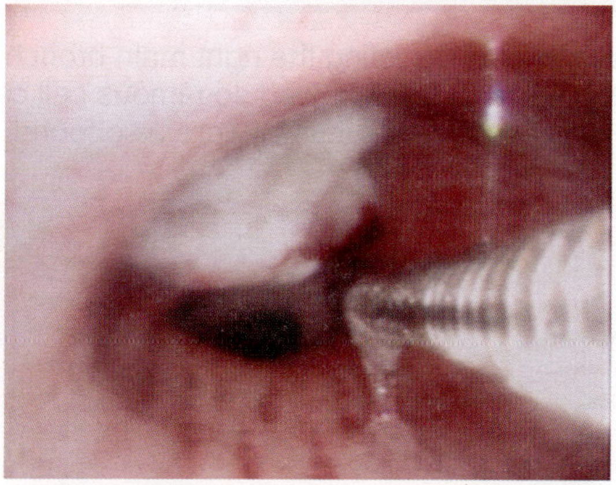

Bronchoscopy shows mass covered with necrotic slough

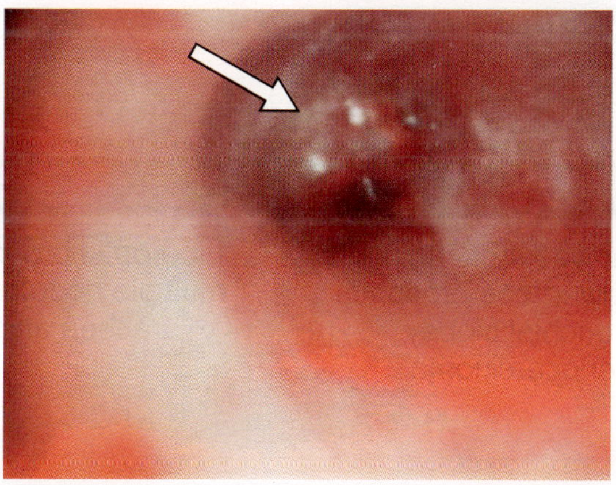

Bronchosopy showed endobronchial growth and endobronchial biopsy showed squamous cell carcinoma with secondaries in brain (stage 4)

PLATE IV

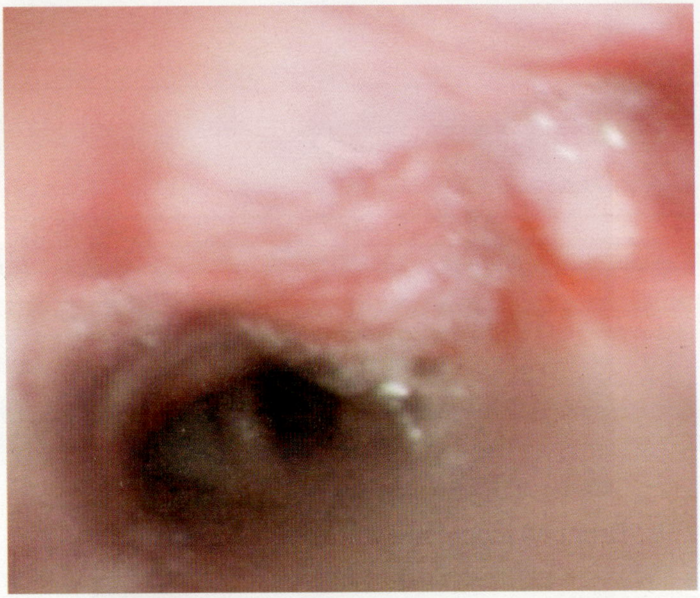

Bronchoscopy shows tumor obstructing the right main bronchus with involvement of carina and endobronchial biopsy showed squamous cell carcinoma (stage IV) and secondaries in liver were also found

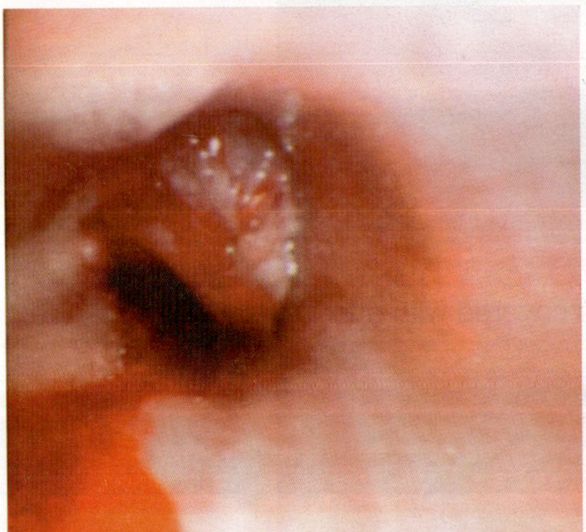

Bronchoscopy shows fungating mass obstructing left lower lobe bronchus and endobronchial biopsy showed adenocarcinoma

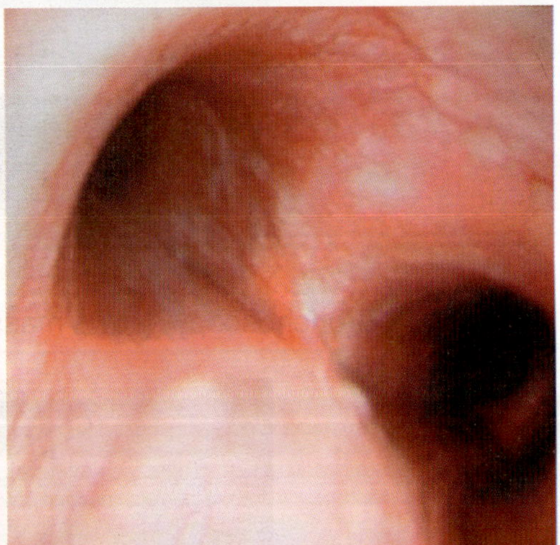

Fiberoptic bronchoscopy shows multiple nodules at lower end of trachea and main carina

Module 3

- **LUNG PARENCHYMA II**
  Miliary Lesions
  Nodular Lesions
  Mass Lesions
  Calcified Lesions
- **PLEURA**

CHAPTER

10

Lung Parenchyma II

Miliary Lesions

Very small from pinpoint to 5 mm size infiltrations which are distributed in both lungs symmetrically and uniformly

Miliary Lesions—*What are Causes?*

- Infection
  - Bacterial: Tubercular, bronchopneumonia, staphylococcal pneumonia
  - Viral: CMV, mycoplasma, varicella
  - Fungal: Coccidiomycosis, histoplasmosis, blastomycosis
  - Parasitic: Malaria, kala-azar, tropical pulmonary eosinophilia
- Pneumoconiosis
  - Anthracosis, silicosis
- Collagen disease
  - Scleroderma, rheumatoid arthritis, systemic lupus erythematosus
- Cardiac
  - Mitral stenosis, pulmonary embolism
- Neoplasm
  - Primary: Alveolar cell carcinoma, lymphoma, leukemia
  - Secondary: Renal carcinoma, thyroid carcinoma
- Others
  - Alveolar microlithiasis, idiopathic haemosiderosis, sarcoidosis

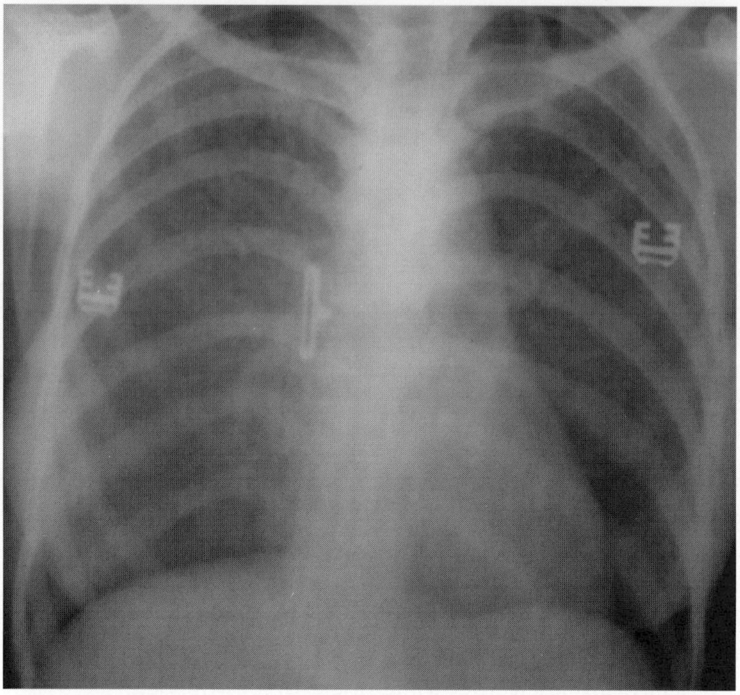

What is this?
See chest X-ray carefully. Patient presented with fever and weakness

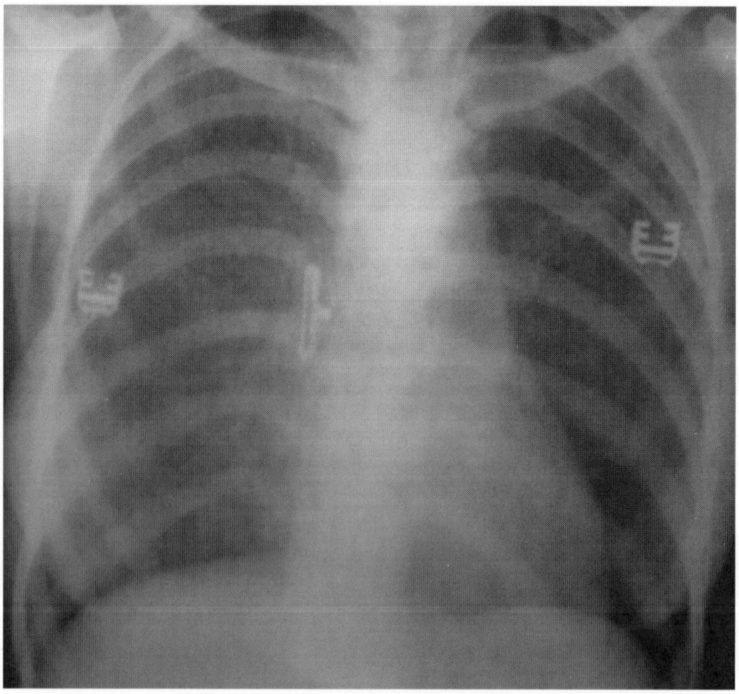

Miliary shadows cause miliary TB

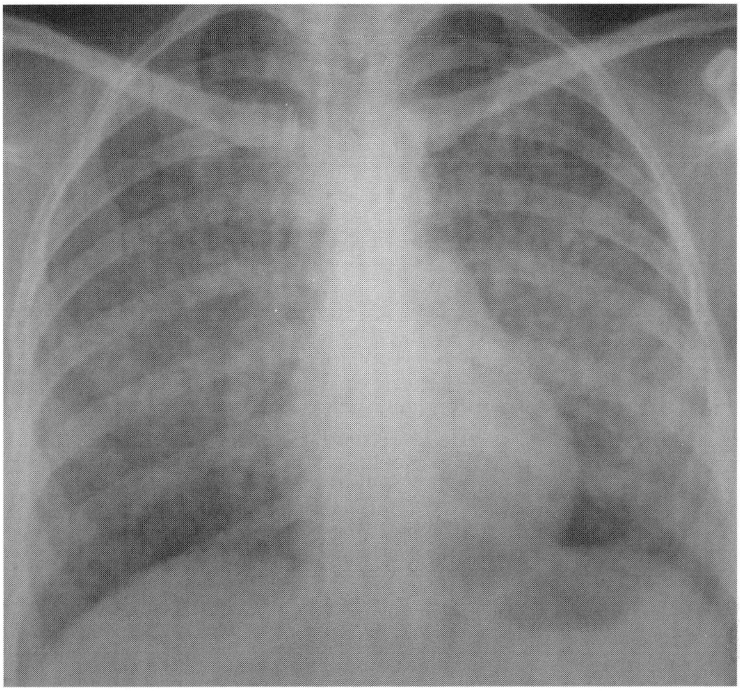

What is this?
See chest X-ray carefully. Patient presented with fever and cough

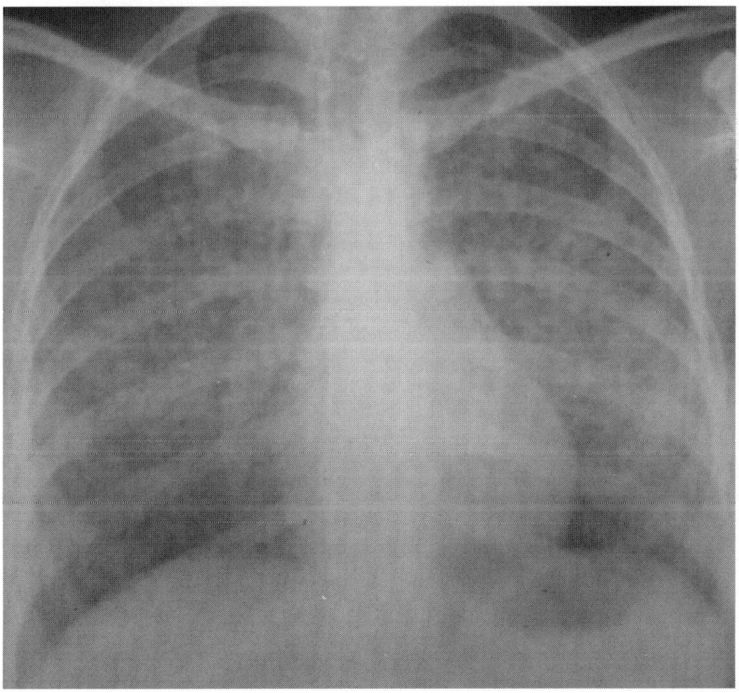

Miliary shadows cause miliary TB

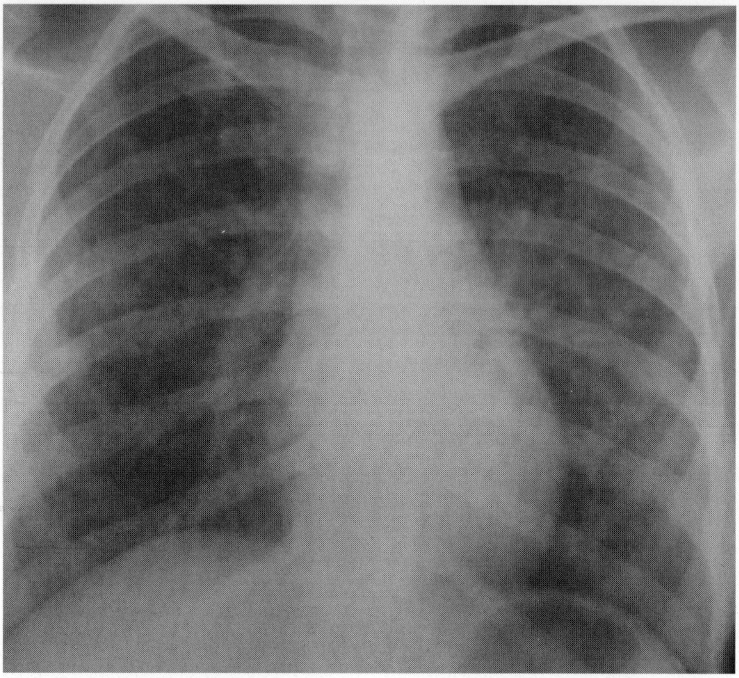

Miliary shadows resolving 2 months after antitubercular treatment

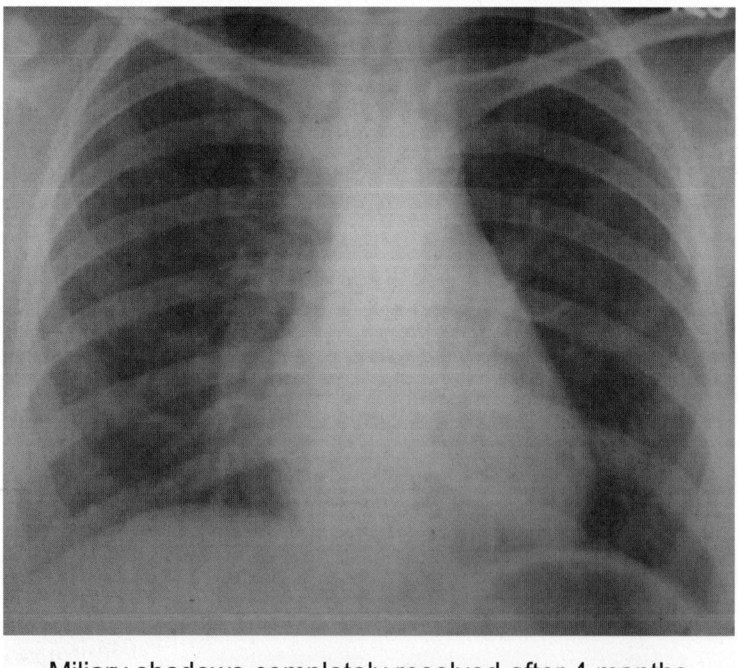

Miliary shadows completely resolved after 4 months of antitubercular treatment

Please note that antituberculosis treatment should be completed

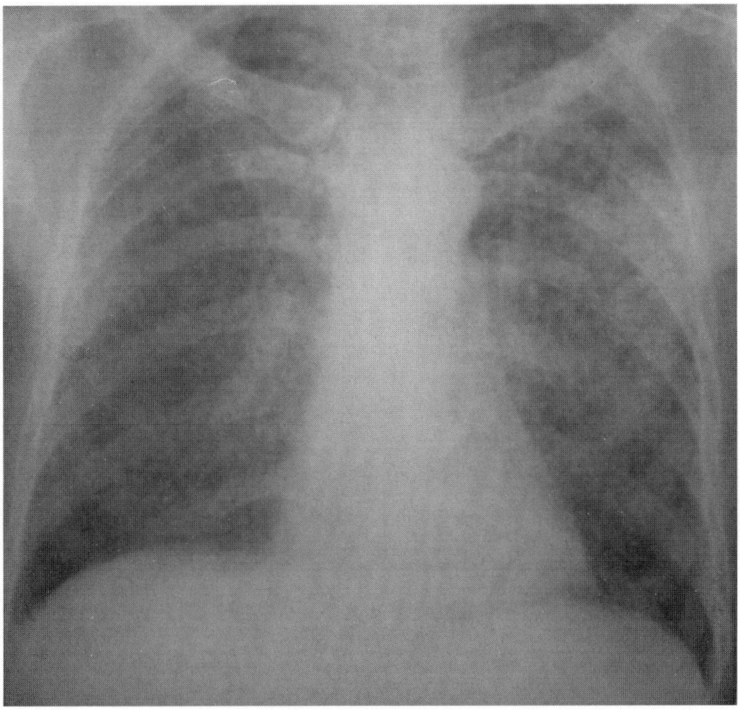

What is this?
A 40-year-old male C/O fever

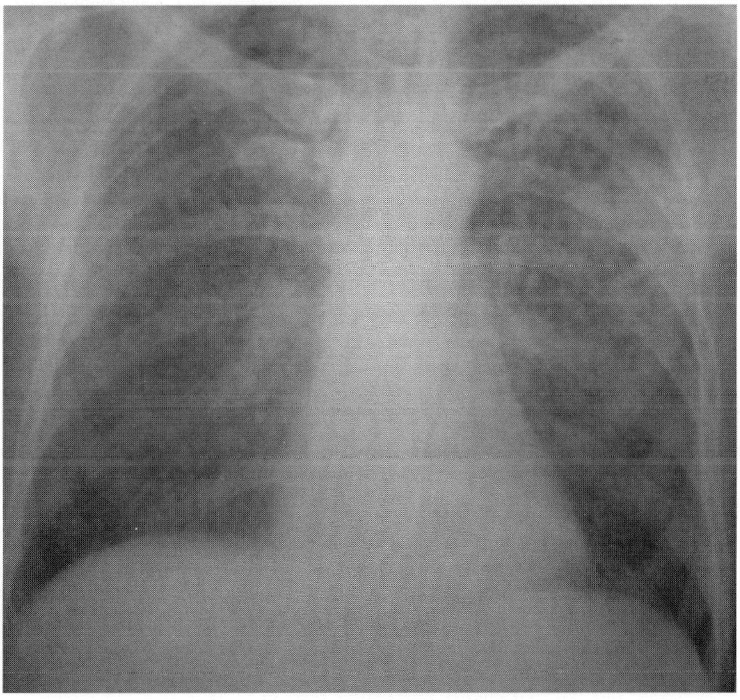

Miliary shadows cause miliary TB

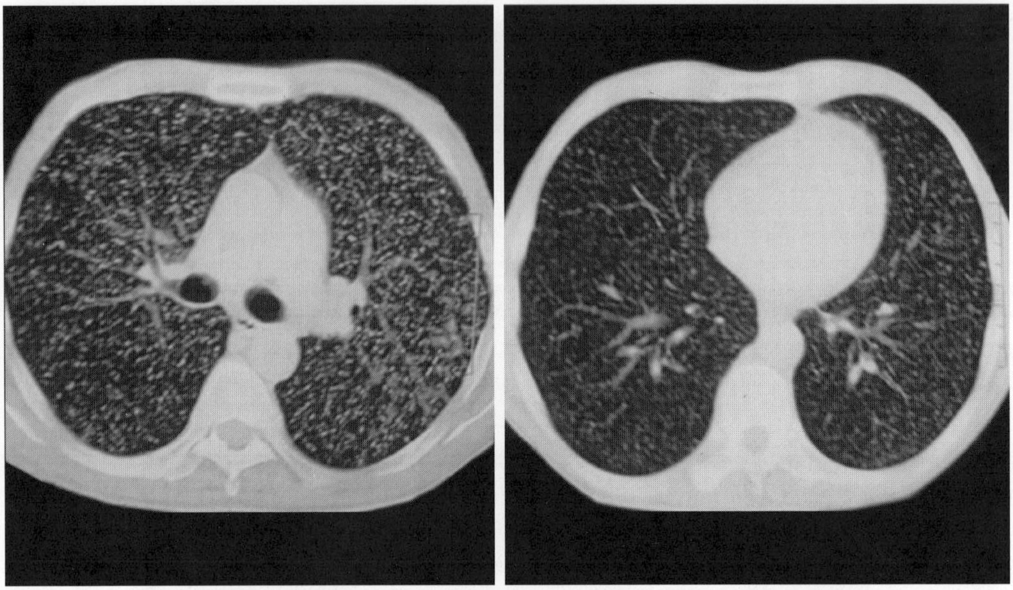

Miliary shadows (miliary TB)

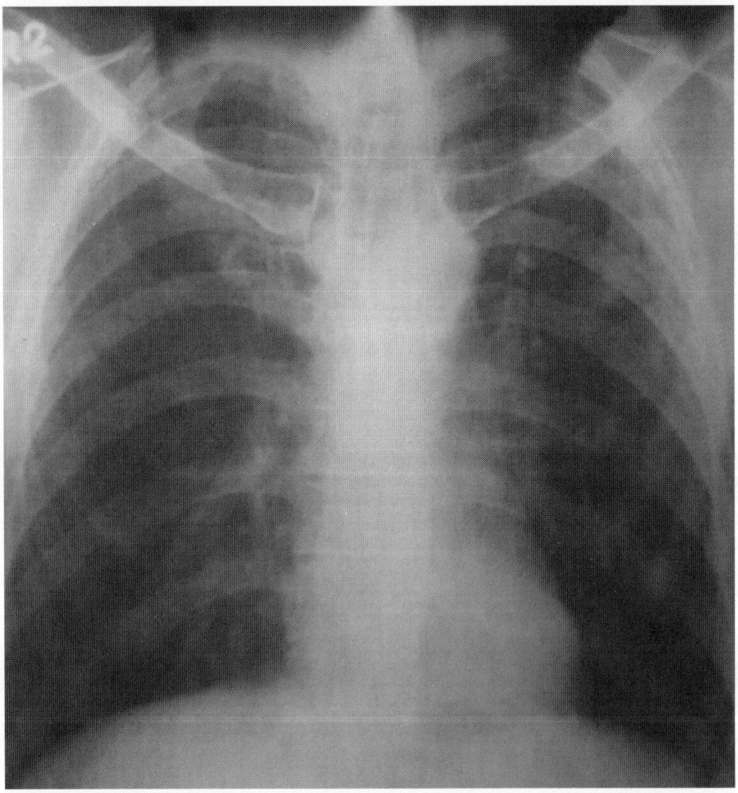

Miliary shadows completely resolved after 4 months of antitubercular treatment

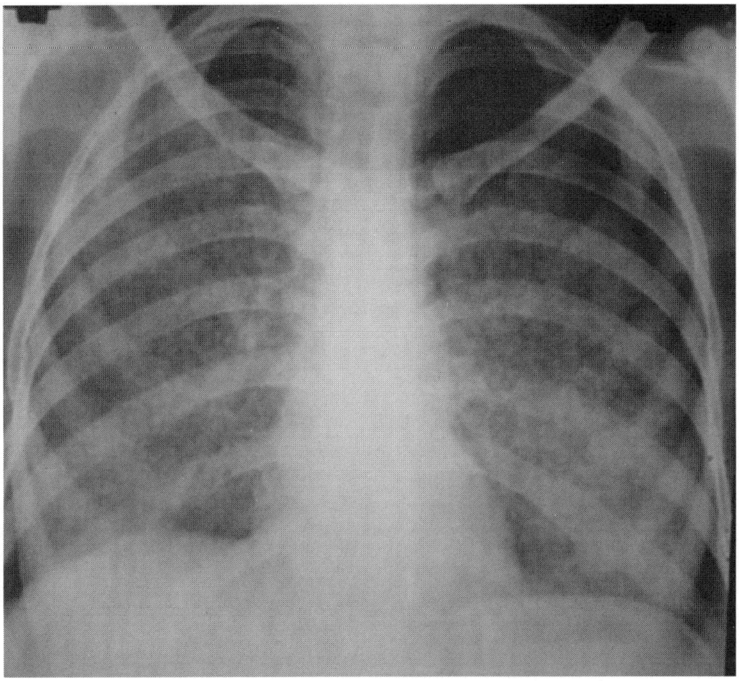

What is this?

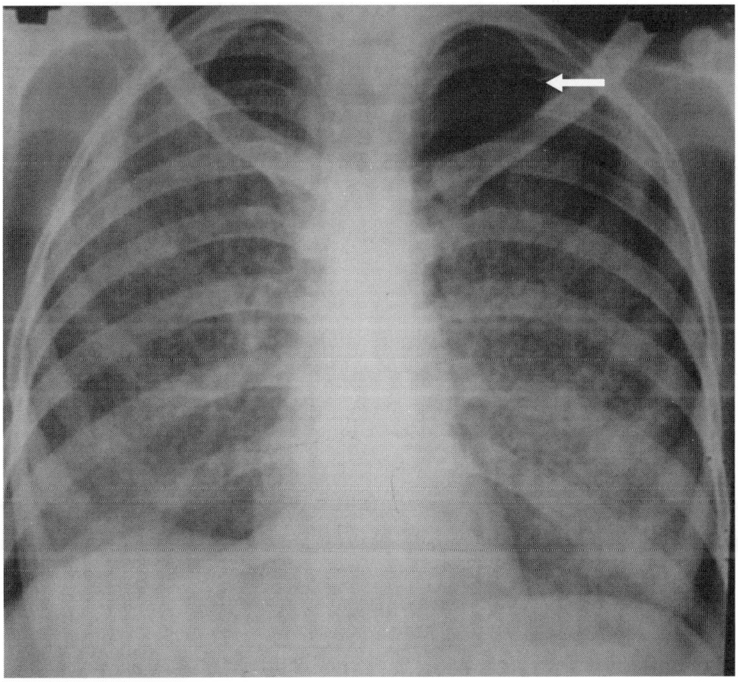

Miliary TB with pneumothorax (left side)

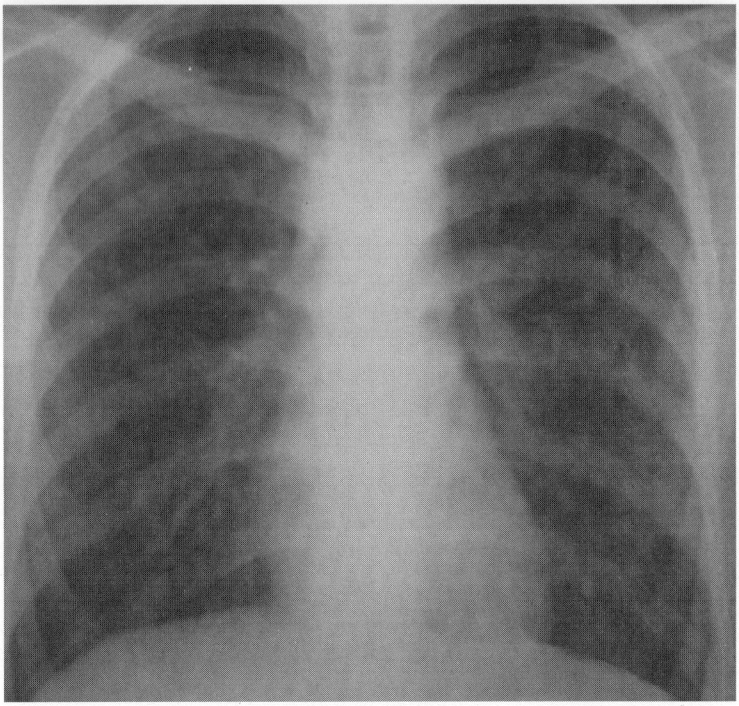

What is this?
C/O cough and high fever for 7 days

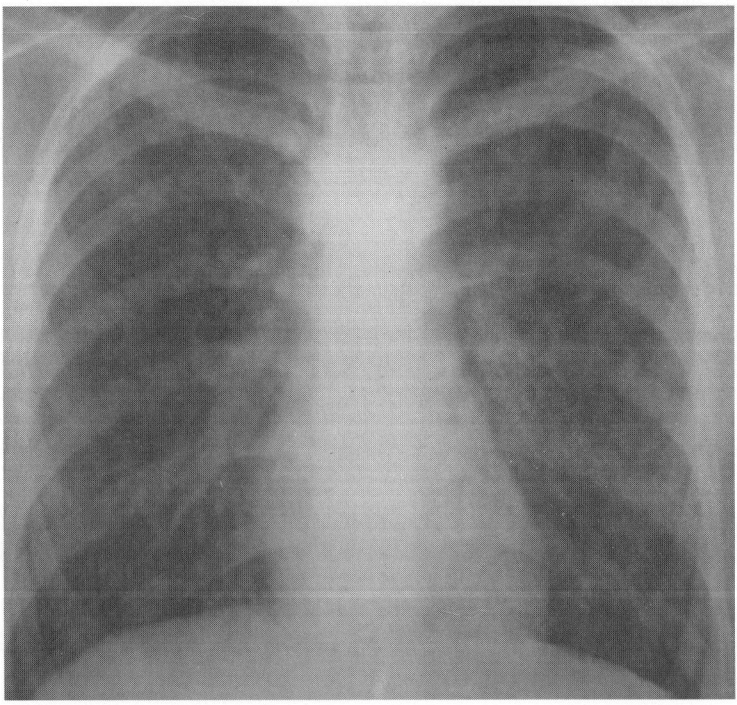

Bronchopneumonia

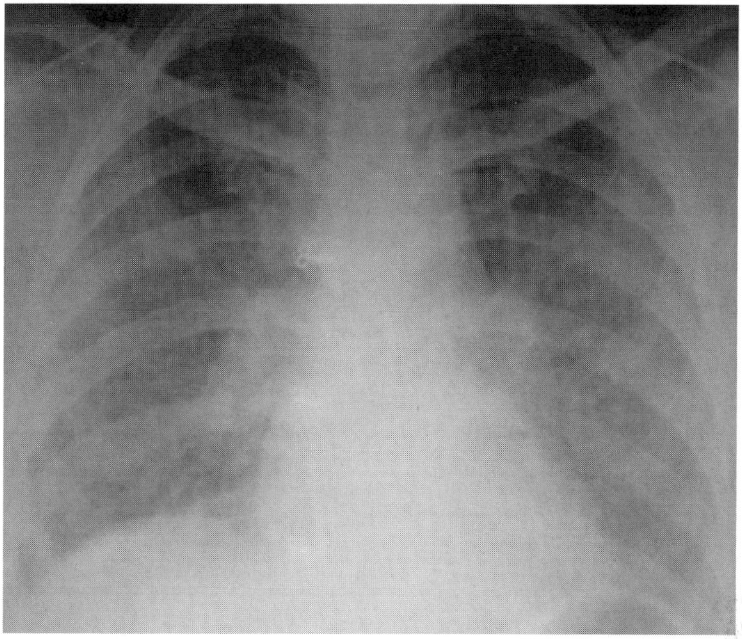

What is this?
A 30-year-old female C/O cough and breathlessness

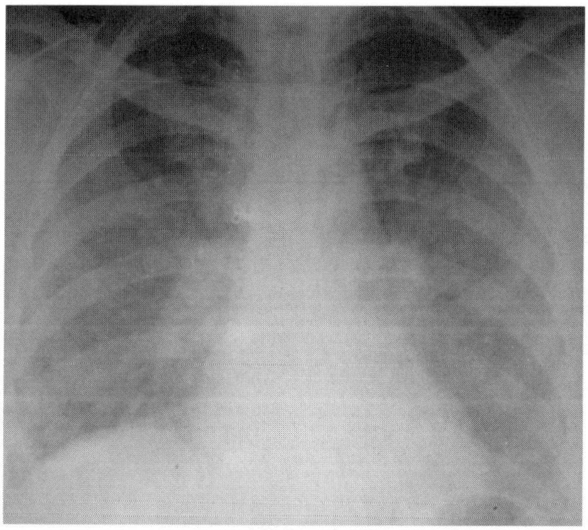

TLC = 13,900, DLC = P30 L22 E48
Absolute eosinophil count = 6672 cells/mm^3

Tropical pulmonary eosinophilia

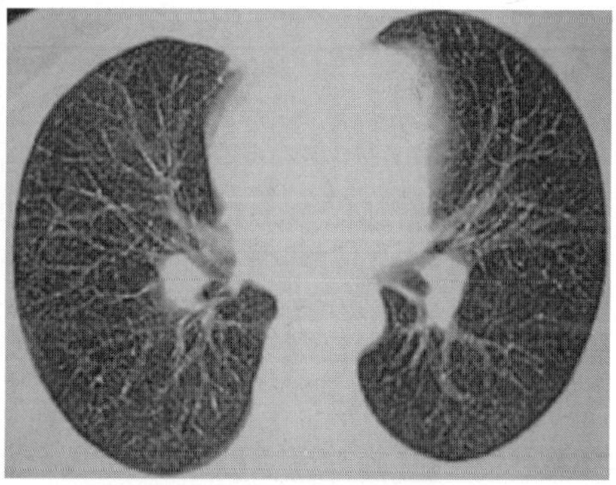

Miliary shadows cause tropical pulmonary eosinophilia

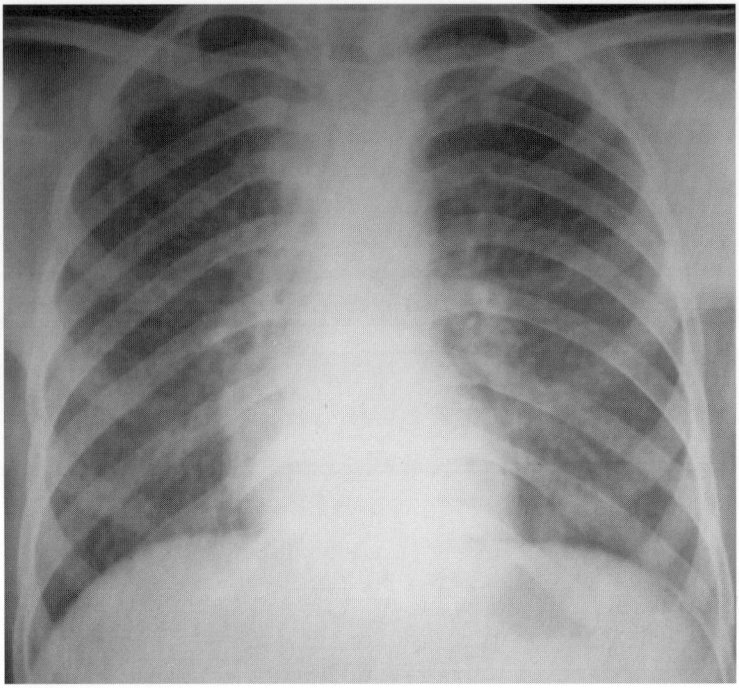

What is this?

A 30-year-old male C/O dry cough, breathlessness, fever for 15 days, PPD:14 mm

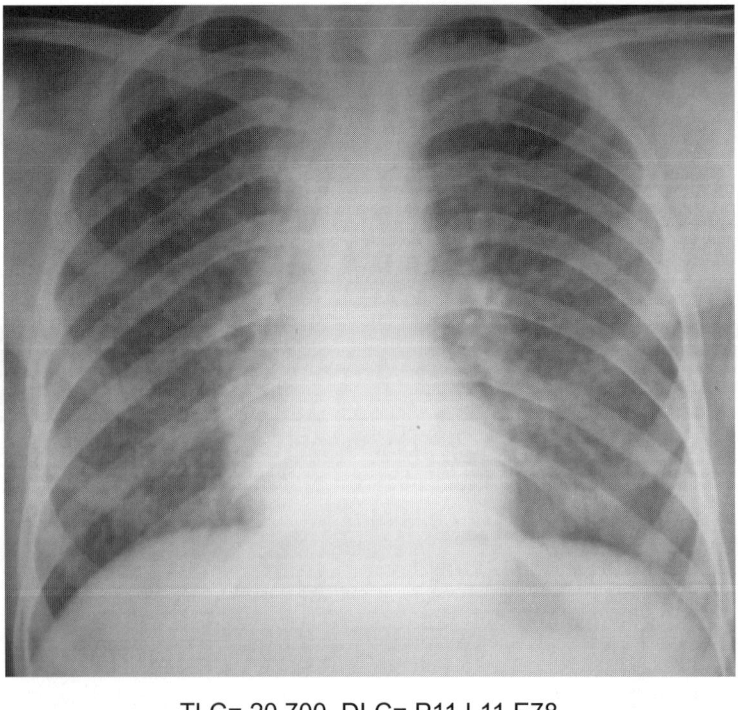

TLC= 20,700, DLC= P11 L11 E78

Miliary shadows cause tropical pulmonary eosinophilia

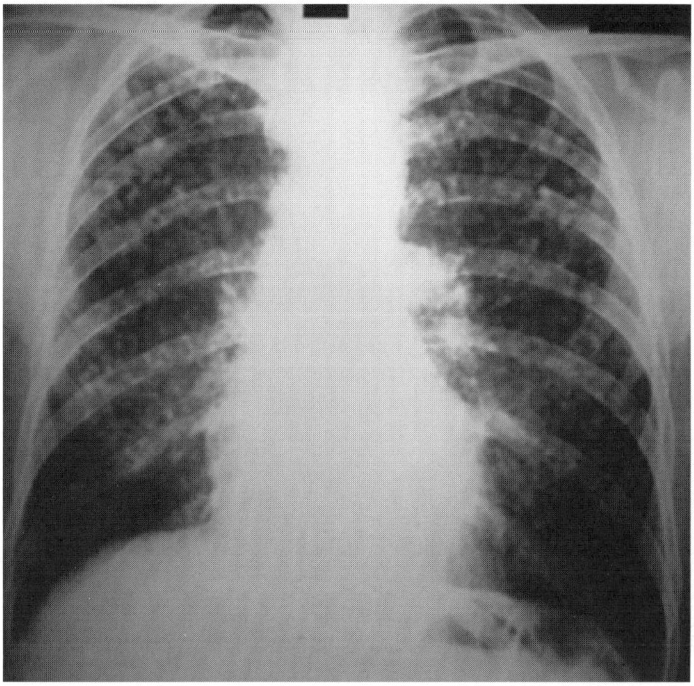

What is this?

C/O breathlessness for 5 years

H/O exposure in coal mine for 20 years

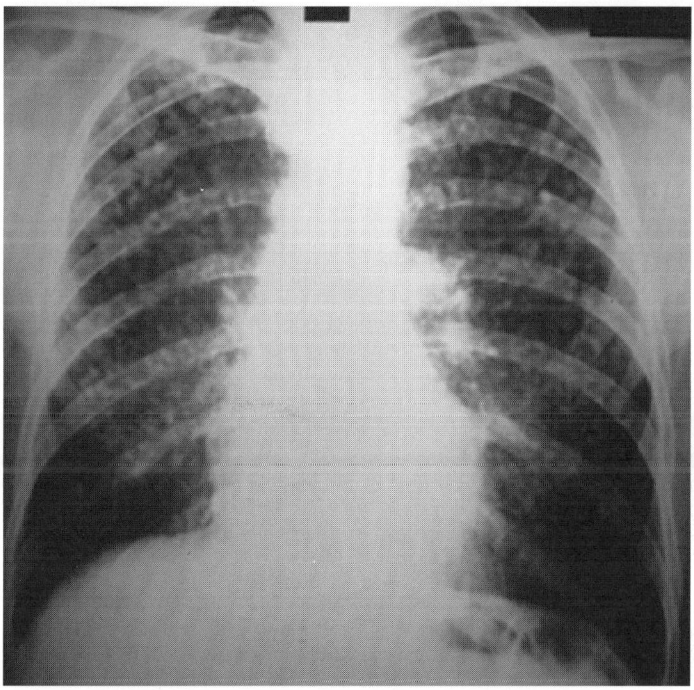

Pneumoconiosis (coal workers lung)

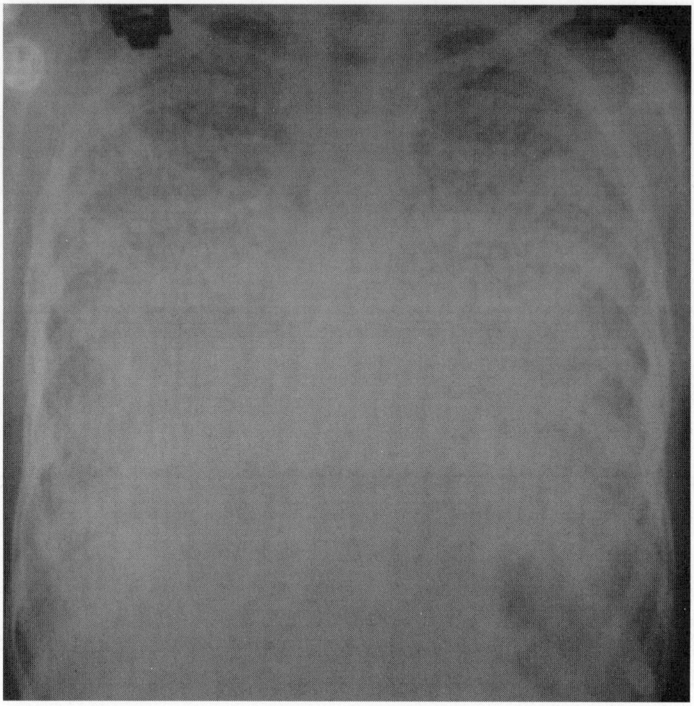

What is this?
An 18-year-old male with no complaints

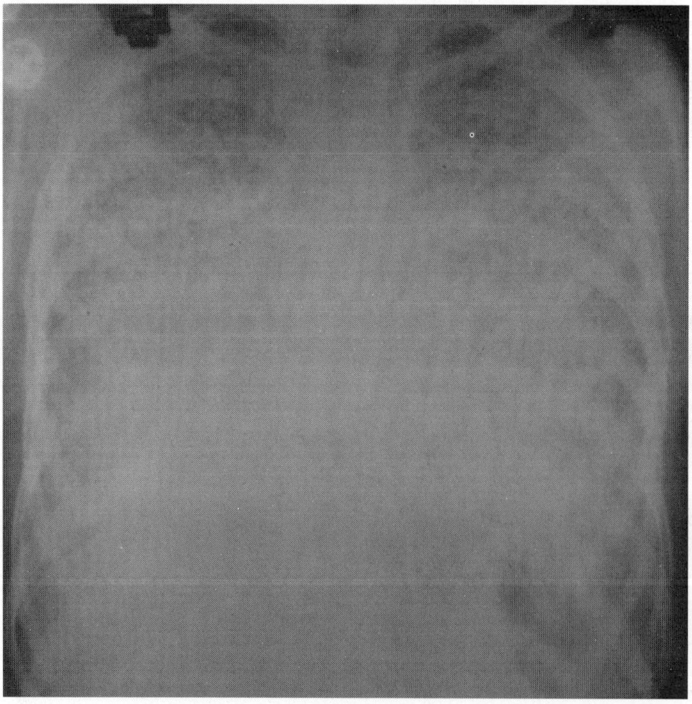

Pulmonary alveolar microlithiasis

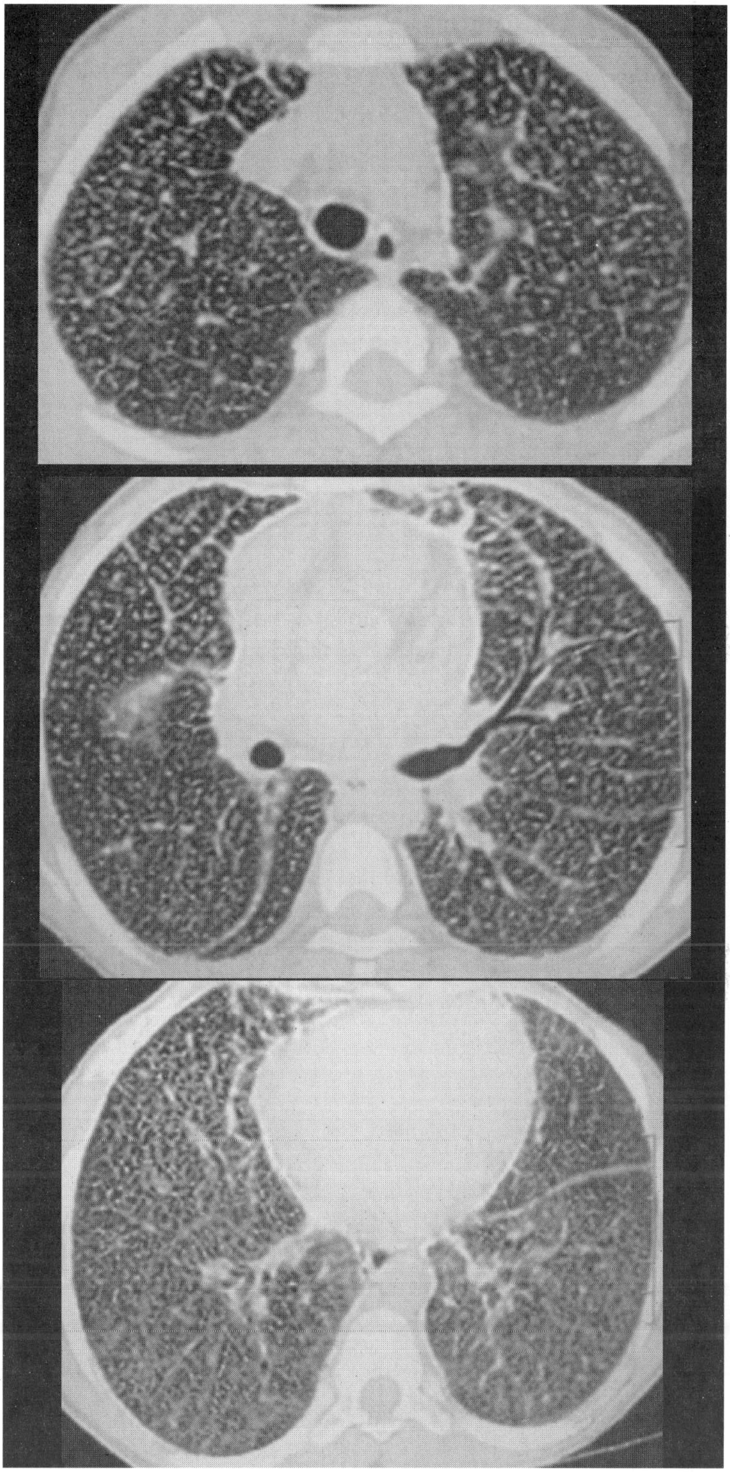

Pulmonary alveolar microlithiasis

Please note that HRCT shows typical numerous sand-like calcification throughout the lung with subpleural and peribronchial distribution

Pulmonary Alveolar Microlithiasis

Pulmonary alveolar microlithiasis (PAM) is a rare idiopathic condition characterized by widespread intra-alveolar deposition of spherical calcium phosphate microliths (calcospherites)

It is usually asymptomatic often discovered incidentally on a chest radiograph which shows sand-like calcification distributed throughout the lungs with black pleura sign

HRCT better shows numerous sand-like calcifications throughout the lungs with subpleural and peribronchial distribution (typically ~1 mm). Additional accompanying HRCT features include:

- Crazy paving pattern
- Calcified interlobular septa (virtually pathognomonic)
- Small subpleural cysts/emphysema
- Black pleura sign
- Ground glass opacities: Tends to be more common in children

Usually requires no treatment but may progress and may require lung transplantation

Nodular Lesions

Nodule: Is a rounded or irregular opacity, which may be well or poorly defined, measuring ≤3 cm in diameter, surrounded by aerated lung on radiological imaging

Nodular Lesions—*What are Causes?*

- Neoplasm
  - Benign: Bronchial adenoma, fibroma, leiomyoma, lipoma
  - Malignant
    - Primary—bronchogenic carcinoma
    - Secondary—lymphoma, sarcoma, mesothelioma
- Granuloma: Tuberculosis, histoplasmosis, coccidioidomycosis, brucella, echinococcus
- Hamartoma
- Simulated pulmonary nodule: Skin tumor, nipple shadow, rib lesion, foreign body, artifact
- Others: Abscess, bulla, hematoma, infarct, loculated effusion

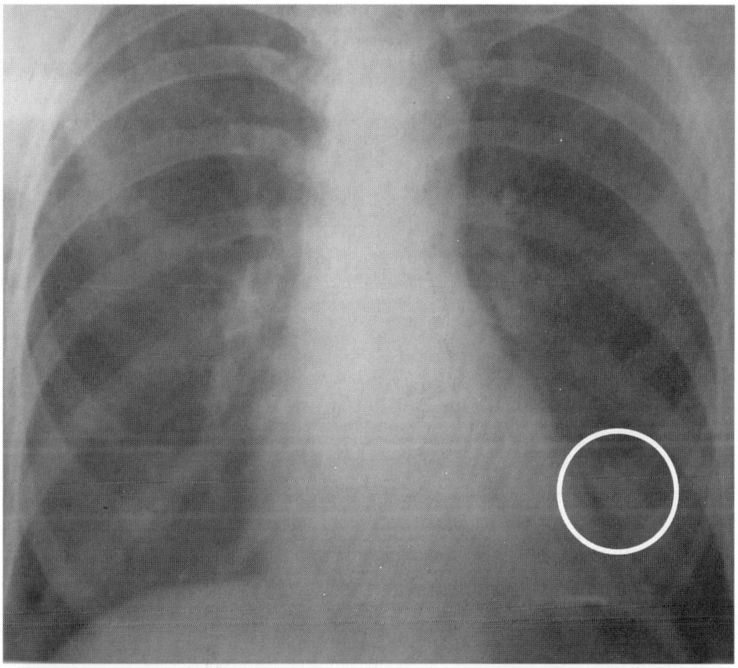

What is this?

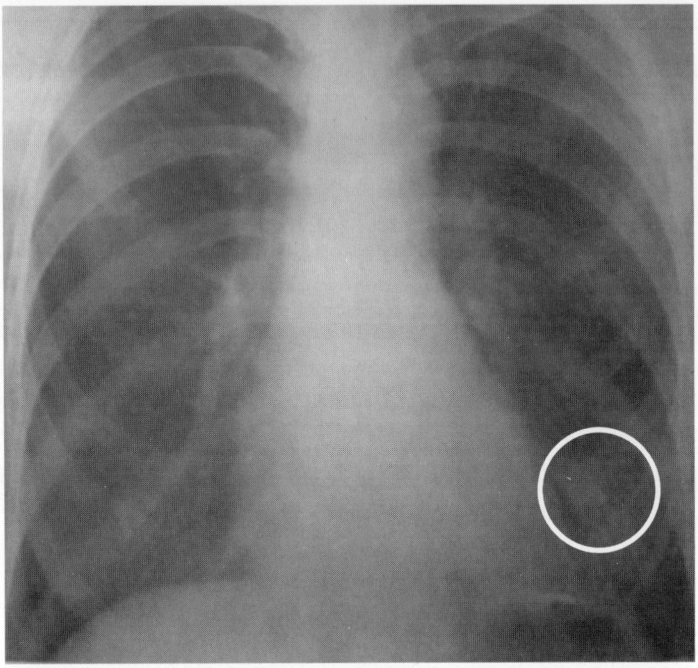

Nipple shadow

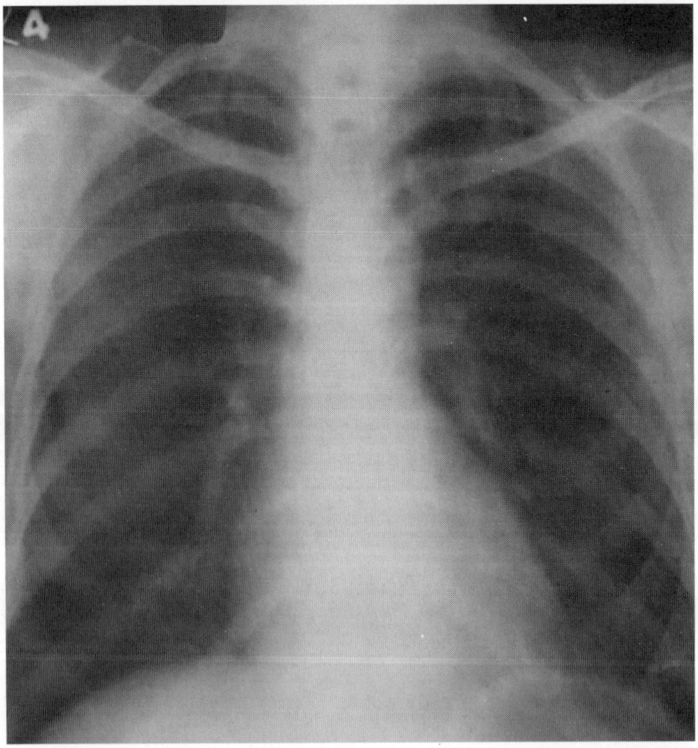

Chest X-ray PA view taken after strapping the breast which shows that nodule in the left lower zone has disappeared

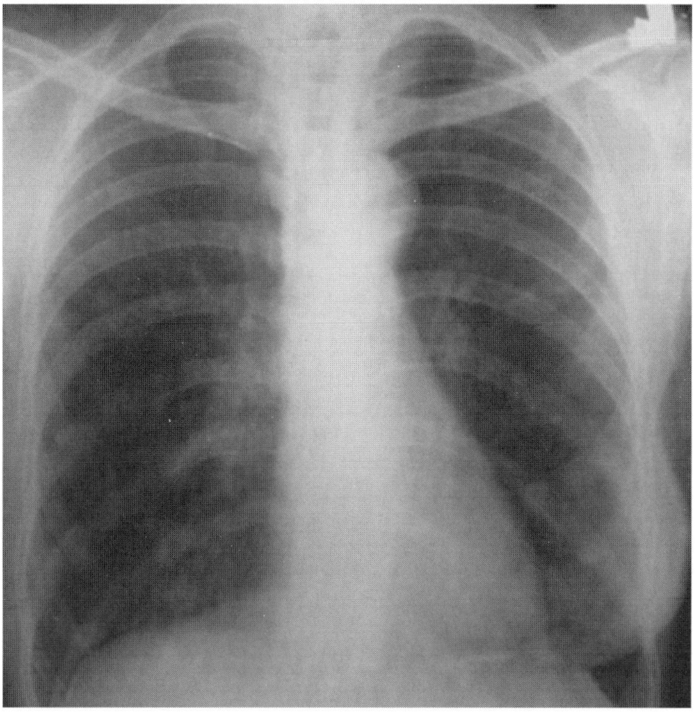

What is this?

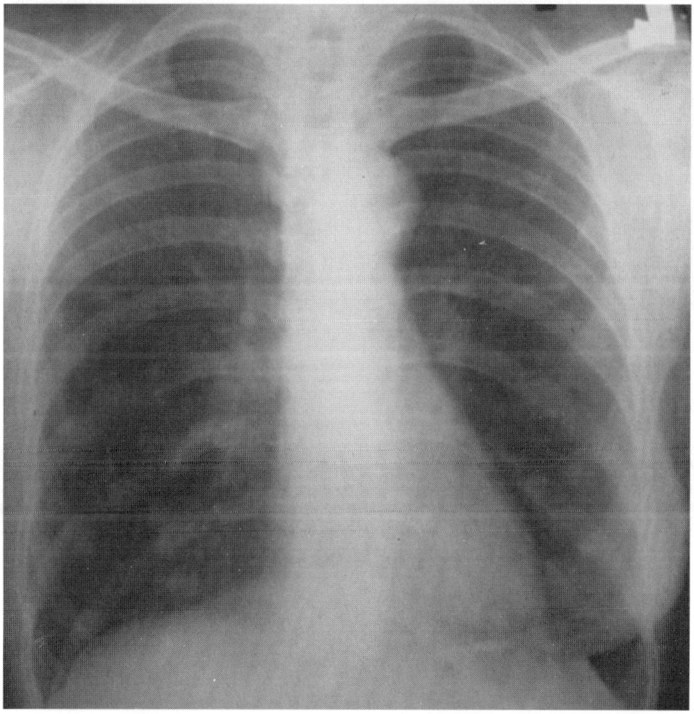

Secondaries from operated carcinoma right breast
(no breast shadow on the right side)

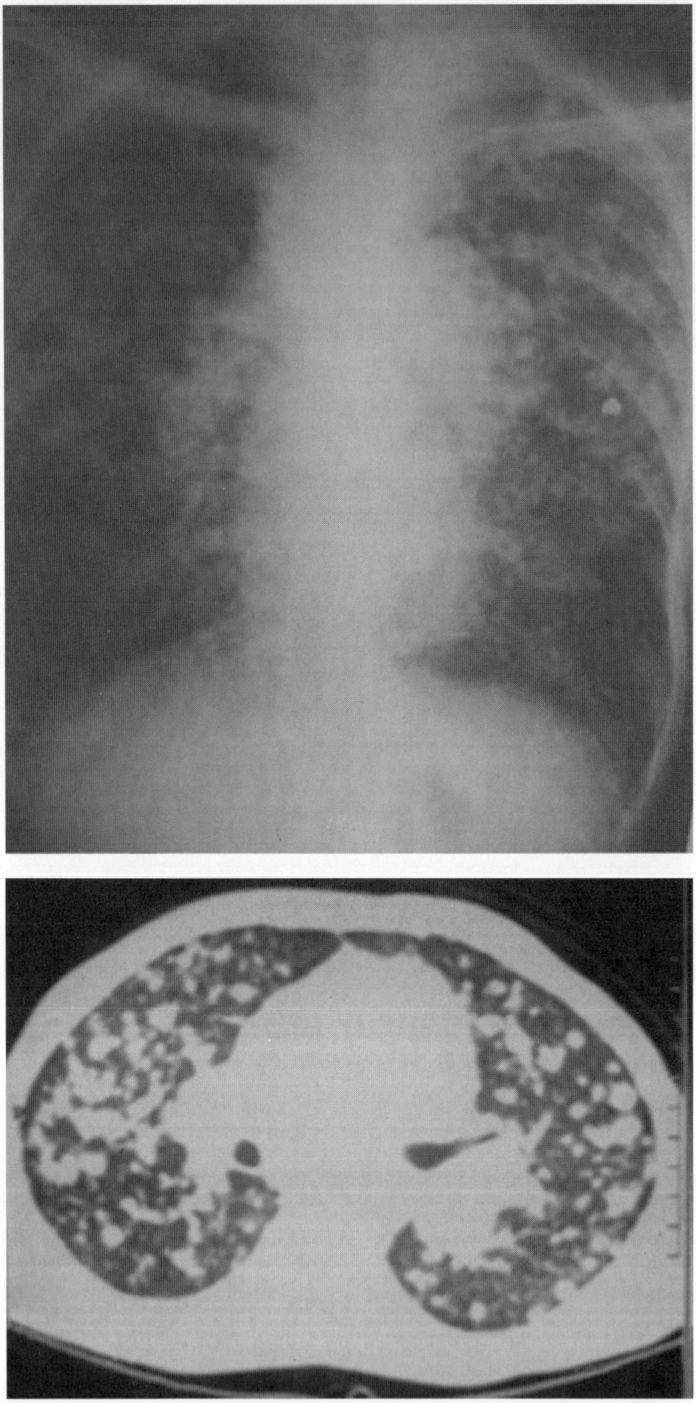

What is this?

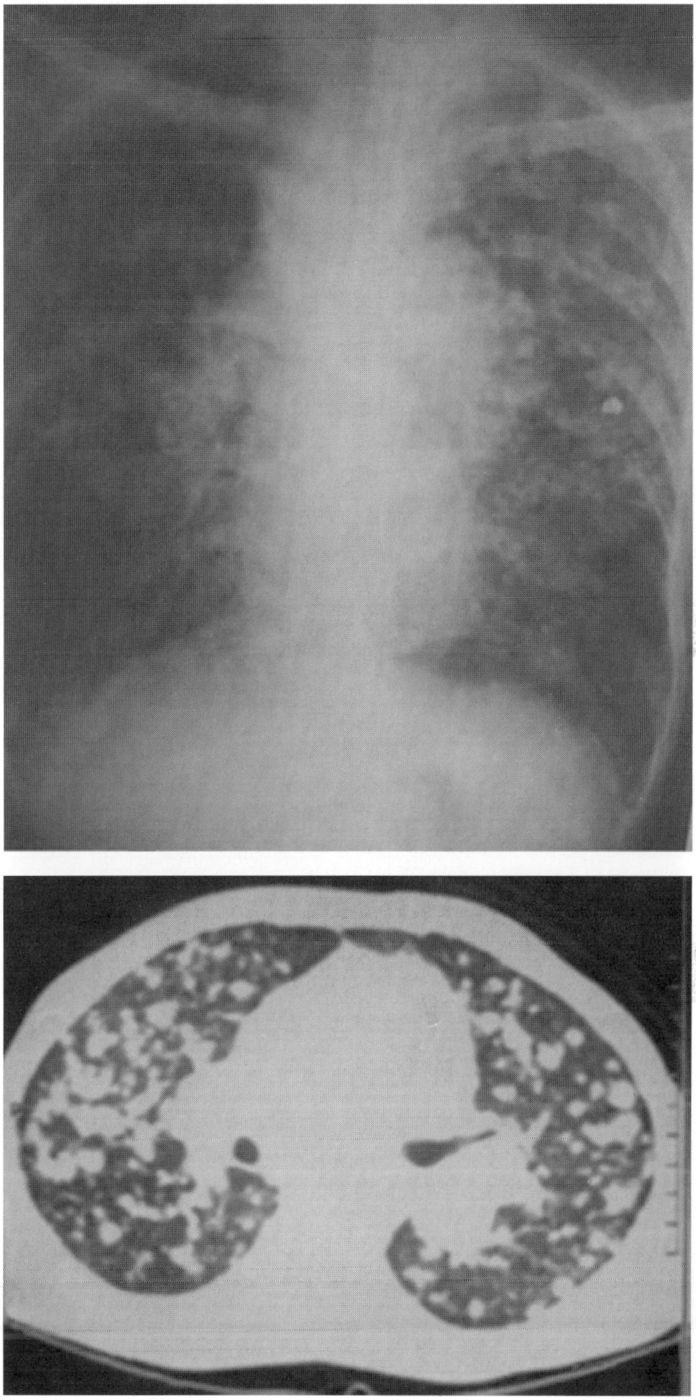

Secondaries from carcinoma thyroid

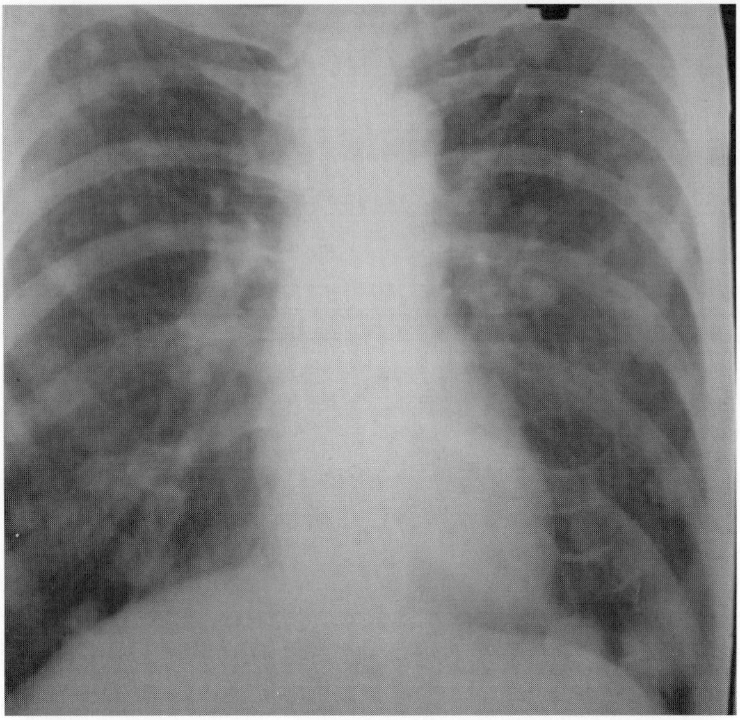

What is this?

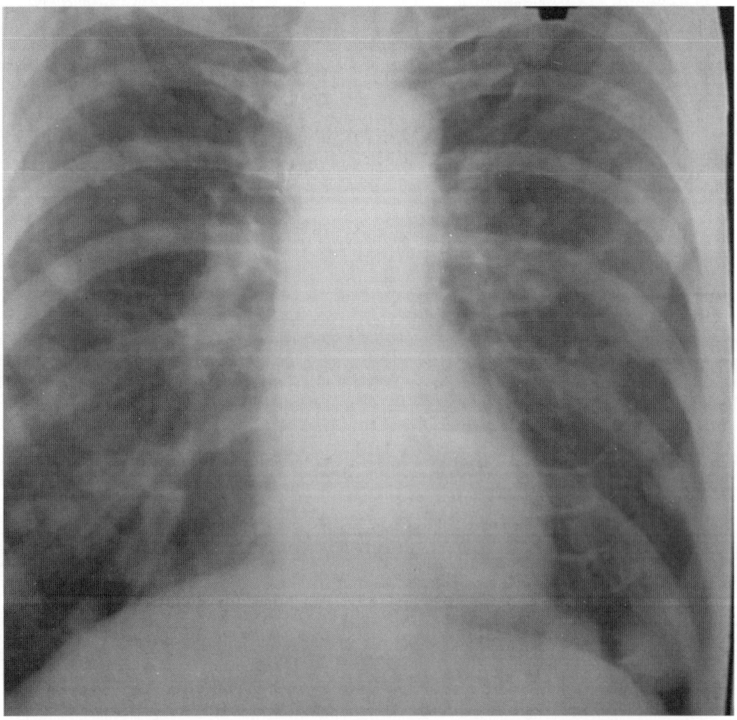

Multiple nodular shadows cause secondaries

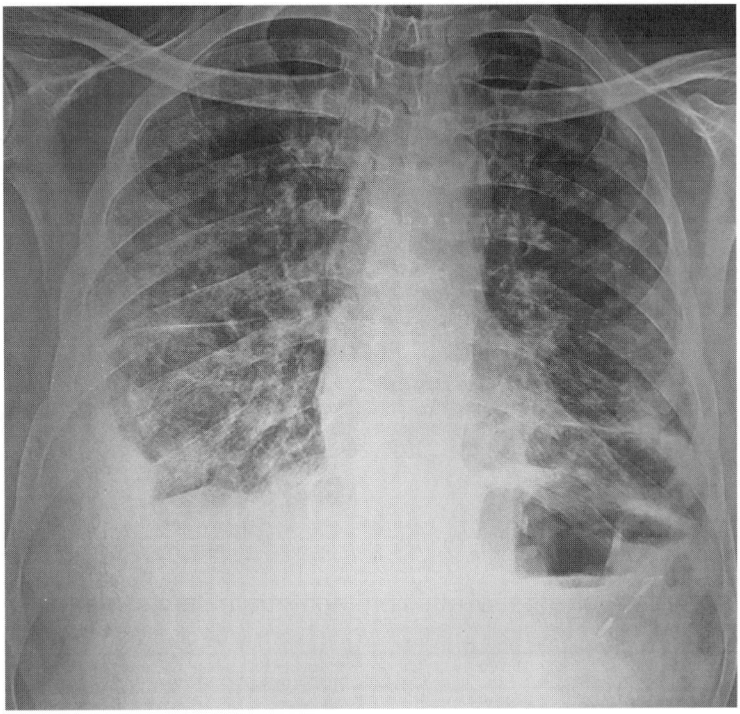

What is this?

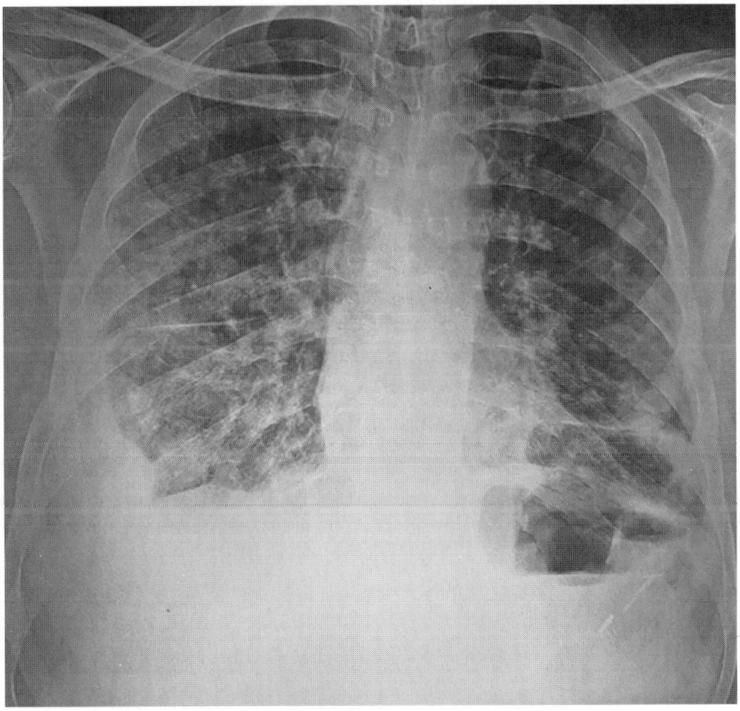

Secondaries with pleural effusion (right) from carcinoma pancreas

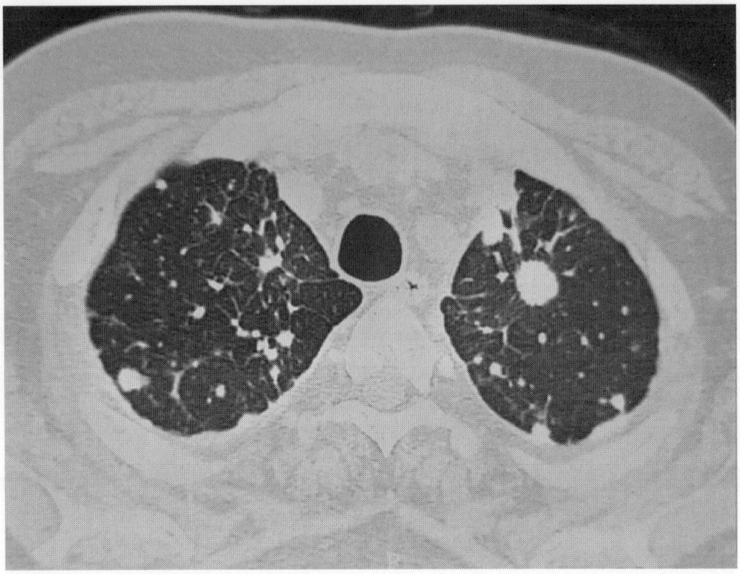

Secondaries with pleural effusion (right) from carcinoma pancreas

Mass Lesions

Mass: A pulmonary mass is any area of pulmonary opacification that measures more than 3 cm in diameter on radiological imaging

Mass Lesions or Rounded Opacity—*What are Causes?*

- Solitary
  - Infection
    - Bacterial: Tuberculoma, lung abscess, pneumonia
    - Fungal: Aspergilloma, histoplasmosis, coccidiomycosis
    - Parasitic: Hydatid cyst
  - Neoplasm
    - Benign: Adenoma, fibroma
    - Malignant: Primary/secondary
  - Developmental
    - Bronchogenic cyst, sequestration of lung, aneurysm
  - Others: Foreign body, pulmonary infarction, encysted effusion

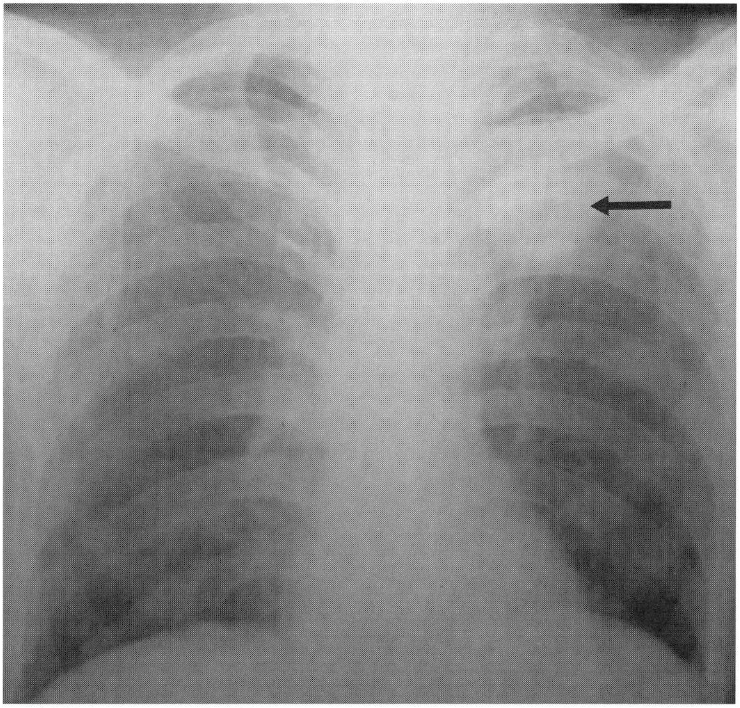

What is this?
C/O fever and cough for 3 months

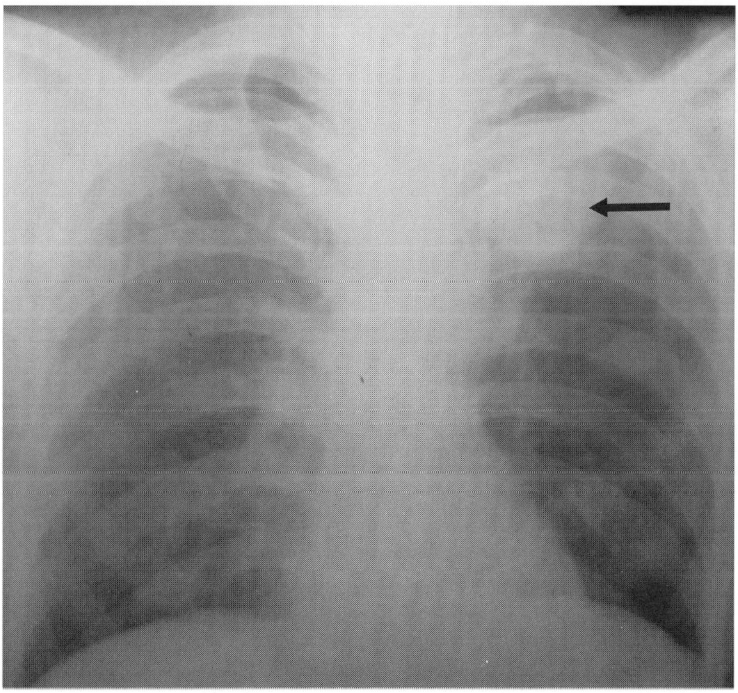

Tuberculoma left upper zone

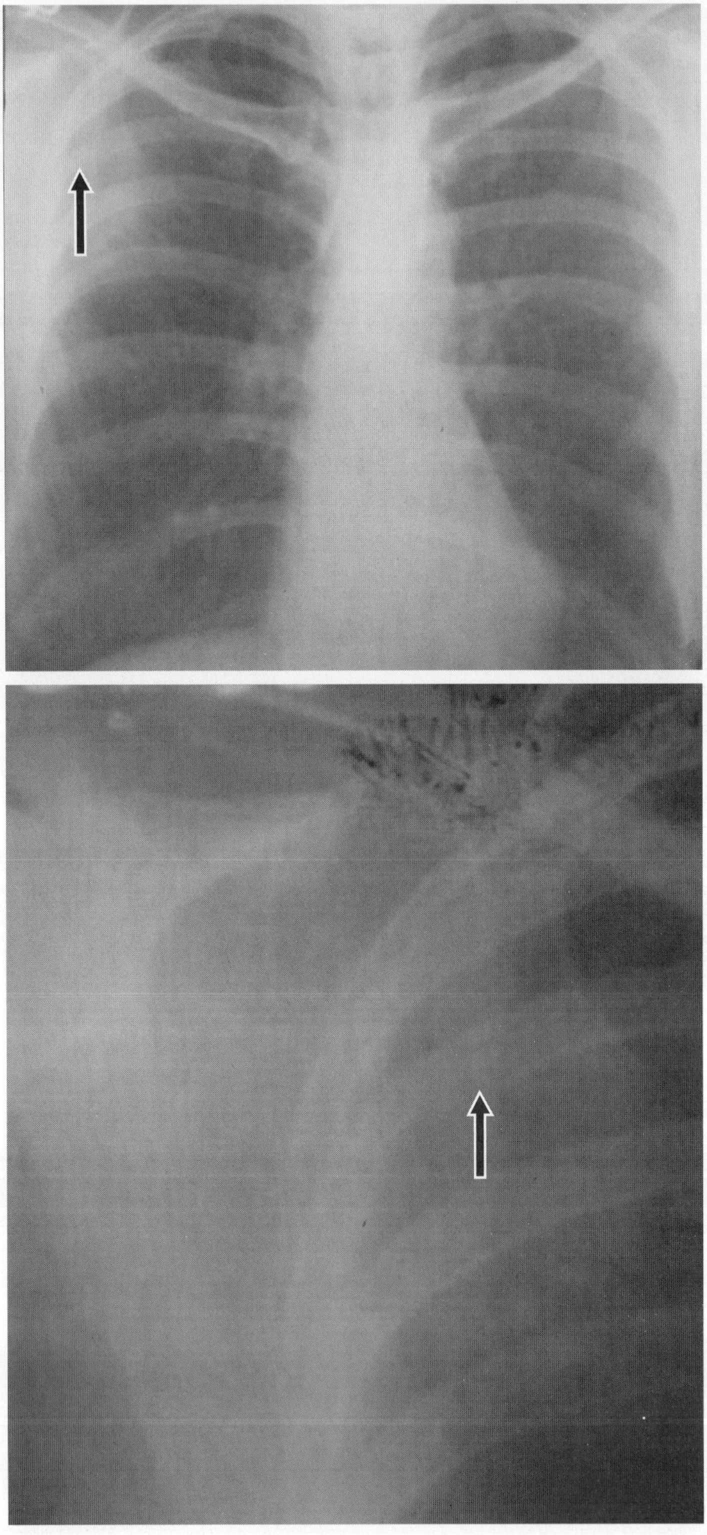

Magnified view
What is this?

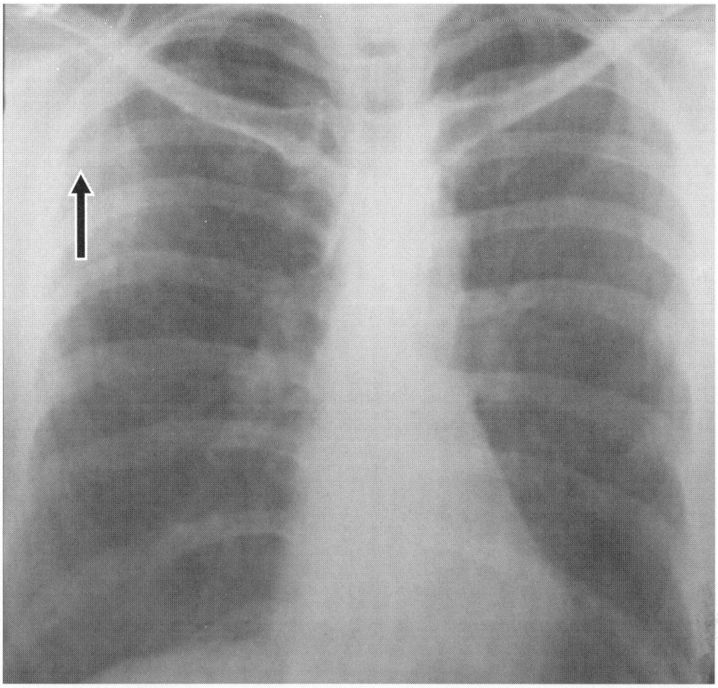

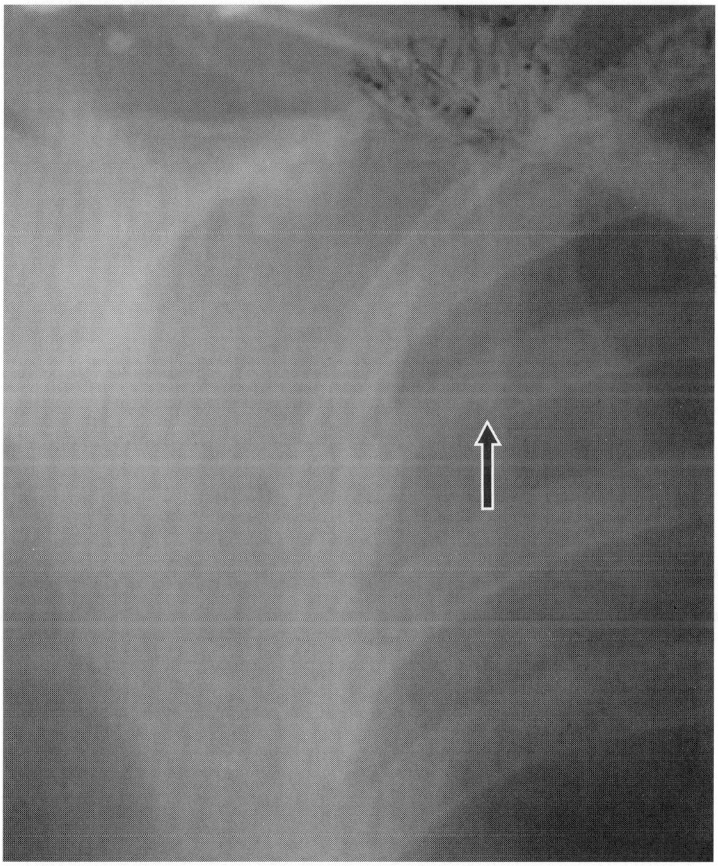

Adenocarcinoma with erosion of posterior end of 4th rib

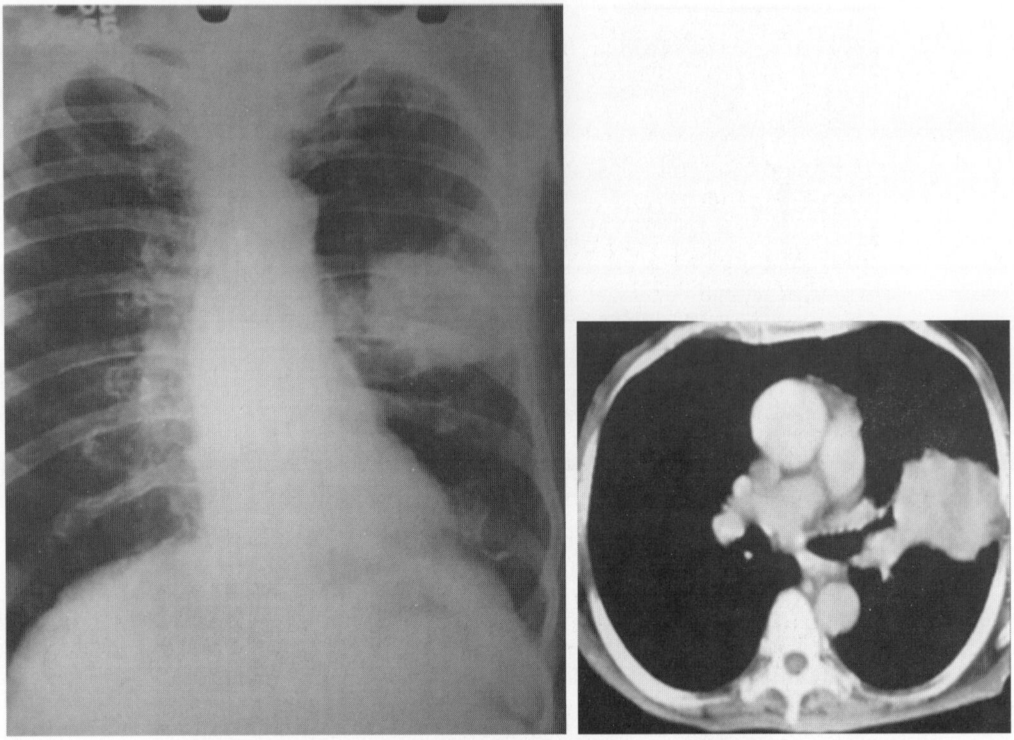

What is this?

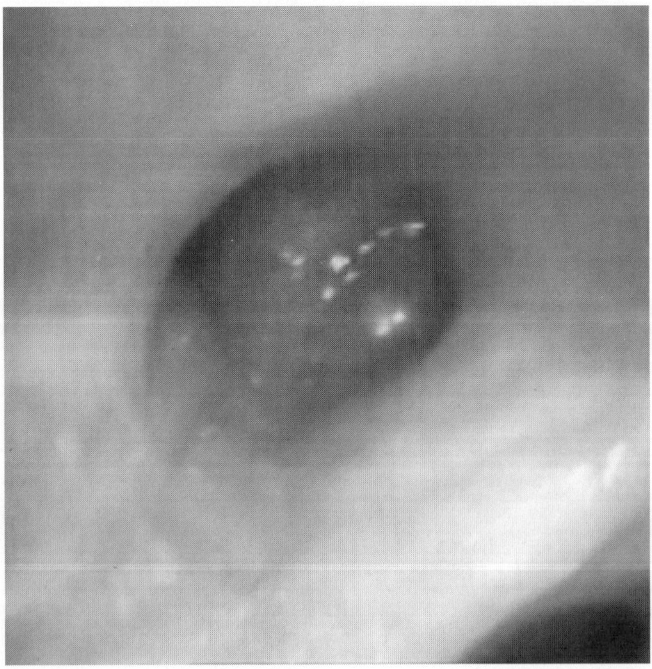

Fiberoptic bronchoscopy shows endobronchial growth (Colour Plate I)

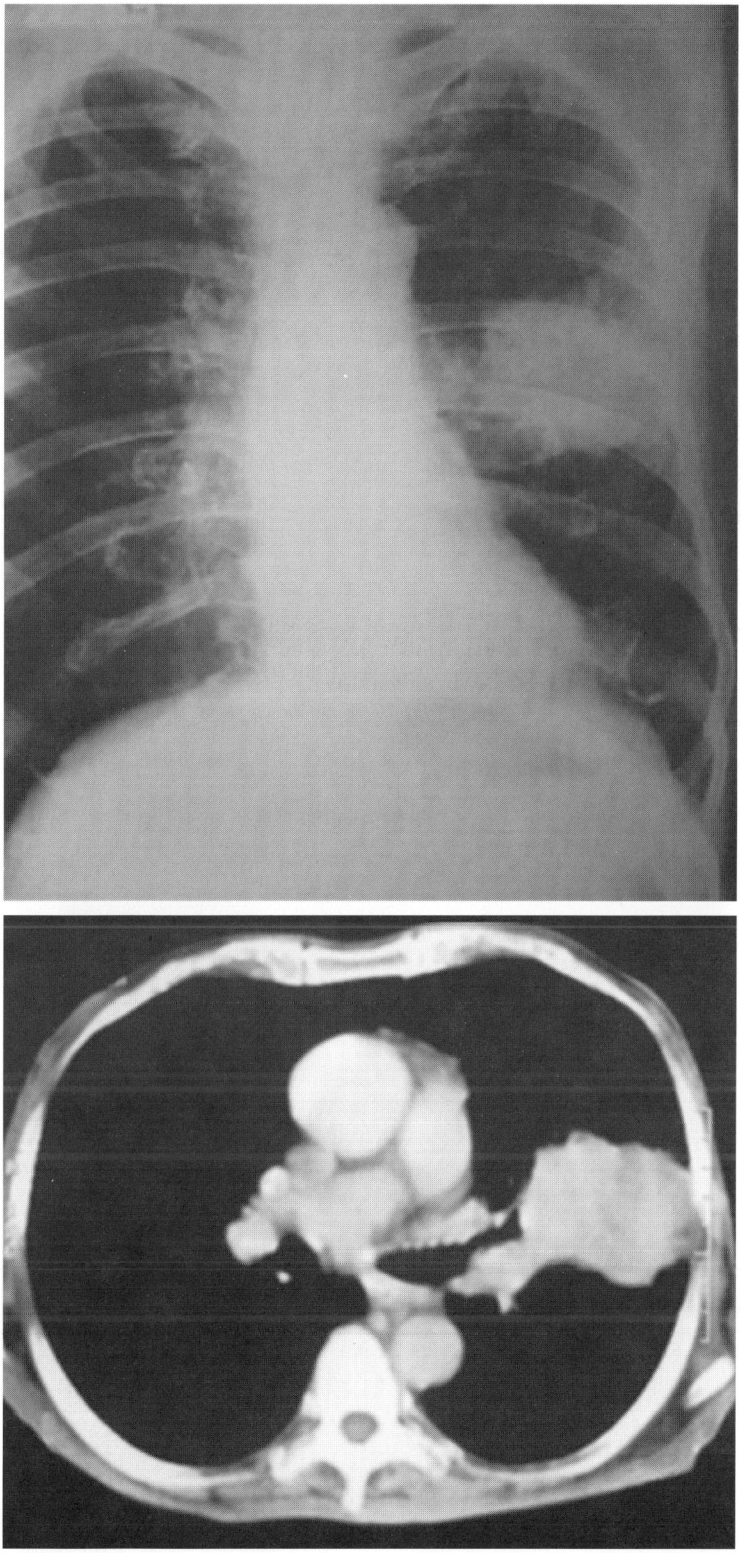

Squamous cell carcinoma

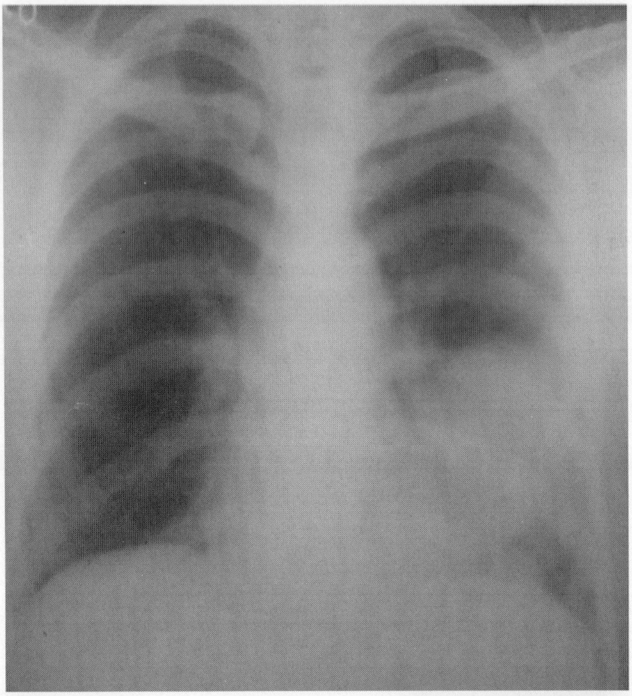

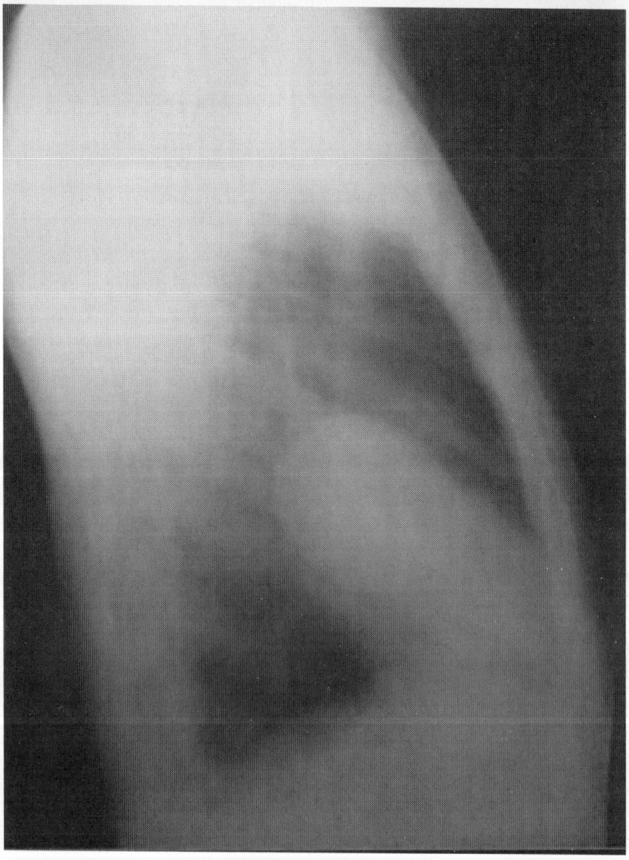

What is this?

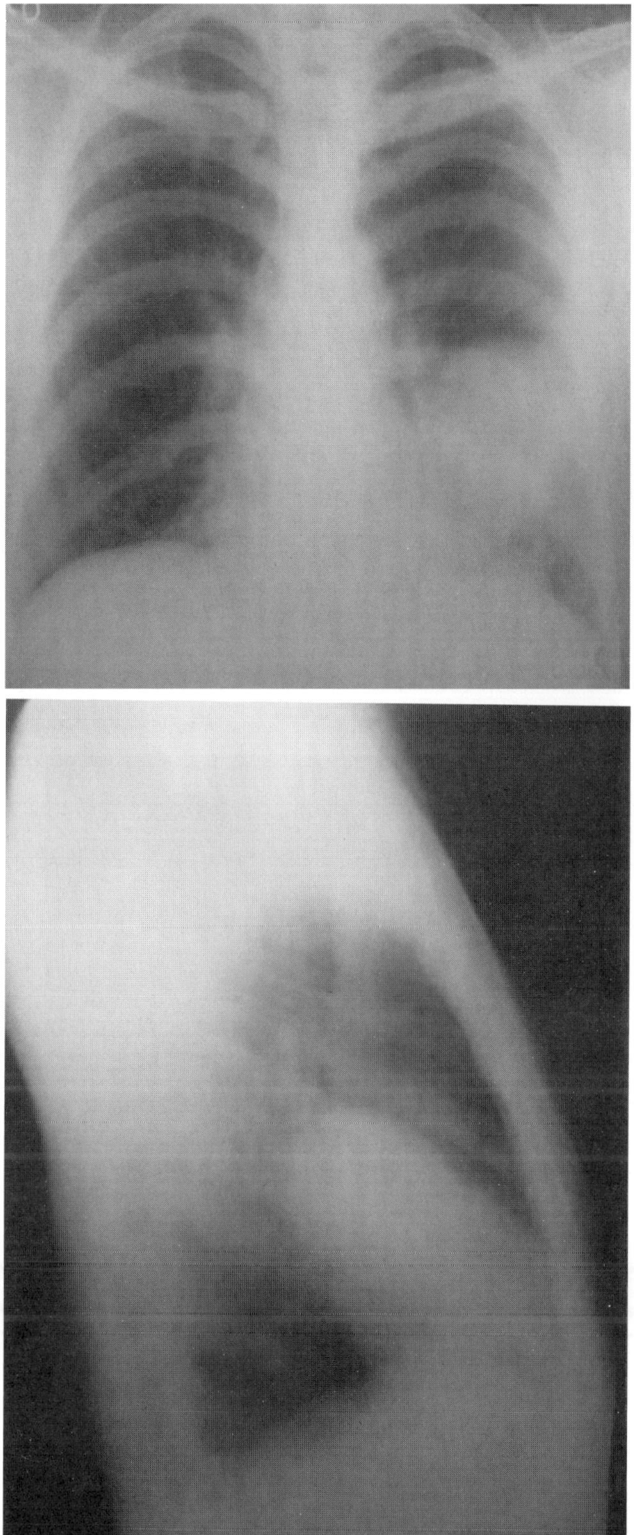

Small cell lung carcinoma

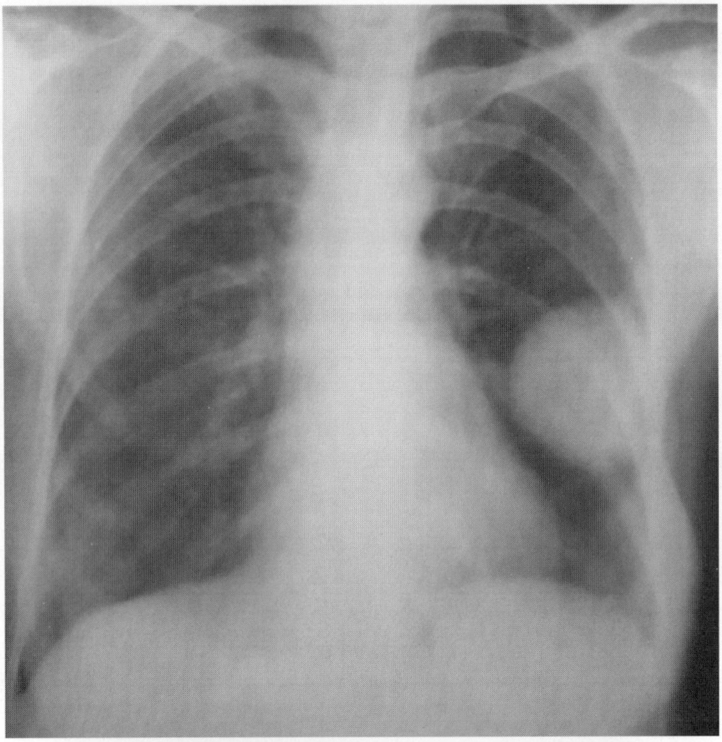

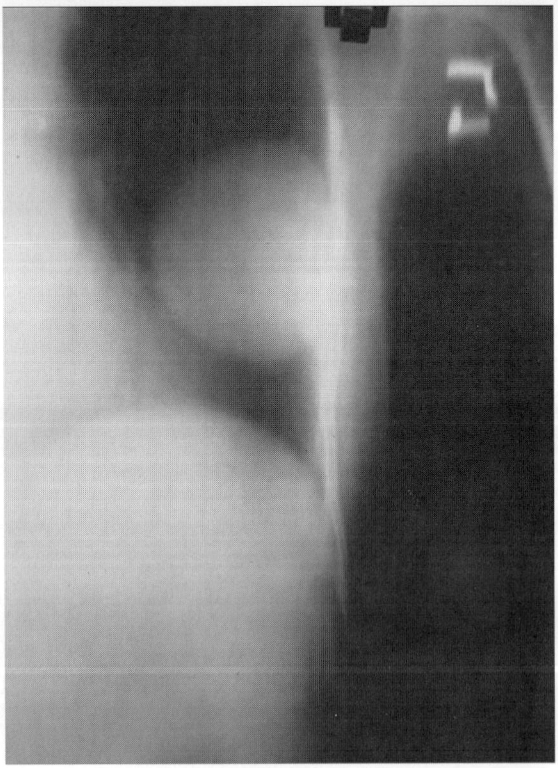

What is this?

See the rounded shadow which has very well-defined borders

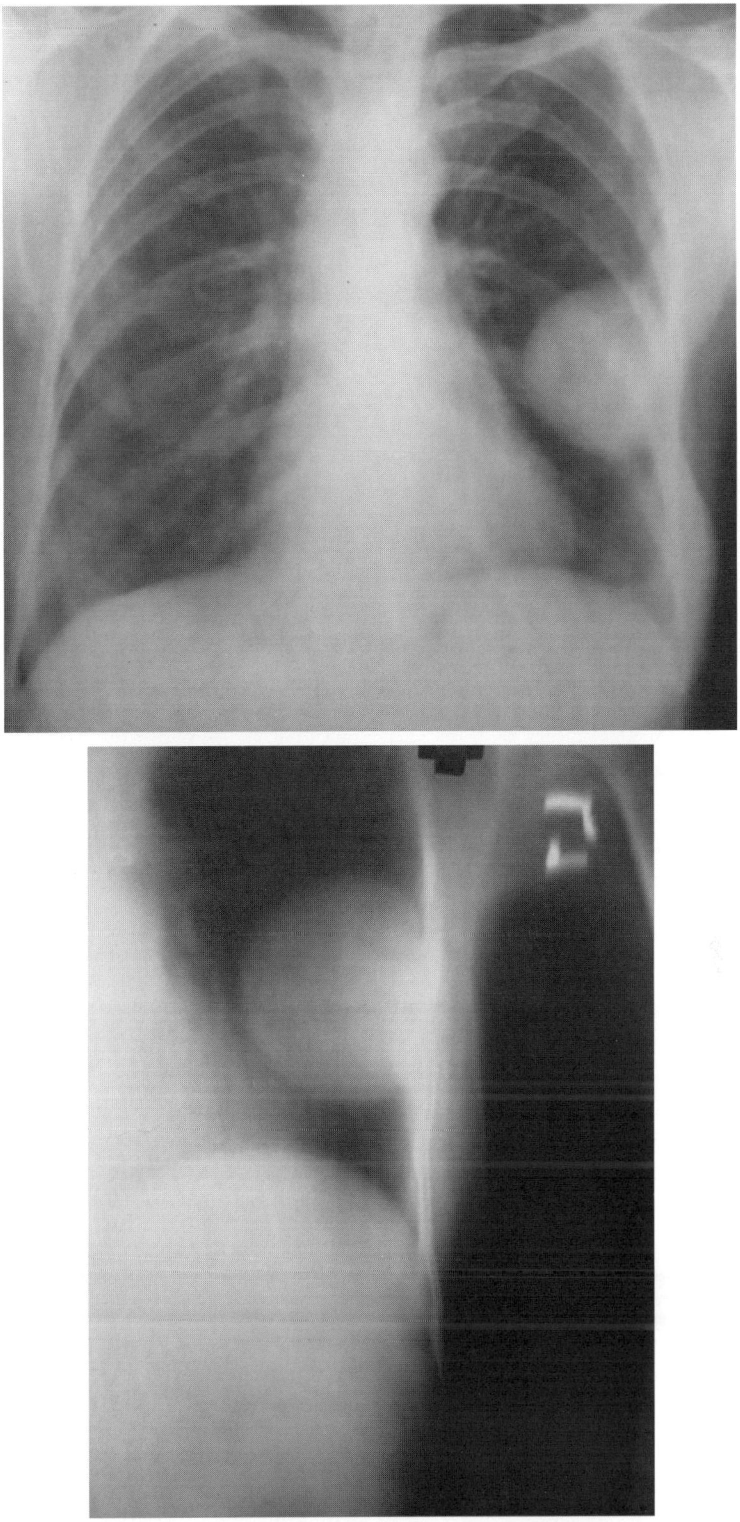

Rounded shadow with well-defined margins
hydatid cyst (left side)

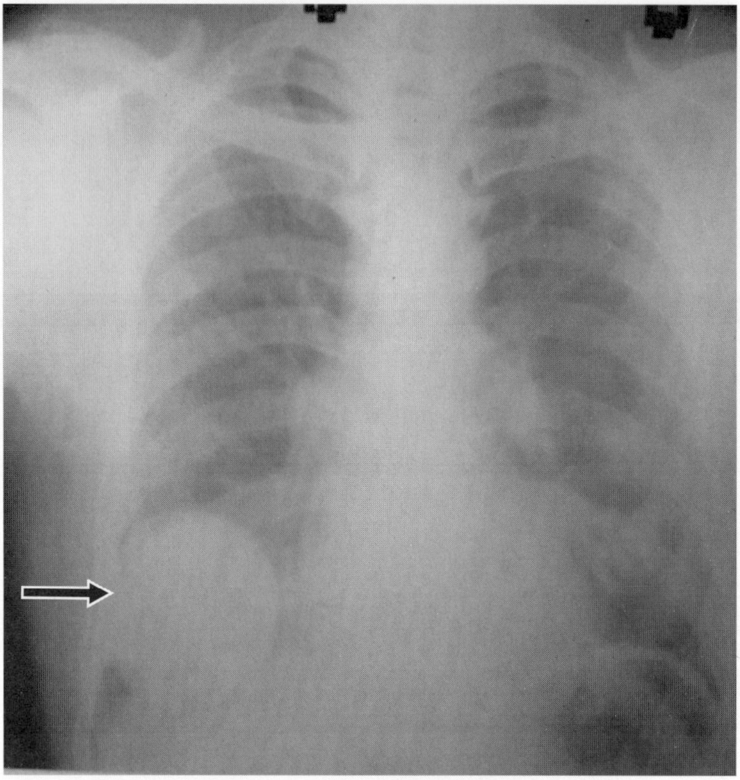

What is this?

A 31-year-old male C/O hemoptysis 1 year back (50–100 ml), right-sided chest pain since 1 year, loss of appetite since 1 month, history of ATT (2 RHEZ/7RH) without any response

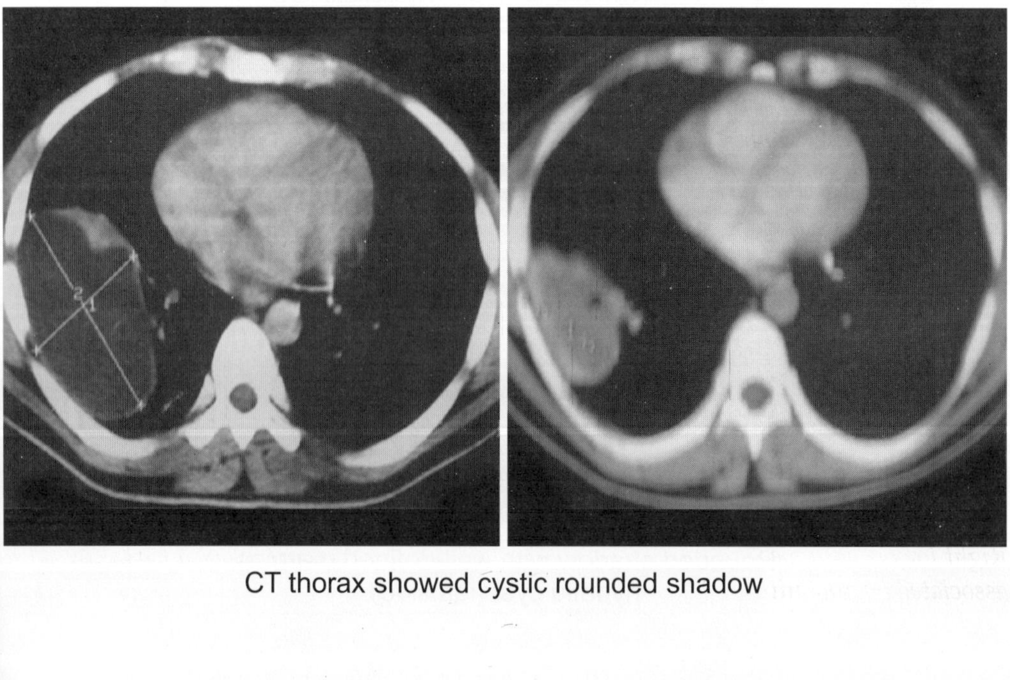

CT thorax showed cystic rounded shadow

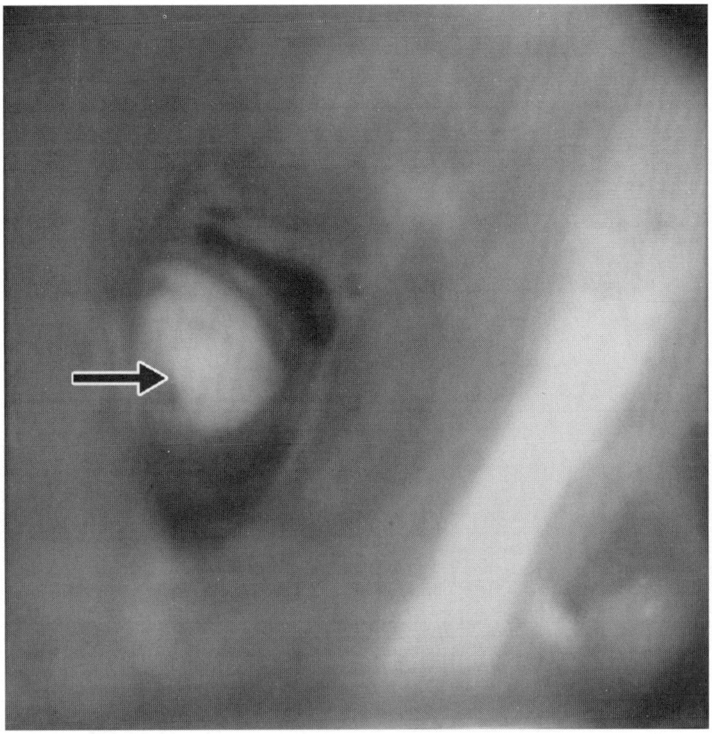

Fiberoptic bronchoscopy showed whitish material in right lower lobe bronchus (Colour Plate I)

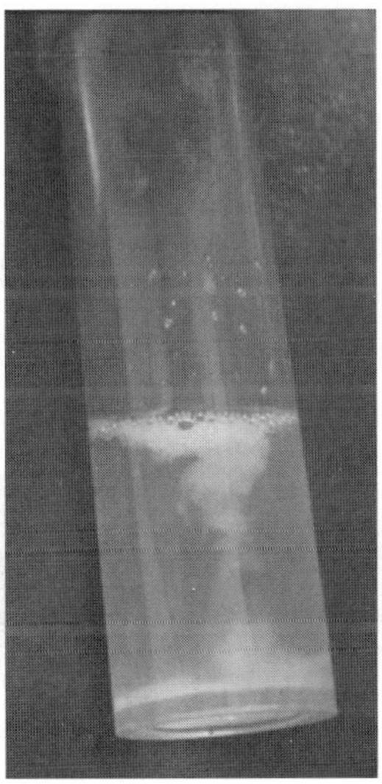

Bronchial aspirate shows membranous structure

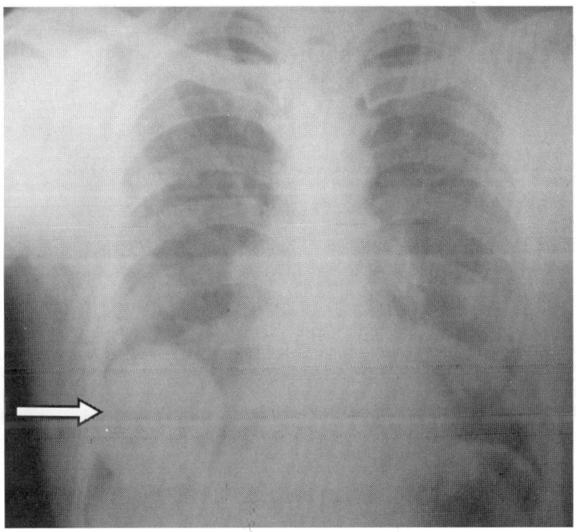

Hydatid cyst which ruptured later on

Right lower lobe lobectomy was done and histopathology revealed hydatid cyst lung with associated pneumonitis

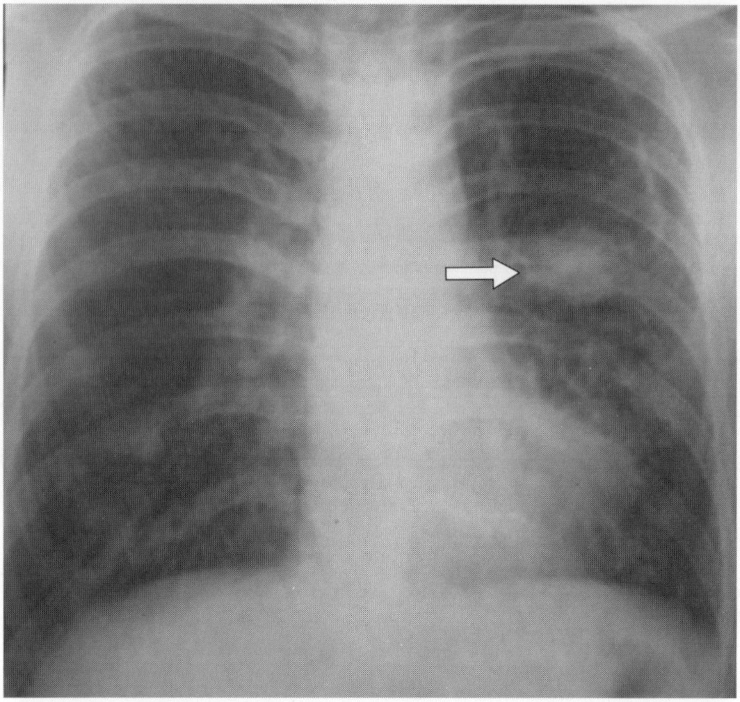

What is this?

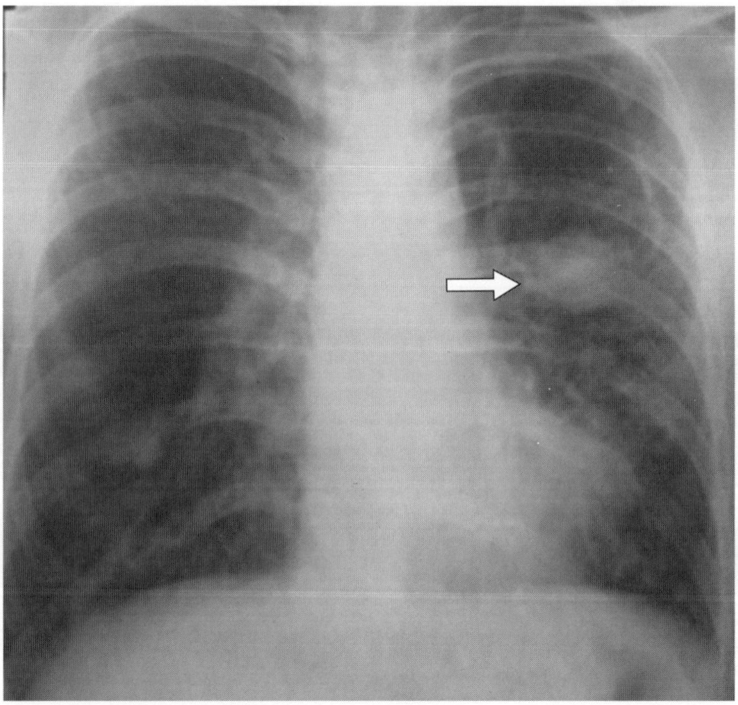

PA view

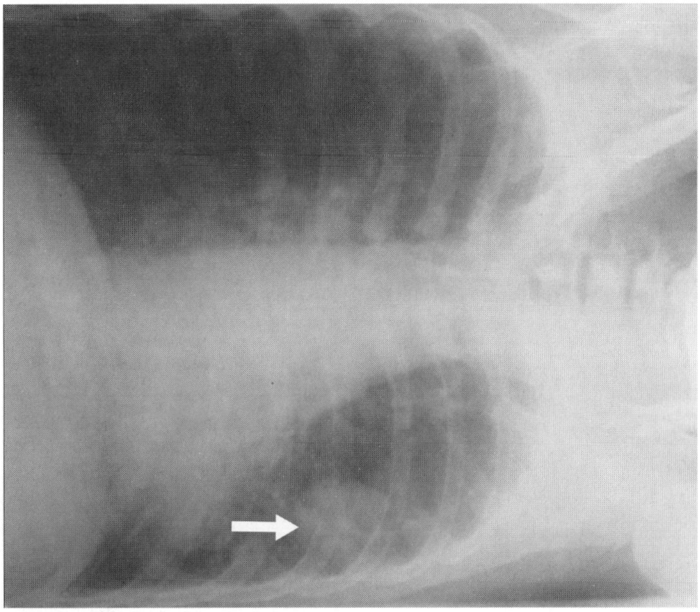

Left lateral decubitus view

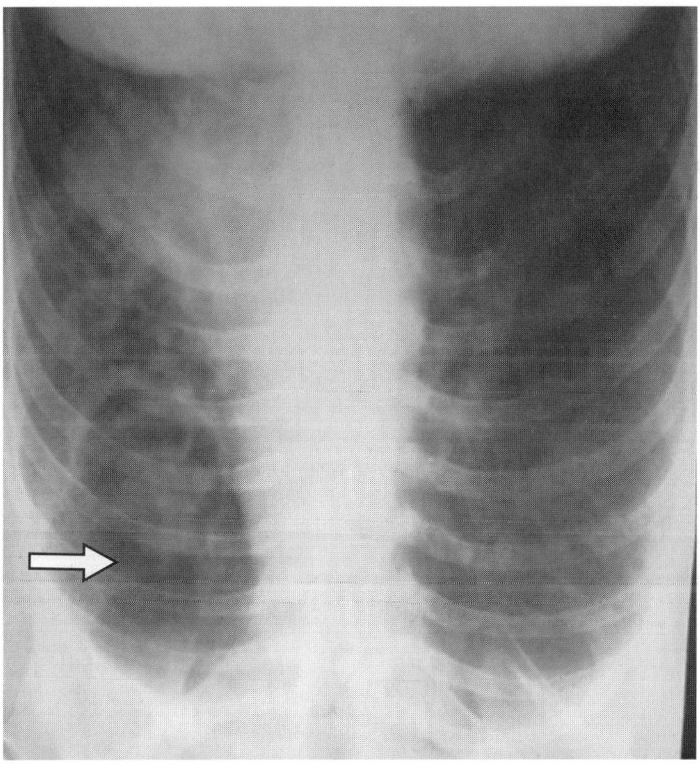

X-ray in Trendelenburg position
Moving Aspergilloma
Please note that ball-like shadow has moved in different views. It is a rare condition

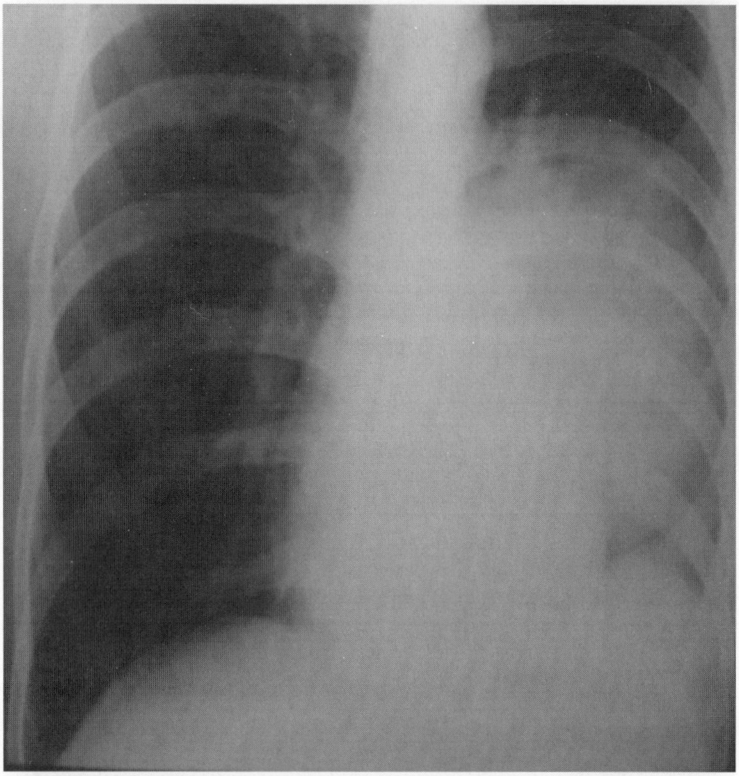

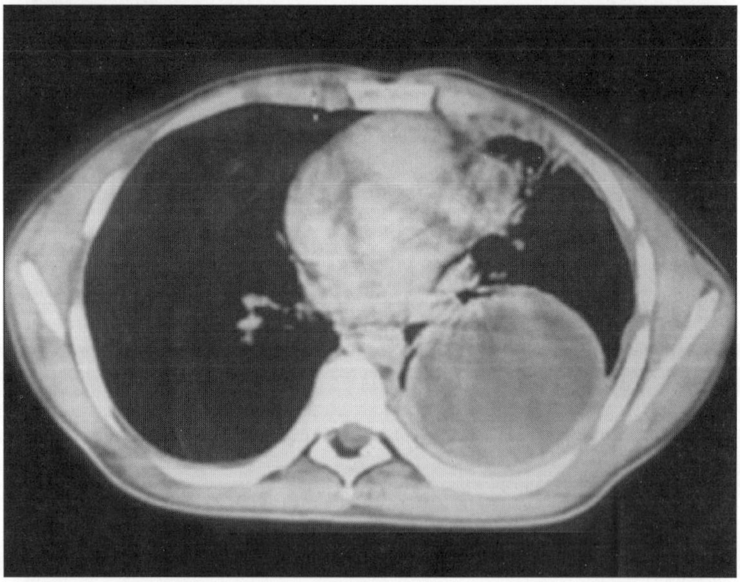

What is this?

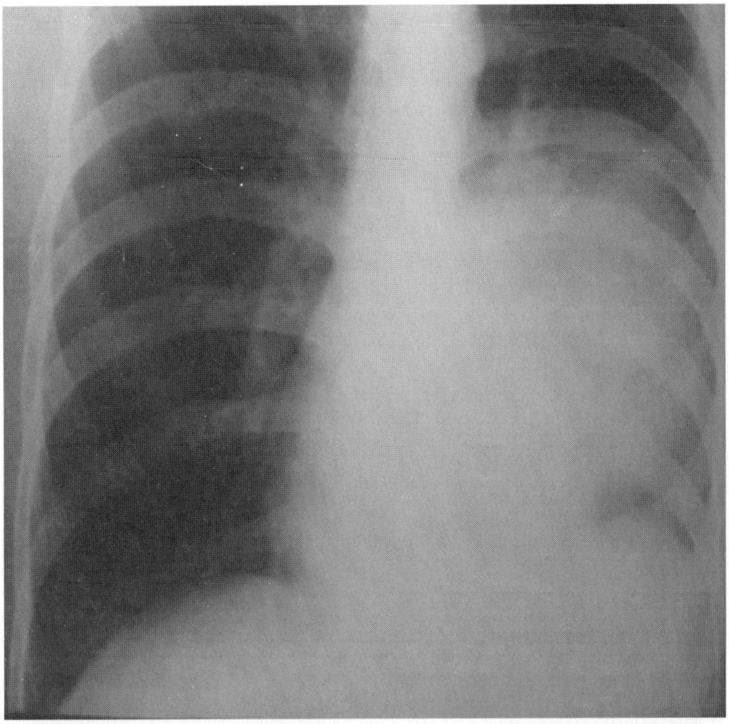

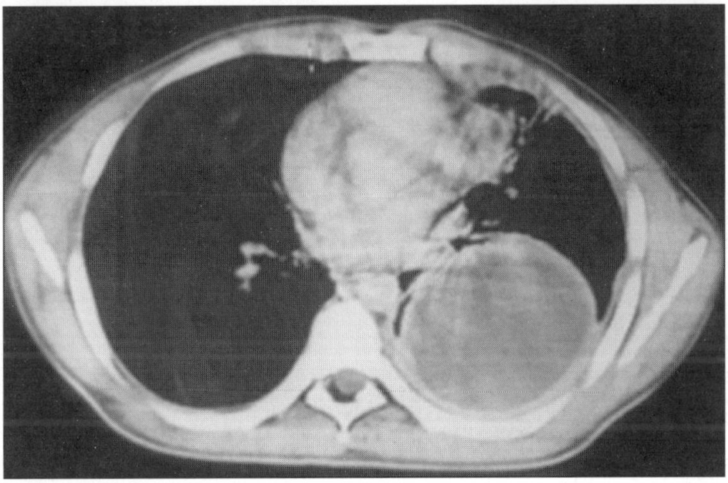

Encysted effusion (left)

Multiple Rounded Opacity—*What are Causes?*

- Secondaries
- Multiple abscess
- Multiple encysted effusion
- Multiple hydatid cyst
- Multiple infarctions
- Rheumatoid arthritis
- Pneumoconiosis

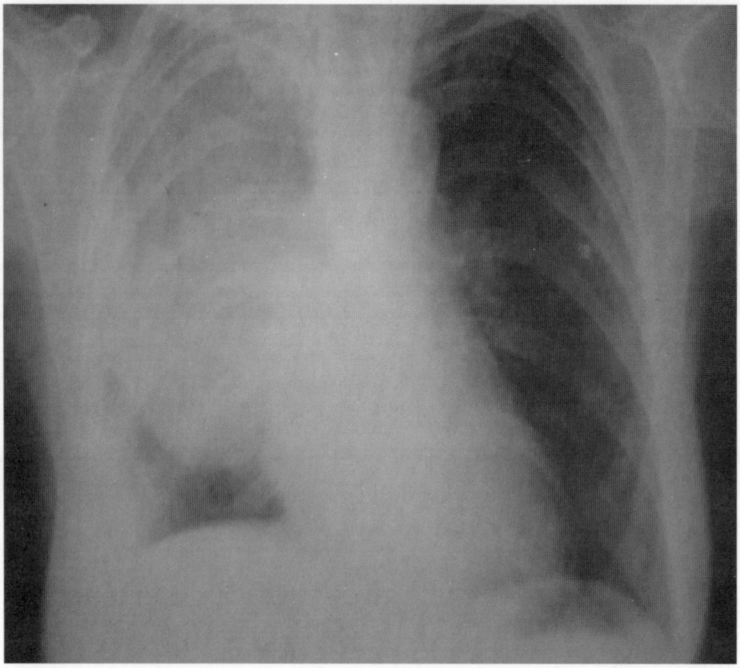

What is this?

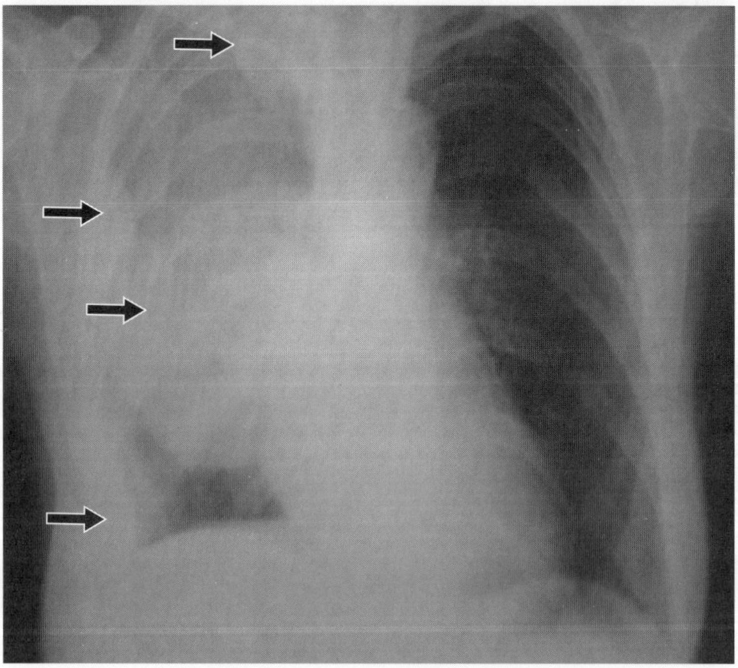

Multiple encysted effusion (left)

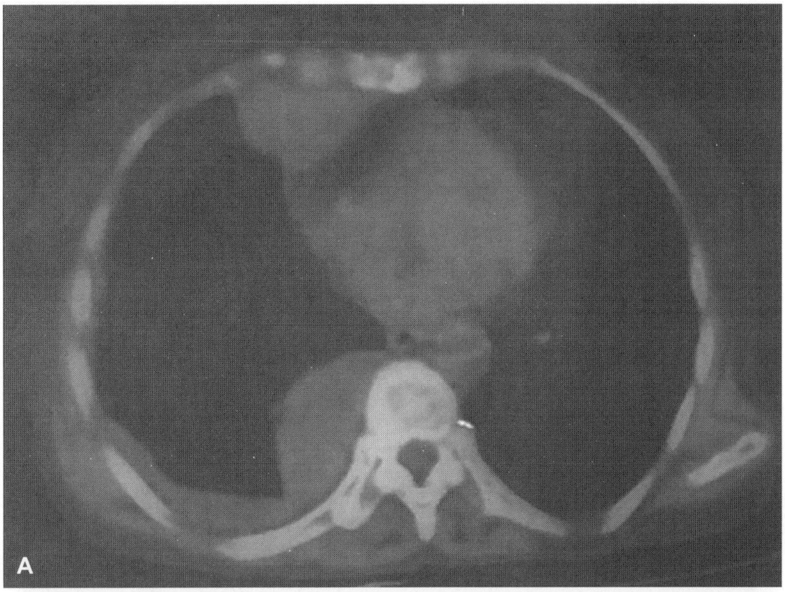
A

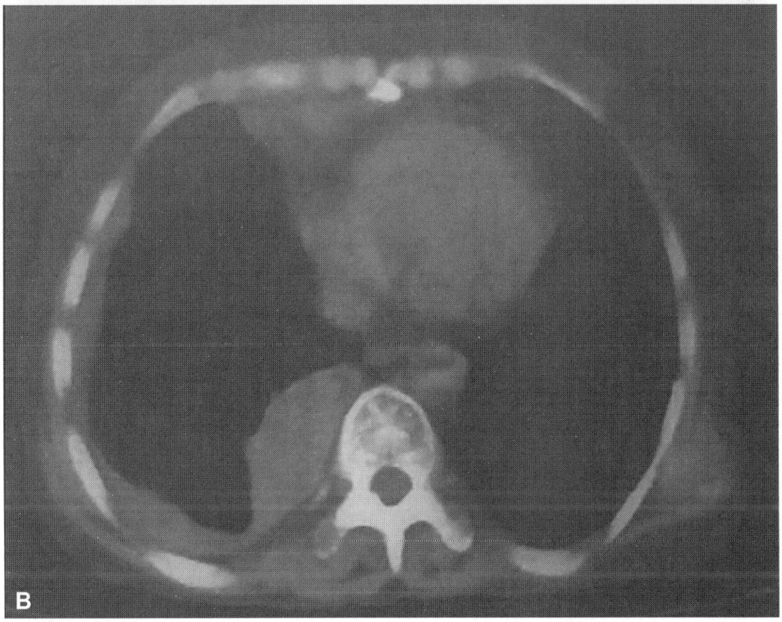
B

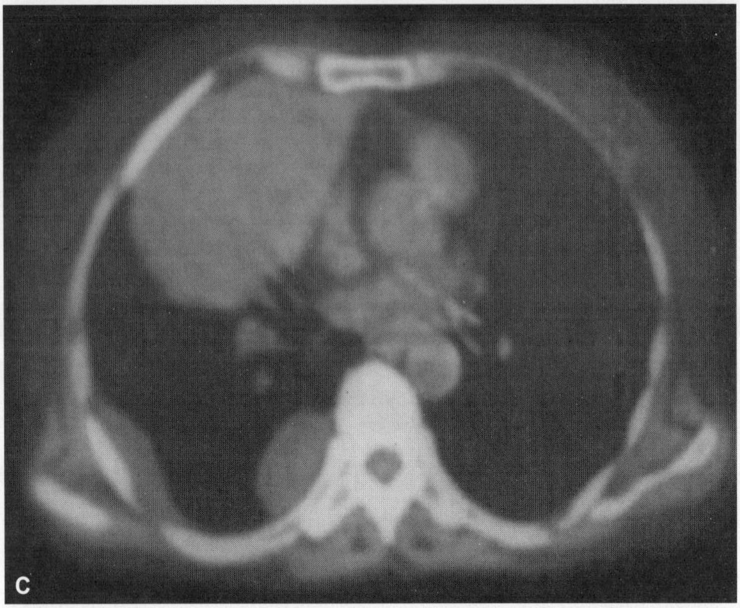

A, B and C: Multiple encysted effusion

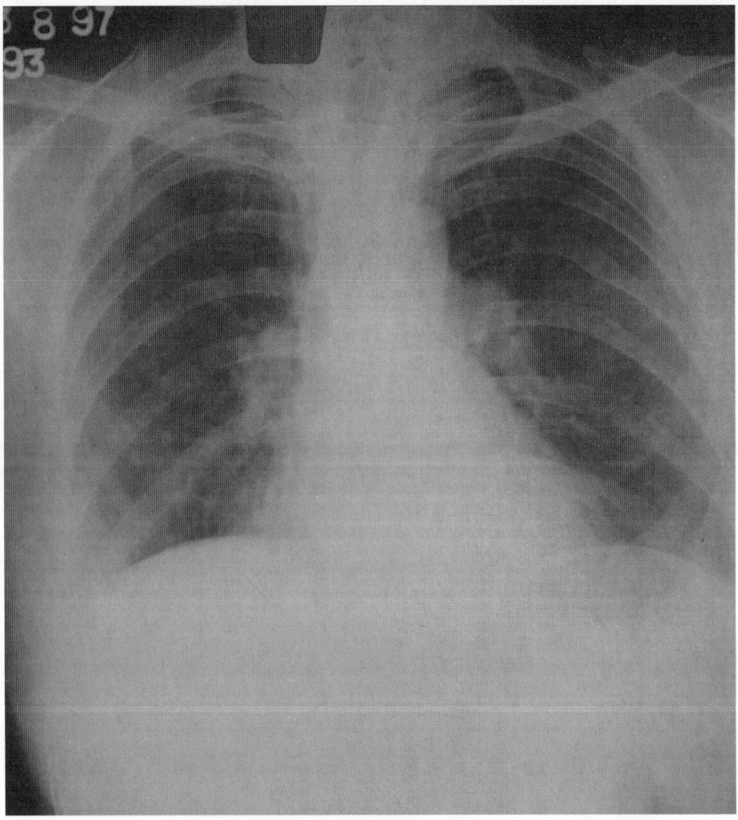

All shadows disappeared after pleural aspiration and antitubercular treatment

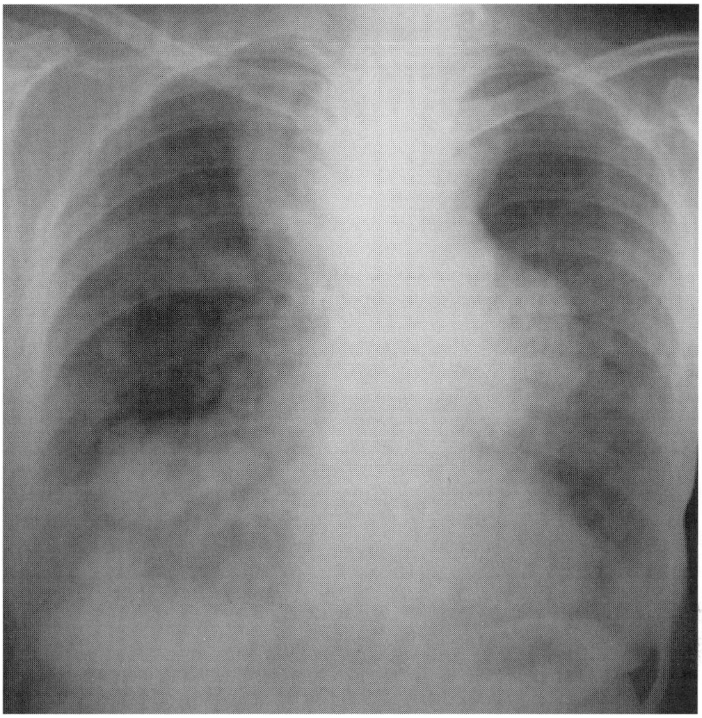

What is this?

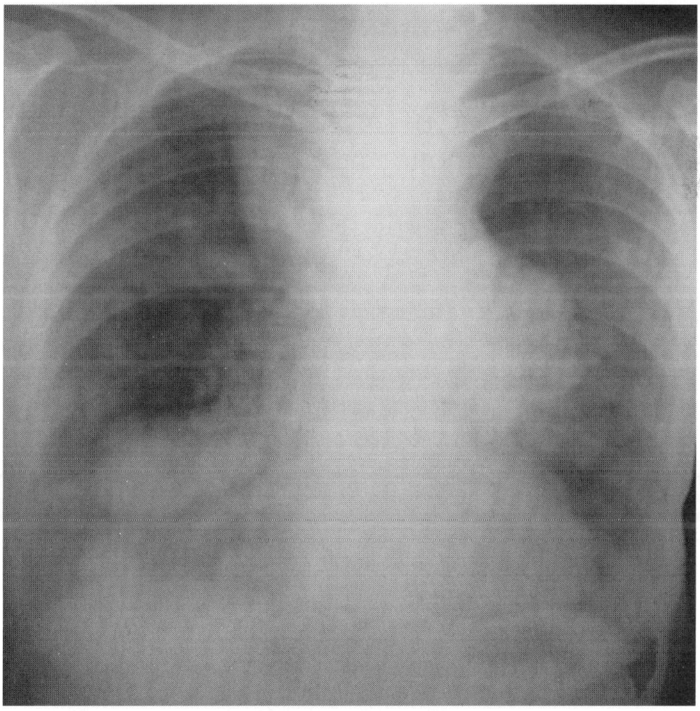

Multiple rounded shadows
secondaries from carcinoma thyroid

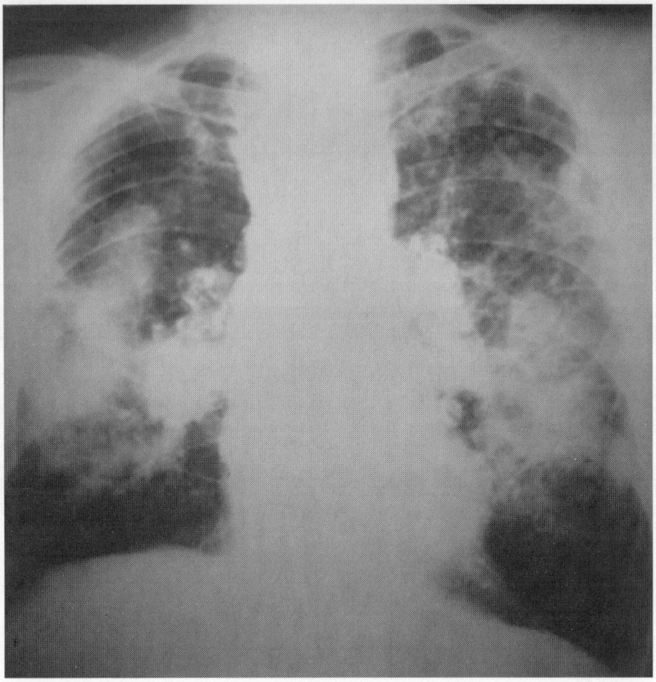

What is this?

C/O breathlessness with significant exposure to coal dust

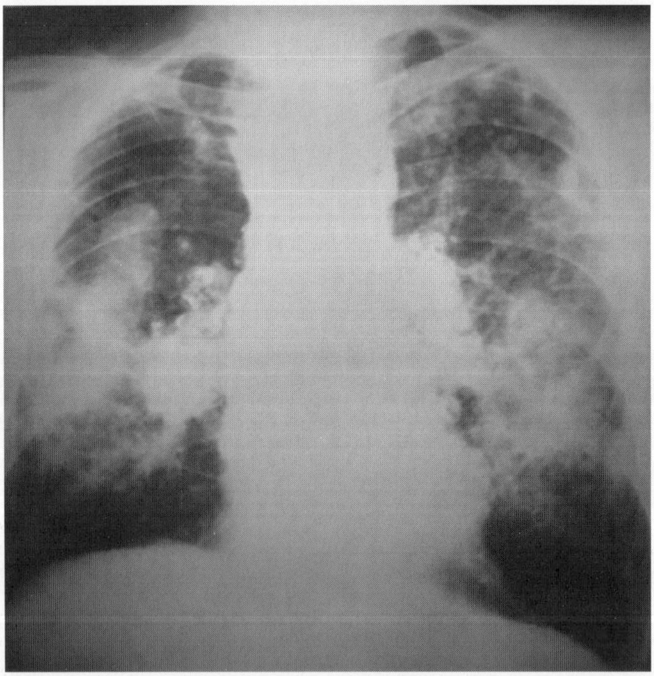

Multiple masses

pneumoconiosis with progressive massive fibrosis

Calcified Lesions

Calcified Lesions—*What are Sources?*

- Endogenous
  - Intrapulmonary
  - Extrapulmonary
- Exogenous

Intrapulmonary Calcification—*What are Sources?*

- Parenchymal calcification
- Pleural calcification
- Vascular calcification
- Lymph nodes calcification
- Mediastinal calcification

Parenchymal

- Granulomatous
  - Tuberculosis
  - Actinomycosis
  - Coccidiomycosis
  - Histoplasmosis
  - Hydatid cyst
  - Chickenpox
- Abscess
- Neoplasm
  - Benign: Hamartoma
  - Malignant
    - Primary: Bronchogenic carcinoma
    - Secondary: Osteogenic sarcoma, chondrosarcoma, thyroid, breast, ovary, GIT
- Others
  - Infarction
  - Broncholith
  - Cavernolith
  - Sarcoidosis
  - Hemosiderosis
  - Silicosis
  - Alveolar microlithiasis
  - Metabolic disorder

Pleural Calcification

- Tuberculosis
- Empyema
- Haemothorax
- Asbestosis
- Talcosis

Vascular Calcification

- Hypertension
- Aneurysm
- Thrombus

Lymph Node Calcification

- Tuberculosis
- Histoplasmosis
- Sarcoidosis
- Silicosis

Mediastinal Calcification

- Thyroid
- Thymus
- Dermoid
- Cardiac

Extrapulmonary Calcification

- Calcified rib
- Calcified costal cartilage
- Callous around fractured rib
- Calcified axillary and cervical lymph node
- Breast tumour calcification
- Fat necrosis
- Parasitic calcification

Exogenous Calcification

- Inhaled foreign body: Pin, metal piece
- Inhaled radiopaque dust: Iron, barium, tin, calcium
- Iodized oil
- Traumatic foreign body

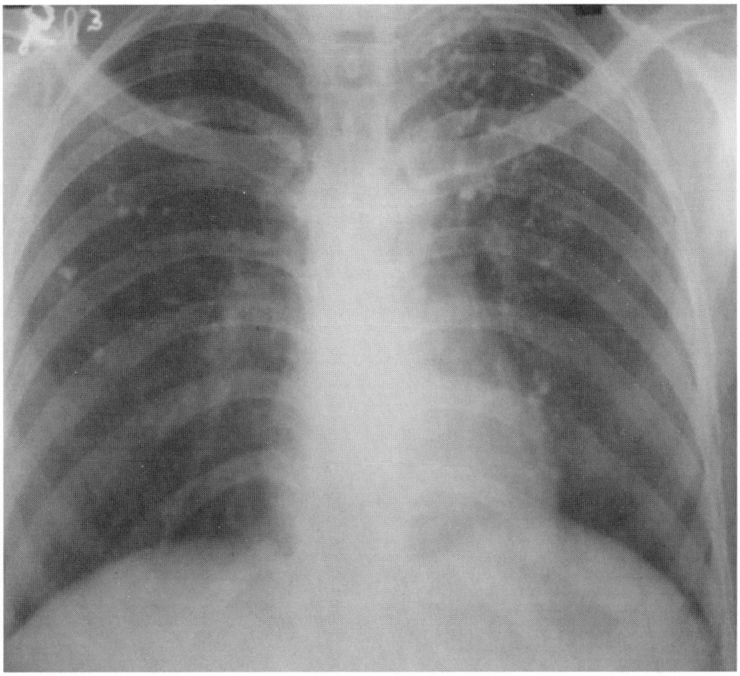

What is this?

C/O massive hemoptysis with history of adequate antitubercular treatment in the past

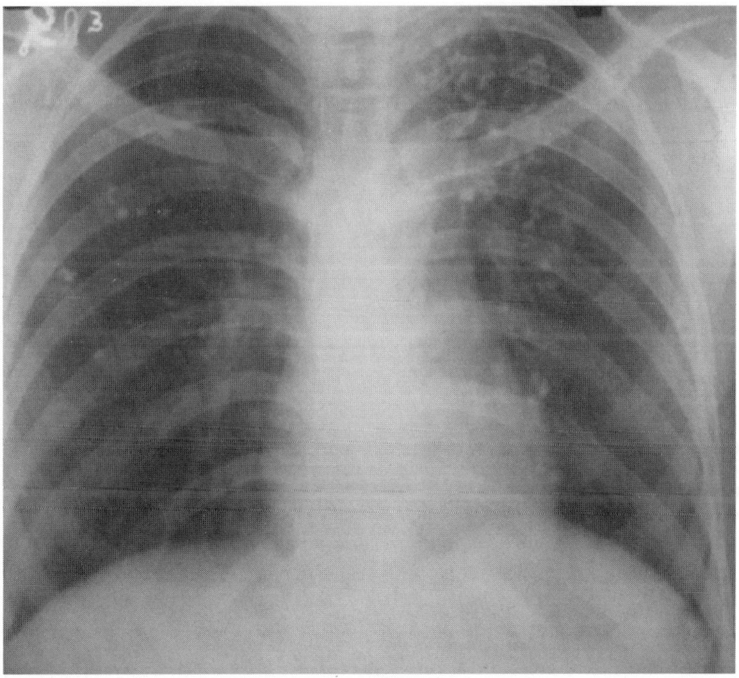

Intrapulmonary calcified shadows (healed pulmonary TB)

Do not forget to ask history of antitubercular treatment in the past

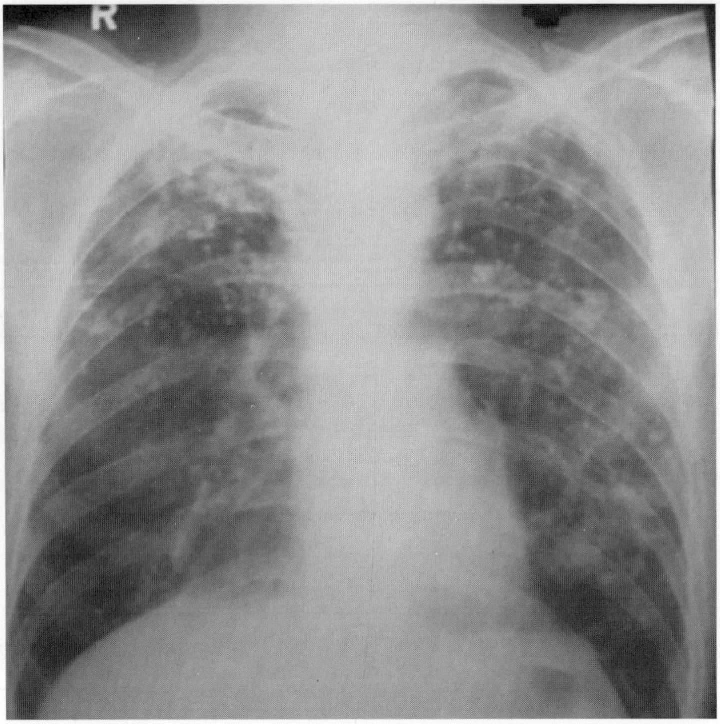

What is this?

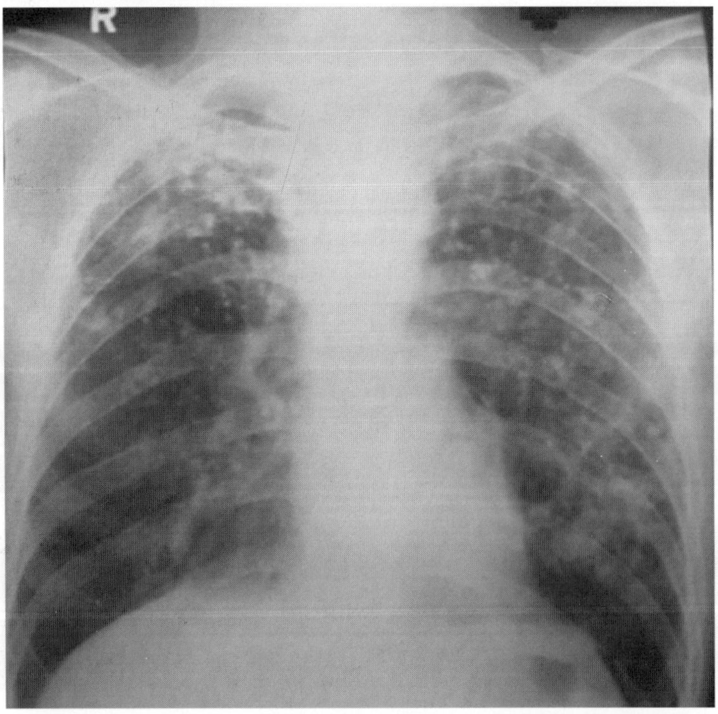

Intrapulmonary calcification (healed pulmonary TB)
Do not forget to ask history of antitubercular treatment in the past

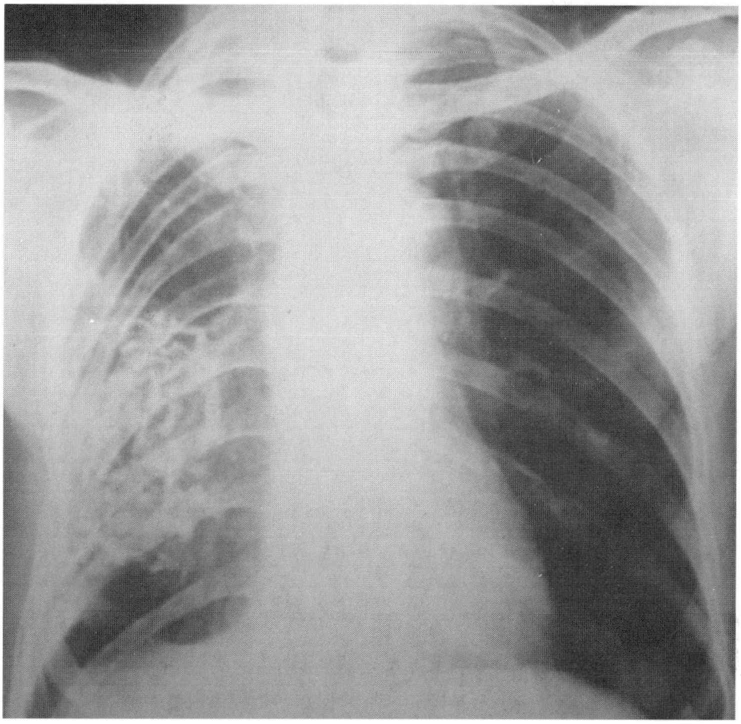

What is this?

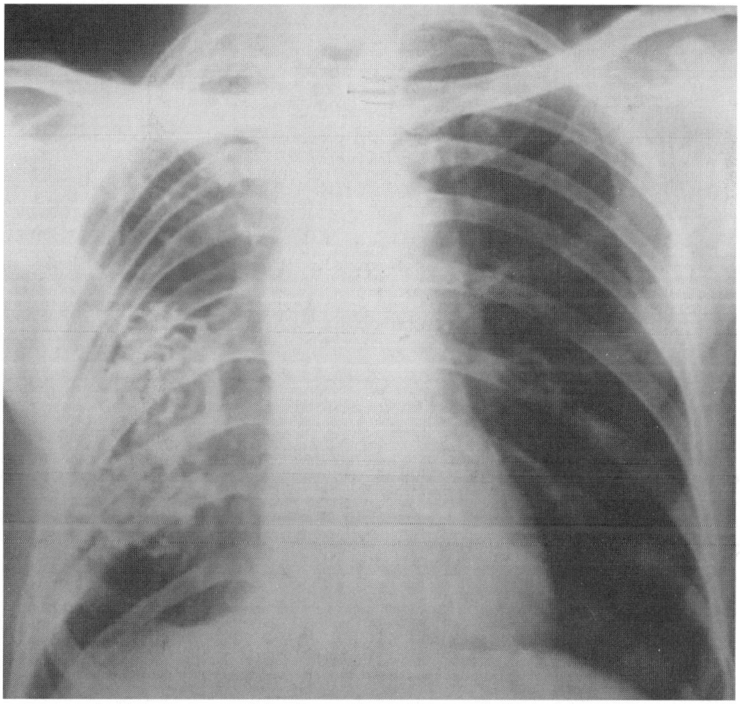

Pleural calcification (right side)
Do not forget to ask history of empyema in the past

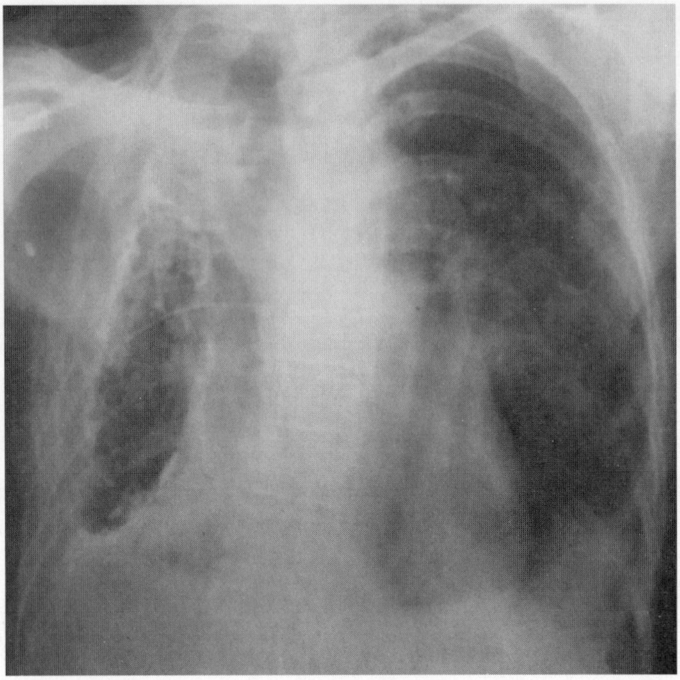

What is this?

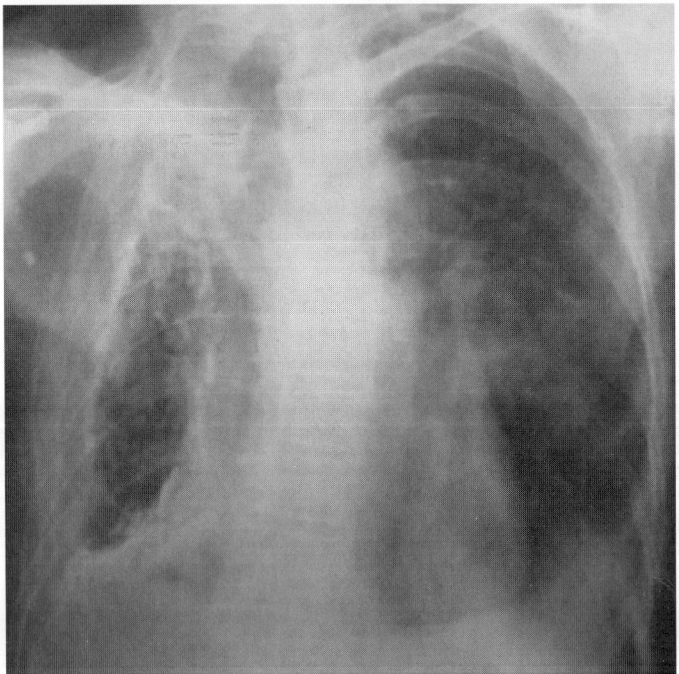

Pleural calcification

Do not forget to ask history of empyema and intercostal tube drainage (ICD) in the past

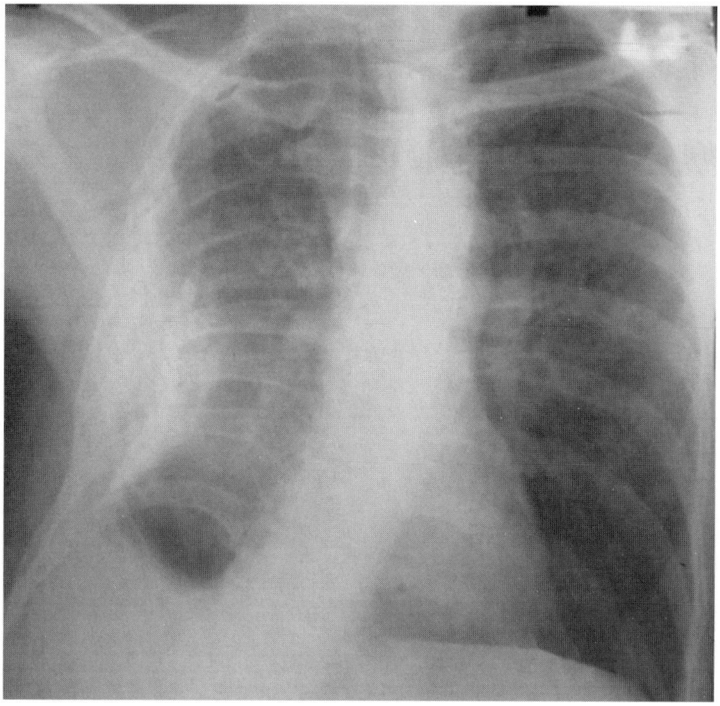

What is this?

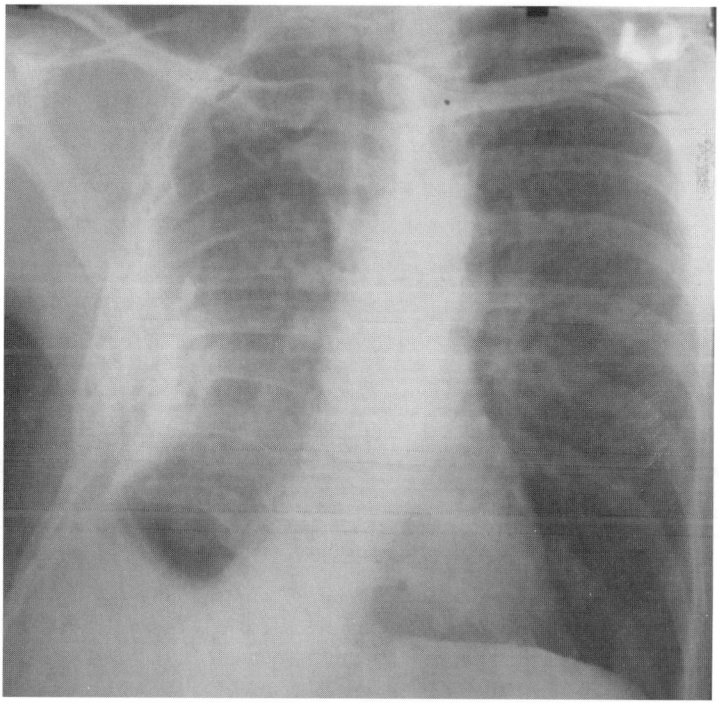

Pleural calcification

Do not forget to ask history of pleural aspiration in the past

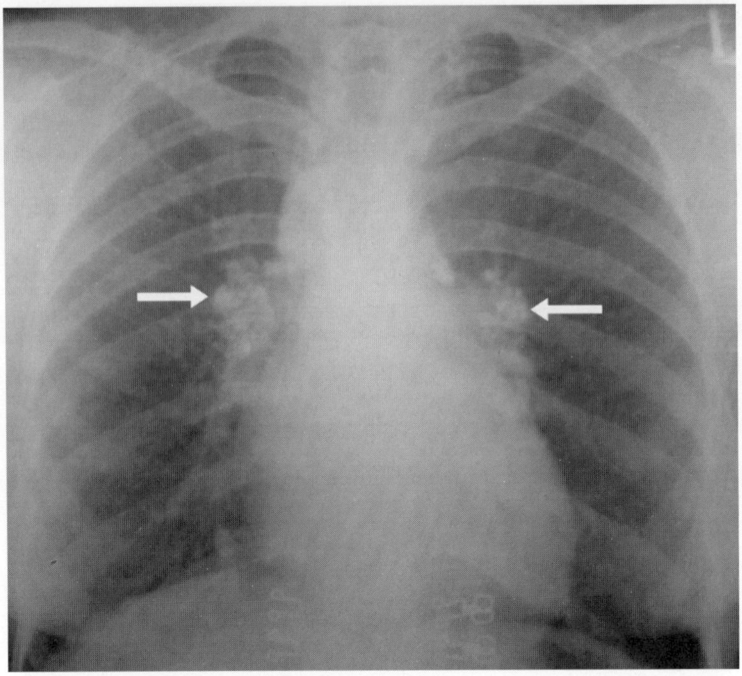

What is this?

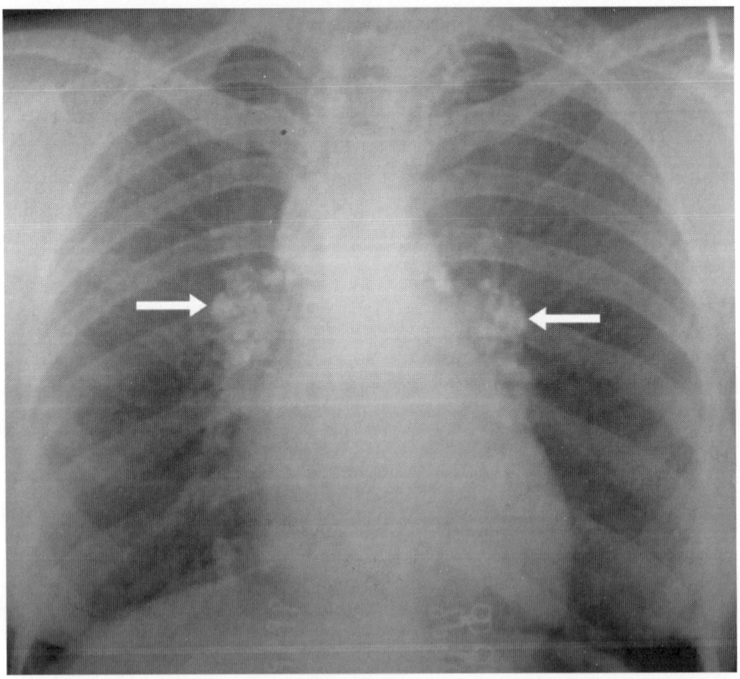

Calcified hilar glands (bilateral)

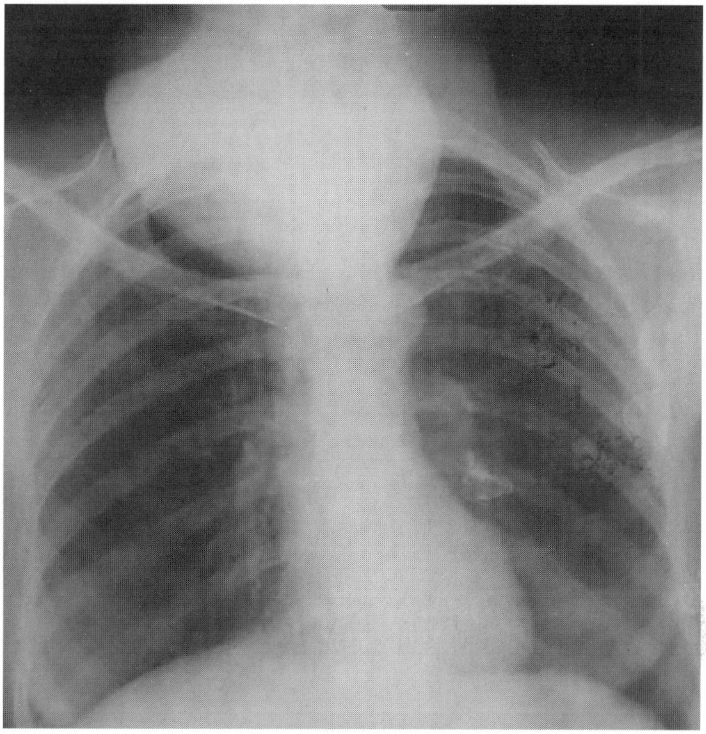

What is this?

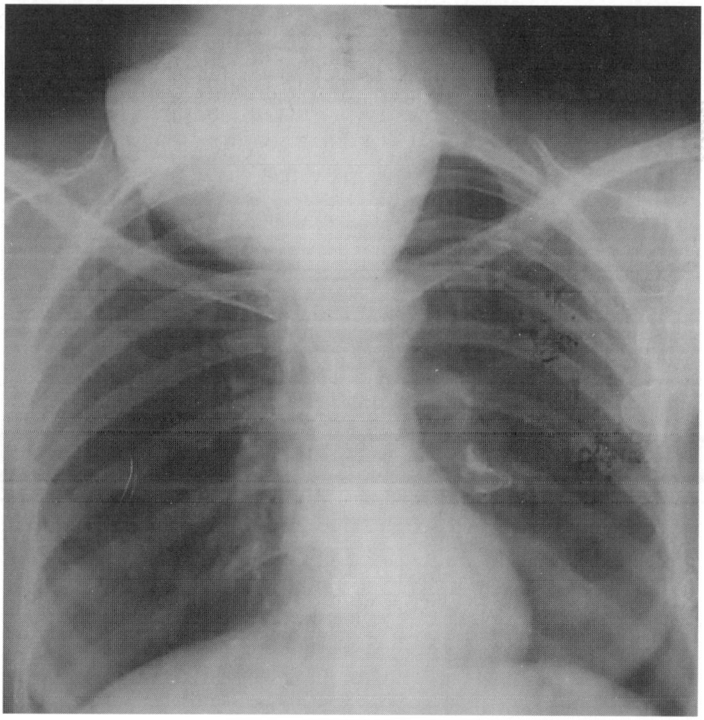

Thyroid calcification

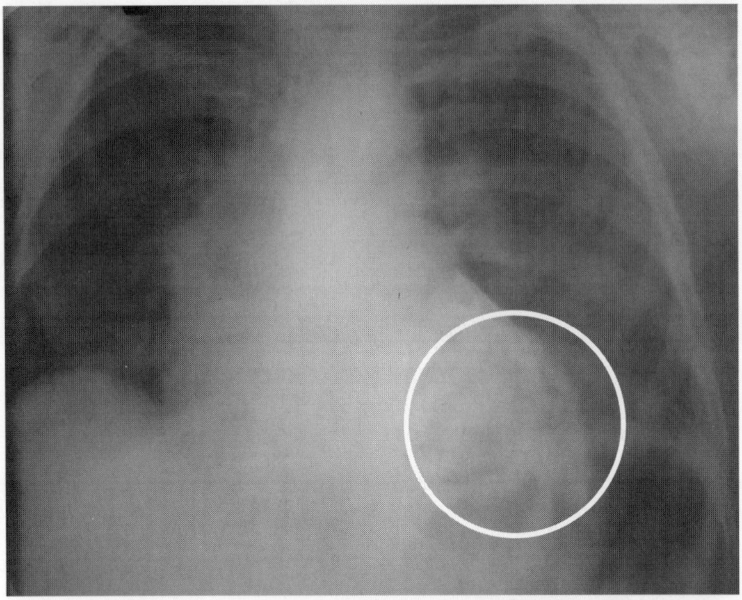

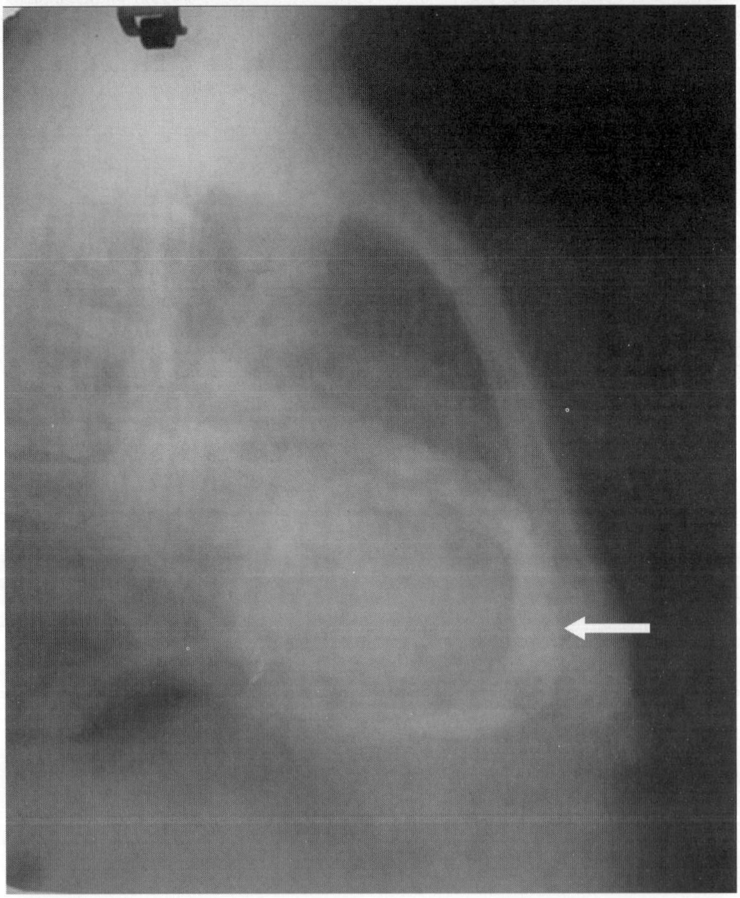

What is this?

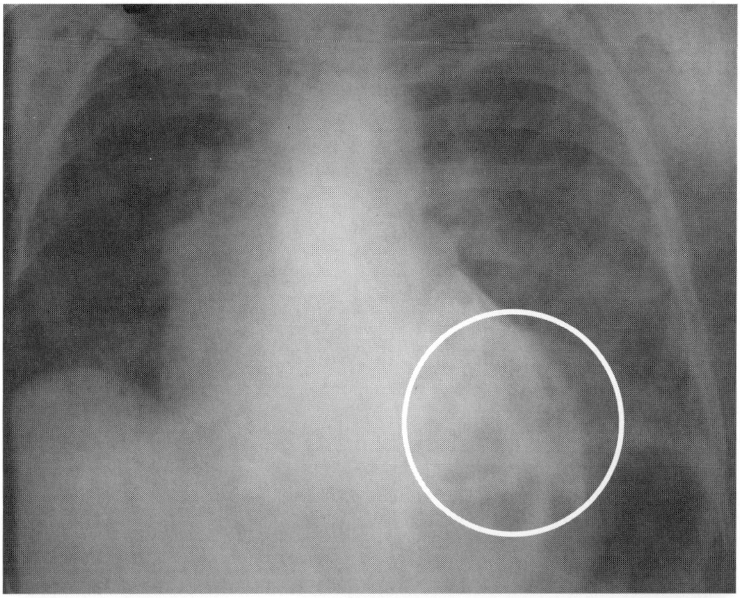

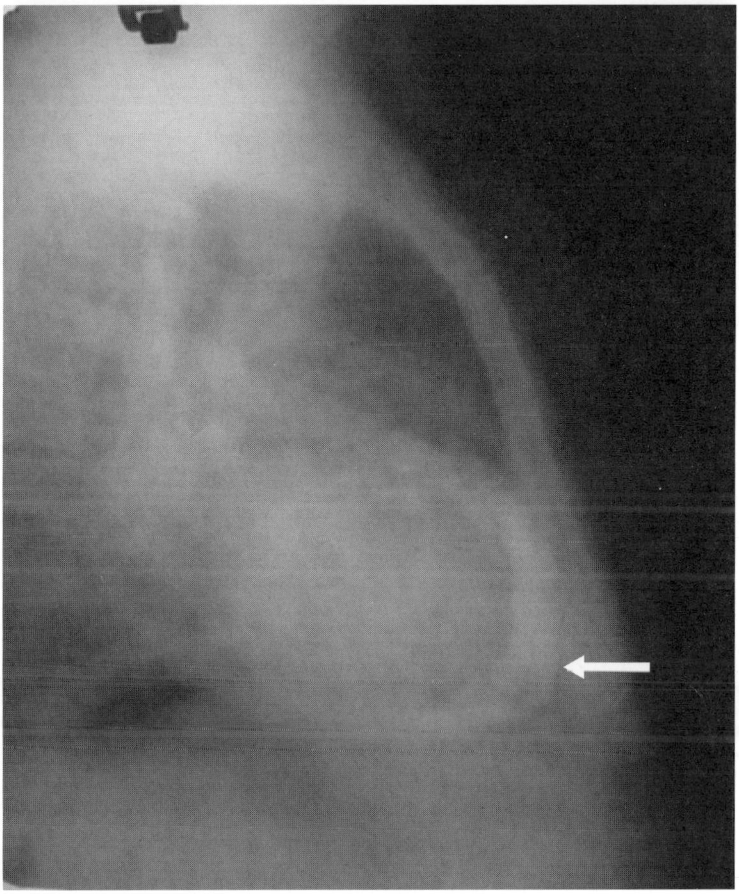

Pericardial calcification

Do not forget to ask history of pericardial effusion and pericardial fluid aspiration. It is a rare condition

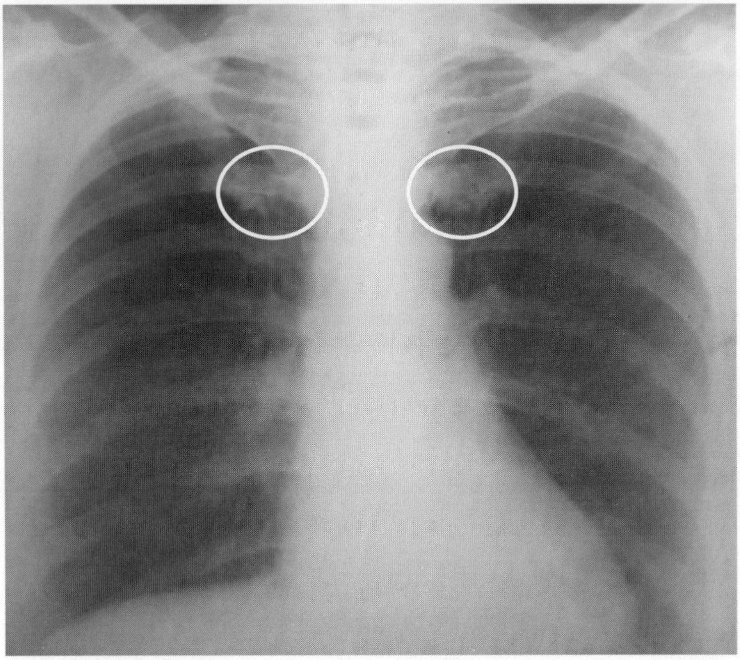

What is this?

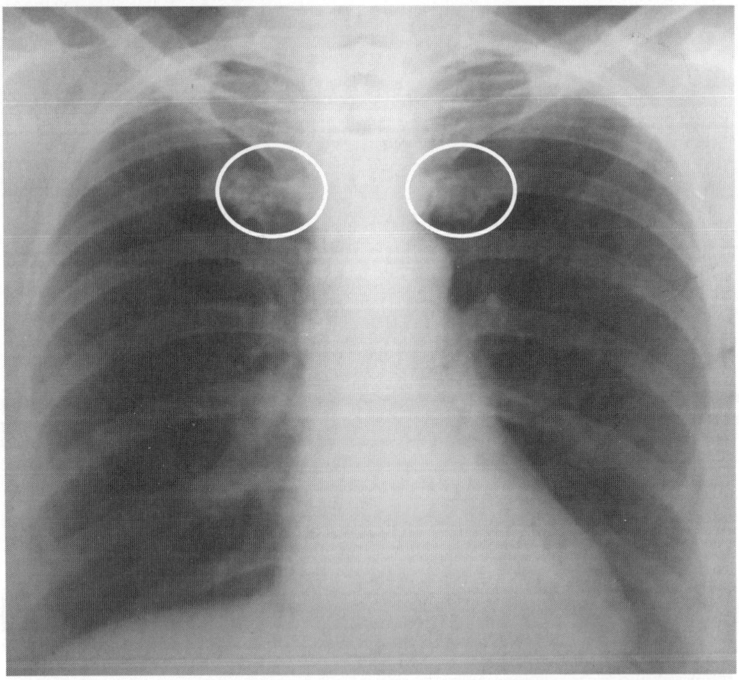

Calcified first costal cartilage

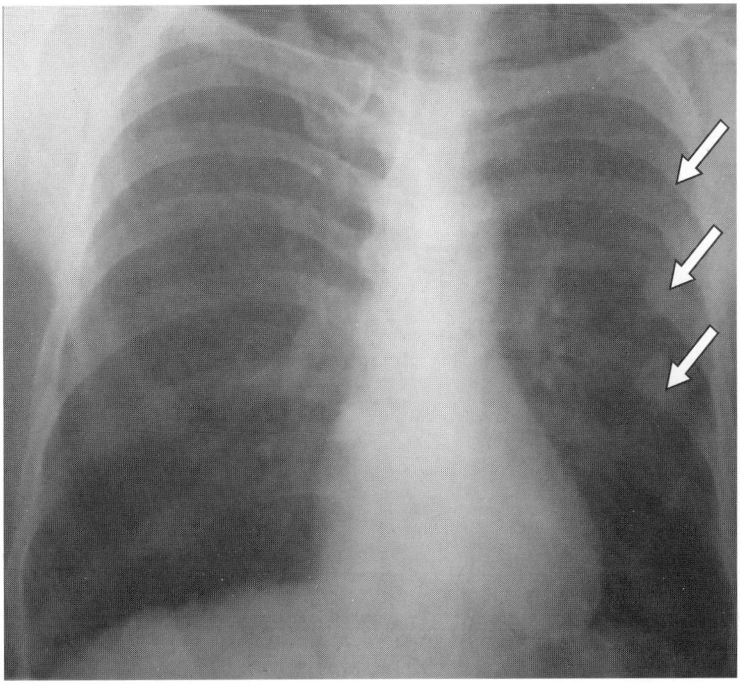

What are these shadows?

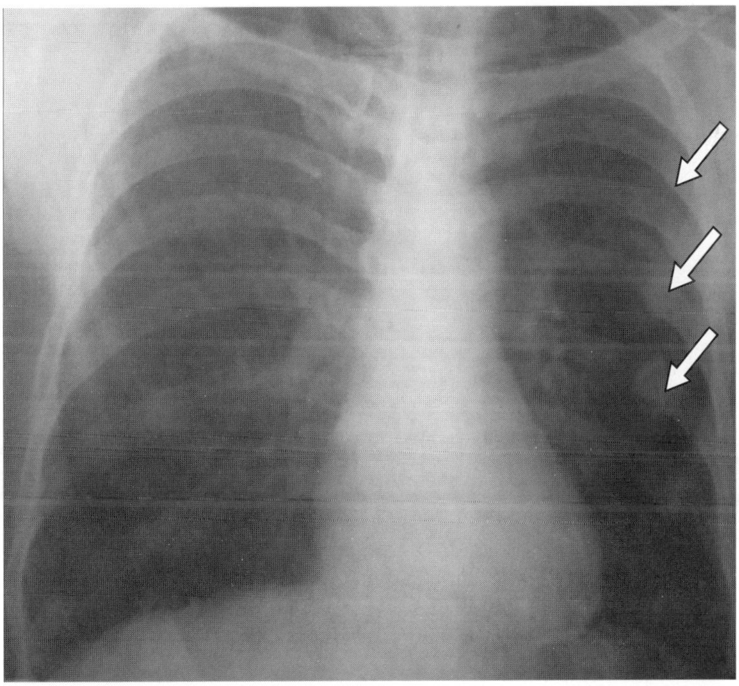

Old multiple fractured ribs with callus formation

Do not forget to ask history of chest trauma in the past

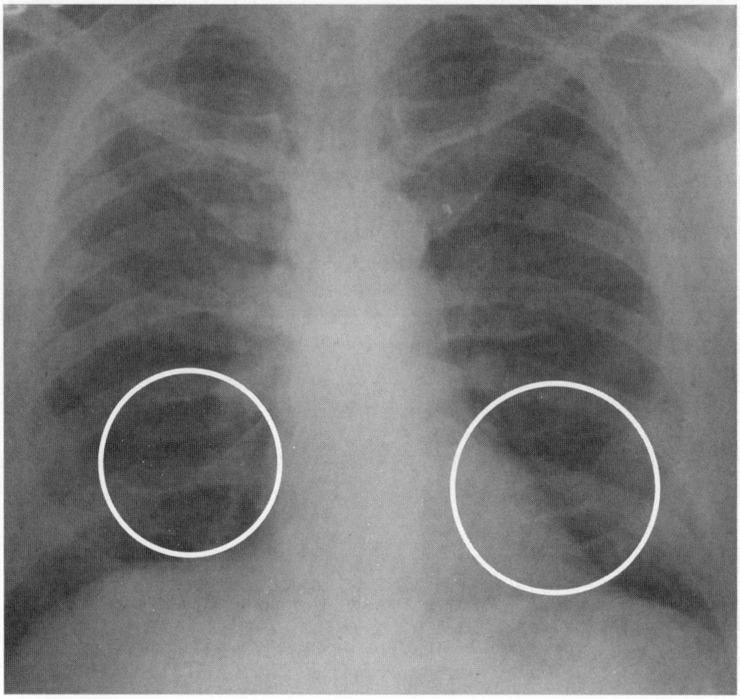

What is this?

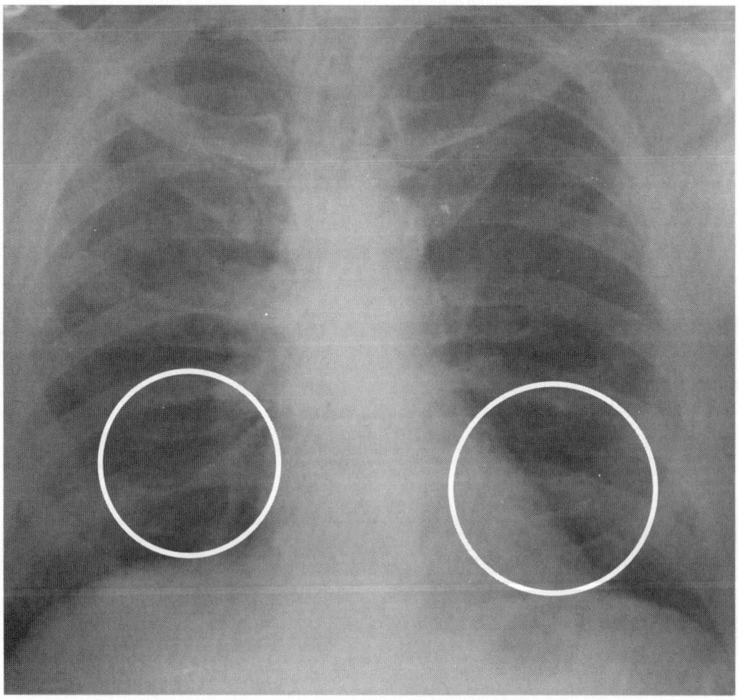

Costal cartilage calcification

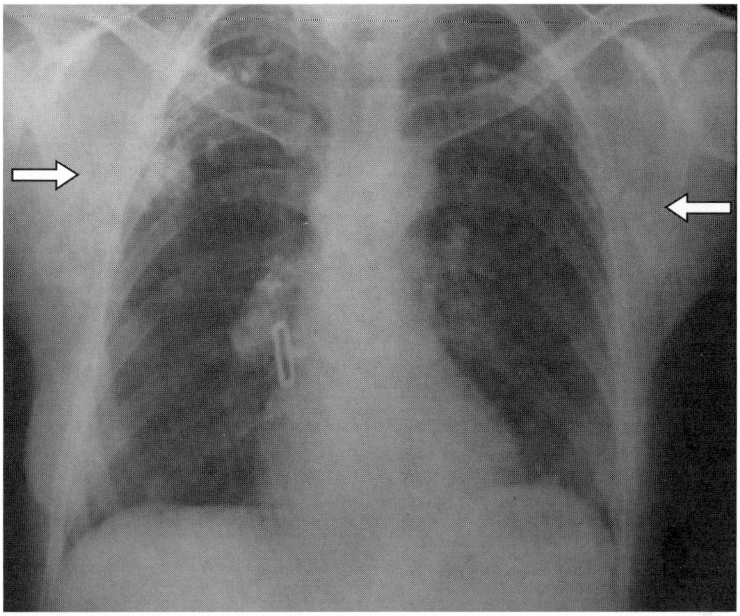

What are these shadows?

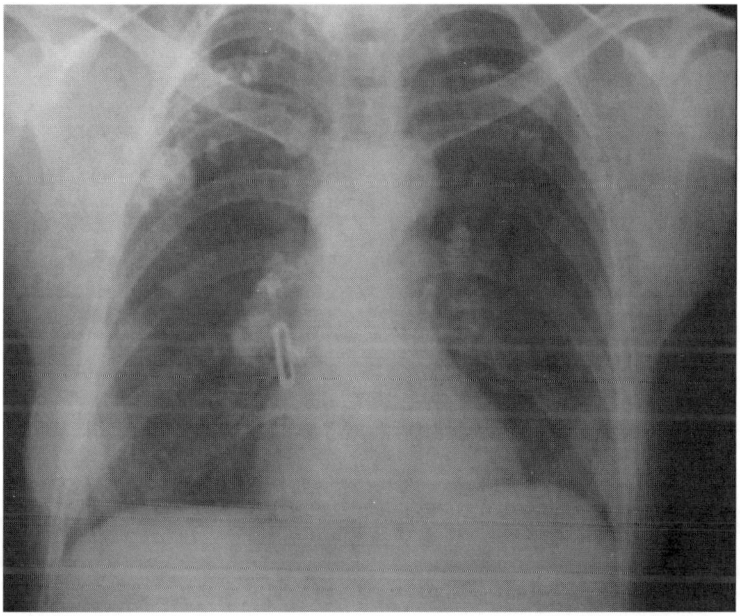

Calcified glands in soft tissue

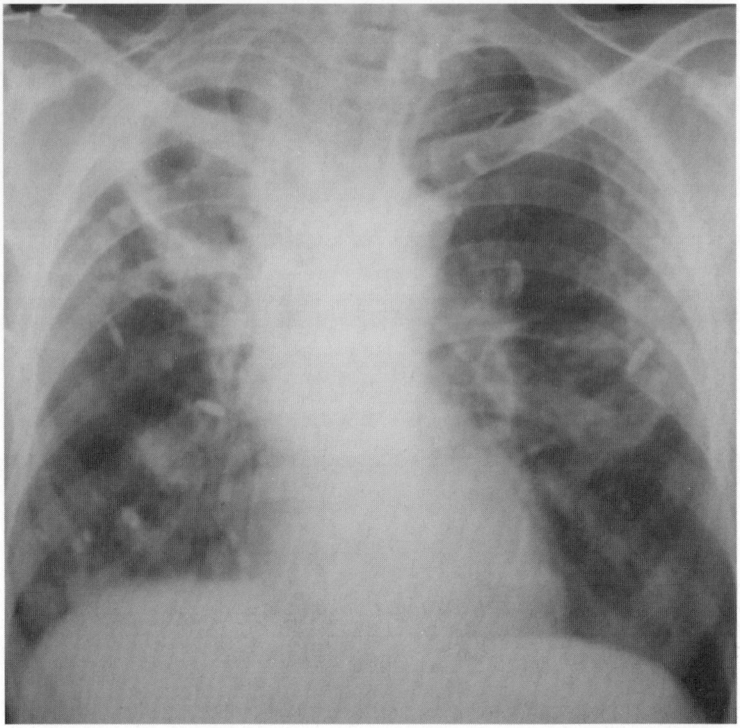

What are these shadows?

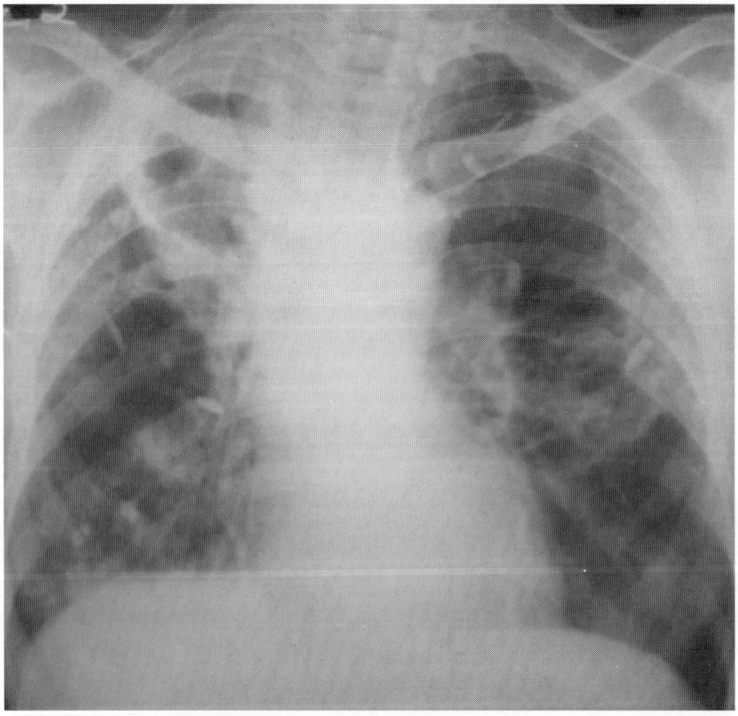

Calcified worms (cysticercosis)

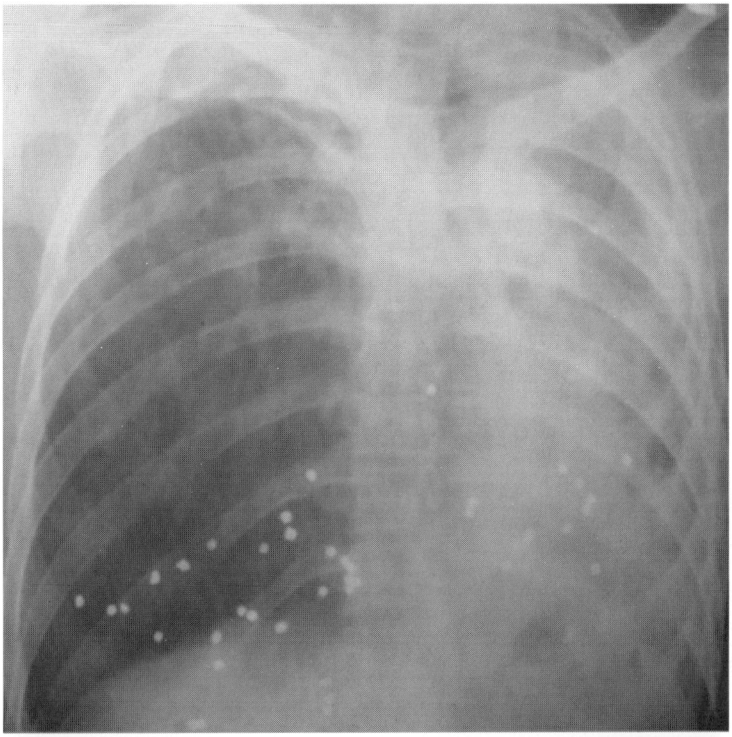

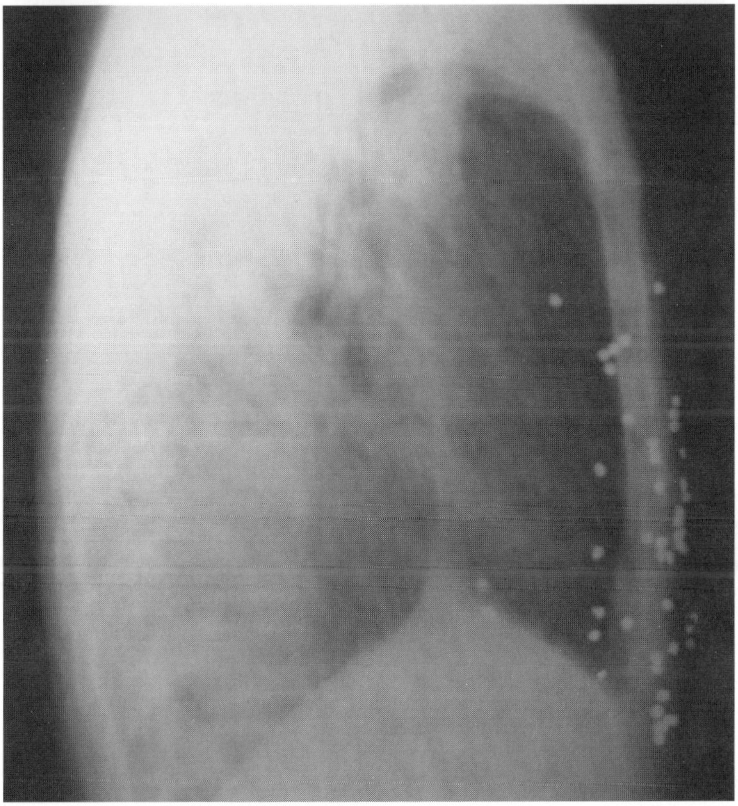

What are these shadows?

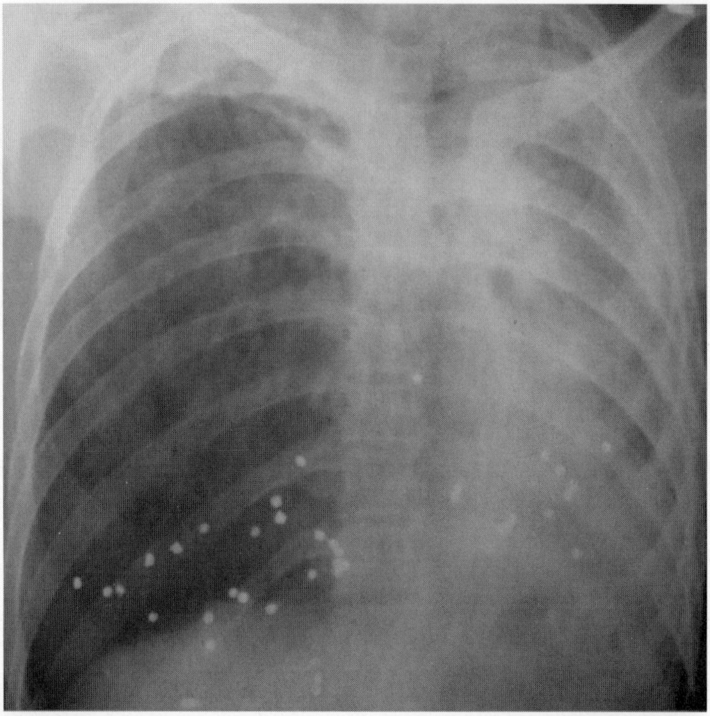

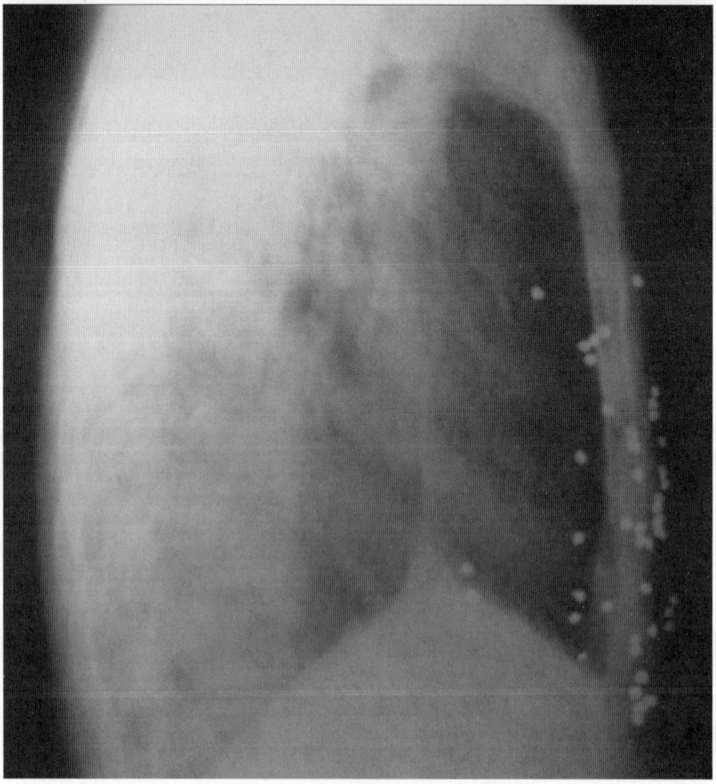

Pellets

Do not forget to ask history of firearm injury in the past

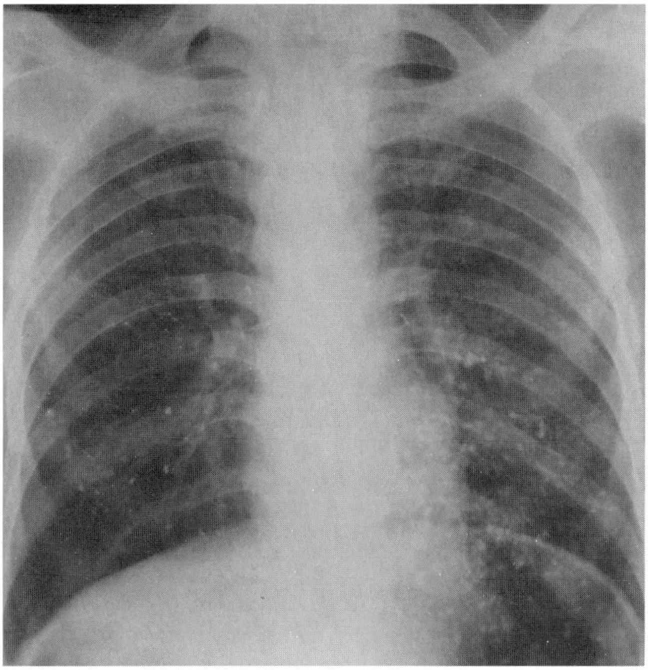

What are these shadows?

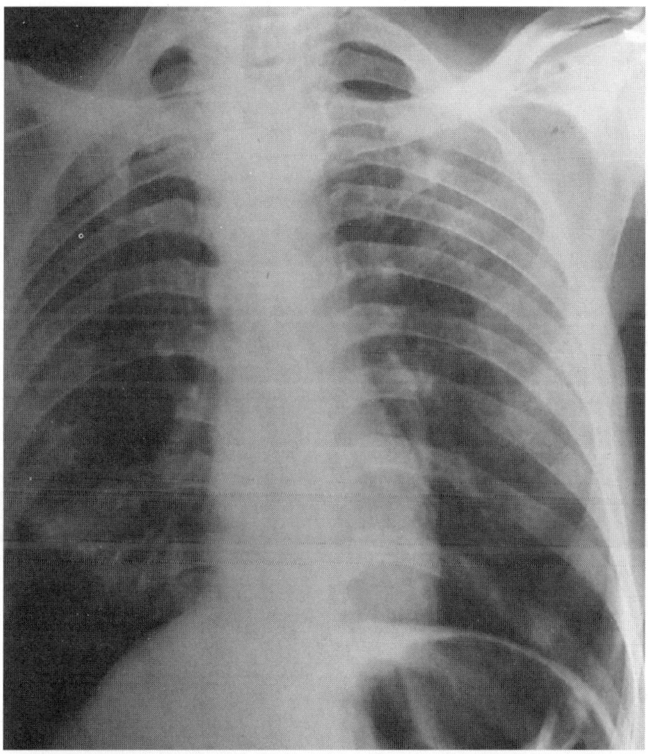

A 46-year-old male with C/o dysphasia, loss of weight and appetite and recurrent haemoptysis

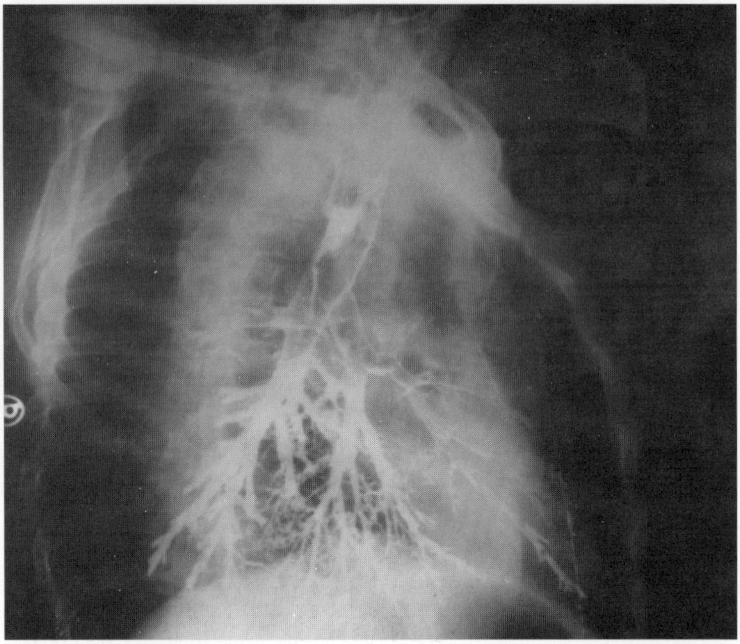

Patient underwent barium swallow to investigate dysphagia but dye enters tracheobronchial tree because of tracheobronchial fistula

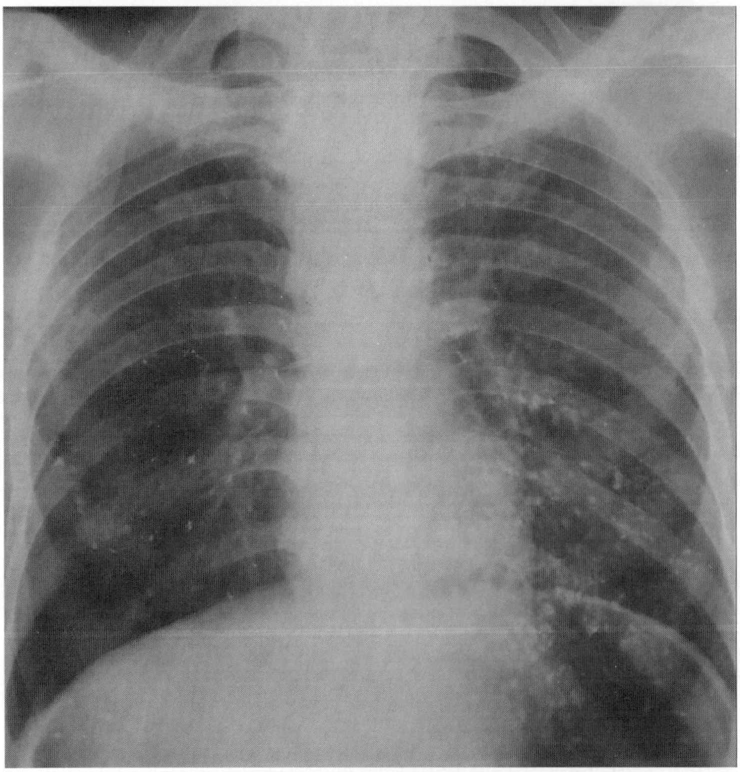

Dye seen in the X-ray after barium swallow

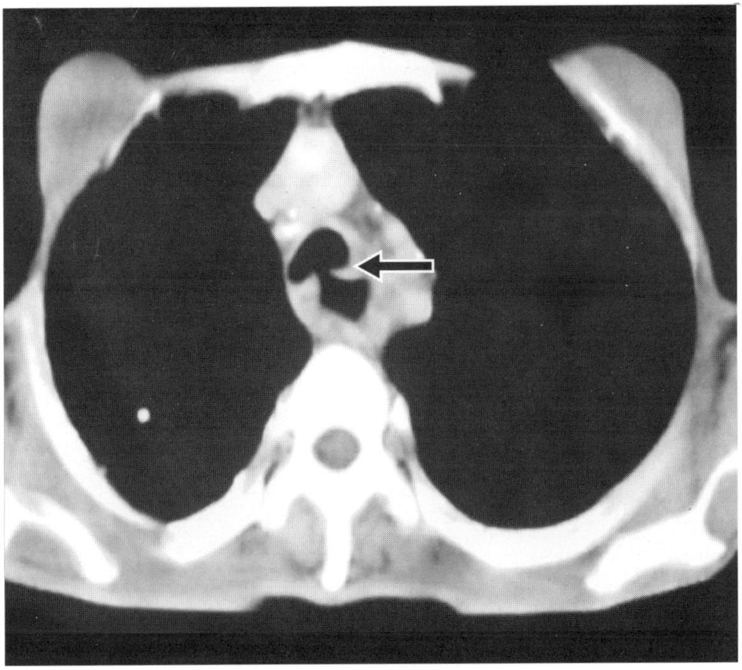

CT shows communication between trachea and oesophagus

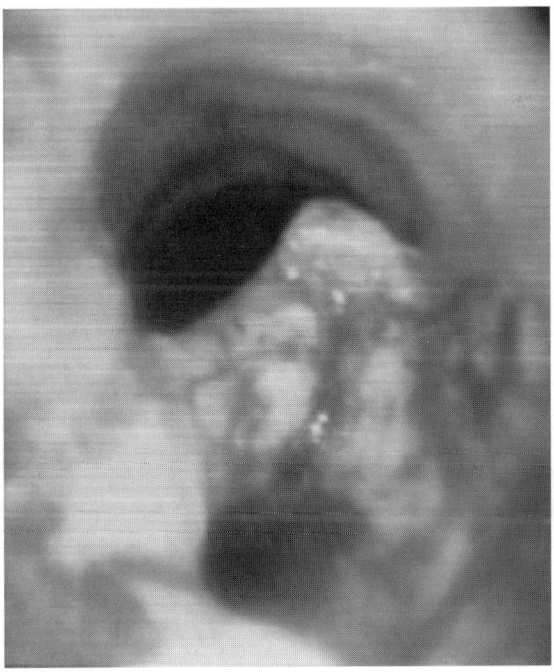

Bronchoscopy shows mass in oesophagus protruding in trachea (Colour Plate I)

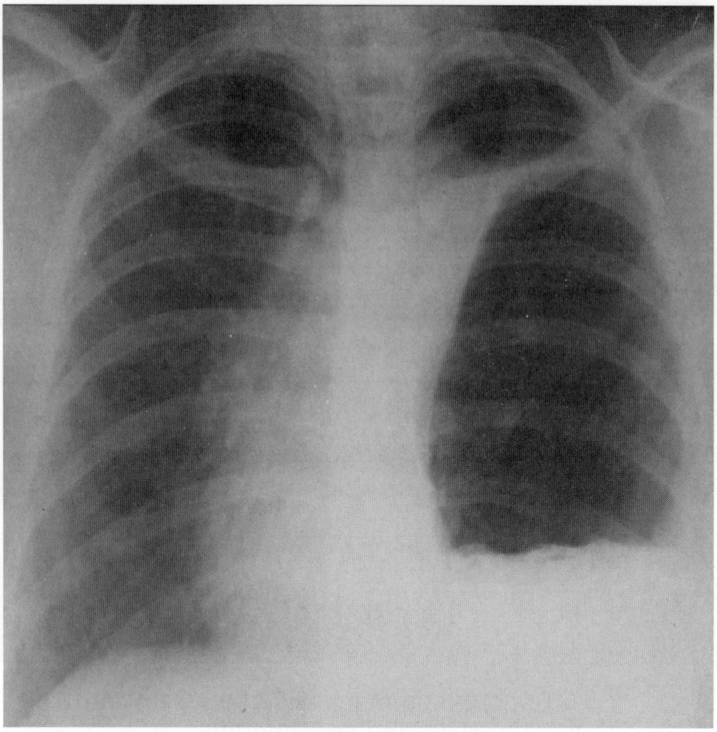

What is this?

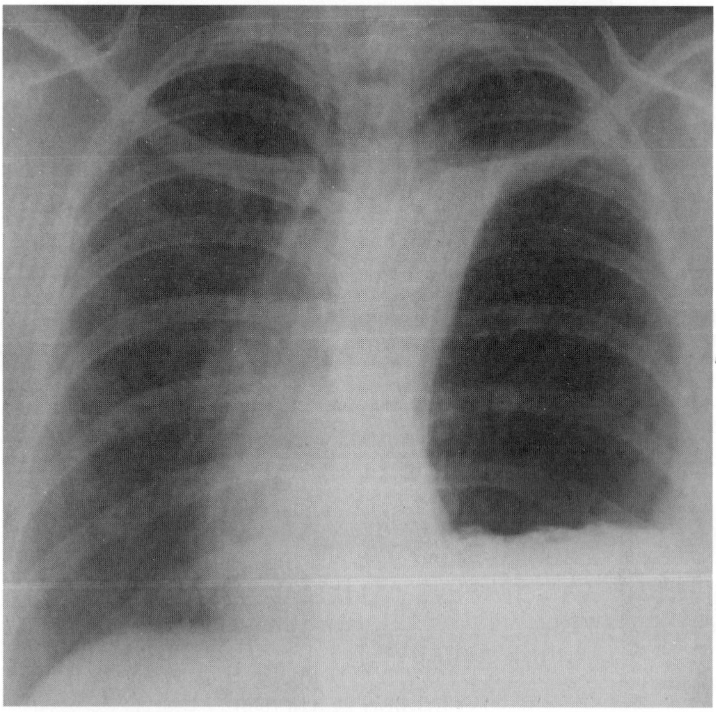

Barium sulphate in stomach causing shadow after barium meal study

CHAPTER

11

Pleura

PLEURA

- Fissure
- Thickened pleura
- Calcified pleura
- Pleural effusion
- Pneumothorax
- Hydropneumothorax

Fissures

- **Minor/Horizontal Fissure**
  - Visible in 70% of PA view, poorly developed or absent in 20% (runs horizontally from the hilum at the lateral margin of right inferior pulmonary artery to meet the 6th rib in axilla)
- **Major/Oblique Fissure**
  - Incomplete in 30%. Seen only in lateral view (lies at level of vertebral end of 5th rib and reaches the diaphragm 2–5 cm behind the cardiophrenic angle)

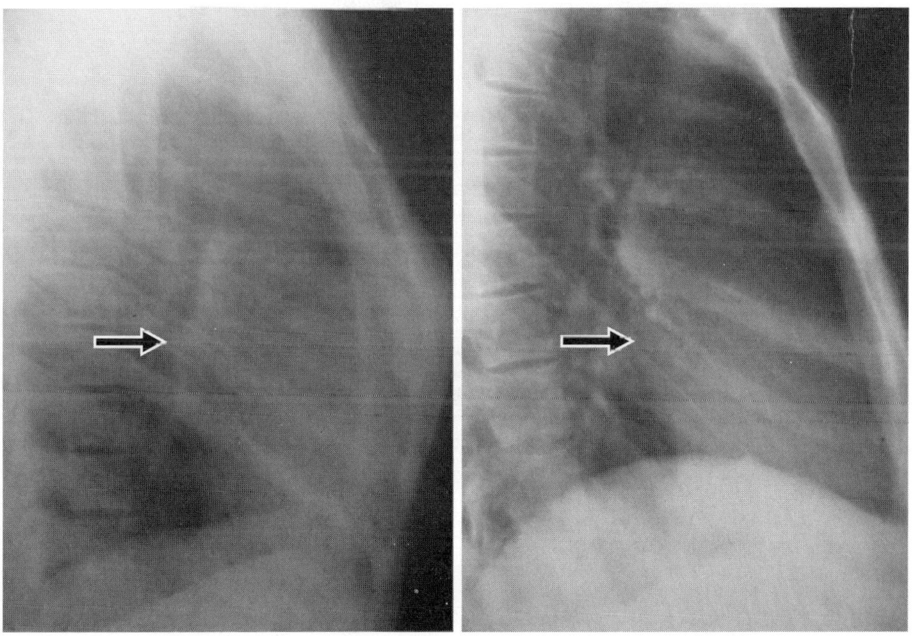

Major/oblique fissure

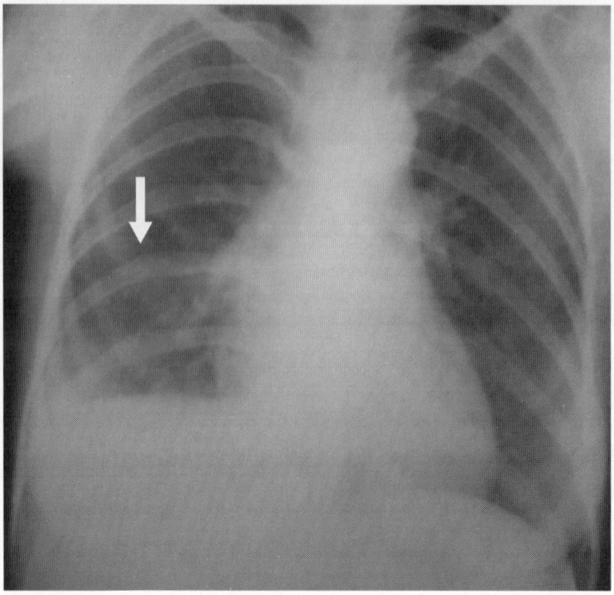

Minor fissure

Accessory Fissures

- Azygos fissure: Visible in 0 .4% of PA view
- Superior accessory fissure: Found in 5% of cases (separates superior segment of lower lobe from other segment)
- Inferior accessory fissure: Found in 5% of cases (separates medial basal segment of lower lobe from other segment)

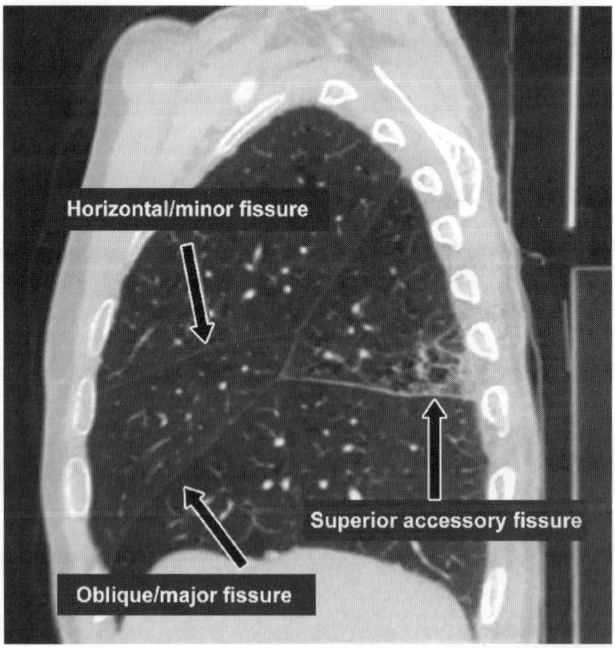

Fissures

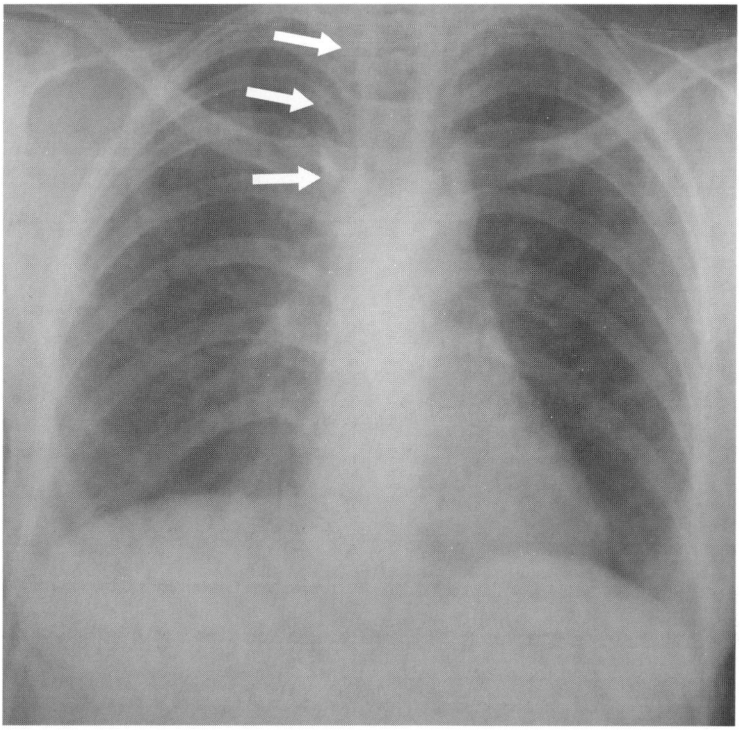

What is this?

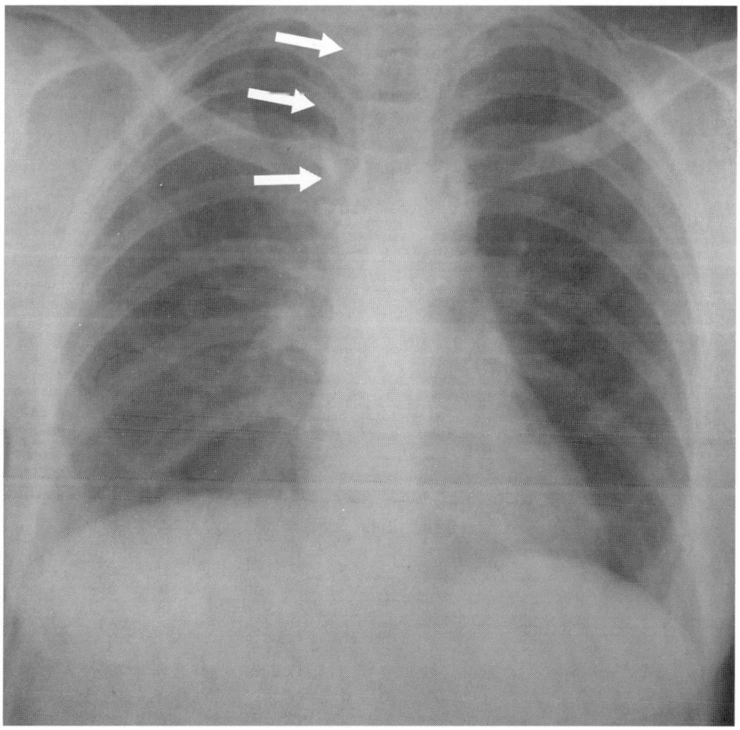

Azygos fissure

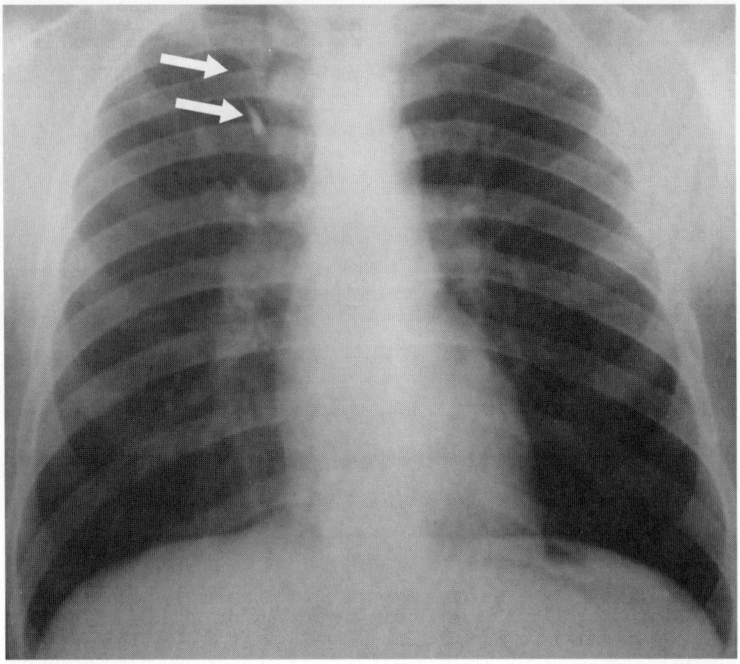

Azygos fissure

Azygos Fissures

A laterally displaced azygos vein creates a deep pleural fissure into the apical segment of the right upper lobe during embryological development known as azygos fissure

It is a normal anatomic variant, due to the invagination of the azygos vein and pleura during development in the fetus

Prevalence—0.4 % in chest X-ray and 1% in autopsy

It divides upper lobe into azygos lobe and rest of the upper lobe

No clinical significance except that it can confuse with other conditions which may be important to surgeon during lung surgery

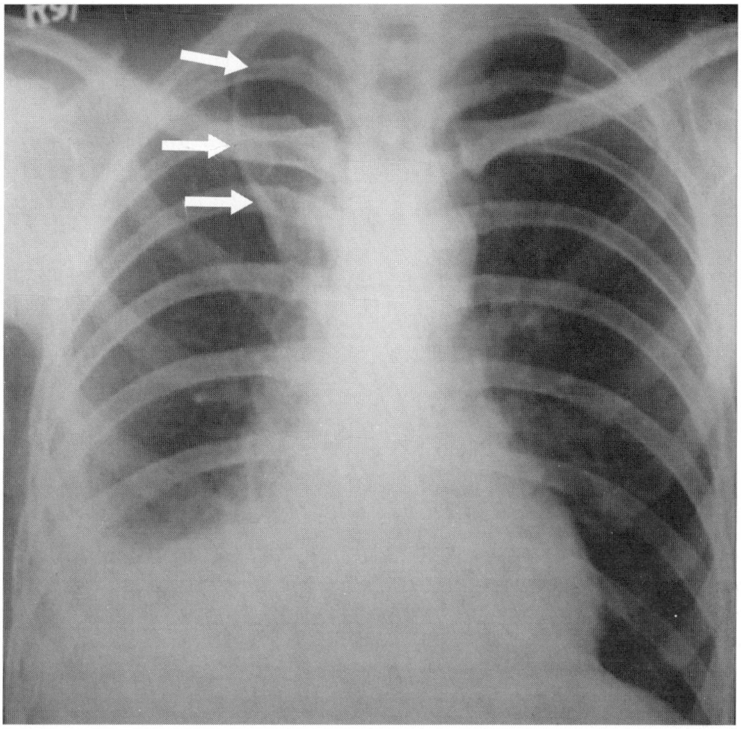

What are these shadows?

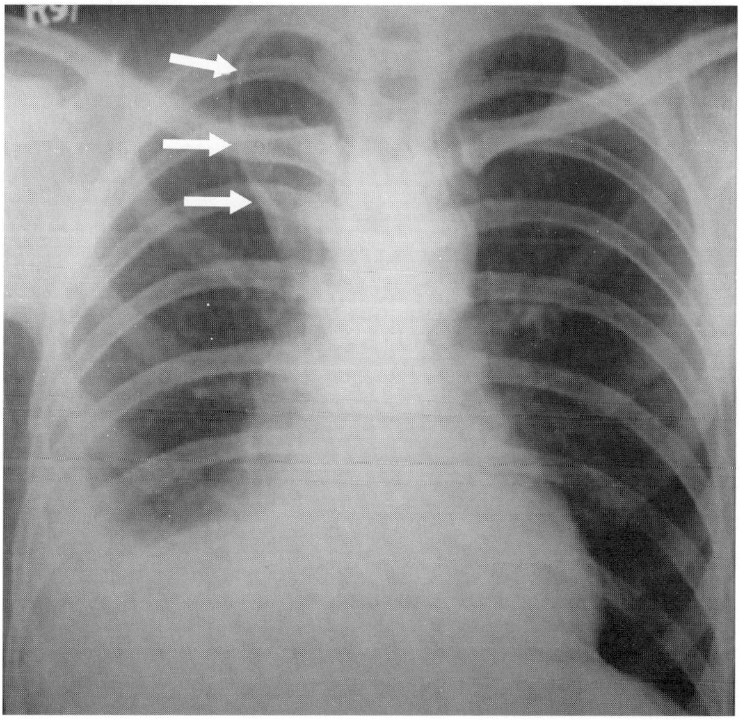

Fluid in azygos fissure with pleural effusion right

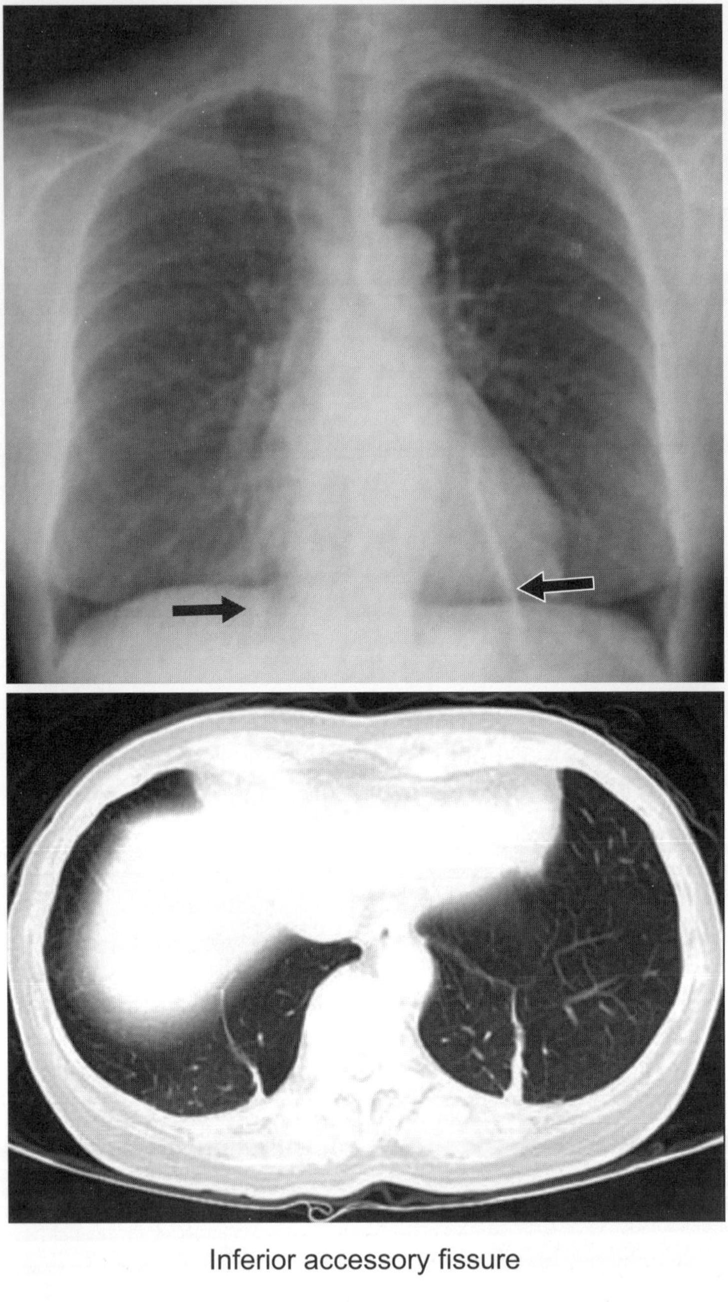

Inferior accessory fissure

Thickened Pleura

- Tubercular effusion
- Old empyema
- Haemothorax
- Radiation therapy
- Systemic disease: SLE, rheumatoid, asbestosis, silicotic massive fibrosis
- Pleural tumors: Fibroma, mesothelioma, sarcoma
- Drugs: Practolol, methysergide

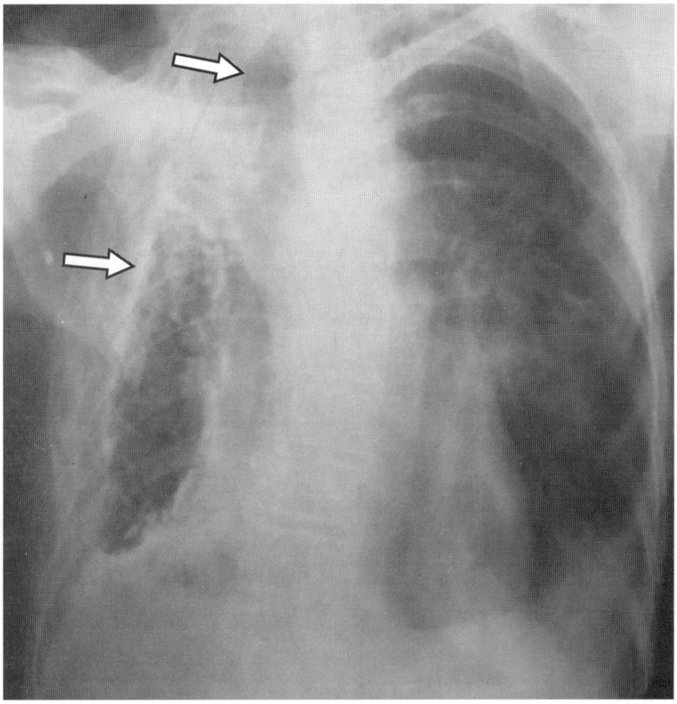

What are these shadows?

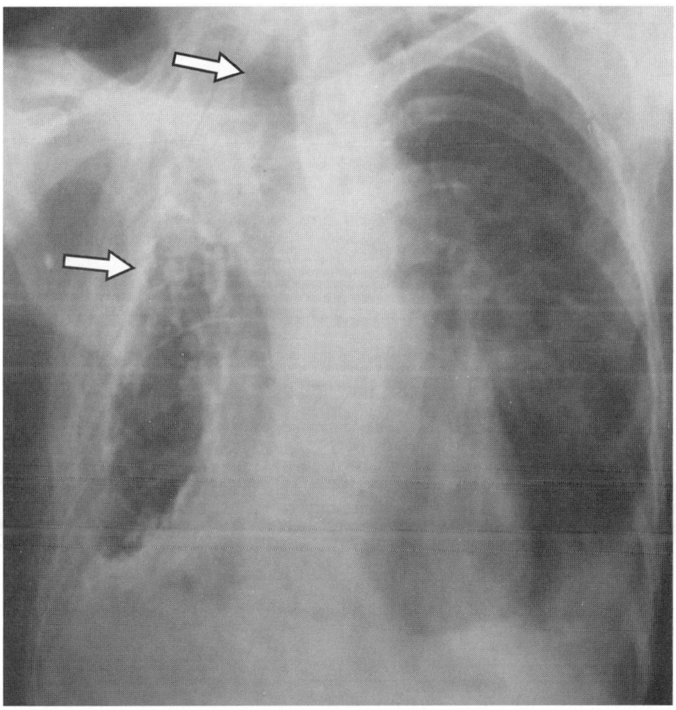

Thickened pleura with pleural calcification

Do not forget to ask history of empyema in the past

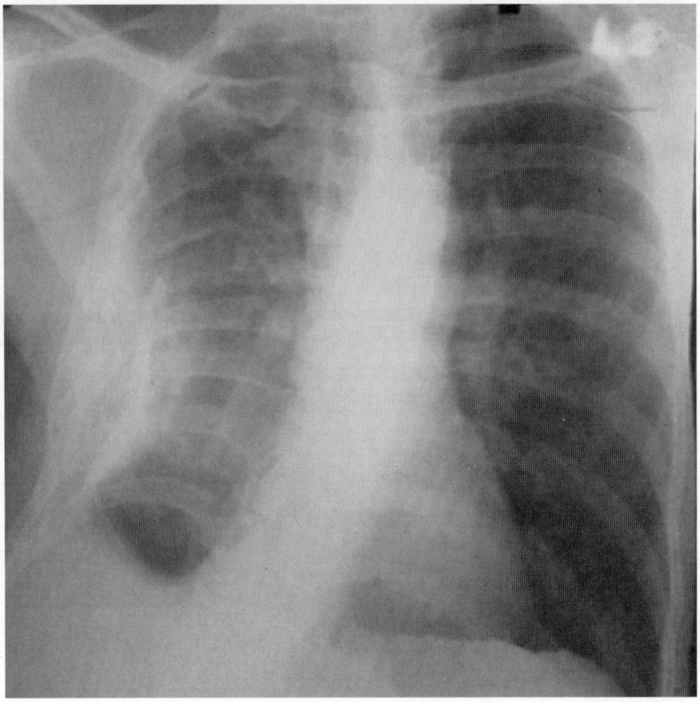

What are these shadows?

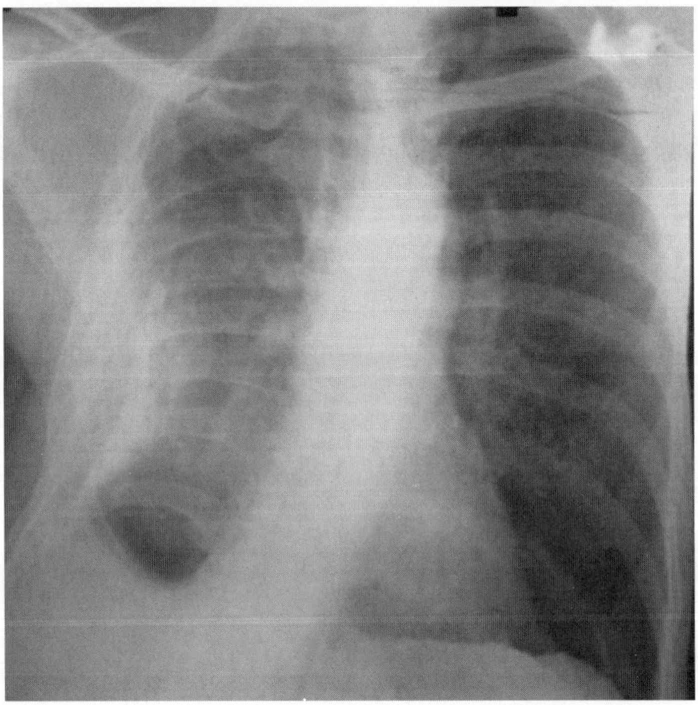

Thickened pleura

Do not forget to ask history of pleural aspiration in the past

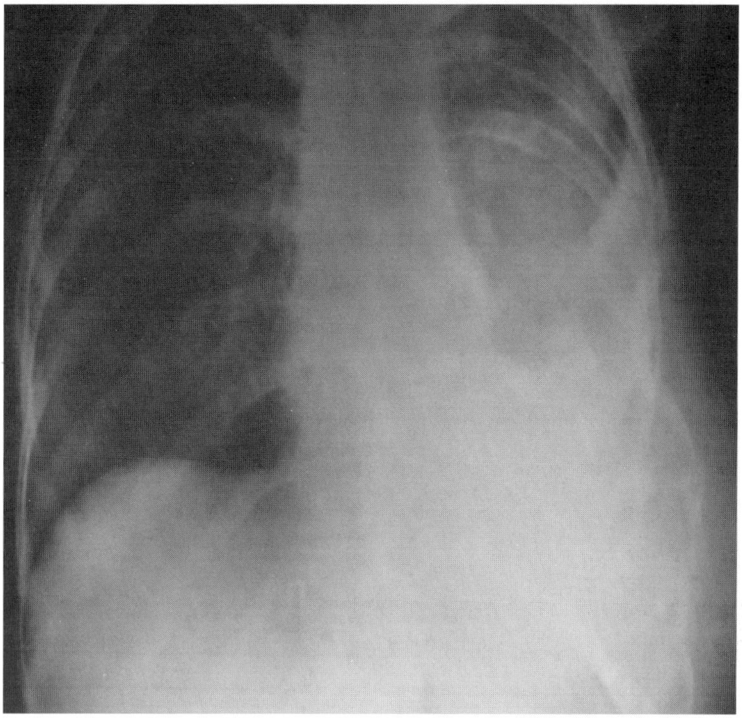

What is this?

C/O severe chest pain on left side and breathlessness

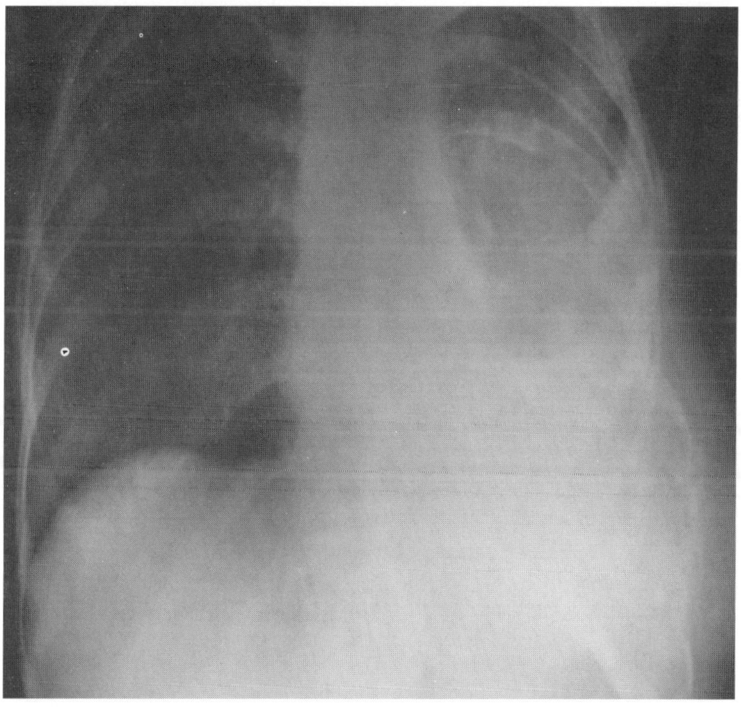

Malignant mesothelioma

Pleural Effusion

Fluid in pleural space. It can be free fluid or loculated

Transudative Effusion—*What are the Causes?*

- Congestive cardiac failure
- Constrictive pericarditis
- Pericardial effusion
- Massive pulmonary embolism
- Cirrhosis
- Nephrotic syndrome
- Malnutrition
- Protein losing enteritis
- Myxoedema
- Peritoneal dialysis
- Transplant of lung

Exudative Effusion—*What are the Causes?*

- Tuberculosis
- Pneumonia
- Post-myocardiac infarction
- Systemic lupus erythematosus (SLE)
- Rheumatoid disease
- Pancreatitis
- Uraemia
- Asbestosis
- Radiation
- Yellow nail syndrome
- Mesothelioma
- Lymphoma
- Metastasis

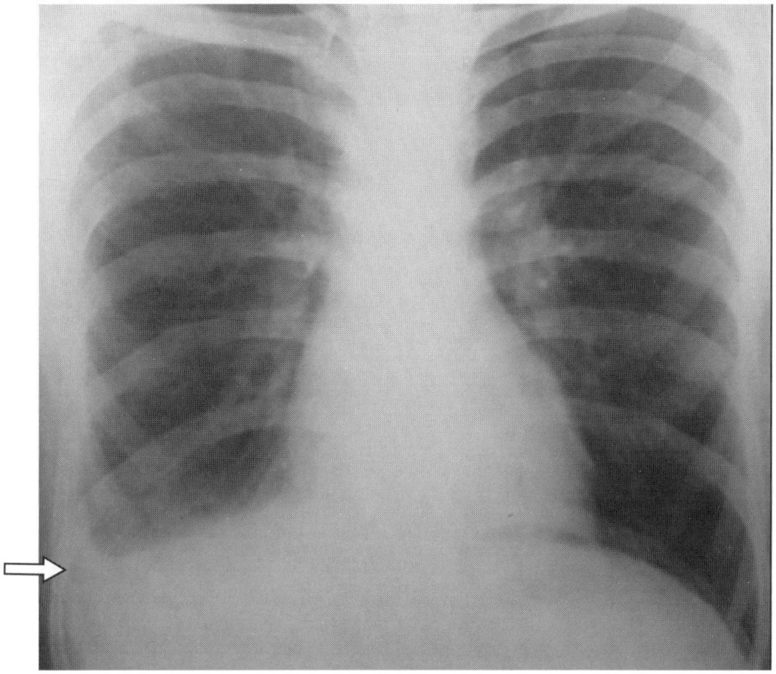

What is this?

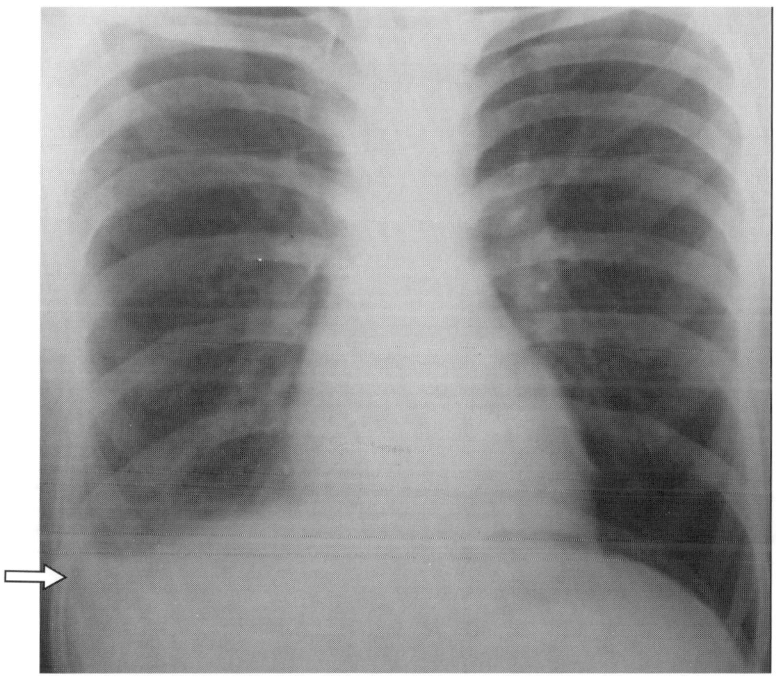

Small pleural effusion (right)

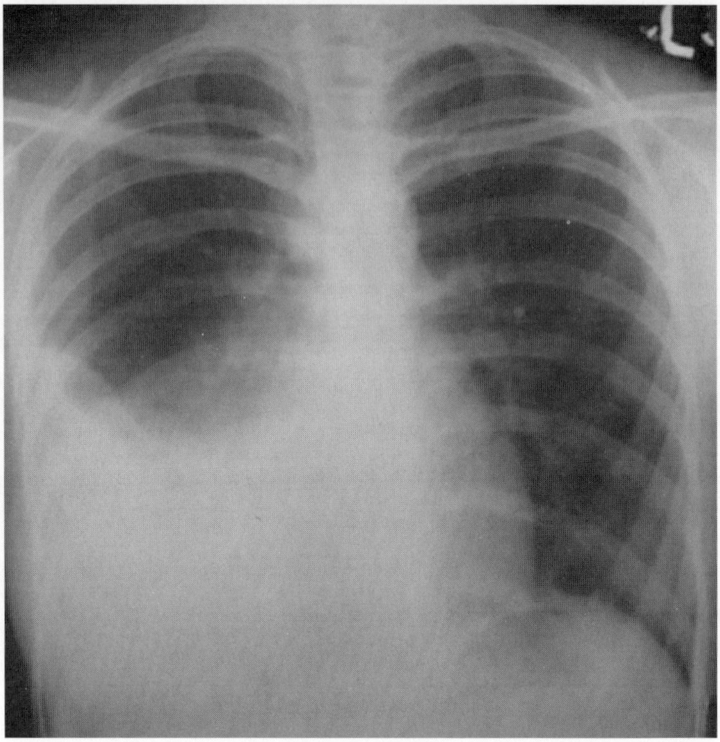

What is this?

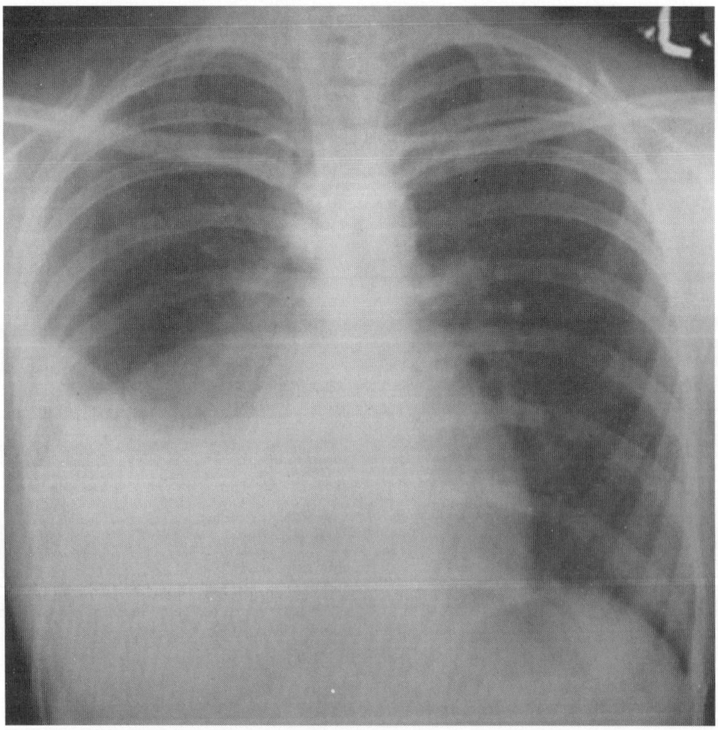

Moderate pleural effusion (right)

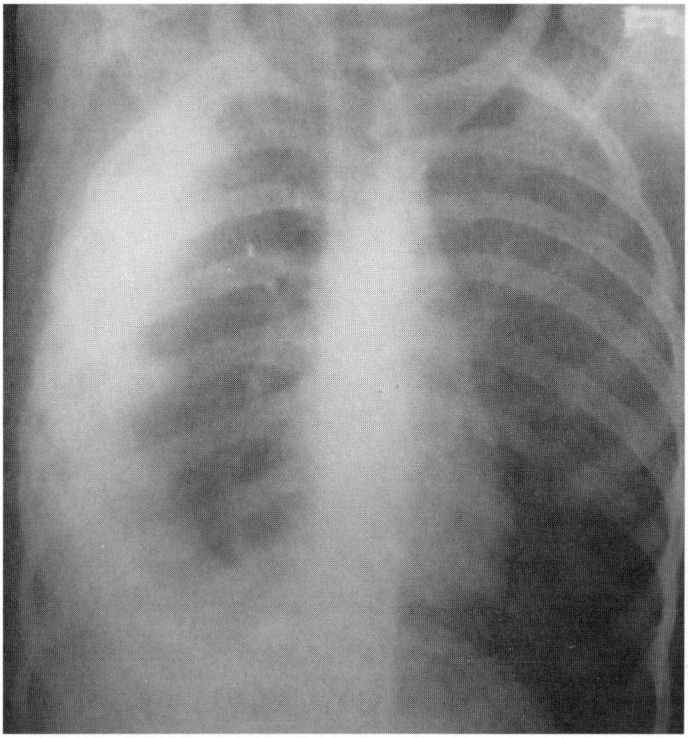

What is this?

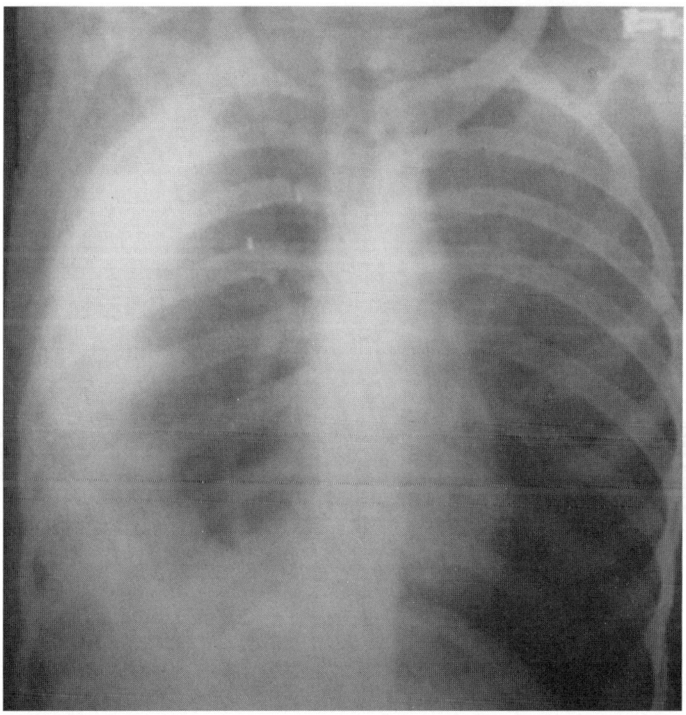

A typical pleural effusion (right)

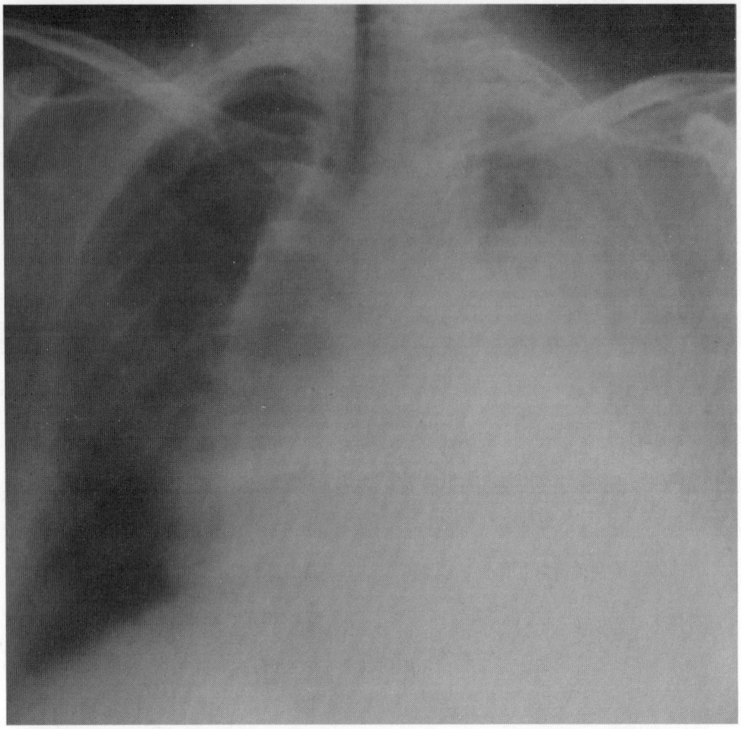

What is this?

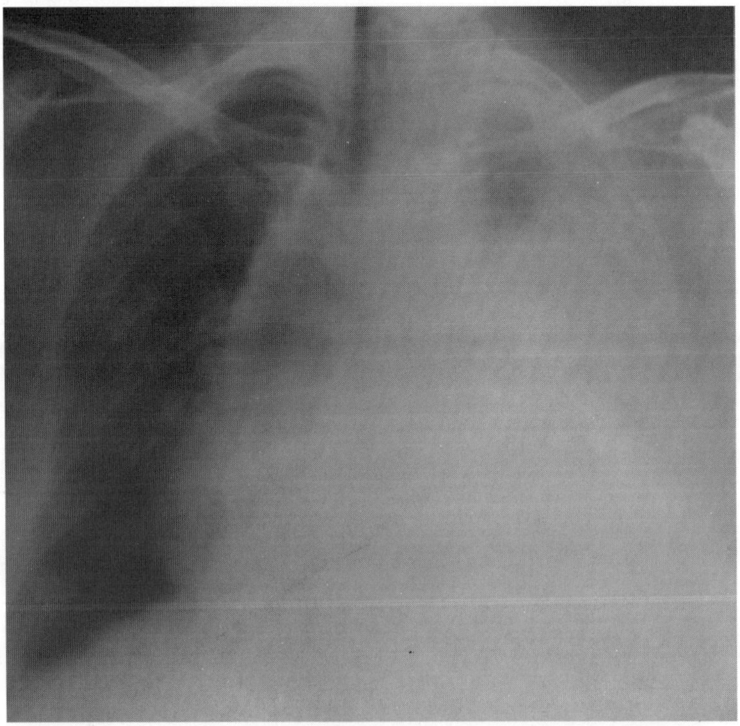

Massive pleural effusion (left)

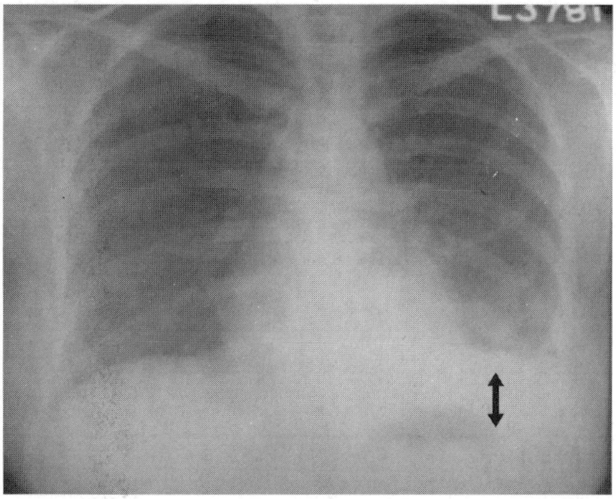

What is this?
Concentrate on left side

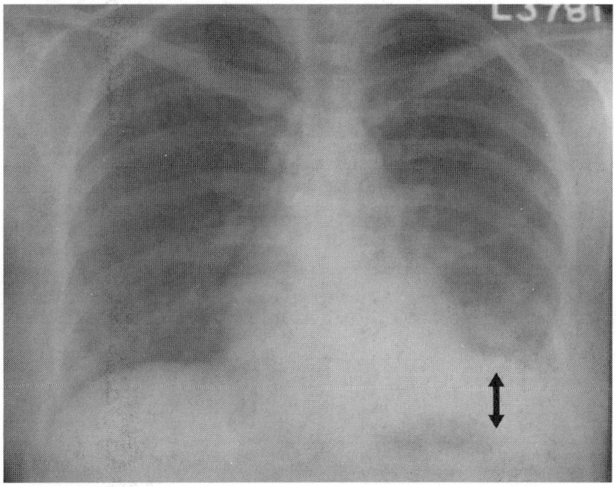

Unilateral raised diaphragm cause infrapulmonary effusion (left)

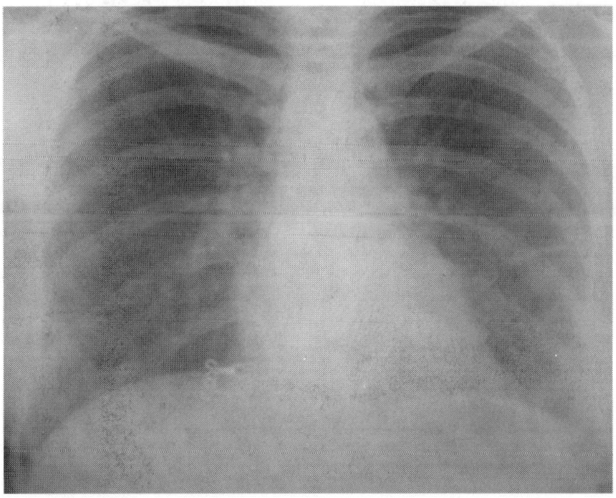

Left diaphragm normal after treatment

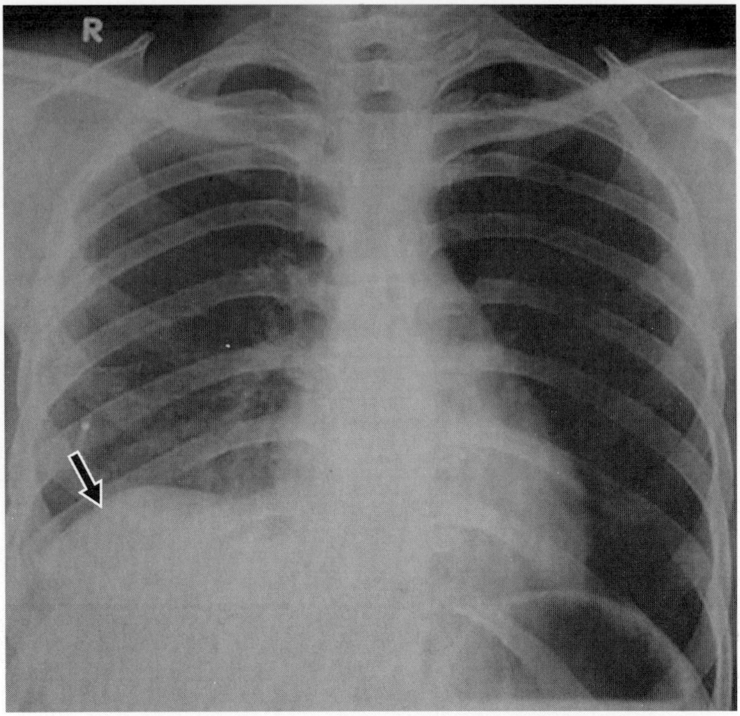

What is this?

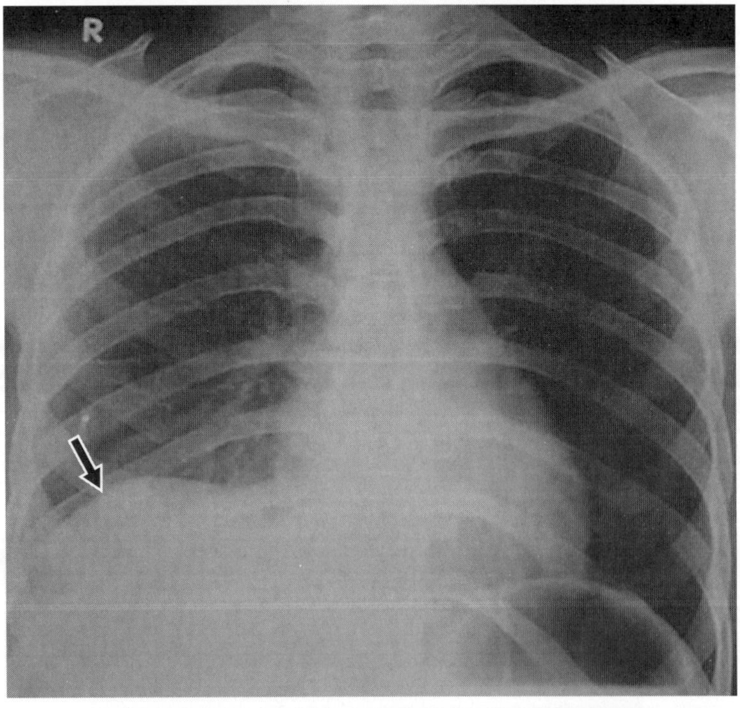

Raised dome of diaphragm with lateral shifting of highest point of diaphragm (right)
Infrapulmonary pleural effusion (right)

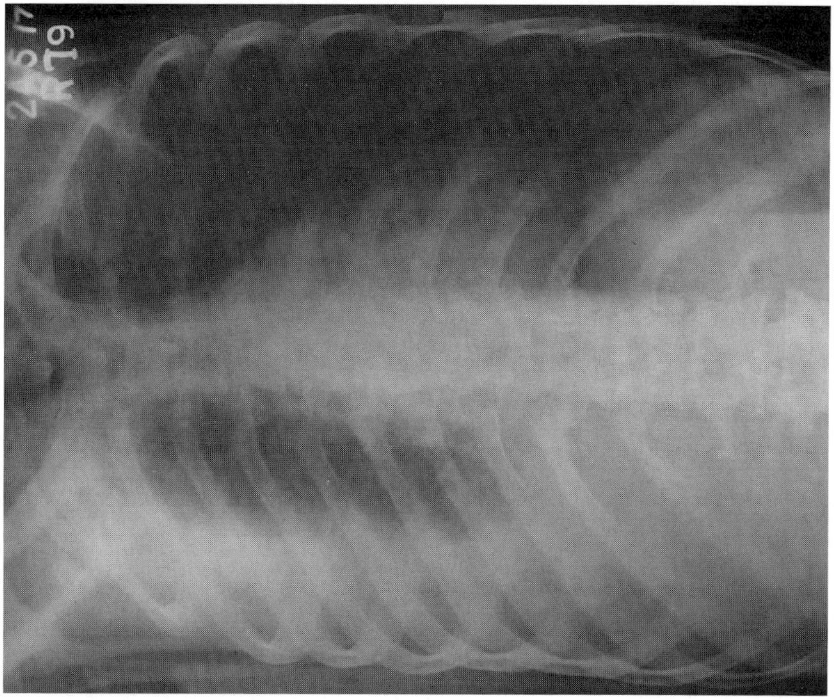

RT lateral decubitus view confirmed infrapulmonary pleural effusion (right)
Please note that fluid has shifted with change of position

Causes of Bilateral Pleural Effusion

Exudative

- Malignancy
- Rheumatologic conditions
- Pneumonia
- Congestive heart failure treated with diuretics
- Renal failure
- Tuberculosis
- Pulmonary embolism

Transudative

- Congestive cardiac failure
- Liver failure
- Constrictive pericarditis
- Hypoalbuminemia
- Hypothyroidism

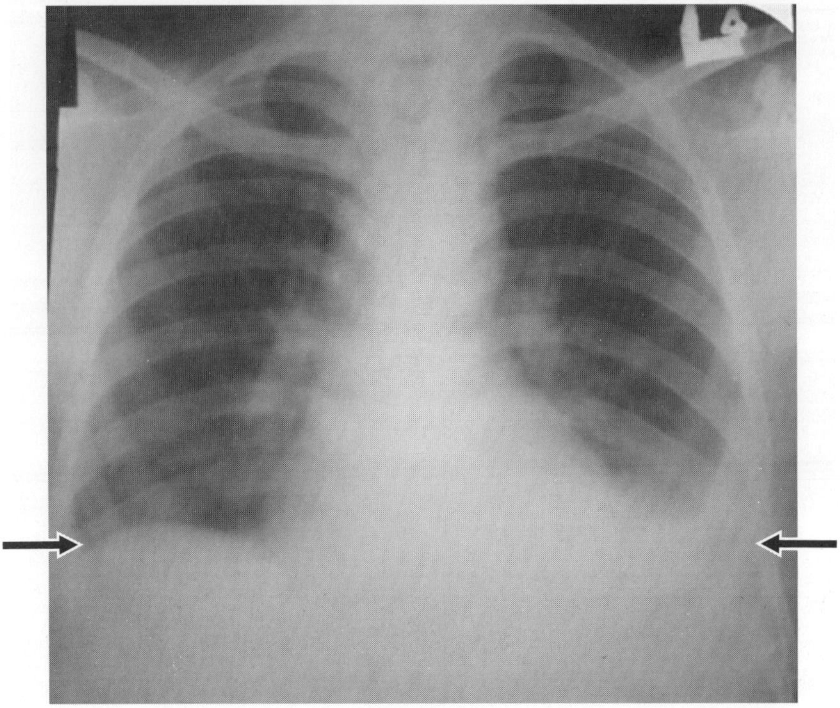

What is this?
See the chest X-ray carefully

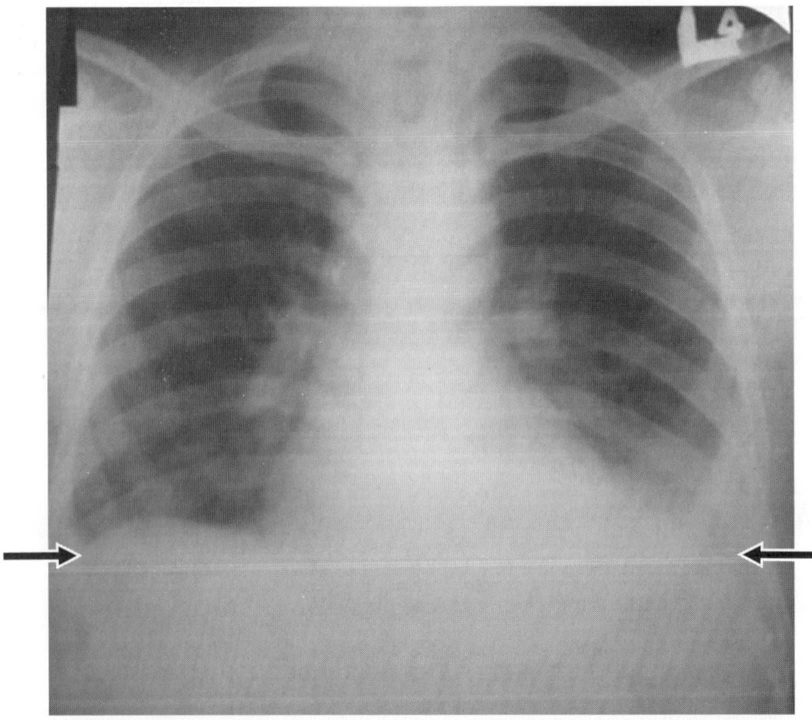

Bilateral pleural effusion

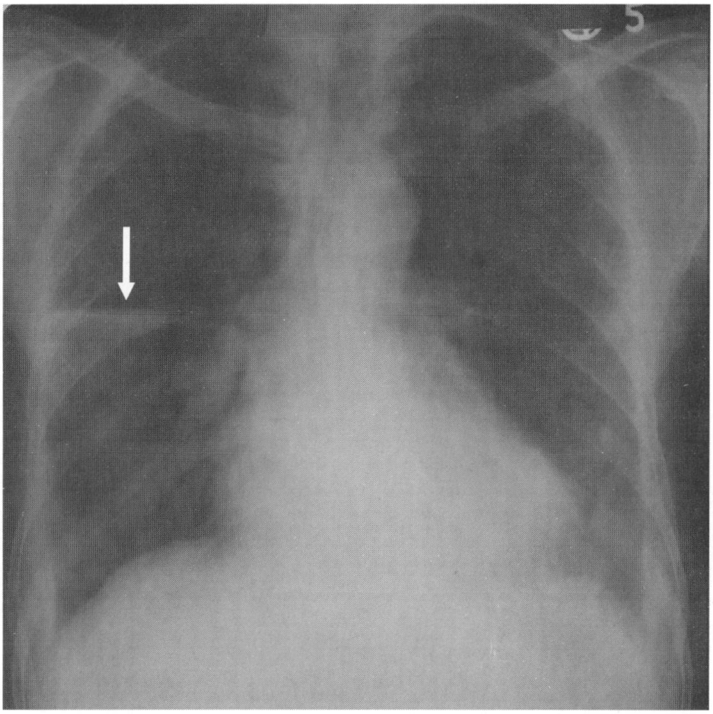

What is this?

See the chest X-ray carefully. It has multiple findings

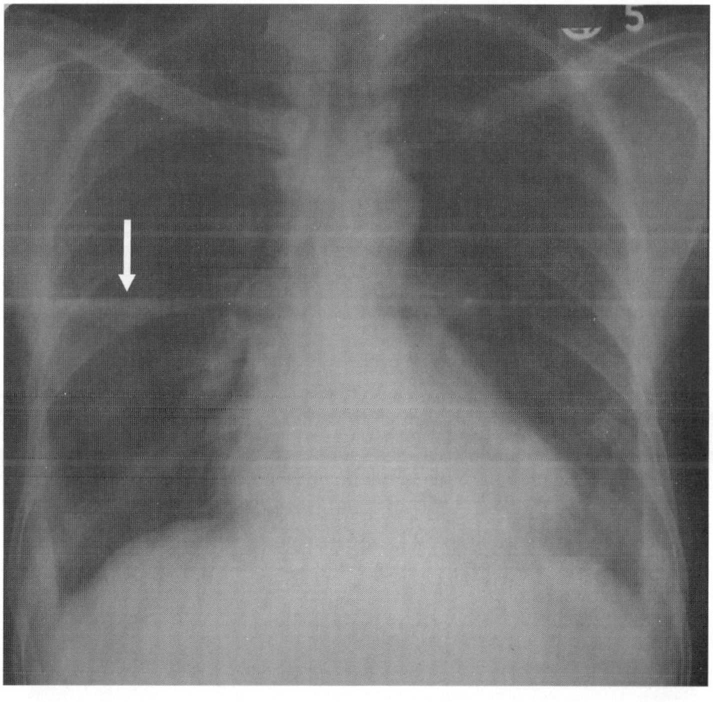

Bilateral pleural effusion with fluid in horizontal fissure

Loculated (Encysted) Pleural Effusion—*What are Types of Loculated Pleural Effusion*

- Parietal
- Diaphragmatic
- Mediastinal
- Interlobar
- Mediastino-interlobar

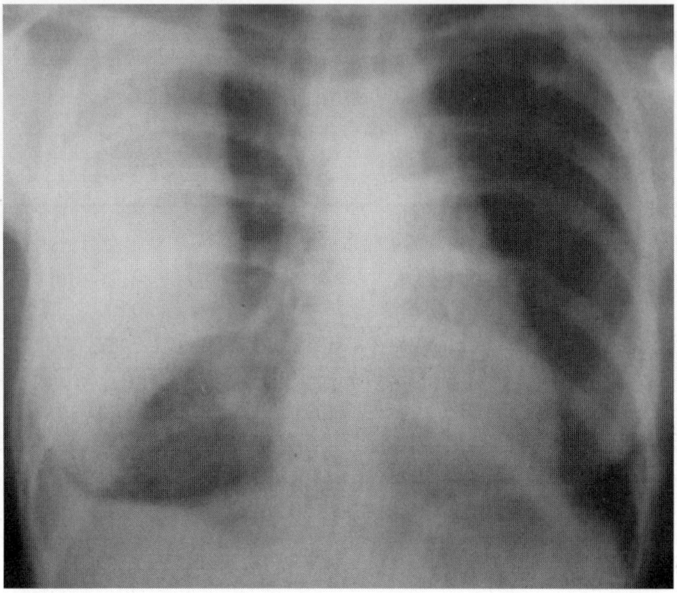

What is this?

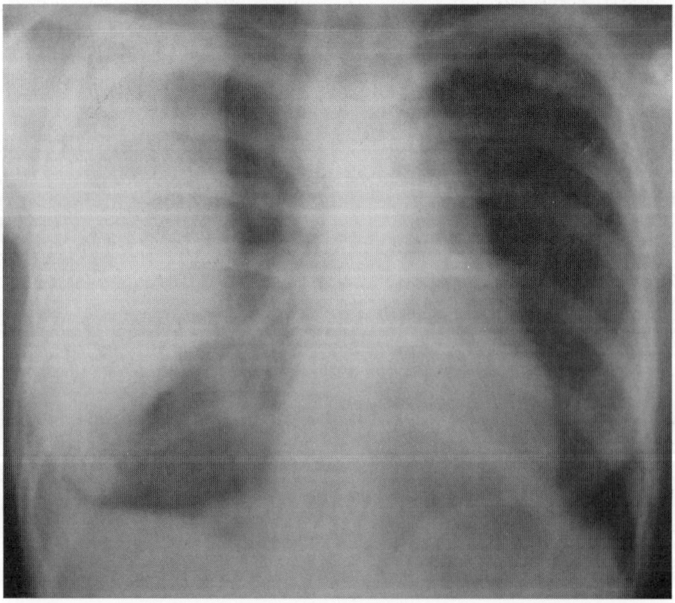

Encysted pleural effusion (parietal)

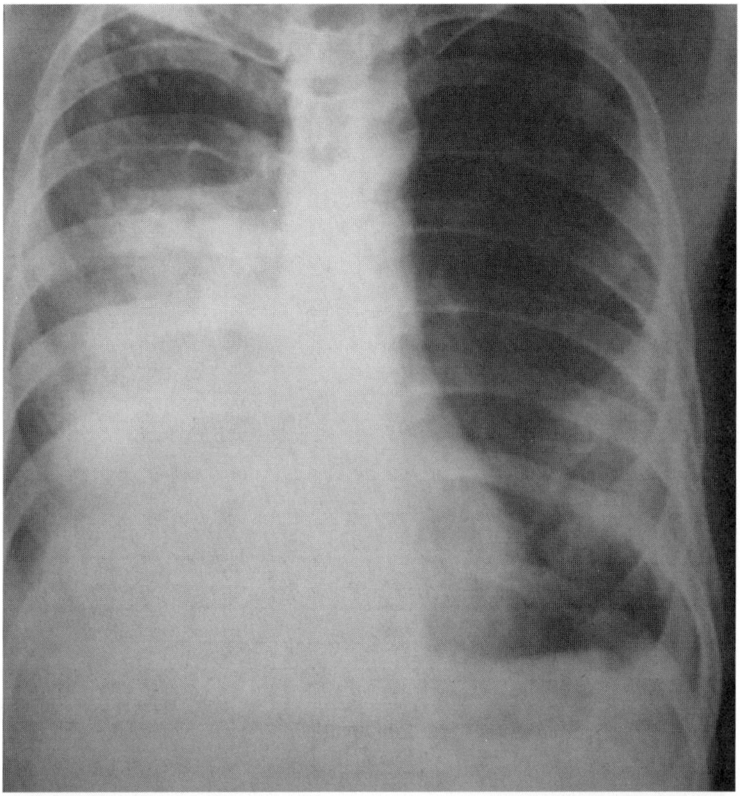

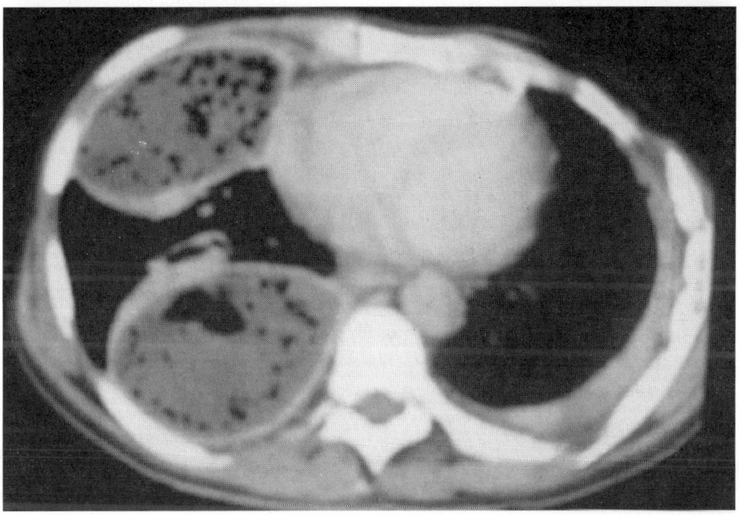

What is this?

See the chest X-ray and CT thorax carefully. It has multiple findings

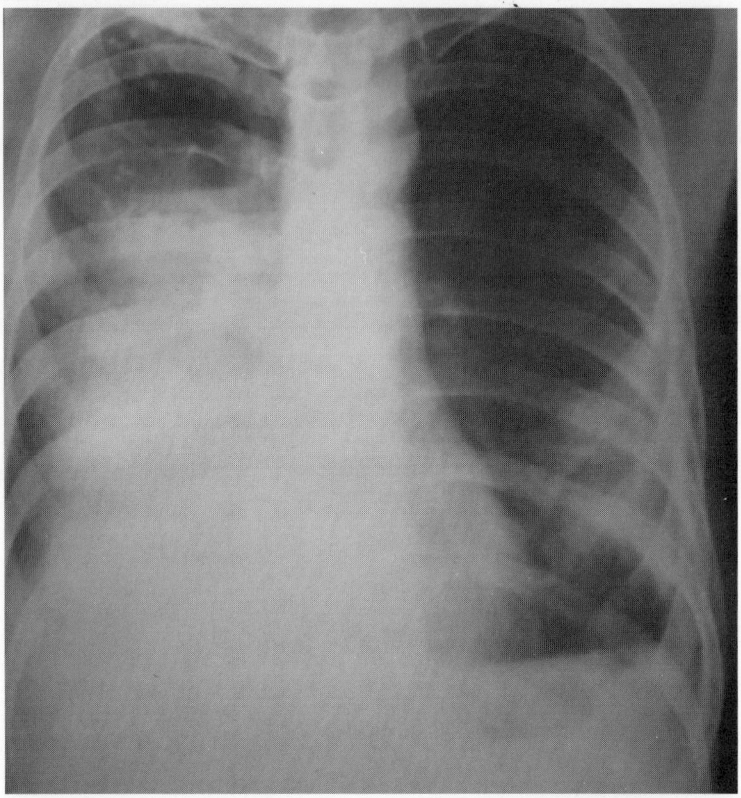

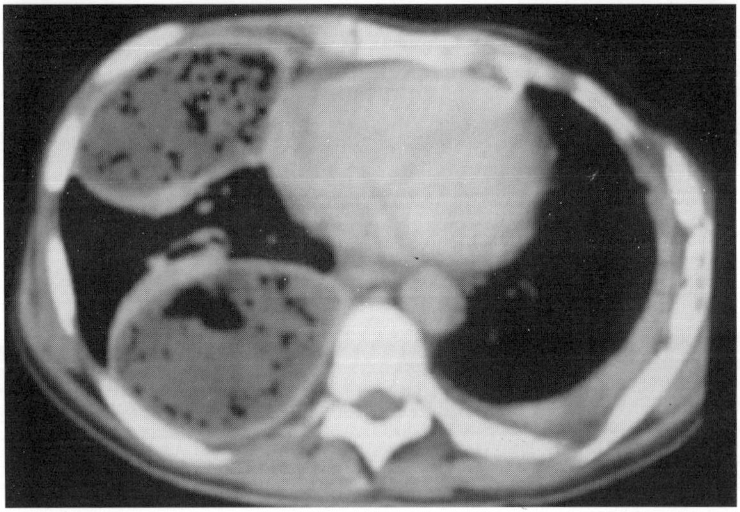

Encysted pleural effusion (right) and small pleural effusion (left)

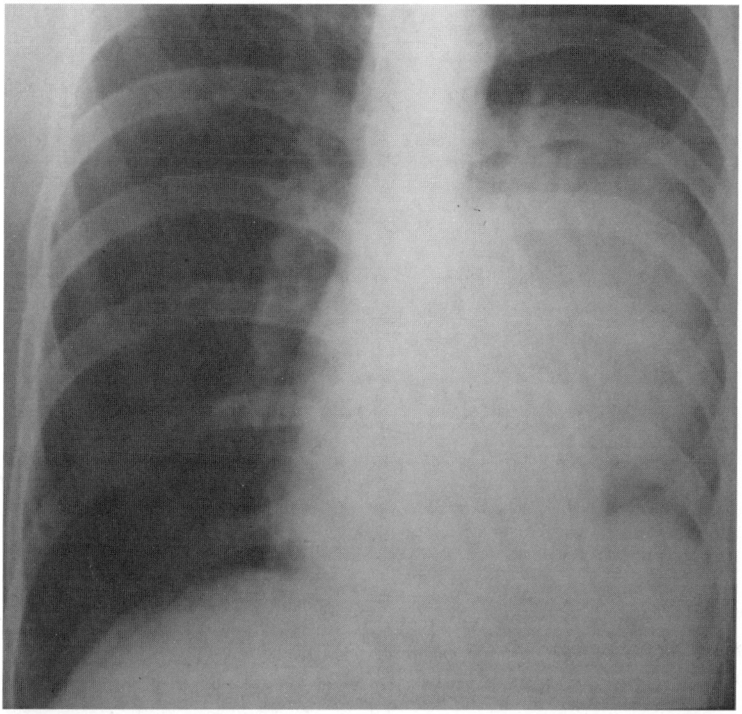

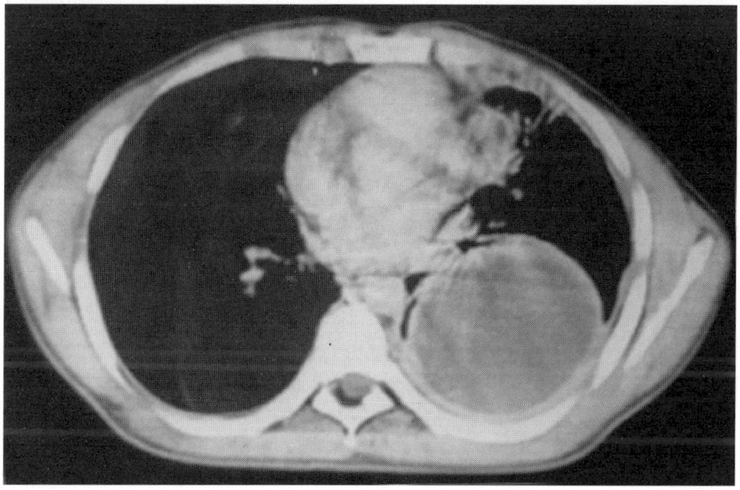

What is this?

See the chest X-ray and CT thorax carefully

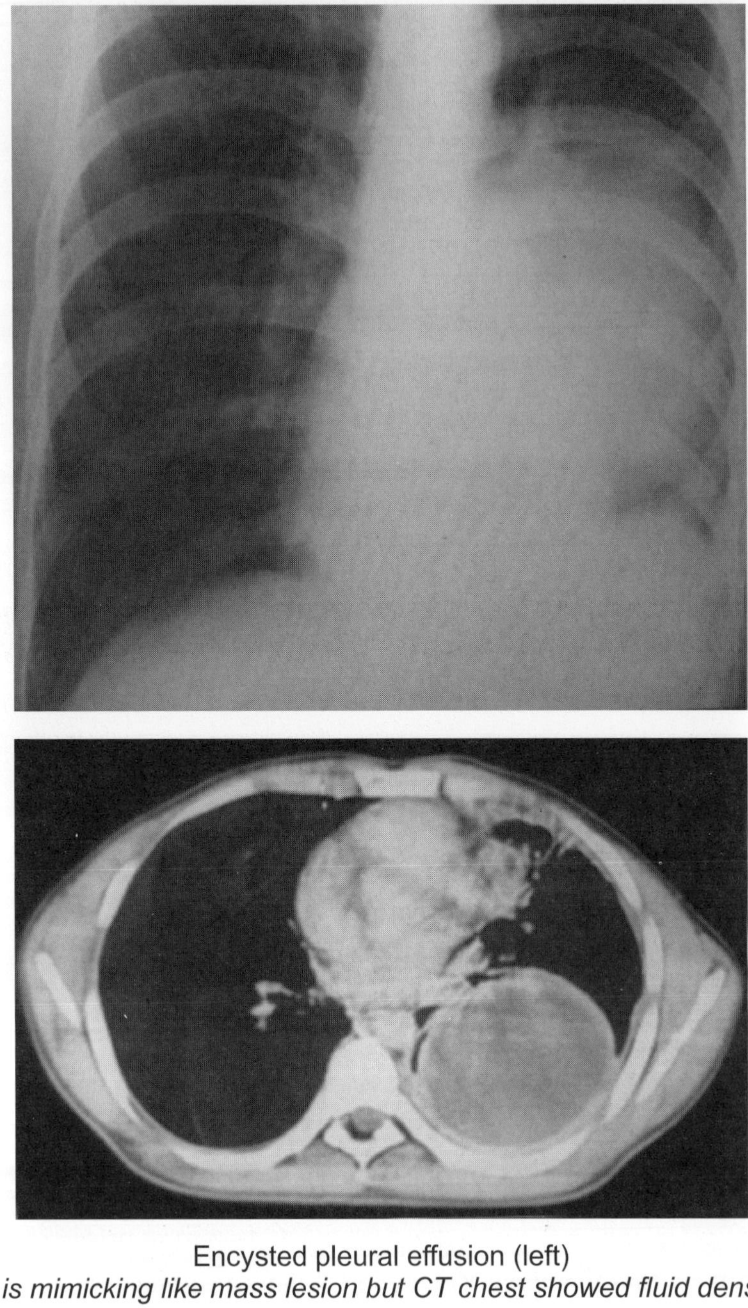

Encysted pleural effusion (left)

It is mimicking like mass lesion but CT chest showed fluid density

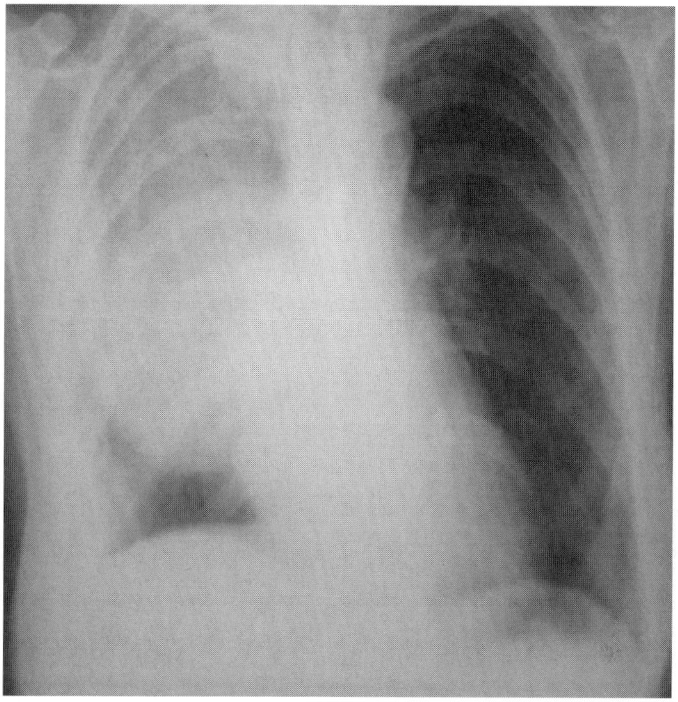

What is this?
See the chest X-ray carefully. It has multiple shadows

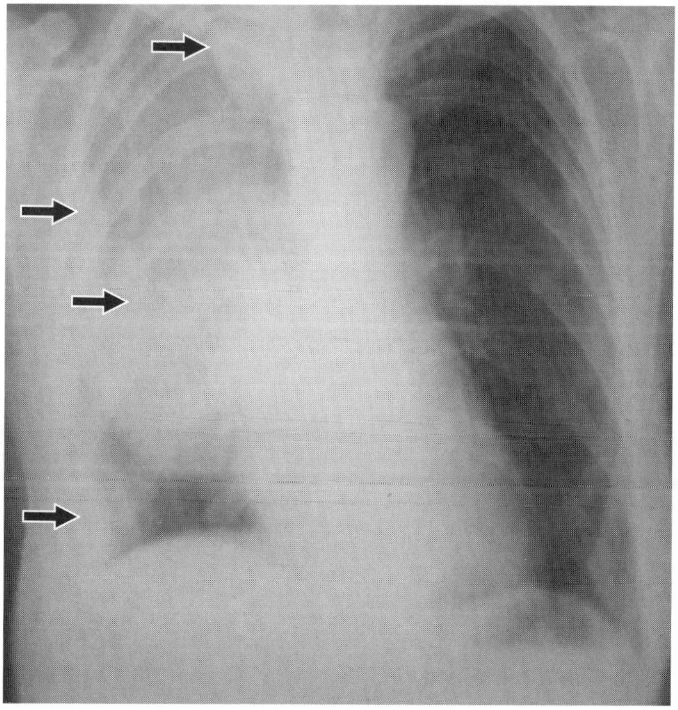

Multiple encysted pleural effusion

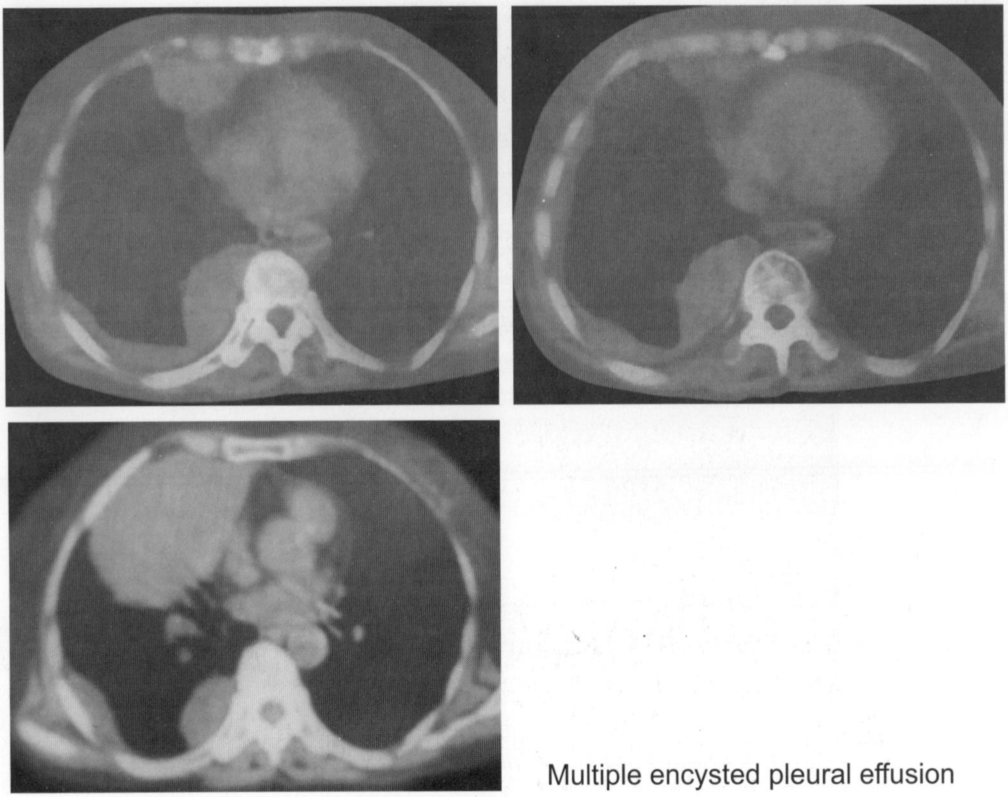

Multiple encysted pleural effusion

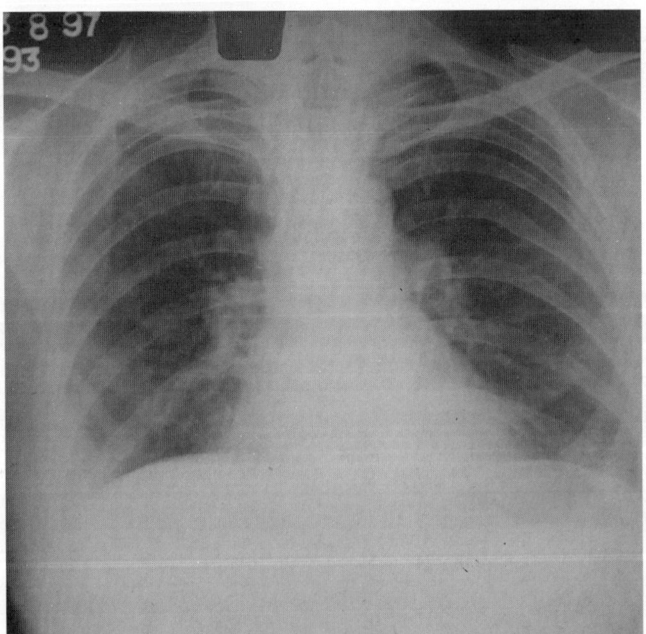

All shadows disappeared after pleural aspiration and antitubercular treatment

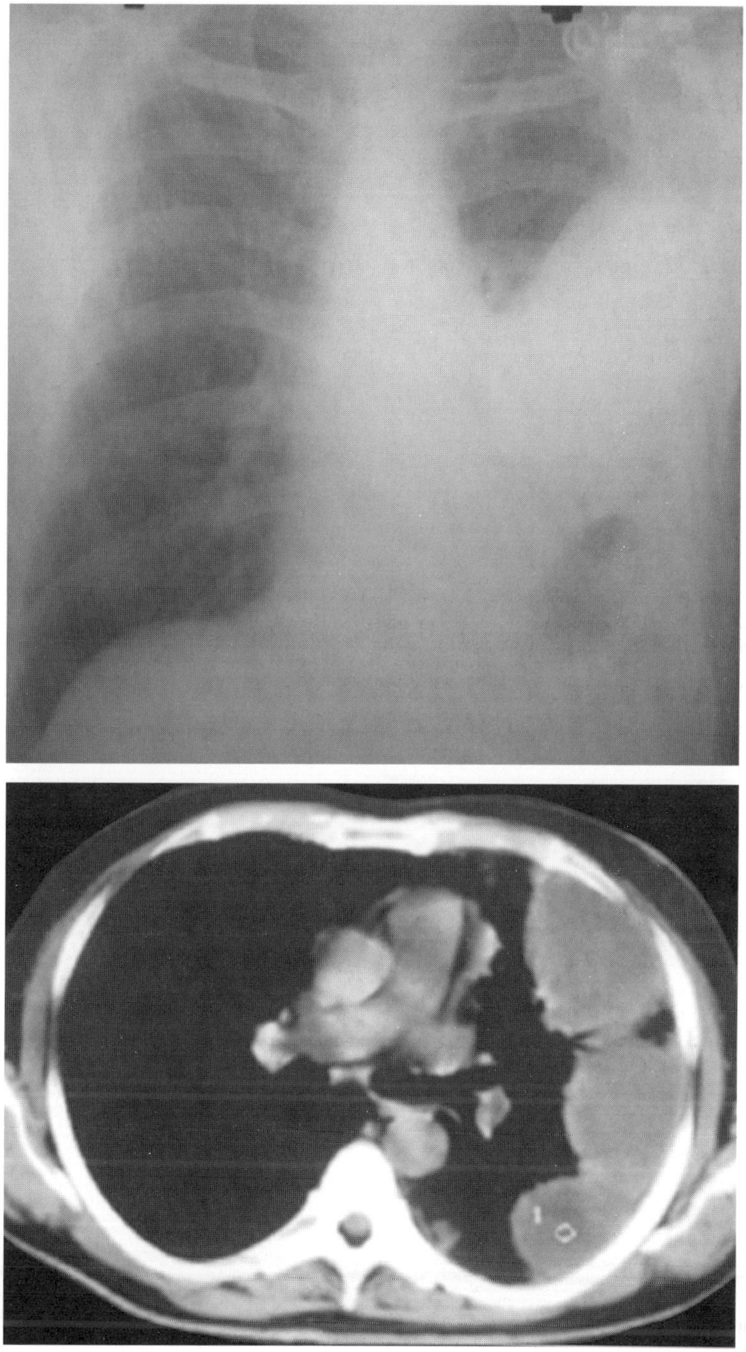

What is this?

See the chest X-ray and CT thorax very carefully and it has multiple findings

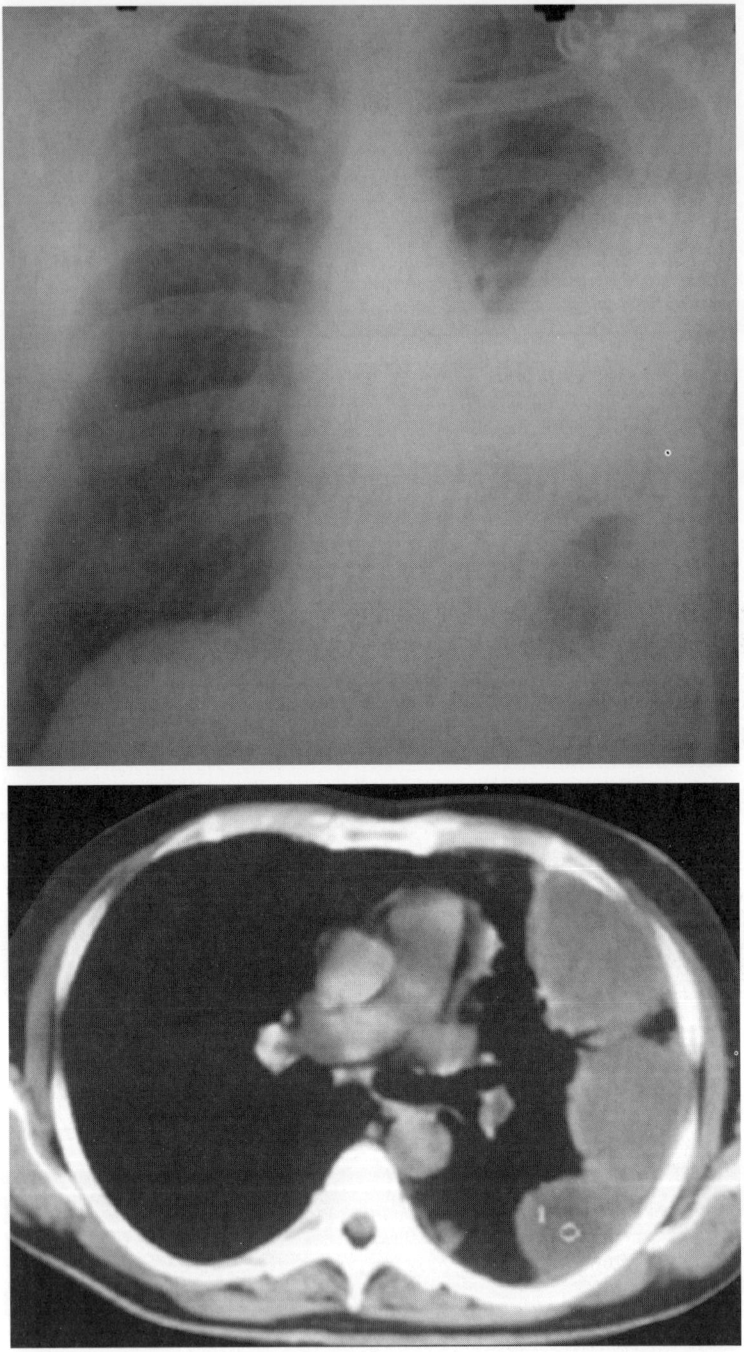

Multiple encysted effusion (parietal) with eventration of diaphragm

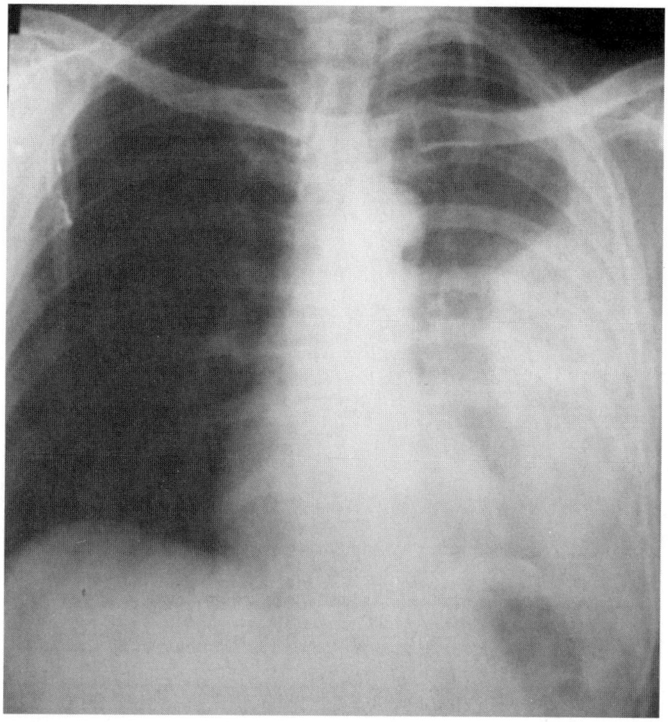

What is this?
See the chest X-ray carefully

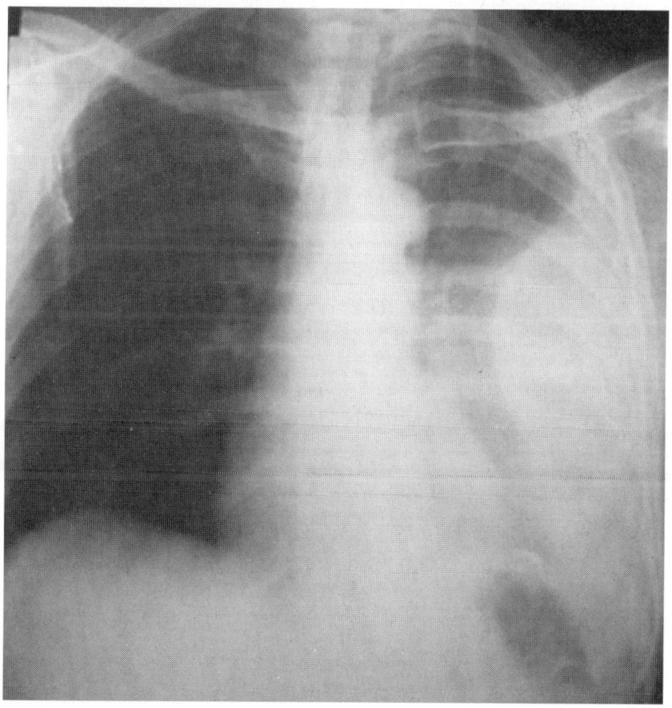

Encysted effusion on left side (parietal)

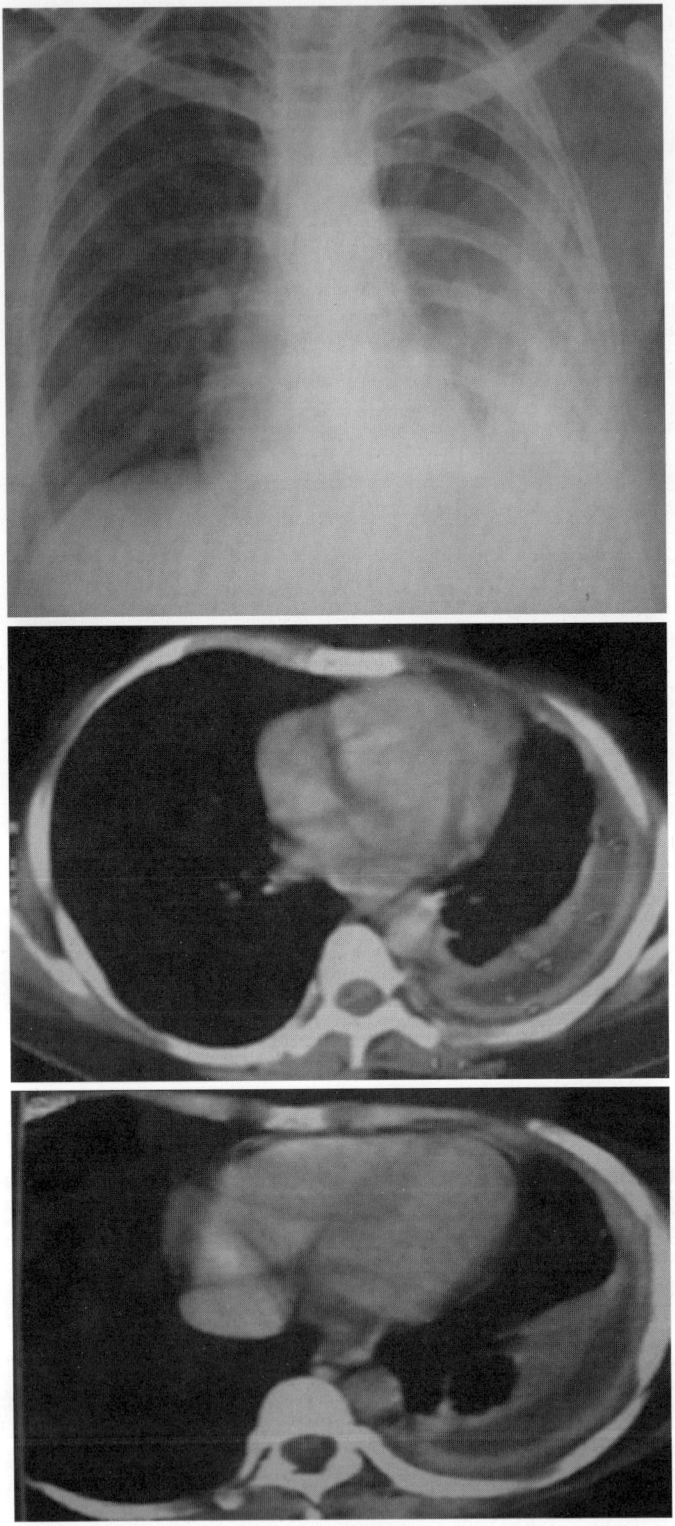

What is this?
See the chest X-ray and CT thorax very carefully

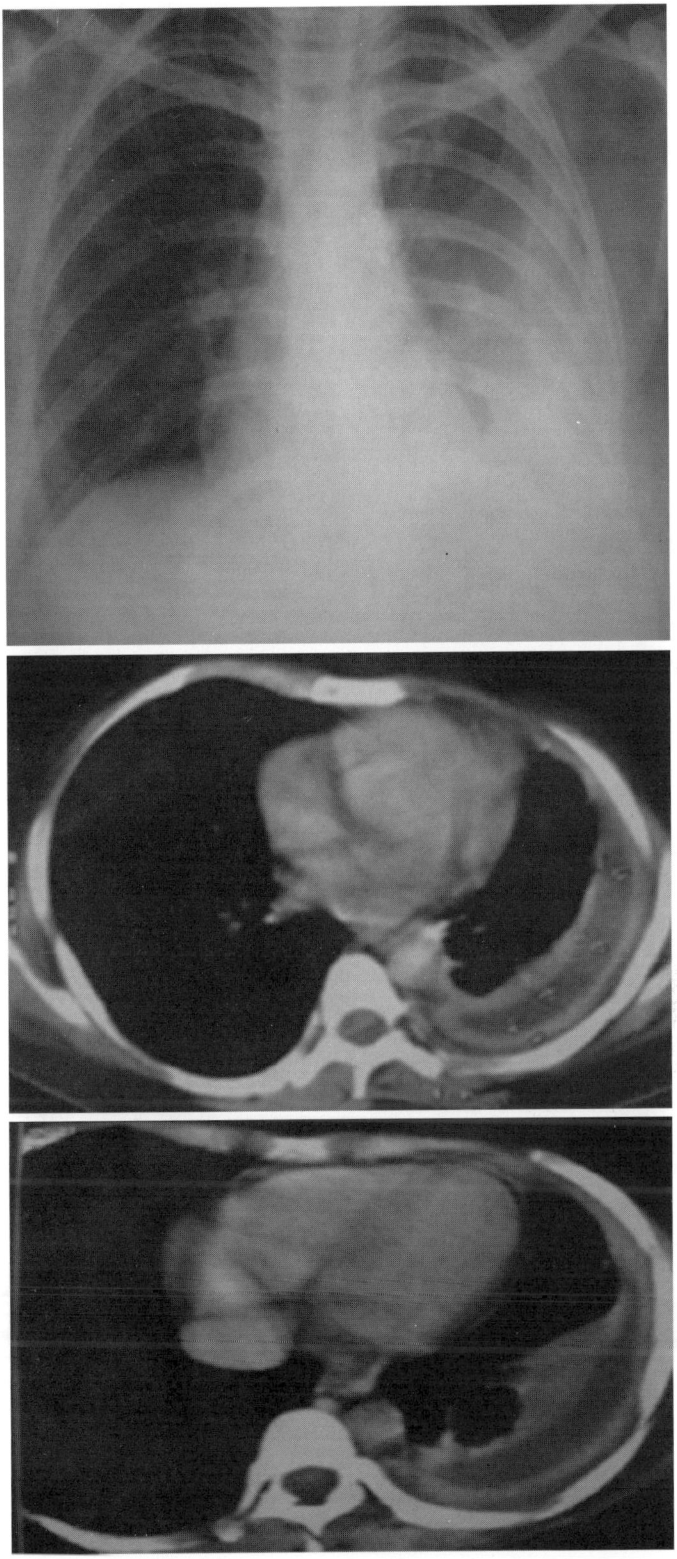

Encysted effusion with split pleura sign (left)

Pneumothorax–*What are Types of Pneumothorax?*

- Spontaneous
  - Primary: Apical blebs, tall stature
  - Secondary: Chronic bronchitis, emphysema, asthma, tuberculosis, pneumonia
- Traumatic
  - Non-iatrogenic: Chest injury, barotrauma
  - Iatrogenic: Paracentesis, pleural biopsy, transbronchial lung biopsy, percutaneous lung biopsy, central venous, cannulation, artificial pneumothorax

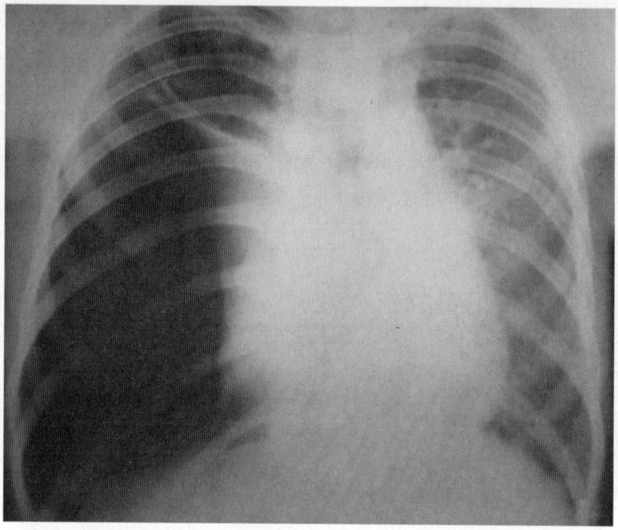

What is this?

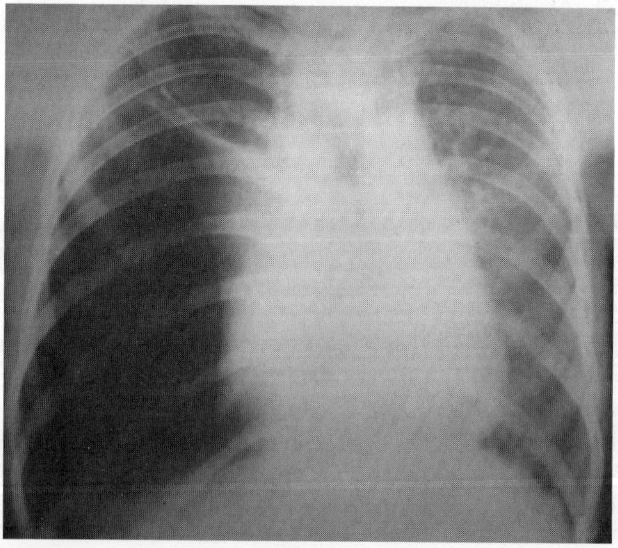

Pneumothorax (right)

To diagnosed pneumothorax you need air in the pleural cavity (radiolucent shadow) and collapsed lung border

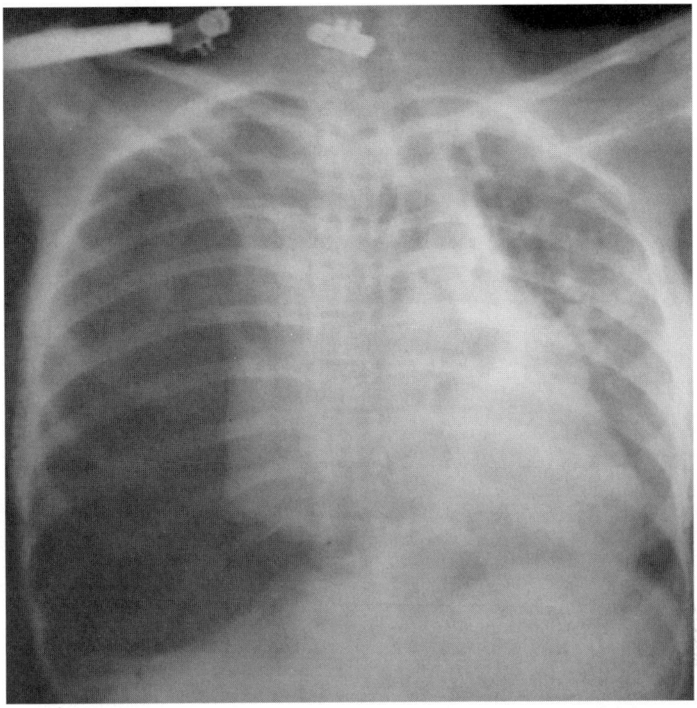

What is this?

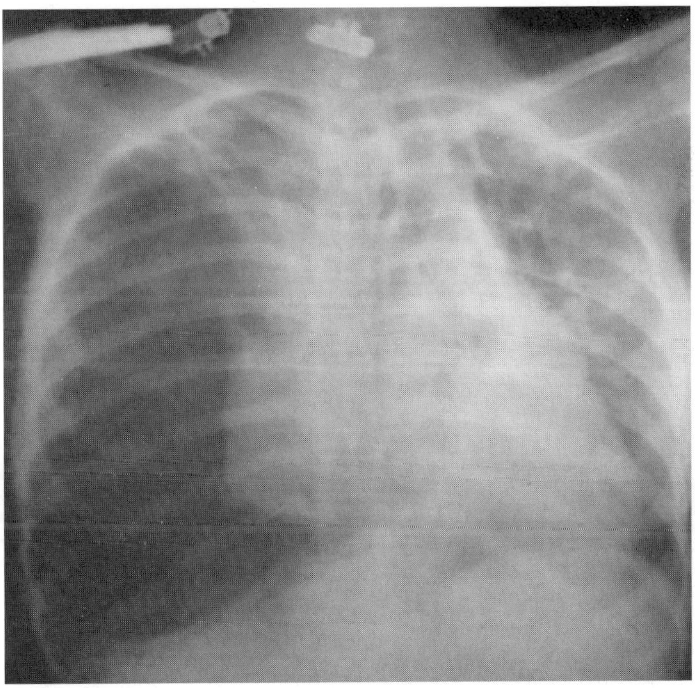

Tension pneumothorax (right)

Radiolucent right lung with collapsed lung border and mediastinal shift to opposite side

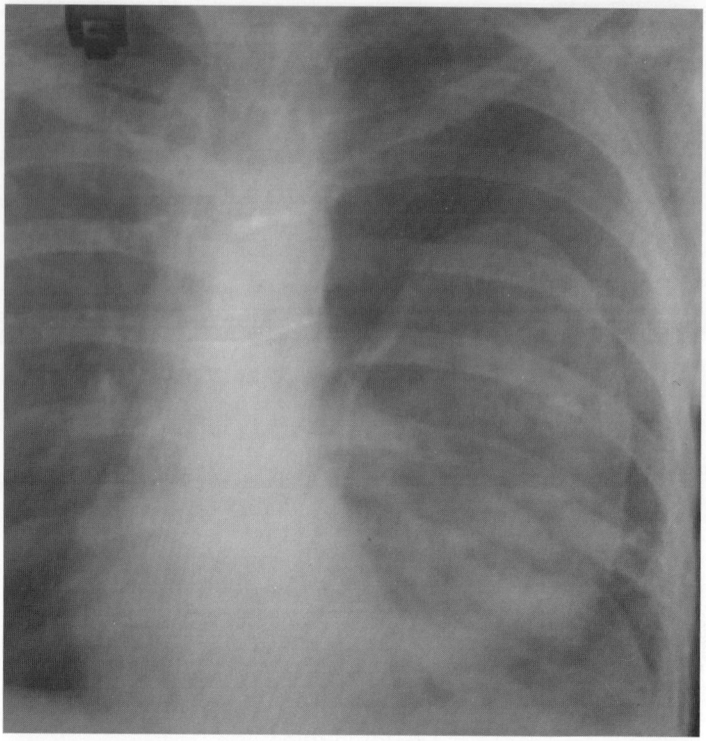

What is this?

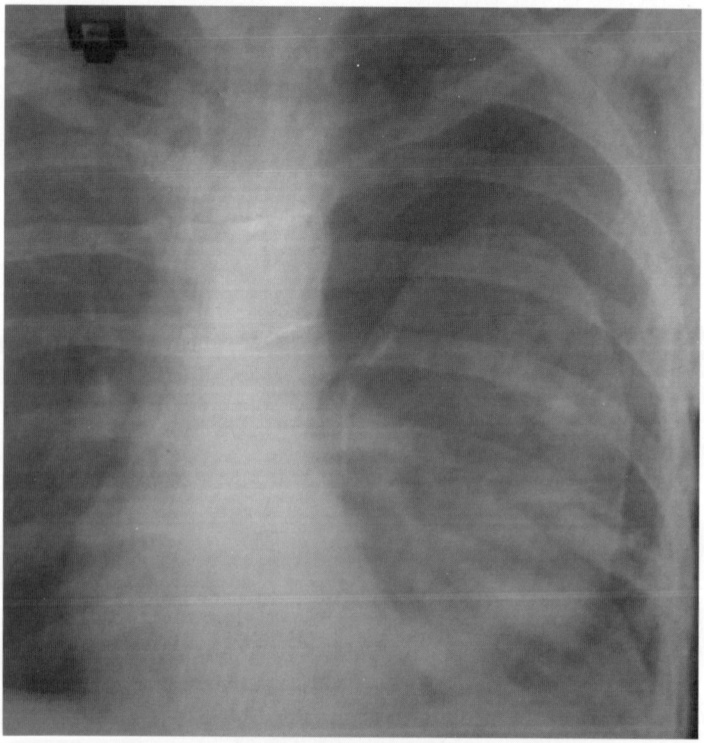

Pneumothorax (left)

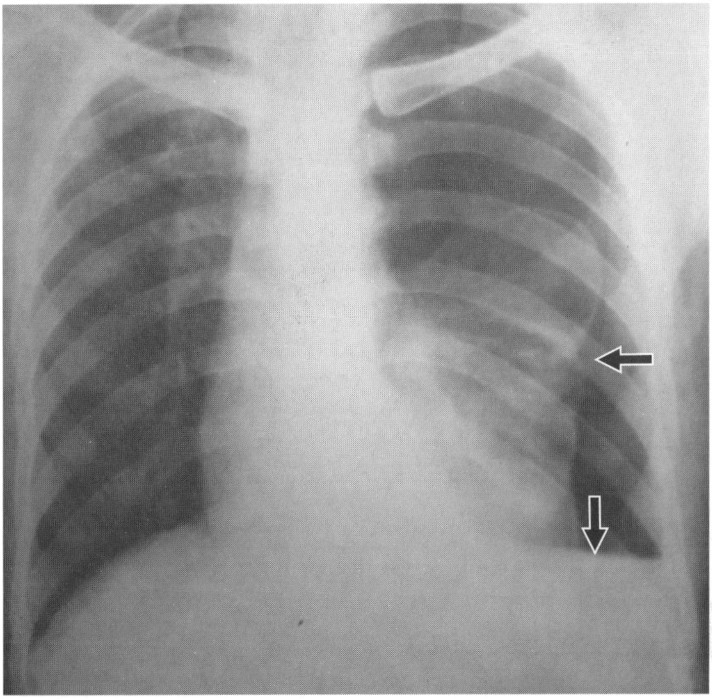

What is this?

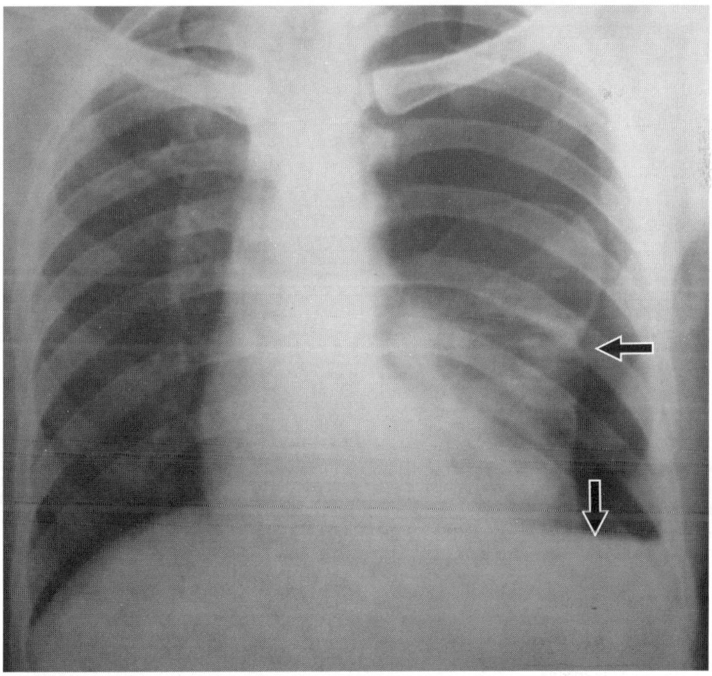

Hydropneumothorax (left)

To diagnose hydropneumothorax you need air in the pleural cavity (radiolucent shadow), collapsed lung border and air-fluid level

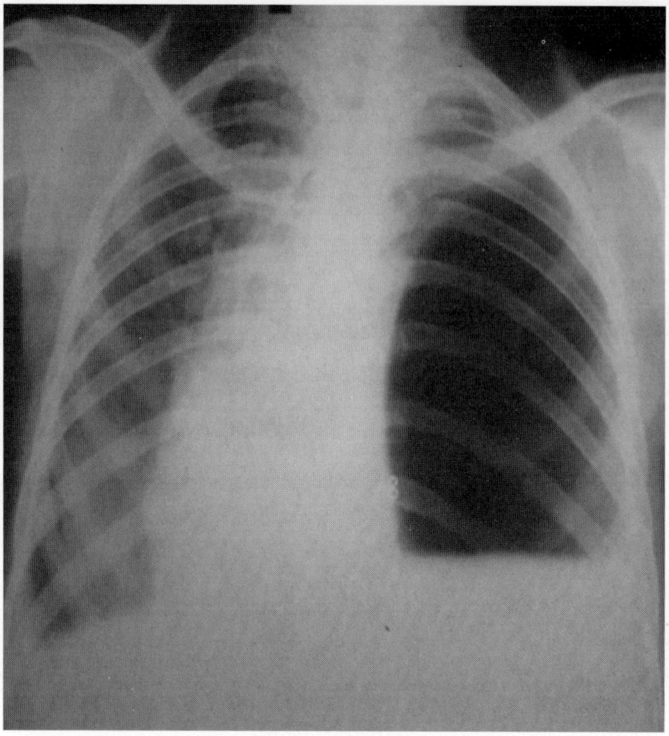

What is this?

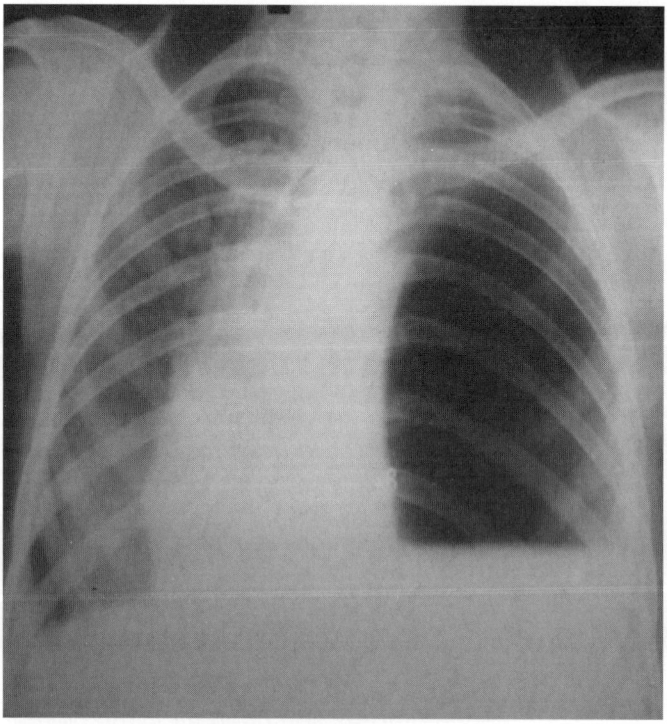

Hydropneumothorax (left)

Module 4

- RADIOLOGY OF TUBERCULOSIS
- RADIOLOGY OF BRONCHIECTASIS
- RADIOLOGY OF CHRONIC OBSTRUCTIVE PULMONARY DISEASE (COPD)
- RADIOLOGY OF ALLERGIC BRONCHOPULMONARY ASPERGILLOSIS (ABPA)
- RADIOLOGY OF LUNG CANCER
- RADIOLOGY OF INTERSTITIAL LUNG DISEASE (ILD)
- RADIOLOGY OF SARCOIDOSIS
- RADIOLOGY OF COVID-19
- RADIOLOGY QUIZ

CHAPTER

12

Radiology of Tuberculosis

Diagnosis of Tuberculosis

Chest X-ray

- Helps in early detection
- Sensitive but not specific
- Identifies persons for further evaluation
- Diagnosis of tuberculosis cannot be established by X-ray alone
- Reliance on CXR alone may result in over diagnosis
- Quality control in terms of technical quality and physician interpretation
- Useful in comparing response to treatment

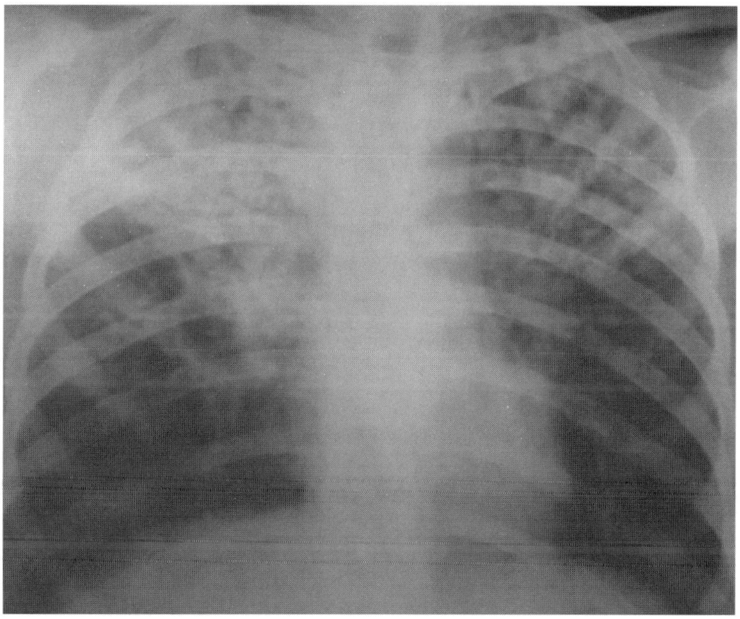

What is this?

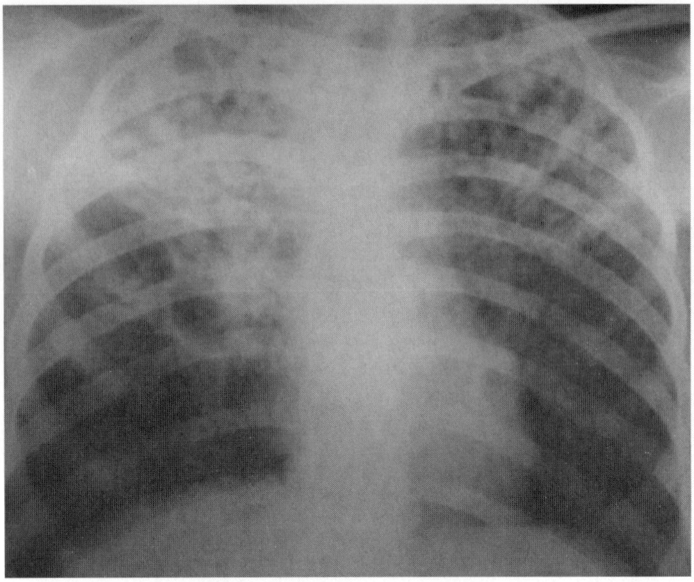

Bilateral pulmonary tuberculosis

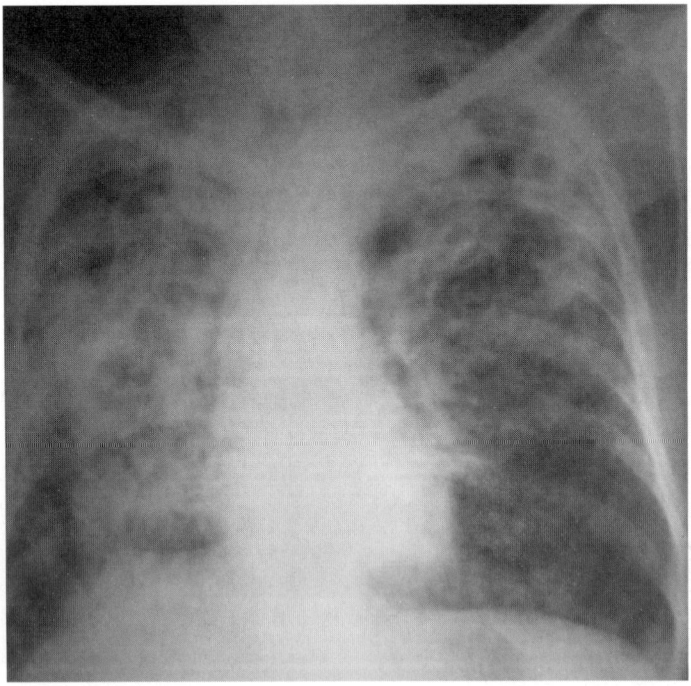

Bilateral pulmonary tuberculosis
Sputum +ve for AFB

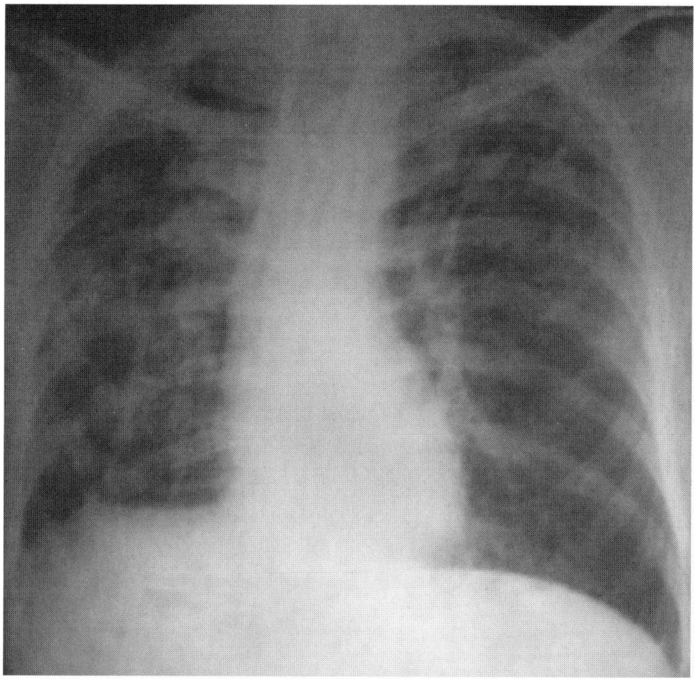

X-ray at the end of 6 months of antitubercular treatment with marked improvement but still there are residual lesions Sputum –ve for AFB

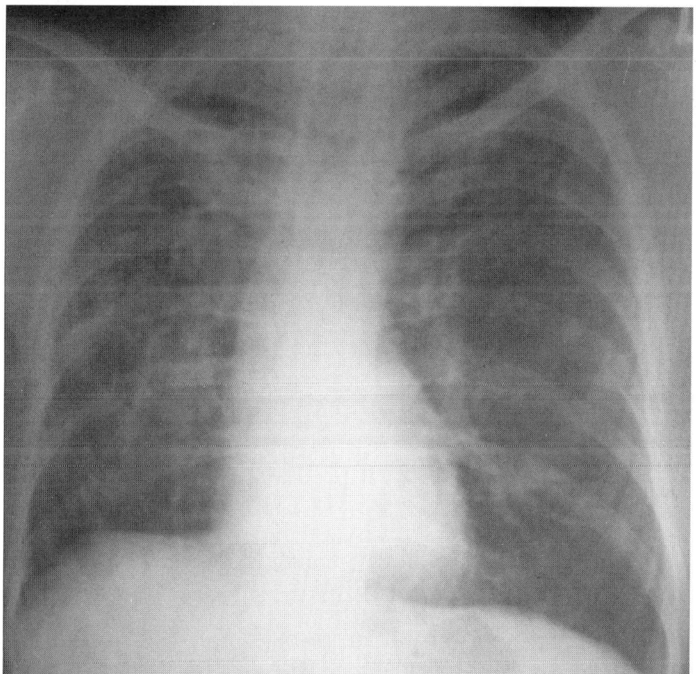

Residual lesions resolved further without any antitubercular treatment

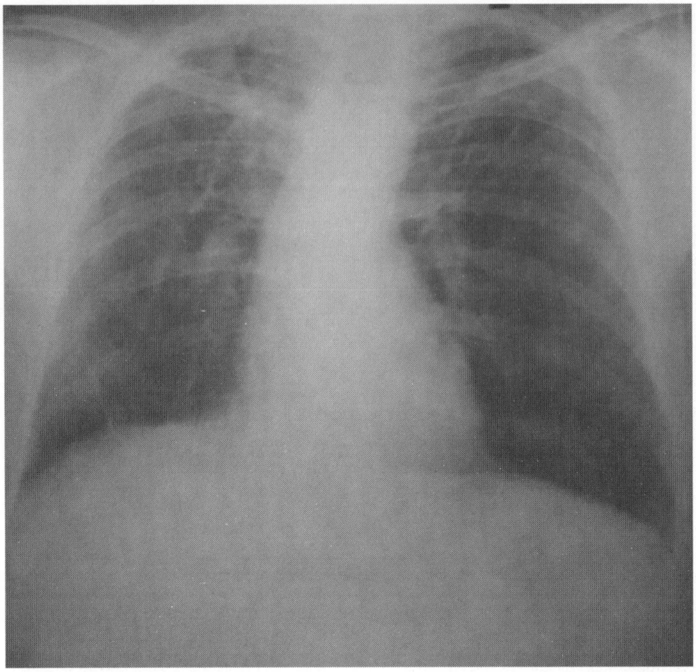

Residual lesions resolved further without any antitubercular treatment

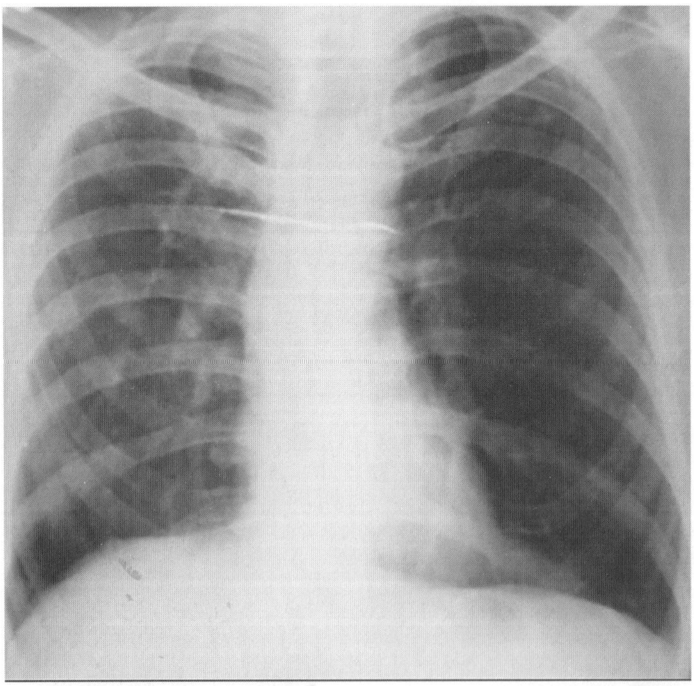

Patient is asymptomatic and chest X-ray is normal
after 2 years of stopping antitubercular treatment
Please remember that radiologically lesions clear late even after stopping the antitubercular treatment

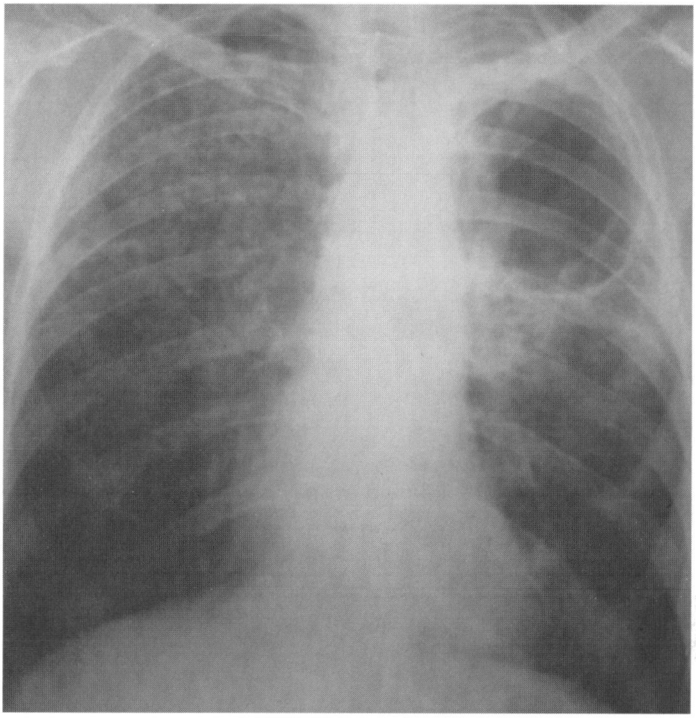

What is this?

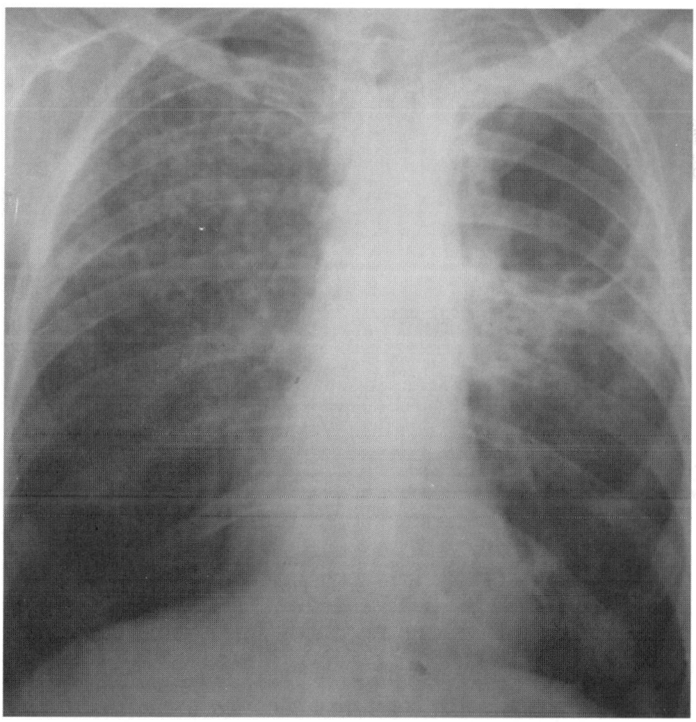

Bilateral pulmonary tuberculosis

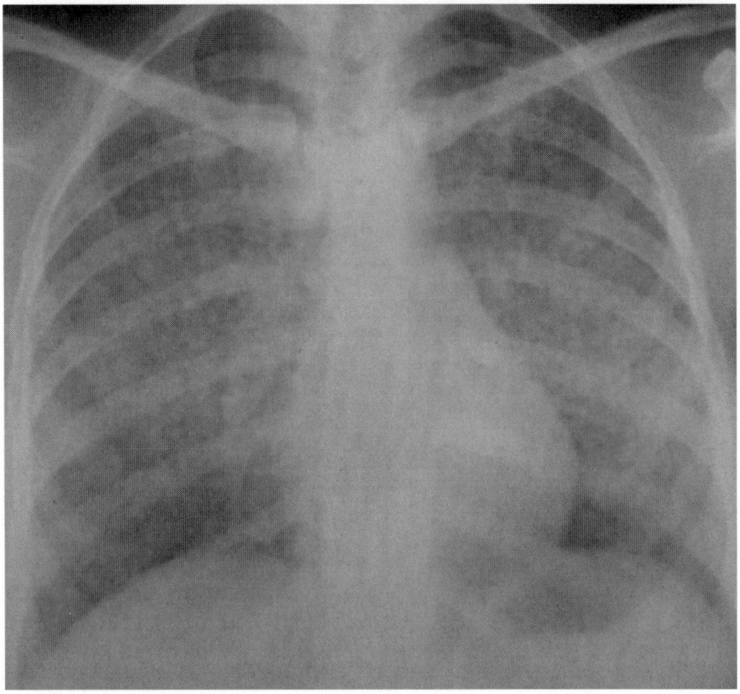

What is this?

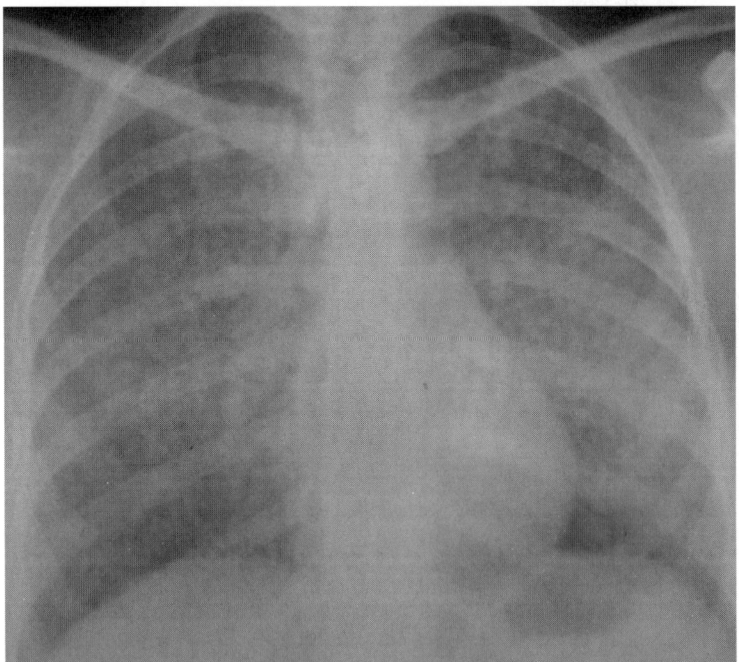

Miliary shadows cause miliary tuberculosis

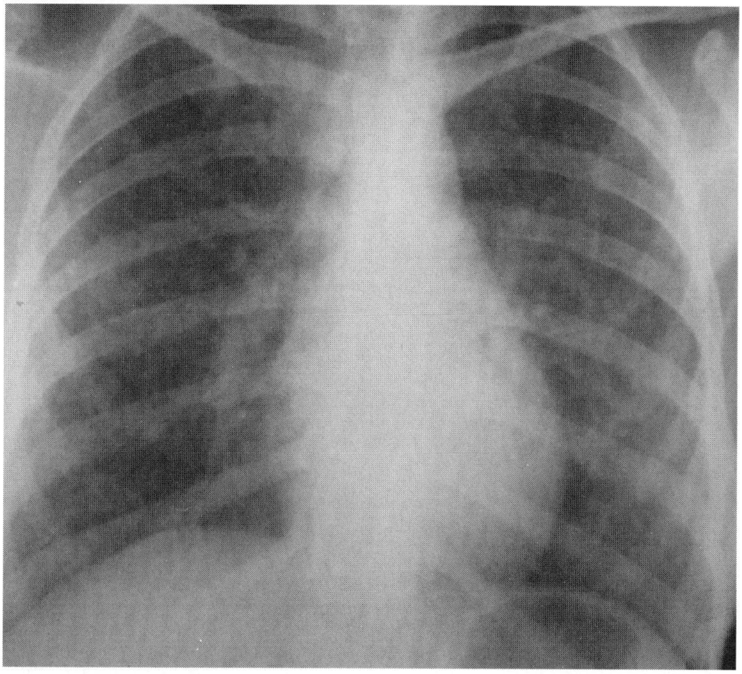

Miliary shadows reduced after 2 months of antitubercular treatment

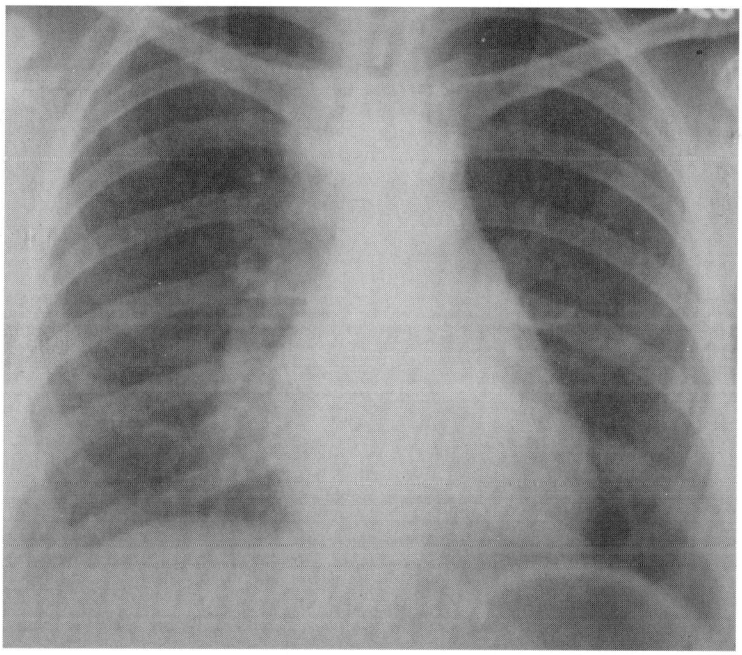

Miliary shadows completely resolved after
4 months of antitubercular treatment
Please note that antitubercular treatment is to be completed and continuation phase is prolonged to 3–6 months

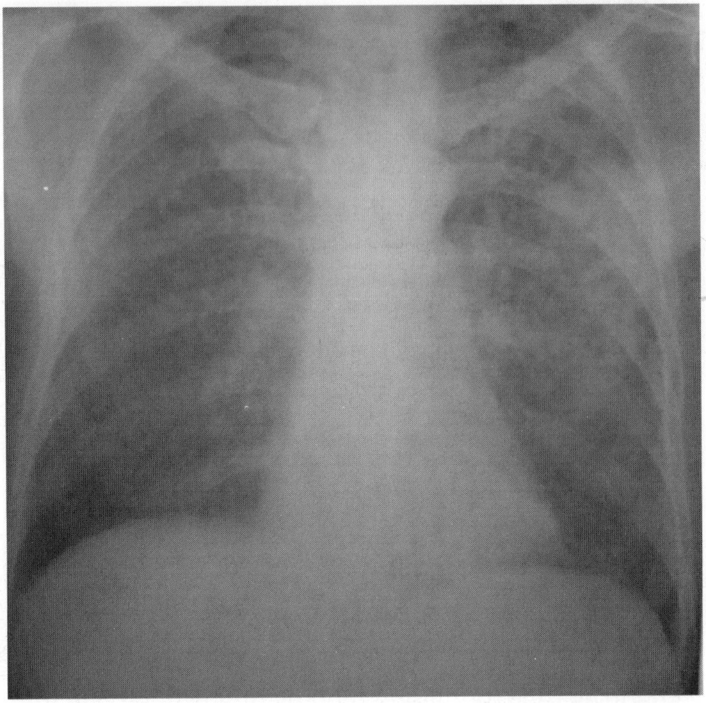

What is this?

A 40-year-old male came with complaints of fever

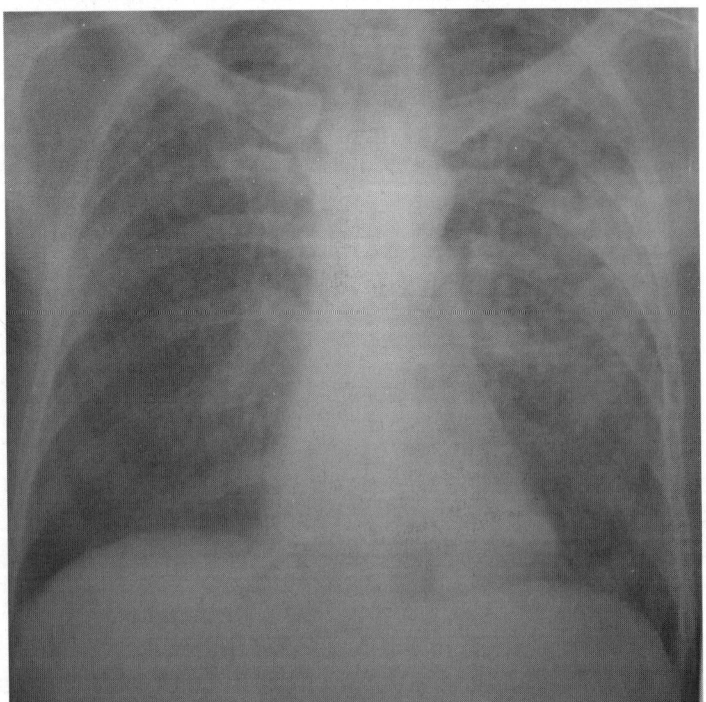

Miliary shadows cause miliary tuberculosis

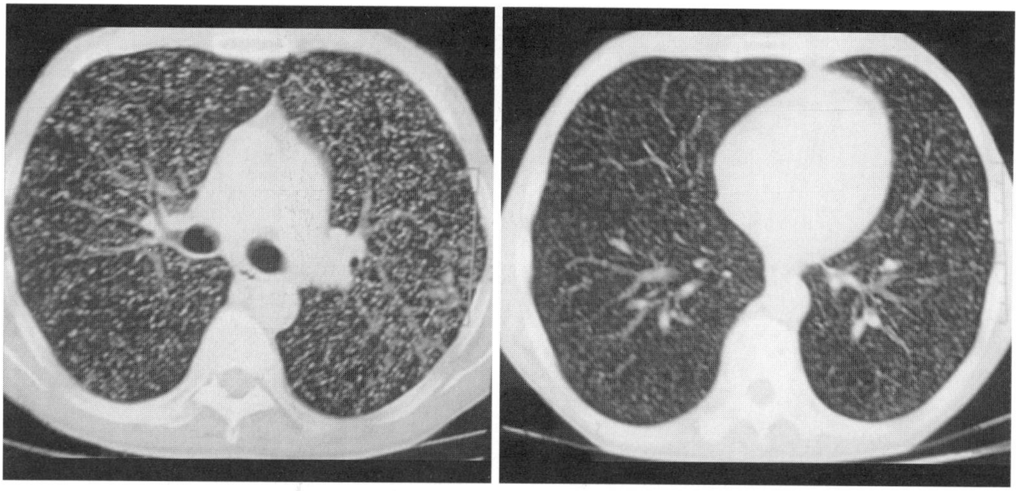

Miliary shadows (miliary tuberculosis)

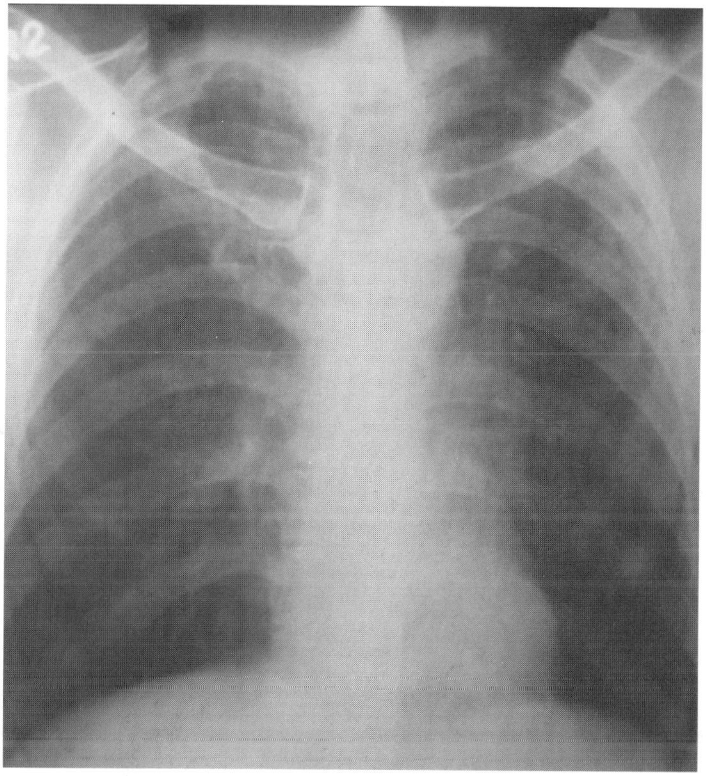

Miliary shadows completely resolved after
4 months of antitubercular treatment

Please note that antitubercular treatment should be completed

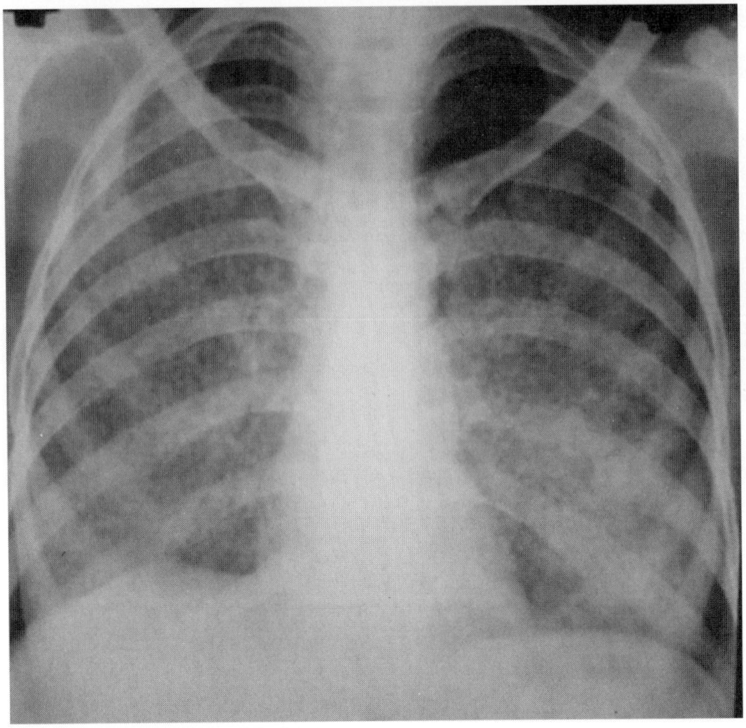

What is this?

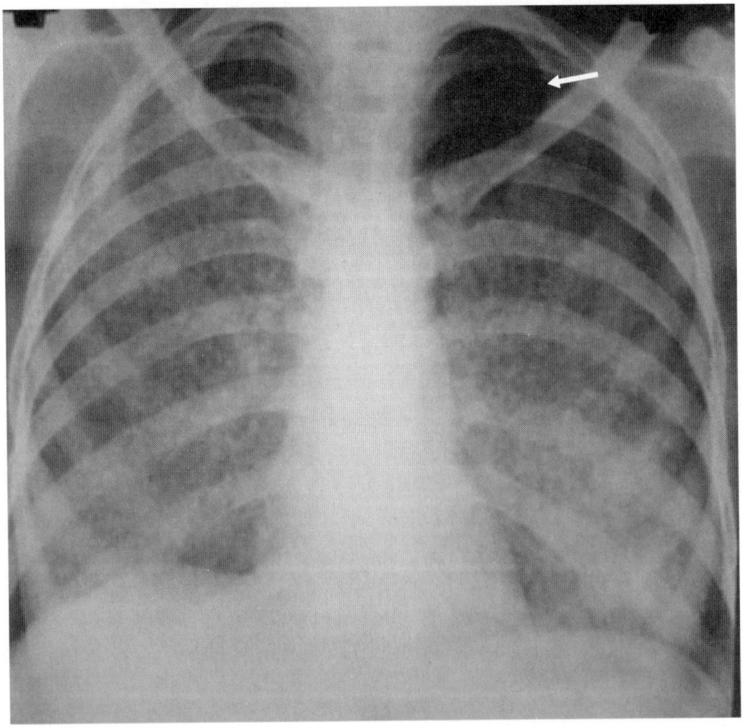

Miliary tuberculosis with pneumothorax (left side)

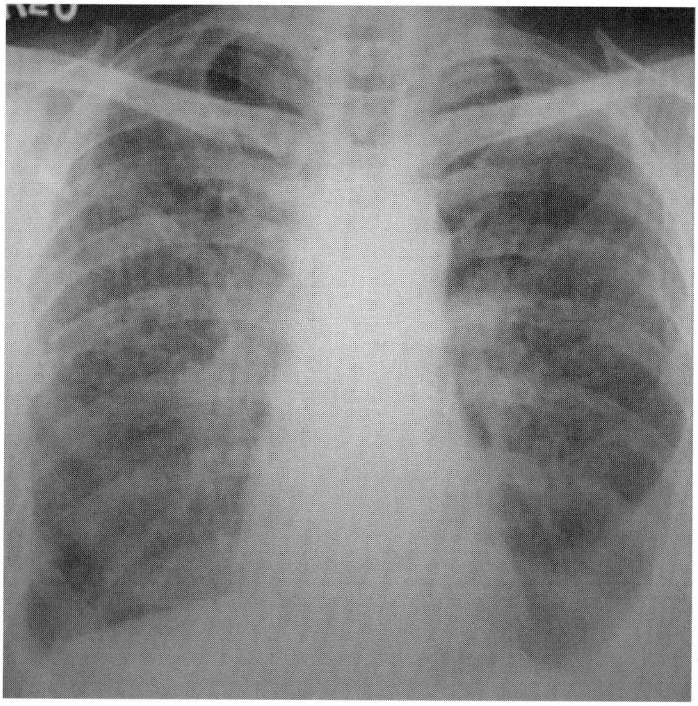

What is this?

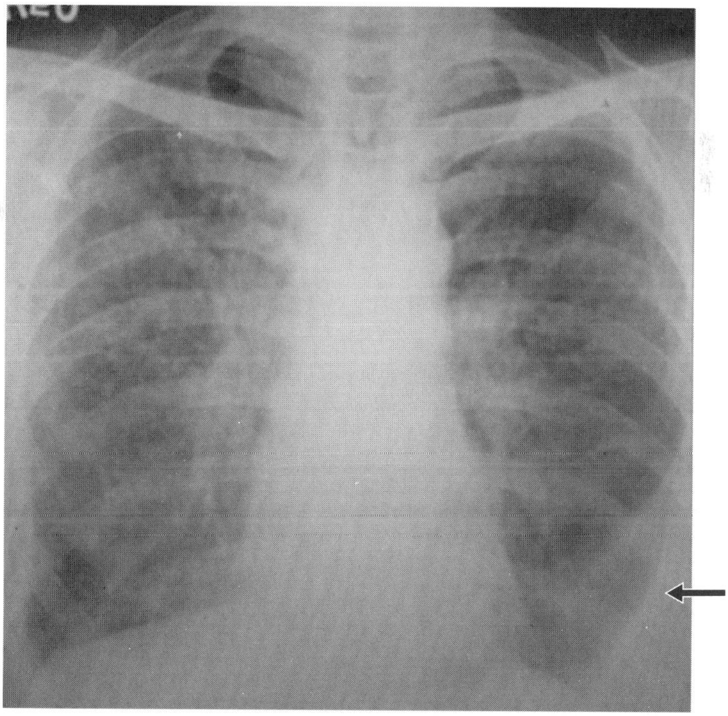

Miliary tuberculosis with pleural effusion (left side)

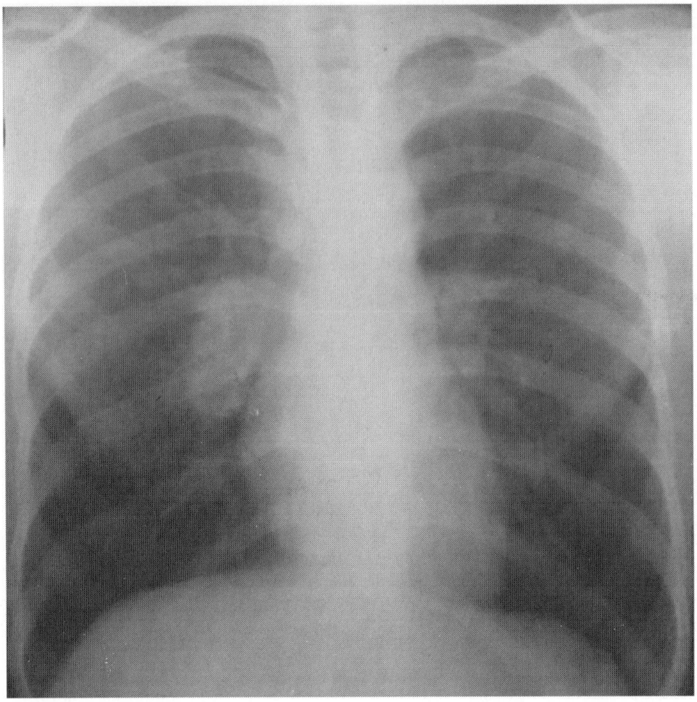

What is this?

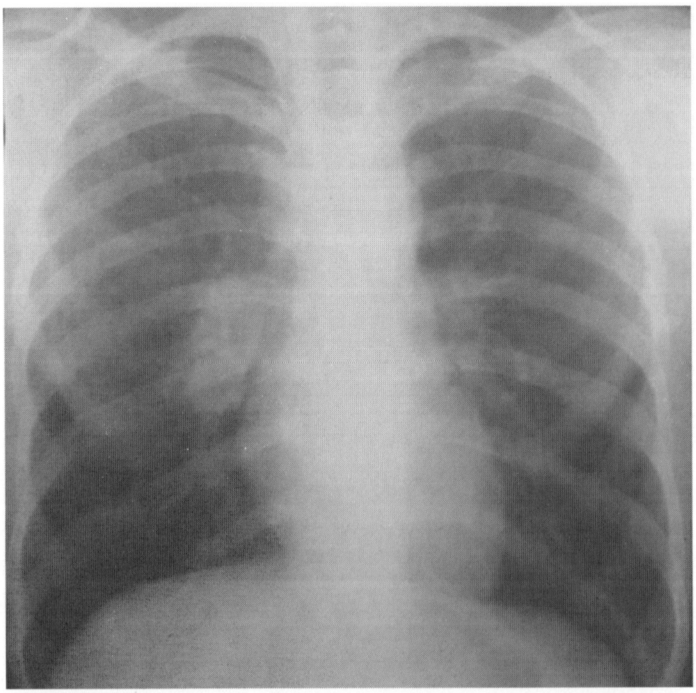

Hilar lymphadenopathy (right) causes tuberculosis

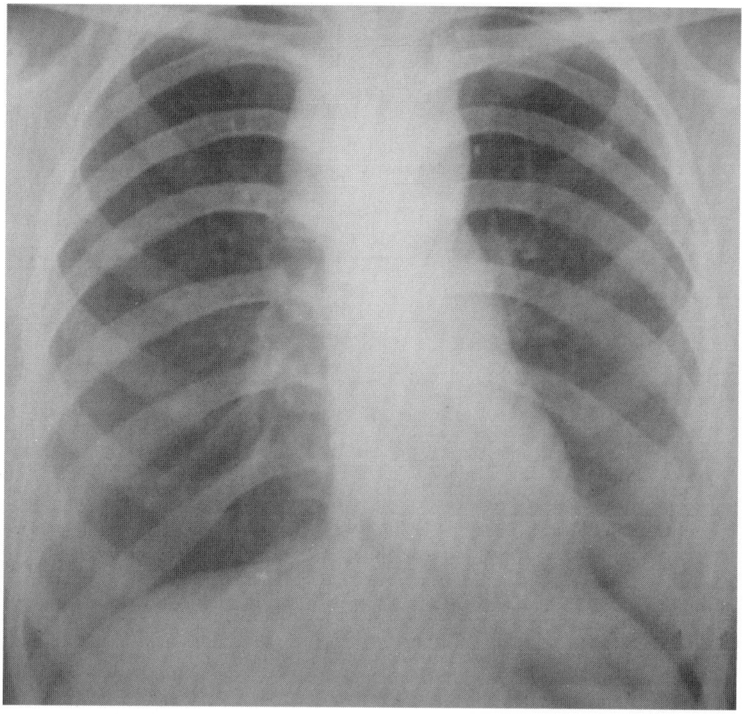

What is this?

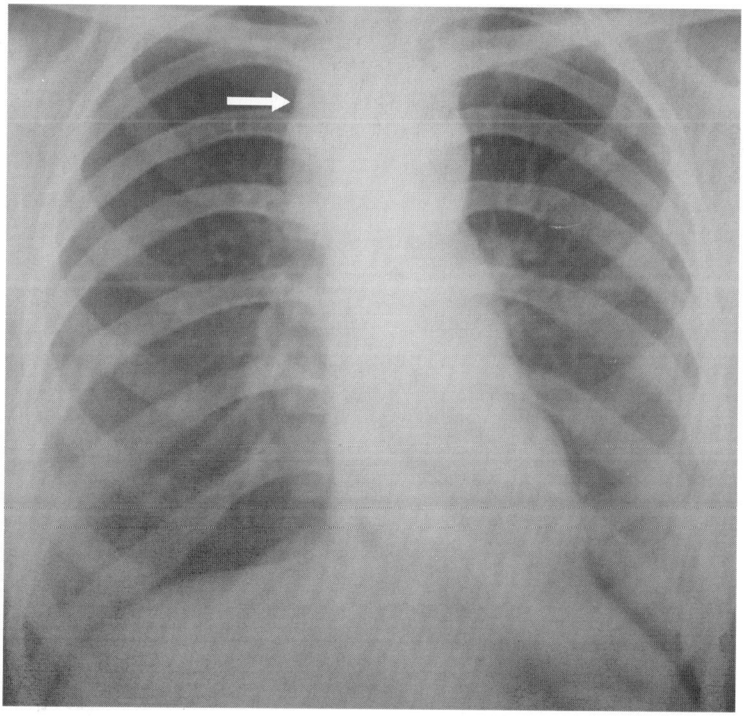

Para-tracheal lymphadenopathy causes tuberculosis

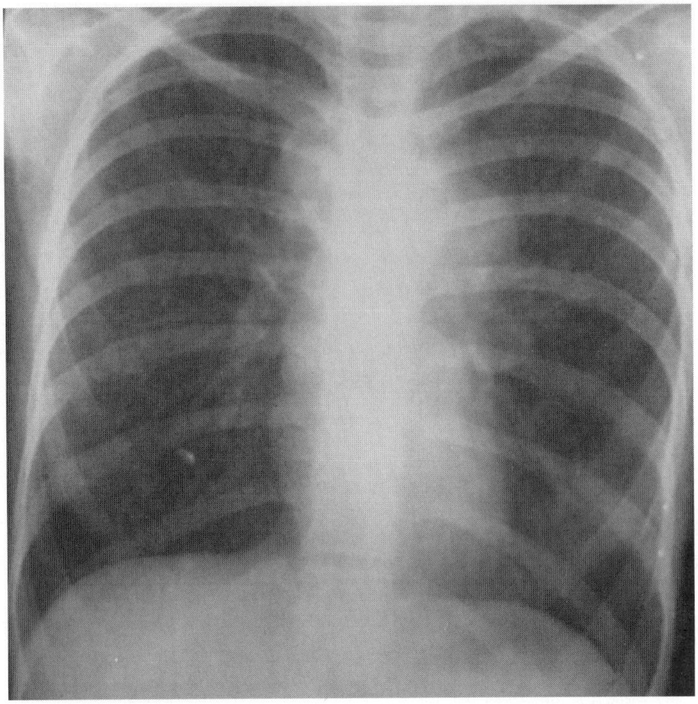

What is this?

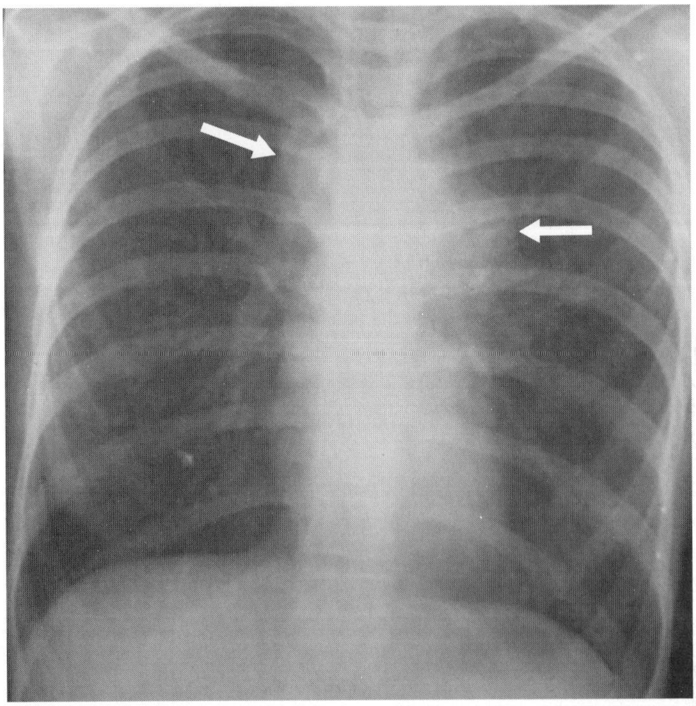

Multiple mediastinal lymph node enlargement cause tuberculosis

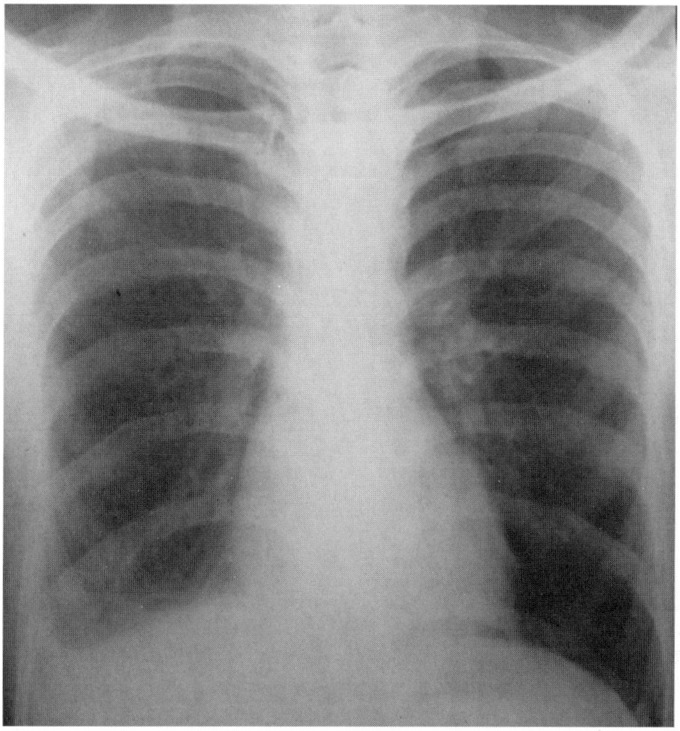

What is this?

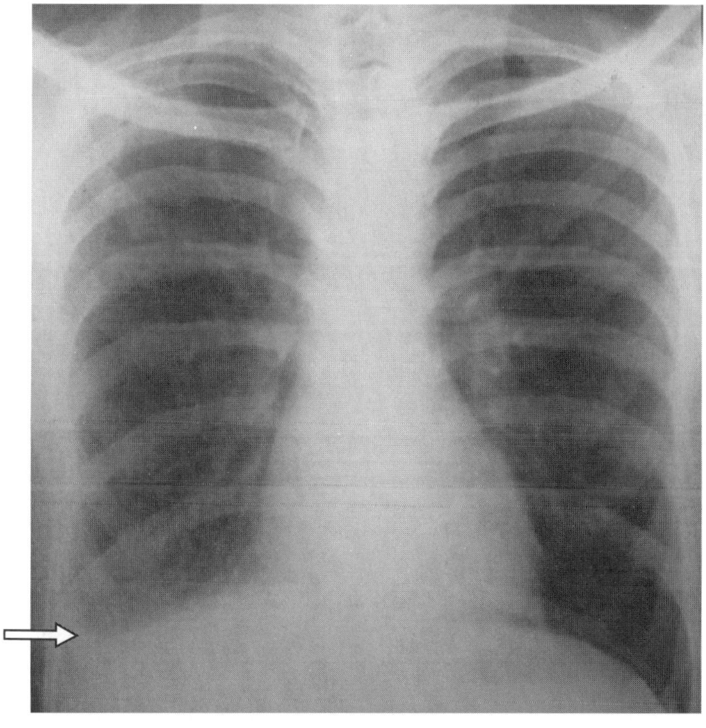

Small pleural effusion (right) cause tuberculosis

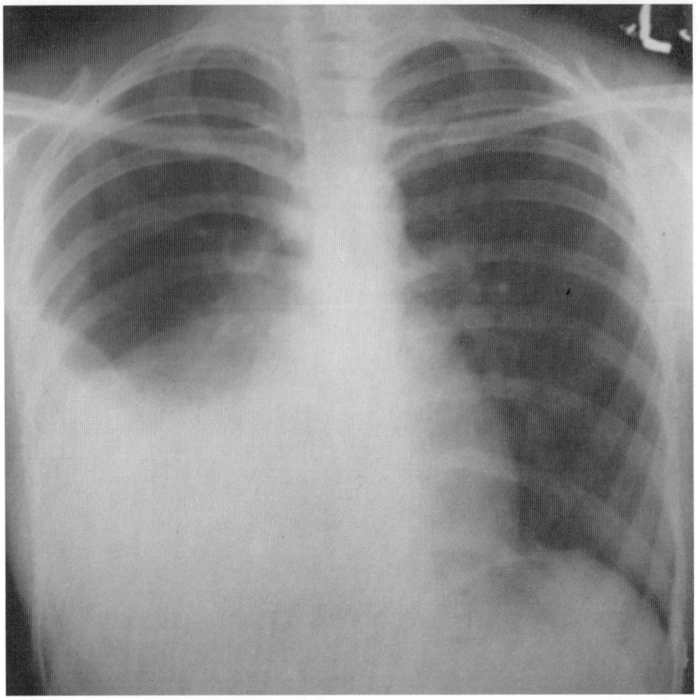

What is this?

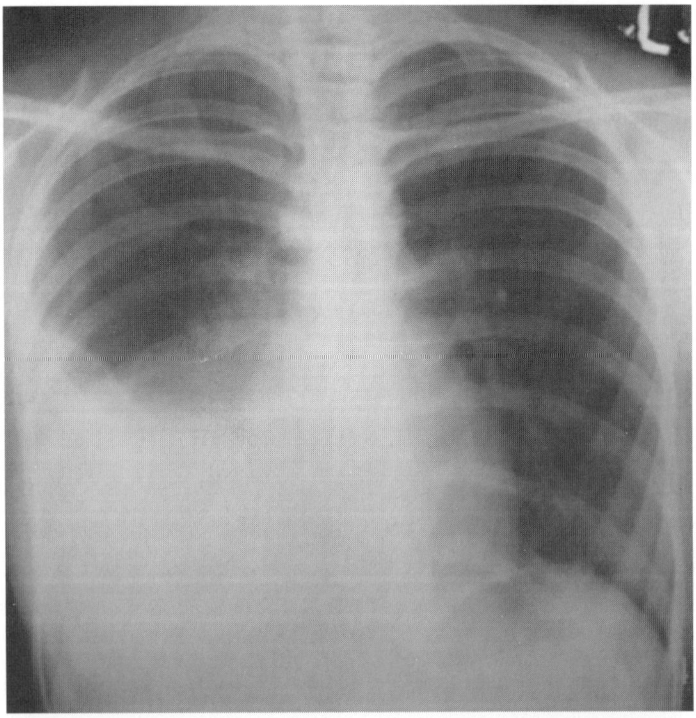

Moderate pleural effusion (right) cause tuberculosis

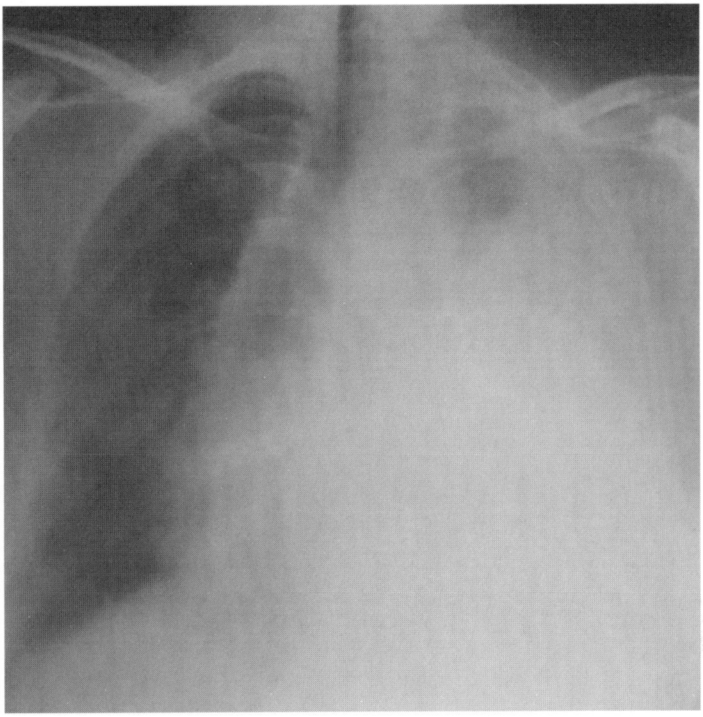

What is this?

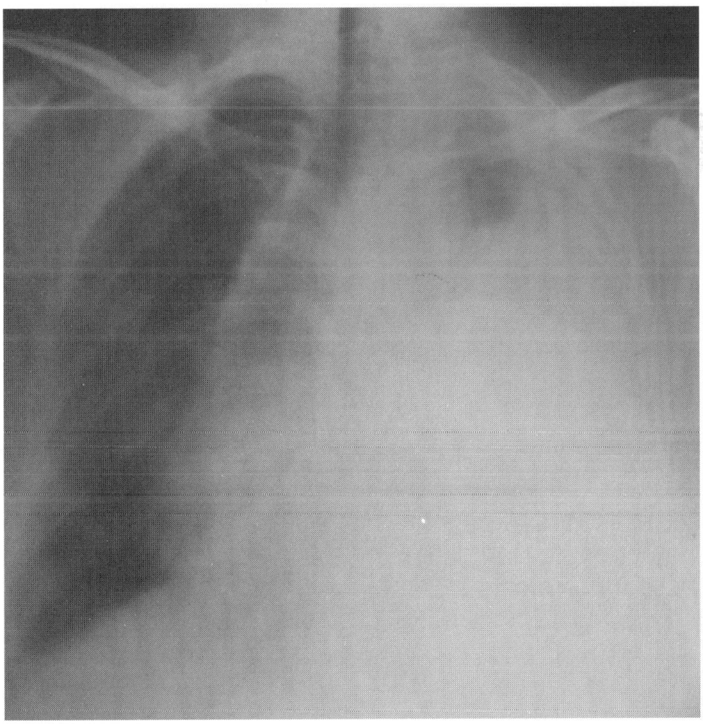

Massive pleural effusion (left) cause tuberculosis

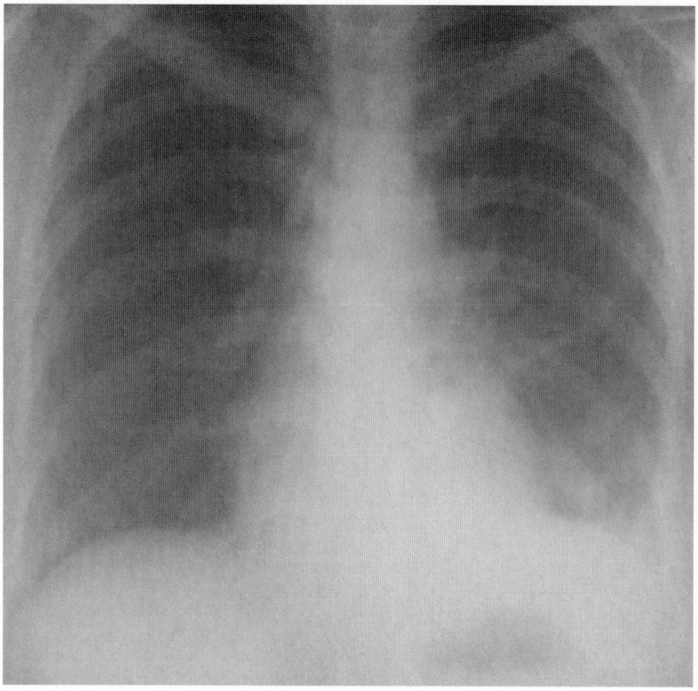

What is this?

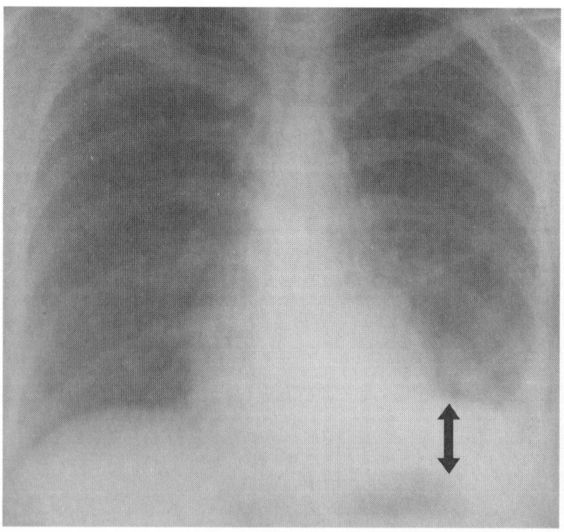

Unilateral raised diaphragm
Infrapulmonary effusion (left)
cause tuberculosis

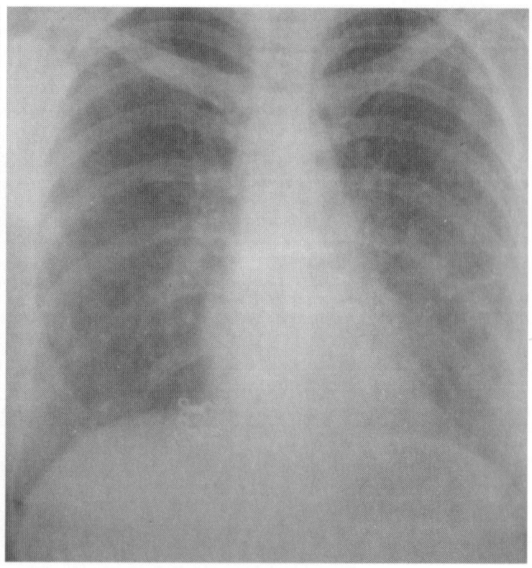

Left diaphragm normal
after treatment

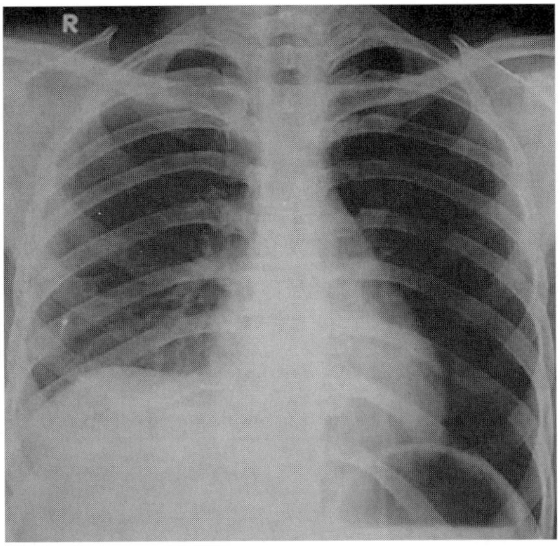

What is this?

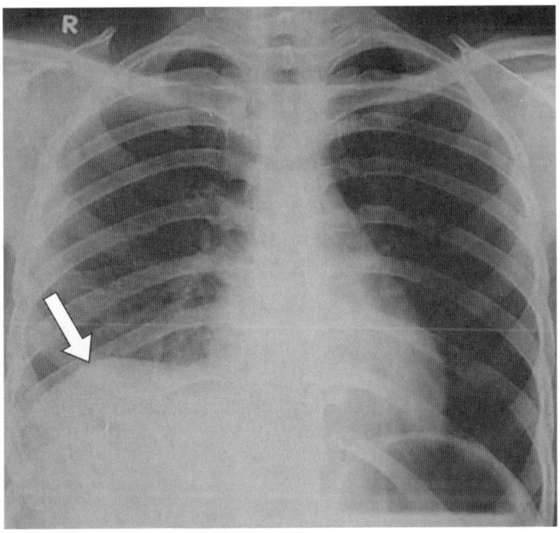

Raised dome of diaphragm with lateral shifting of highest point of diaphragm (right) Infrapulmonary pleural effusion cause tuberculosis

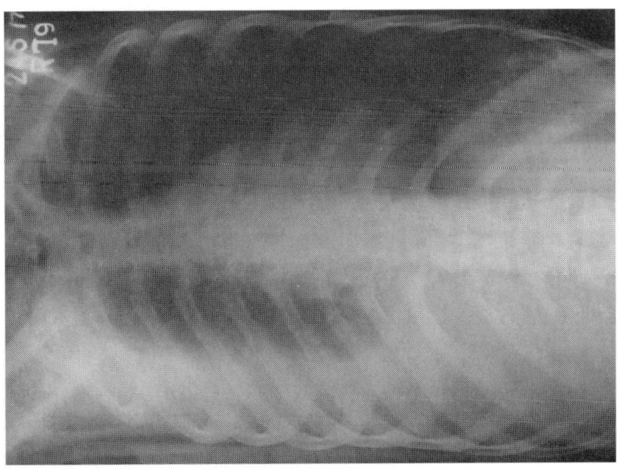

Right lateral decubitus view shows infrapulmonary pleural effusion (right) cause tuberculosis

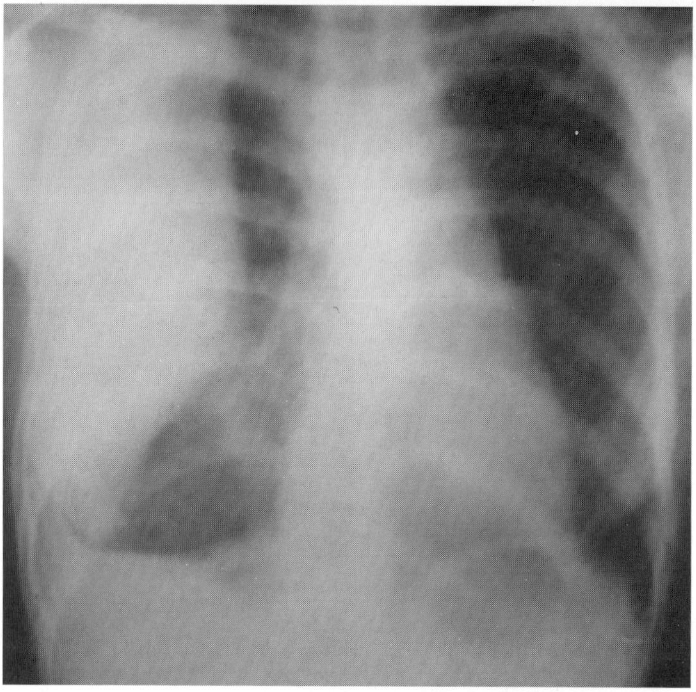

What is this?

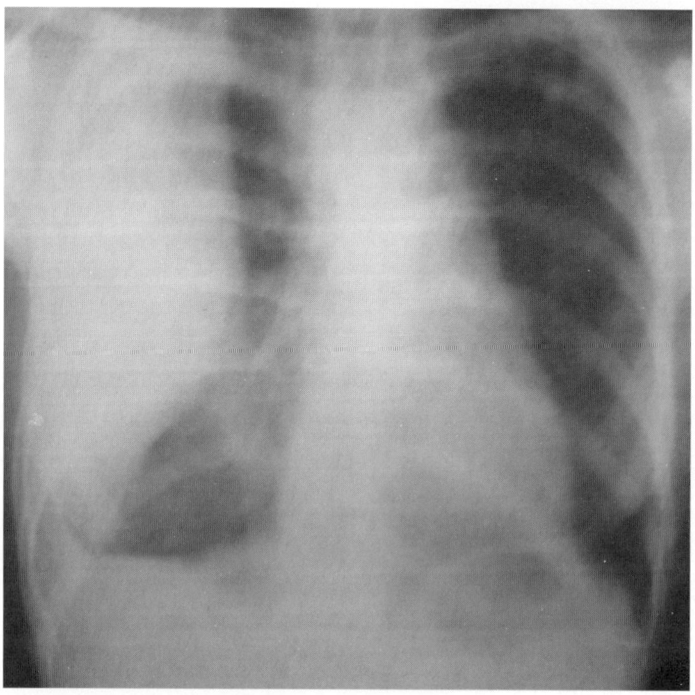

Encysted pleural effusion (right) cause tuberculosis

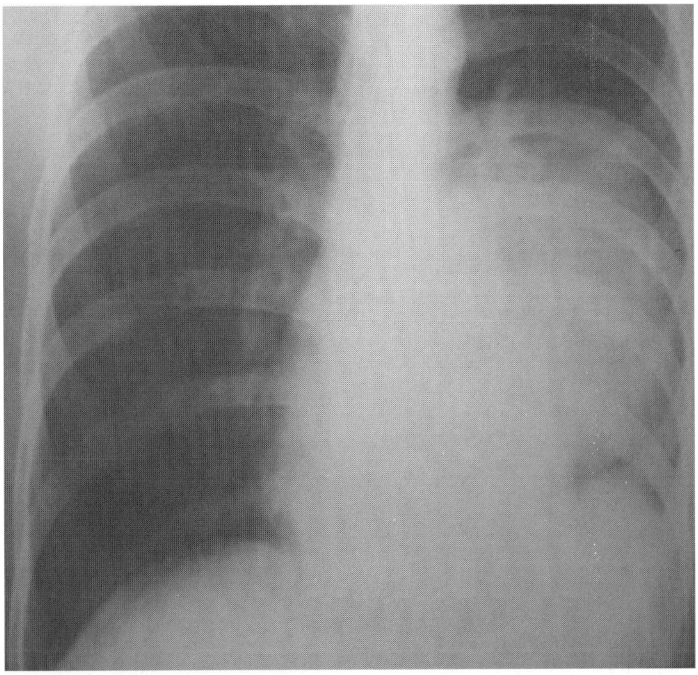

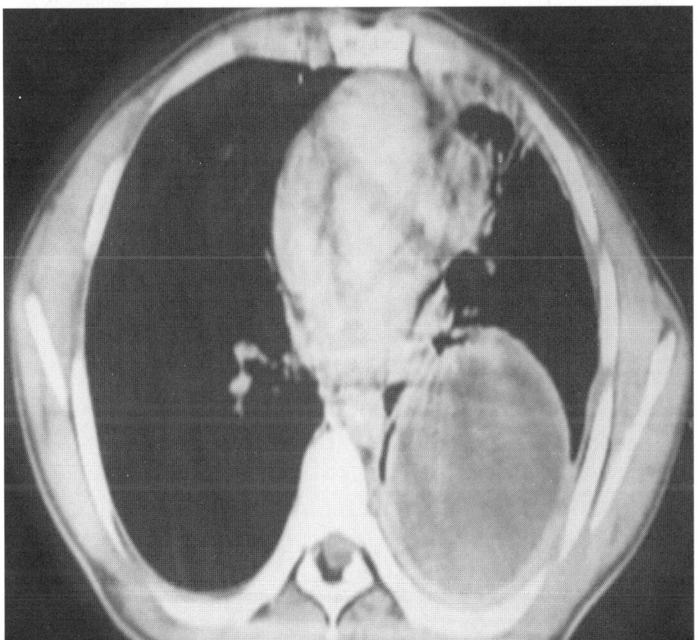

What is this?

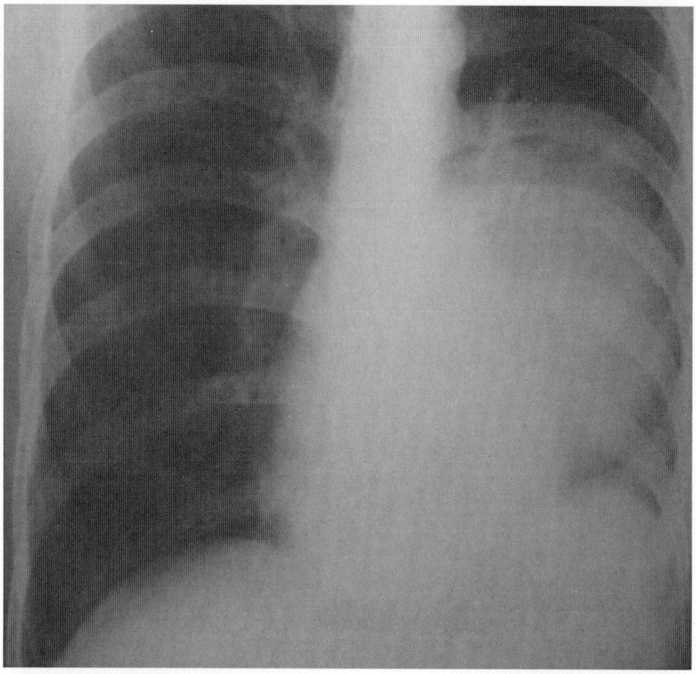

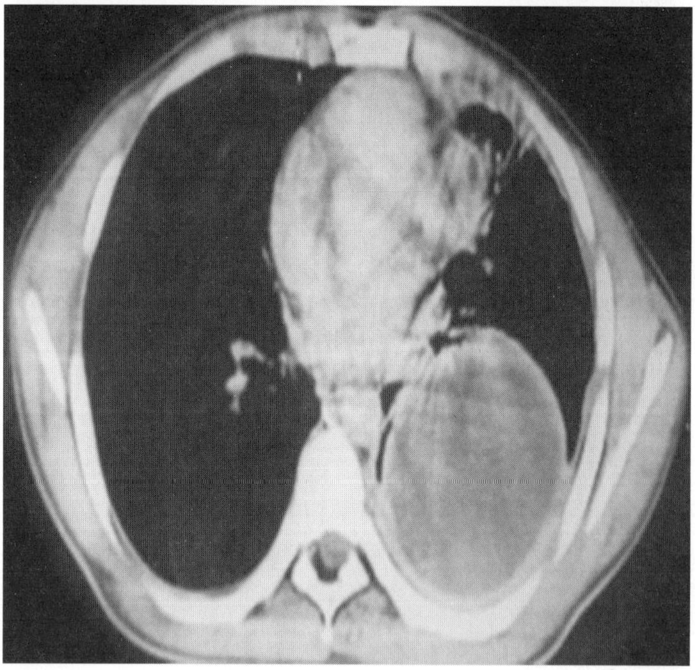

Encysted pleural effusion (left)
cause tuberculosis

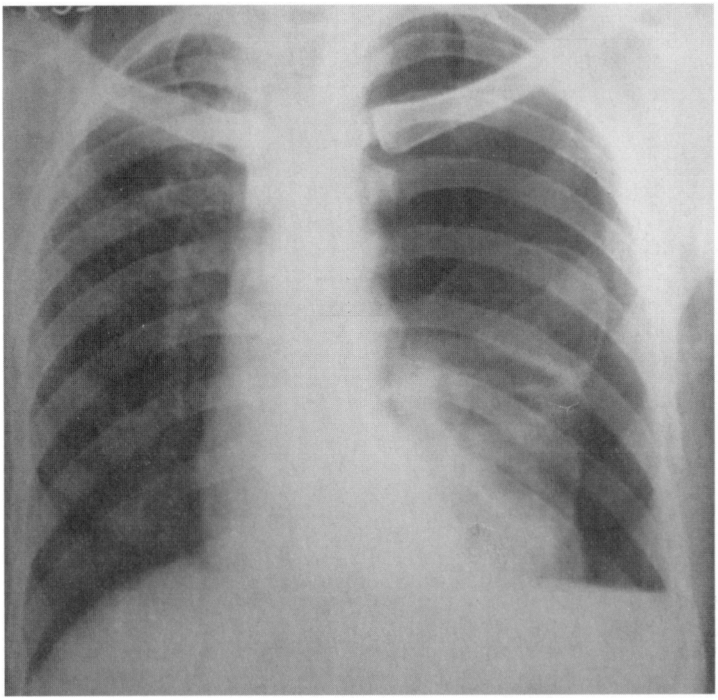

What is this?

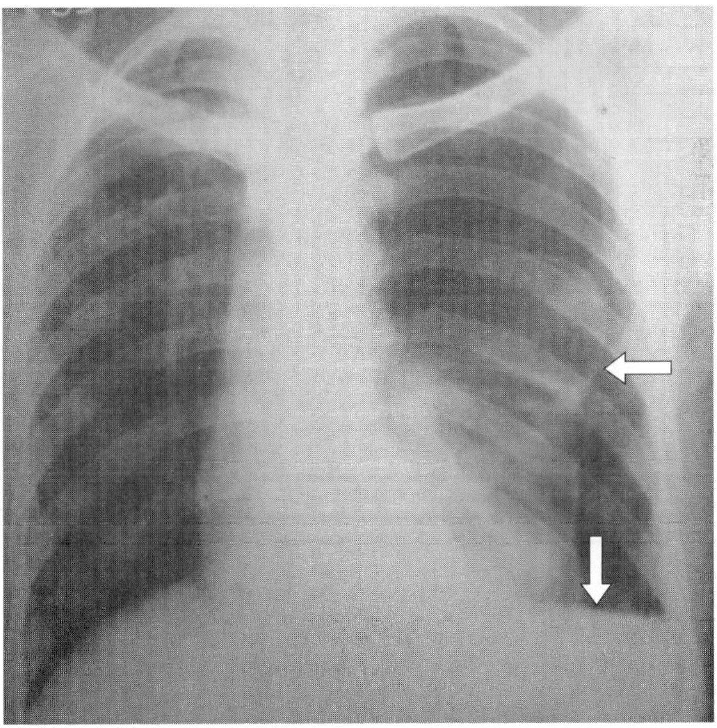

Hydropneumothorax (left) cause tuberculosis

Healing in Pulmonary Tuberculosis

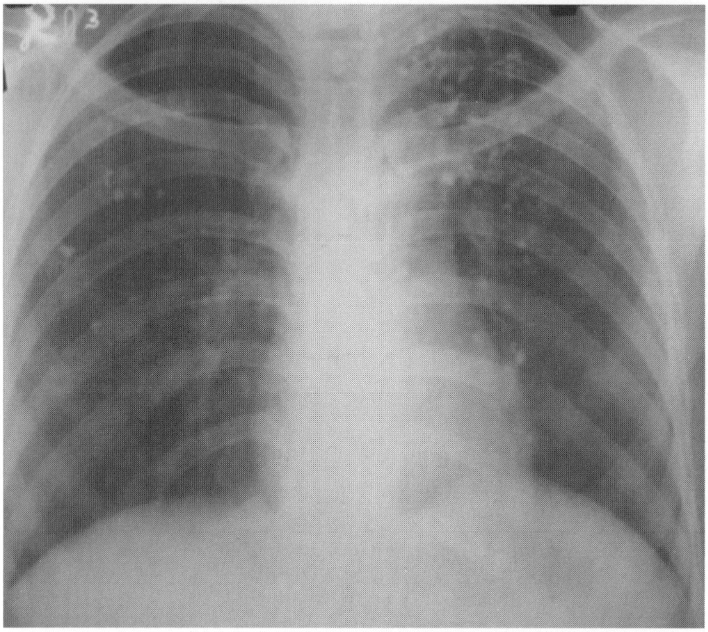

What is this?

C/O massive hemoptysis with history of adequate antitubercular treatment in the past

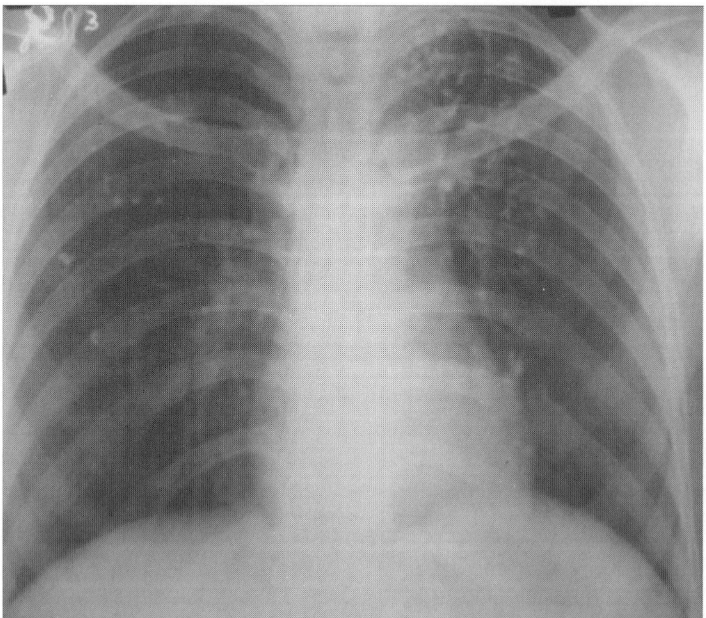

Intrapulmonary calcified shadows (healed pulmonary tuberculosis)

Please note that patients with such healed lesions should not be prescribed antitubercular treatment and only haemoptysis should be managed

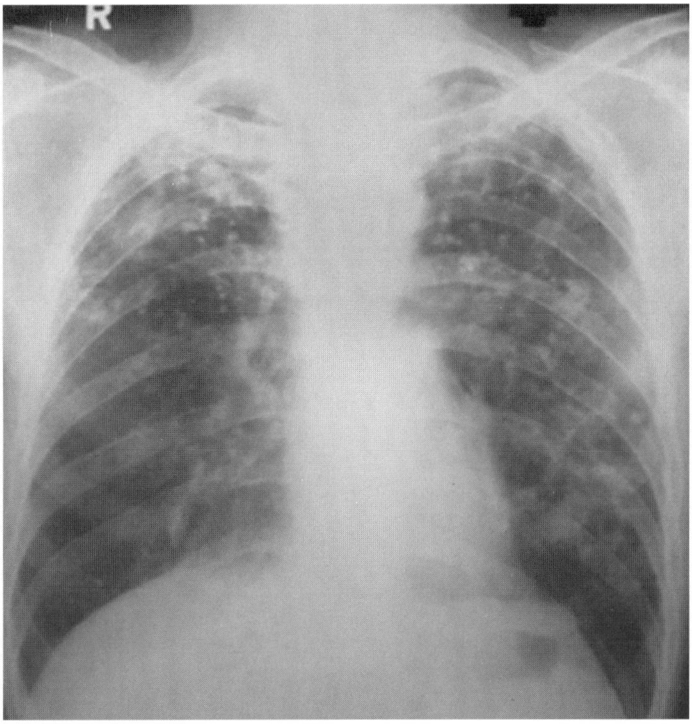

What is this?

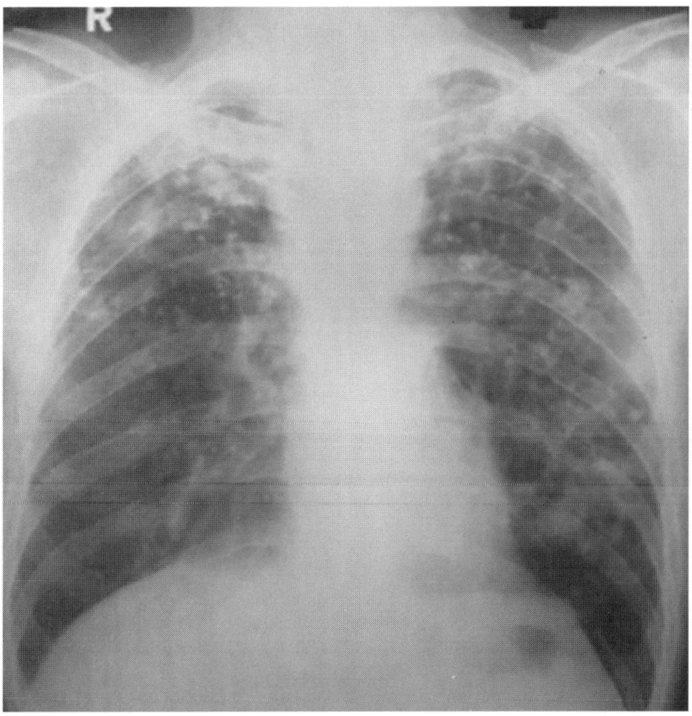

Intrapulmonary calcification (healed pulmonary tuberculosis)

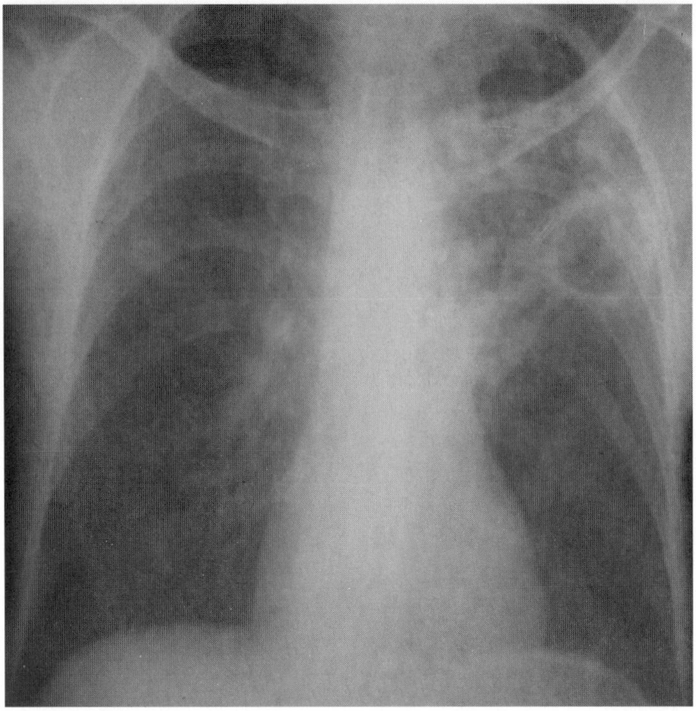

Cavity with infiltration left upper zone cause pulmonary tuberculosis

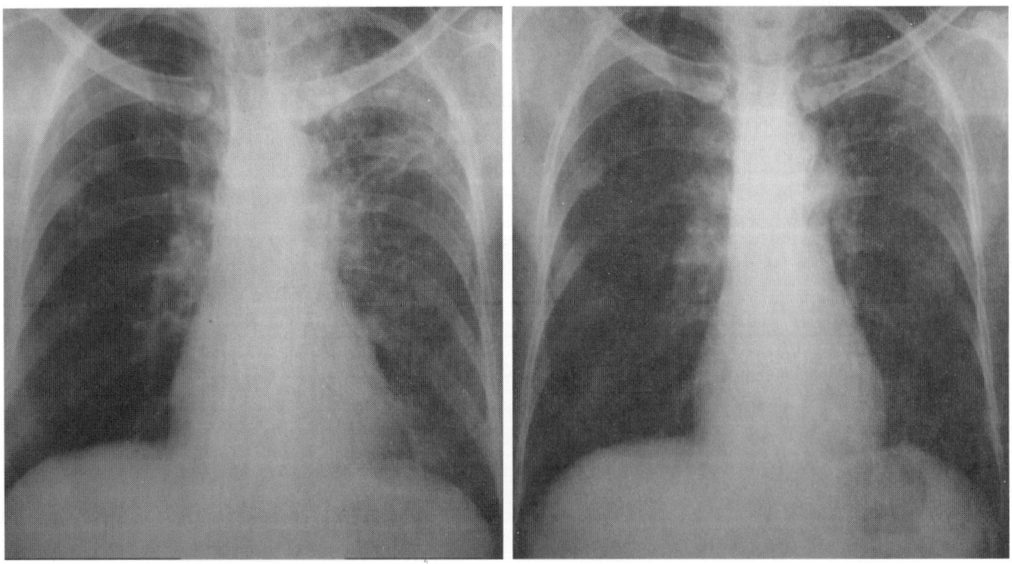

Healing of cavity under effective antitubercular treatment after 6 months. Cavity has completely disappeared, this is an example of a close healing of cavity

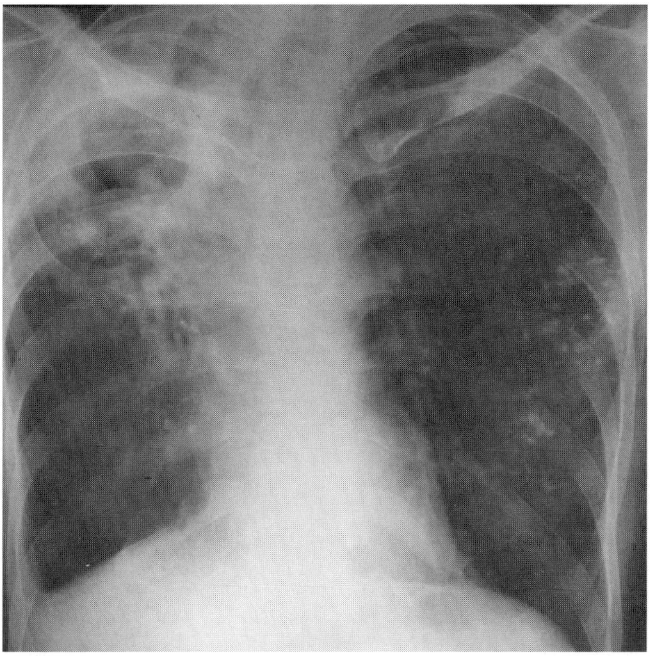

Cavity right upper zone cause sputum positive pulmonary tuberculosis

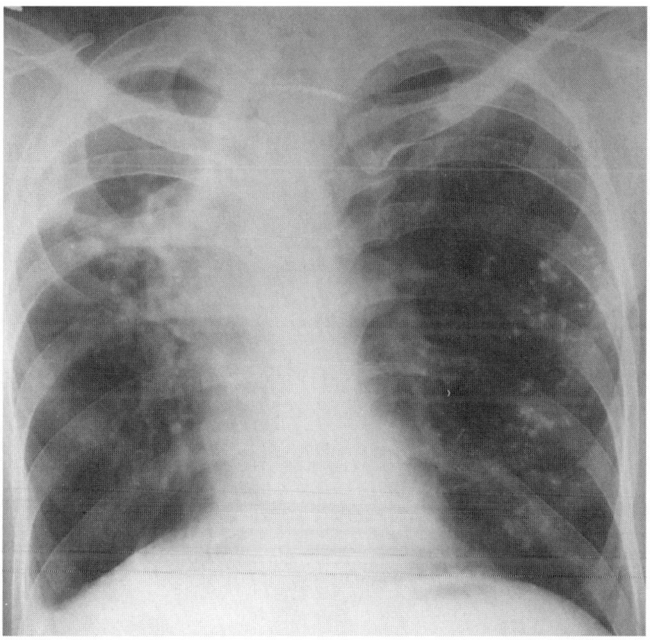

After 6 months of effective antitubercular treatment cavity became thin walled and is persisting but sputum became negative for AFB. This is an example of open healing of cavity (open negative syndrome)

Please remember that such healed cavity will persist throughout the life and do not require antitubercular treatment. Such healed cavity may have recurrent haemoptysis

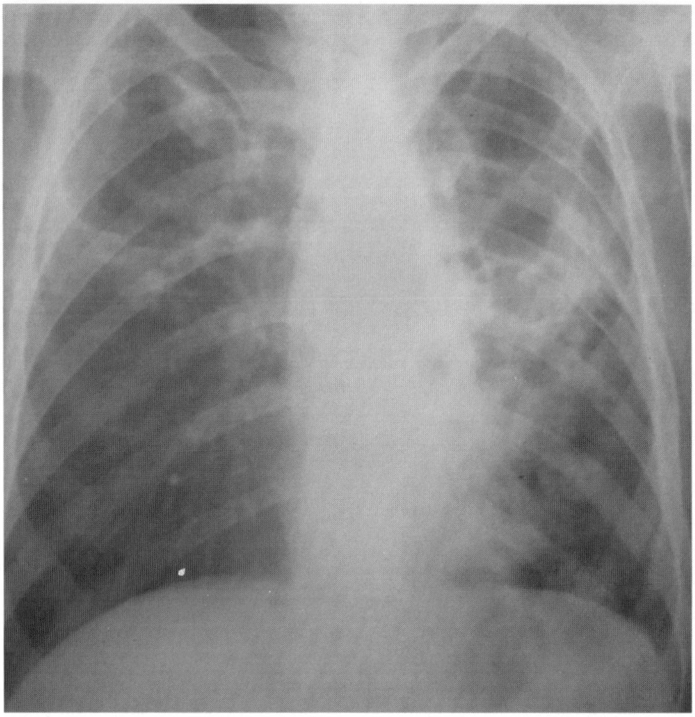

A 50-year-old male with cough and haemoptysis—6 months (off and on) with history of adequate antitubercular treatment in the past and sputum for AFB is negative

What is this?

Bilateral upper zone thin-walled cavities open negative syndrome (healed cavity)

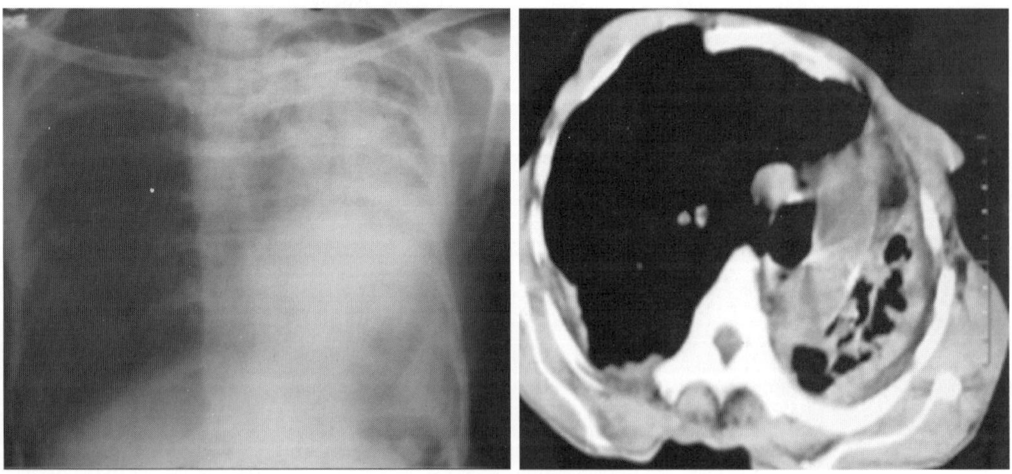

A 35-year-old male with fever, cough, haemoptysis—1 month with history of adequate antitubercular treatment in the past and sputum is negative for AFB

What is this?

Fibrocavitary disease left side with herniation of right lung

Healed pulmonary tuberculosis

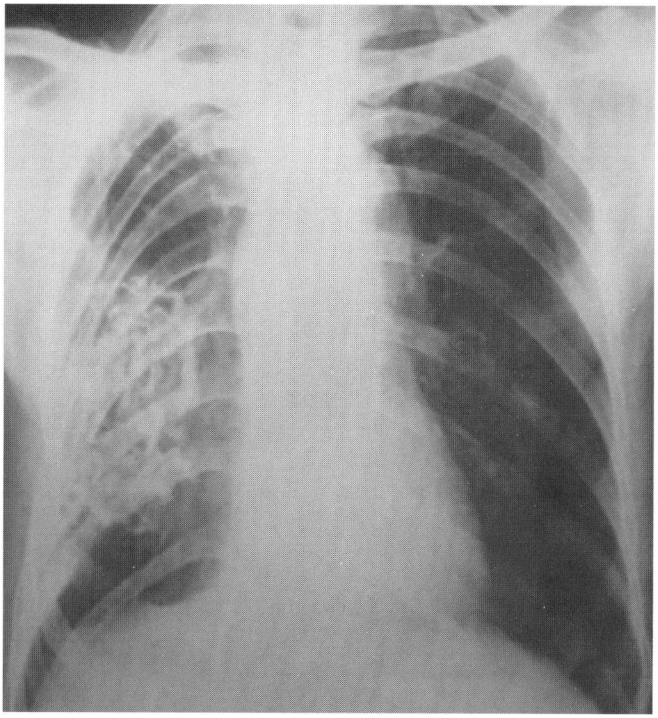

What is this?

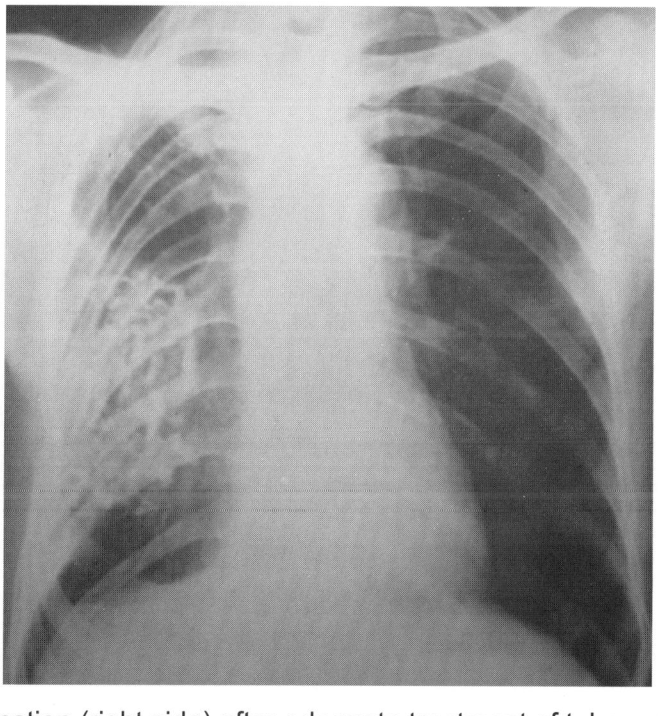

Pleural calcification (right side) after adequate treatment of tubercular empyema
Please note that such lesions will persist and patients are usually asymptomatic

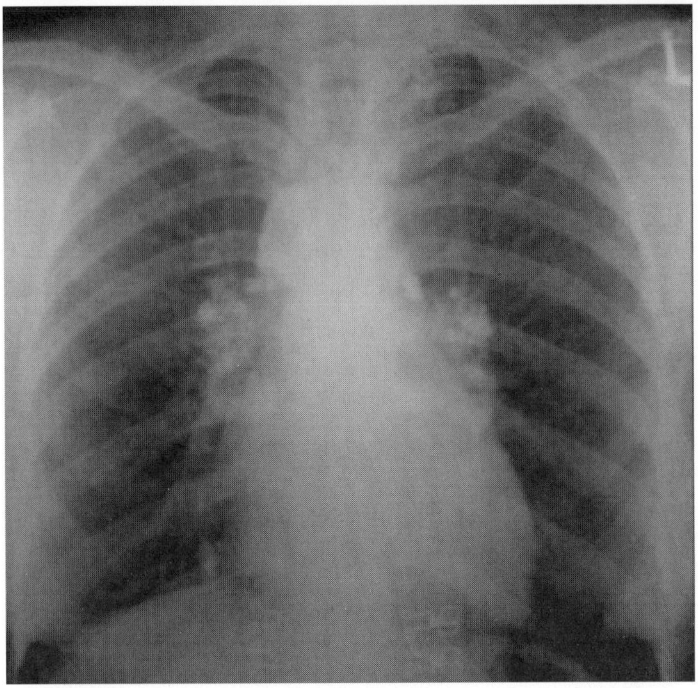

What is this?

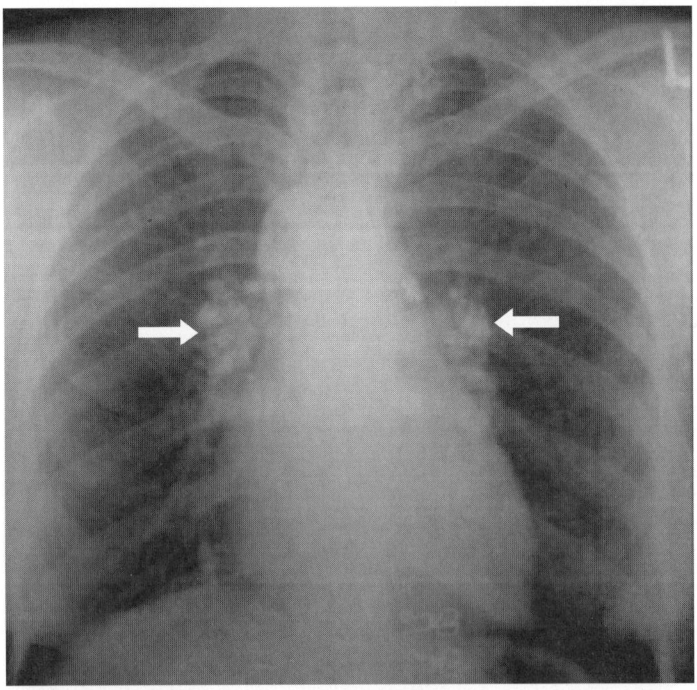

Calcified hilar glands (bilateral)

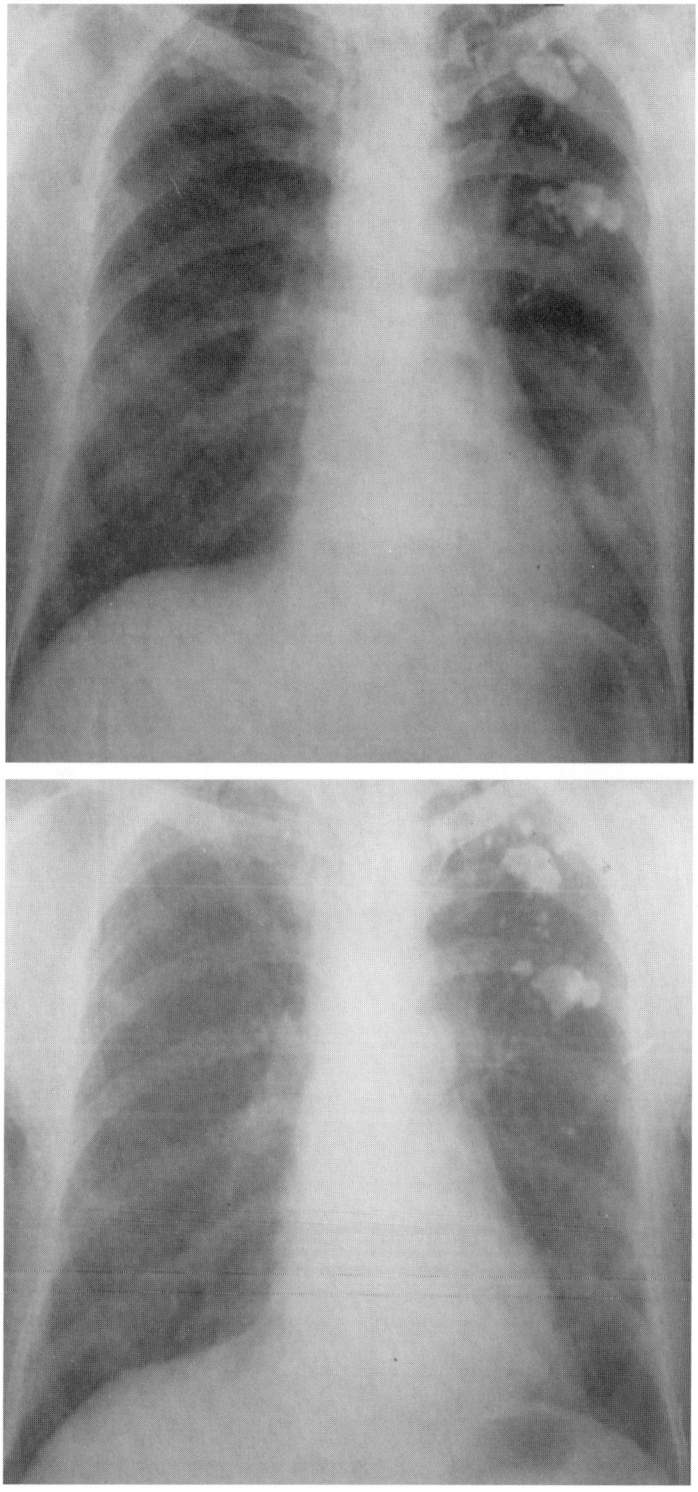

A 65-year-old presented with fever, cough and a large amount of yellow sputum
What is this?

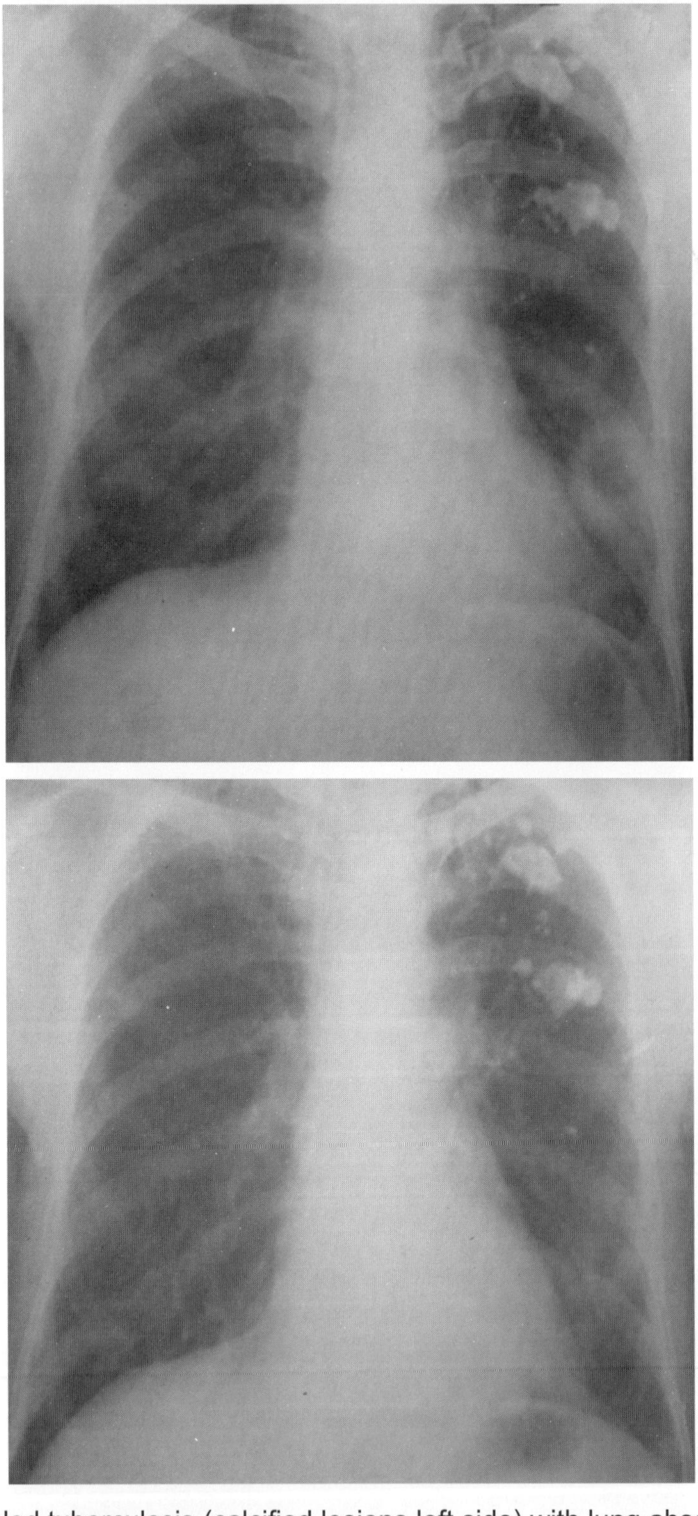

Healed tuberculosis (calcified lesions left side) with lung abscess which disappeared after 3 weeks of antibiotics
Patient gave history of adequate antitubercular treatment in past

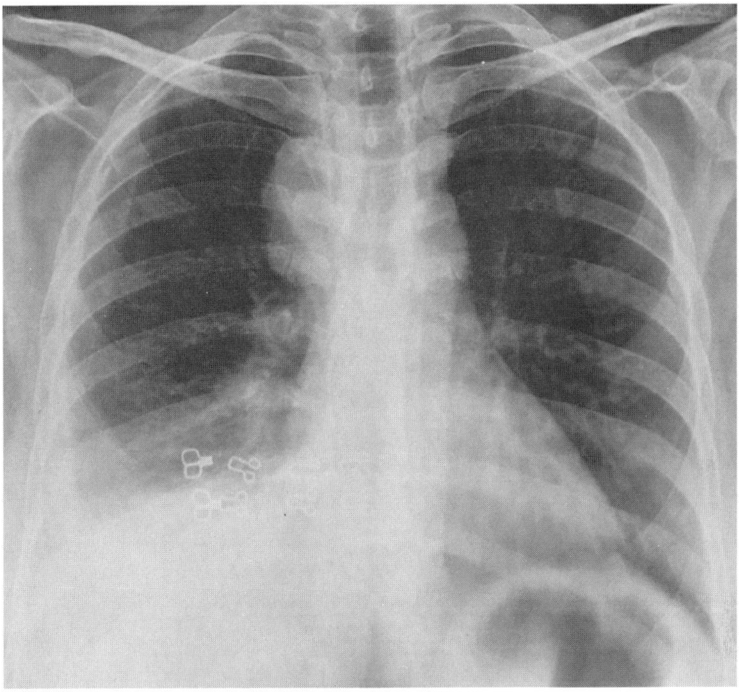

A 30-year-old female with fever and chest pain (right side) since 3 months
What is this?

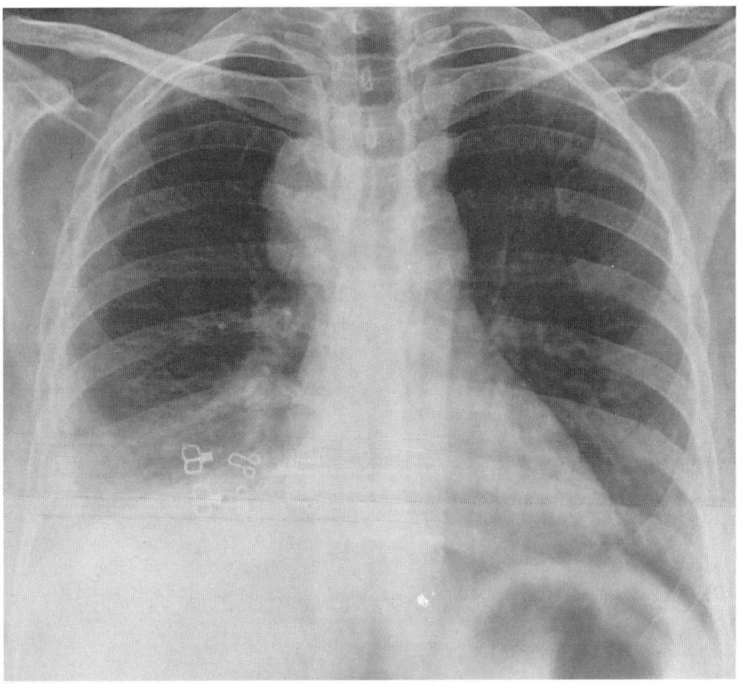

Pleural effusion (Right) with mediastinal lymph nodes cause tuberculosis
Patient denied for pleural aspiration and was given antitubercular treatment with Rifampicin (R), Isoniazid (H), Ethambutol (E) and Pyrizinamide (Z)

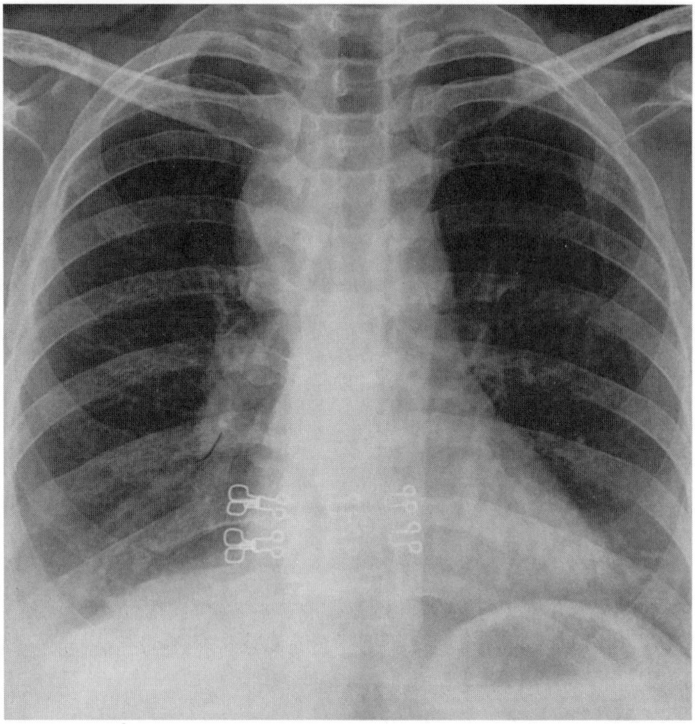

After 6 weeks of antitubercular treatment (RHEZ) patient developed jaundice, so rifampicin and pyrizinamide were stopped and treatment continued with streptomycin, isoniazid and ethambutol. Rifampicin was started once again when LFT became normal but patient again developed jaundice so rifampicin and pyrizinamide were stopped permanently and continued with only streptomycin, isoniazid and ethambutol

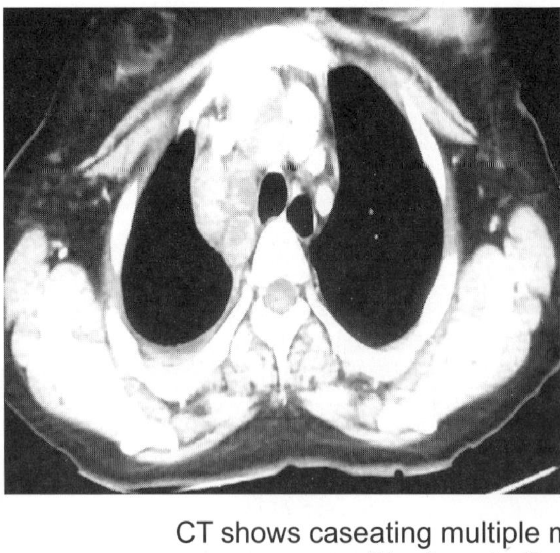

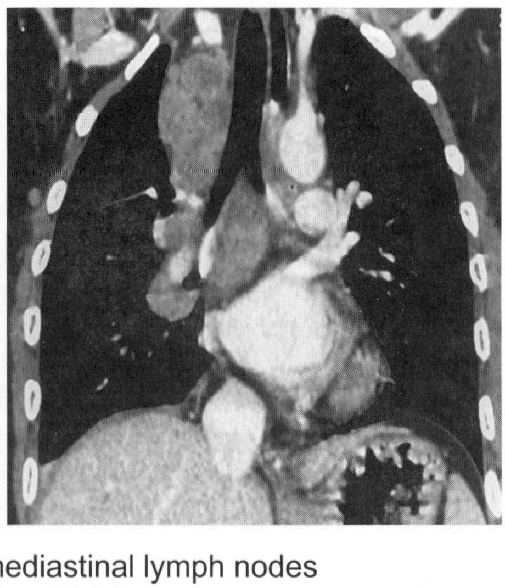

CT shows caseating multiple mediastinal lymph nodes with pleural effusion (right)

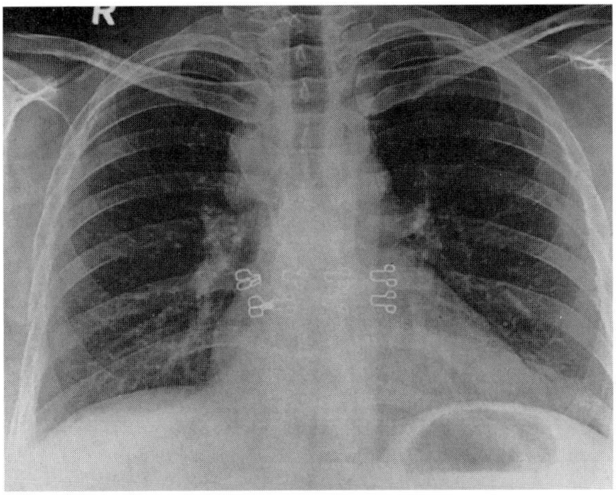

After 6 months of antitubercular treatment. Pleural effusion disappeared but mediastinal lymph nodes persisted so oral steroids were added for 6 weeks

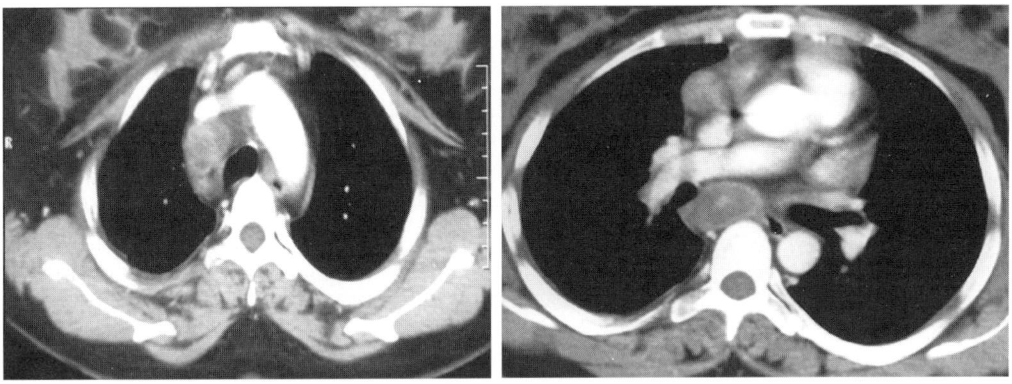

CT shows persistent caseating multiple mediastinal lymph nodes

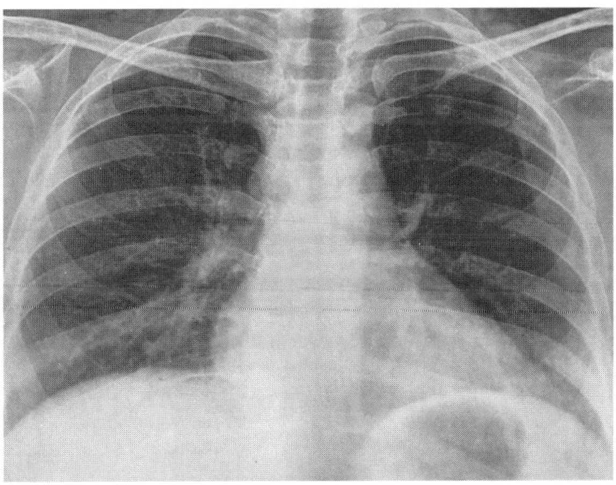

After 1 year of streptomycin (2 months), isoniazid and ethambutol and oral steroids (for 6 weeks in tapering doses), lymph nodes also disappeared and she was followed for next 2 years without any recurrence

Reader's Notes

CHAPTER

13

Radiology of Bronchiectasis

Presence of permanent and abnormal dilatation of one or more of the conducting bronchi or airways

Types of Bronchiectasis

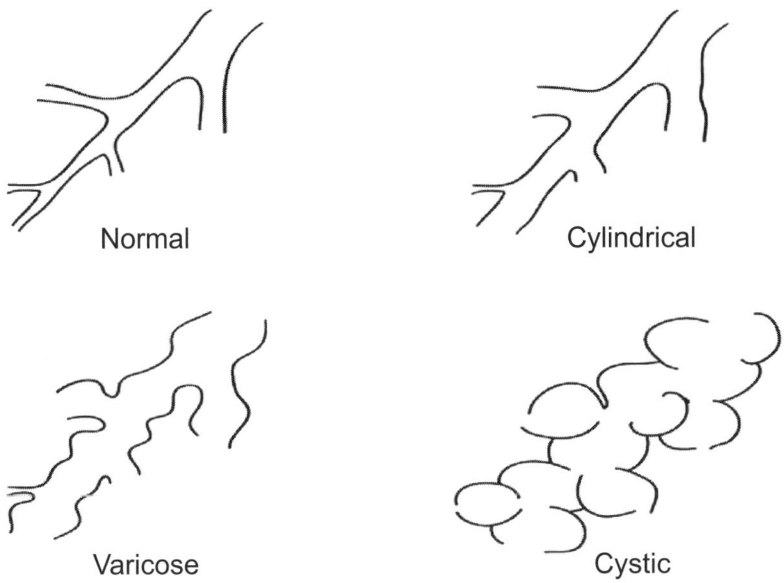

Chest X-ray Findings of Bronchiectasis

- Not sensitive for diagnosing bronchiectasis
- May be normal in 12–15% of the cases
- Increased bronchovascular markings with conglomeration of vessels in a localized area
- Bronchial dilatation and thickening (tram-track sign)
- Signet ring shadows (dilated end-on bronchi)
- Reticulonodular opacities
- Cystic lesions, often with air–fluid levels
- Mucoid impaction
- Consolidation particularly recurrent and slow resolving pneumonia
- Fibrosis/collapse
- Compensatory overinflation of the less affected lobe/lung

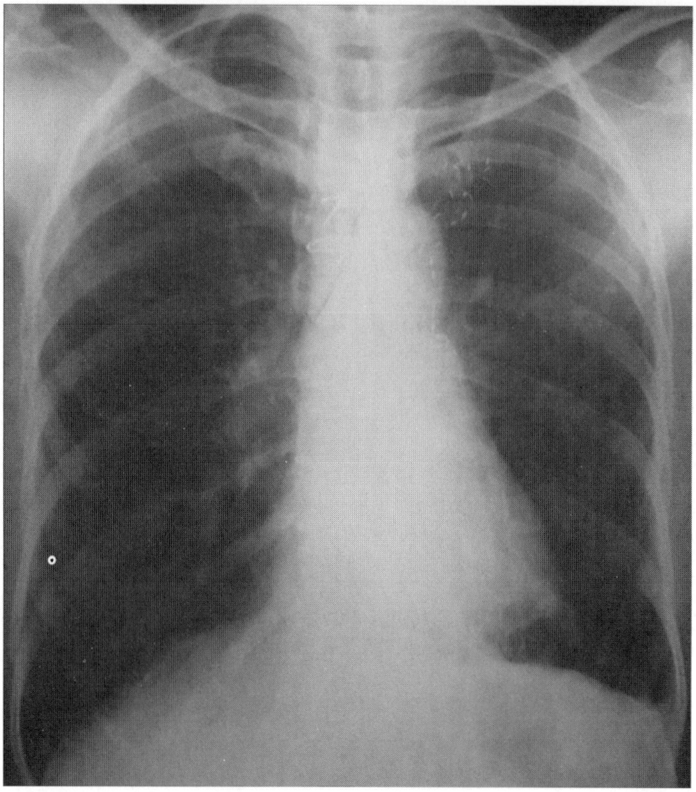

Chest X-ray PA view normal looking with evidence of overinflated chest

A 65-year-old male came with recurrent cough with expectoration and recurrent hemoptysis for 40 years and was chronic smoker (10 cigarettes/day for 30 years) and received many courses of antitubercular treatment without any response. On auscultation there were coarse crepts present in left infrascapular area

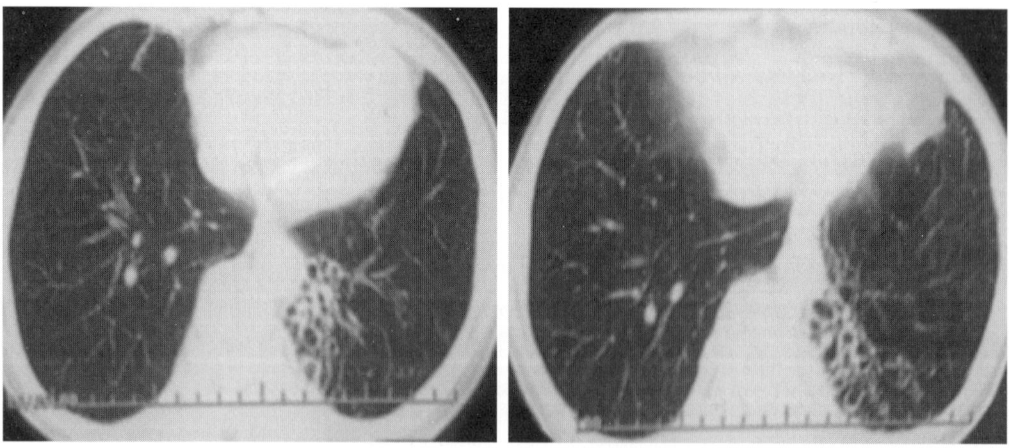

CT thorax shows bronchiectasis left lower lobe

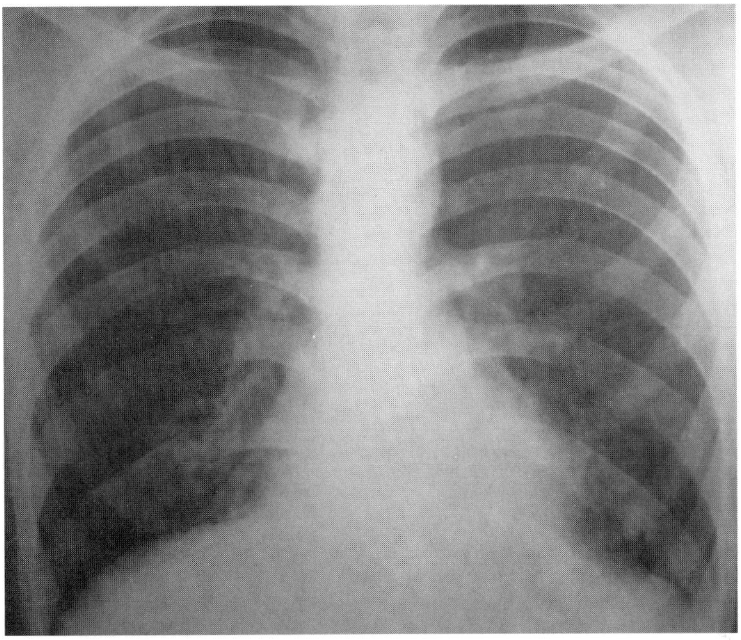

What is this?

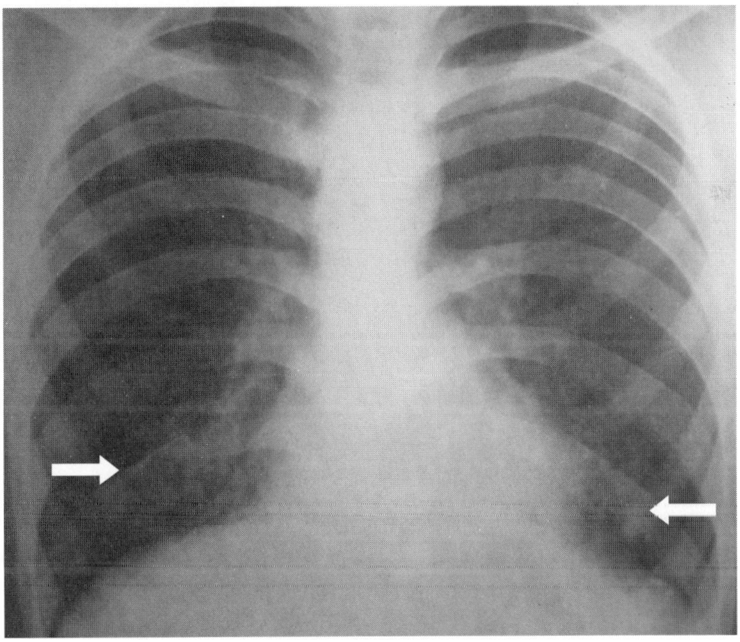

Increased bronchovascular markings in both lower zones suggestive of bronchiectasis

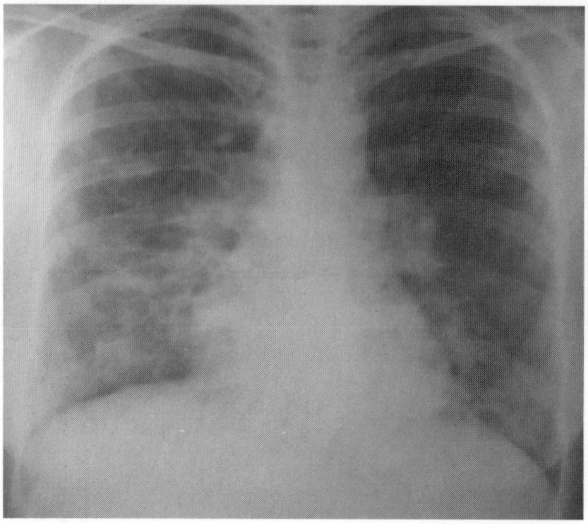

What is this?

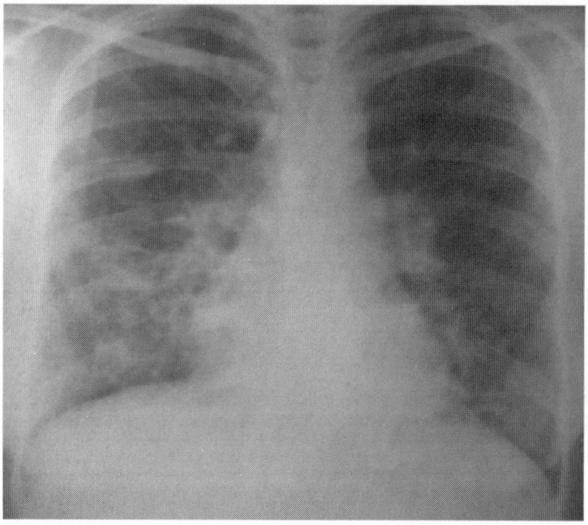

Multiple cystic spaces in lower zones (bilateral)

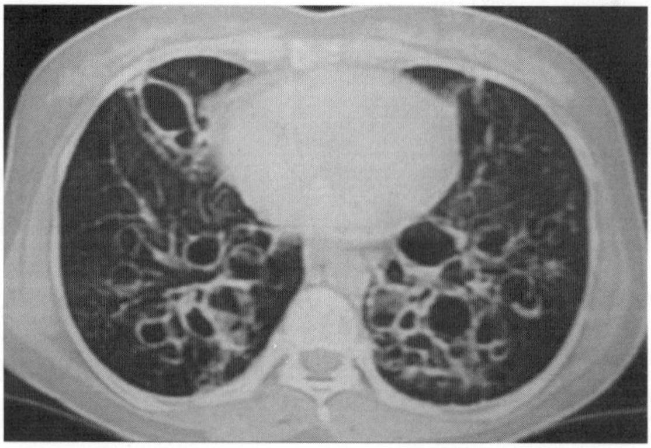

CT thorax shows bilateral lower lobe cystic bronchiectasis

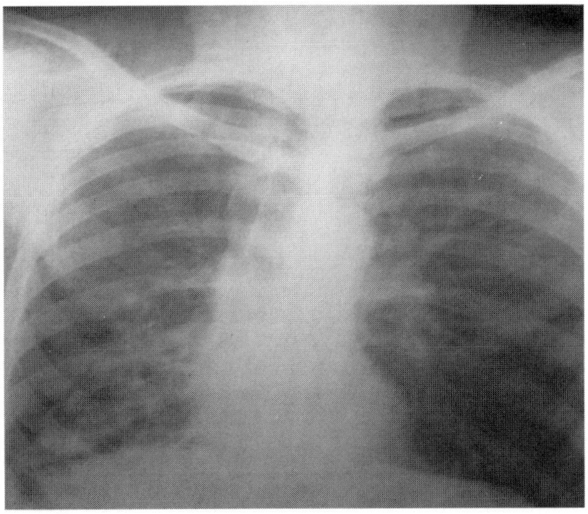

What is this?

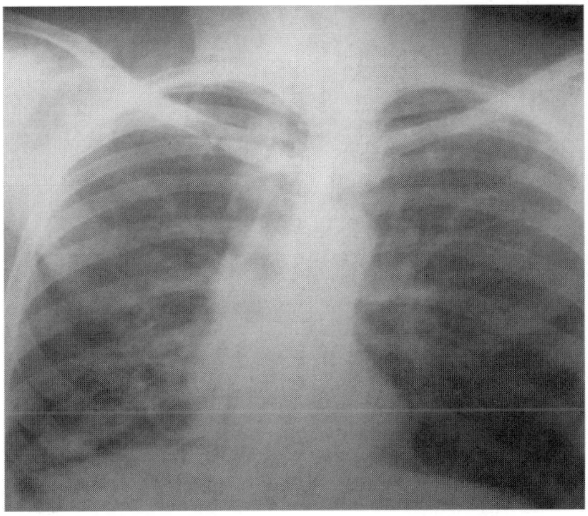

Cystic spaces right lower zone

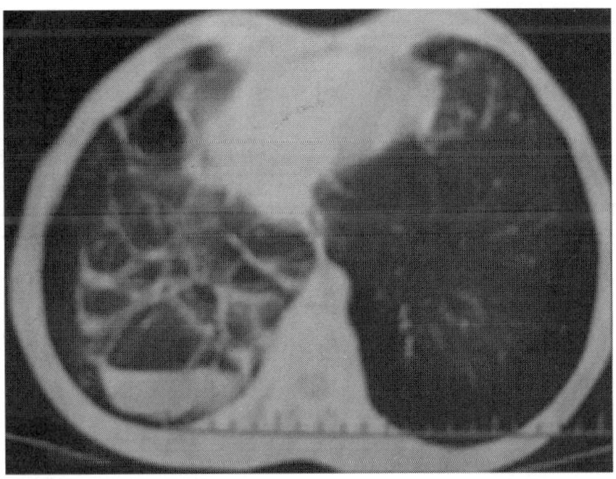

CT thorax shows cystic bronchiectasis in right lower lobe

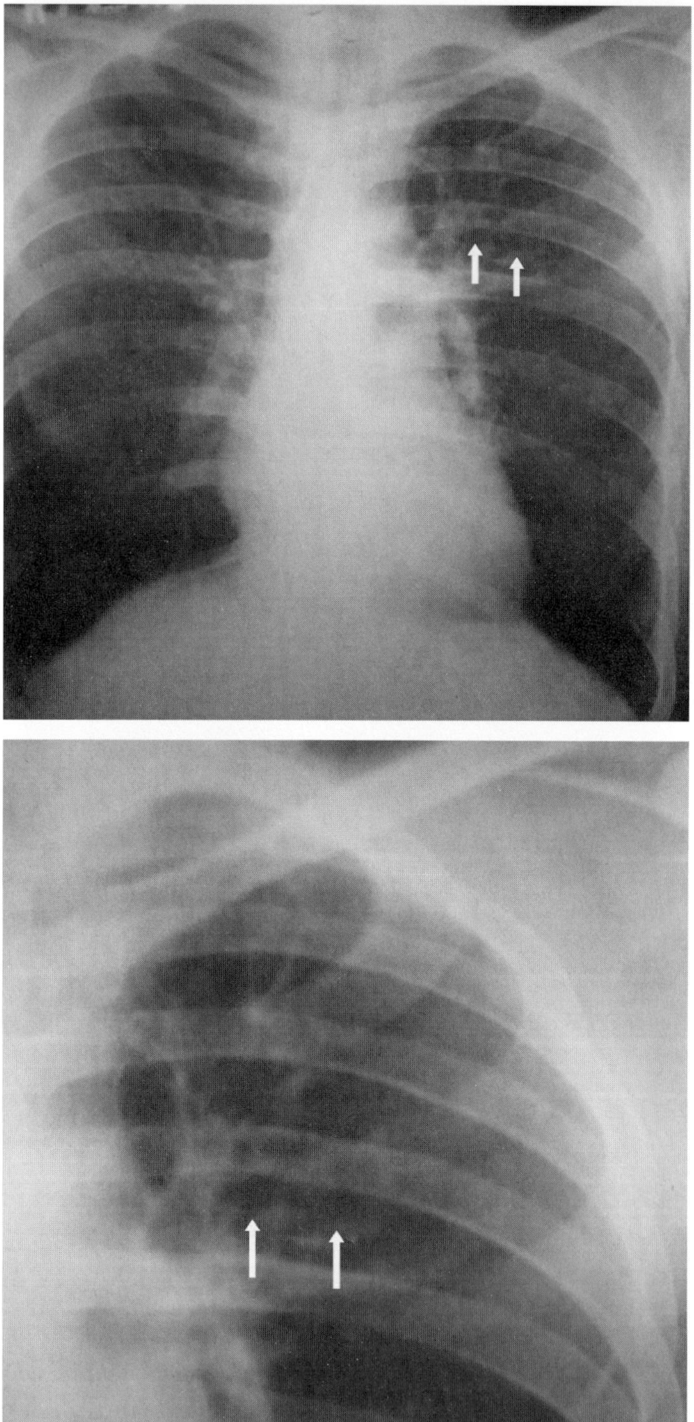

What is this?

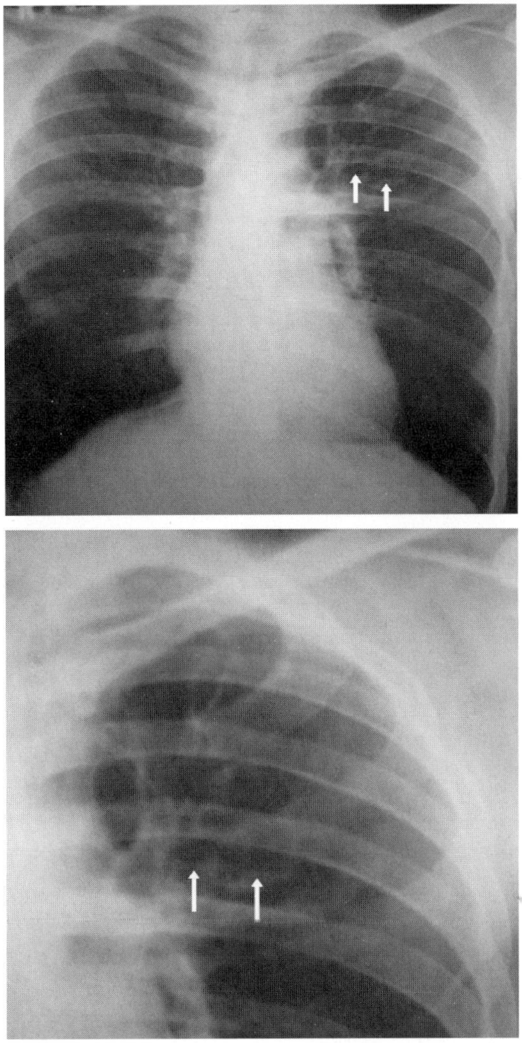

Cystic spaces in left upper zone

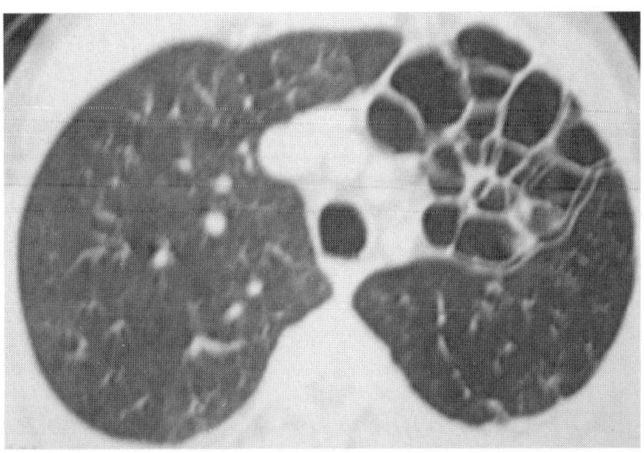

CT thorax shows bronchiectasis in left upper lobe

Please remember that bronchiectasis is uncommon in upper lobes

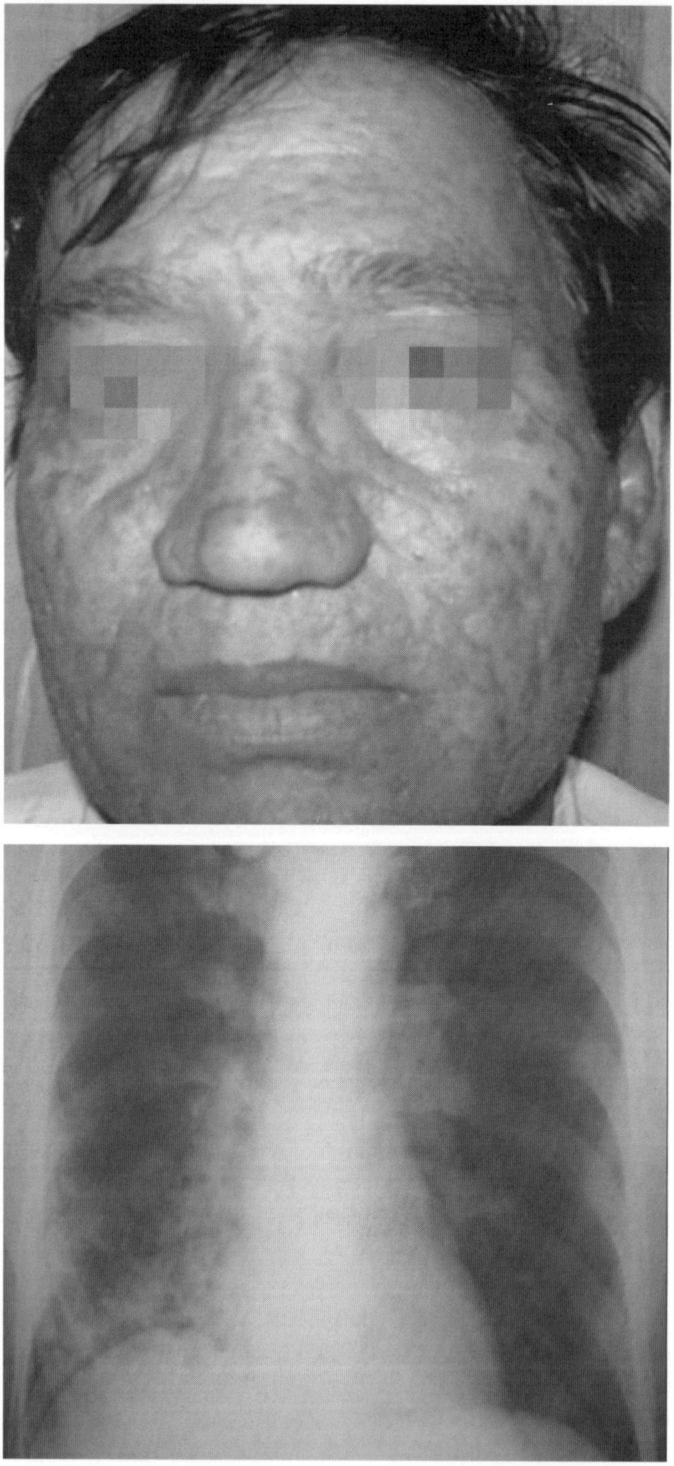

Patient with past history of smallpox during childhood with recurrent cough, a large amount of expectoration and recurrent hemoptysis for the last 15 years with 3 courses of antitubercular treatment without any response
What is this?

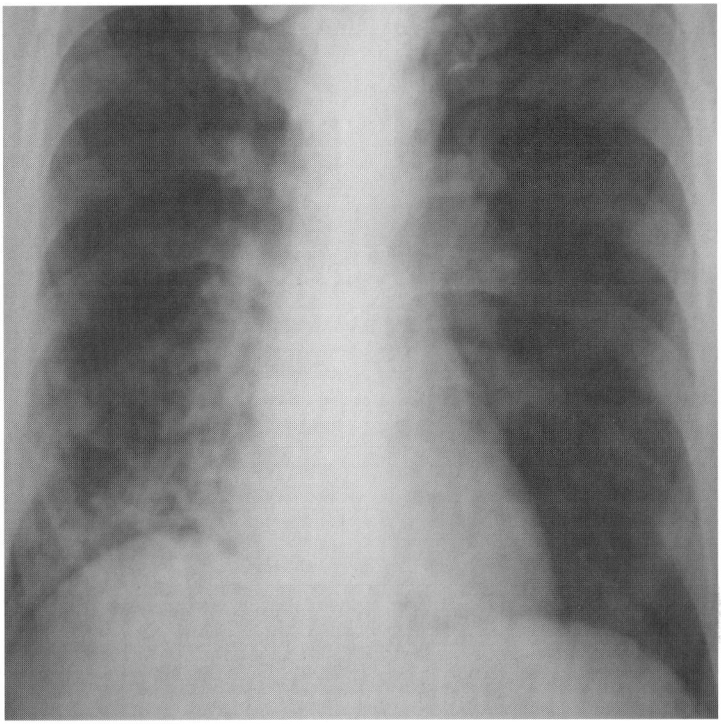

X-ray shows heterogenous shadows in right lower zone? bronchiectasis

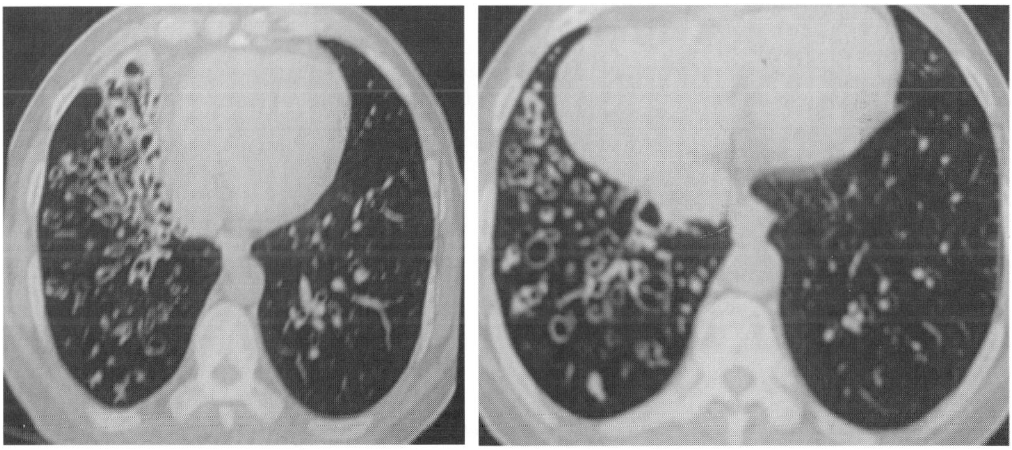

CT thorax shows bronchiectatic changes in right middle and lower lobe

Please remember that bronchiectasis is permanent disease and a lot of anti-tubercular drugs are misused. If such patients have life-threatening symptoms, surgery is a choice

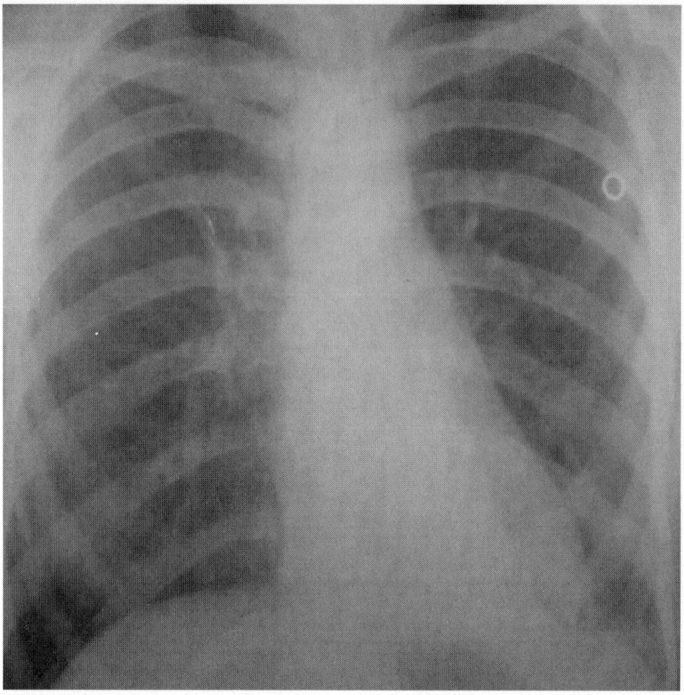

A 35-year-old female presented with cough with expectoration and recurrent hemoptysis for the last 10 years with history of many courses of antitubercular treatment without any response

What is this?

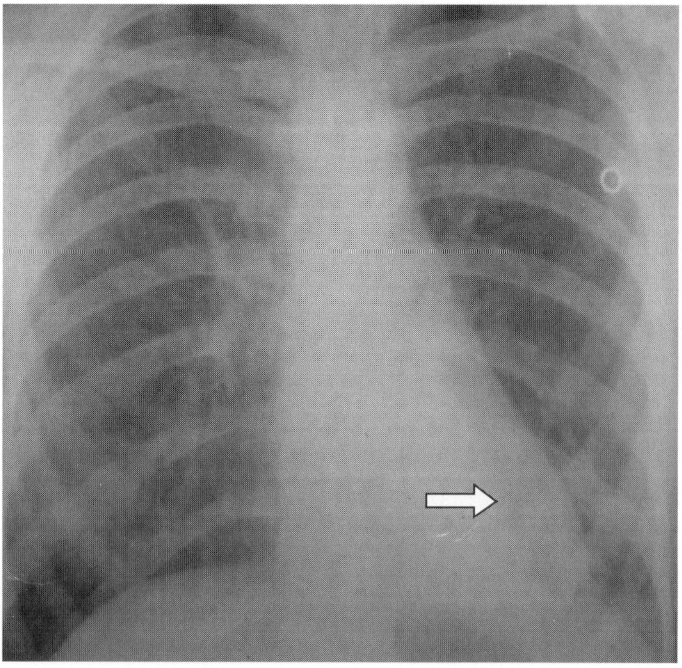

X-ray shows shadow in retrocardiac area

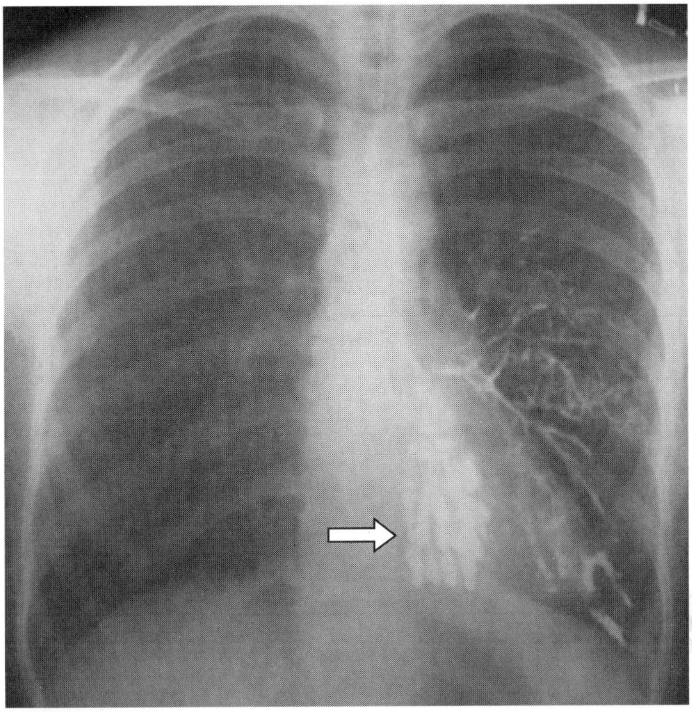

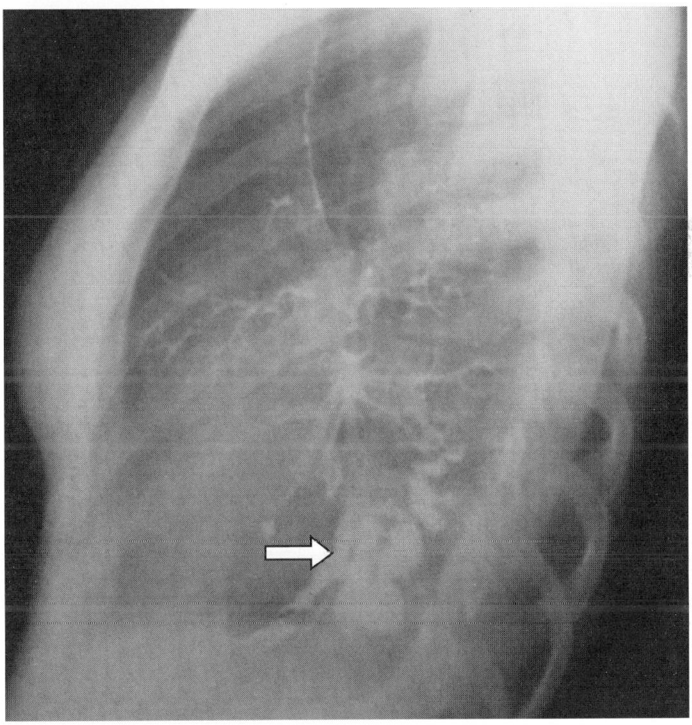

Bronchogram shows bronchiectatic changes in left lower lobe and patient underwent left lower lobe lobectomy and followed up for next 3 years without any recurrence

Reader's Notes

CHAPTER

14

Radiology of Chronic Obstructive Pulmonary Disease (COPD)

COPD

Obstructive airway disease, emphysema and chronic bronchitis as separate disease entities were first defined in CIBA Guest symposium in 1958

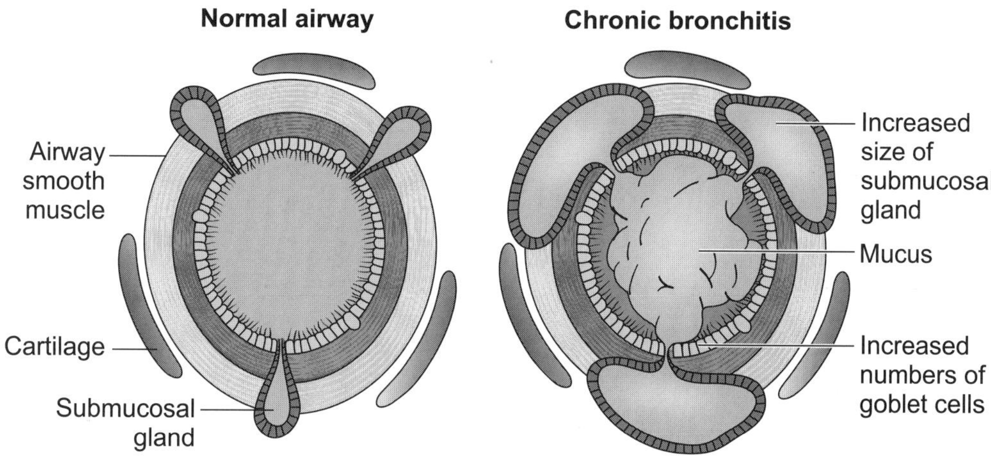

Chronic cough with excessive mucus secretion for most days out of 3 months in each of two or more successive years without other specific cause of cough (asthma, bronchiectasis, tuberculosis)

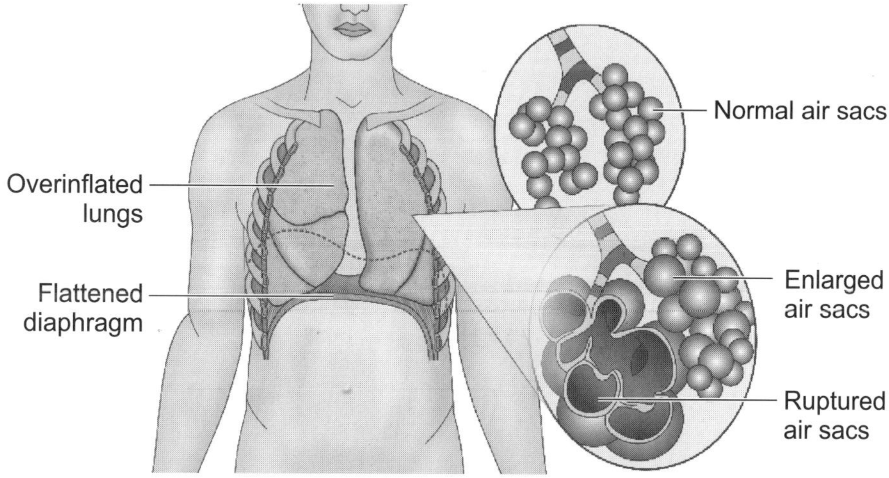

Abnormal enlargement of the air spaces distal to the terminal bronchioles accompanied by destruction of their walls, and without obvious fibrosis

Definition of COPD

COPD is a common, preventable and treatable disease that is characterized by persistent respiratory symptoms and airflow limitation that is due to airway and/or alveolar abnormalities usually caused by significant exposure to noxious particles or gases and influenced by host factors. Significant comorbidities may have impact on morbidity and mortality (GOLD – 2022)

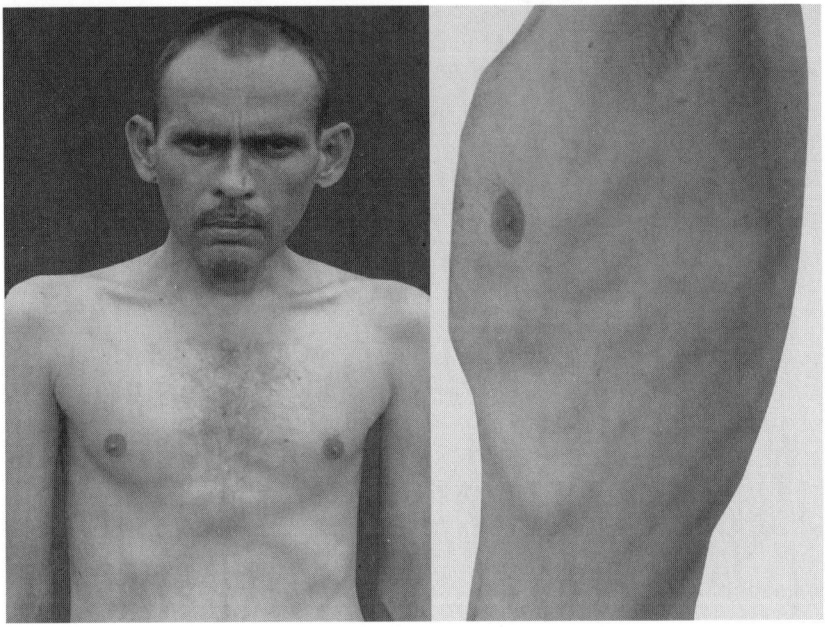

Barrel-shaped chest

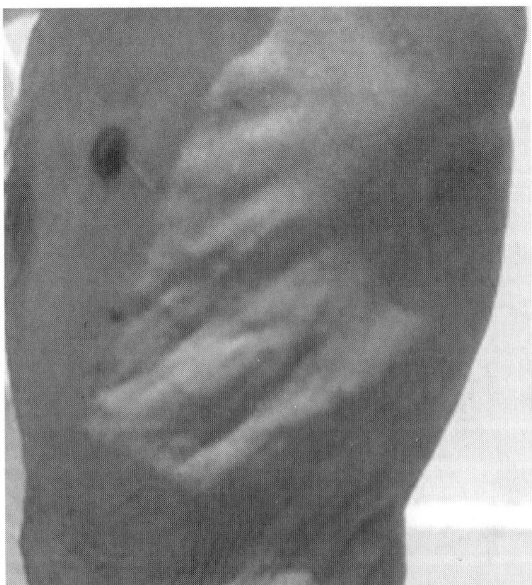

Indrawing of intercostal spaces during inspiration (Hoover's sign)

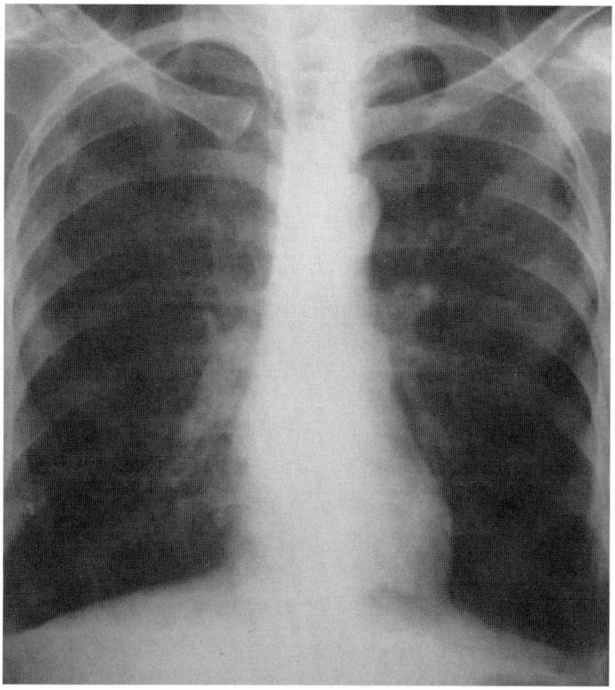

What is this?

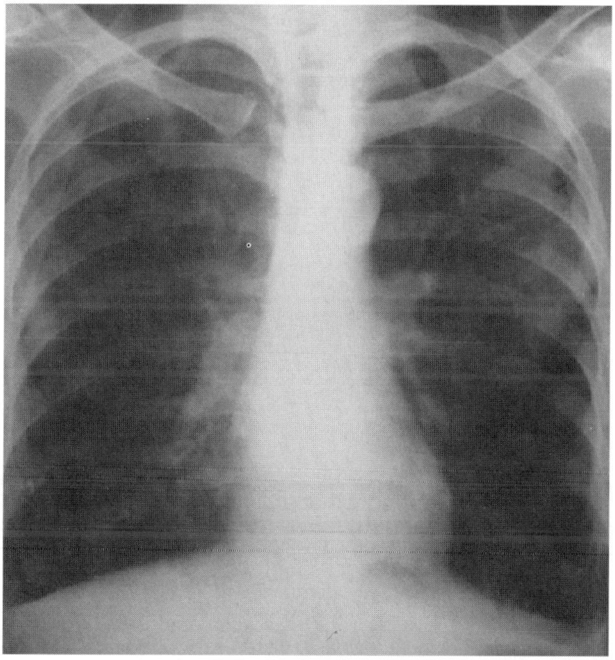

X-ray shows hyperinflation of lung, flattening of diaphragm and pendular heart suggestive of COPD

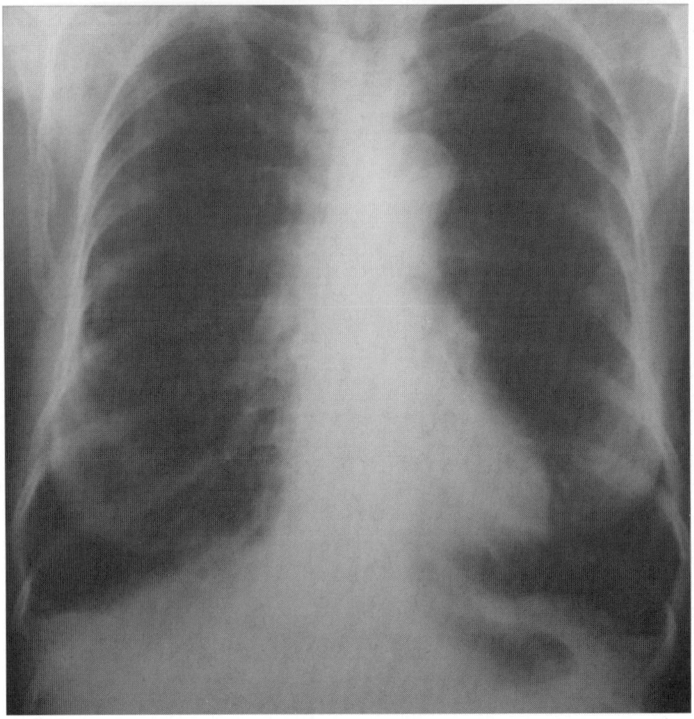

What is this?

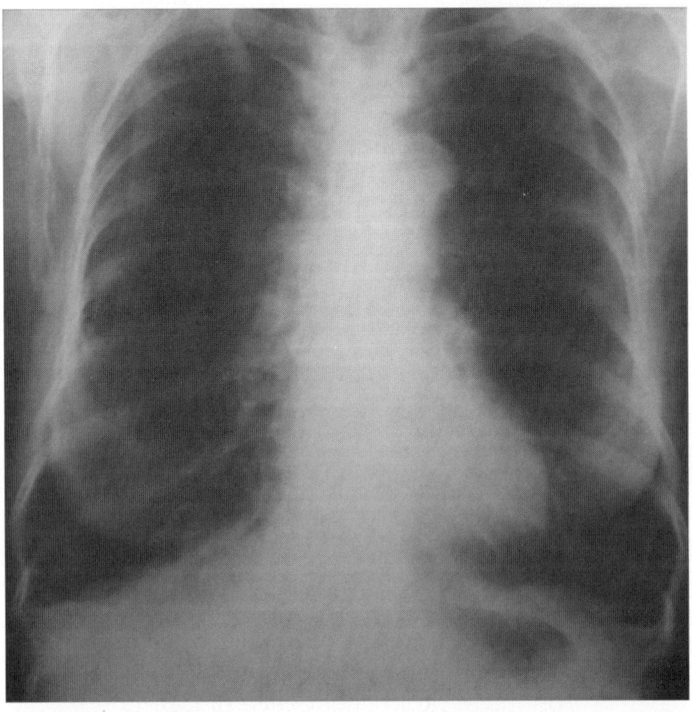

Overinflated chest with depressed diaphragms suggestive of COPD with obliteration of both CP angles giving false impression of bilateral pleural effusion

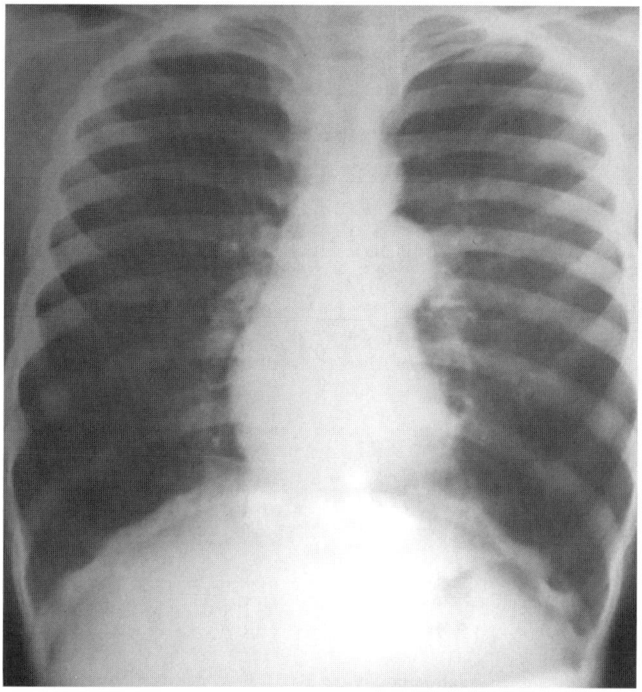

What is this?

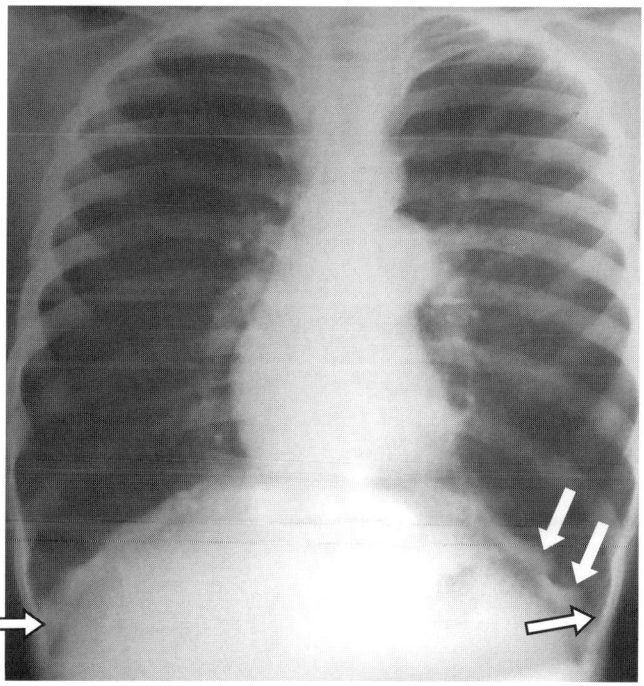

Depressed both diaphragms with costophrenic muscle slips obliterating both CP angles giving false impression of pleural effusion
Never try pleural aspiration

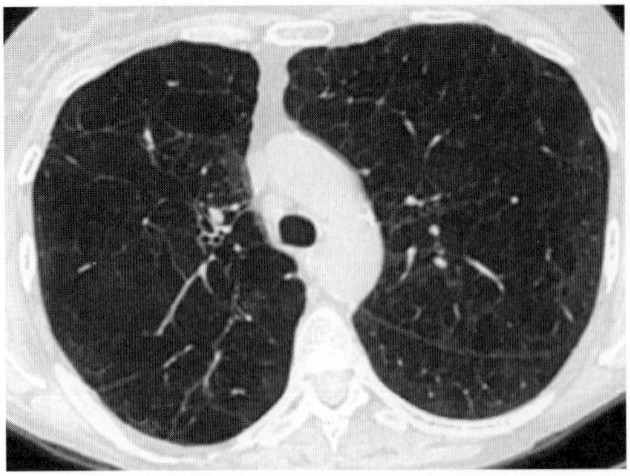

What is this?

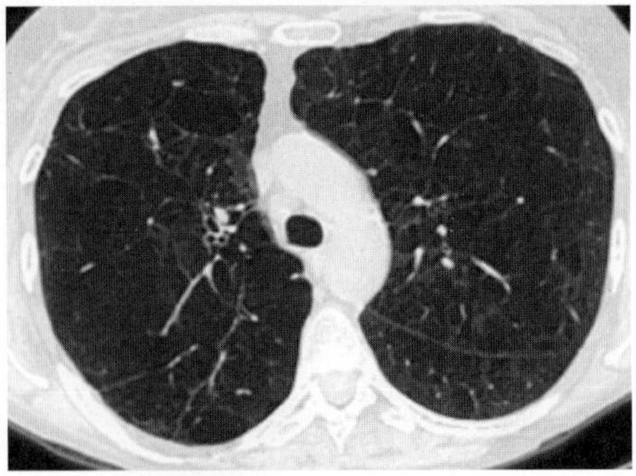

Centrilobular emphysema

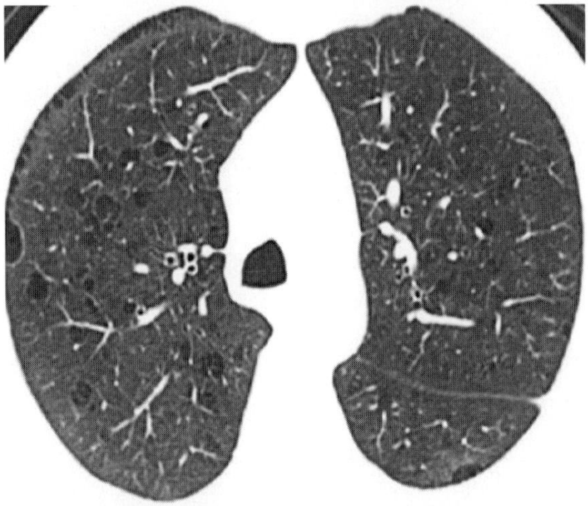

What is this?

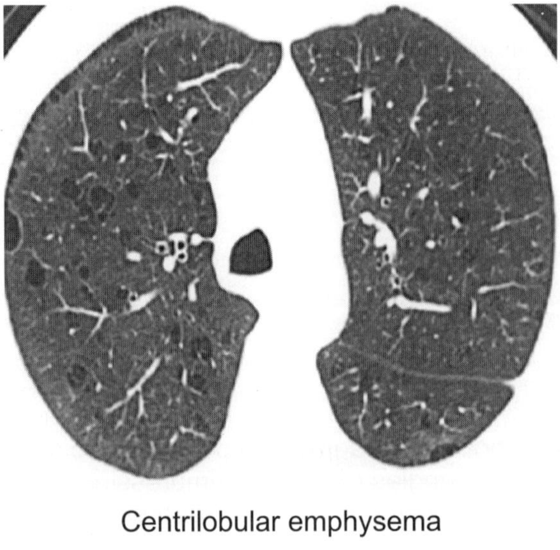

Centrilobular emphysema

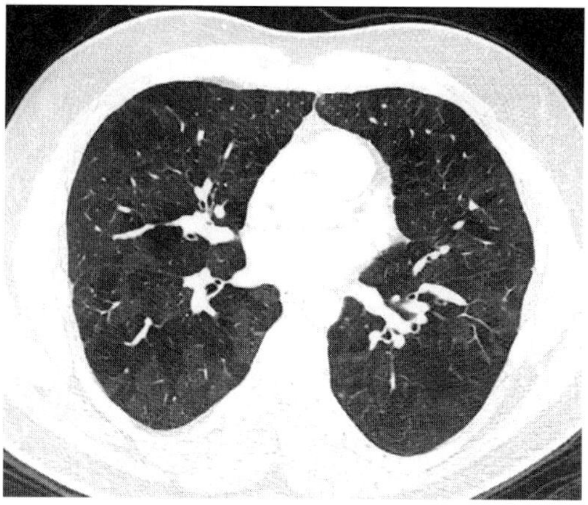

What is this?

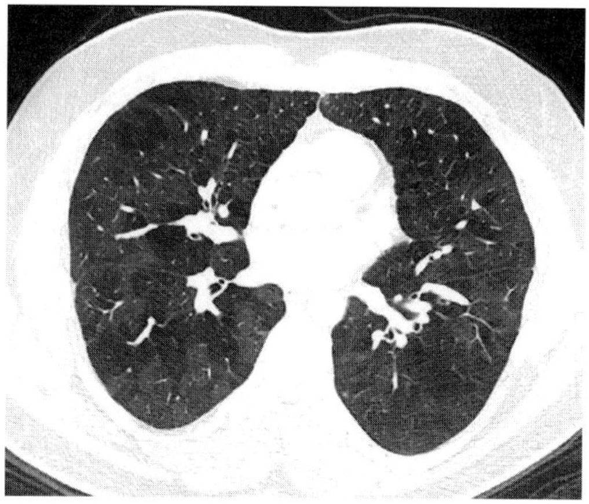

Panlobular emphysema

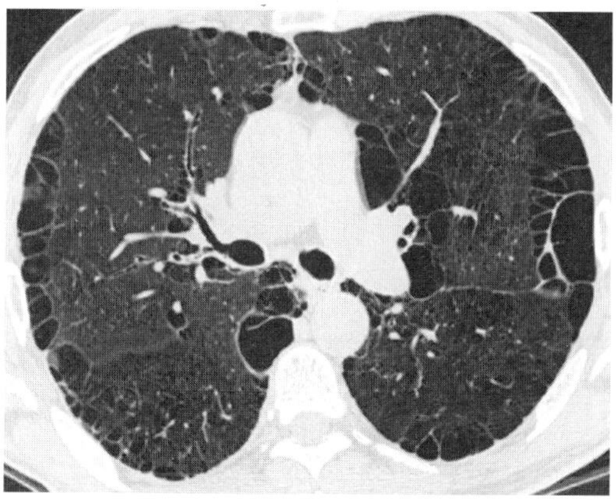

What is this?

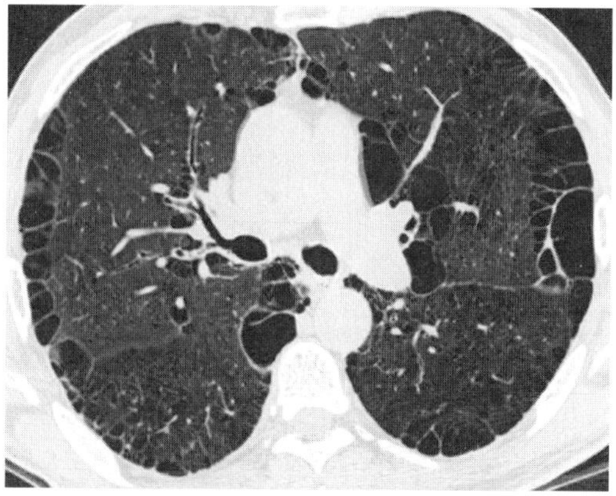

Paraseptal emphysema with subpleural blebs

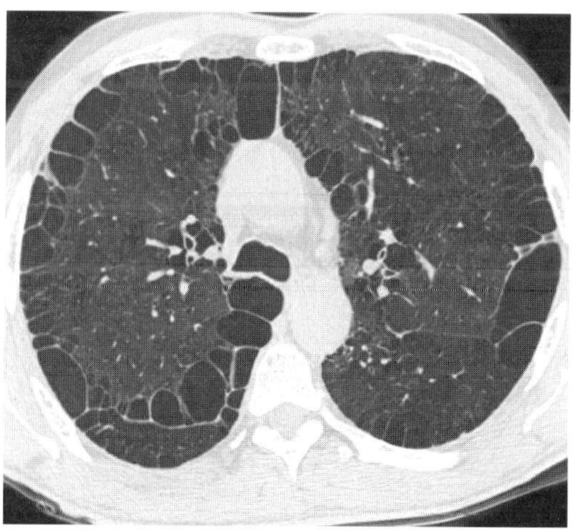

What is this?

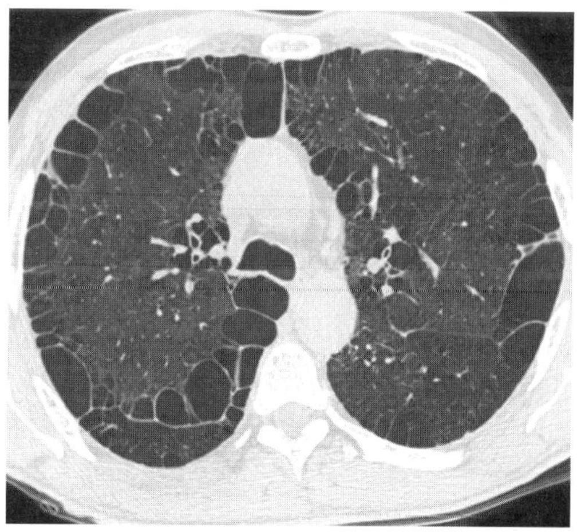

Paraseptal emphysema

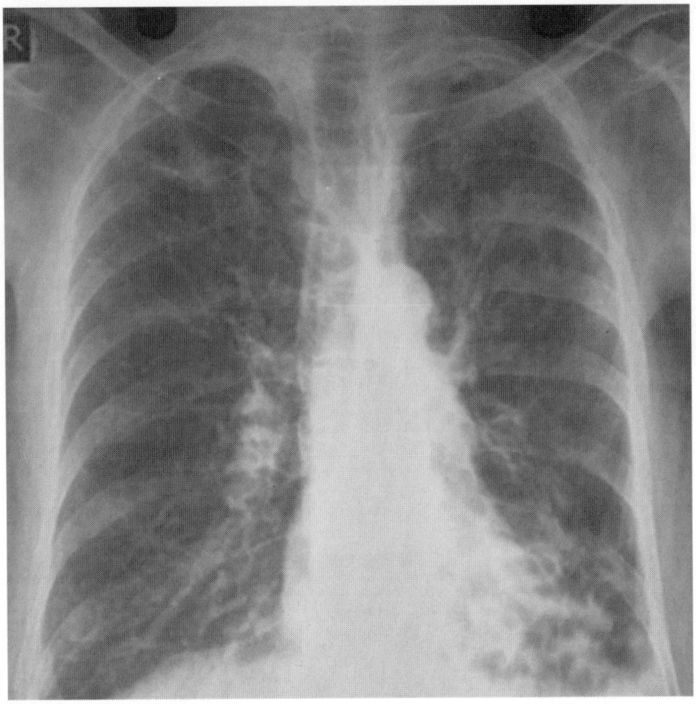

What is this?

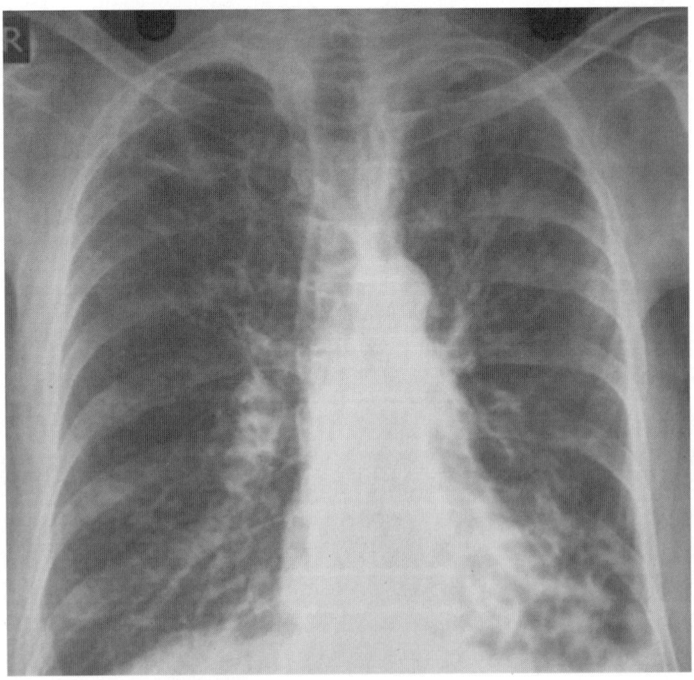

COPD with bronchiectasis
Chest X-ray shows a bulla, signs of hyperinflation in the right upper zone and cystic shadows in the left lower zone

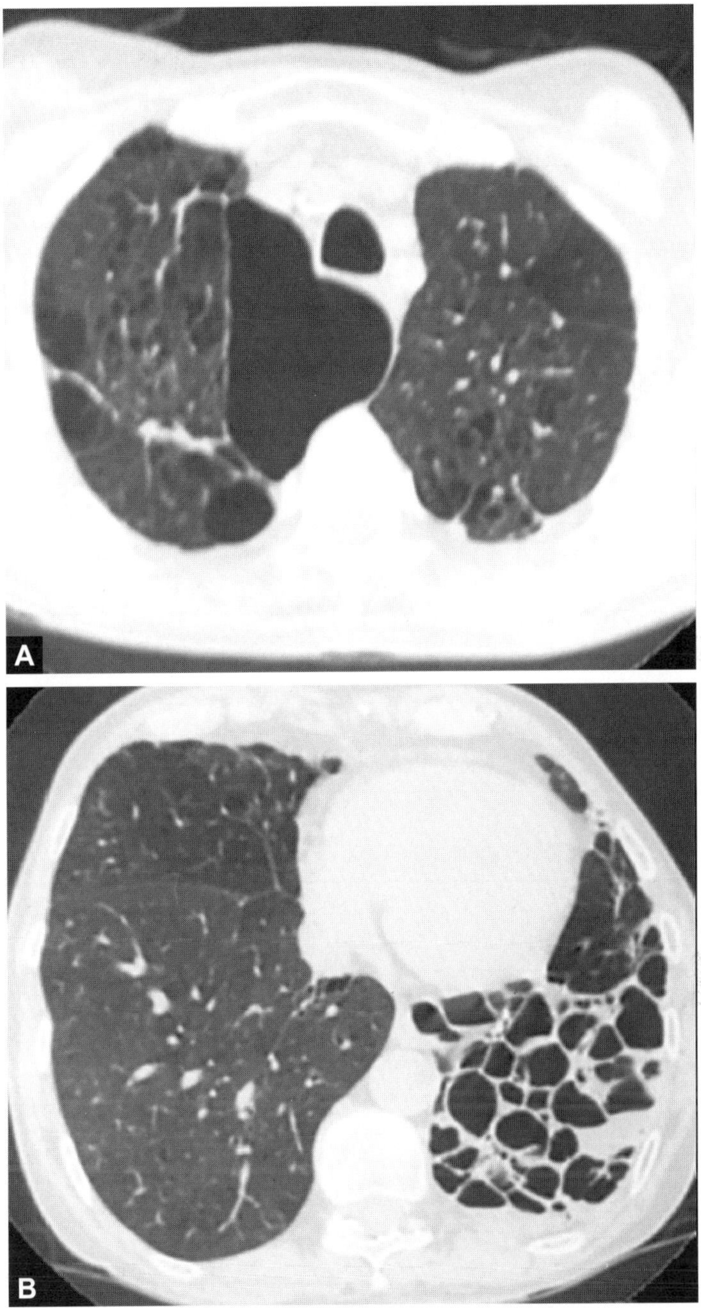

HRCT thorax shows (A) right upper lobe bulla with emphysematous changes and (B) left lower lobe cystic bronchiectasis
COPD and bronchiectasis existing together and is a rare condition

Reader's Notes

CHAPTER

15

Radiology of Allergic Broncho-pulmonary Aspergillosis (ABPA)

Clinical Spectrum of Bronchopulmonary Aspergillosis

- Saprophytic
  - Aspergilloma
- Allergic
  - Allergic asthma
  - Allergic bronchopulmonary aspergillosis
  - Allergic aspergillus sinusitis
  - Hypersensitivity pneumonitis
- Invasive
  - Airway invasive aspergillosis
  - Chronic necrotising pulmonary aspergillosis
  - Invasive aspergillosis

Allergic Bronchopulmonary Aspergillosis (ABPA)

Allergic pulmonary disorder caused by hypersensitivity to *Aspergillus fumigatus*, clinically manifested as chronic asthma, recurrent pulmonary infiltrates and bronchiectasis. The condition has immunological features of immediate hypersensitivity (Type I), antigen–antibody complexes (Type III) and eosinophil rich inflammatory cell response (Type IVb)

Allergic Bronchopulmonary Aspergillosis (ABPA)	
	Causative organism
• Characterised by asthmatic symptoms, recurrent shadows on the chest X-ray and blood eosinophilia in atopics • Allergic bronchopulmonary mycosis (ABPM) syndrome similar to ABPA but caused by fungi other than *Aspergillus fumigatus*	• *A. fumigatus* • *A. niger* • *A. flavus* • *A. clavatus* • *A. nidulans* • *A. glaucus* • *A. oryzae* • *A. sydowi*

Prevalence of ABPA

- Schwartz and Greenberger (1991): 2.5–7%
- Indian studies: 3.7–16%

Diagnosis of ABPA

- Asthma (mild or severe) or cystic fibrosis
- Immediate cutaneous reactivity to *Aspergillus antigen*
- Current or previous pulmonary infiltrates
- Elevated total IgE concentration (>1 mg/L)
- Preciptin antibodies to *A. fumigatus*
- Peripheral blood eosinophilia
- Elevated serum IgE against *Aspergillus fumigatus* and/or IgG against *Aspergillus fumigatus*
- Proximal bronchiectasis

ISHAM Criteria for ABPA-2013

- <u>**Predisposing conditions:**</u>
  - Bronchial asthma, cystic fibrosis
- <u>**Obligatory criteria (both should be present):**</u>
  - Type I aspergillus skin test positive or
  - Elevated IgE levels against *Aspergillus fumigatus*
- <u>**Other criteria (at least two of three):**</u>
  - Presence of precipitating or IgG antibodies against *A. fumigatus* in serum
  - Radiographic pulmonary opacities consistent with ABPA
  - Total eosinophil count >500 cells/lL in steroid naıve patients (may be historical)

Treatment of ABPA

<u>Oral Steroids</u>

Regime-1

- Prednisolone 0.5 mg/kg/day for 2 weeks, then on alternate day for 6–8 weeks, then taper by 5–10 mg every 2 weeks and discontinue
- Repeat the eosinophil count, chest X-ray and total serum IgE in 6–8 weeks

Regime-2

- Prednisolone 0.75 mg/kg for 6 weeks, 0.5 mg/kg for 6 weeks, then taper 5 mg every 6 weeks to continue for a total of at least 6–12 months
- Repeat the eosinophil count, chest X-ray and total serum IgE in 6–8 weeks

Follow-up and Monitoring of ABPA

- With chest X-ray, eosinophil count and serum IgE every 6–8 weeks
- Clearing/improvement in chest X-ray and decrease in eosinophil count—satisfactory response
- 35 % decline in serum IgE level—satisfactory response
- Doubling of serum IgE levels signify a silent ABPA exacerbation
- Monitor for adverse effects of steroids
- Prophylaxis for osteoporosis

Role of Anti-Fungal Drugs in ABPA

- Itraconazole 400 mg daily in stable ABPA patients for 16 weeks
- Decrease in eosinophil count (35% per week)
- Decrease in serum IgE and IgG levels against *Aspergillus fumigatus*
- A few exacerbations requiring oral steroids
- Itraconazole treatment in stable ABPA reduces eosinophilic airway inflammation, systemic immune activation and exacerbation
- Potential adjunctive treatment for ABPA

A Randomized Trial of Itraconazole vs Prednisolone in Acute Stage ABPA

Oral glucocorticoids were more effective than itraconazole monotherapy in producing treatment response in ABPA

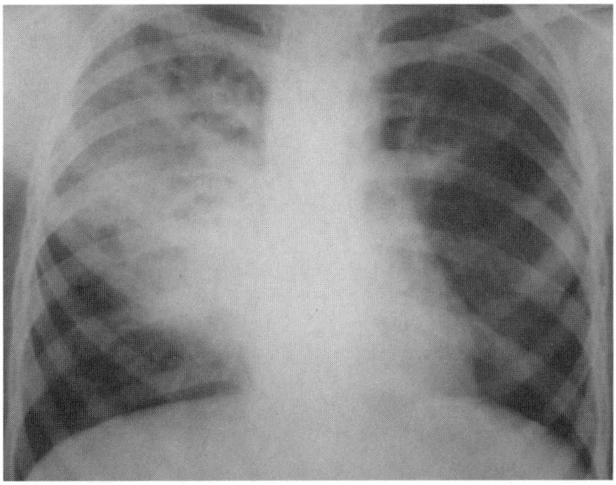

A 20-year-old male C/o breathlessness: 10 years, fever and cough: 2 months, hemoptysis (streaking): 15 days
Radiopaque shadow in right upper and middle zones

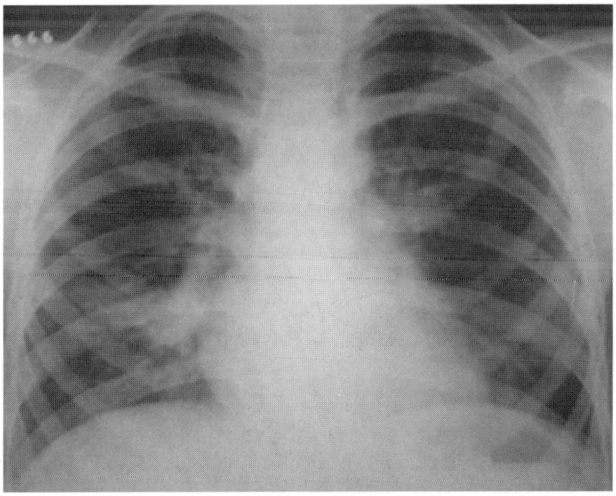

Shadows cleared after 6 weeks of oral steroid treatment

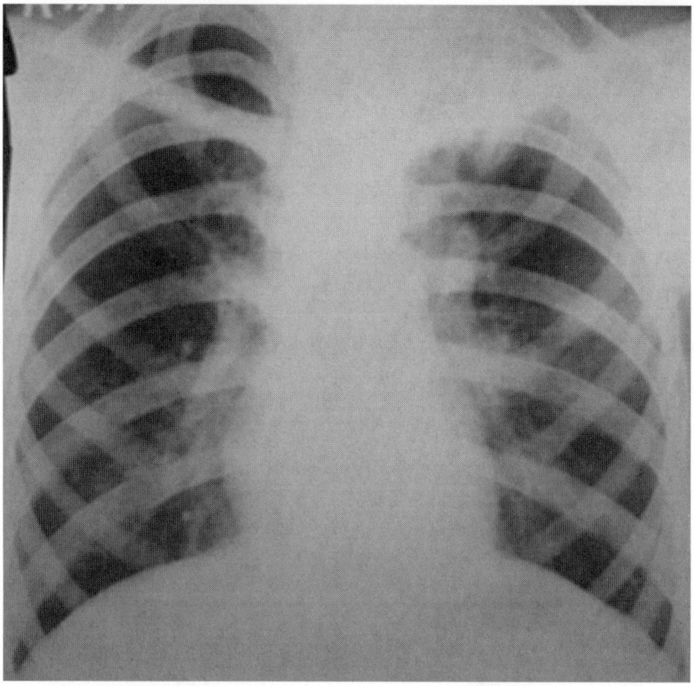

Shadow reappeared in left upper zone

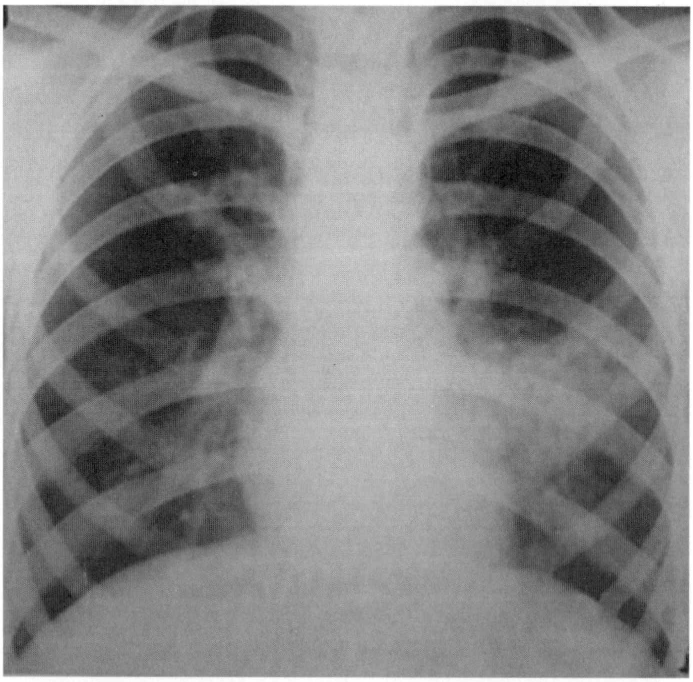

Shadow cleared from left upper zone and reappeared in left middle zone

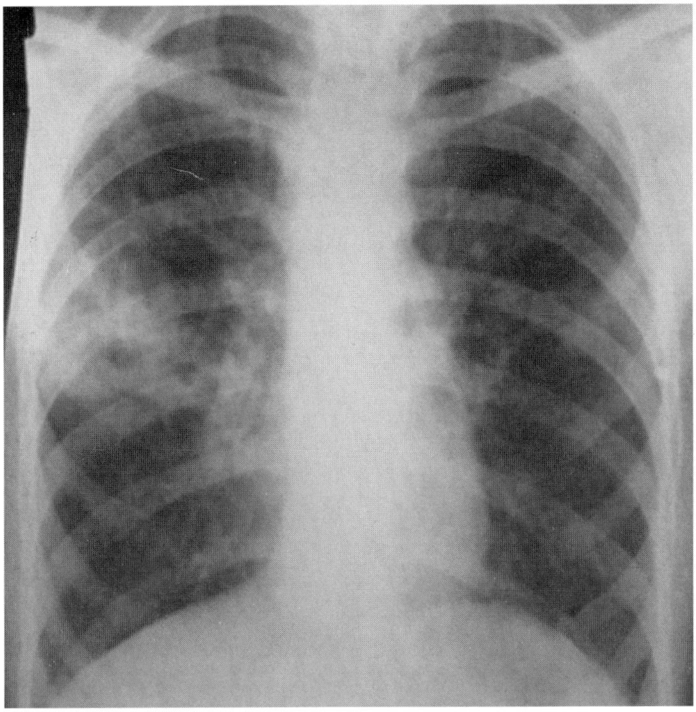

Shadow cleared from left middle zone
and reappeared in right middle zone

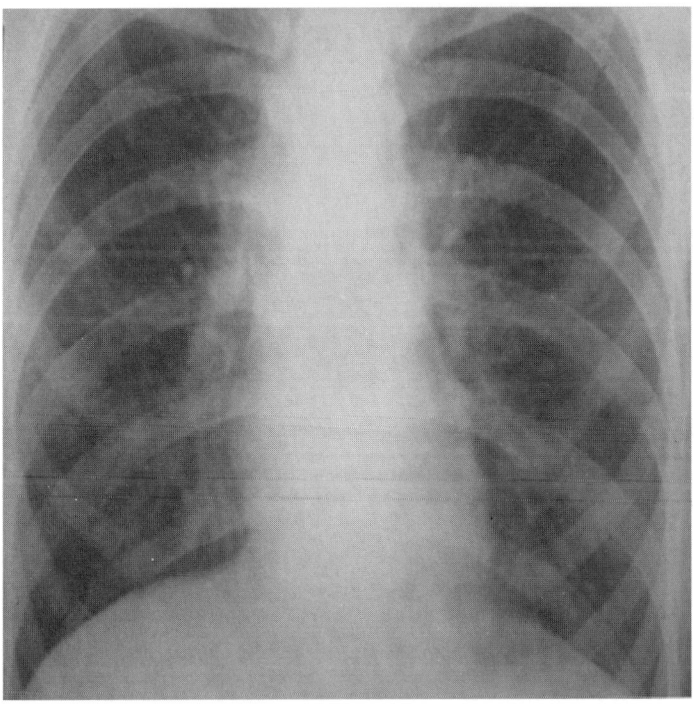

Shadow cleared after 3 weeks of steroid treatment

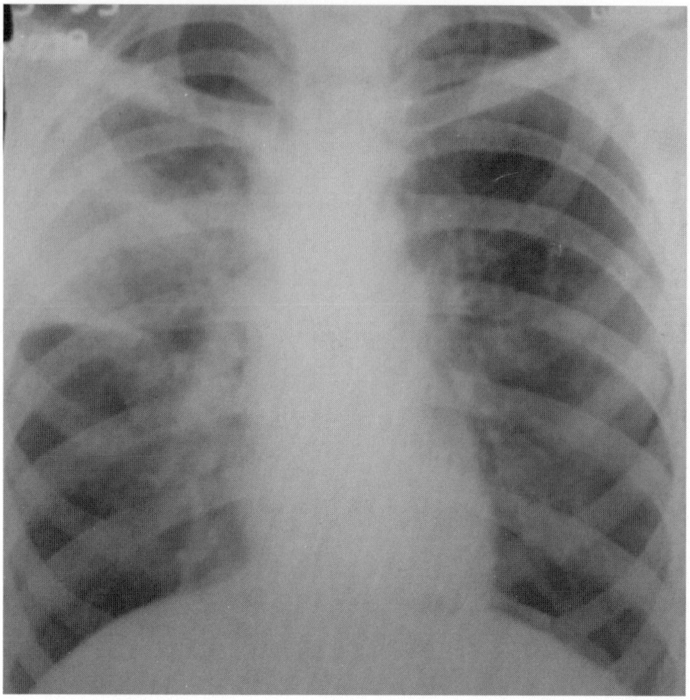

Shadow reappeared in right middle zone

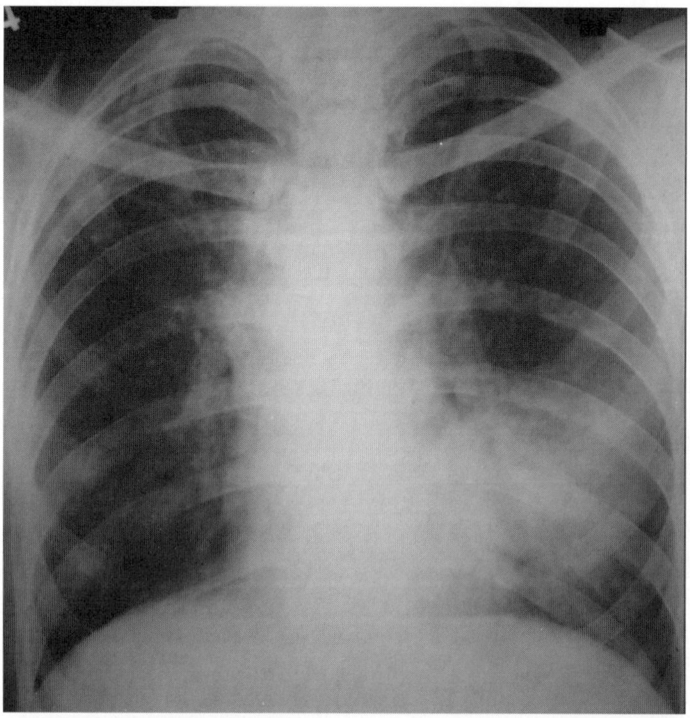

Shadow cleared from right middle zone and reappeared in left middle zone

Walking pneumonia or fleeting shadows

Investigations

TLC: 8600/mm^3 DLC: P_{56} L_{30} E_{14}
Absolute eosinophil count: 1204/cmm
Mantoux test: 6 mm
Sputum smear for AFB: Negative
Sputum culture for *M. tuberculosis*: Negative
Sputum smear for fungus: Positive
Sputum culture showed growth of *Aspergillus fumigatus*

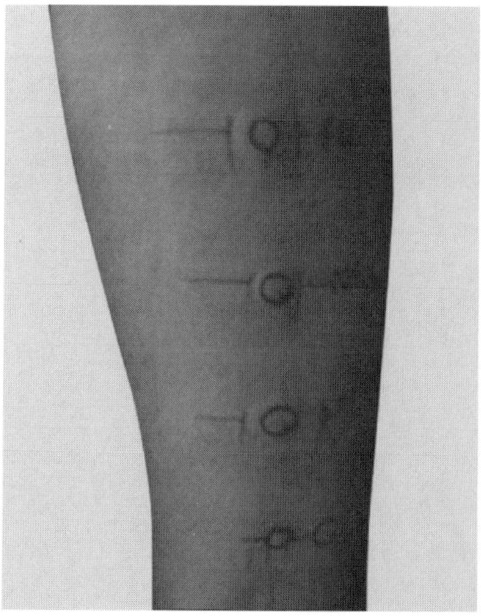

Positive skin test against *Aspergillus fumigatus* after 20 minutes (type I)

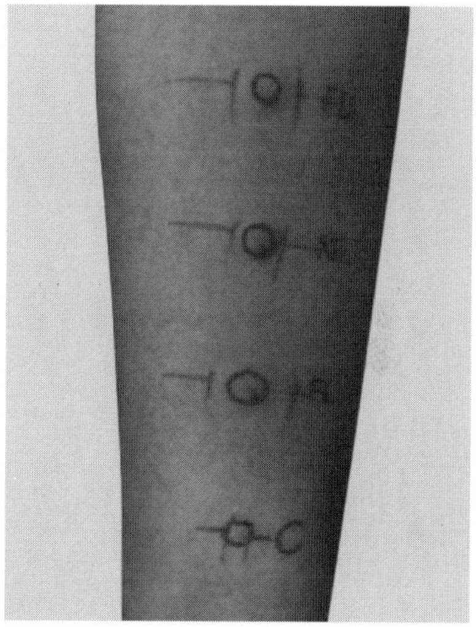

Positive skin test against *Aspergillus fumigatus* after 6 hours (type III)

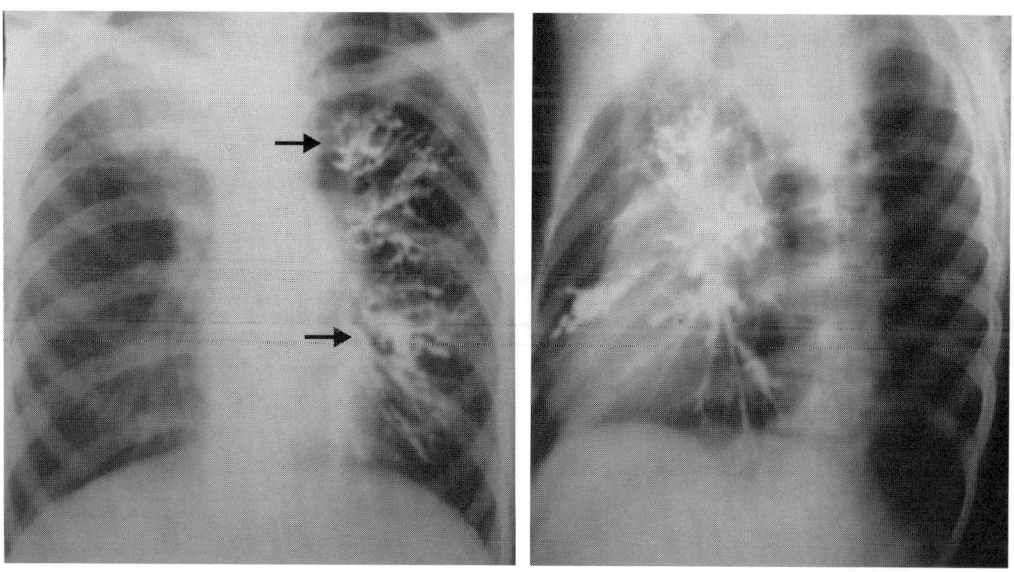

Bronchogram shows proximal bronchiectasis

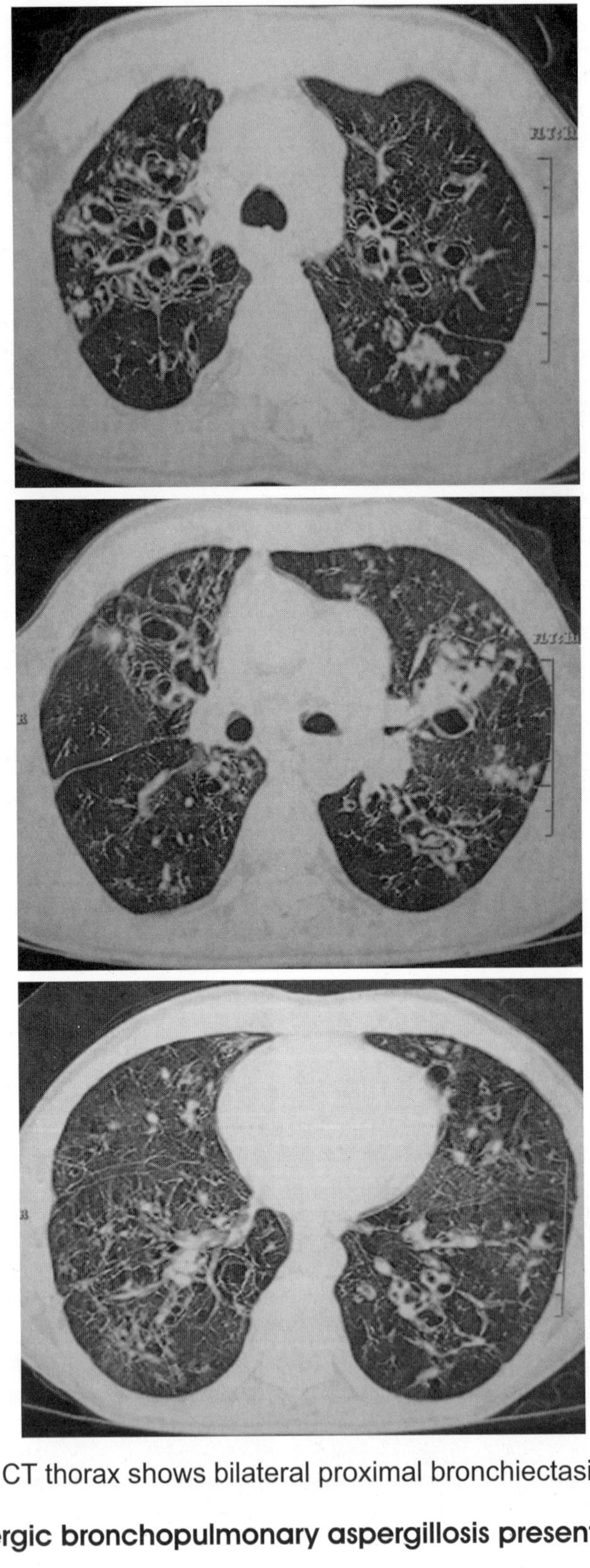

CT thorax shows bilateral proximal bronchiectasis

Diagnosis: Allergic bronchopulmonary aspergillosis presented as walking pneumonia

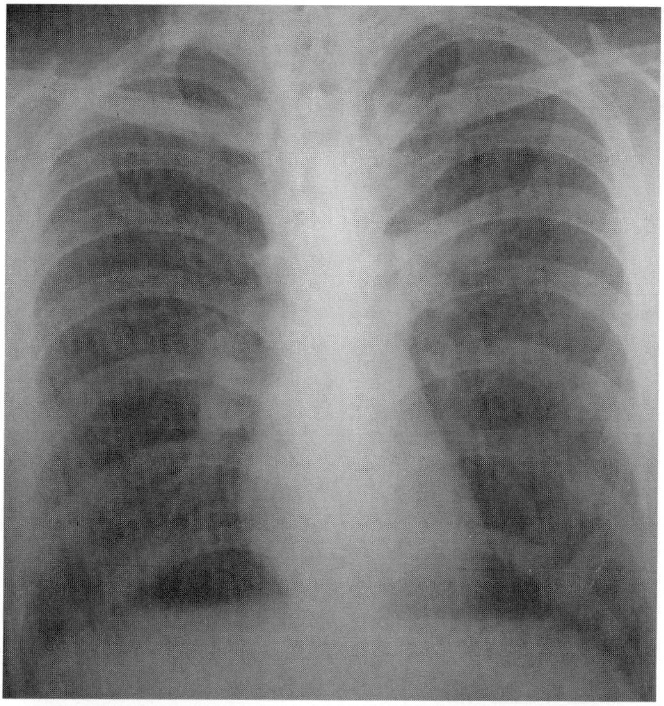

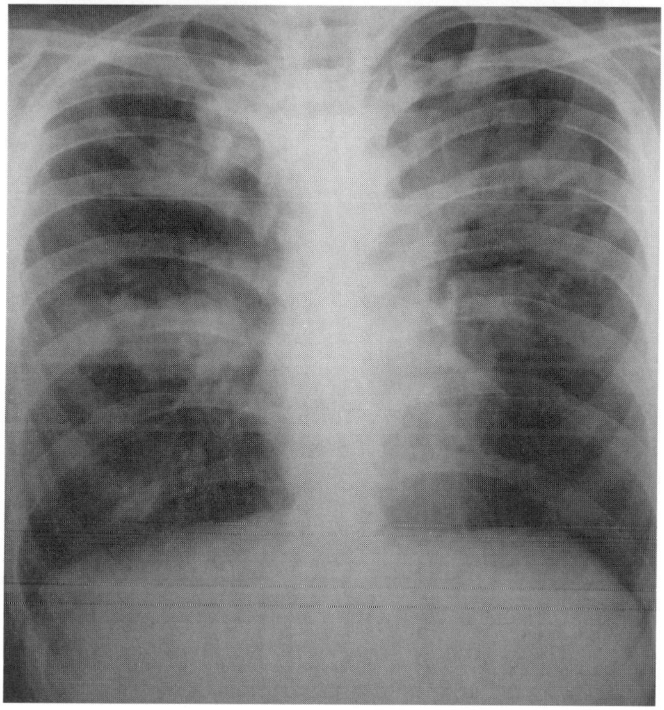

A 22-year-old male, nonsmoker presented with cough and episodic breathlessness—7 years, recurrent streaking—6 months, loss of appetite and weakness—2 months and received bronchodilators and oral steroids off and on after and was also given antitubercular treatment for 6 months (2RHEZ/4RHE) without any response and was suspected as MDR-TB

Investigations

- Sputum for AFB: Negative (three times)
- TLC: 12,700, DLC: P_{47} L_{23} E_{30}
- Absolute eosinophil count: 3710/cubic mm
- Skin test to Aspergillus antigen: Positive (type I and III)
- Total serum IgE: 34228 IU/ml
- IgE against *Aspergillus fumigatus*: 21.50 U/ml (N <.38 U/ml)
- IgG against *Aspergillus fumigatus*: 118 U/ml (N <8 U/ml)

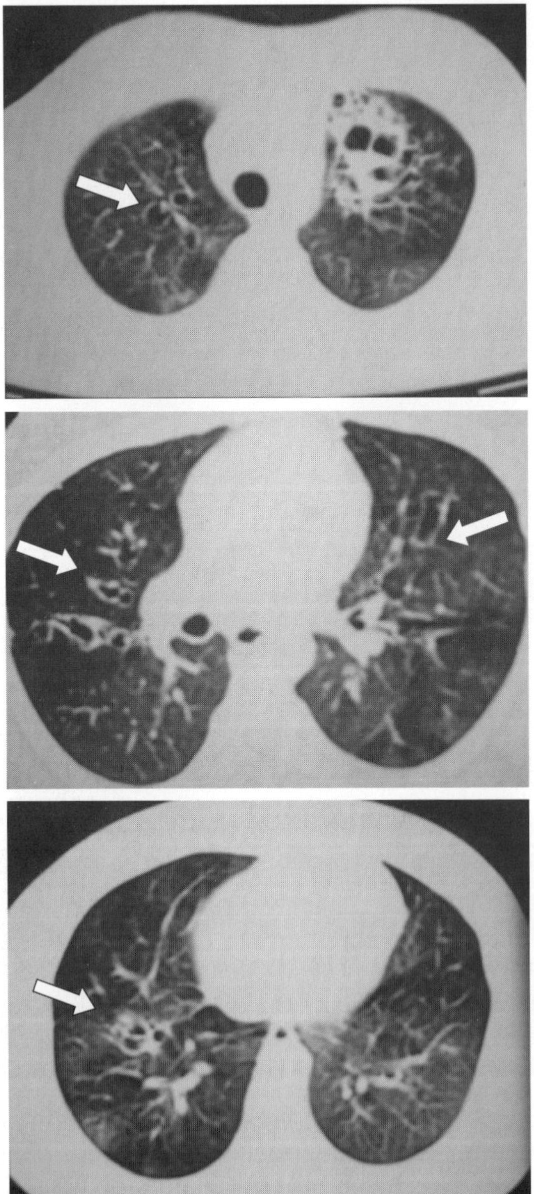

CT thorax shows bilateral proximal bronchiectasis

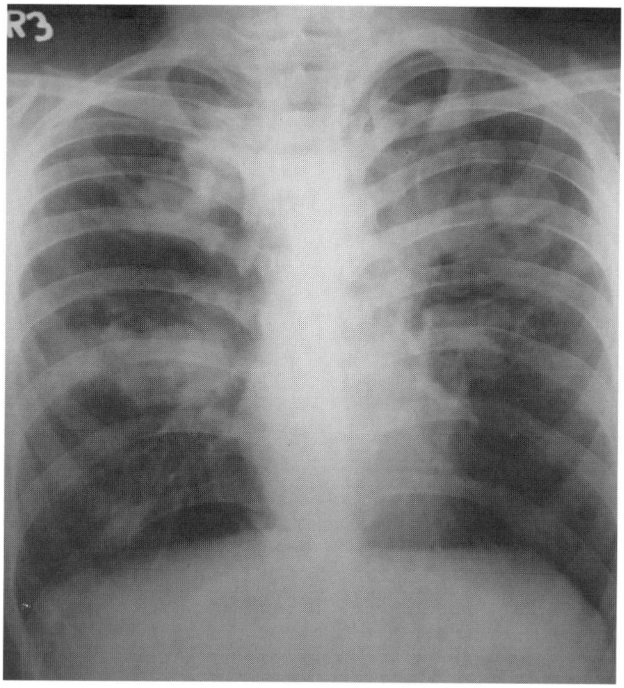

Chest X-ray before treatment

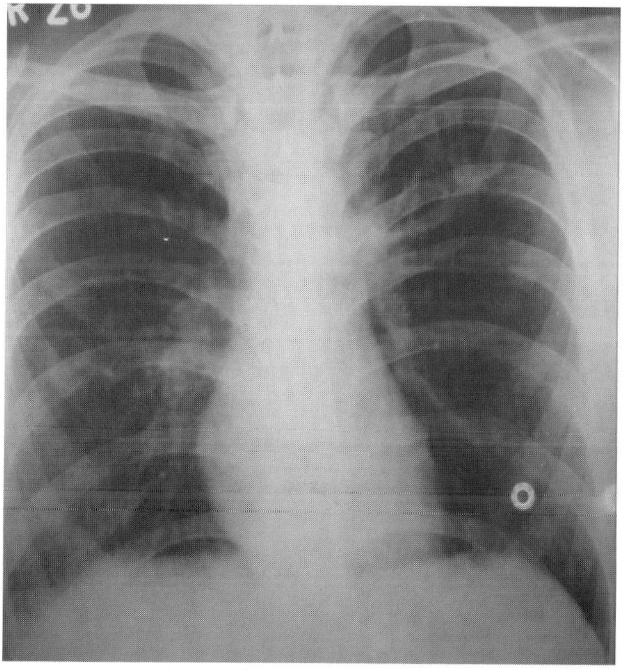

Chest X-ray after 8 weeks of steroid treatment in tapering doses shows complete resolution of shadows

Diagnosis: Allergic Bronchopulmonary Aspergillosis

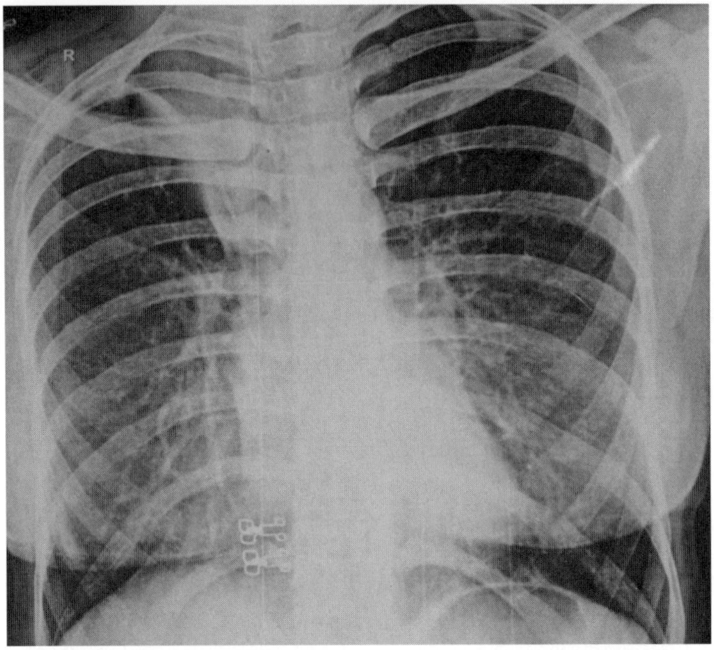

A 23-year-old female presented with complaints of breathlessness (on/off) since childhood, recurrent nasal block and rhinorrhoea since 3 years. Functional endoscopic sinus surgery (FESS) was done in April 2017
Chest X-ray shows collapse of right upper lobe

Investigations

- Sputum AFB: Negative
- Eosinophil count: 14% (November 2003)
- Eosinophil count: 15% (August 2017)
- Total serum IgE: 6420 IU/ml
- Serum IgE specific for *Aspergillus fumigatus*: 16.30 U/ml
- Serum IgG specific for *Aspergillus fumigatus*: 24.78 U/ml (N-< 8) (17/09/2017)
- Skin prick test positive for *Aspergillus fumigatus*

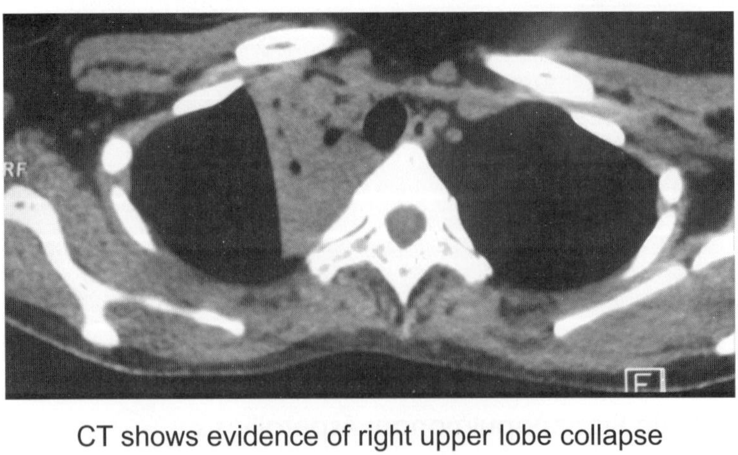

CT shows evidence of right upper lobe collapse

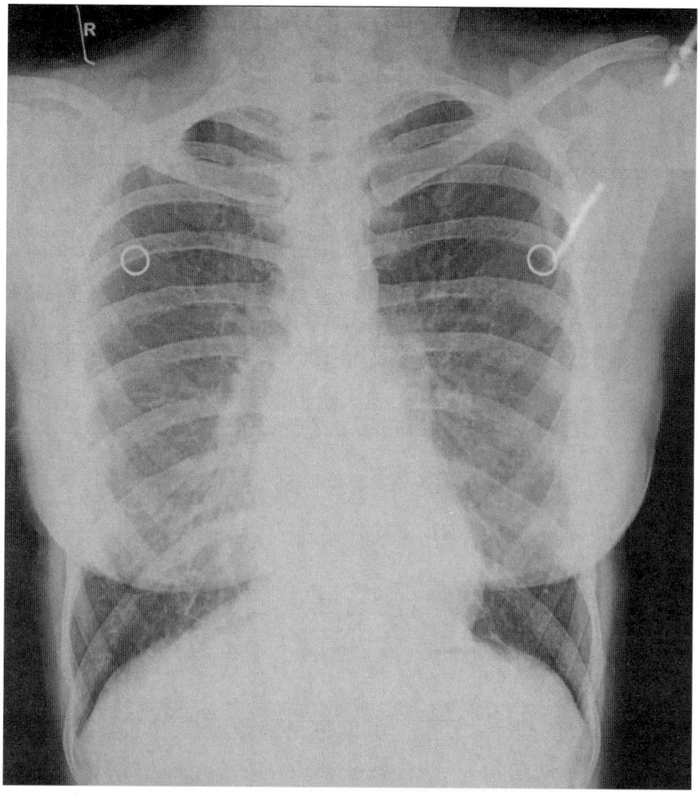

Patient was diagnosed as ABPA. Collapse opened up after treatment with oral steroids for 6 weeks
Please remember that ABPA rarely can present has collapse of lung

Allergic Bronchopulmonary Aspergillosis (ABPA)

- Not rare condition and seen in day-to-day clinical practice often misdiagnosed as pulmonary tuberculosis
- Early diagnosis and appropriate treatment of ABPA is important in view of preventing lung damage/fibrosis, worsening of asthma and preventing mis-diagnosis with pulmonary tuberculosis
- Asthma patients with pulmonary shadows and peripheral blood eosinophilia (1000–2000/cmm) should be suspected for ABPA and further investigated to confirm ABPA

Reader's Notes

CHAPTER

16

Radiology of Lung Cancer

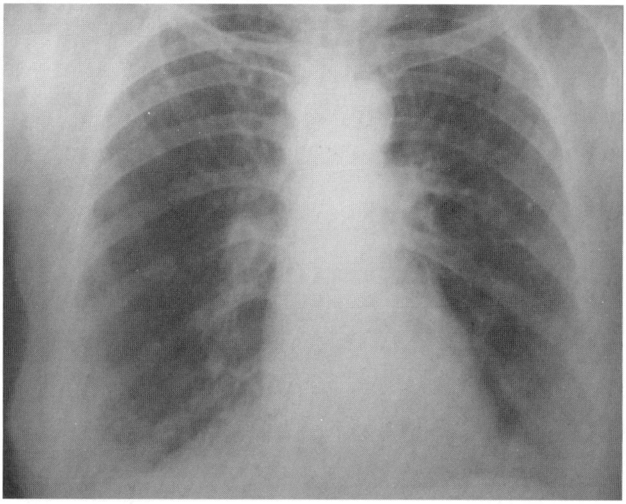

A 61-year-old female presented with complaints of cough with expectoration—5 years, breathlessness—3 years with history of smoking—15 bidi/day for 35 years
Past history of antitubercular treatment for 1 year without any response
Patient was diagnosed as COPD with normal chest X-ray

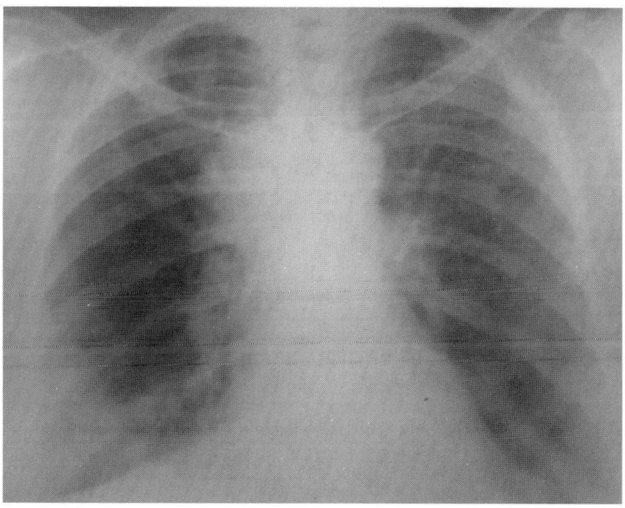

Patient developed chest pain on right side and recurrent hemoptysis for last 1 year
Since patient developed new symptoms and X-ray changes (mediastinal shadows) she was investigated further

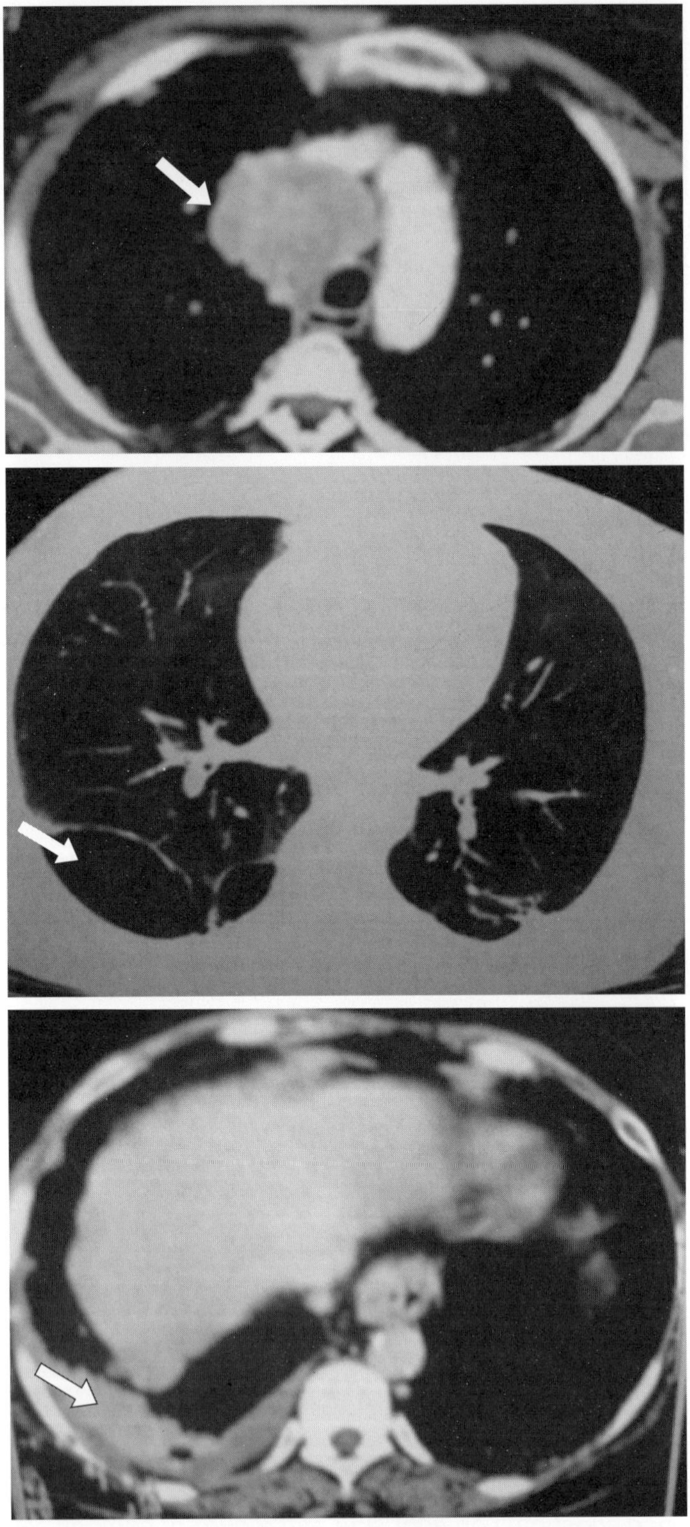

CT shows lobulated mass in mediastinum, bullous lesions in both lungs and pleural effusion right side

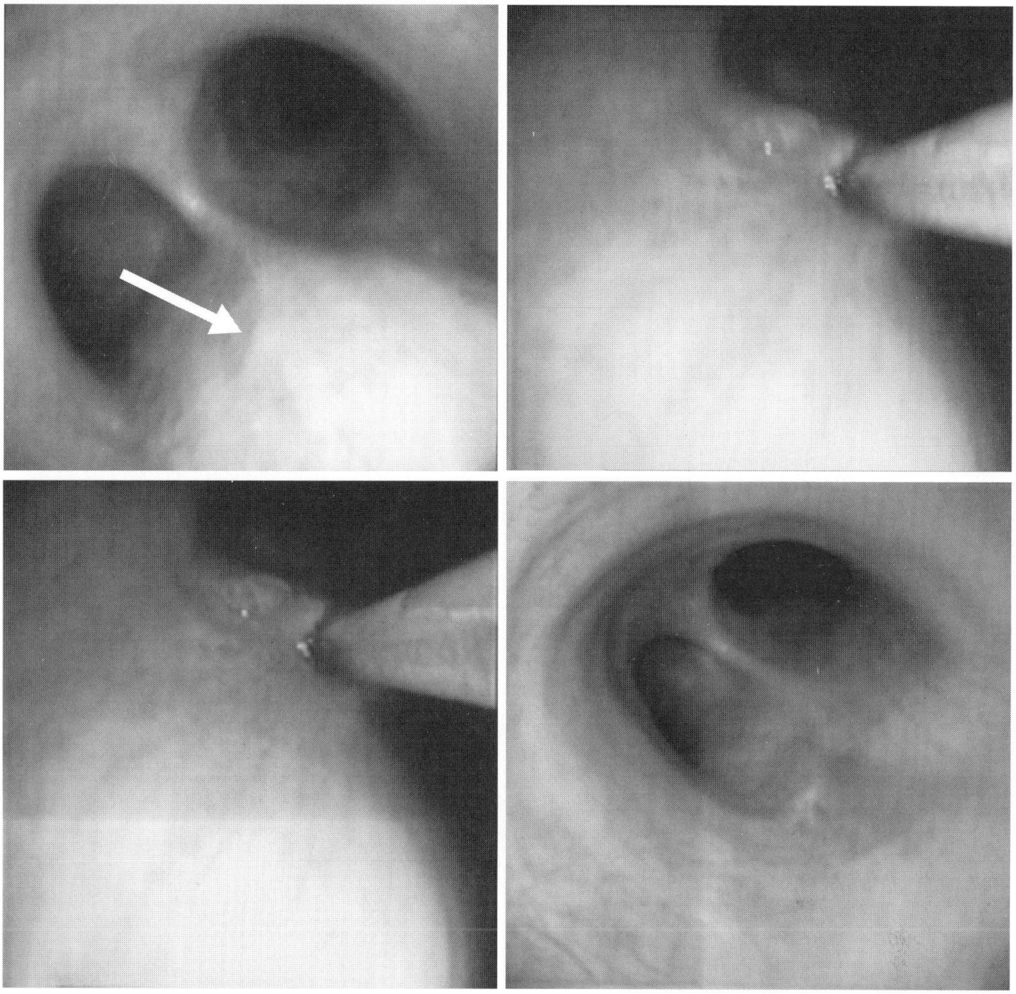

Fiberoptic bronchoscopy showed bulging near lower end of trachea just before the main carina, transtracheal needle aspiration was done which showed squamous cell carcinoma and bone scan suggestive of skeletal metastasis in sacrum and patient was diagnosed as squamous cell carcinoma stage IV with COPD (Colour Plate II)

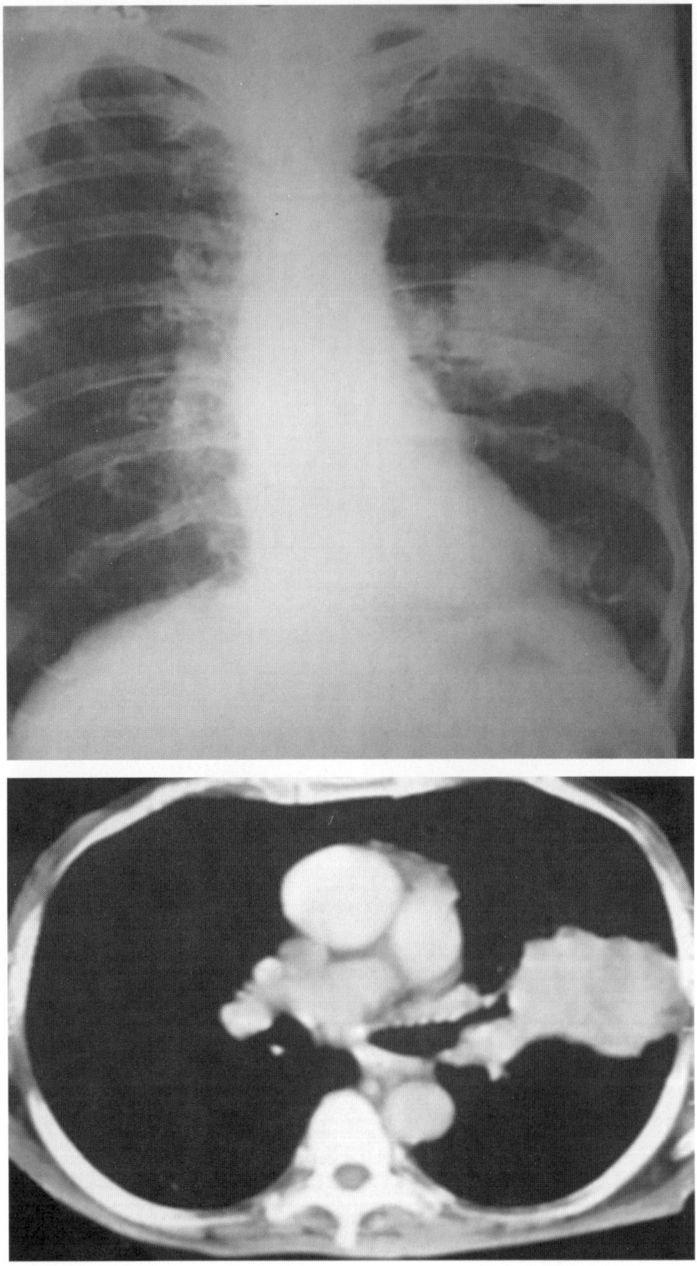

What is this?

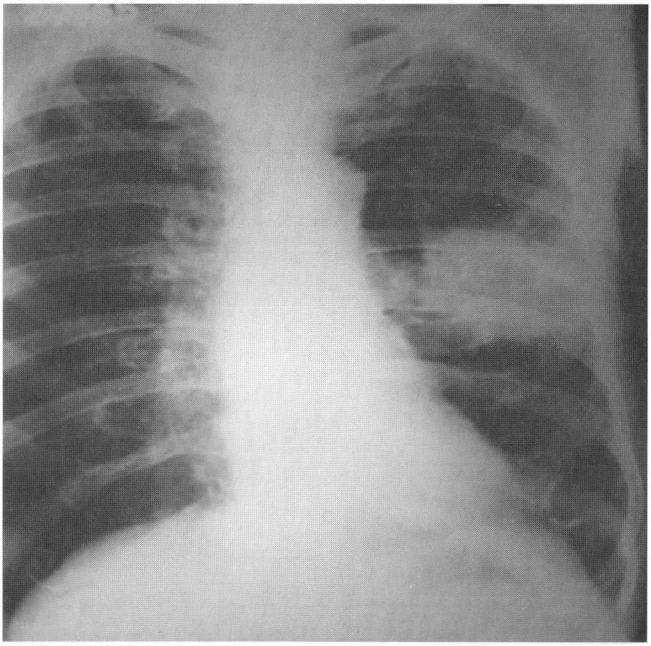

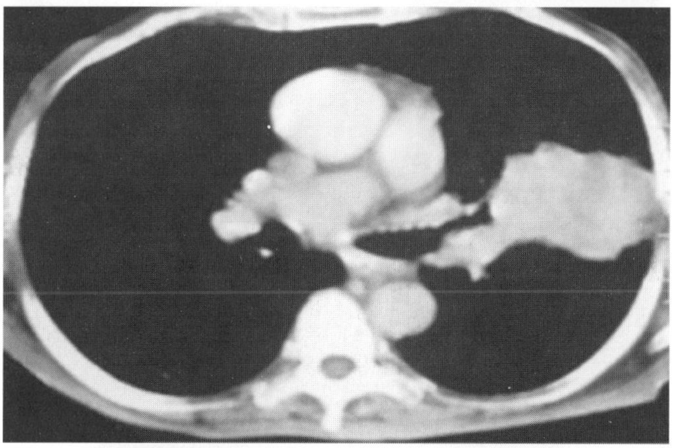

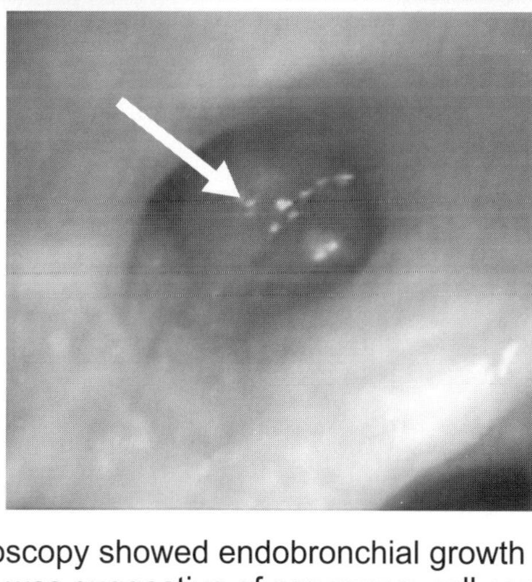

Fiberoptic bronchoscopy showed endobronchial growth and endobronchial biopsy was suggestive of squamous cell carcinoma
(Colour Plate II)

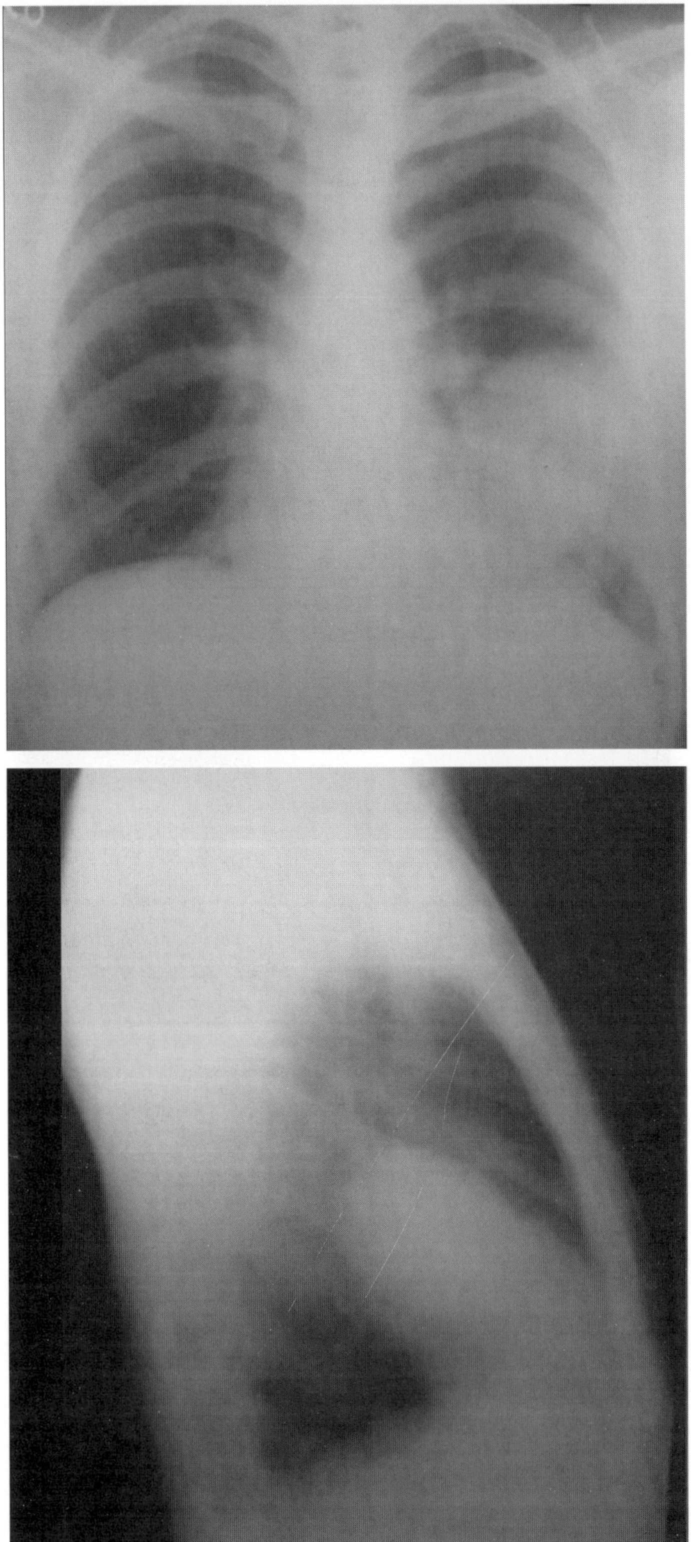

What is this?

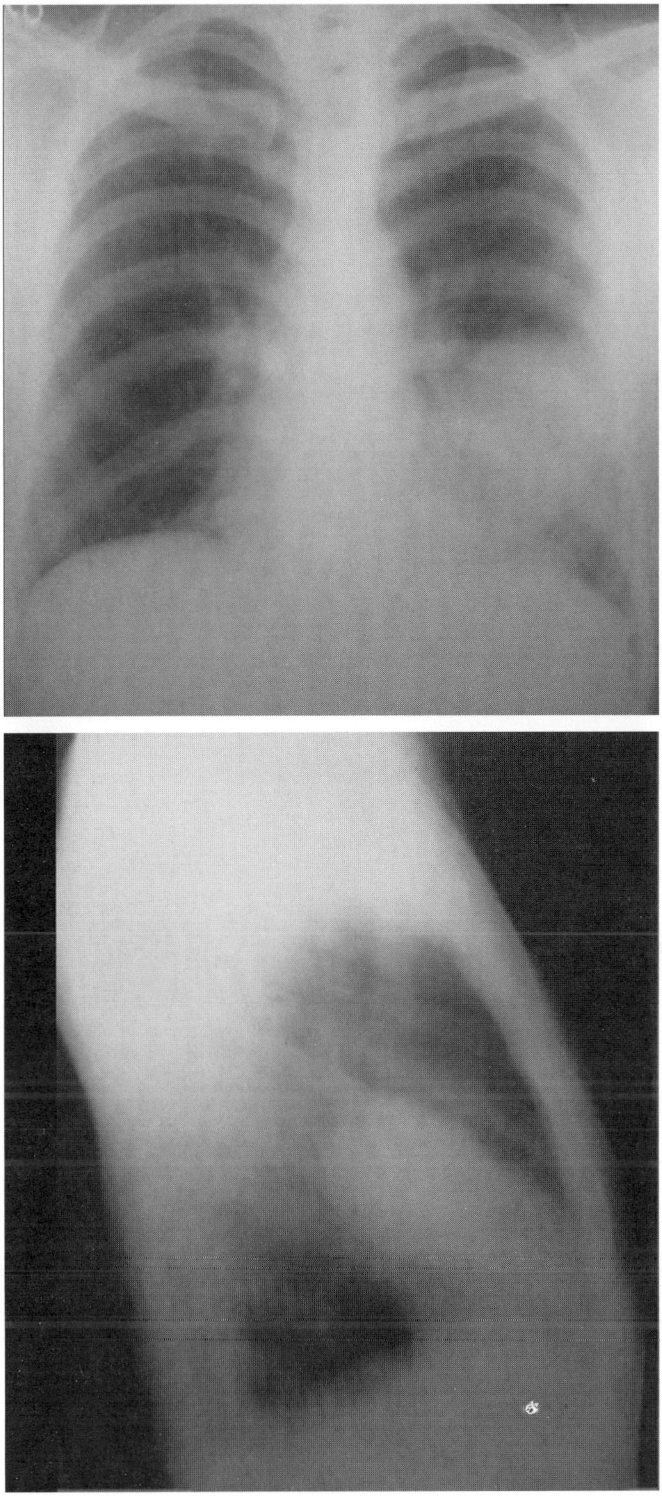

Mass lesions proven as small cell lung carcinoma

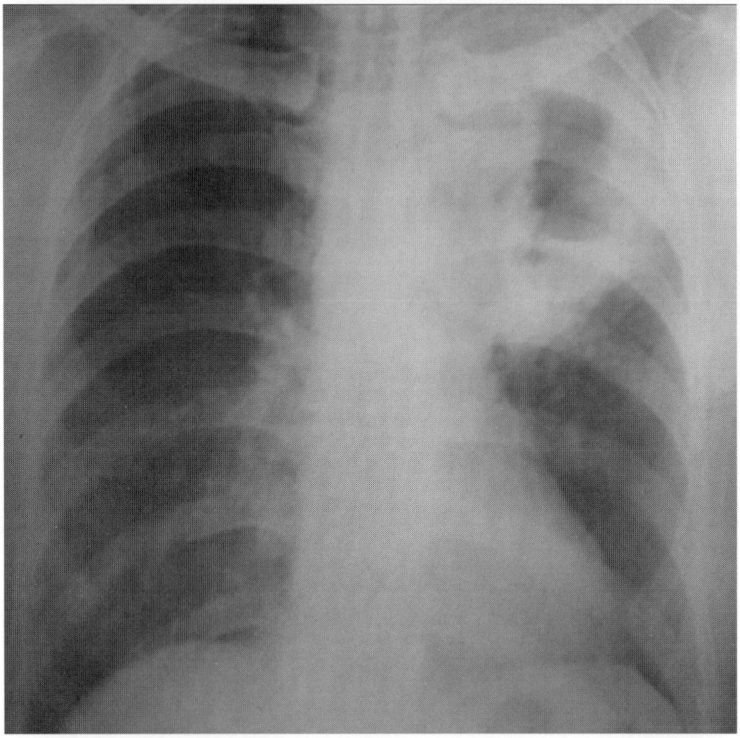

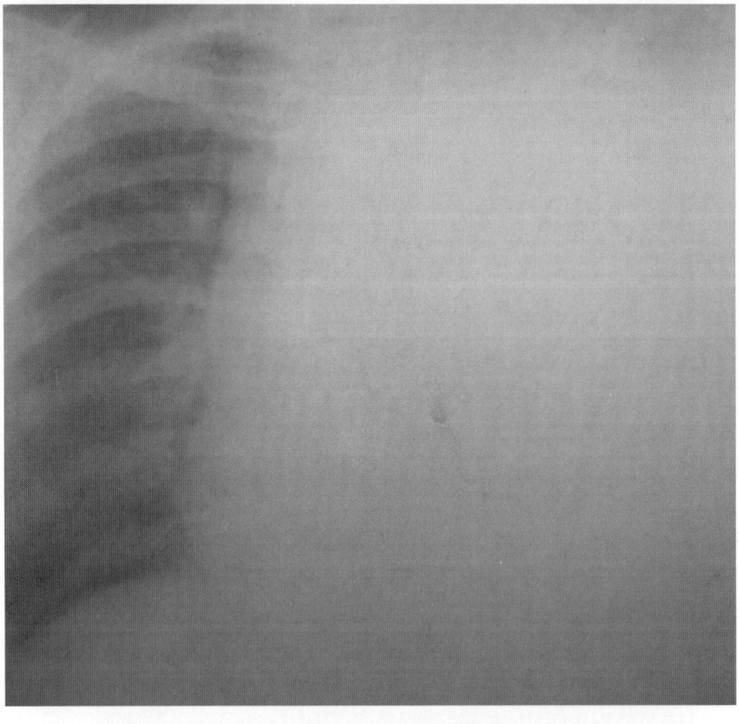

Patient presented with thick-walled cavity of left upper zone. Sputum was negative for AFB and was treated for sputum negative pulmonary tuberculosis without any response. After 3 months of antitubercular treatment, disease progressed further

What is this?

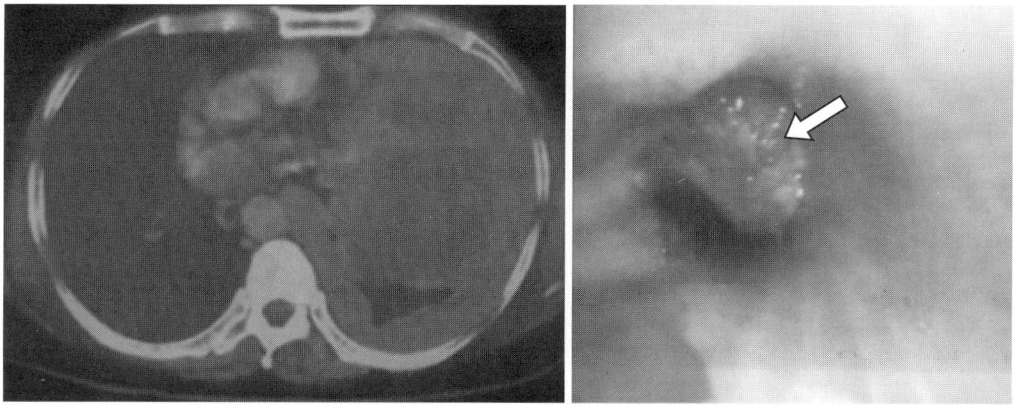

CT shows mass with cavitation and
bronchoscopy shows endobronchial growth (Colour Plate III)

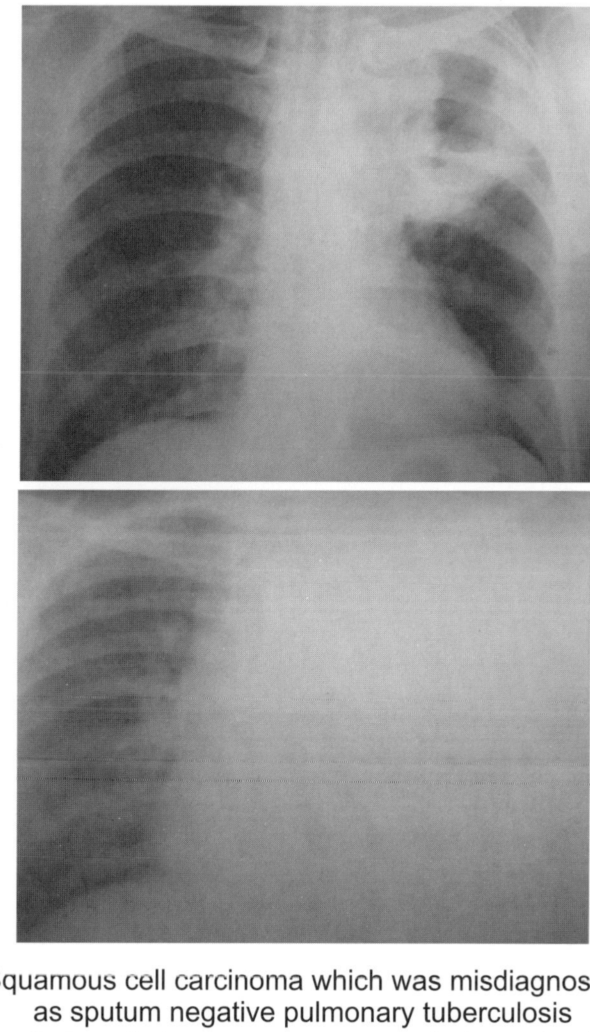

Squamous cell carcinoma which was misdiagnosed
as sputum negative pulmonary tuberculosis
Please remember that cavity in upper zone may not always be due to tuberculosis

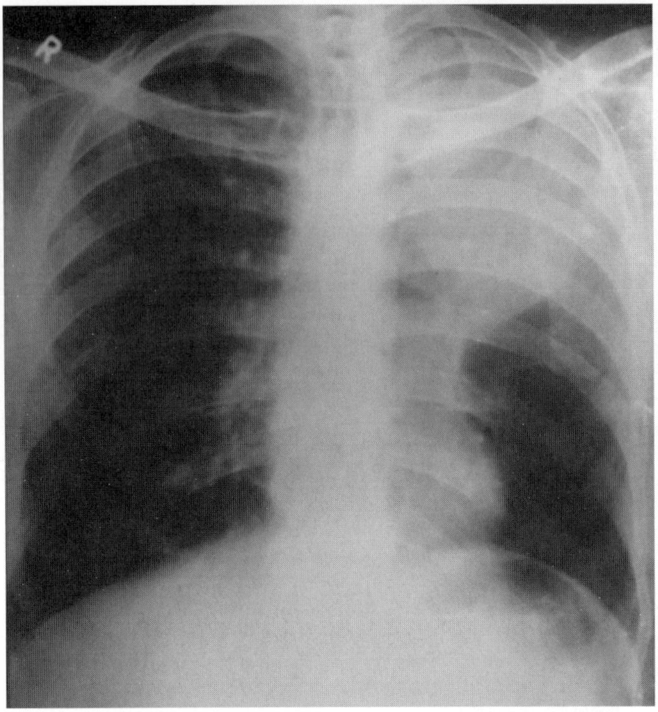

A 65-year-old male presented with breathlessness—8 years, cough with expectoration—6 years, loss of weight—6 years, fever—4 years and hemoptysis—12 days and smoked bidi 10/day for 40 years

What is this?

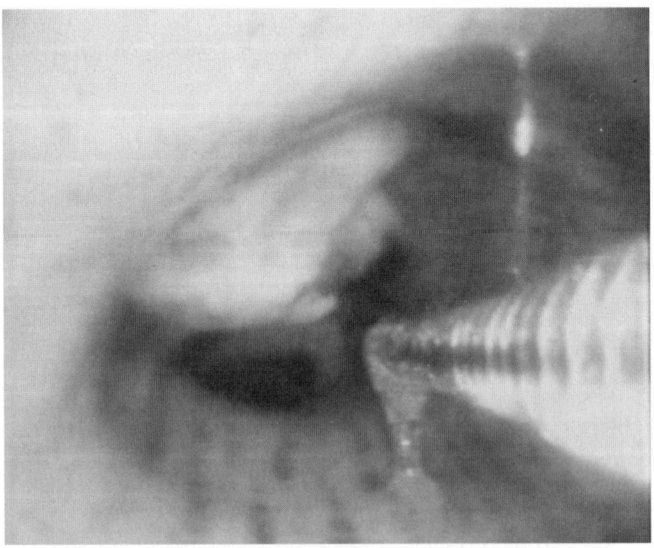

Bronchoscopy shows mass covered with necrotic slough and endobronchial biopsy was performed which confirmed the diagnosis of squamous cell carcinoma. Patient also had evidence of COPD for the last 8 years

(Colour Plate III)

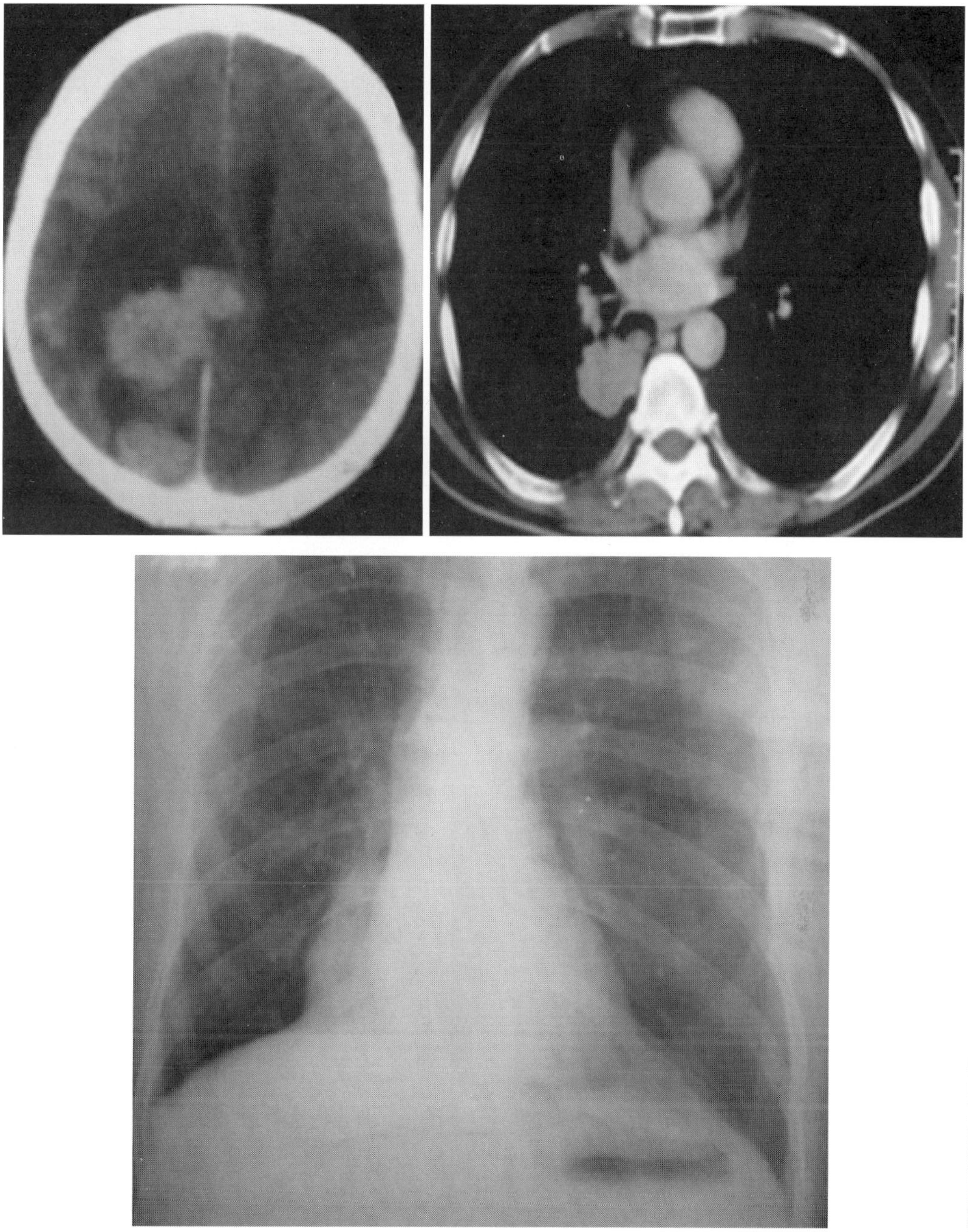

A 55-year-old male came with neurological symptoms—4 months, loss of weight and appetite 3 months with history of cigarette smoking—10/day for 30 years
What is this?

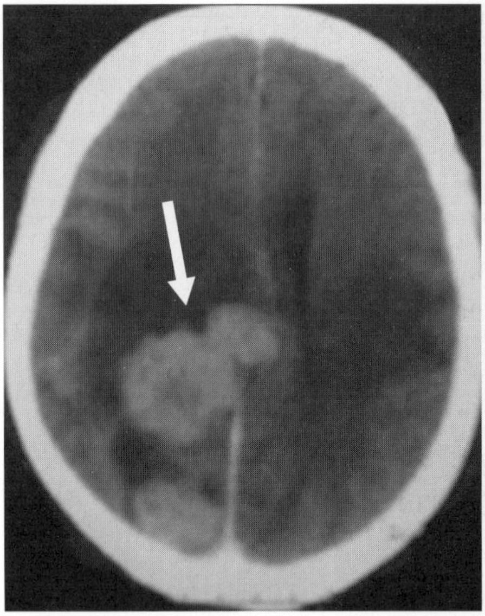

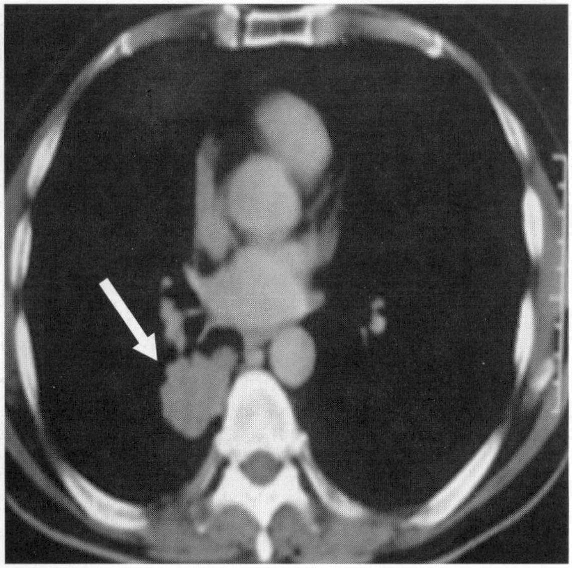

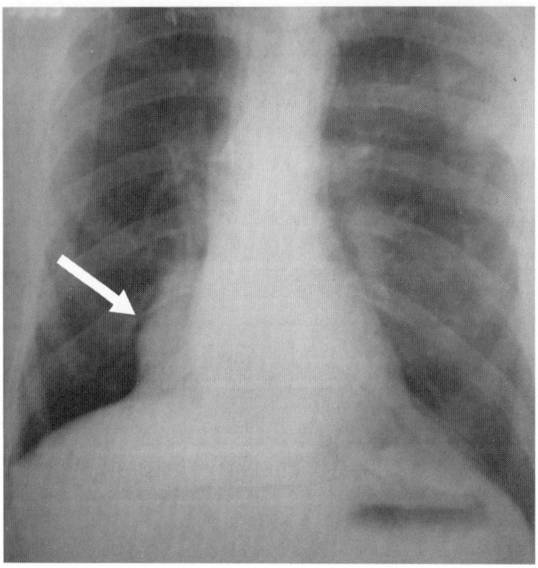

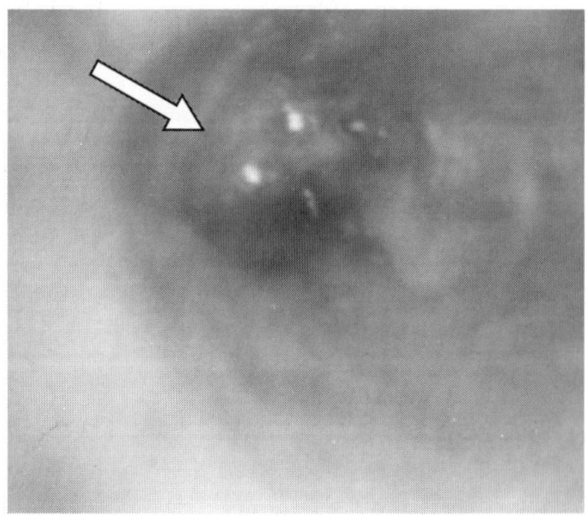

CT head showed multiple secondaries and chest X-ray and CT thorax which was done later on showed mass lesion in the right lung

Bronchoscopy showed endobronchial growth and endobronchial biopsy showed squamous cell carcinoma with secondaries in brain (stage 4) (Colour Plate III)

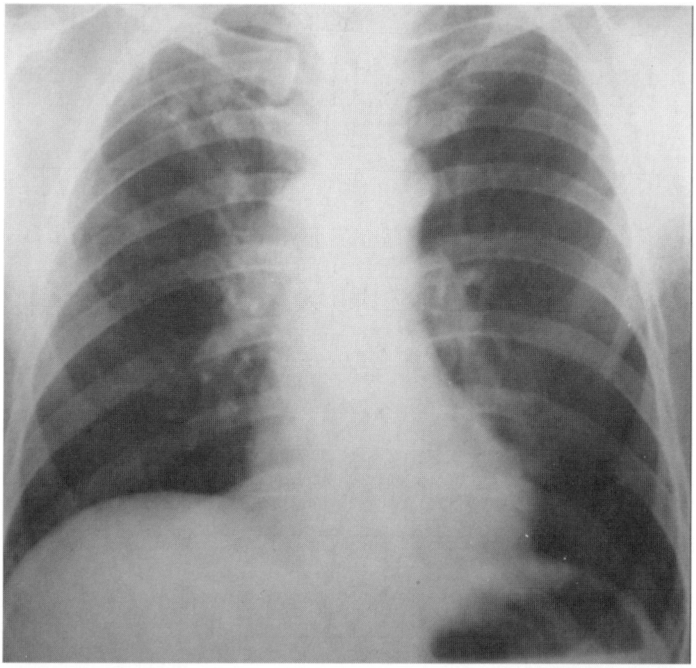

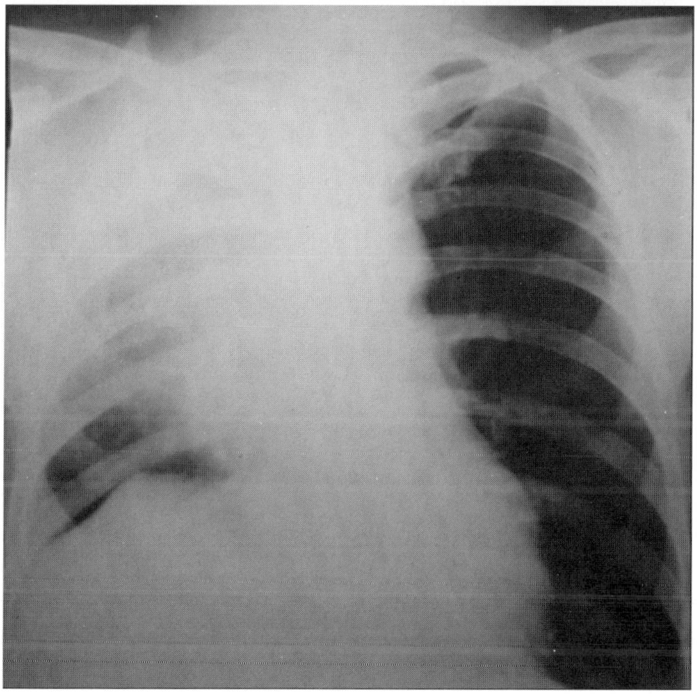

A 45-year-old male, chronic smoker (40 bidis x 25 years), presented with cough with expectoration, recurrent hemoptysis (streaking), loss of appetite and weight and fever off and on from last 7 months with history of antitubercular treatment (2 RHEZ/4RH) for 6 months without any response
What is this?

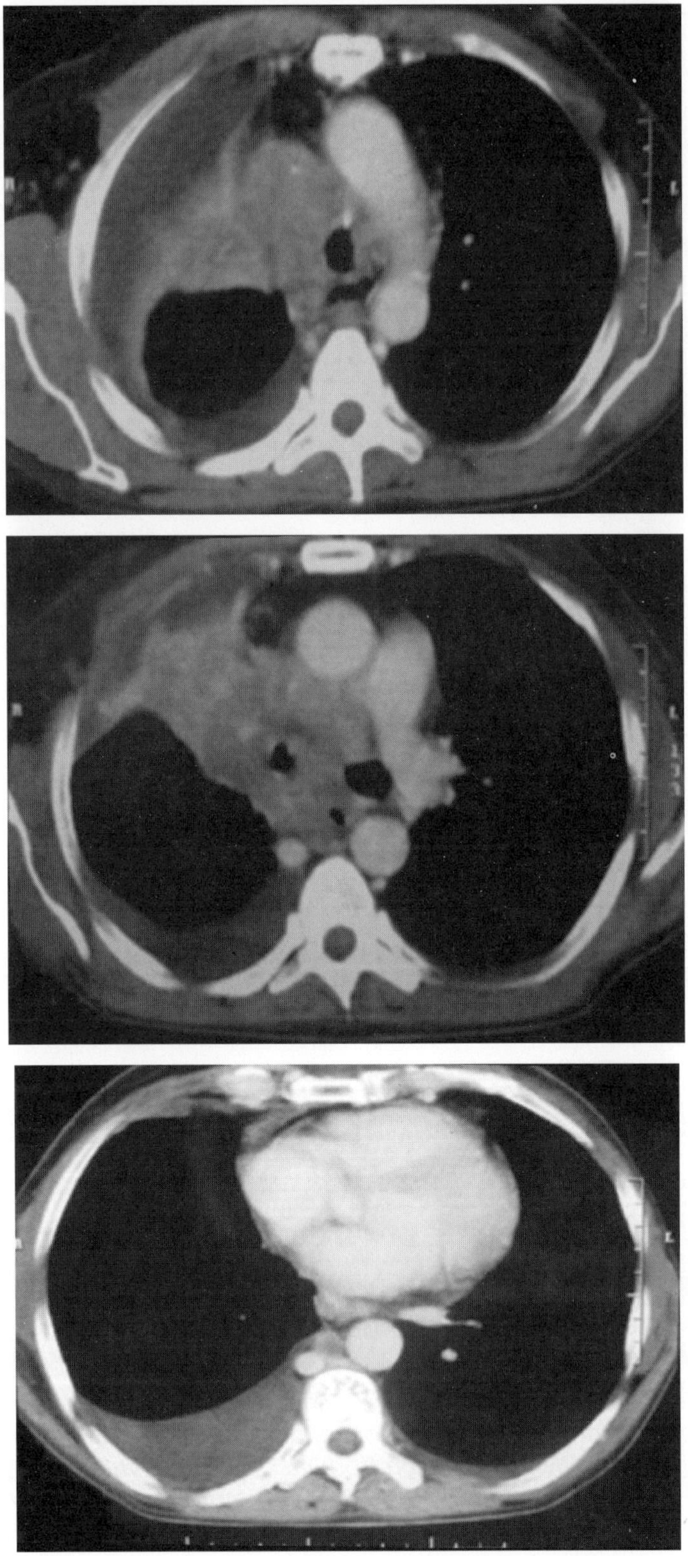

CT thorax shows mass with pleural effusion right lung

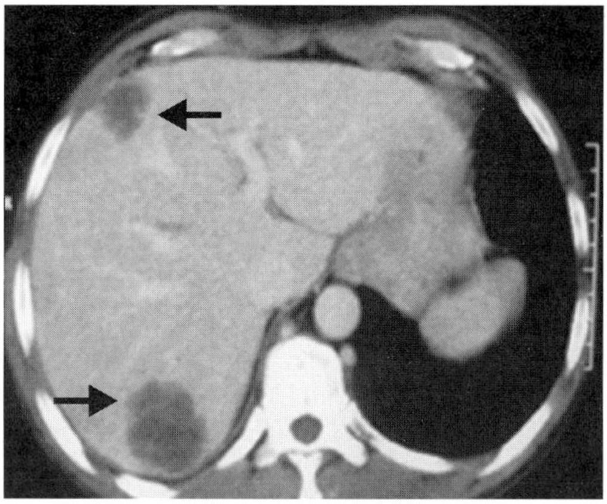

CT thorax shows multiple secondaries in liver

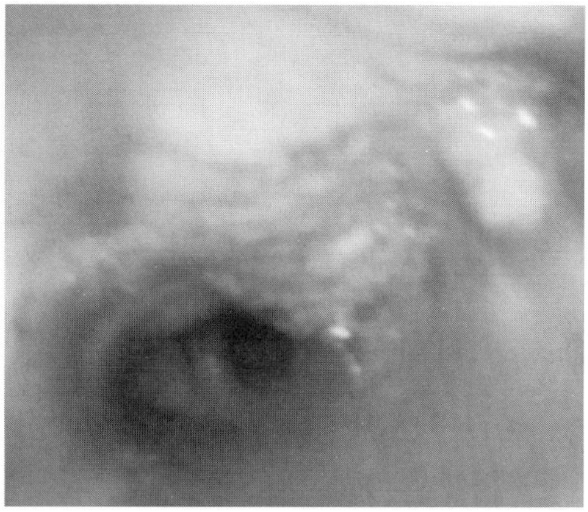

Bronchoscopy shows tumor obstructing the right main bronchus with involvement of carina and endo-bronchial biopsy showed squamous cell carcinoma (stage IV) and secondaries in liver were also found (Colour Plate IV)

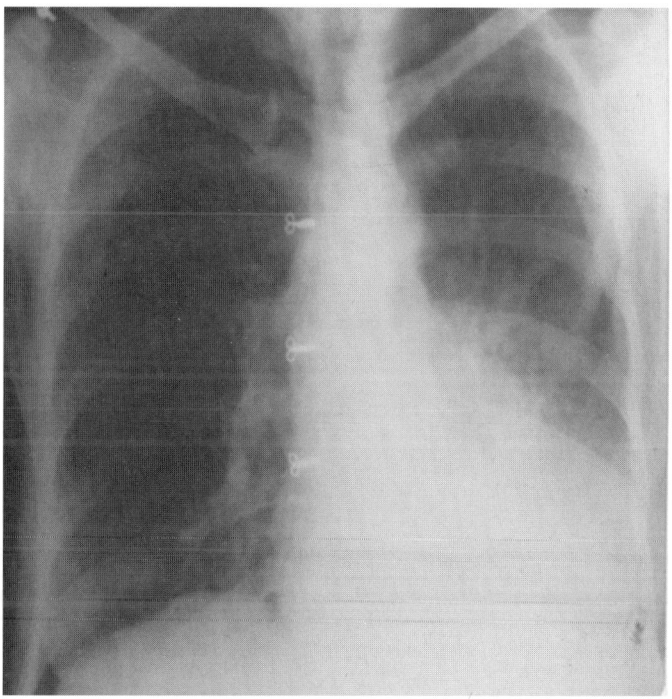

A 57-year-old female, chronic smoker (40 bidis x 25 years), presented with cough with expectoration, recurrent hemoptysis (streaking), loss of appetite and weight and fever (off and on) for 7 months

Chest X-ray showed pleural effusion left side which was aspirated and was exudative in nature

What is this?

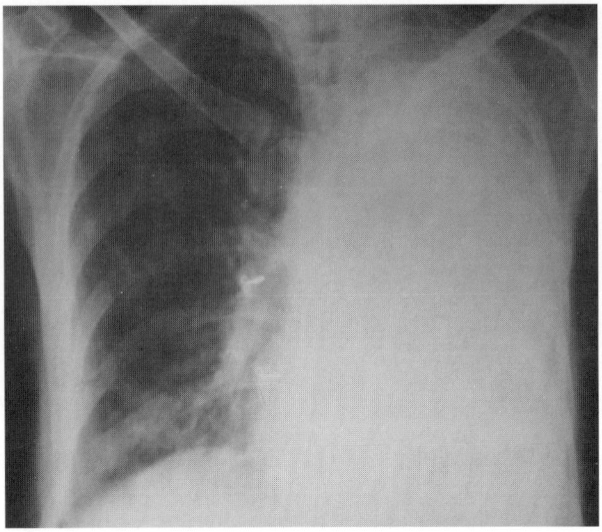

Patient was given antitubercular treatment for 3 months without any response. Effusion increased without any mediastinal shift

Massive effusion without mediastinal shift, suspect endobronchial lesion and perform fiber optic bronchoscopy

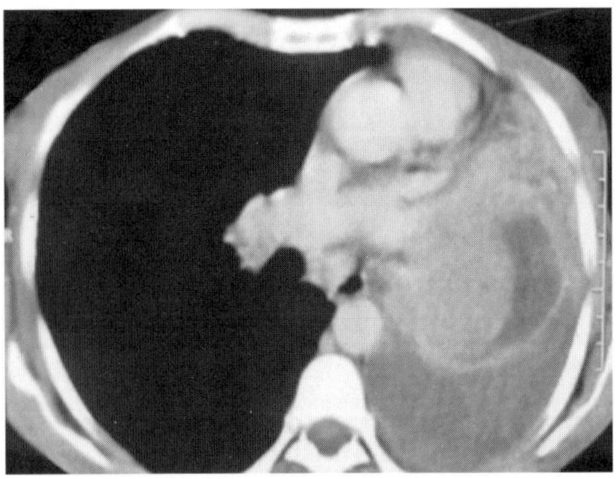

CT thorax shows cavitating mass with pleural effusion left side

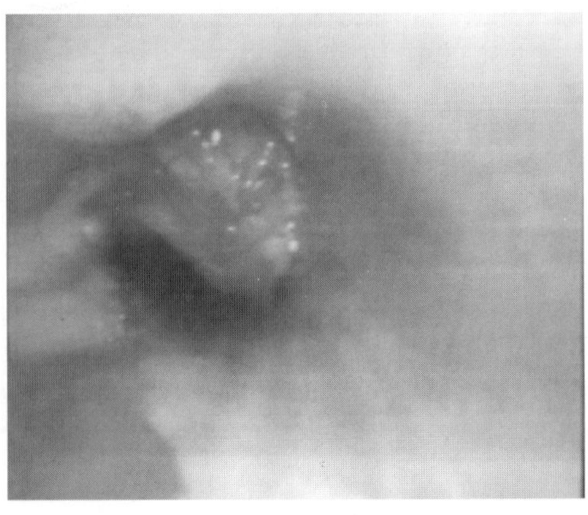

Bronchoscopy shows fungating mass obstructing left lower lobe bronchus and endobronchial biopsy showed adenocarcinoma (Colour Plate IV)

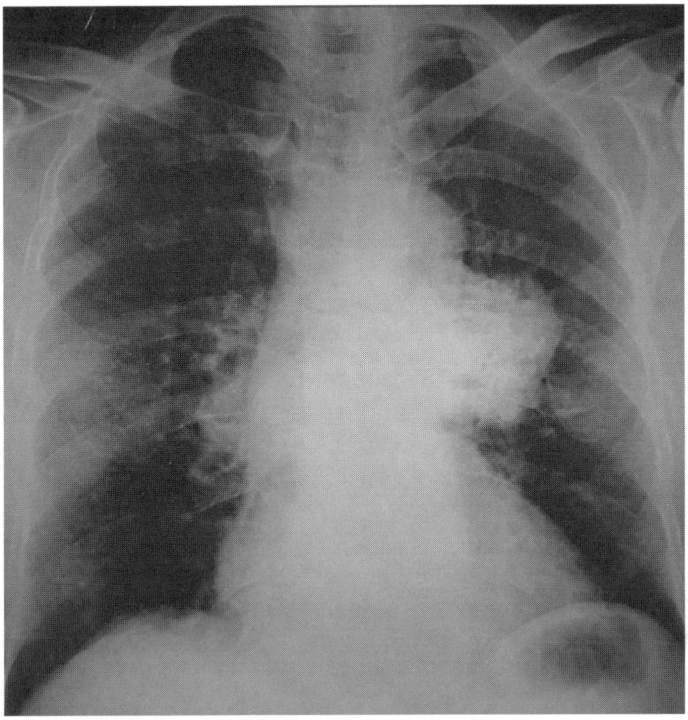

What is this?

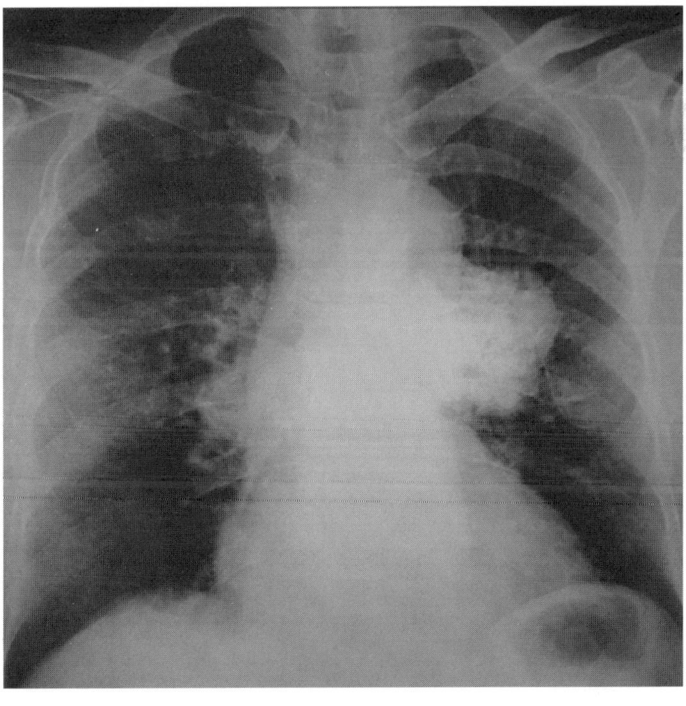

Chest X-ray PA view shows a mediastinal mass with calcification ?Hamartoma

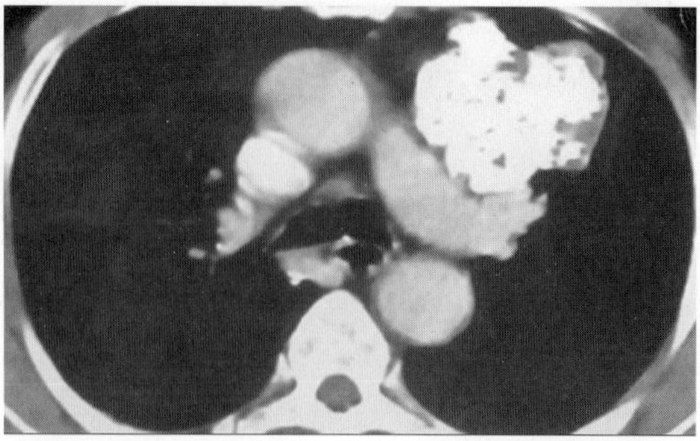

CT thorax shows an anterior mediastinal mass with chunky calcification and diagnosed as hamartoma

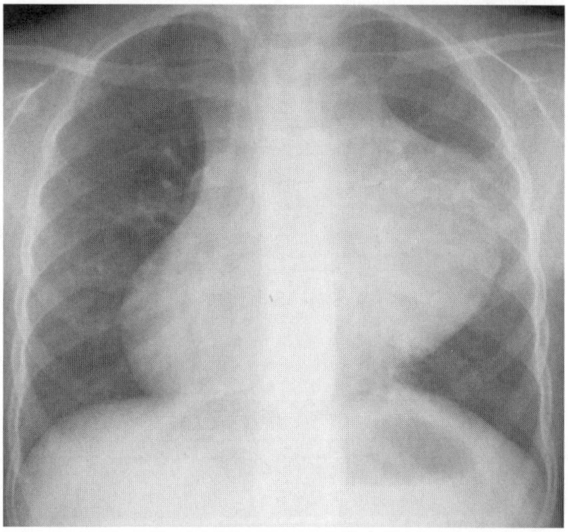

What is this?

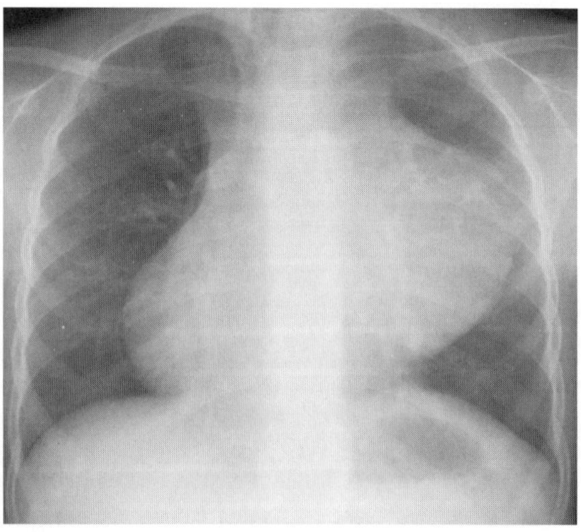

Chest X-ray PA view shows large anterior mediastinal mass with calcification

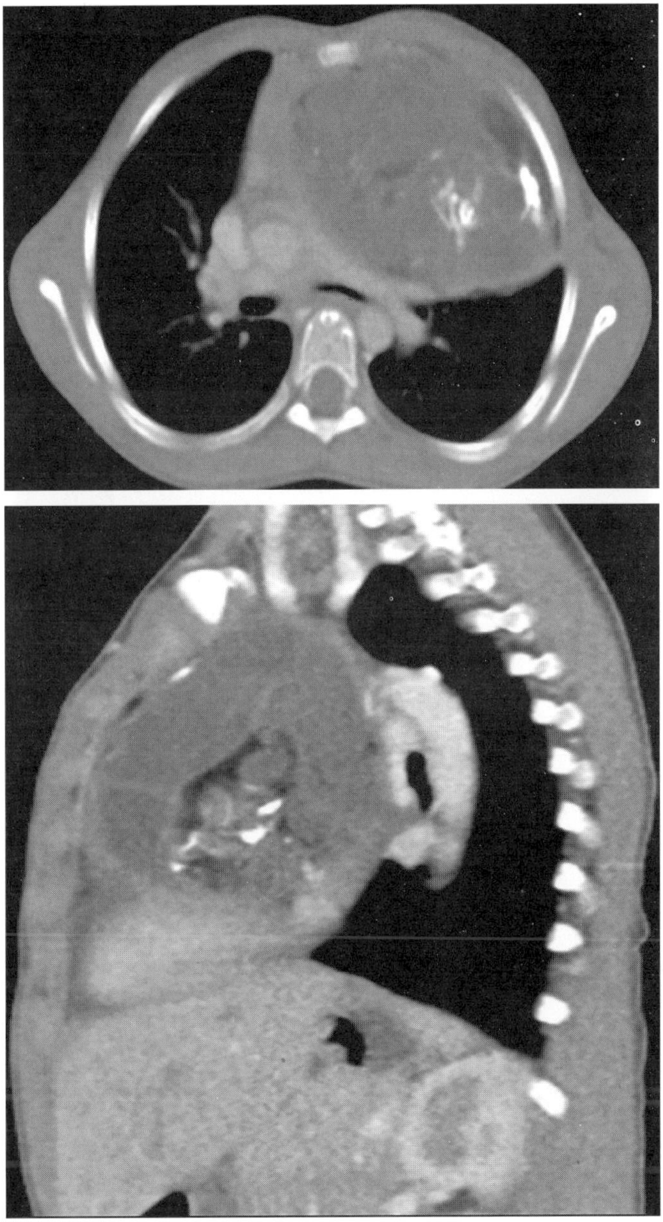

CT thorax shows anterior hypodense, left-sided mediastinal mass with calcification and fat within and diagnosed as teratoma

Reader's Notes

CHAPTER 17

Radiology of Interstitial Lung Disease (ILD)

Interstitial Lung Disease (ILD)

ILD is a heterogenous group of acute and chronic inflammatory and fibrotic lung diseases involving the distal lung parenchyma, of known and unknown causes with different prognosis. It is diverse collection of more than 300 lung disorders

Types of interstitial lung disease (ILD) most likely to have a progressive-fibrosing phenotype (indicated in bold); IIPs: idiopathic interstitial pneumonias. #Stage IV sarcoidosis only

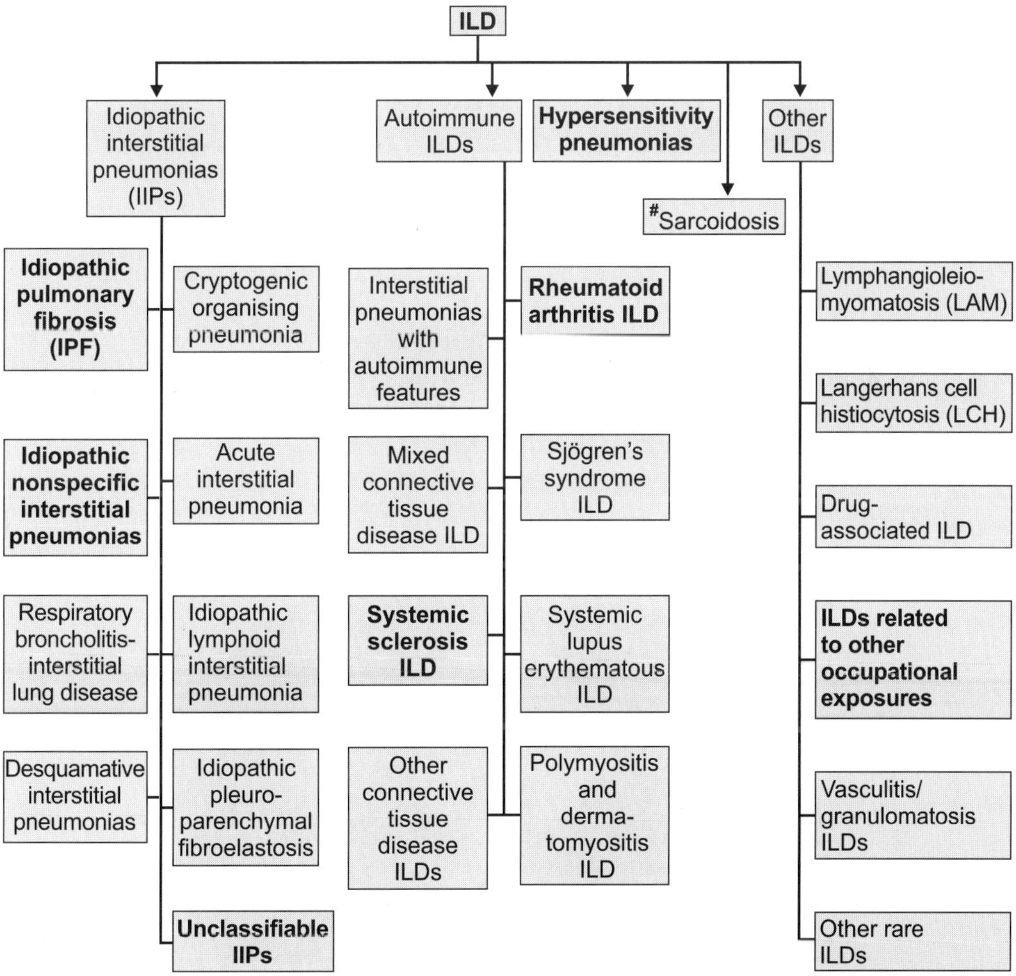

The top 4 ILDs in India are: IPF, CHP, CTD-ILD* and sarcoidosis

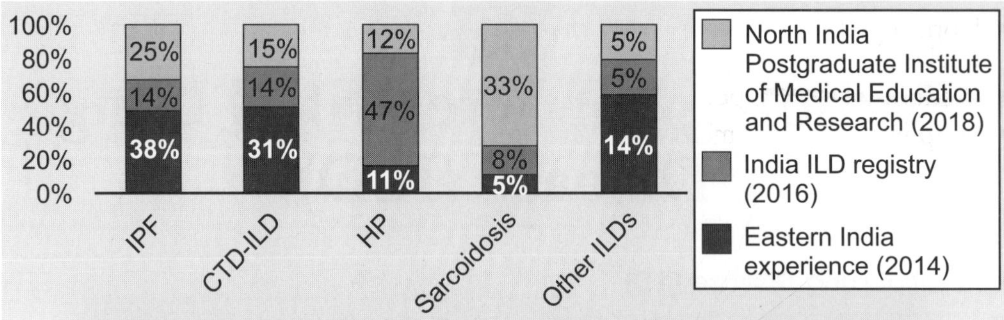

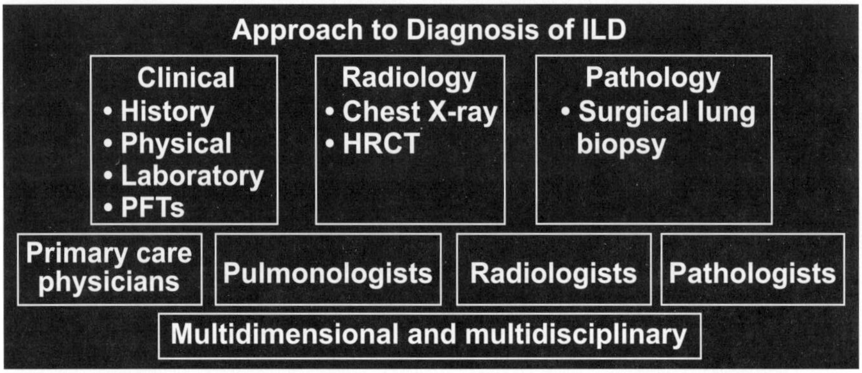

*IPF: Idiopathic pulmonary fibrosis; CHP: Chronic hypersensitivity pneumonitis; CTD-ILD: Connective tissue disorder related ILD

High Resolution Computed Tomography (HRCT) Thorax Common Patterns

Reticular Shadows

- Caused by thickened interlobular or intralobular septa
- Infiltration by fibrosis, abnormal cells, or fluid
- Interlobular septal thickening is usually described as smooth or irregular
- Manifests as a fine reticular pattern on HRCT
- Late stage—honeycombing, characterized by cystic airspaces surrounded by irregular walls

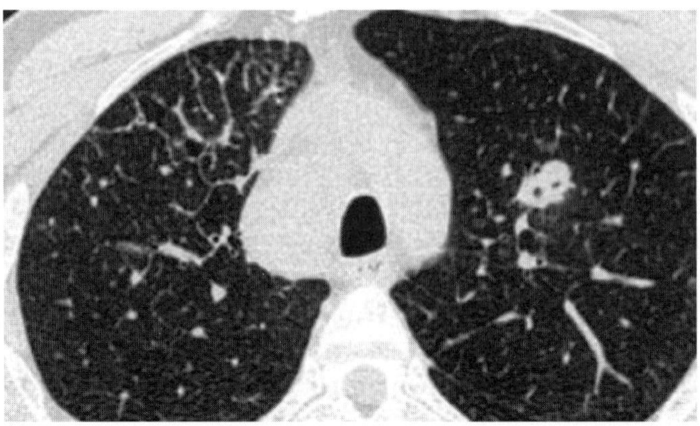

Focal septal thickening

Honeycombing

- Honeycombing is defined by the presence of small cystic spaces with irregularly thickened walls composed of fibrous tissue
- Predominate in the peripheral and subpleural lung regions
- Subpleural honeycomb cysts occur in several contiguous layers

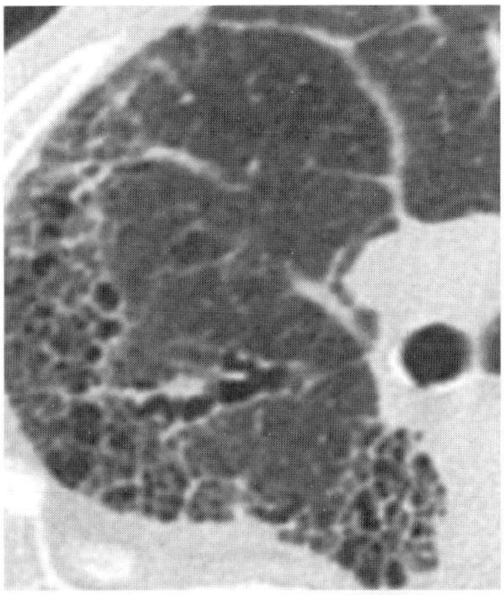

Honeycombing

Causes of Honeycombing

Lower lobe predominance
UIP or interstitial fibrosis
Connective tissue disorders
Hypersensitivity pneumonitis
Asbestosis
NSIP (rare)
Upper lobe predominance
End stage sarcoidosis
Radiation
Hypersensitivity pneumonitis
End stage ARDS

Nodular Shadows

- Feature of both interstitial and airspace disease
- Perilymphatic nodules within the lung interstitium, especially those related to the lymphatic vessels, are seen in the interlobular septa, subpleural and peribronchovascular regions
- Centrilobular nodules
- Random

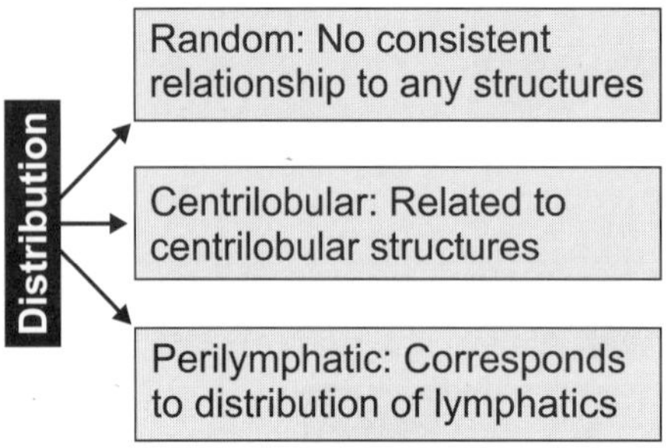

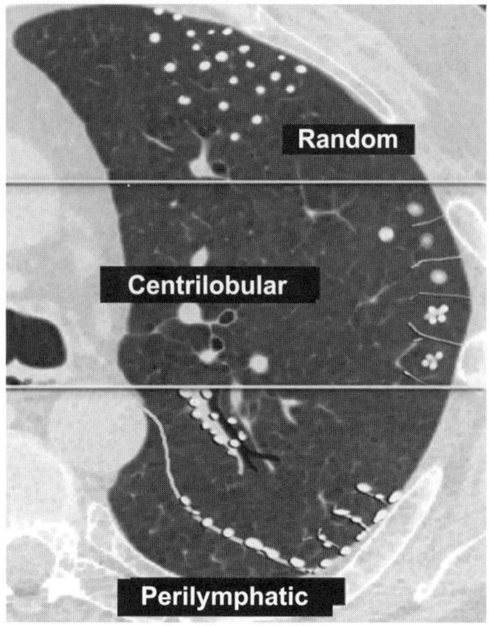

Centriacinar Nodules

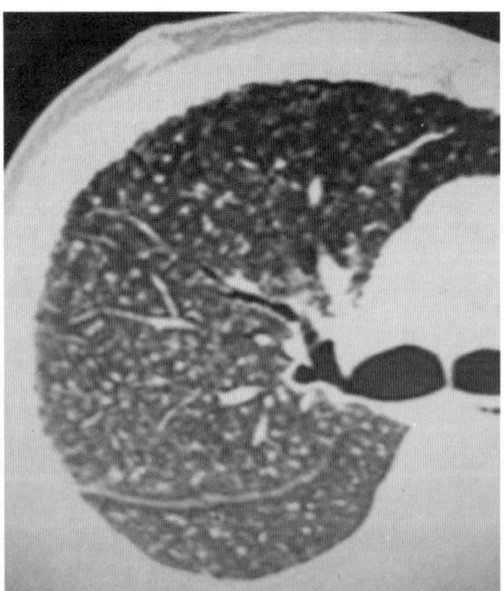

Centrilobular nodules in a patient with subacute hypersensitivity pneumonitis

Perilymphatic Nodules

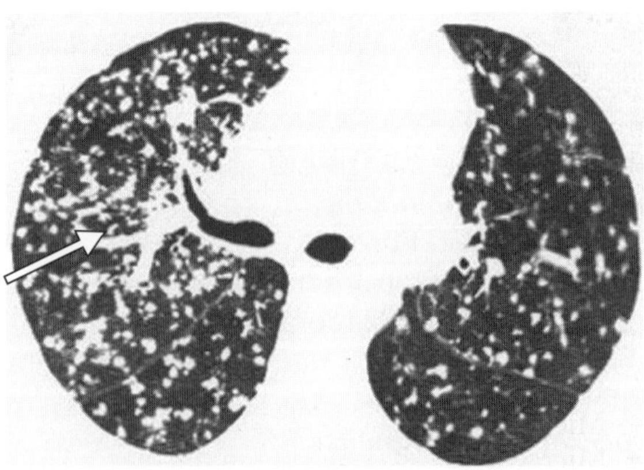

Perilymphatic and random distribution of nodules, seen in sarcoidosis

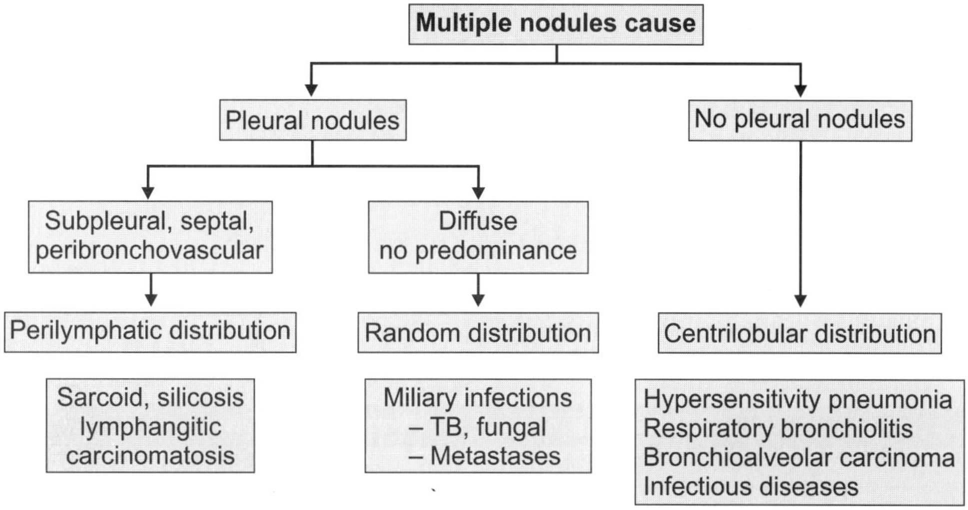

Ground Glass Opacity (GGO)

- Generalized increase in opacity that does not obscure pulmonary vessels
- Include partial filling of the airspaces, considerable thickening of the interstitium, or a combination of the two
- Hazy increased attenuation of lung, with preservation of bronchial and vascular margins
- ***Pathology***: It is caused by partial filling of air spaces, interstitial thickening, partial collapse of alveoli, normal expiration, or increased capillary blood volume

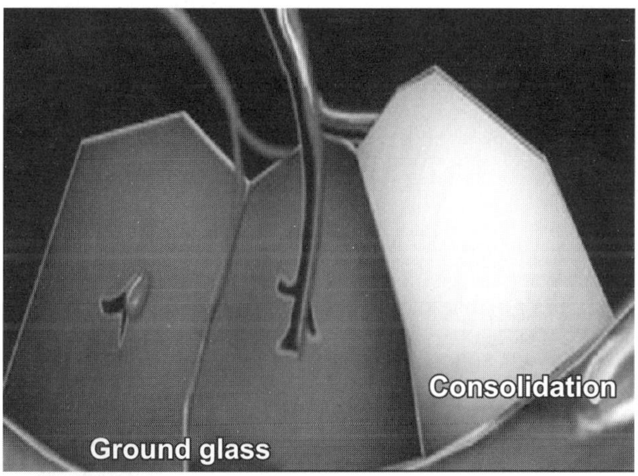

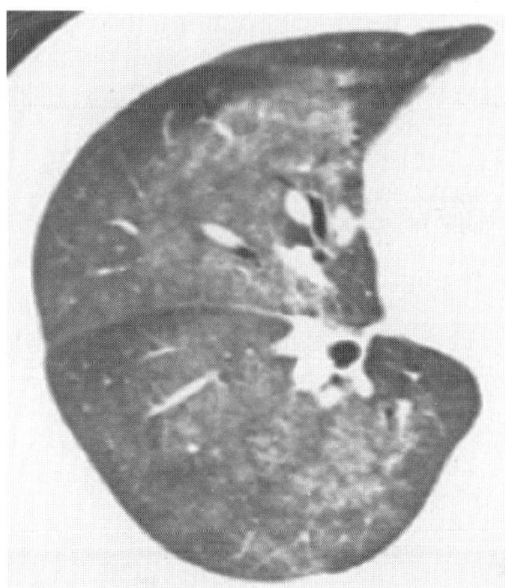

Importance of GGO

- Can represent
  - Microscopic interstitial disease (alveolar interstitium)
  - Microscopic alveolar space disease
  - Combination of both
- In the absence of fibrosis, mostly indicates the presence of an ongoing, active, potentially treatable process

Differential Diagnosis: GGO	
Ground glass opacity	
Acute	**Chronic**
Pulmonary edema • Heart failure • ARDS	Hypersensitivity pneumonitis Organizing pneumonia (BOOP, COP) Chronic eosinophilic pneumonia
Pulmonary hemorrhage pneumonia • Viral • Mycoplasma • *Pneumocystis jiroveci* pneumonia (PJP)	Alveolar proteinosis Lung fibrosis • UIP • NSIP
Acute eosinophilic pneumonia	Bronchoalveolar carcinoma

HRCT Patterns in Idiopathic Pulmonary Fibrosis		
	UIP pattern	Probable UIP pattern
• Level of confidence for UIP histology	• Confident (>90%)	• Provisional high confidence (70–89%)
• Distribution	• Sub-pleural and basal predominant • Often heterogeneous (areas of normal lung interspersed with fibrosis) • Occasionally diffuse • May be asymmetric	• Sub-pleural and basal predominant • Often heterogeneous (areas of normal lung interspersed with reticulation and traction bronchiectasis/ bronchiolectasis)
• CT features	• Honeycombing with or without peripheral traction bronchiectasis/bronchiolectasis • Presence of irregular thickening of interlobular septa • Usually superimposed with a reticular pattern, mild GGO • May have pulmonary ossification	• Reticular pattern with traction bronchiectasis or bronchiolectasis • May have mild GGO • Absence of subpleural sparing
	Indeterminate for UIP	Alternative diagnosis
• Level of confidence for UIP histology	• Provisional low confidence (51–69%)	• Low to very low confidence (<50%)
• Distribution	• Diffuse distribution without subpleural predominance	• Peribronchovascular predominant with subpleural sparing (consider NSIP) • Perilymphatic distribution (consider sarcoidosis) • Upper or mid-lung (consider fibrotic HP, CTD-ILD, and sarcoidosis) • Subpleural sparing (consider NSIP or smoking-related IP)
• CT features	• CT findings of lung fibrosis that do not suggest any specific etiology	• Lung findings ◆ Cysts (consider LAM, PLCH, LIP, and DIP) ◆ Mosaic attenuation or three-density sign (consider HP) ◆ Predominant GGO (consider HP, smoking-related disease, drug toxicity, and acute exacerbation of fibrosis) ◆ Profuse centrilobular nodules (consider HP or smoking-related disease) ◆ Nodules (consider sarcoidosis) ◆ Consolidation (consider organizing pneumonia, etc.) • Mediastinal findings ◆ Pleural plaques (consider asbestosis) ◆ Dilated esophagus (consider CTD)
IPF (an update) and Progressive Pulmonary Fibrosis in Adults, American Journal of Respiratory and Critical Care Medicine, May 1 2022		

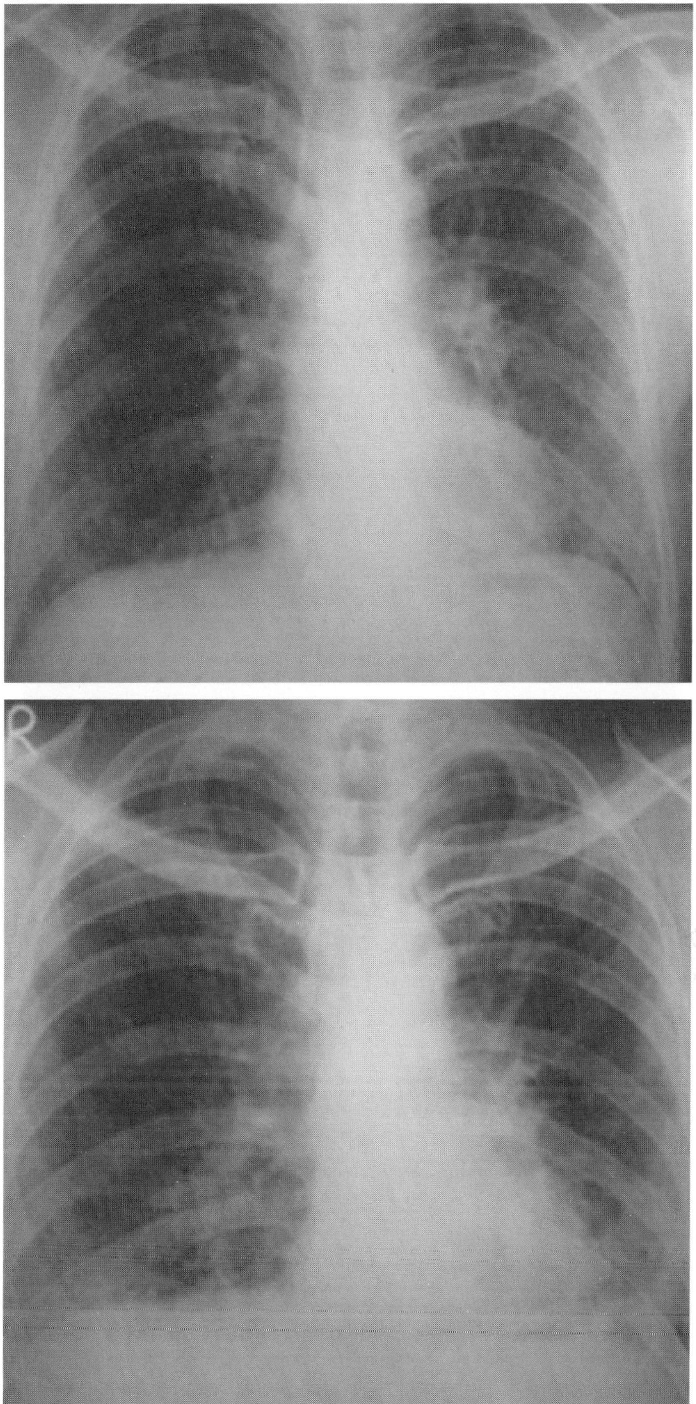

A 63-year-old male presented with breathlessness (exertional) and dry cough for 6 months treated as asthma with inhaled medications for 3 years without any response

What is this?

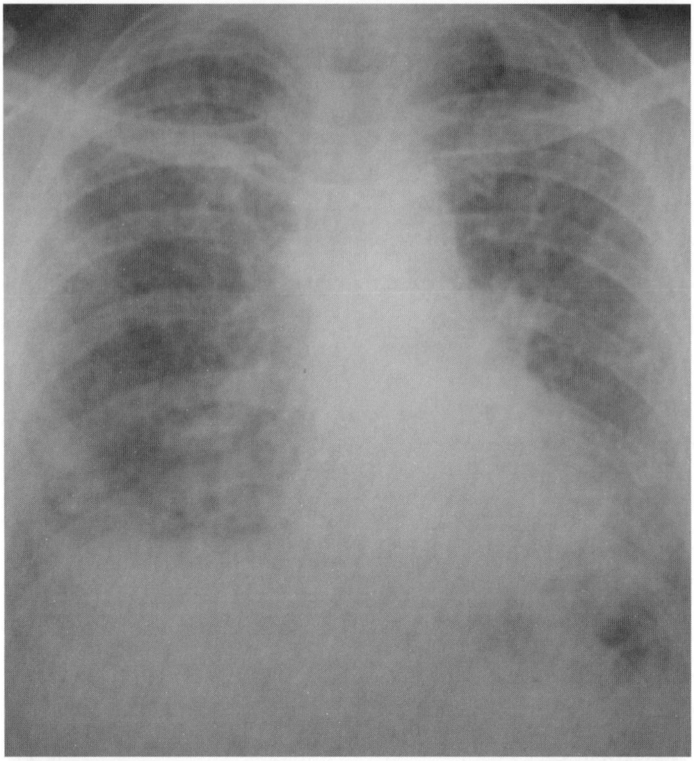

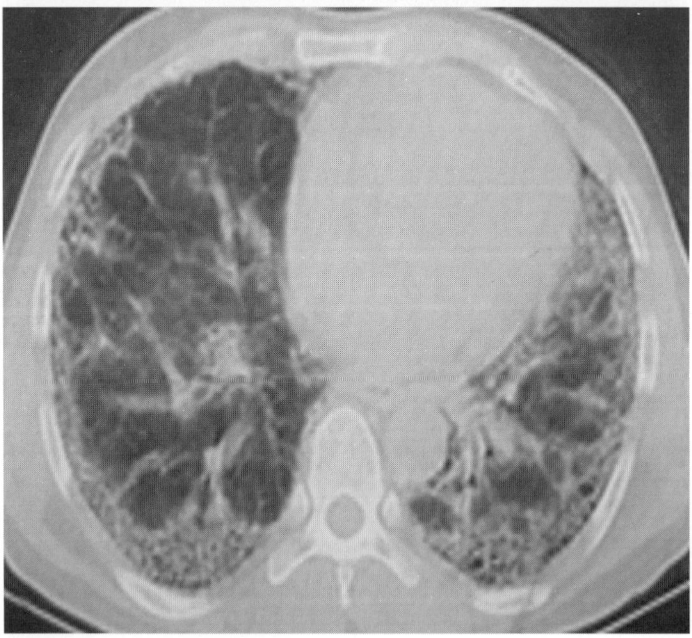

Spirometry shows restrictive disorder (FVC: 1.3 L [48% of predicted value])

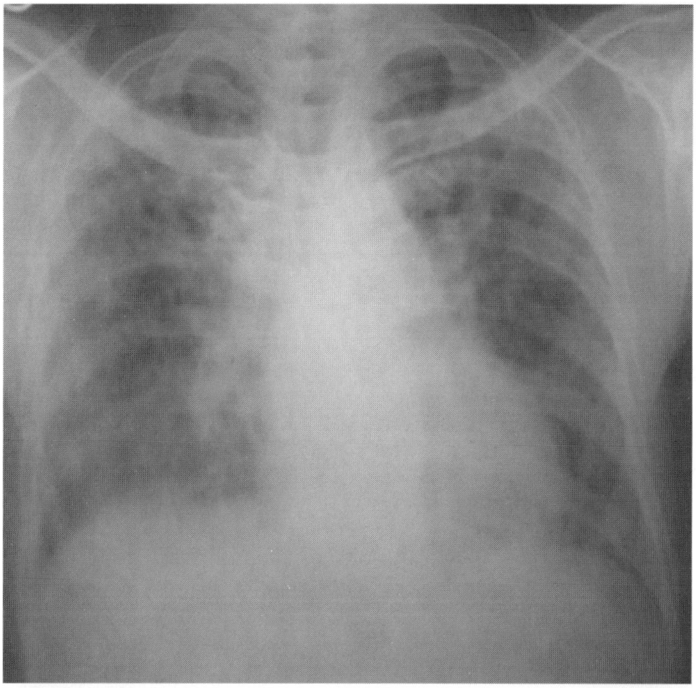

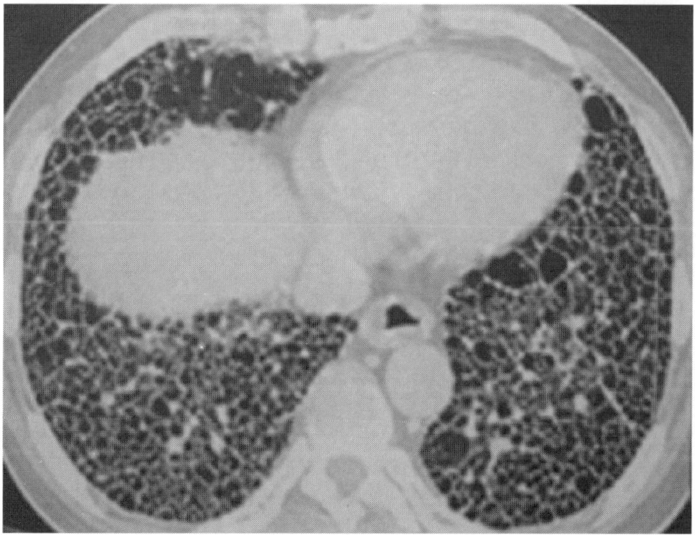

Spirometry shows restrictive disorder (FVC: 0.78 L [29% of predicted value])
In spite of adequate treatment patient progressed to extensive honeycombing and died in 2004
Diagnosis: Idiopathic pulmonary fibrosis (IPF)
Please note that typical IPF has poor prognosis and survival rate is like lung cancer

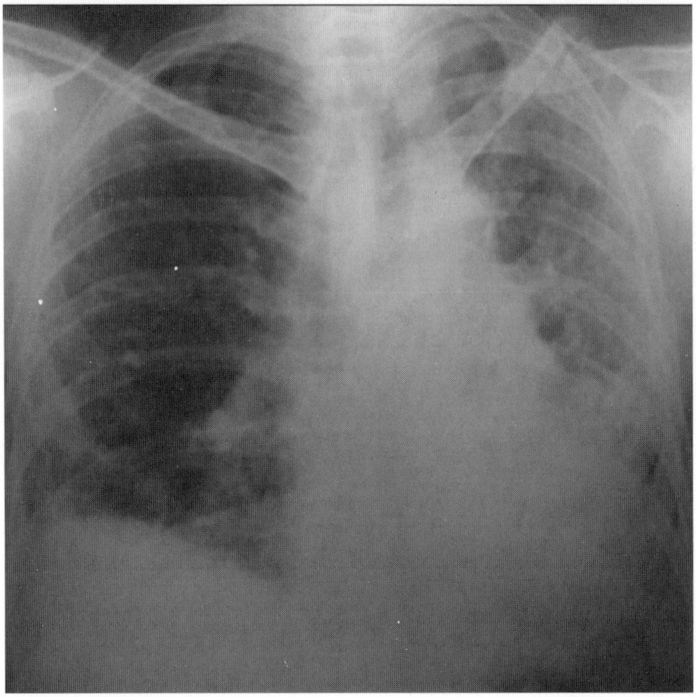

What is this?

A 56-year-old male, known case of rheumatoid arthritis, smoker 20 bidi/day—35 years presented with fever—1 year, cough with minimal expectoration—1 year, breathlessness—3 months, right-sided chest pain—10 days, decrease appetite—5 days
Had taken antitubercular treatment but without any response

Investigations

Serum-rheumatoid factor: 452 IU/ml

Pleural Fluid

Protein: 4.6 g/dl, sugar: 74 mg/dl
TLC: 1000, DLC-neutrophilic predominant (P84%)
Rheumatoid factor: 49.4 IU/ml
AFB: Negative

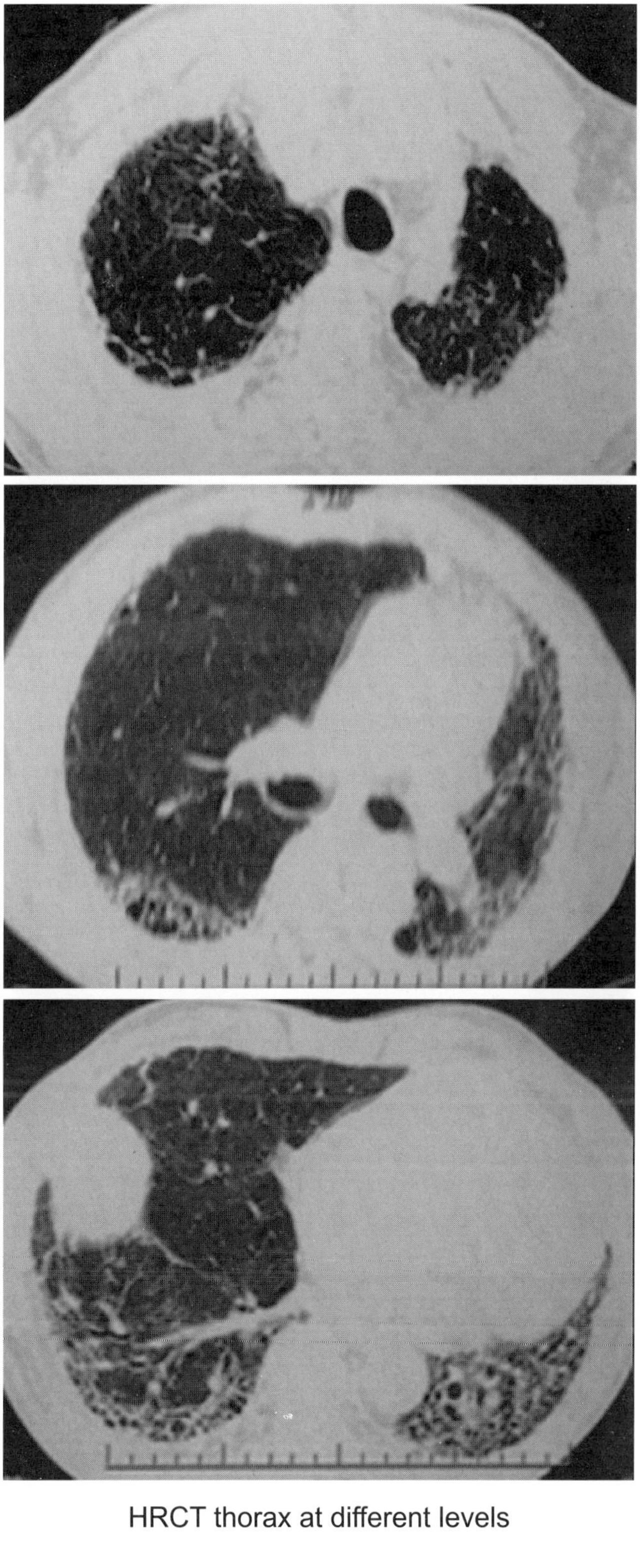

HRCT thorax at different levels

Diagnosis: Interstitial Lung Disease Cause Rheumatoid Arthritis

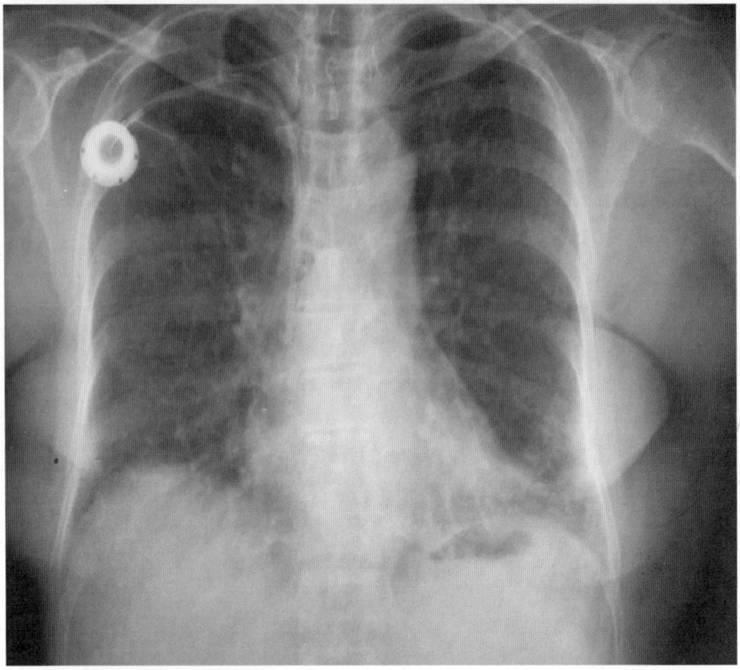

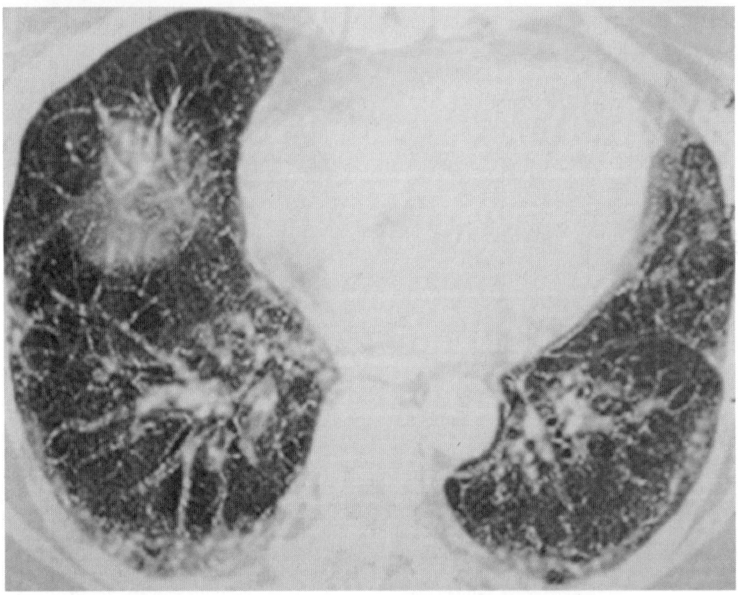

A 63-year-old female presented with progressive breathlessness and dry cough for 1 month. Patient had past history of adenocarcinoma colon and was given oxaloplatin, 5-FU and leucovorin for six cycles 4 months ago

What is this?

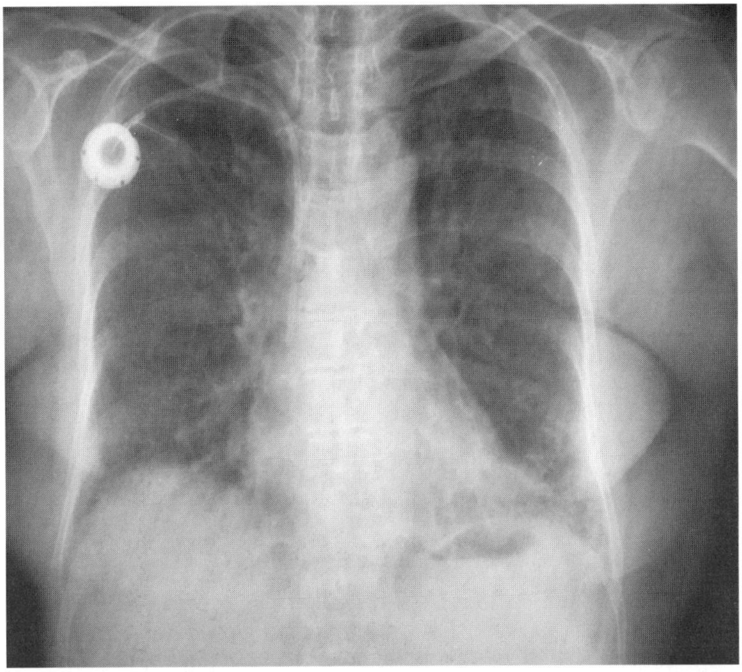

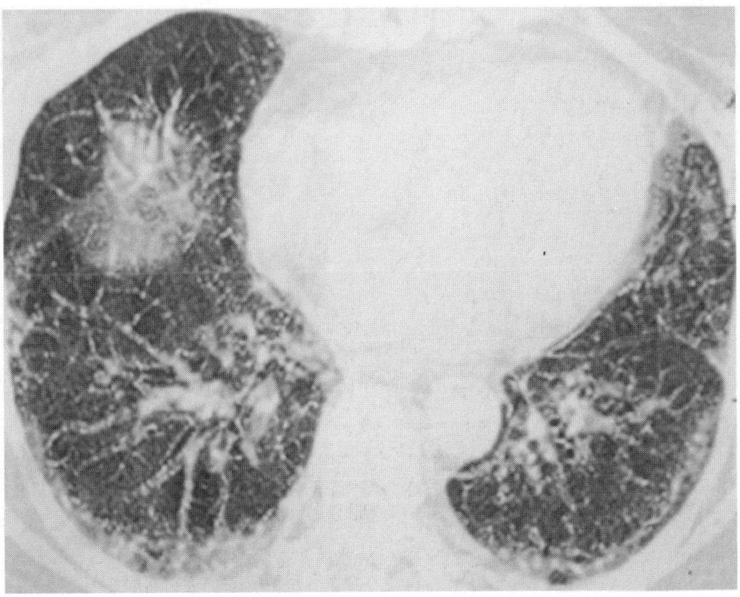

Chest X-ray and HRCT thorax

Spirometry and arterial blood gases (ABG)

FVC	FEV1	FEV1/FVC	PaO_2	$PaCO_2$
1.51 (66%)	1.25 (66%)	82%	36 mmHg	28 mmHg

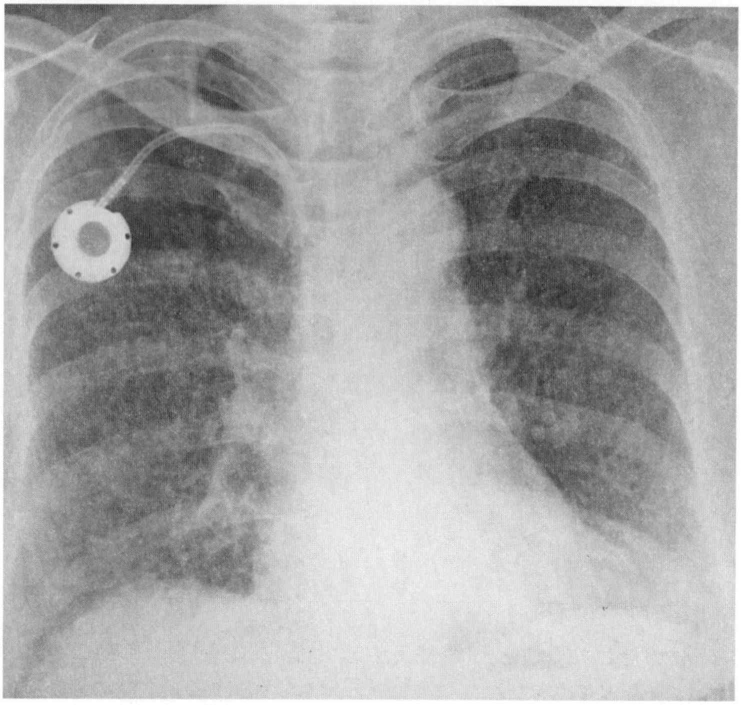

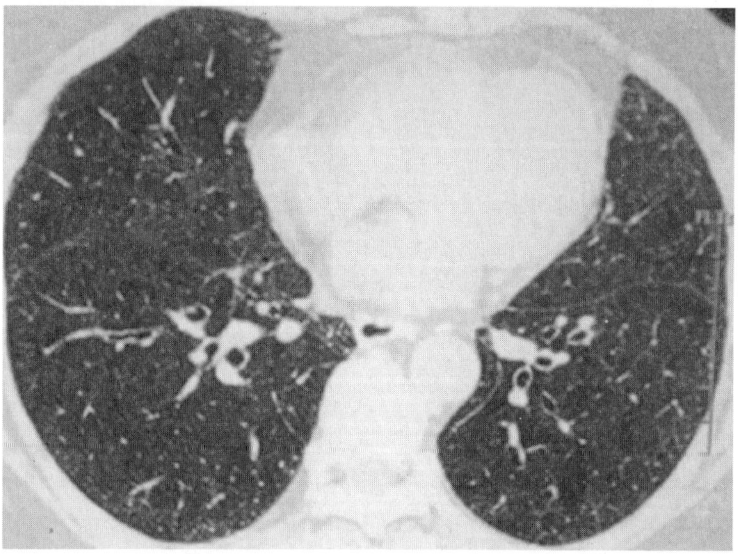

Chest X-ray and HRCT thorax

Drug (oxaloplatin) induced ILD was diagnosed and patient was started on deflazacort 30 mg BD and tapered to 6 mg OD over 6 months

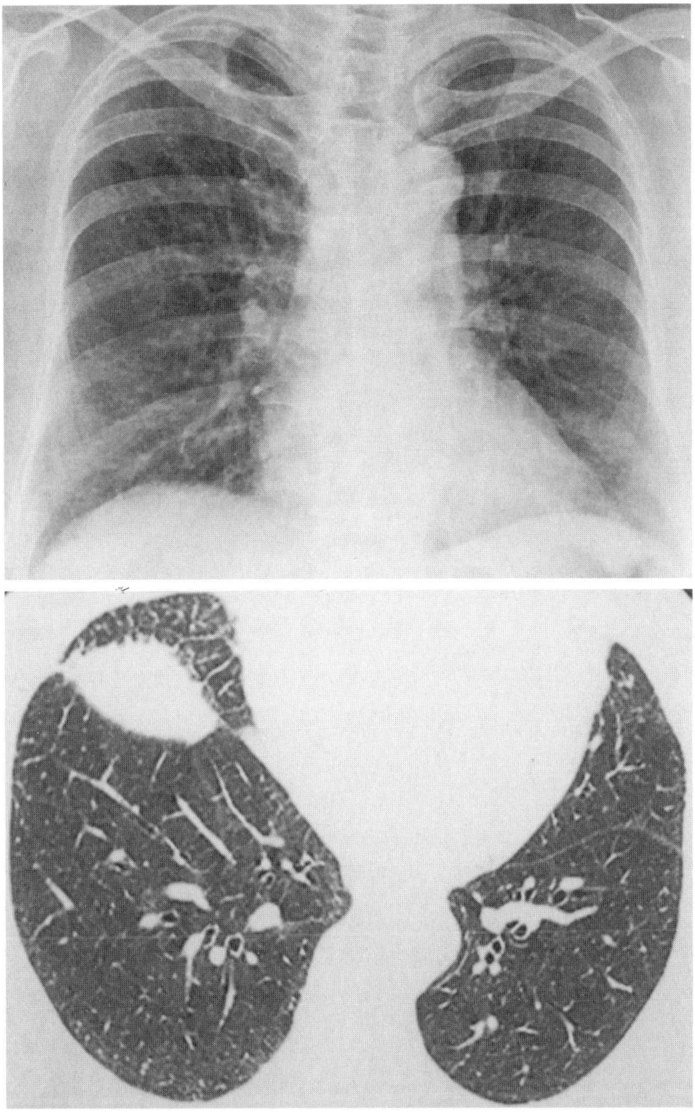

Chest X-ray and HRCT thorax after 6 months of oral steroid treatment

Spirometry and arterial blood gases (ABG) After 6 months of treatment

FVC	FEV1	FEV1/FVC	PaO_2	$PaCO_2$
2.28 (99%)	1.77 (93%)	80%	84 mmHg	29 mmHg

Patient improved clinically, radiologically (chest X-ray, HRCT thorax) and in spirometric parameters (FVC 1.51 L to 2.28 L)

Diagnosis: Drug-induced ILD

Please note that drug-induced ILD is treatable and has better prognosis if detected early and treated

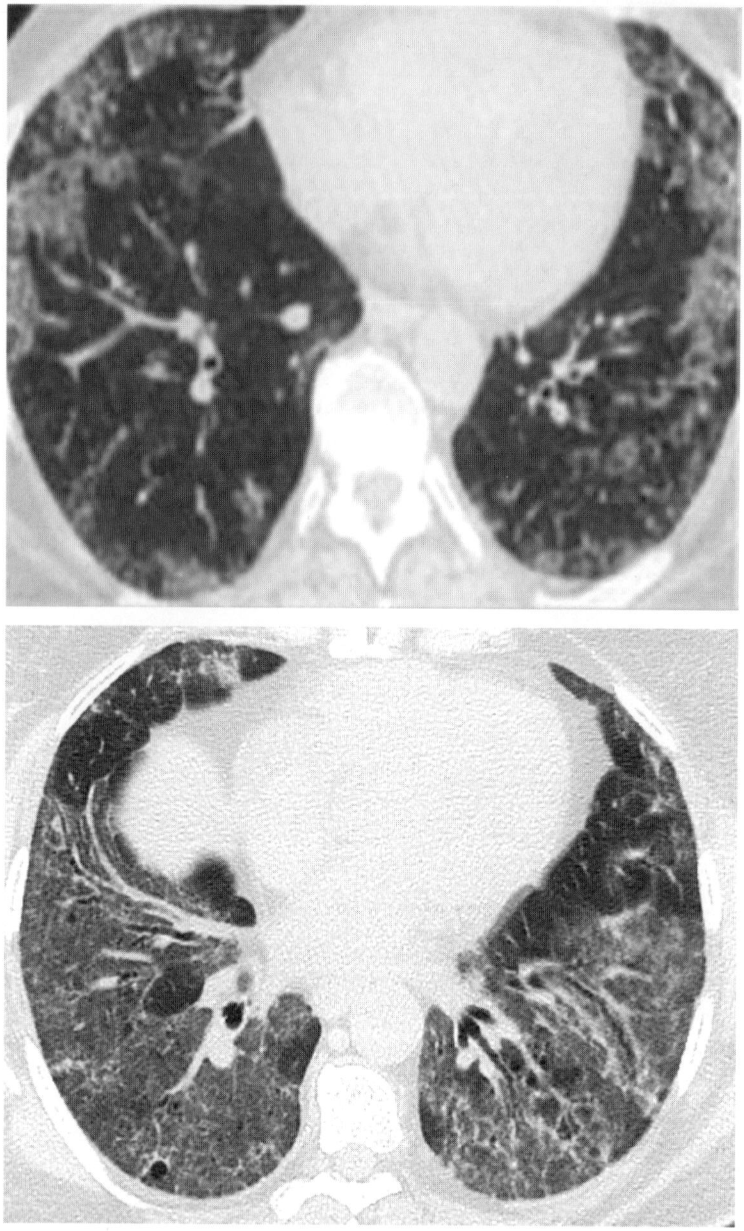

A 50-year-old female presented with cough and breathlessness for last 3 months
What is this?

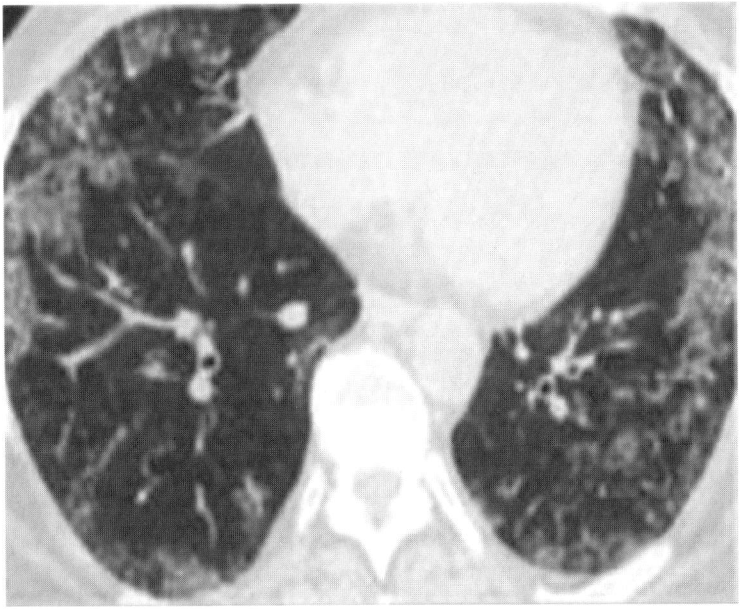

Ground glass opacities with a superimposed fine reticular densities without any honeycombing

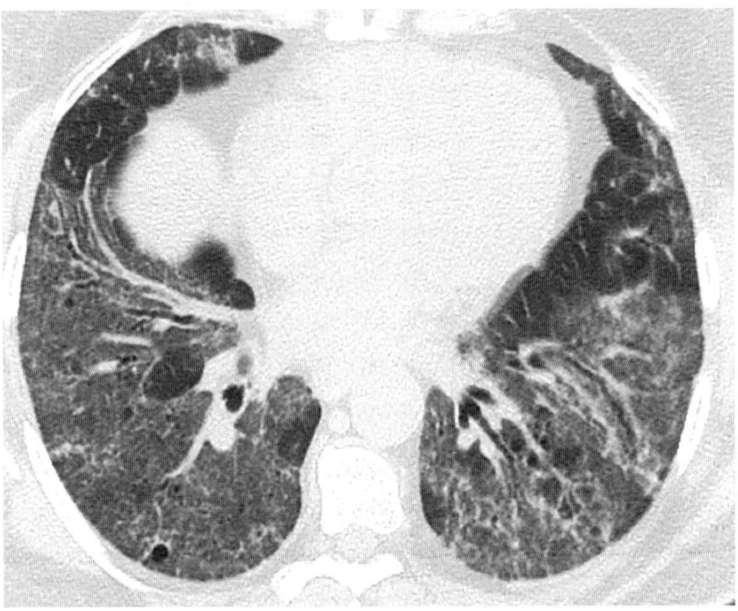

Ground glass opacities with reticulation and traction bronchiectasis without any honeycombing

Diagnosis: Non-specific Interstitial Pneumonia (NSIP)

Please note that NSIP has better prognosis if detected early and effectively treated

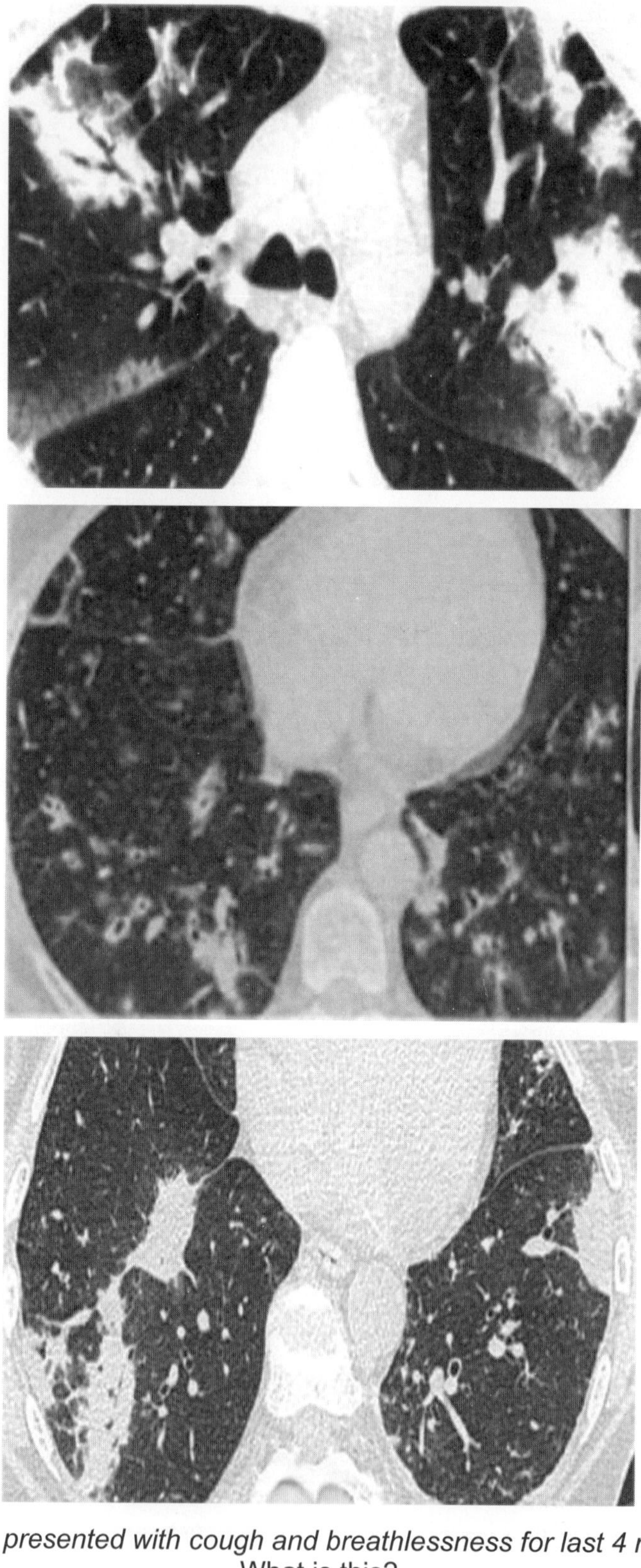

Patient presented with cough and breathlessness for last 4 months
What is this?

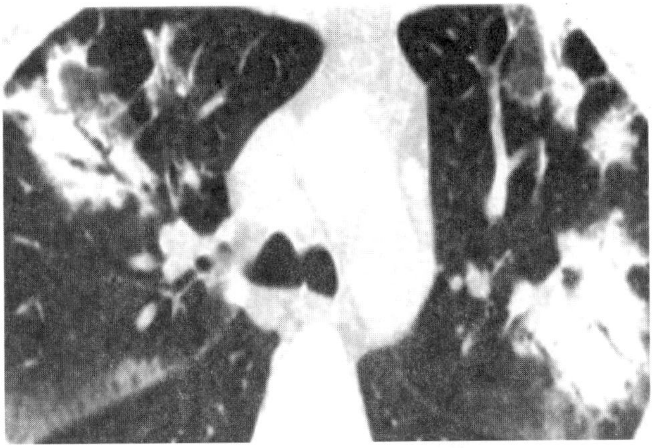

Typical bilateral peripheral consolidation

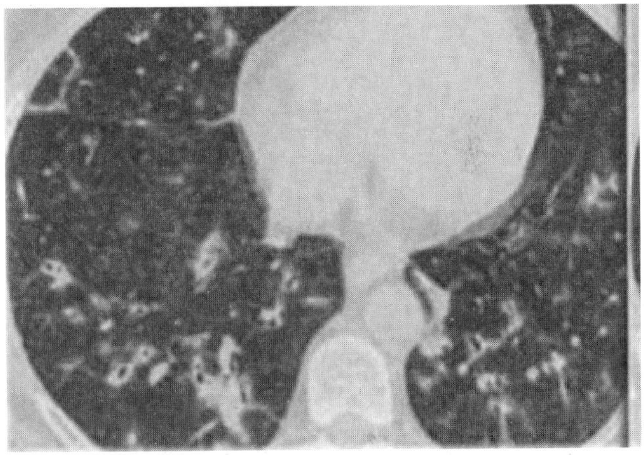

Patient with collagen vascular disease with multiple small bilateral peripheral consolidations

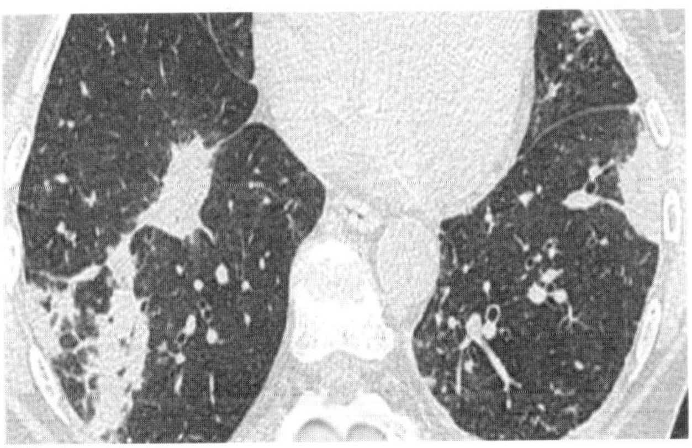

Patient with rheumatoid arthritis and bilateral peripheral consolidations

Diagnosis: Cryptogenic Organizing Pneumonia

Cryptogenic organizing pneumonia (COP) used to describe as bronchiolitis obliterans with organizing pneumonia (BOOP) in an earlier version of the classification of idiopathic interstitial pneumonias. It is an inflammatory process in which the healing process is characterized by organization of the exudate rather than by resorption

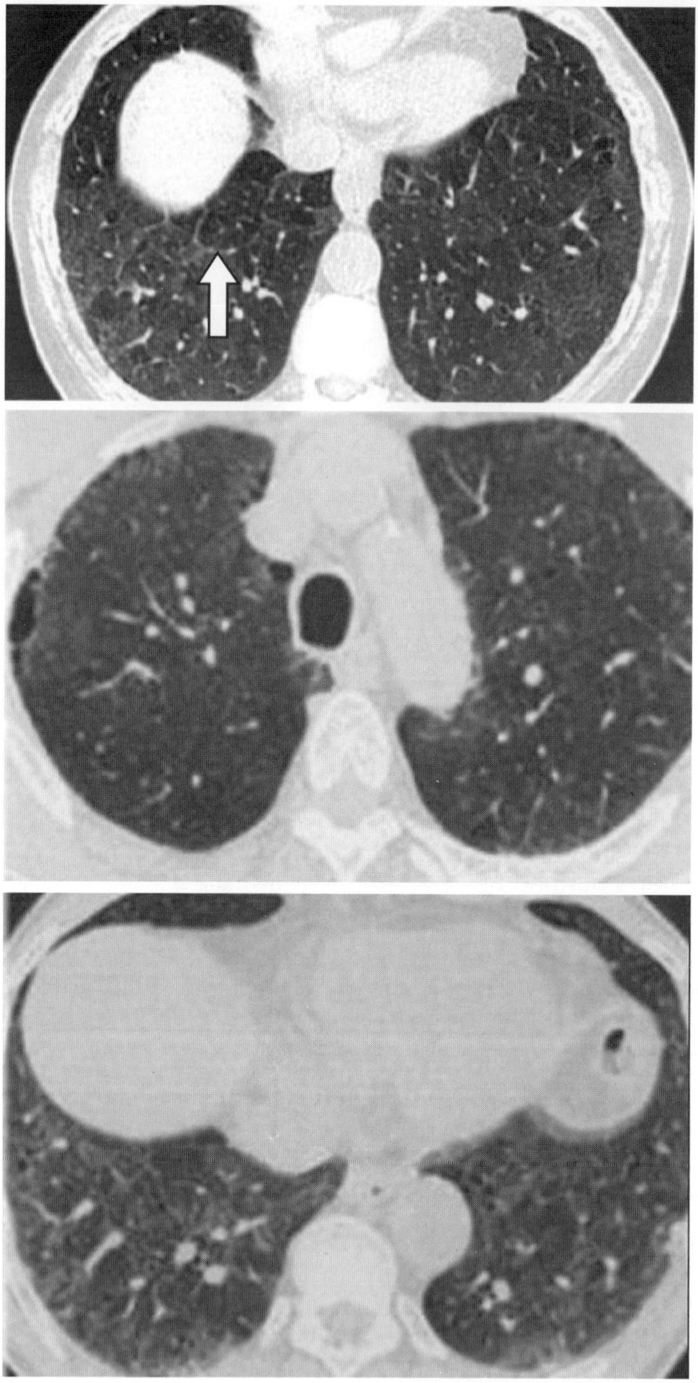

Chronic smoker presented with breathlessness
What is this?

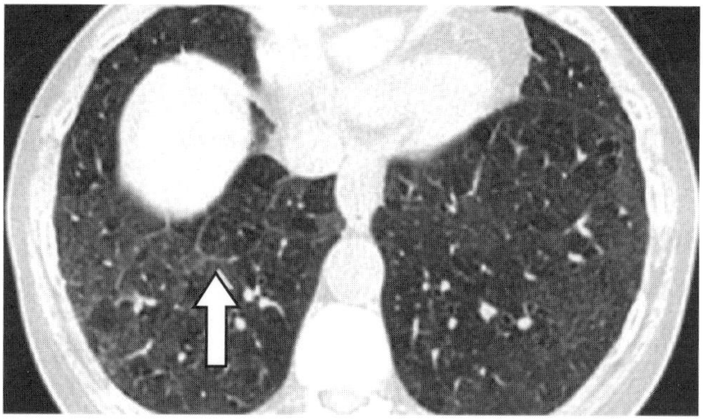

Ground glass opacification with thickened interlobular septa (arrow)

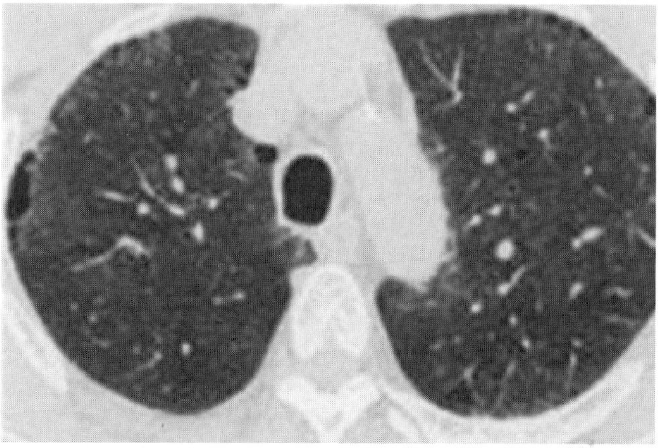

Ground glass opacification with paraseptal emphysema in the upper lobes

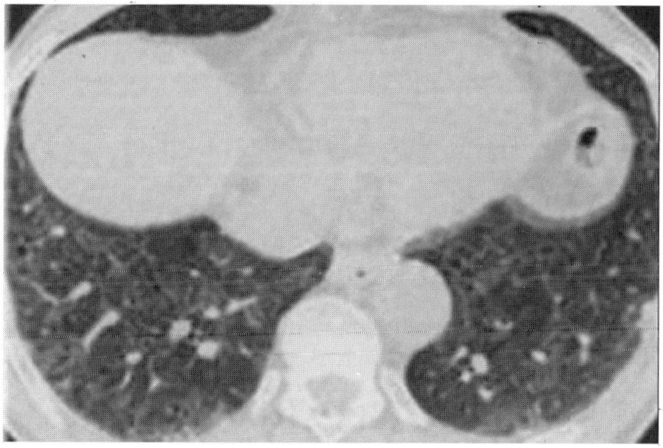

Multiple bilateral ground glass opacifications with some septal thickening

Diagnosis: Respiratory Bronchiolitis-associated Interstitial Lung Disease (RB-ILD)

RB-ILD is a treatable condition and has better prognosis if detected early. It is mandatory to stop smoking

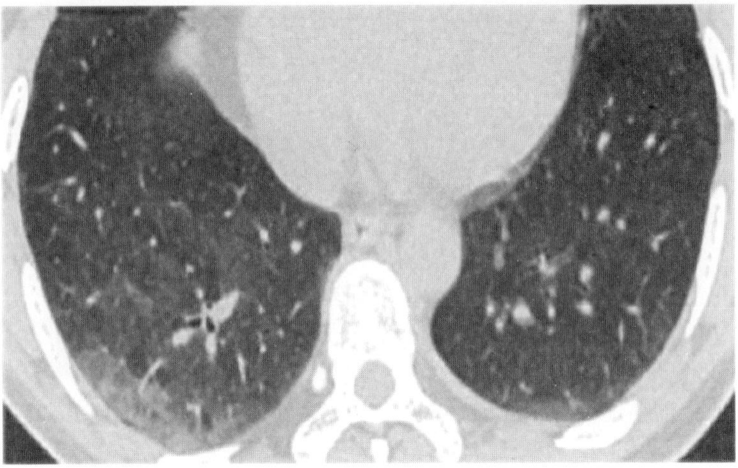

What is this?

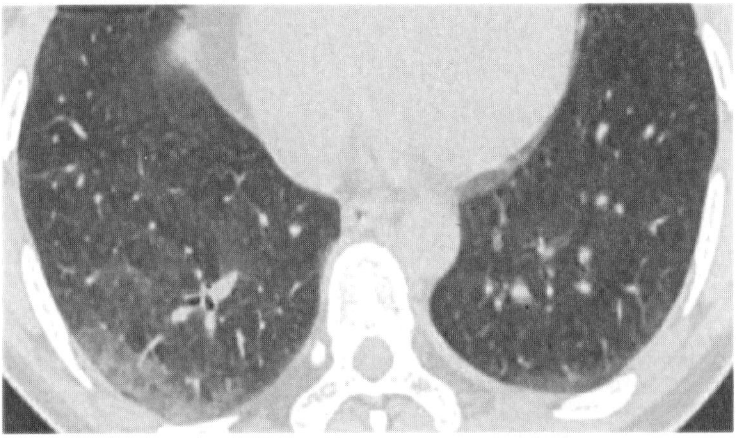

HRCT shows diffuse areas of ground-glass opacification in the lower lobes and some mosaic pattern as the sole abnormality

Diagnosis: Desquamative Interstitial Pneumonia (DIP)

Respiratory Bronchiolitis-associated Interstitial Lung Disease (RB-ILD), and Desquamative Interstitial Pneumonia (DIP)

- Respiratory bronchiolitis (RB), respiratory bronchiolitis-associated interstitial lung disease (RB-ILD), and desquamative interstitial pneumonia (DIP) represent different degrees of severity of small airway and parenchymal reaction to cigarette smoke
- All smokers have various degrees of respiratory bronchiolitis, but it is usually asymptomatic
- HRCT findings in RB-ILD: Centrilobular nodules of ground glass opacity with upper lobe predominance, bronchial wall thickening and secondary lobule with decreased attenuation (air trapping)

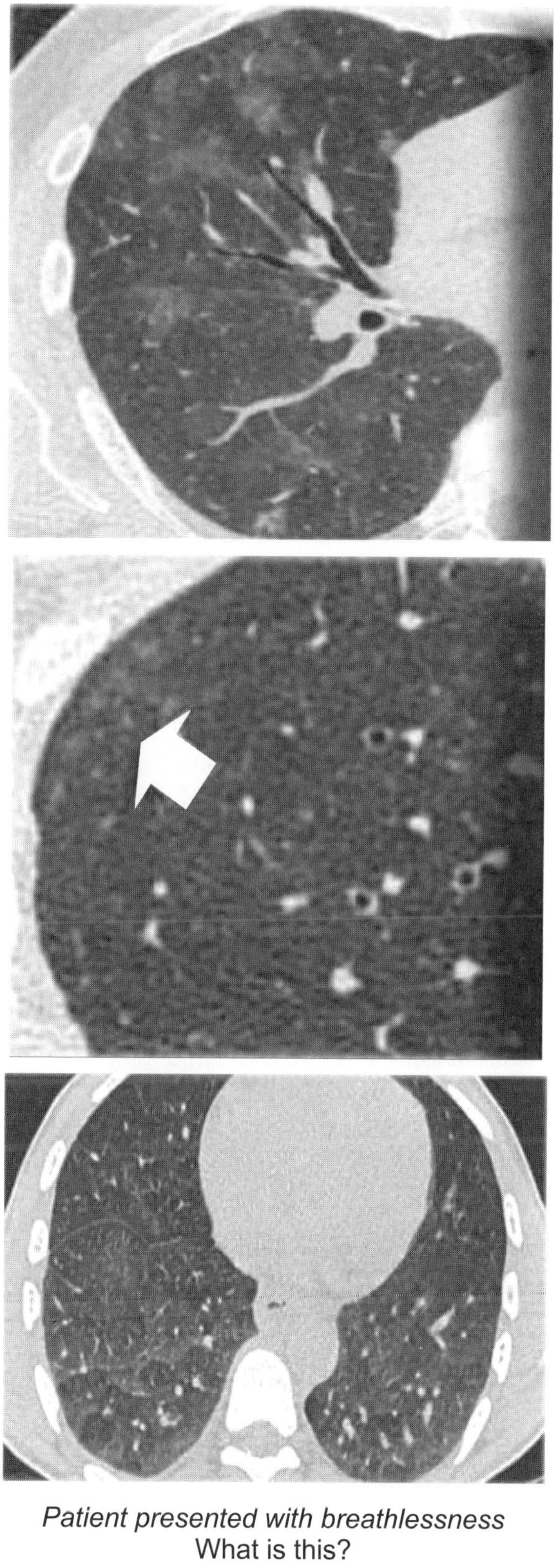

Patient presented with breathlessness
What is this?

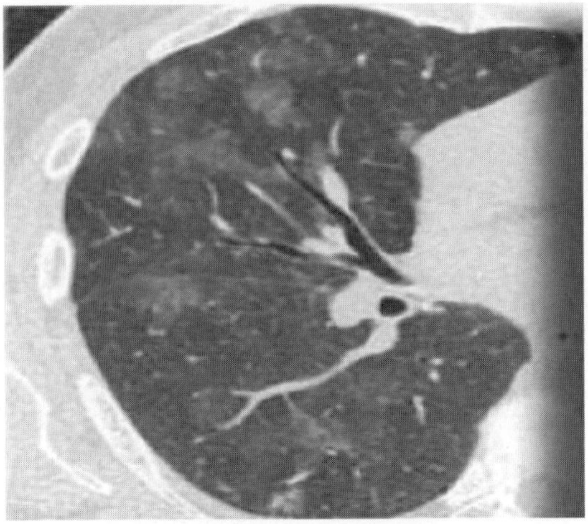

HRCT shows lobular areas of ground glass attenuation
Acute hypersensitivity pneumonitis

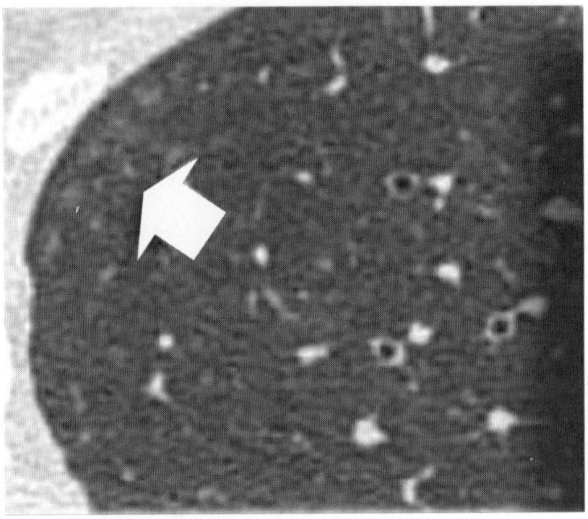

HRCT shows ill-defined centrilobular nodules

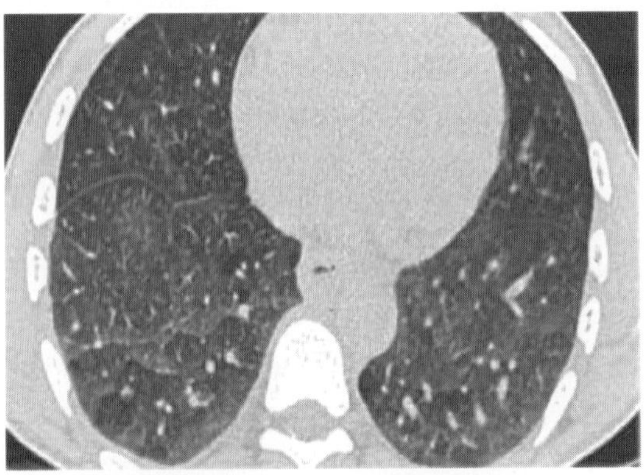

HRCT shows ill-defined centrilobular nodules with mosaic pattern
Subacute hypersensitivity pneumonitis

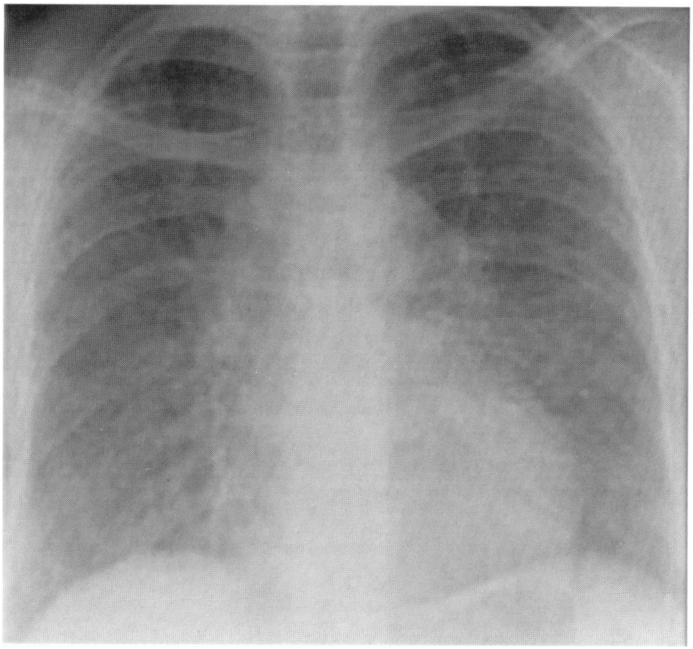

Patient presented with breathlessness
What is this?

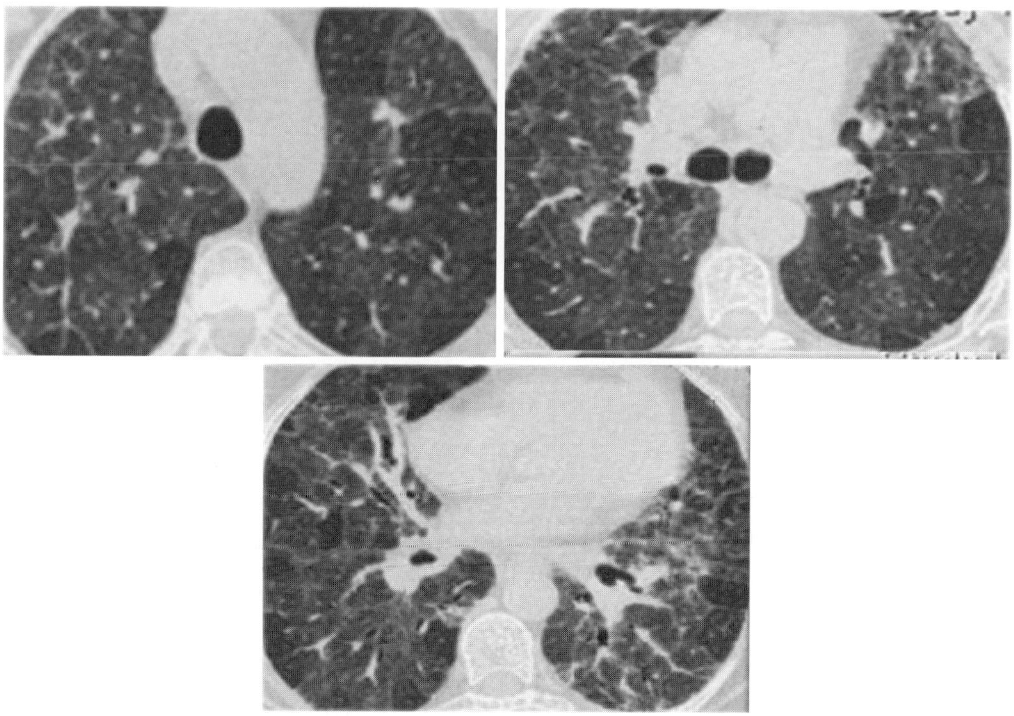

HRCT thorax at different levels

Diagnosis: Chronic Hypersensitivity Pneumonitis

Hypersensitivity Pneumonitis

- Hypersensitivity pneumonitis (HP) is also known as extrinsic allergic alveolitis (EAA)
- The radiographic and pathologic abnormalities in patients can be classified into acute, sub-acute, and chronic stages. Recently hypersensitivity pneumonitis is classified as fibrotic or nonfibrotic based on presence or absence of fibrosis on high resolution CT thorax
- Mostly HRCT is performed in the sub-acute stage of HP, weeks to months following the first exposure to the antigen or in the chronic phase
- HRCT shows a mosaic pattern with hyperaerated secondary nodules of increased attenuation, additionally there is a septal and interlobular reticular thickening, indicating already existing irreversible fibrosis

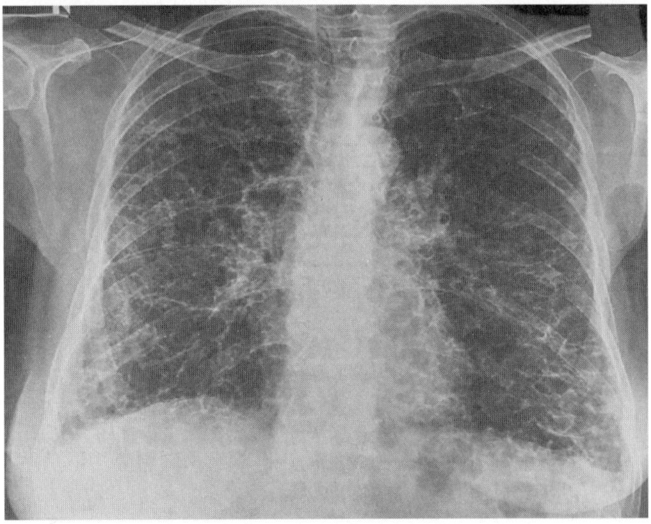

A 50-year-old female presented with breathlessness
What is this?

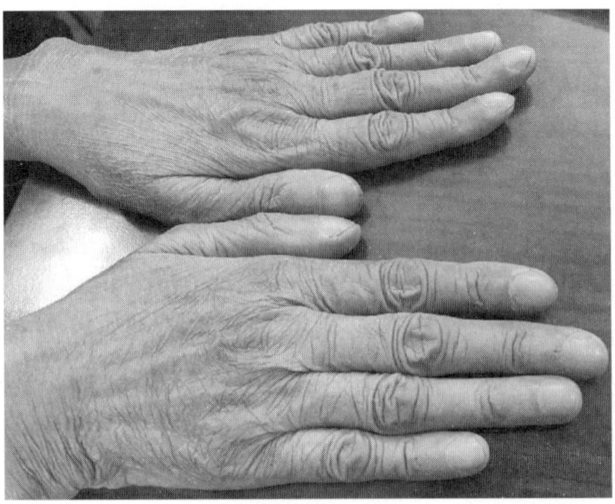

Clubbing

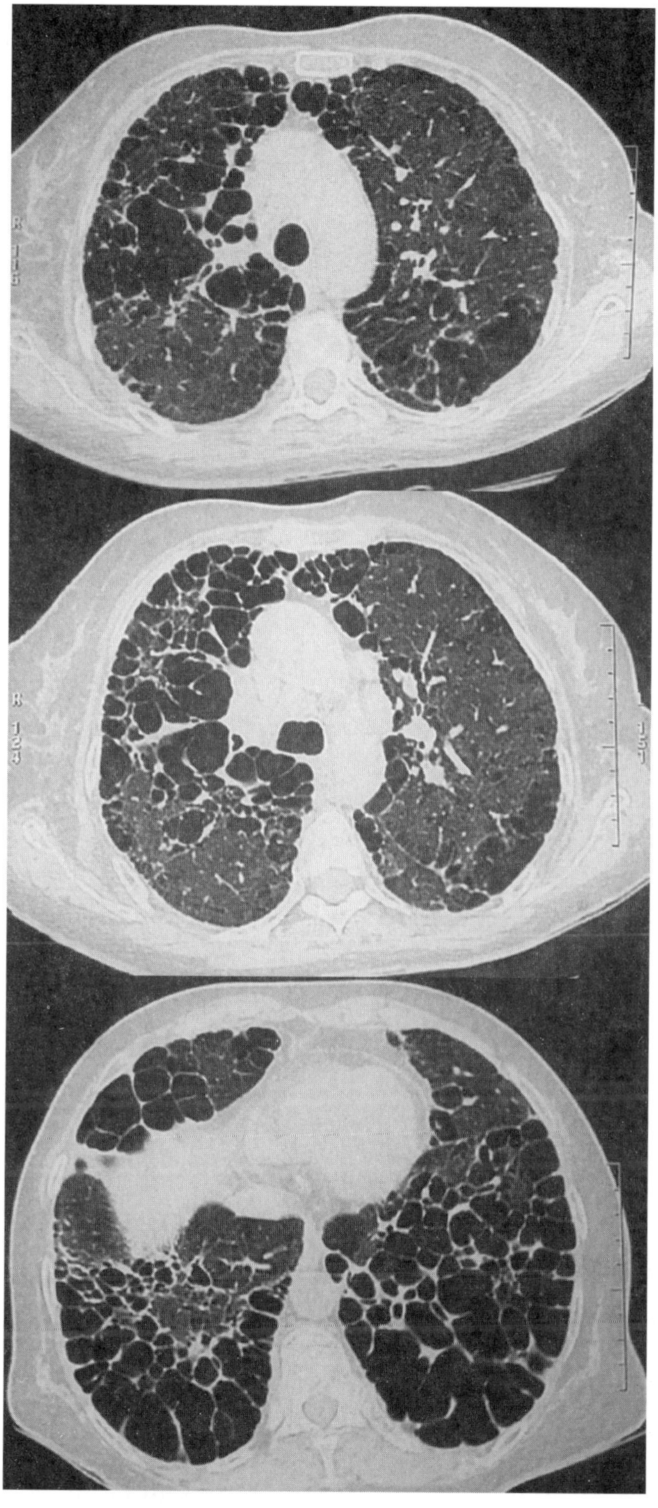

HRCT thorax at different level showing numerous thin-walled cysts

Diagnosis: Lymphangioleiomyomatosis (LAM)

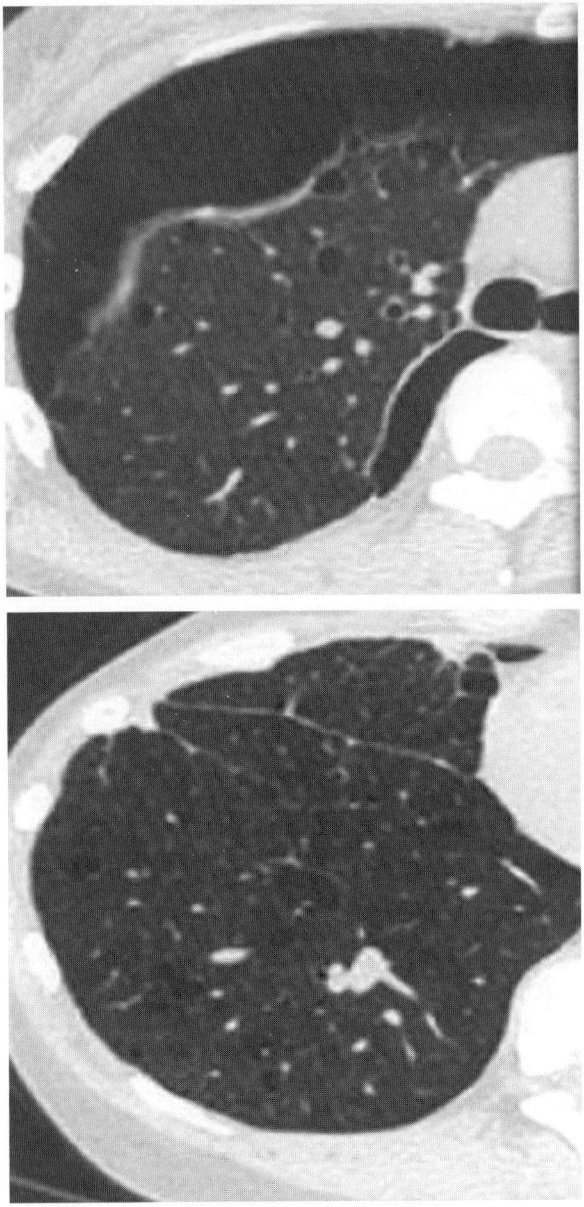

Multiple evenly spread thin-walled cysts complicated by a pneumothorax

Diagnosis: Lymphangioleiomyomatosis (LAM)

Lymphangioleiomyomatosis (LAM)

- Rare disease, that occurs only in premenopausal women
- Numerous thin-walled cysts, surrounded by normal parenchyma
- Cysts range from 2 mm to 5 cm in diameter, are round in shape and more or less uniform
- Cysts are distributed diffusely throughout the lungs and upper and lower lobes are involved to a similar degree

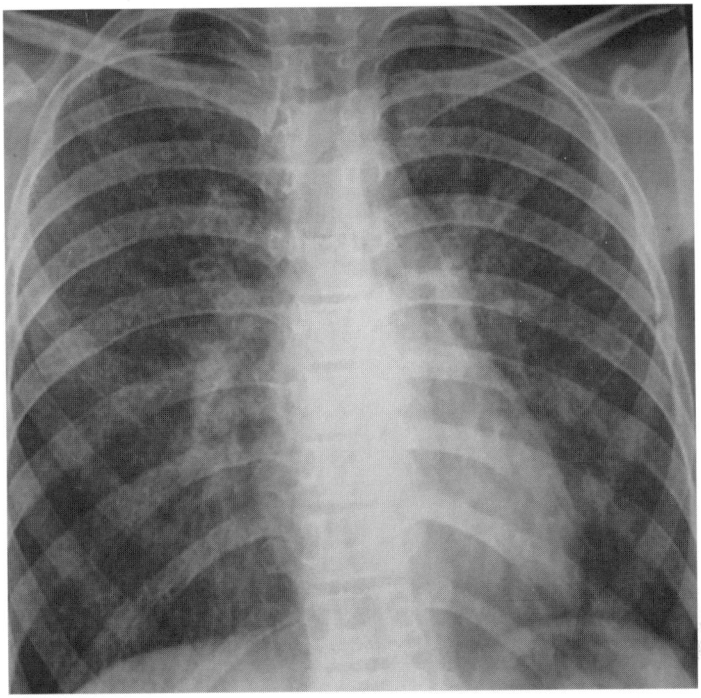

A 15-year-old male, nonsmoker, nonalcoholic, came with cough since 10 years and shortness of breath since 3 years with history of antitubercular treatment two years back without improvement. Grade IV clubbing with bilateral end inspiratory crepts

What is this?

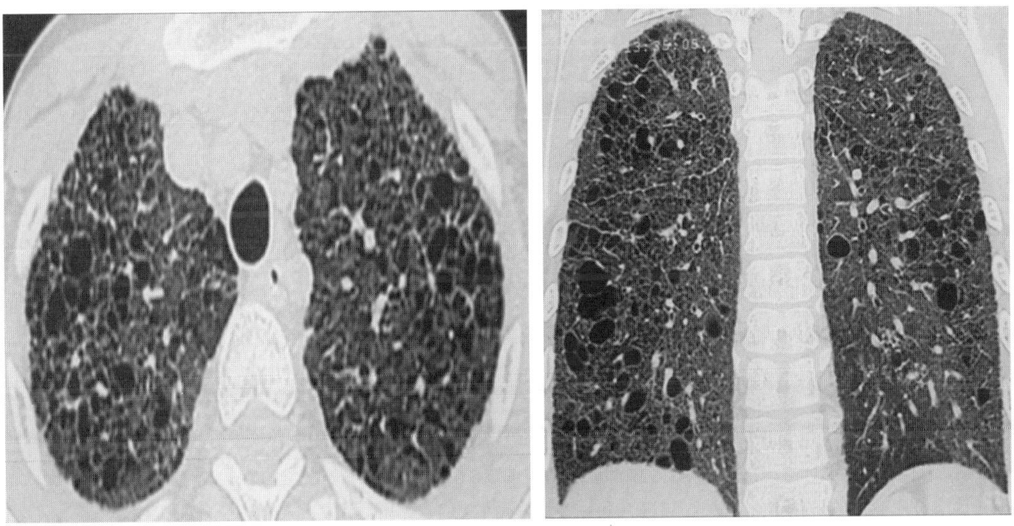

HRCT thorax showing cystic air spaces with bizarre shapes

Diagnosis: Pulmonary Langerhans Cell Histiocytosis (PLCH)

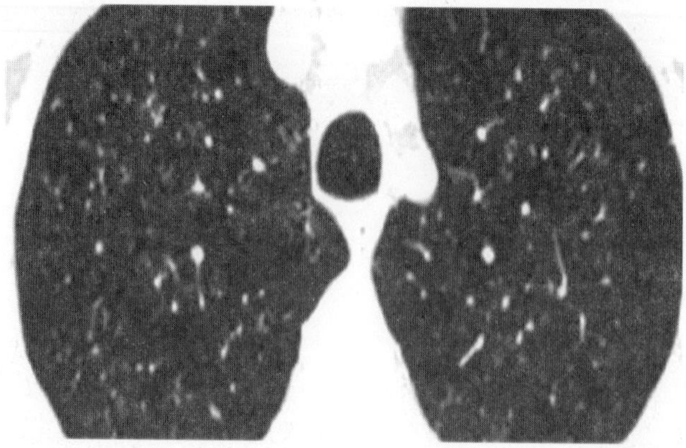

Early stage Langerhans cell histiocytosis with small nodules

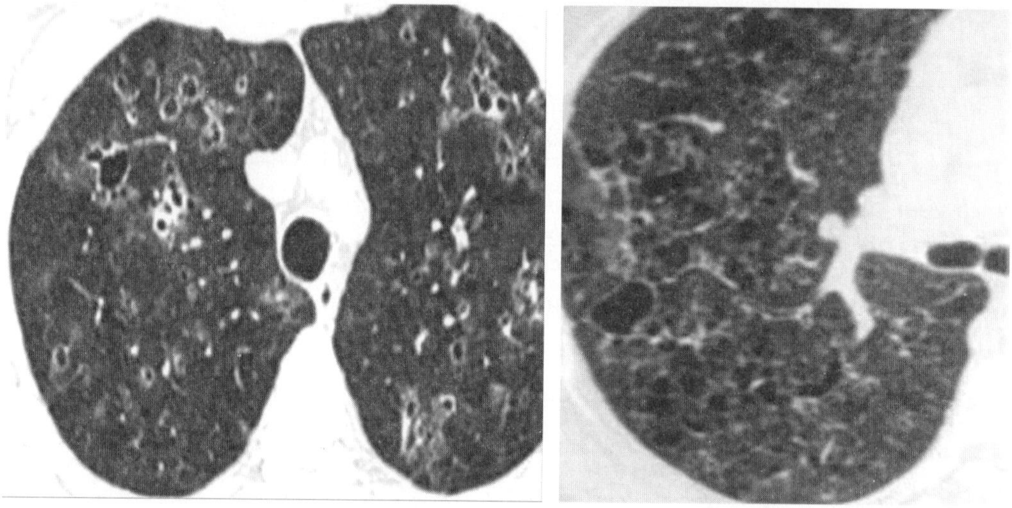

Late stage Langerhans' cell histiocytosis.
Cysts progress to typical bizarre-shaped cysts

Diagnosis: Pulmonary Langerhans Cell Histiocytosis (PLCH)

Pulmonary Langerhans Cell Histiocytosis (PLCH)

Also known as pulmonary histiocytosis X or eosinophilic granuloma

HRCT findings

- Early stage: Small irregular or stellate nodules in centrilobular location
- Late stage (more commonly seen): Cystic airspaces cysts have bizarre shapes, they may coalesce and then become larger, upper and midlobe predominance and recurrent pneumothorax

CHAPTER

18

Radiology of Sarcoidosis

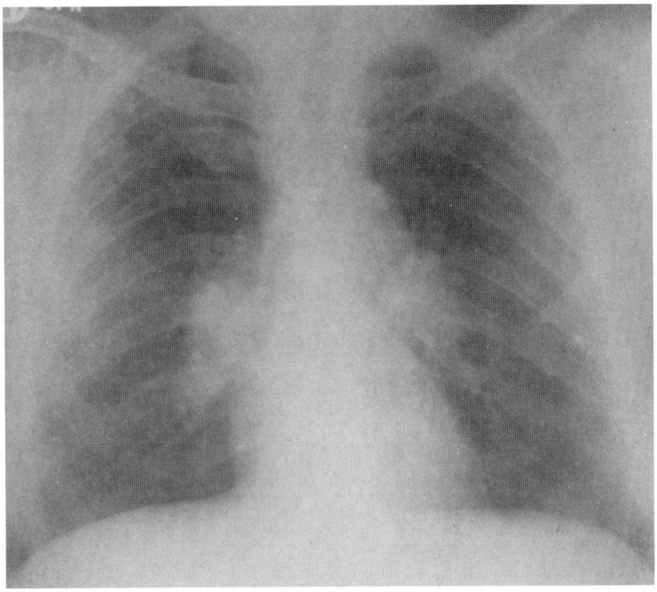

What is this?

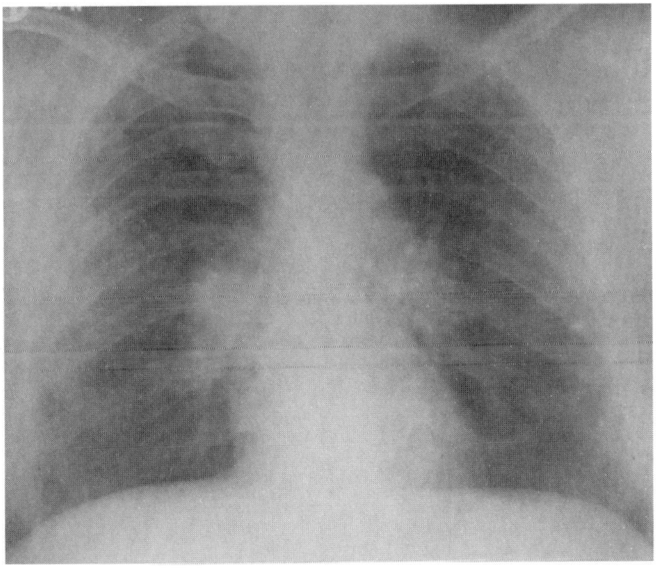

Bilateral hilar lymph node enlargement cause sarcoidosis stage 1

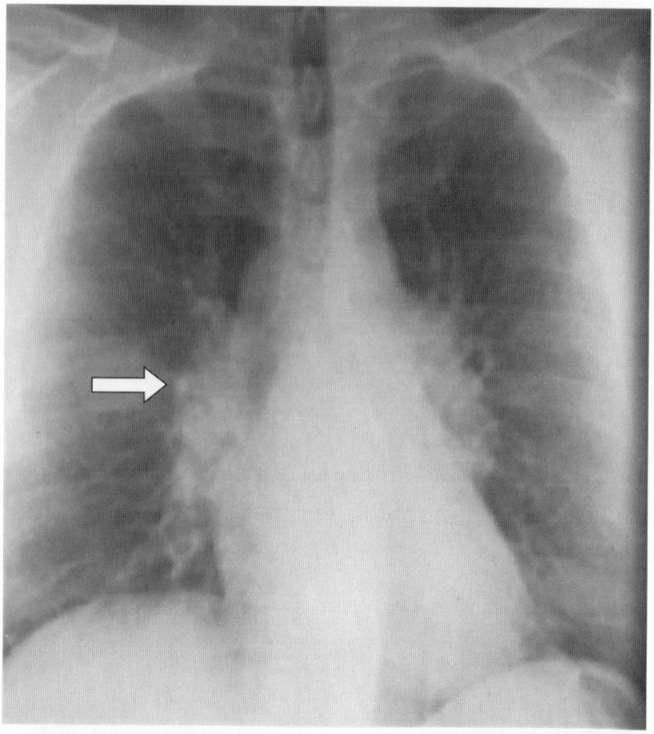

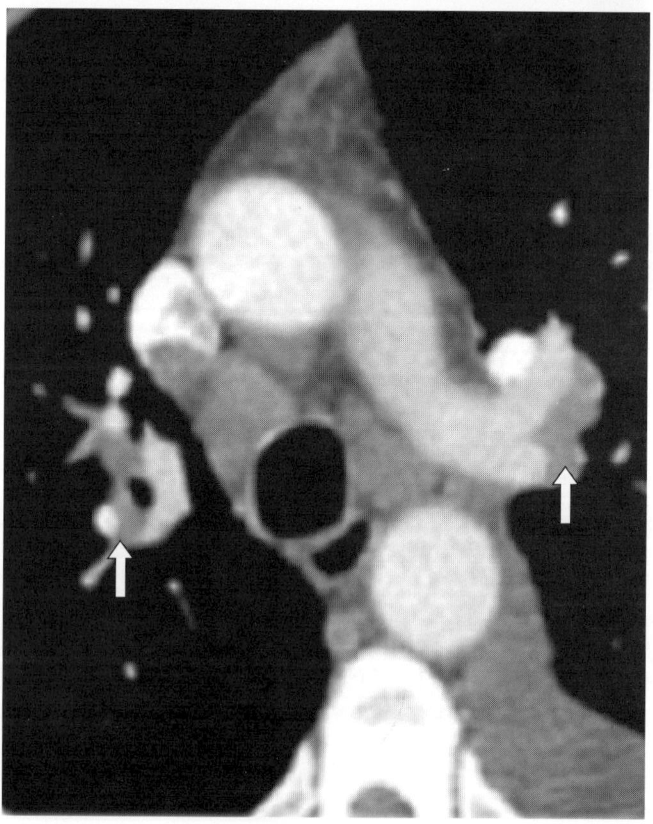

What is this?

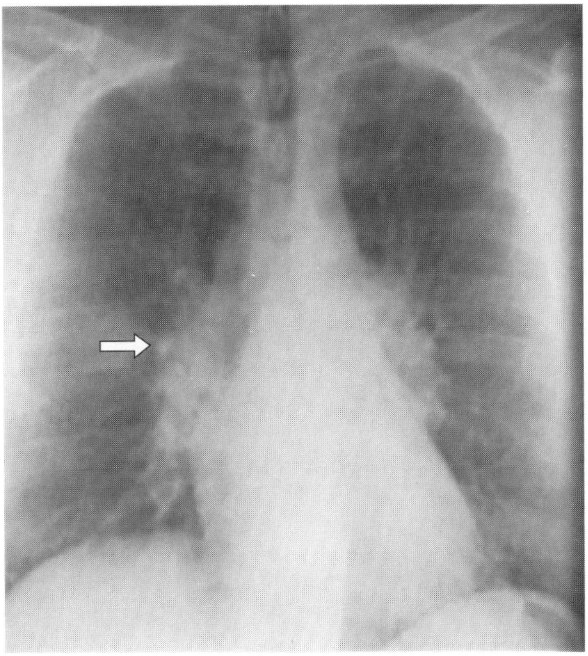

Left and right hilar adenopathy

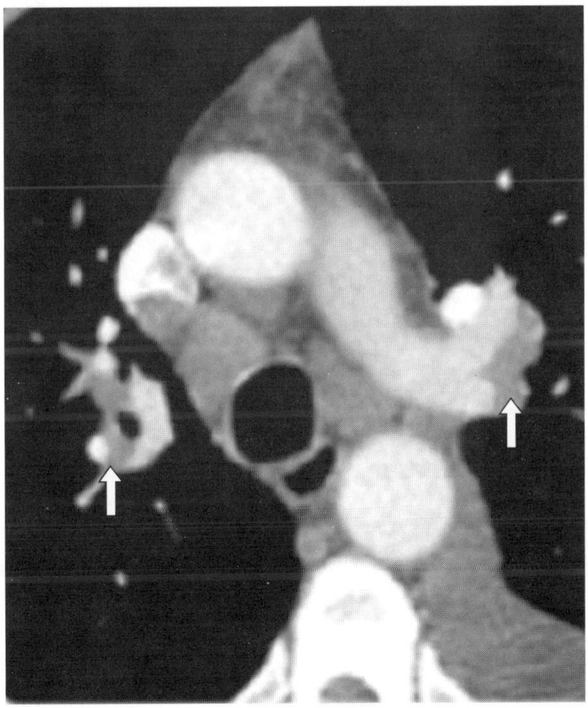

Left and right hilar and paratracheal adenopathy (1-2-3 sign)

Diagnosis: Sarcoidosis Stage I

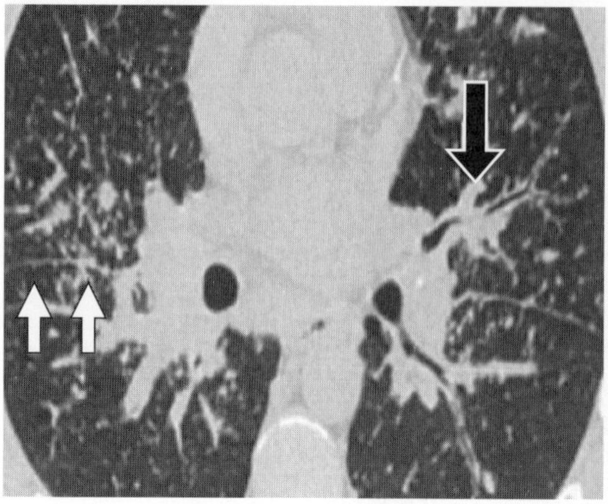

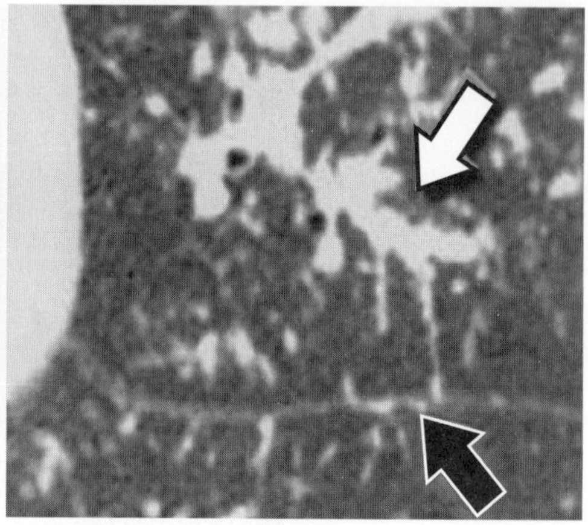

What is this?

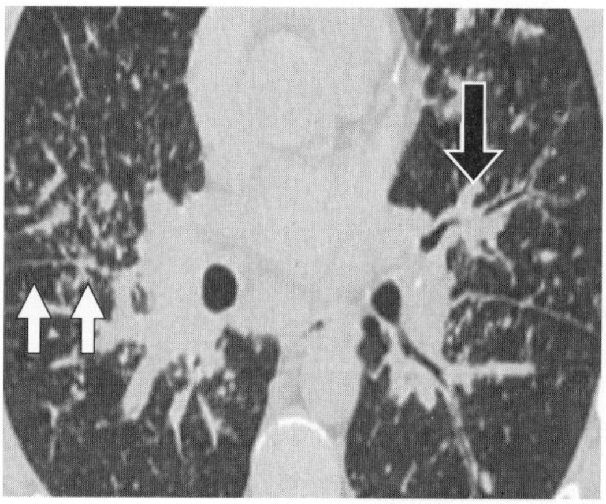

CT picture shows nodules along the bronchovascular bundle and fissures

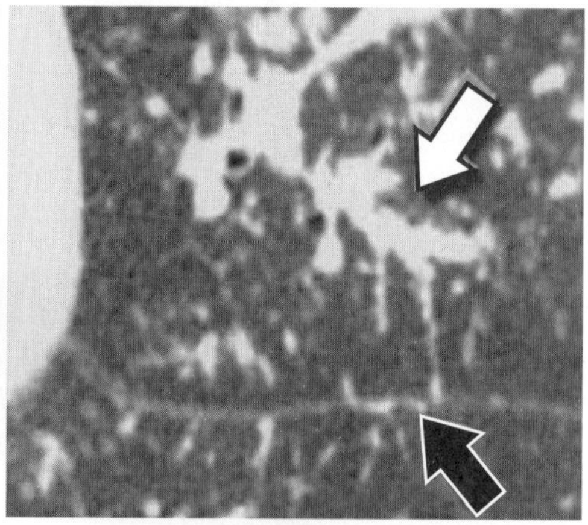

HRCT shows nodules along bronchovascular bundle (white arrow) and fissures (black arrow), this is the typical perilymphatic distribution of the nodules

Diagnosis: Sarcoidosis Stage III

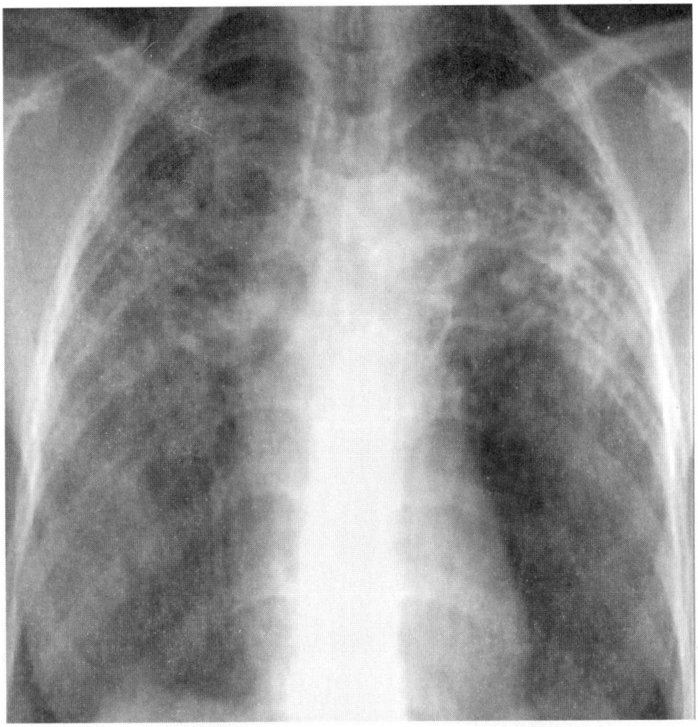

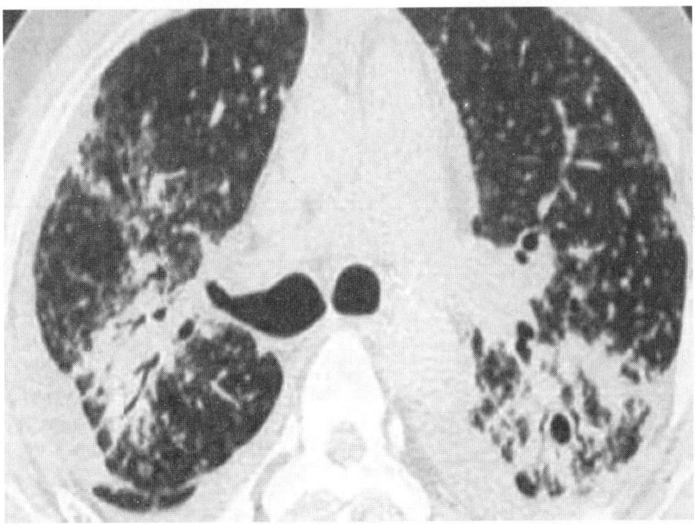

What is this?

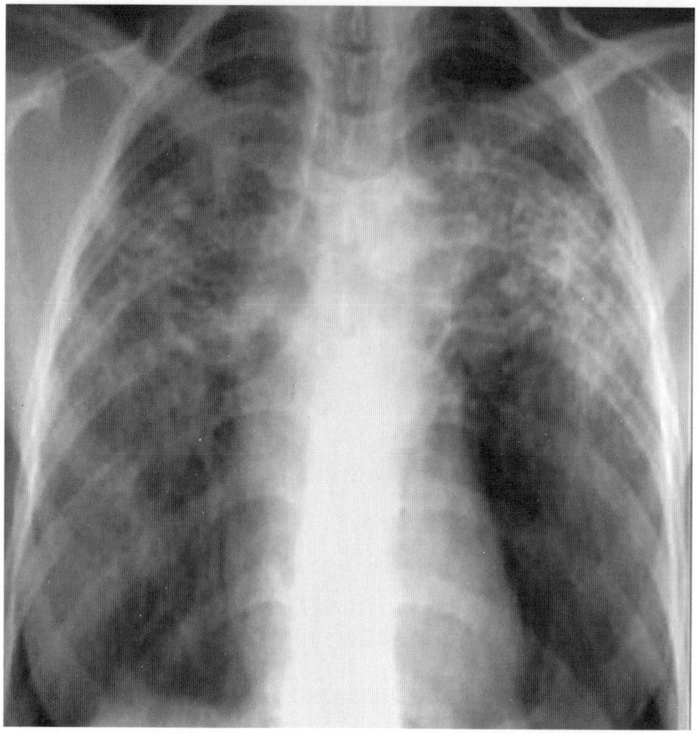

Long standing sarcoidosis with fibrosis in upper zones

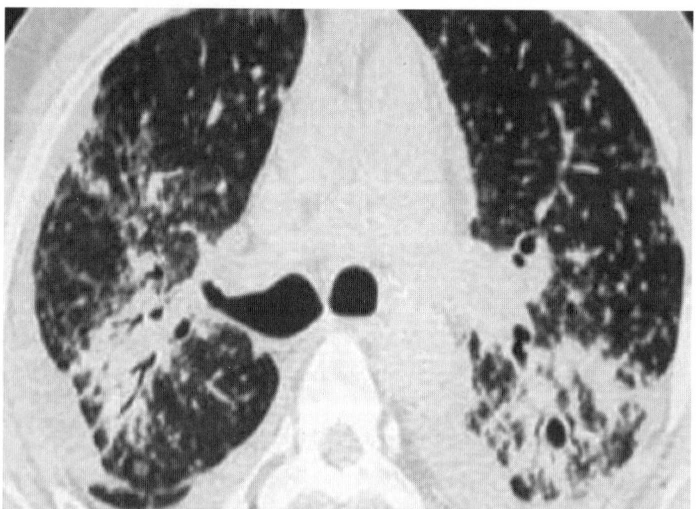

CT shows conglomerate masses of fibrosis in posterior part of lungs with multiple small well-defined nodules with subpleural distribution

Diagnosis: Sarcoidosis with Fibrosis Stage IV

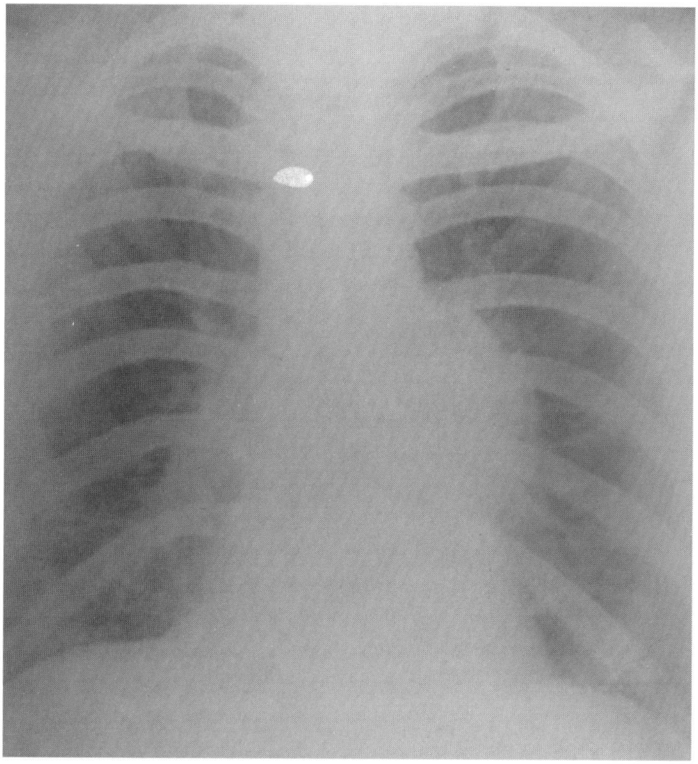

What is this?

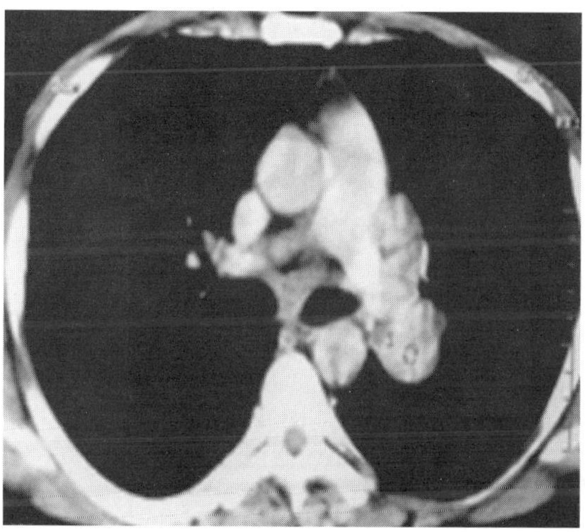

CT thorax left hilar lymphadenopathy

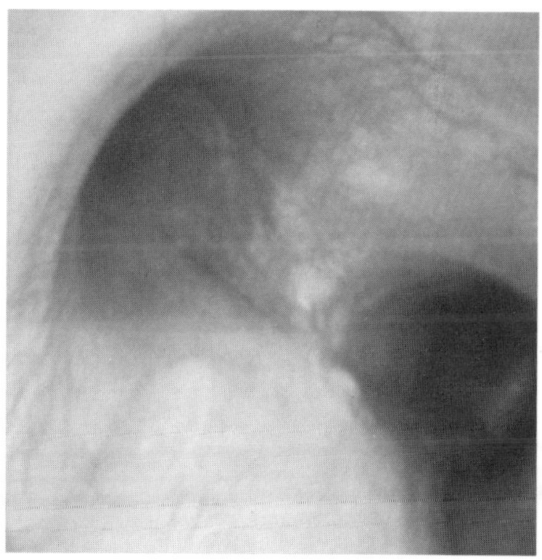

Fiberoptic bronchoscopy shows multiple nodules at lower end of trachea and main carina (Colour Plate IV)

Diagnosis: Sarcoidosis Stage II

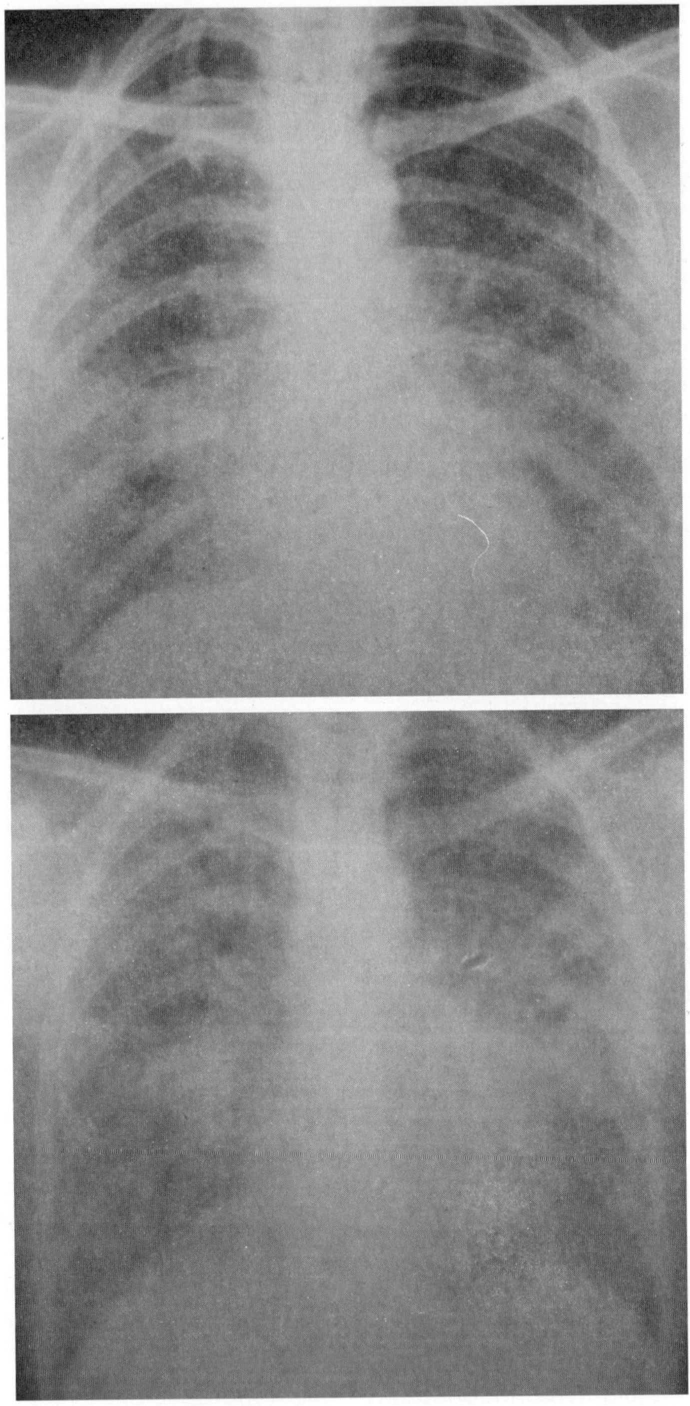

A 38-year-old female presented with dry cough—1 year, breathlessness—10 months, PPD and sputum for AFB negative. 5 years back patient had supraclavicular lymph node, histopathology showed epitheloid granuloma with caseous necrosis, had antitubercular treatment for 8 months with good response patient received antitubercular treatment again for 10 months with no response

What is this?

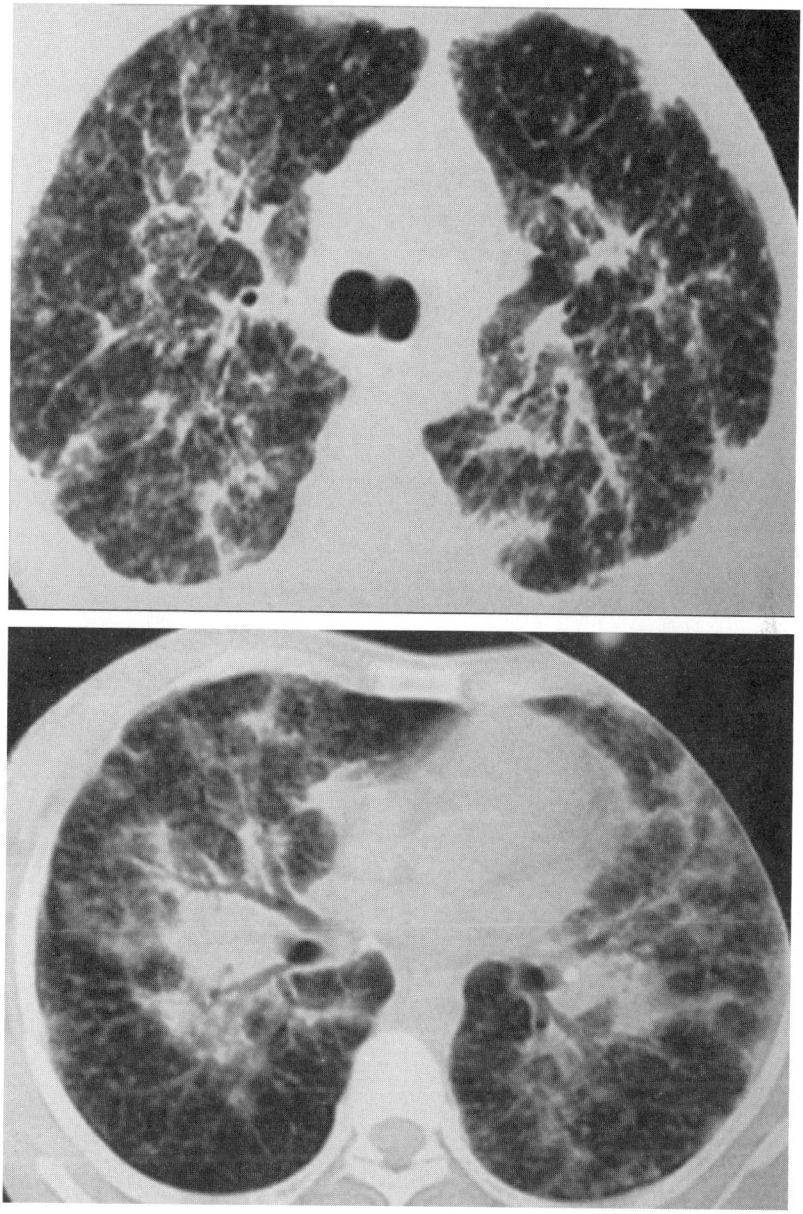

HRCT thorax
Serum ACE-144 IU/L transbronchial lung biopsy (TBLB) showed evidence of epitheloid ganuloma without caseous necrosis

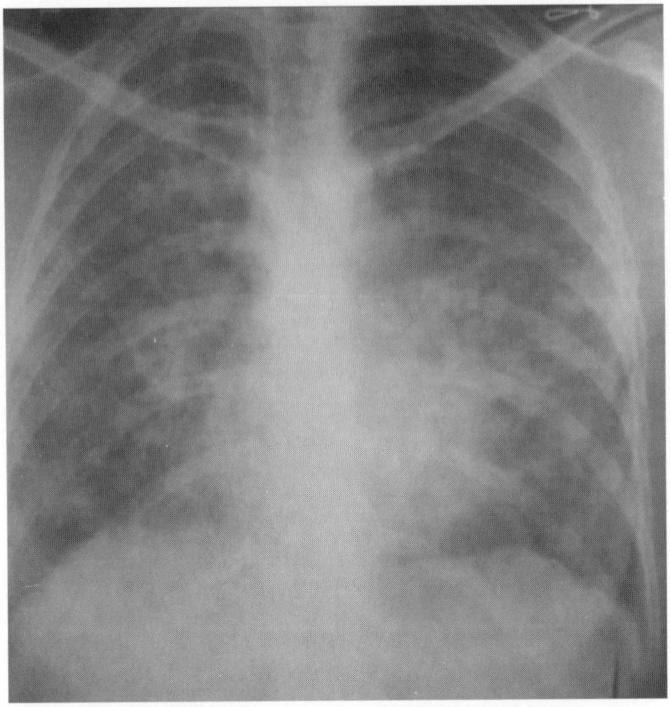

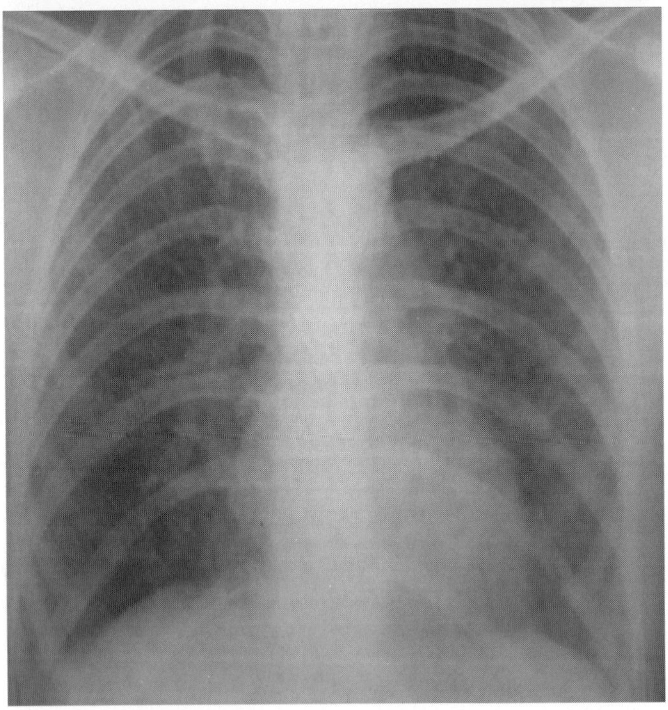

Clinical and radiological improvement after 6 months of steroid treatment

Diagnosis: Sarcoidosis Stage III

Please note that this was a rare case in which tuberculosis and sarcoidosis diagnosed in same patient at different time

CHAPTER

19

Radiology of Covid-19

CO-RADS Classification

Based on the CT findings, level of suspicion of Covid-19 infection is graded from very low or CO-RADS 1 to very high or CO-RADS 5 and severity and stage of disease is determined with remarks on comorbidity and a differential diagnosis

CO-RADS Level of suspicion Covid-19 infection		
		CT findings
CO-RADS 1	No	Normal or non-infectious abnormalities
CO-RADS 2	Low	Abnormalities consistent with infections other than Covid-19
CO-RADS 3	Indeterminate	Unclear whether Covid-19 is present
CO-RADS 4	High	Abnormalities suspicious for Covid-19
CO-RADS 5	Very high	Typical Covid-19
CO-RADS 6	PCR +	

Covid-19	
Typical findings	**Atypical findings**
Multifocal ground glass opacities	Central or peribronchovascular
Peripheral and basal distribution	More apical distribution
Unsharp demarcation	Lymphadenopathy
Vascular thickening	
Round shadow	**Very atypical findings**
Crazy paving	Cavitation, calcification
Ground glass and consolidations reversed halo sign	Tree-in-bud, bronchiolitis
Spider web	Nodular pattern
	Mass
	Pleural thickening

CO-RADS 1

- Covid-19 is highly unlikely
- CT is normal or there are findings that indicate non-infectious disease like congestive heart failure, sarcoid, histoplasmosis, malignancy, ILD

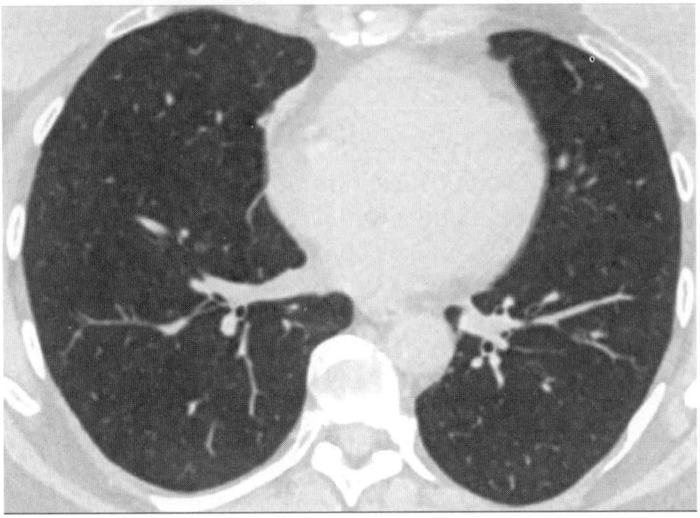

HRCT thorax showing nonspecific finding

CO-RADS 2

- Level of suspicion of Covid-19 infection is low
- Findings consistent with other infections like typical bronchiolitis with tree-in-bud and thickened bronchus walls
- No typical signs of Covid-19

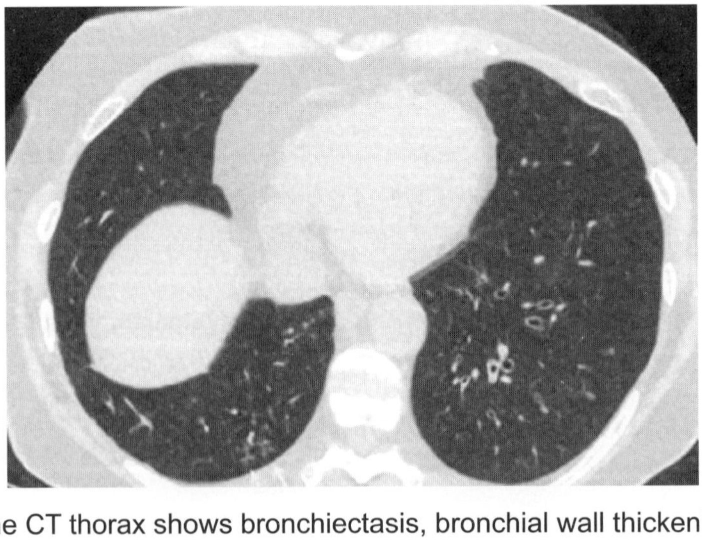

The CT thorax shows bronchiectasis, bronchial wall thickening and tree-in-bud, there are no ground glass opacities

CO-RADS 2

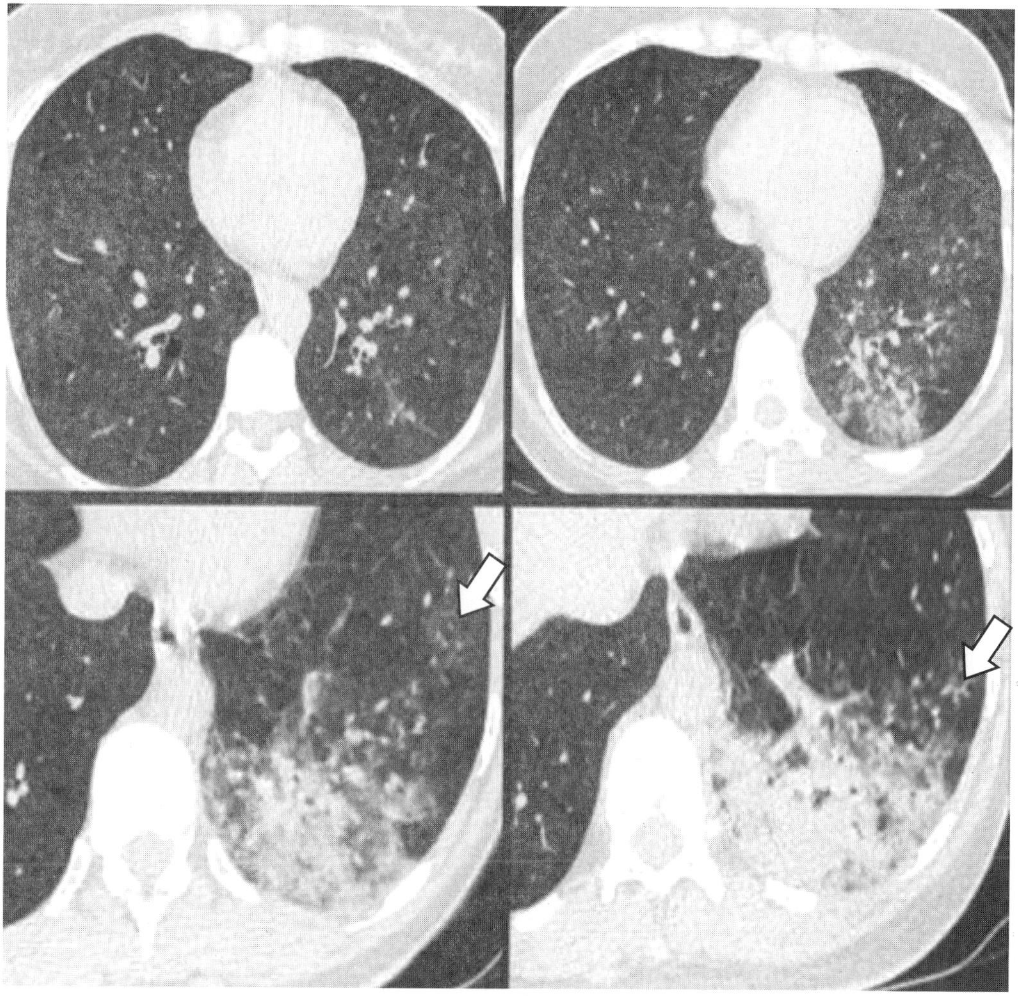

CT thorax shows lobar consolidation and tree-in-bud consistent with a bacterial infection, Covid-19 unlikely

CO-RADS 3

- Covid-19 unsure or indeterminate
- CT abnormalities indicating infection, but unsure whether Covid-19 is involved, like widespread bronchopneumonia, lobar pneumonia, septic emboli with ground glass opacities

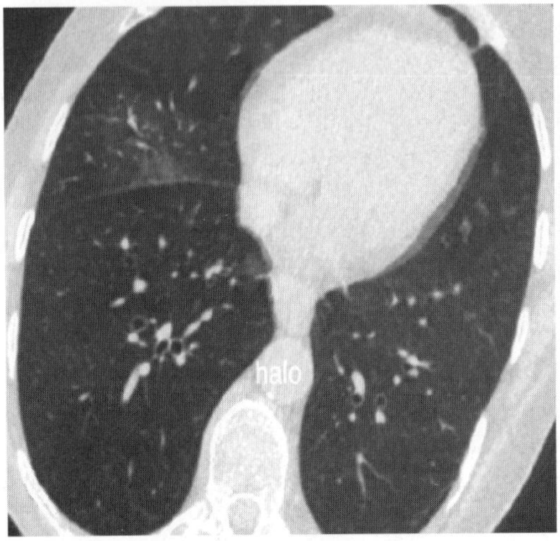

One day complaints
CT: Unifocal ground glass opacities
PCR negative

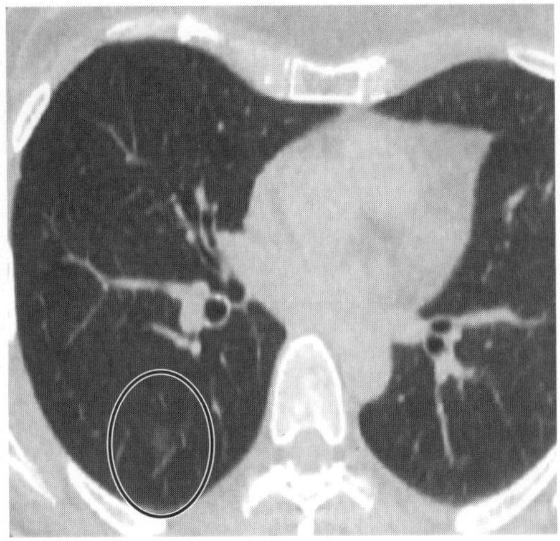

CT: Unifocal ground glass opacities

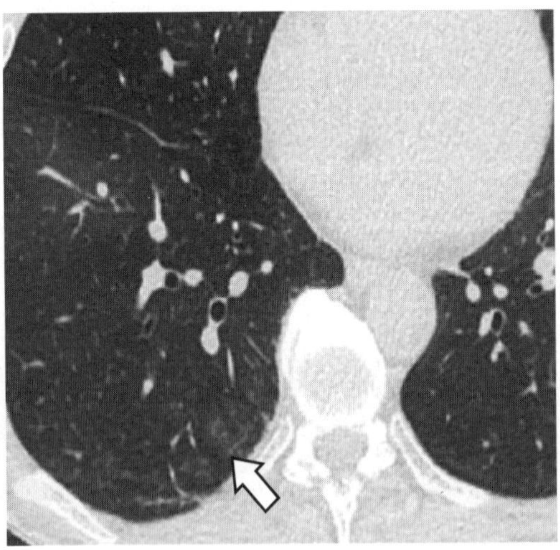

CT: Unifocal ground glass opacities

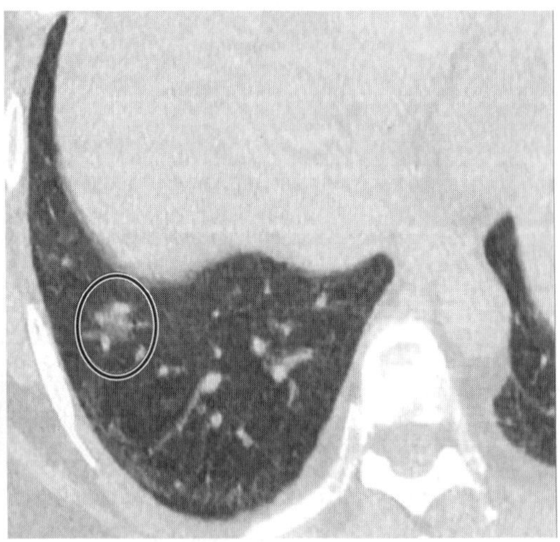

CT: Unifocal ground glass opacities

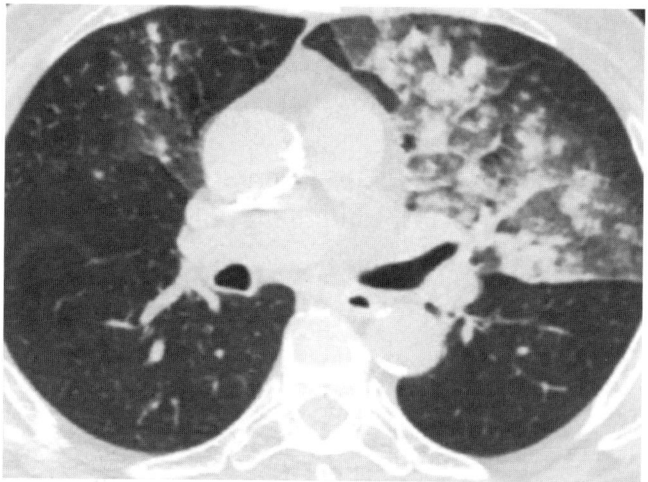

HRCT shows multifocal consolidations with surrounding ground glass opacities. Covid-19 PCR negative

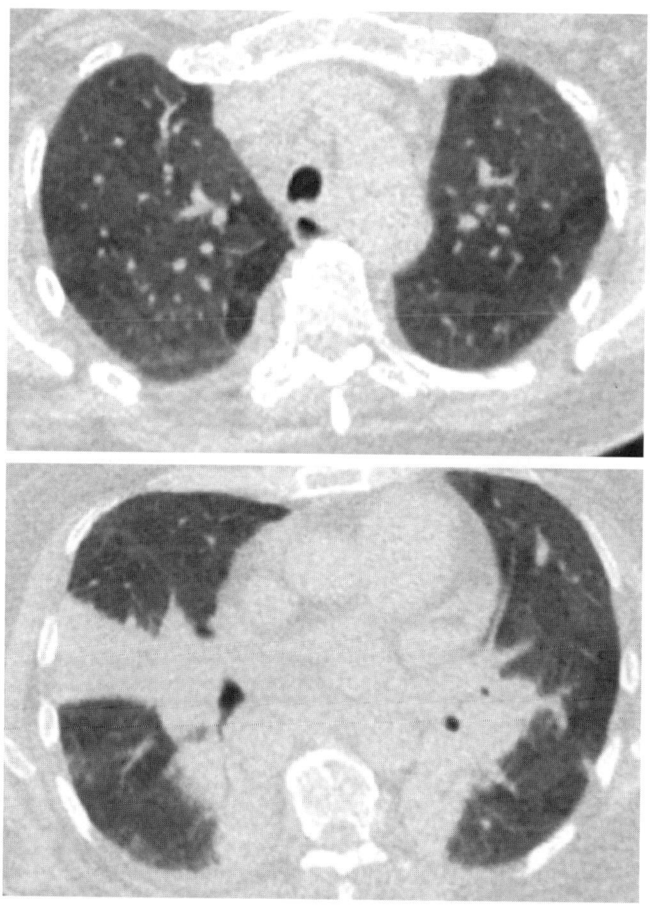

HRCT shows bilateral central consolidations with diffuse ground glass opacities Covid-19 PCR negative and influenza A positive

CO-RADS 4

- In CO-RADS 4 level of suspicion is high
- Mostly these are suspicious CT findings but not extremely typical
- Unilateral ground glass
- Multifocal consolidations without any other typical finding
- Findings suspicious of Covid-19 in underlying pulmonary disease

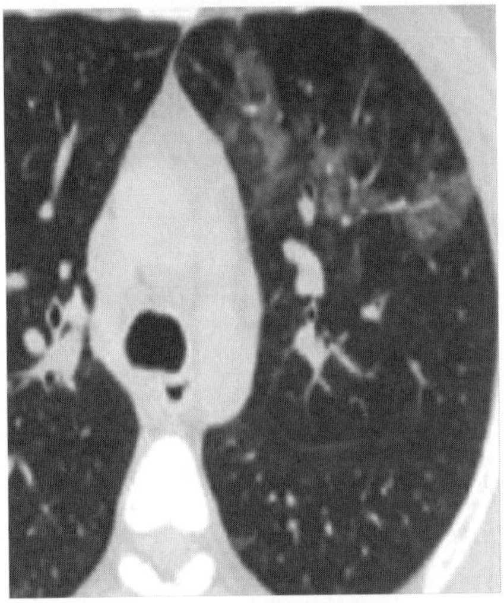

CT shows unilateral areas of ground glass opacities in left upper lobe, PCR positive

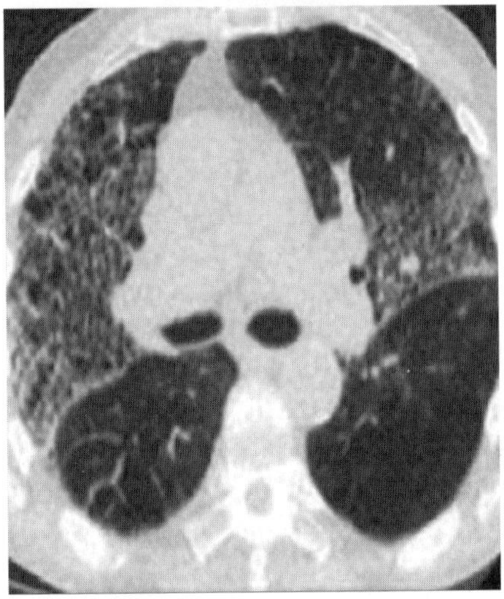

CT shows bilateral ground glass opacities in a patient with emphysema

CO-RADS 5

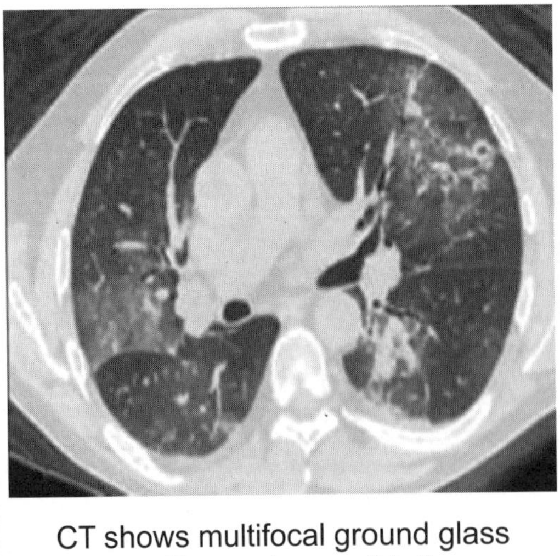

CT shows multifocal ground glass opacities and consolidation

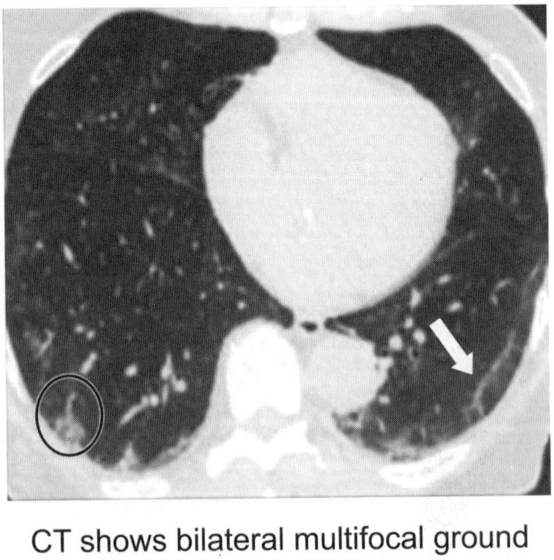

CT shows bilateral multifocal ground glass opacities, vascular thickening, subpleural bands, Covid PCR positive

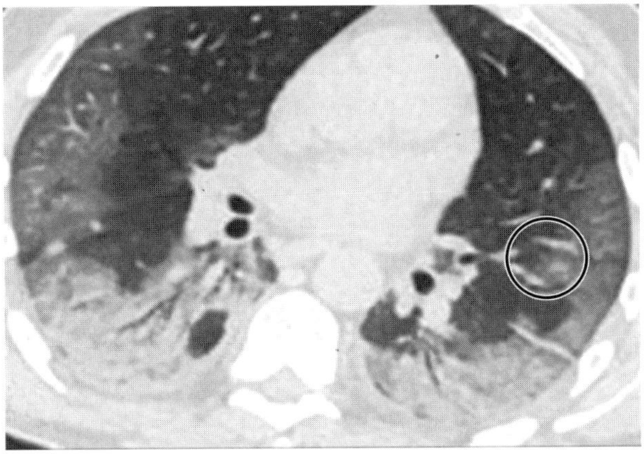

CT shows bilateral ground glass opacities and consolidation, basal preference, vascular thickening (circle), Covid-19 PCR positive

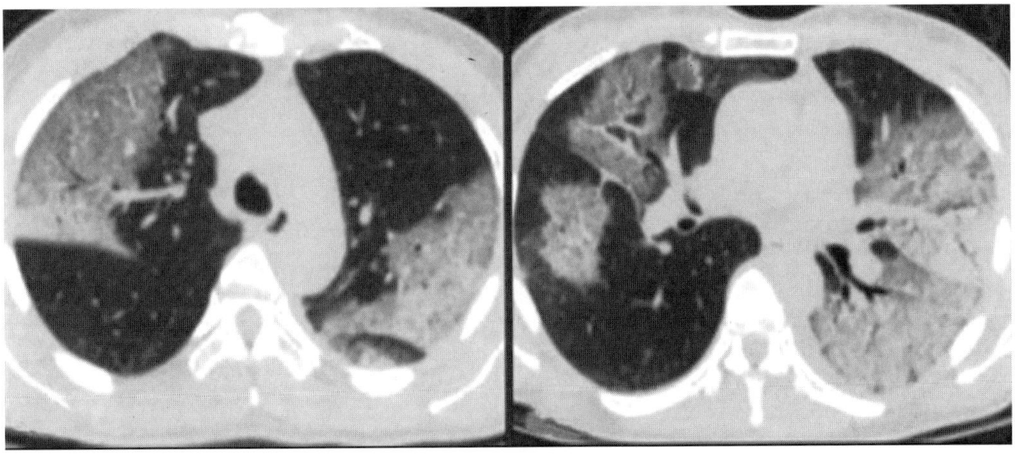

CT shows multifocal areas of ground glass and consolidation

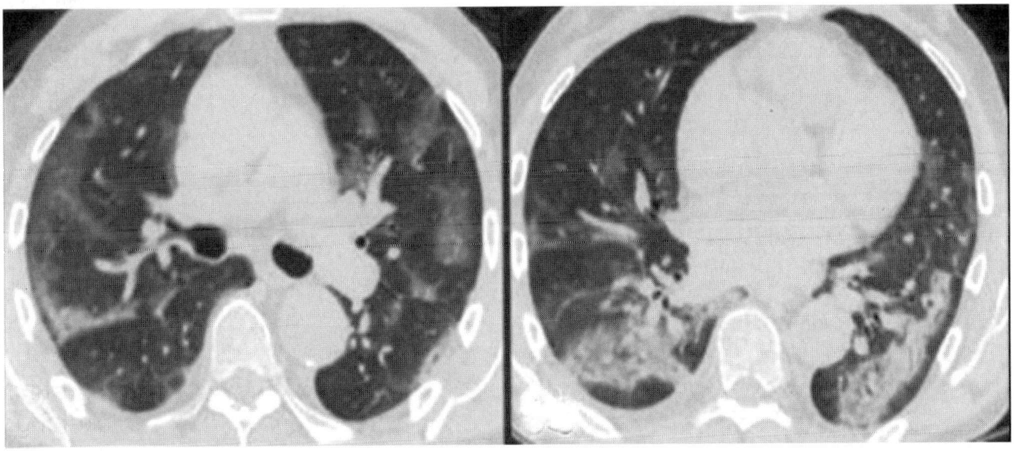

CT shows multifocal areas of ground glass and consolidation

CO-RADS 6

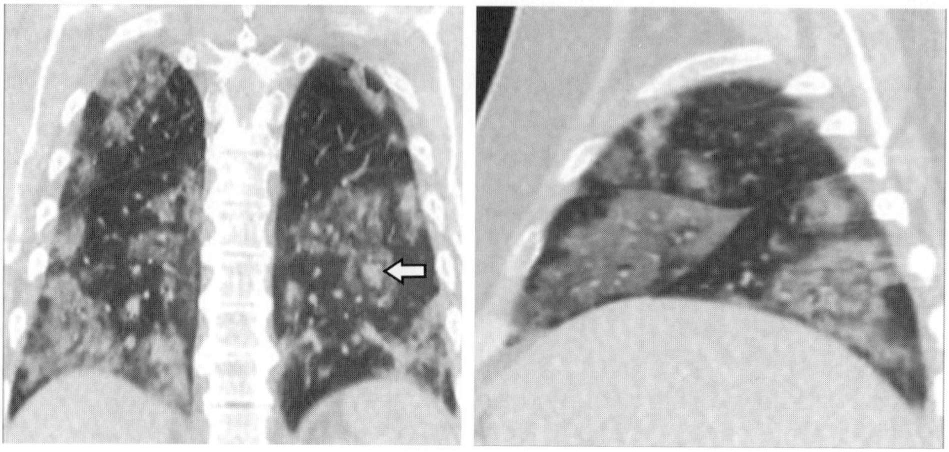

CT shows bilateral ground glass opacities with halo sign

CT Changes Over Time

Stage	Time	CT changes
Early	0 to 4 days	GGO Partial crazy paving
Progressive	5 to 8 days	Extension of GGO Increased crazy paving
Peak	10 to 13 days	Consolidation
Absorption	>14 days	Gradual resolution

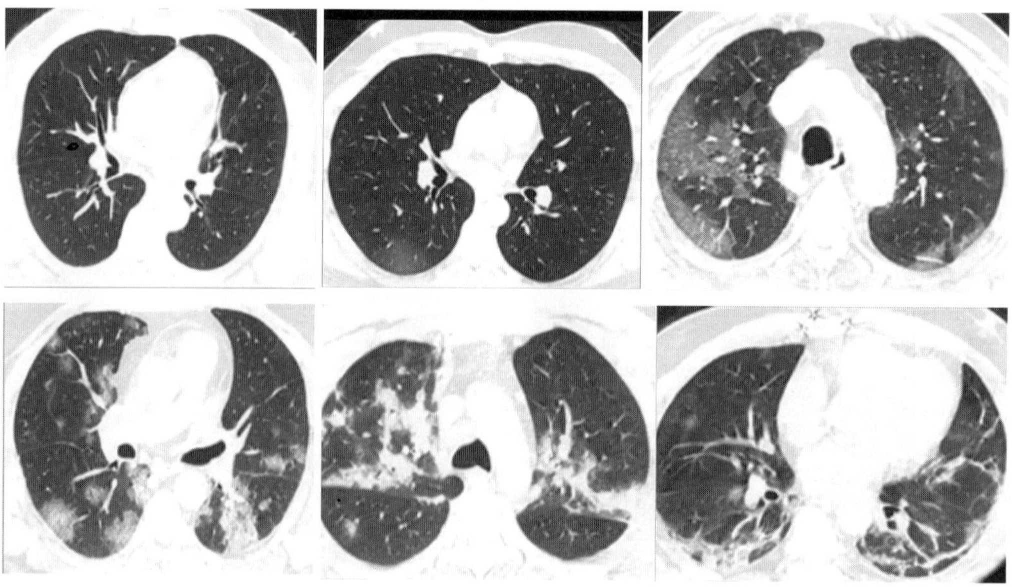

HRCT thorax showing lesions at different times

CT-Severity Score

- Semi-quantitative scoring system
- Estimates the pulmonary involvement of Covid-19 related abnormalities
- Ranges from 0 (no involvement) to 25 (maximum involvement)

Lung lobes

- **Right lung**
  - Upper lobe
  - Middle lobe
  - Lower lobe
- **Left lung**
  - Upper lobe
  - Lower lobe

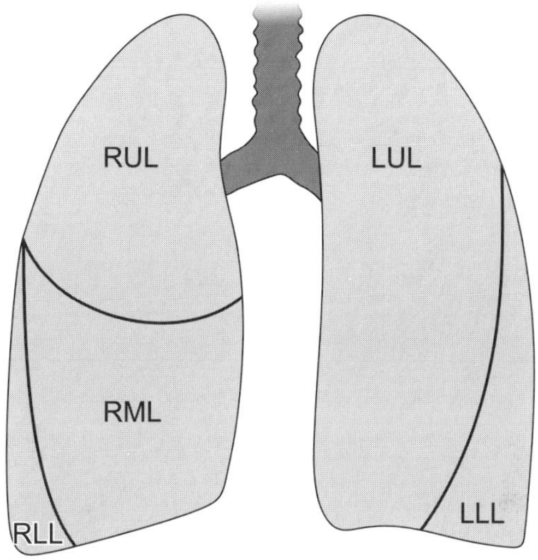

For Each Lobe, Calculate Score	
Score	**Lung involvement**
0	Absent
1	<5%
2	5 to 25%
3	25 to 50%
4	50 to 75%
5	>75%

CT Severity Score Calculation			
Lobe	**Patient lung involvement**	**Patient score**	**Maximum score**
Right upper lobe	<5%	1	5
Right middle lobe	<5%	1	5
Right lower lobe	<5%	1	5
Left upper lobe	<5%	1	5
Left lower lobe	<5%	1	5
Total	**<5%**	**5**	**25**

Reader's Notes

CHAPTER

20

Radiology Quiz

Radiology Quiz

You can score your performance by providing 1 mark for each correct answer—*Do not cheat*

Quiz No. 1

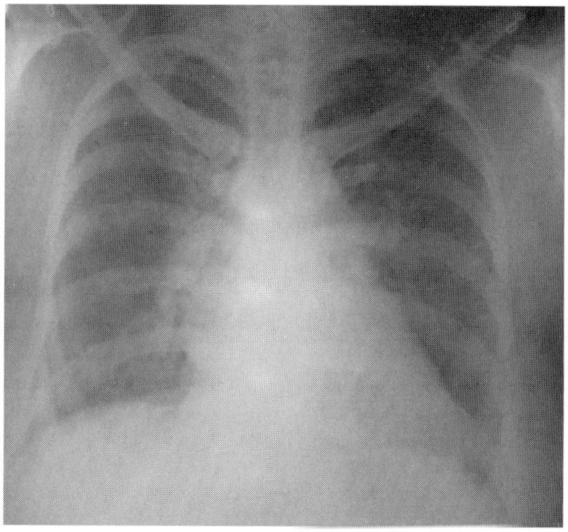

What is this?

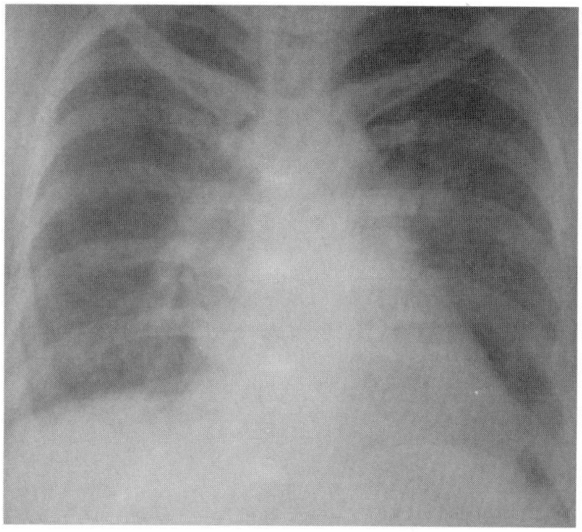

Cardiomegaly with hilar prominence as X-ray was taken in expiratory phase

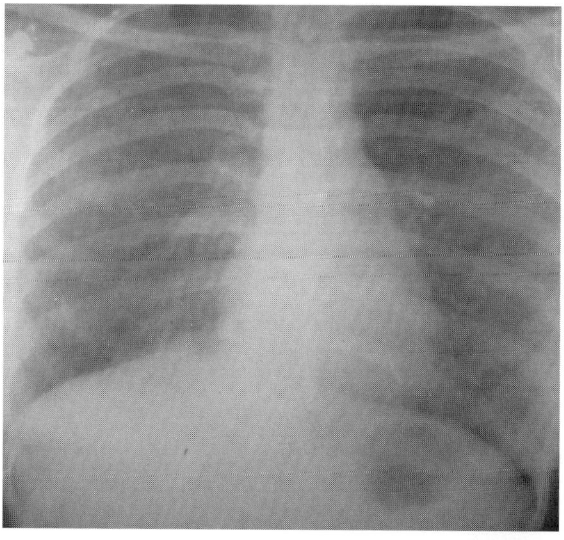

X-ray became normal when taken in inspiratory phase

Never try to read X-ray done in expiratory phase

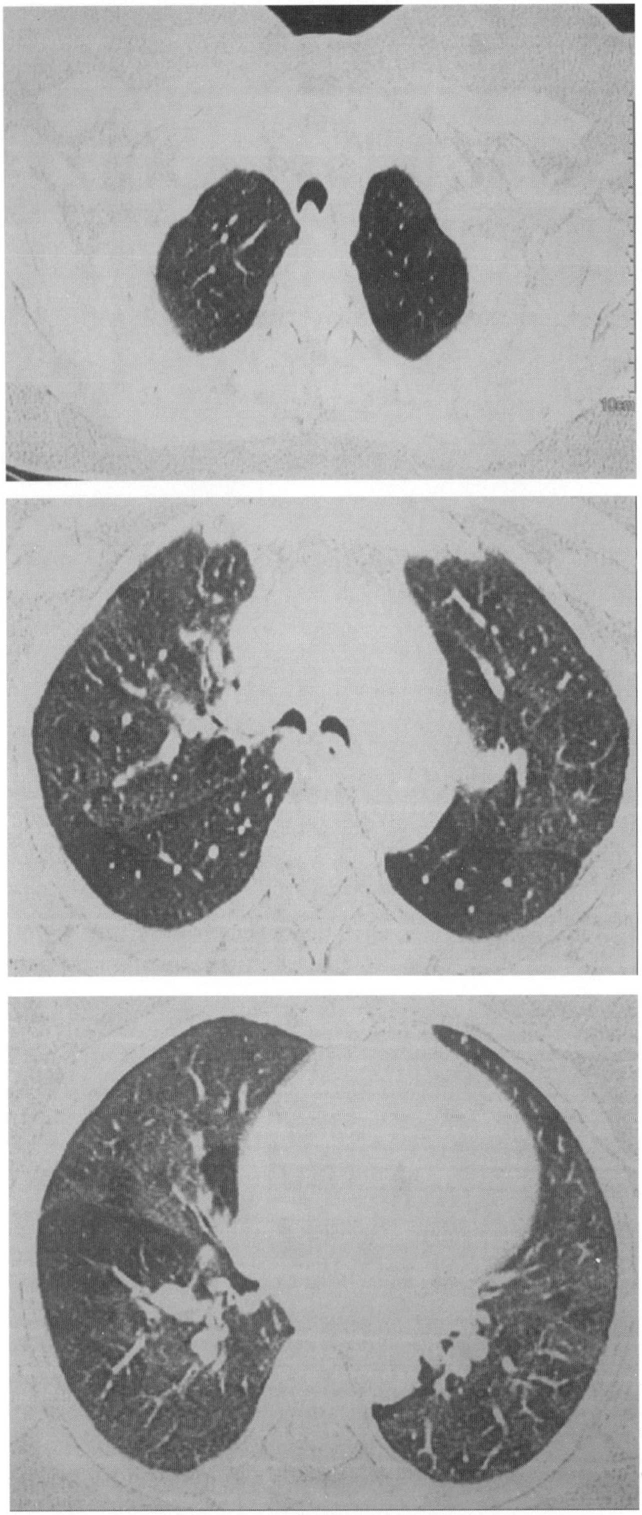

What is the diagnosis?

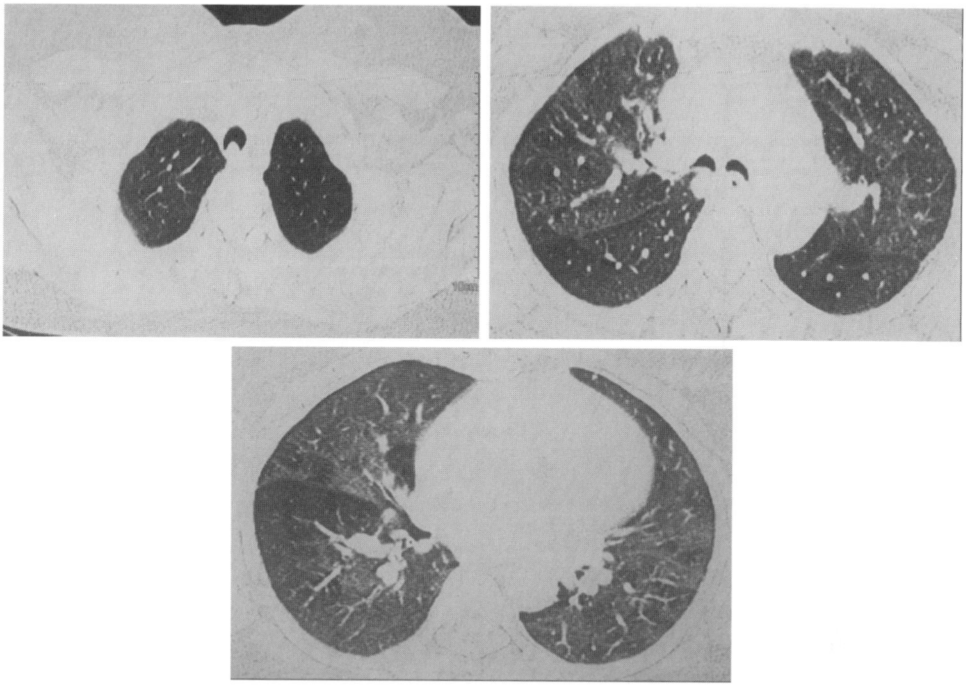

CT done in expiratory phase (see the shape of trachea) shows a lot of shadows

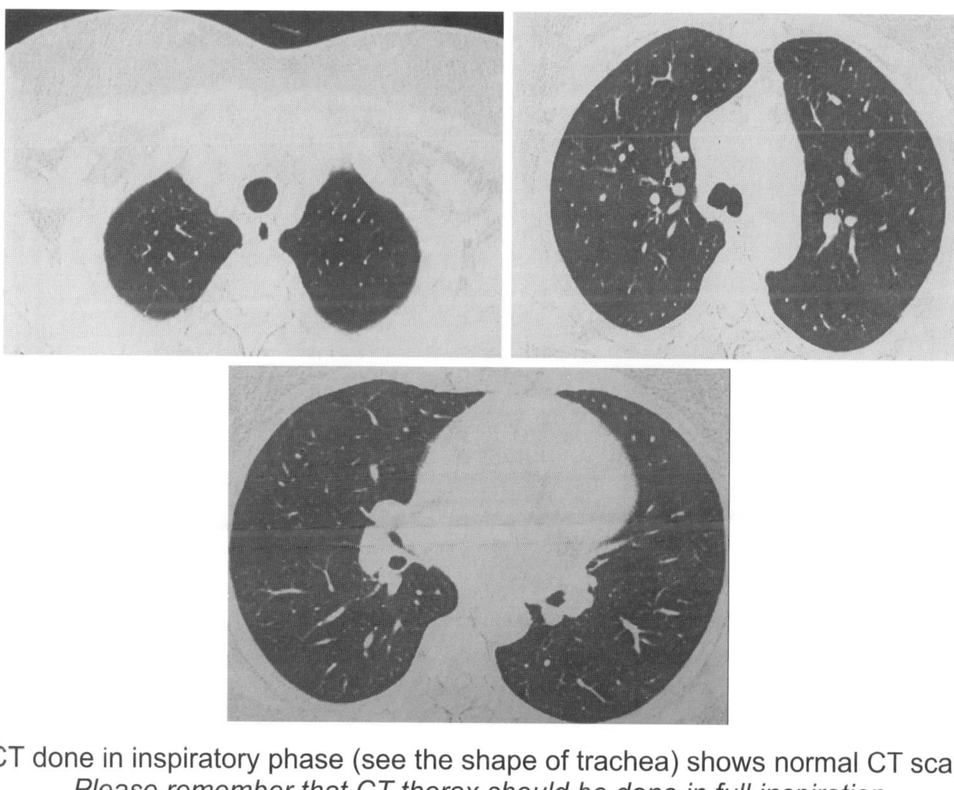

CT done in inspiratory phase (see the shape of trachea) shows normal CT scan
Please remember that CT thorax should be done in full inspiration

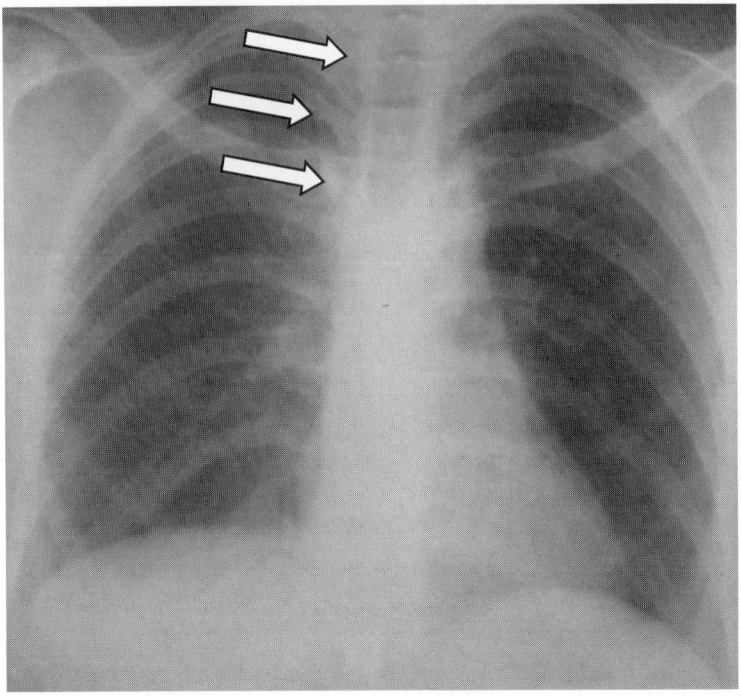

What is this?

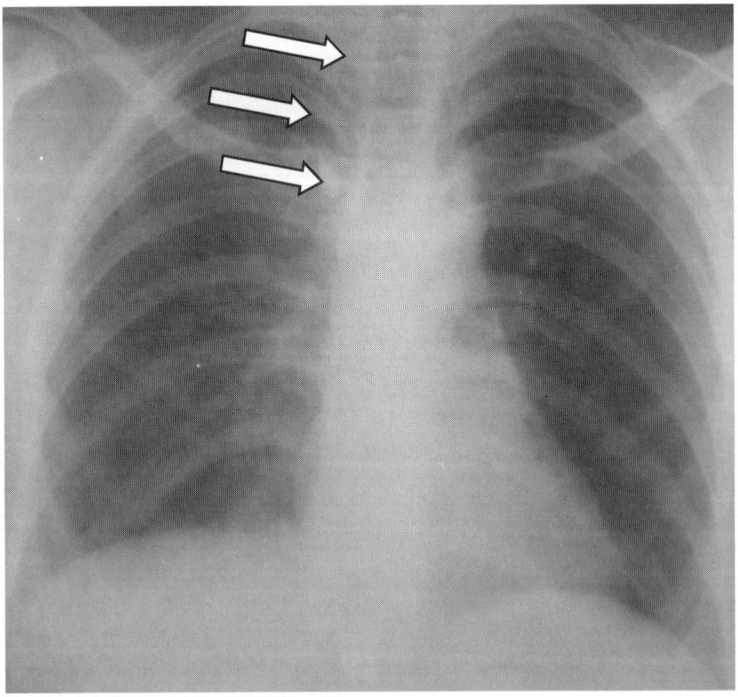

Azygos fissure

Quiz No. 4

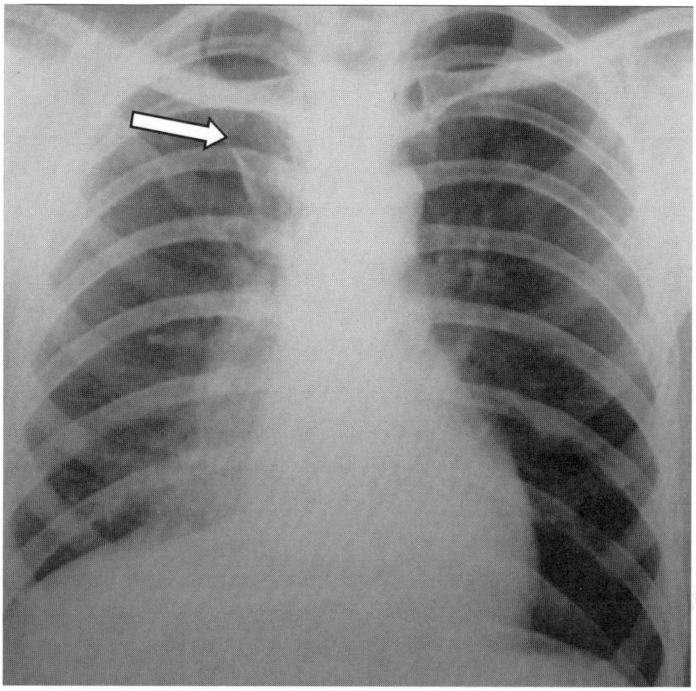

What is this?

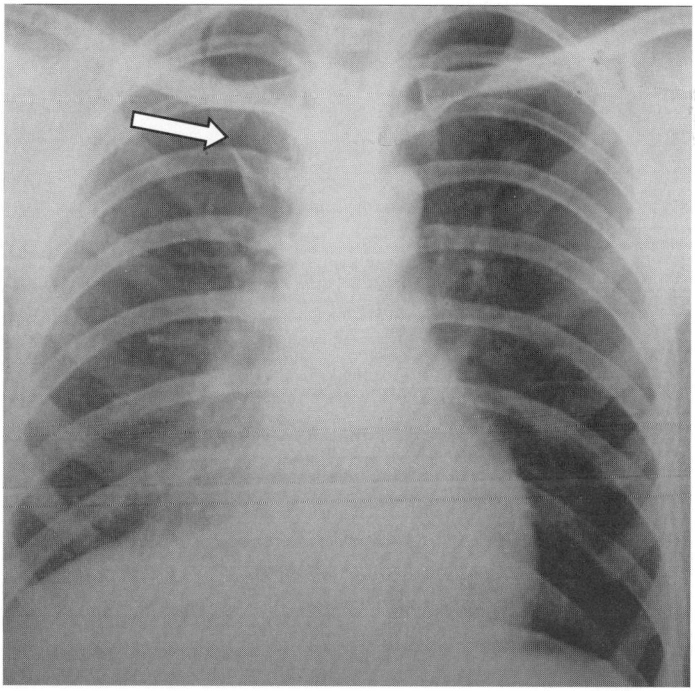

Azygous fissure

Quiz No. 5

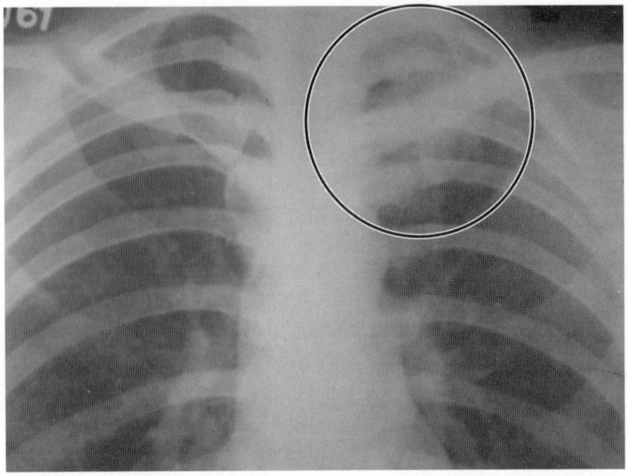

What is this shadow?

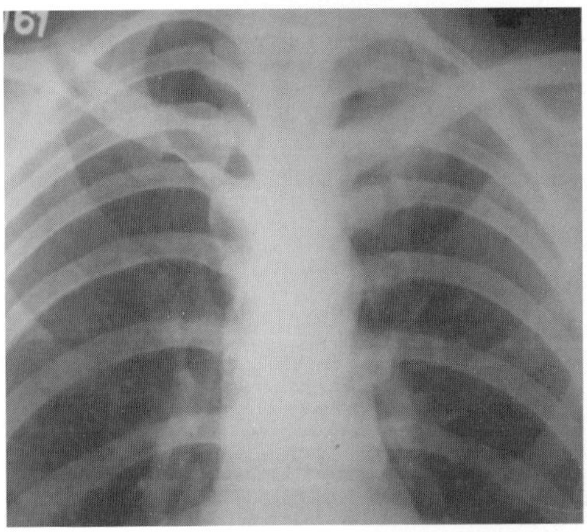

Plaits of hairs (extra thoracic shadow)

Plaits of hairs

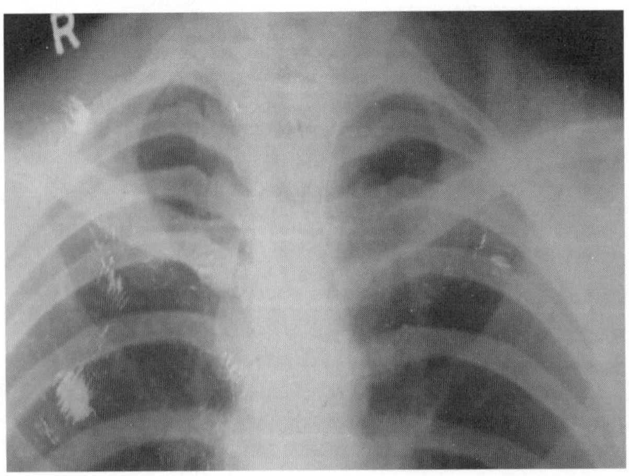

Shadow in left upper zone disappeared when plaits of hair displaced

Quiz No. 6

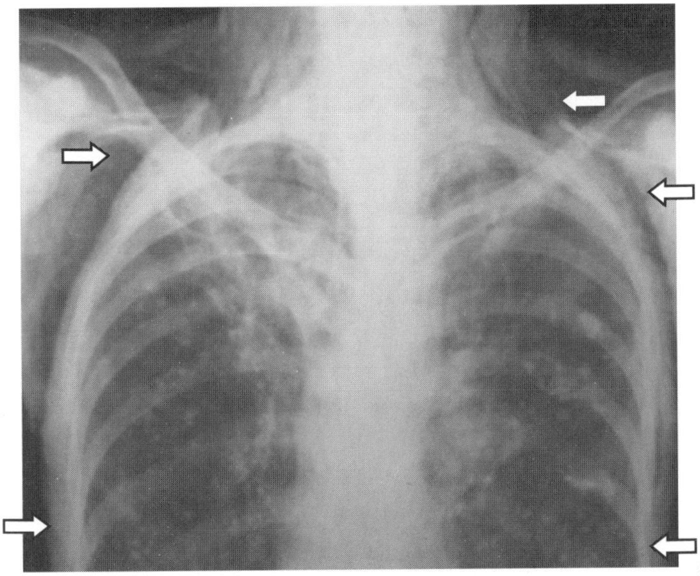

What are these shadows?

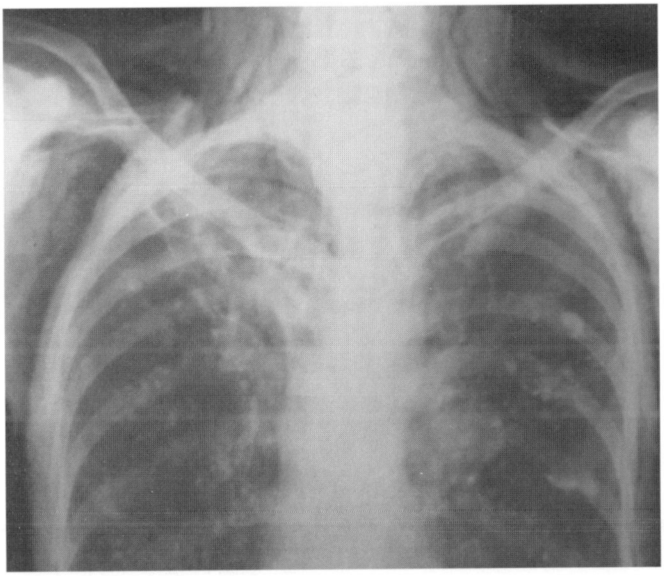

Subcutaneous emphysema

Quiz No. 7

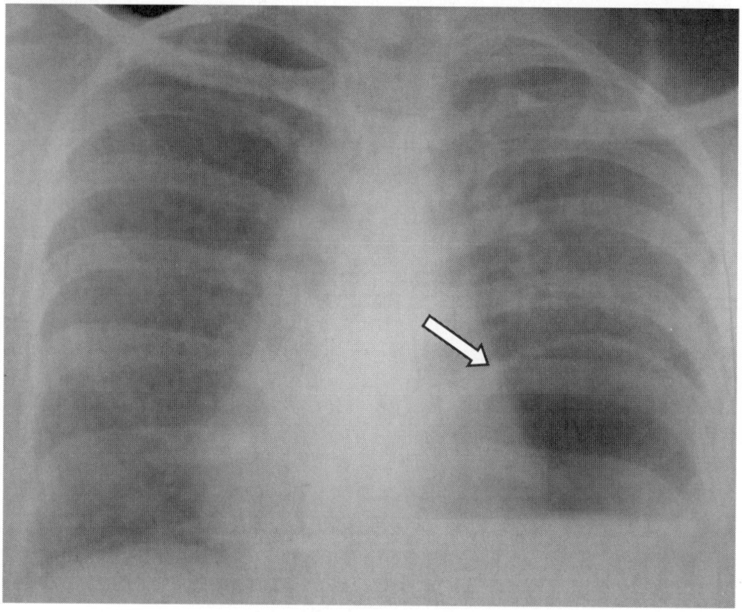

What is this?

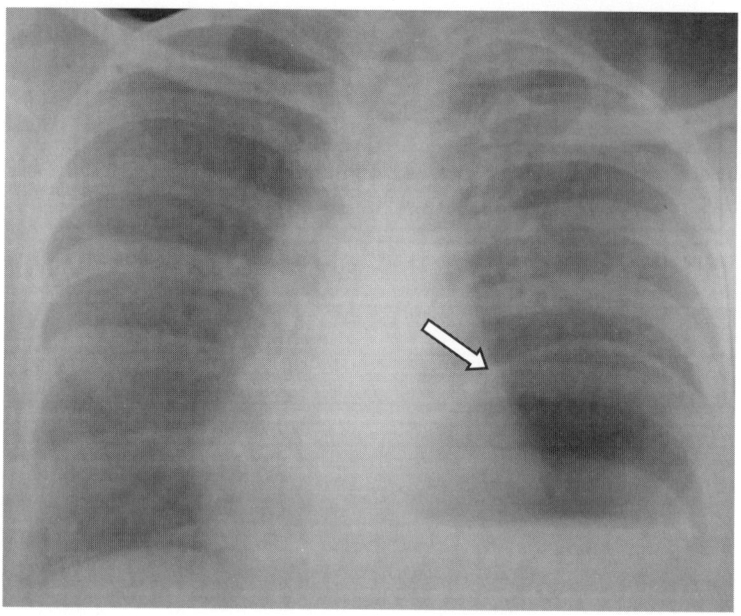

Raised left dome of diaphragm
(eventration of diaphragm)

Quiz No. 8

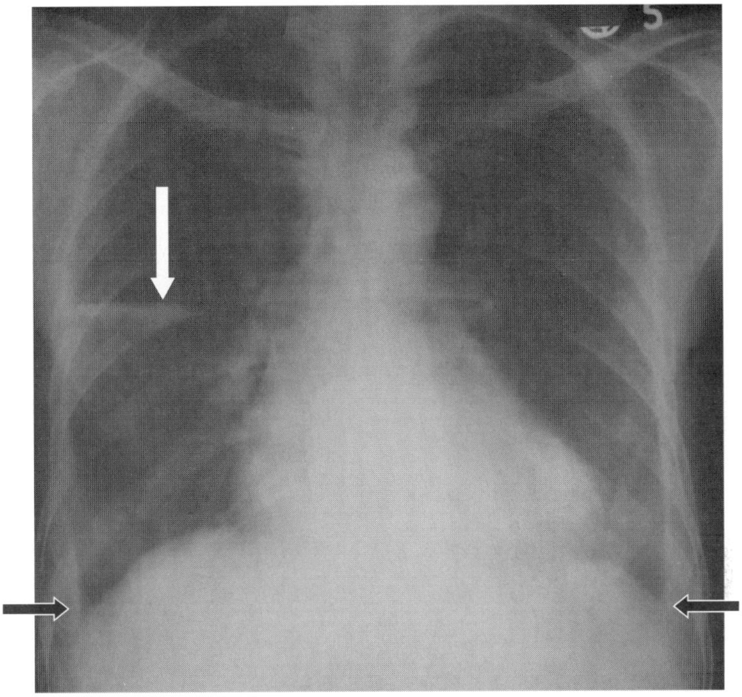

What is this?

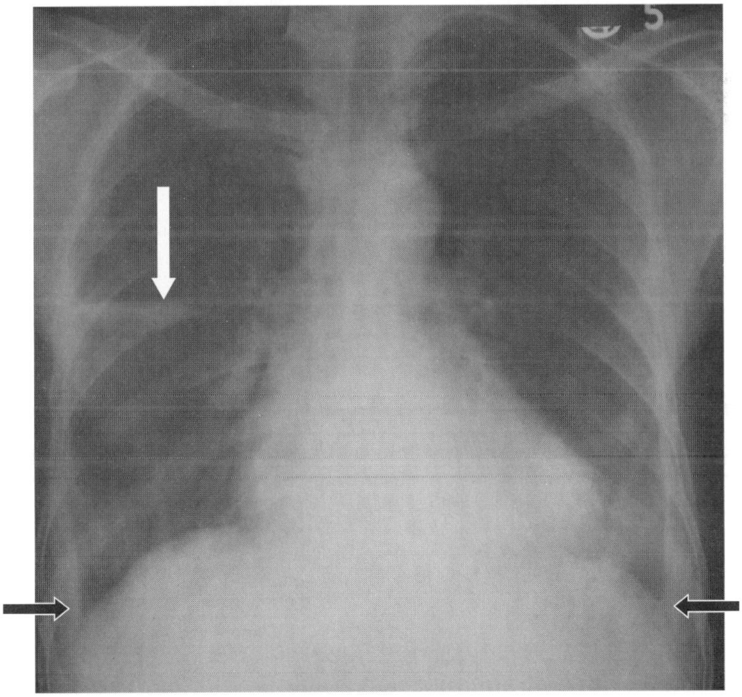

Bilateral pleural effusion with fluid in horizontal fissure

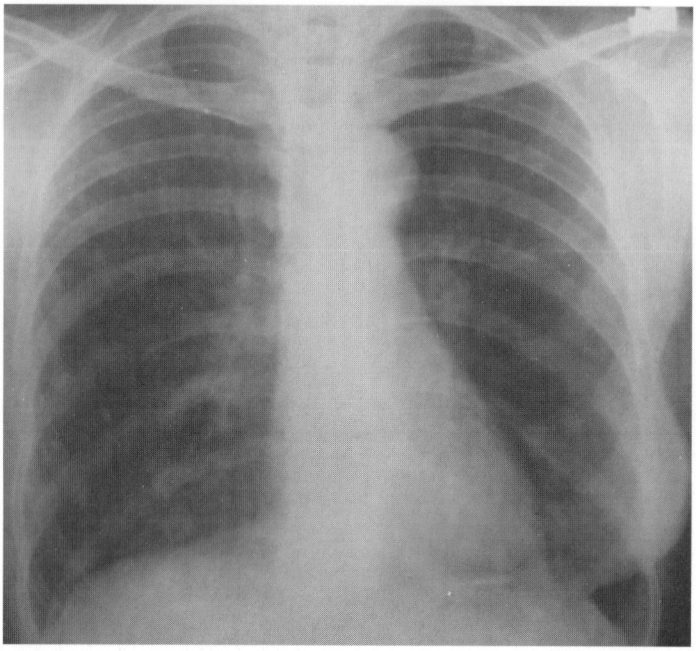

What is this?

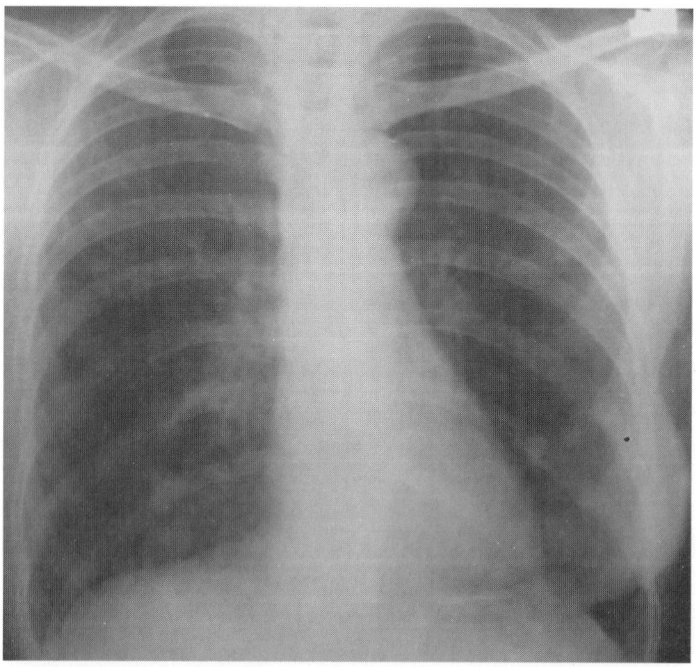

Multiple bilateral nodular shadows cause secondaries from operated carcinoma right breast (no breast shadow on the right side)

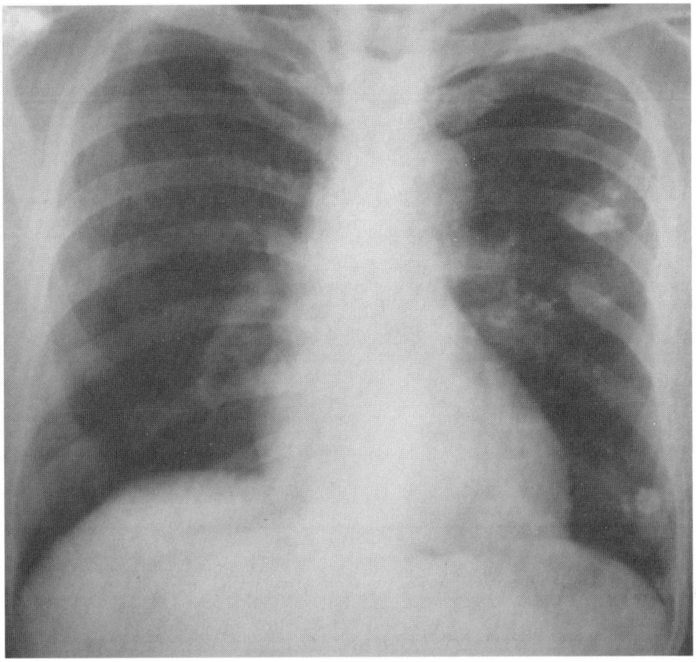

What is this?

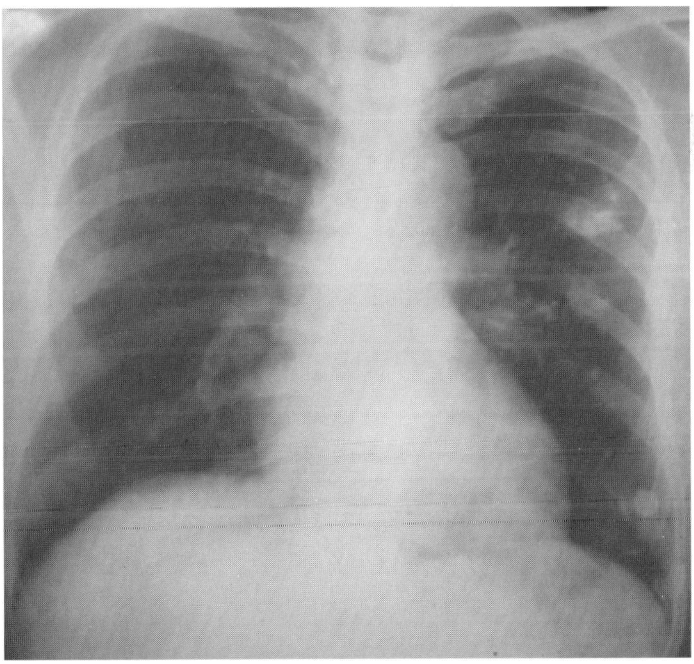

Callus formation around multiple fractured ribs

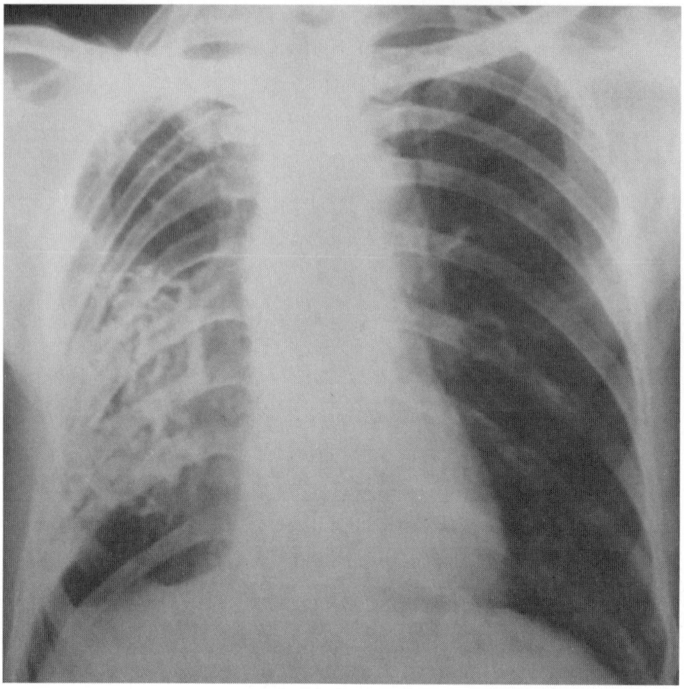

What is this?

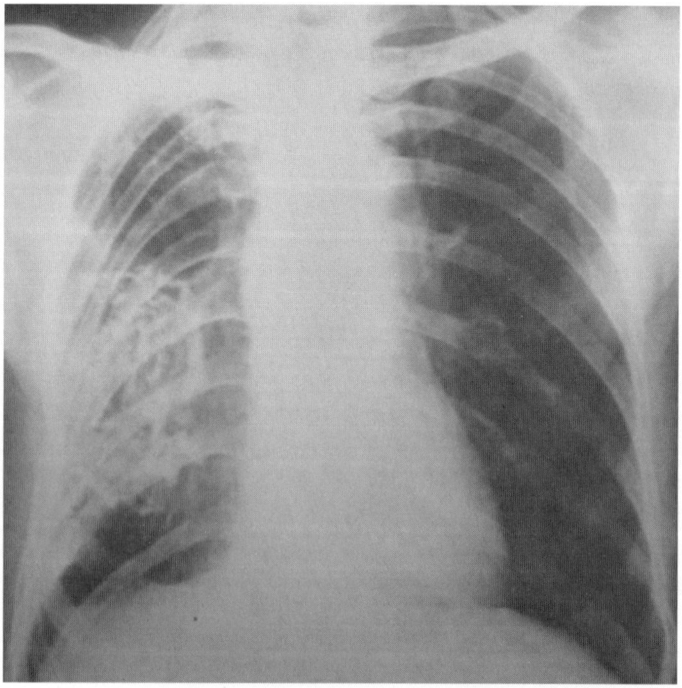

Pleural calcification (right side)
(there was past history of empyema on right side)

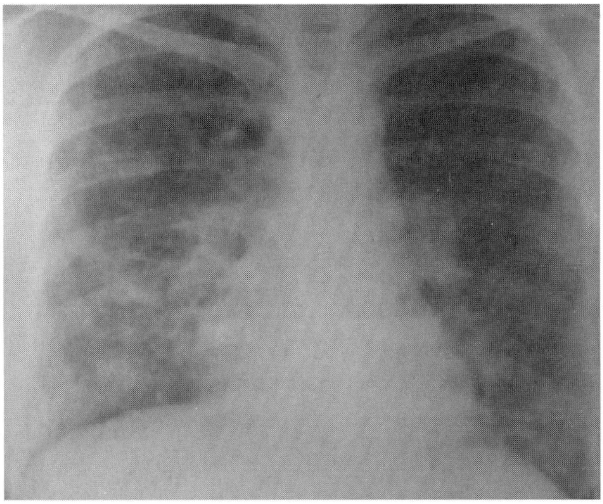

What is this?

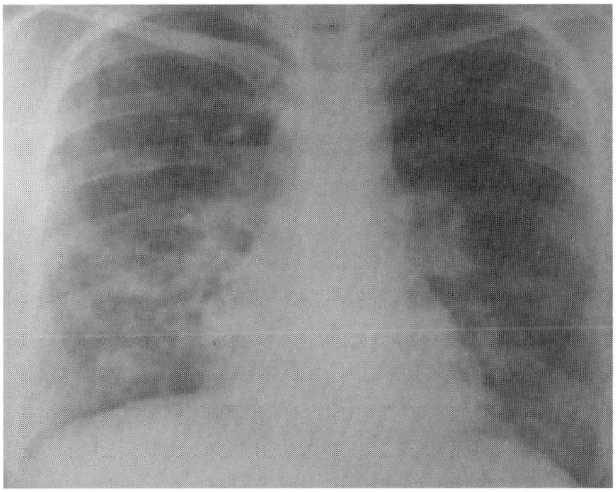

Multiple cystic spaces lower zones (bilateral)

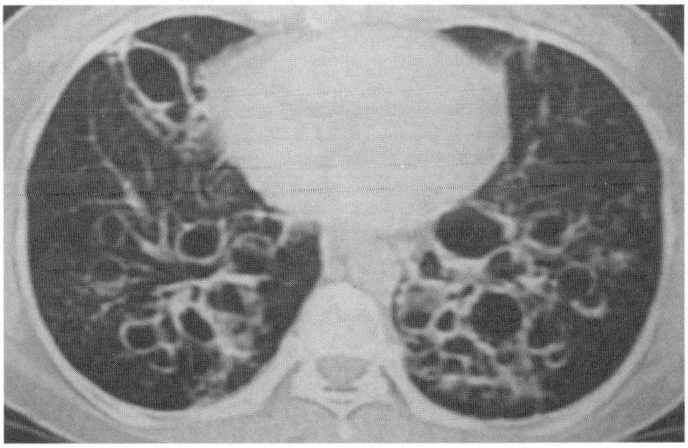

Bilateral lower lobe cystic bronchiectasis

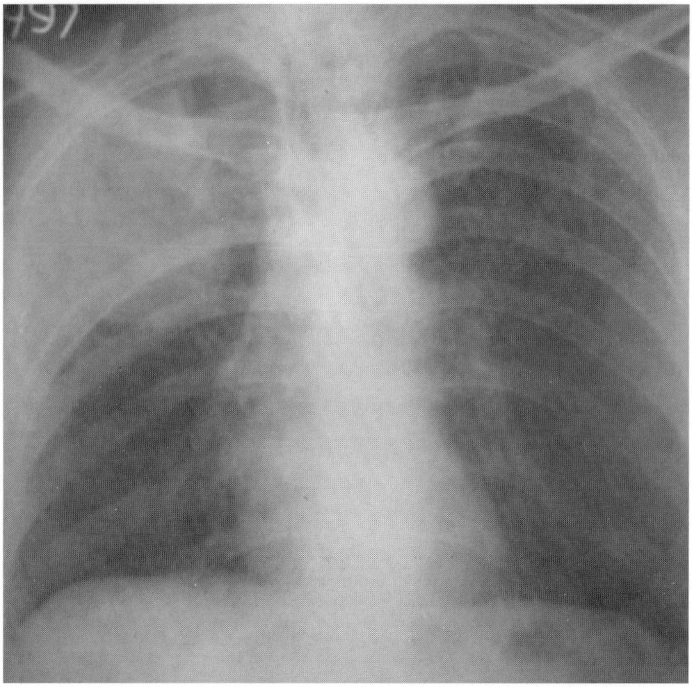

What is this?

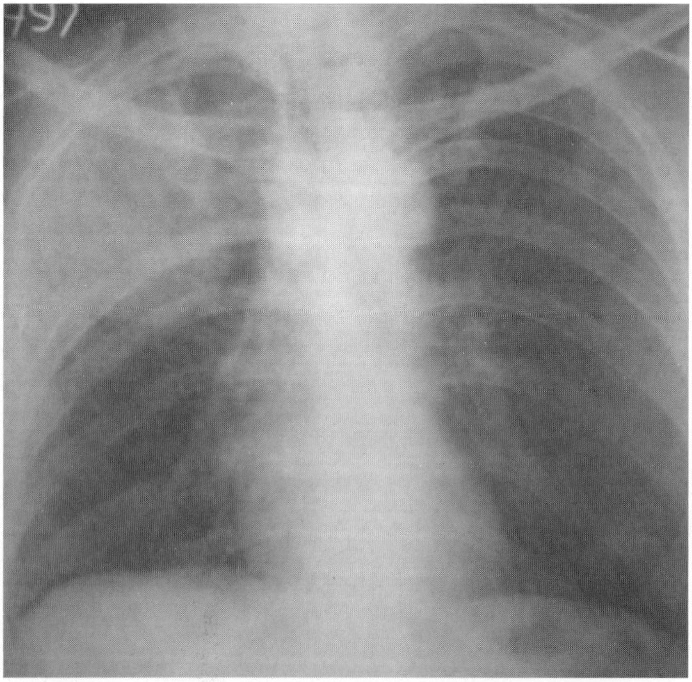

Rounded shadows with destruction of posterior ends of right 4th and 5th ribs cause bronchogenic carcinoma

Quiz No. 14

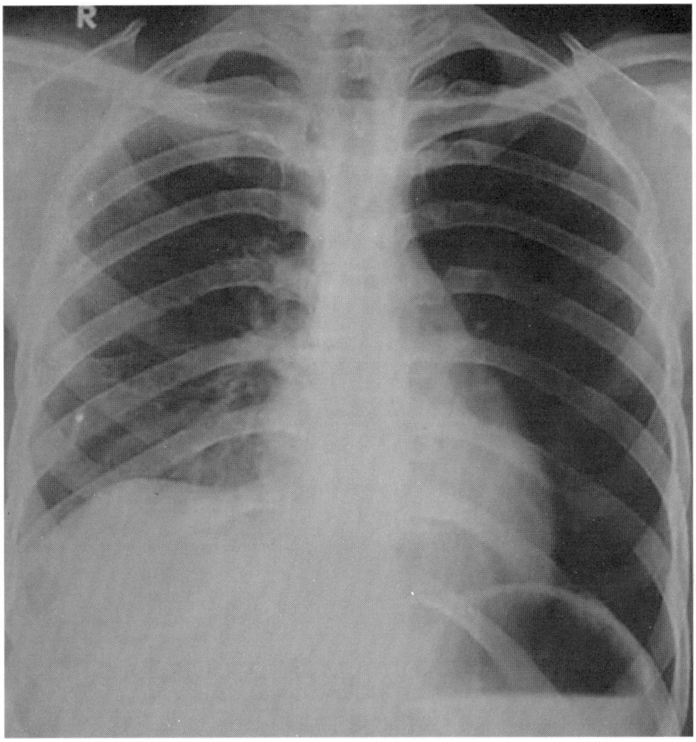

What is this?

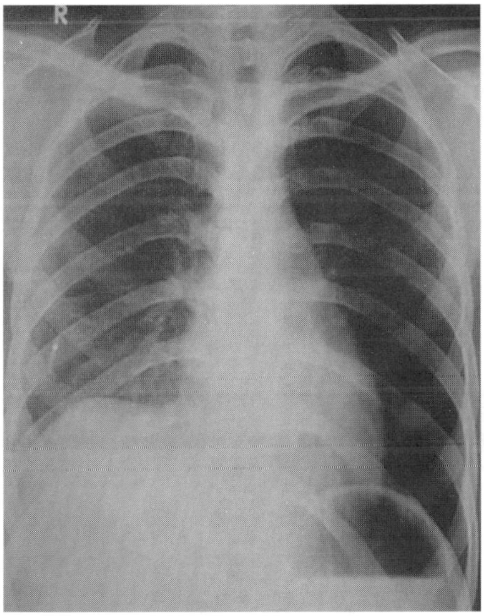

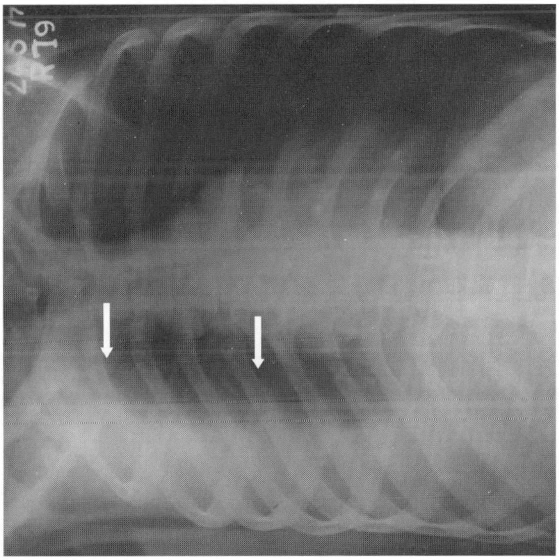

Right lateral decubitus view

Infrapulmonary pleural effusion (right)

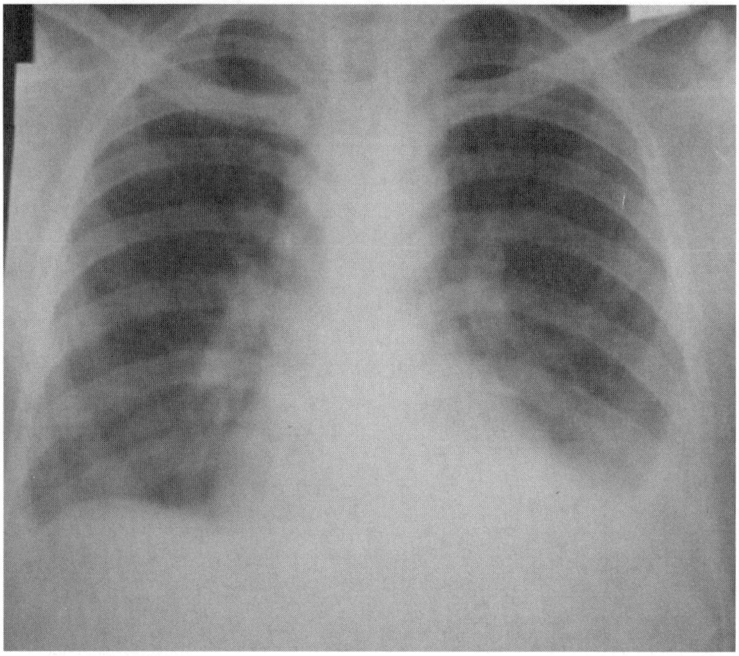

What is this?

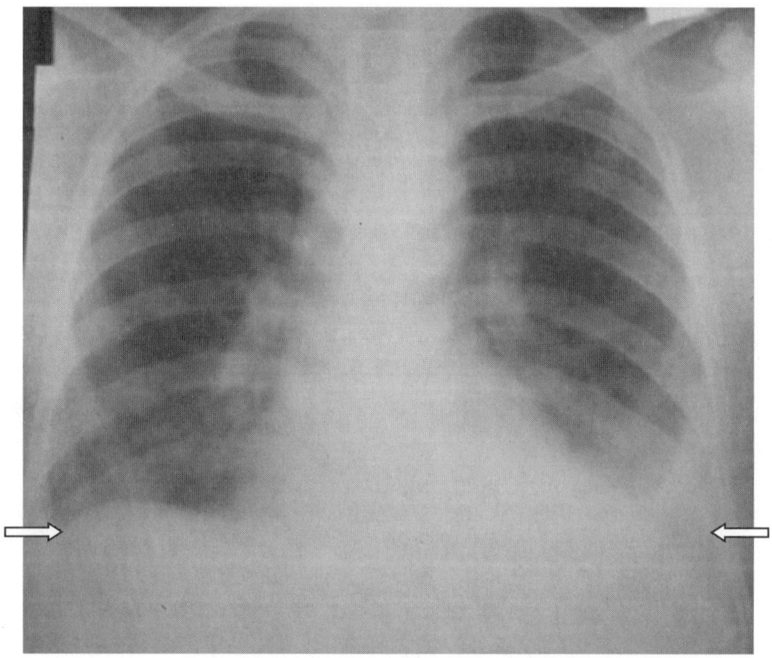

Bilateral pleural effusion

Quiz No. 16

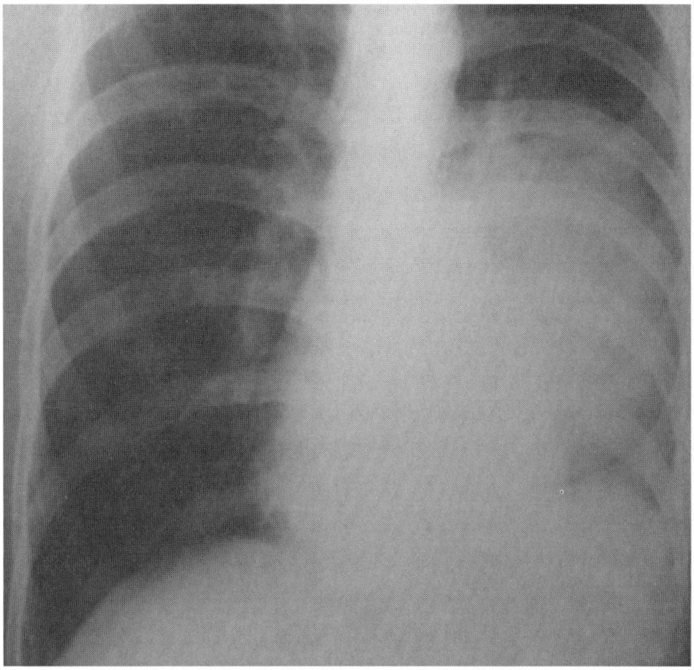

What is this?

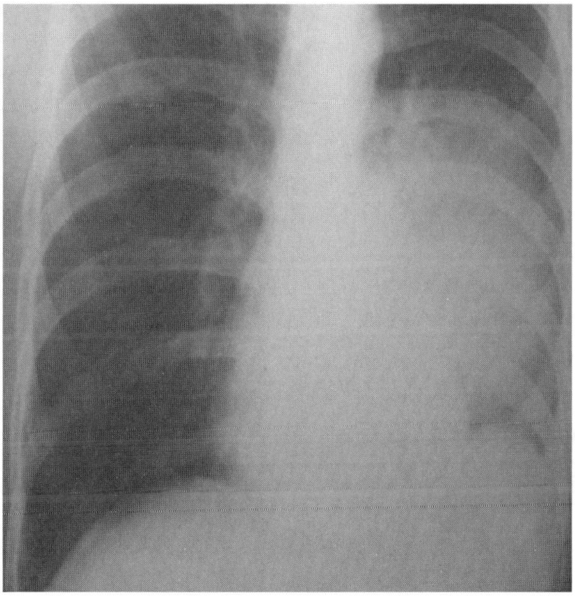

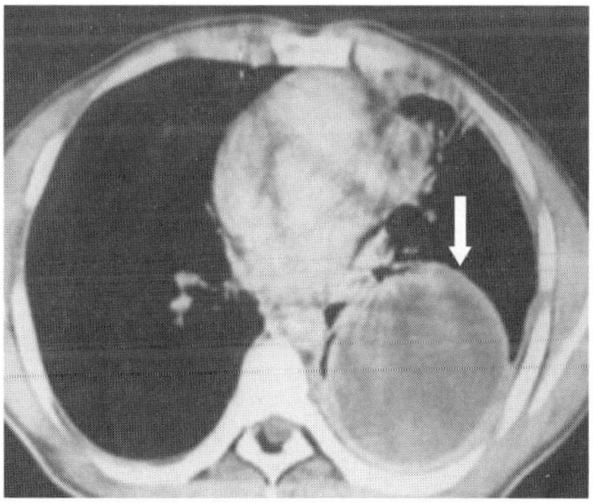

Encysted pleural effusion (left)

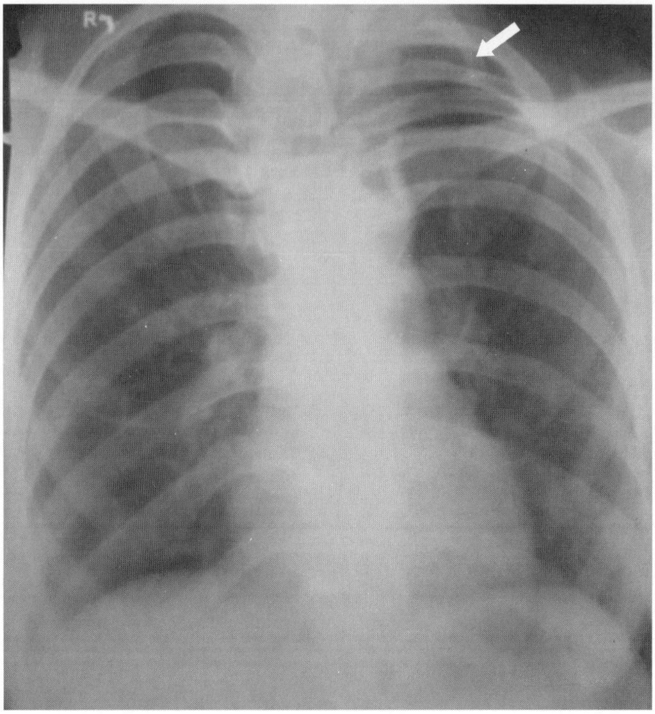

What is this?

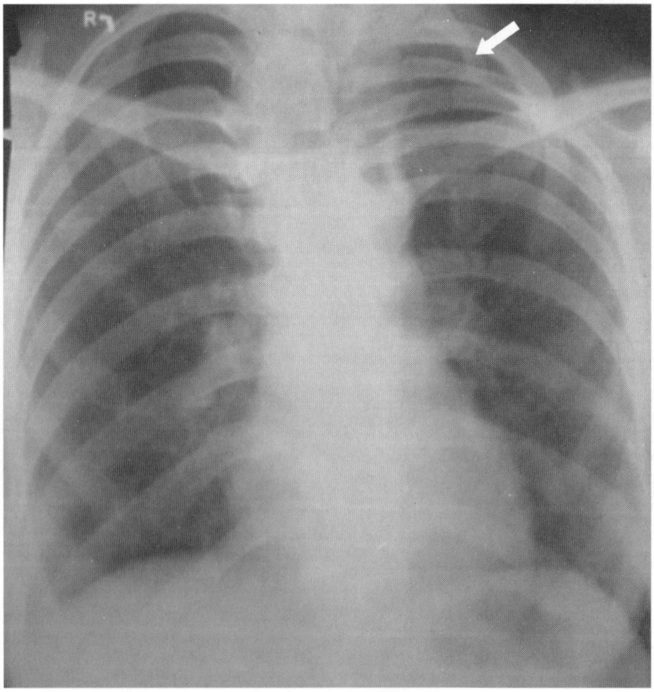

Cervical ribs (unilateral)

Quiz No. 18

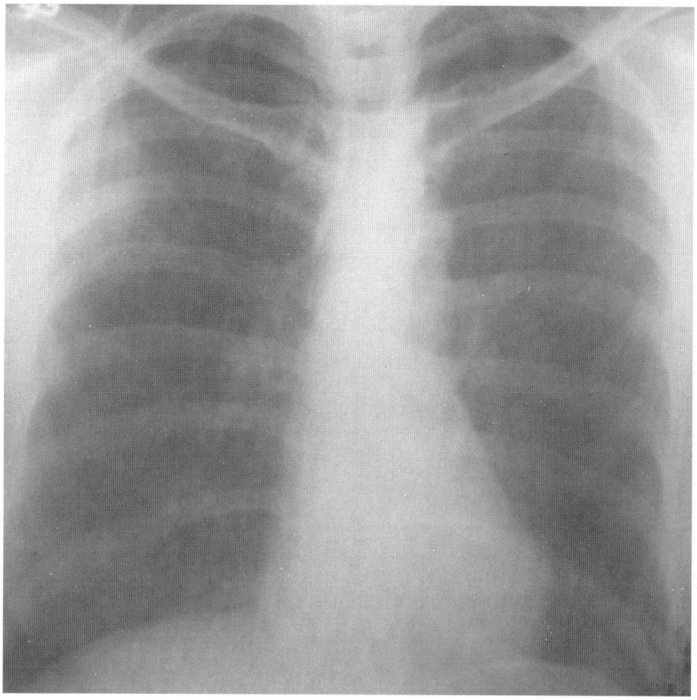

What is this?

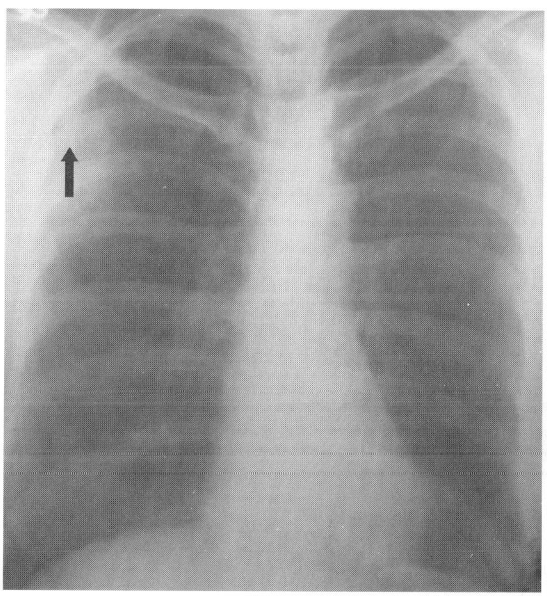

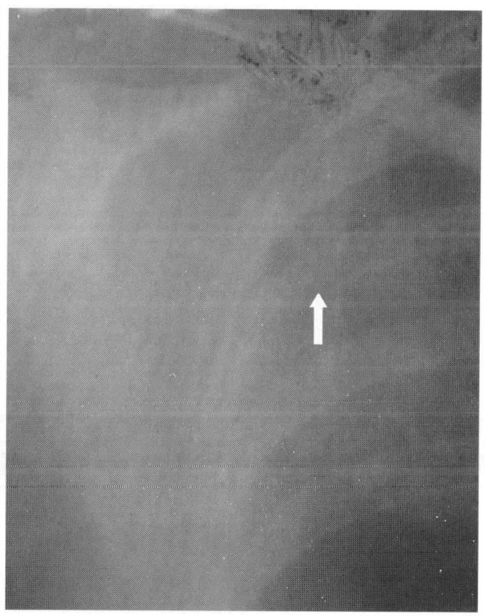

Adenocarcinoma with erosion of posterior end of 4th rib

Quiz No. 19

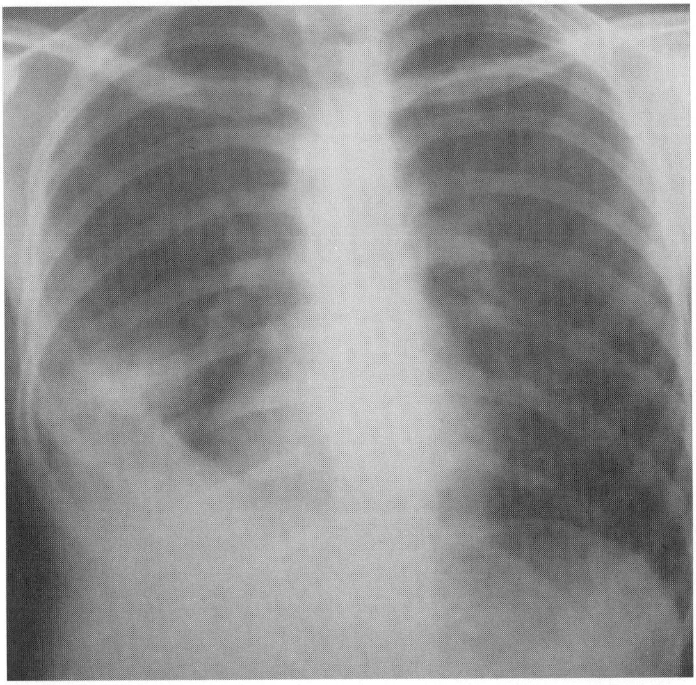

What are these shadows and which ribs are missing?

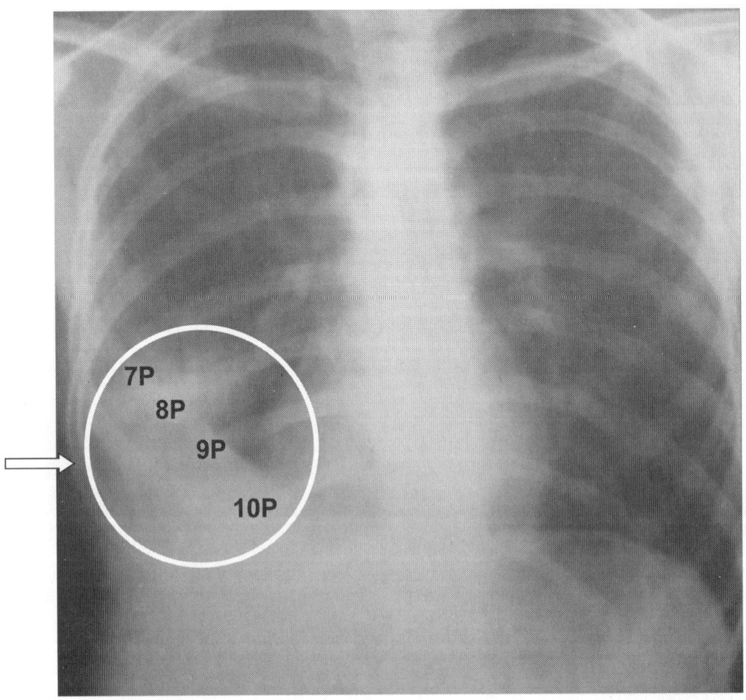

Posterior ends of 7th, 8th, 9th and 10th ribs are missing with soft tissue bulging (Sarcoma)

Quiz No. 20

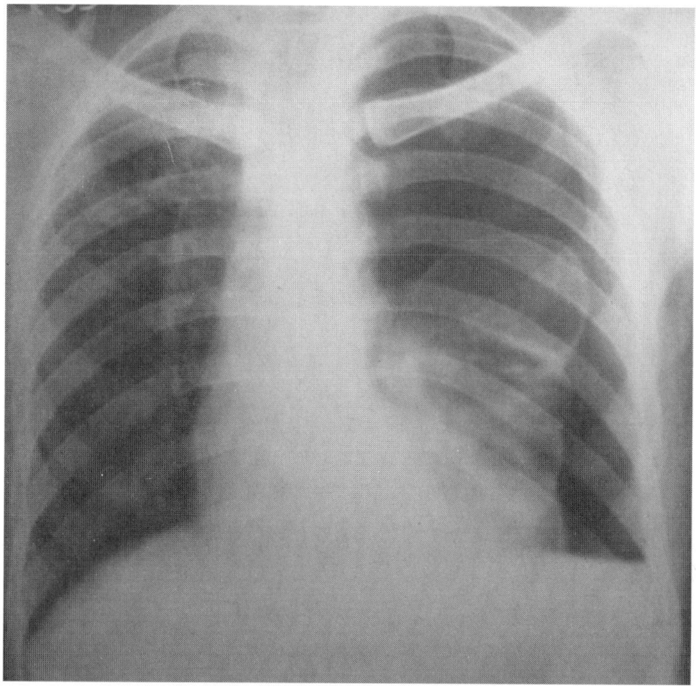

What is this?

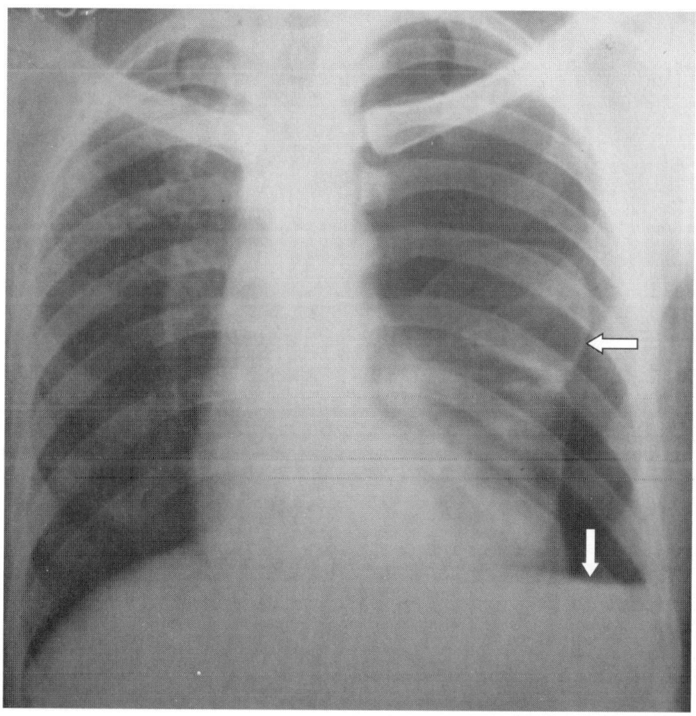

Hydropneumothorax (left)

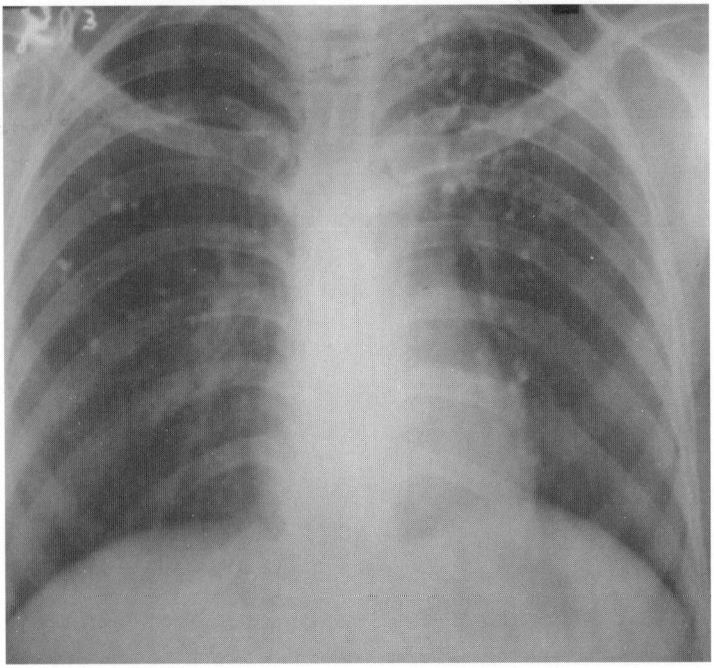

C/O massive hemoptysis with history of adequate antitubercular treatment in the past
What is this?

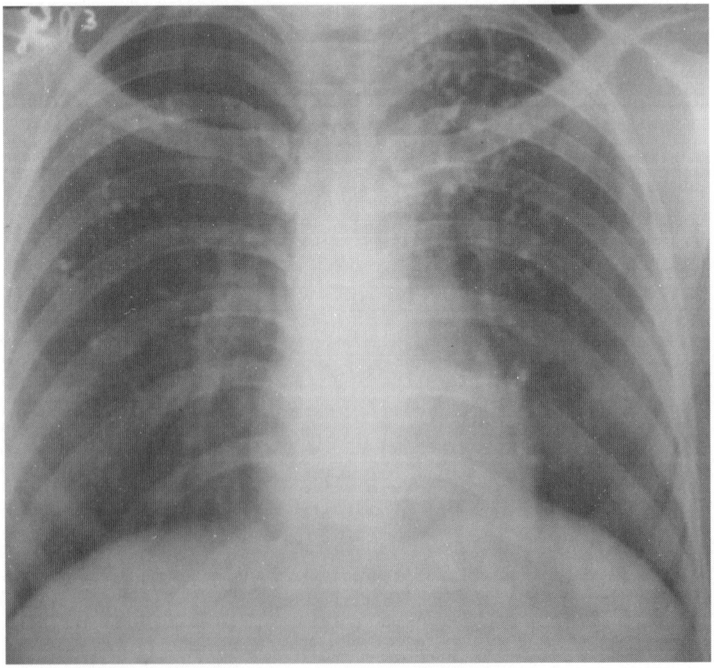

Calcified shadows (healed pulmonary tuberculosis)

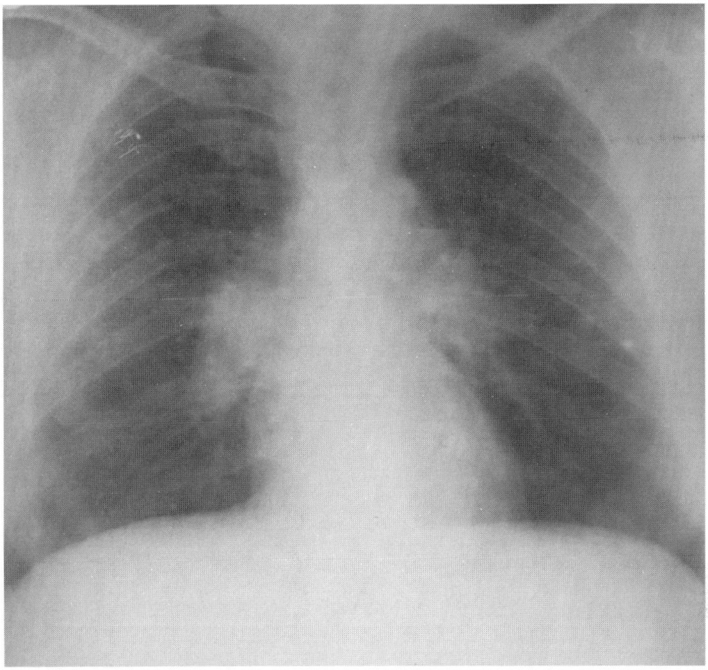

Patient is practically asymptomatic
What is this?

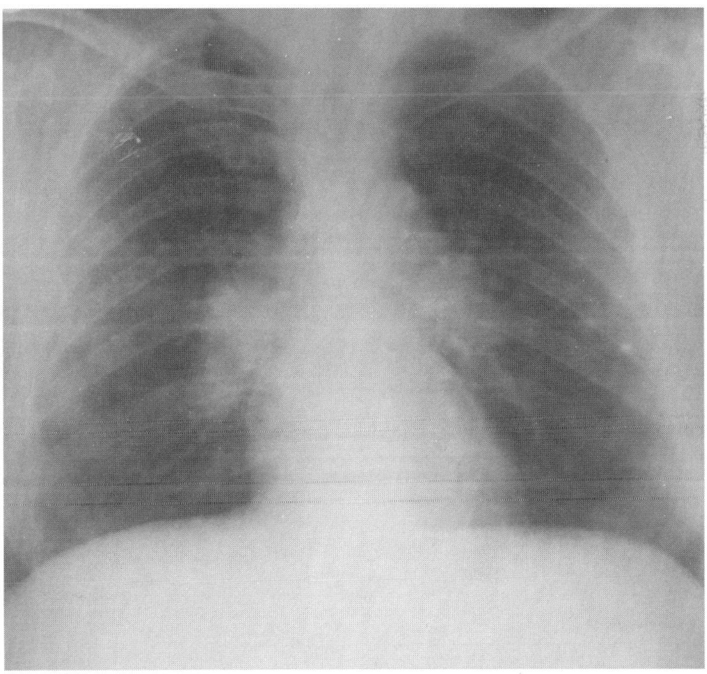

Bilateral hilar lymph node enlargement causes sarcoidosis

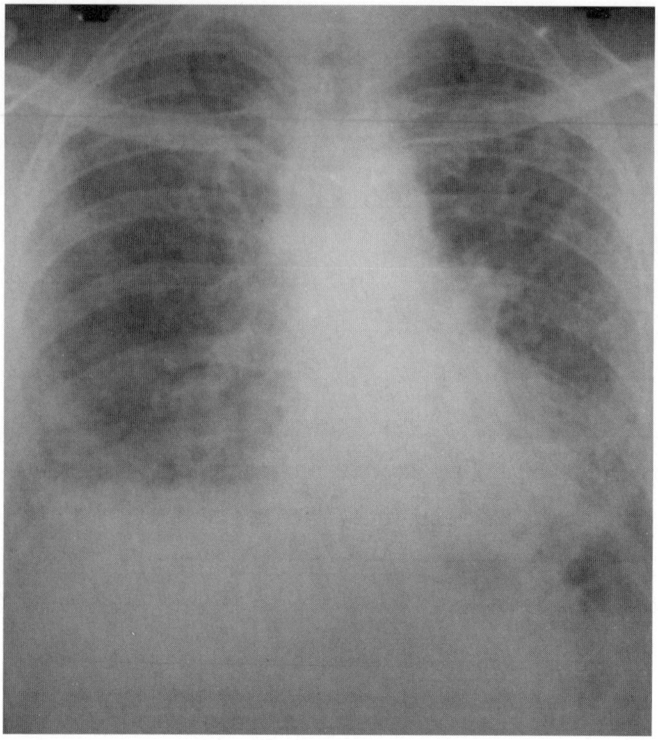

Patient presented with breathlessness for last 6 months
FVC–1.3 L (48% pred.), FEV1/FVC= 90%
What is this?

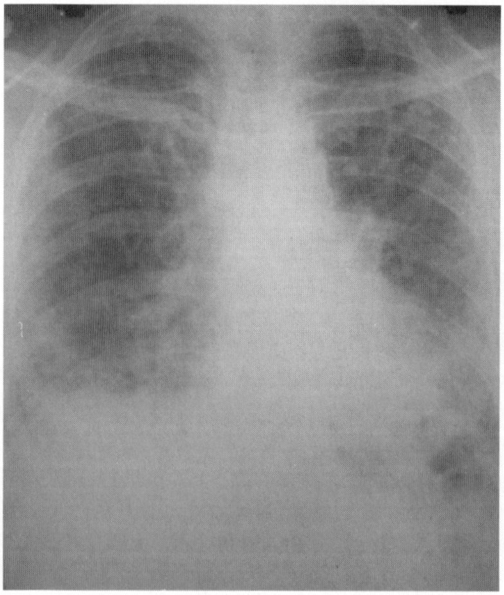

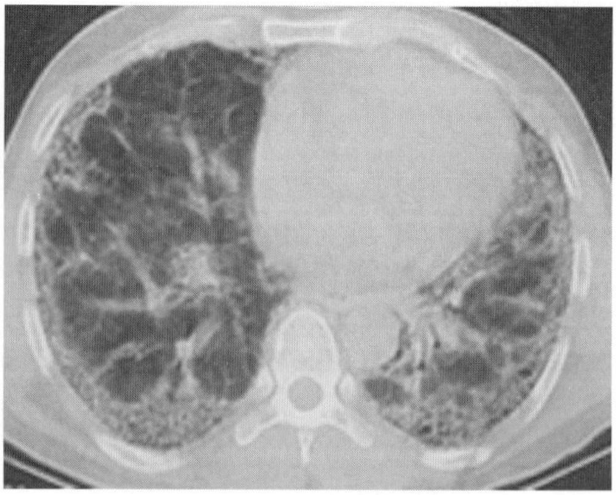

Interstitial lung disease (idiopathic pulmonary fibrosis)

Quiz No. 24

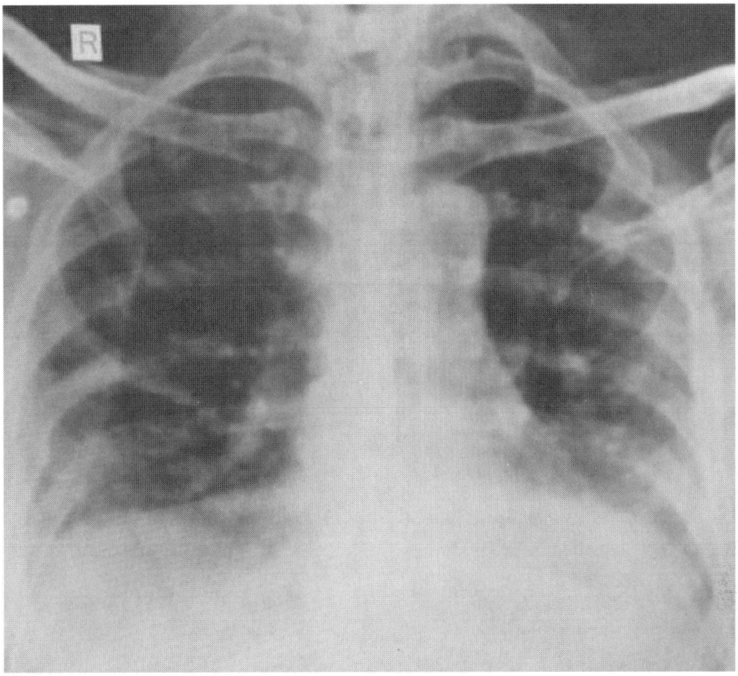

Patient complaining of fever and cough for 8 days
What is this?

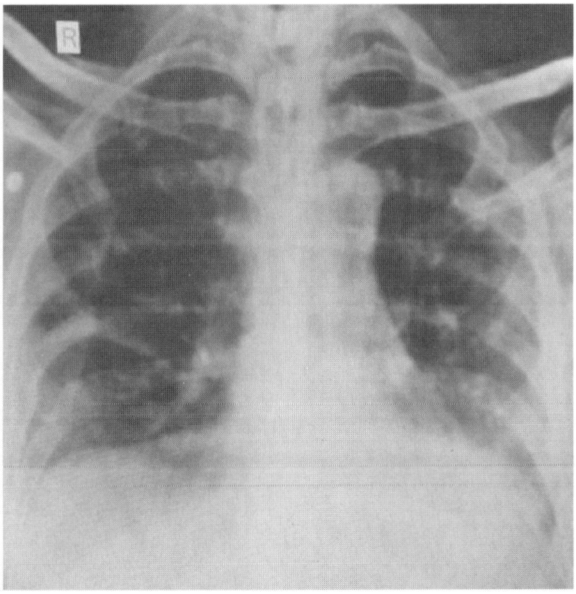

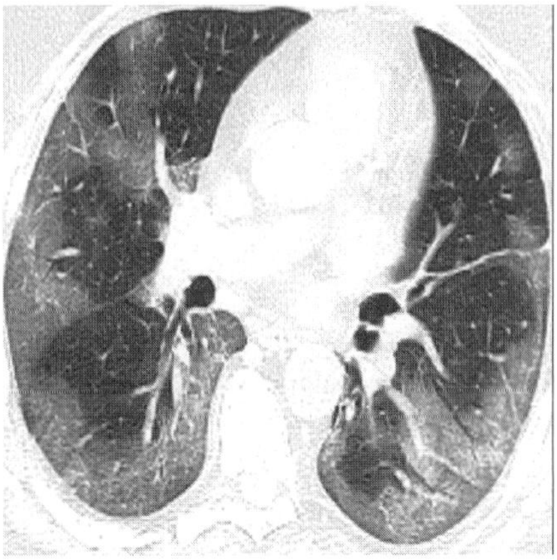

Covid-19 pneumonia
(Covid RT-PCR positive)

Quiz No. 25

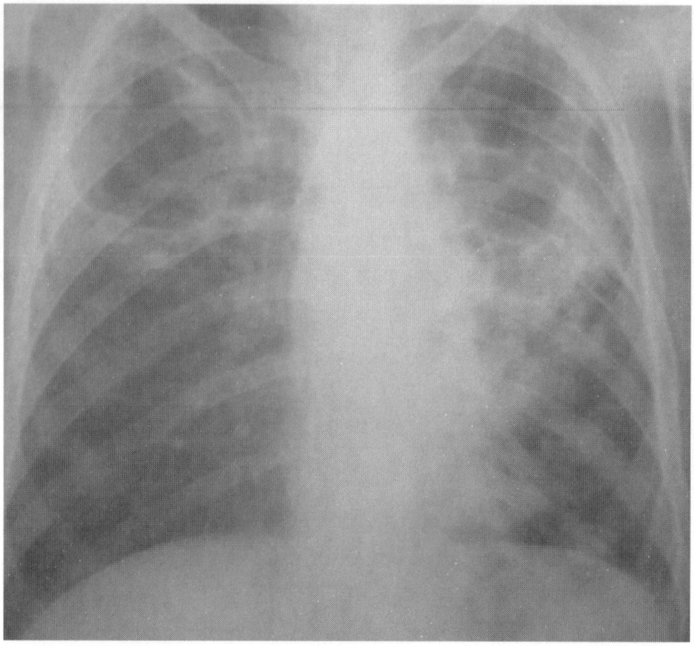

A 50-year-old male presented with cough and hemoptysis for 6 months with history of adequate antitubercular treatment

What is this?

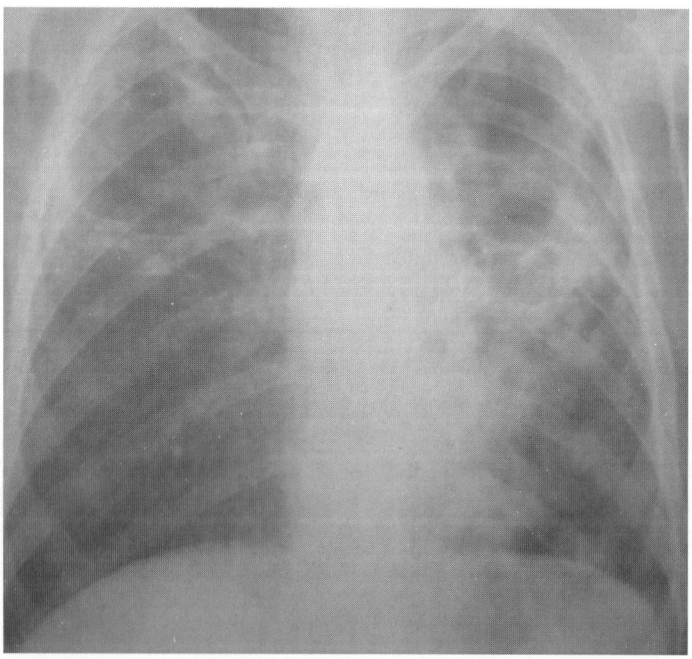

Healed pulmonary tuberculosis (bilateral healed cavities) sputum AFB negative
Open negative syndrome

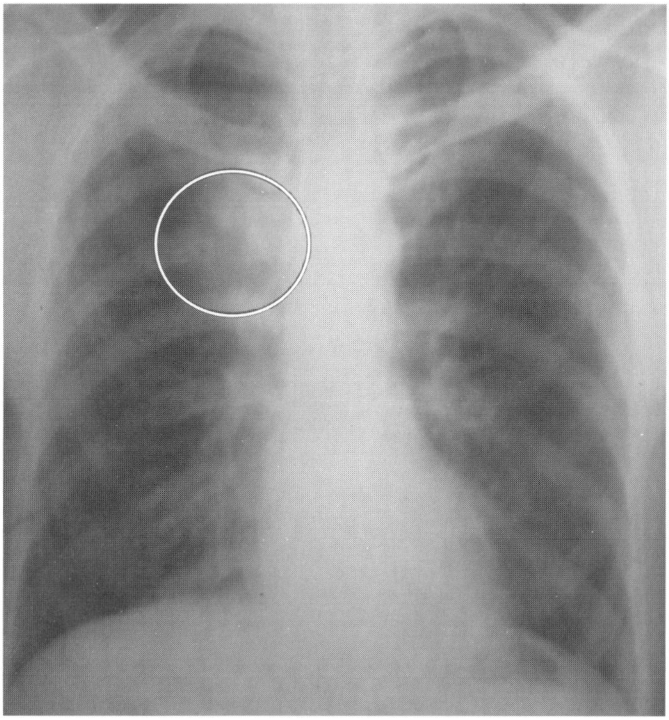

What is this?

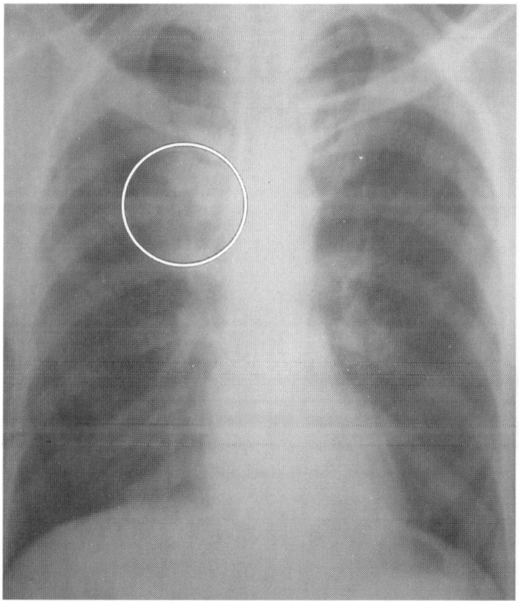

Paravertebral shadow with rib erosion (posterior end of 6th rib) causes tuberculosis

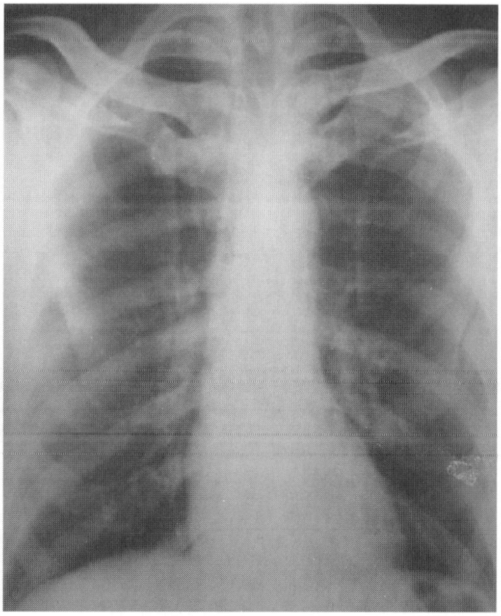

Rib regenerated after a course of antitubercular treatment

You can Score your performance by providing 1 mark for each correct answer—*Please be honest*

Check Your Performance

Please tick ✓/x for your answer

Answers

1	2	3	4	5	6	7
8	9	10	11	12	13	14
15	16	17	18	19	20	21
22	23	24	25	26		

Total Score

If you have scored 26/26, your performance is Excellent

If you have scored 22/26, your performance is Very Good

If you have scored 18/26, your performance is Good

If you have scored 14/26, your performance is Satisfactory

If you have scored 10/26, your performance is Poor (improve yourself)

If you have scored 6/26, your performance is Very Poor (improve yourself)

Manual of Chest X-ray: Take Home Messages

- Approach the X-ray systematically
- Single X-ray not sufficient
- Think of other views
- Think of old X-rays
- Think of other radiological investigations
- Think of other investigations
- Think of clinical picture

Index